Pattern Recognition, Recent Advances

PATTERN RECOGNITION, RECENT ADVANCES

Edited by
ADAM HEROUT

Pattern Recognition, Recent Advances

Edited by Adam Herout

CBS, Edition **2017**

Published by InTech

Janeza Trdine 9, 51000 Rijeka, Croatia

Notice

Statements and opinions expressed in the chapters are these of the individual contributors and not necessarily those of the editors or publisher. No responsibility is accepted for the accuracy of information contained in the published chapters. The publisher assumes no responsibility for any damage or injury to persons or property arising out of the use of any materials, instructions, methods or ideas contained in the book.

Additional hard copies can be obtained from orders@intechopen.com

Pattern Recognition, Recent Advances,
Edited by Adam Herout
p. cm.
ISBN 978-953-7619-90-9

Preface

Pattern recognition is a very wide research field. It involves factors as diverse as sensors, feature extraction, pattern classification, decision fusion, applications and others. The signals processed are commonly one, two or three dimensional, the processing is done in real-time or takes hours and days, some systems look for one narrow object class, others search huge databases for entries with at least a small amount of similarity. No single person can claim expertise across the whole field, which develops rapidly, updates its paradigms and comprehends several philosophical approaches.

This book reflects this diversity by presenting a selection of recent developments within the area of pattern recognition and related fields. It covers theoretical advances in classification and feature extraction as well as application-oriented works. Authors of these 25 works present and advocate recent achievements of their research related to the field of pattern recognition.

The editors would like to thank the authors, who have invested so much effort to the publication of this book.

Editor

Adam Herout

Brno University of Technology

Czech Republic

Contents

Contents

Contents

1

Learning multiclass rules with class-selective rejection and performance constraints

Nisrine Jrad, Pierre Beauseroy and Edith Grall-Maës
Université de Technologie de Troyes ICD (FRE CNRS 2848), LM2S
France

1. Introduction

The task of classification occurs in a wide range of human activity. The problem concerns learning a decision rule that allows to assign a pattern to a decision option on the basis of observed attributes or features. Contexts in which a classification task is fundamental include, sorting letters on the basis of machine-read postcodes, the preliminary diagnosis of a patient's disease or the fraud currency and documents detection. In the classical framework, decision options are given by the pre-defined classes and a decision rule is designed by optimizing a given loss function, for instance the misclassification rate.

In some cases, the loss function should be more general.

First, for some applications, like face identification or cancer diagnosis, one may favor withholding decision instead of taking a wrong decision. In such cases, the introduction of rejection options should be considered in order to ensure a higher reliability Ha (1997); Horiuchi (1998); Jrad, Grall-Maës & Beauseroy (2008); Jrad et al. (2009d). Basic rejection consists of assigning a pattern to all classes which means that no decision is taken. More advanced rejection methods enable to assign a pattern ambiguously to a subset of classes. In this class-selective rejection scheme, decision options are given by the pre-defined classes as well as by defined subsets of different combinations among these classes. In order to define a decision rule, a general loss function can be defined by costs that penalize differently the wrong decisions and the ambiguous ones.

Some applications may require to control the performance of the decision rule or more specifically, the performance measured by indicators related to the decision rule. These latter could be formulated as the performance constraints. Hence, the decision problem should also take into account these constraints. A general formulation of this problem was proposed in Grall-Maës & Beauseroy (2009). The decision problem is formulated as an optimization problem with constraints. It was shown that the optimal rule can be obtained by optimizing its Lagrangian dual function which consists of finding the saddle point of this Lagrangian function. This optimal theoretical rule is applicable when the probability distributions are known. However, in many applications, only amounts of training set is available. Therefore, one should infer a classifier from a more or less limited set of training examples. In the classical decision framework, referred as the classical framework, many historical strands of research can be identified: statistical, Support Vector Machines, Neural Network Bishop (2006); Guobin & Lu (2007); Hao & Lin (2007); Husband & Lin (2002); Vapnik (1998); Yang et al. (2007)... In the class-selective rejection scheme, fewer works have been done Ha (1997); Horiuchi (1998).

One approach based on v-1-SVM was proposed in Jrad, Grall-Maës & Beauseroy (2008) and tested on five cancer genes datasets in Jrad et al. (2009d). A cascade of classifiers with class-selective rejection learned on different feature sets was used as a good way to provide improved supervised diagnosis. In this chapter, multiclass problem is studied in the general framework of class-selective rejection subject to constraints. Two approaches are presented and discussed; a class-modeling approach and a boundary based approach.

The class-modeling approach is defined within the statistical community. It exploits flexible classes of models to provide an estimate of the joint distribution within each class, which in turn provides a classification rule. Estimators may be either parametric or not. In the parametric case, an additional hypothesis about the underlying probability density function should be made. To illustrate that approach, a parametric estimator, Gaussian Mixture Models (GMM) Titterington et al. (1985), and a non-parametric estimator, Parzen Windows estimator (PW) Emanuel (1962), are explored. The proposed approach Jrad et al. (2009c) consists of optimizing the class-conditional density estimates on the basis of a goodness of fit criterion. The GMM and PW densities are plugged into the hypothesis tests framework to get the decision rule associated to the estimates. The decision rule is selected by optimizing the Lagrangian function.

The boundary based approach is defined in the SVM community. It avoids the estimation of the complete density functions which is unnecessary since only densities in the neighborhood of borders need to be precisely known. A multiclass support vector machine algorithm (MSVM), based on v-1-SVM, is used. The proposed method divides the multiple class problem into several unary classification problems and train one v-1-SVM for each class Scholkopf et al. (2001); Scholkopf & Smola (2001); Tax (2001) coupled with its regularization path Hastie et al. (2004); Rakotomamonjy & Davy (2007). The winning class or subset of classes is determined using a prediction function that takes into consideration the different costs. The parameters of all the v-1-SVMs are optimized jointly in order to minimize the Lagrangian function. Taking advantage of the regularization path method, the entire parameters searching space is considered. Compared to similar approaches Bottou et al. (1994); Hao & Lin (2007); Yang et al. (2007), since the searching space is widely extended, the selected decision rule is more likely to be the optimal one. Note that standard multiclass learning strategy is a particular case of the proposed approaches where the different decision options are given by the pre-defined classes, the loss function is given by the error rate and no constraint is considered. We will refer to this case as the classical framework.

The class-conditional approach and the boundary based approach were applied to several artificial datasets or toy problems. The datasets were constructed such that they differ in modal complexity and sample size. By using toy problems, the characteristics of the datasets can be exactly set and the performances of the supervised rule can be deduced by a simple comparison to the theoretical ones. General comments about the behavior of the different approaches can be made by analyzing these results. As a final example, the boundary approach is tested on five well-known cancer genes data sets, LEUKEMIA72 Golub et al. (1999), OVARIAN Welsh et al. (2001), NCI Ross et al. (2000); Scherf et al. (2000), LUNG CANCER Garber et al. (2001) and LYMPHOMA Alizadeh et al. (2000) in order to study the performance of this approach on real world datasets.

This chapter is outlined as follows. Paragraph 2 introduces the general framework of multiclass problems with class-selective rejection and performance constraints. It presents the optimal solution in the statistical theory framework. After describing the problem, we turn to an exploration of a supervised solution in the class-modeling framework by exploiting the non-parametric Parzen Windows estimator and the parametric Gaussian Mixture Models in paragraph 3. The boundary strategy based on ν-1-SVM is presented in paragraph 4. The efficiency of the latter approach is illustrated through a supervised cancer diagnosis. Results on the five genes datasets are reported in paragraph 5. The last paragraph discusses and compares the class-conditional and boundary based approaches.

2. Classification with class selective rejection and performance constraints

This section addresses the problem of multiclass decision with class-selective rejection and performance constraints. It gives a general framework for specifying such a problem. The optimal solution is presented in the statistical hypothesis testing framework.

2.1 Multiclass problem

Let us consider a multiclass decision problem with N classes. A given pattern $x \in \Re^d$ belongs to the class j noted w_j, for $j = 1, \ldots, N$, with the class-conditional probability density function $P(x/w_j)$. Each class is characterized by its a priori probability $P_j = P(w_j)$. The unconditional probability function (mixture density) $P(x)$ and the posterior probabilities $P(w_j/x)$ are provided through the total probability theorem and Bayes' formula.

The proposed general framework, introduced in Grall-Maës et al. (2006a) and developed in Grall-Maës & Beauseroy (2009), allows to define a multiclass decision problem subject to performance constraints using three kinds of criteria:

- the decision options: they correspond to the assignment subsets of classes that are deemed as admissible for the problem. In the class-selective rejection scheme, there are $2^N - 1$ assignment subsets of classes. They correspond to the possible subsets in a set of N elements excluding the empty set. They can be referred to ψ_i with $i = 1, \ldots, 2^N - 1$. For example, assigning a pattern to $\psi_i = \{1; 3\}$ means that it is assigned to both classes w_1 and w_3 with ambiguity.

  Thus, the decision options are defined by the set Ψ composed of only the admissible subsets of classes ψ_i:

  $$\Psi = \{\psi_1, \psi_2, \ldots, \psi_I\},$$

  where $I \leq 2^N - 1$ is the number of decision options. Any decision rule $Z : \Re^d \rightarrow [1, 2, \ldots, I]$ is defined such that $Z(x) = i$ when x is assigned to the set ψ_i.

  The probability of deciding that an element of the class j belongs to the set ψ_i is $P(D_i/w_j)$:

  $$P(D_i/w_j) = \int_{\{x|Z(x)=i\}} P(x/w_j)dx.$$

- the performance constraints to be satisfied. They are defined by inequalities, each of them defining a threshold on a linear combination of class conditional decision probabilities. Any performance constraint $C^{(k)}$ where k is a integer between 1 and the number of constraints K is defined by its expression $e^{(k)}(Z)$ and its threshold $\gamma^{(k)}$:

$$C^{(k)} : e^{(k)}(Z) = \sum_{i=1}^{I} \sum_{j=1}^{N} \alpha_{i,j}^{(k)} P_j P(D_i/w_j) \leq \gamma^{(k)} \tag{1}$$

with $e^{(k)}(Z)$ a linear combination of class conditional decision probabilities, $\alpha_{i,j}(k)$, for $i = 1, \ldots, I$ and $j = 1, \ldots, N$, is the cost of deciding that an element x belongs to the set ψ_i when it is assigned to the class j, in the expression of the kth constraint.

- the average expected loss: it corresponds to the cost function to be minimized. It is also expressed as a linear combination of class-conditional decision probabilities:

$$\bar{c}(Z) = \sum_{i=1}^{I} \sum_{j=1}^{N} c_{i,j} P_j P(D_i/w_j), \tag{2}$$

where $c_{i,j}$, for $i = 1, \ldots, I$ and $j = 1, \ldots, N$, is the cost of deciding to assign an element x to the set ψ_i when it belongs to the class j. The values of $c_{i,j}$ are relative since the aim is to minimize $\bar{c}(Z)$, thus, without loss of generality, the values are defined in the interval $[0; 1]$.

In this framework, finding the optimal decision rule consists in determining the decision rule Z^* so that the cost $\bar{c}$ is minimum and the constraints given by equation (1) are satisfied. The decision problem to be solved is expressed by the following optimization problem:

$$\min_Z \bar{c}(Z)$$

$$\text{s.t. } e^{(k)}(Z) \leq \gamma^{(k)} \quad \forall k = 1, \ldots, K.$$

Given this primal problem, the Lagrangian dual problem is defined by:

$$\max_{\mu \in \Re^{K+}} \{\min_Z \{L(Z, \mu)\}\} \tag{3}$$

in which $\mu = [\mu_1, \mu_2, \ldots, \mu_K]^T$ is the vector of Lagrangian multipliers associated with the constraints and $\gamma = [\gamma^{(1)}, \gamma^{(2)}, \ldots, \gamma^{(K)}]^T$ is the vector of the constraint thresholds and

$$L(Z, \mu) = \bar{c}(Z) + \sum_{k=1}^{K} \mu_k (e^{(k)}(Z) - \gamma^{(k)})$$

$$= \sum_{i=1}^{I} \sum_{j=1}^{N} \left(c_{i,j} + \sum_{k=1}^{K} \mu_k \alpha_{i,j}^{(k)} \right) P_j P(D_i/w_j) - \sum_{k=1}^{K} \mu_k \gamma^{(k)} \tag{4}$$

2.2 Theoretical optimal decision rule

According to Grall-Maës & Beauseroy (2009) the optimal objective values of the primal and dual problems are equal. Thus, solving the dual problem provides the optimal decision rule. The Lagrangian $L(Z, \mu)$ can be rewritten as:

$$L(Z, \mu) = \sum_{i=1}^{I} \int_{\{x|Z(x)=i\}} \lambda_i(x, \mu) dx - \mu^T \gamma \tag{5}$$

where $\lambda_i(x, \mu)$ is given by:

$$\lambda_i(x, \mu) = \sum_{j=1}^{N} P_j P(x/w_j) \left(c_{i,j} + \mu^T \alpha_{i,j} \right)$$

with $\alpha_{i,j} = [\alpha_{i,j}^{(1)}, \alpha_{i,j}^{(2)}, \ldots, \alpha_{i,j}^{(K)}]^T$. For a given μ the minimum value of $L(Z, \mu)$ is obtained when the integrated expression is minimum, that is by choosing the decision rule $\tilde{Z}_\mu$ so that:

$$\tilde{Z}_\mu(x) = i \quad \text{if} \quad \lambda_i(x, \mu) < \lambda_l(x, \mu), \quad \forall i = 1, \ldots, I, \quad l = 1, \ldots, I, \quad l \neq i. \tag{6}$$

The solution of the dual problem (3), which defines the optimal decision rule Z^* is obtained with μ^* that maximizes $L(\widetilde{Z}_\mu, \mu)$ as follows:

$$Z^* = \widetilde{Z}_{\mu^*} \quad \text{with} \quad \mu^* \quad \text{given by} \quad \mu^* = arg \max_{\mu \in \Re^{K+}} L(\widetilde{Z}_\mu, \mu)$$

Note that the same decision rule could be obtained by minimizing a modified loss function:

$$c_{modif}(Z) = \bar{c}(Z) + \sum_{k=1}^{K} \mu_k^*(e^{(k)}(Z) - \gamma^{(k)}) = L(Z, \mu^*) \tag{7}$$

If μ^* is known, the optimal rule Z^* is obtained by minimizing $\bar{c}(Z) + \sum_{k=1}^{K} \mu_k^* e^{(k)}(Z)$.
A particular case of the stated rule can be given by the non constrained rule for which decision options are given by the admissible classes and the loss function is defined by the probability of error. We will refer to this case as the classical case.
In the supervised learning framework, P_j and $P(D_i/w_j)$ are unknown, the process is described by a training sample set. To tackle the decision problem in that case, two approaches are developed and tested in the following: one is based on density estimation and the other based on boundary methods. For each of the two approaches, different models can be designed. In the following, we will present and discuss some of these methods and their characteristics.

3. Class-modeling approach

The most straightforward method to obtain a multiclass rule is to estimate the density of the training data and exploit them within the decision theory framework to provide a classification rule. We will refer to this approach as class-modeling approach. It exploits flexible classes of models which attempt to provide an estimate of the joint distribution of the features within each class. The decision rule is determined by plugging these estimations in the statistical hypothesis framework and solving the latter optimization problem (3). Many estimators may be used Bishop (2006).
In this section we consider that the data is described by a set of observations $\{x_1, \ldots, x_n\}$ drawn from a given class w. Two estimators, the non-parametric Parzen Windows estimator PW Emanuel (1962) and the parametric Gaussian Mixture Models GMM Titterington et al. (1985) are investigated. Simulations on artificial datasets were carried out to study the efficiency of the proposed method and discuss its sensibility to estimator choice. In the coming subsections PW and GMM estimators will be presented, followed by the description of the supervised learning method. Then two different data sets are introduced. They show very specific features in order to illustrate the advantages and disadvantages of the proposed methods.

3.1 Parzen Windows estimator
Let us suppose that n observations are being drawn from some unknown probability density $P(x)$ in some d-dimensional space, which we shall take to be Euclidean, and we wish to estimate the value of $P(x)$. Suppose that, for some particular applications, no specific hypothesis about the probability law can be made. In this case, a non-parametric density estimator should be used. Kernels or Parzen Windows estimator (PW) Emanuel (1962) is exploited in this study. It contains parameters that control the model complexity rather than the form of the distribution. Thus the density model is obtained by placing kernels over each data point and adding up the contributions over the whole dataset. Most often, Gaussian kernels are

chosen with a mean m centered on the individual training objects ($m = x_p$) and diagonal covariance matrices $S = hI$, where h is the smoothness parameter of the windows width. This choice gives rise to the following density model:

$$\widehat{P}(x;h) = \frac{1}{n} \sum_{p=1}^{n} G(x;x_p,hI) \tag{8}$$

where G is a gaussian component given by:

$$G(x;m,S) = \frac{1}{(2\pi)^{\frac{d}{2}} \mid S \mid^{\frac{1}{2}}} \exp[-0.5(x-m)^T S^{-1}(x-m)] \tag{9}$$

in which x is a given pattern, m is the mean and S is the covariance matrix of the kernel. When the covariance matrix S is set equal to hI, the Parzen density estimator assumes equally weighted features. The estimation of the density only depends on one parameter h and on the sample set. Thus, training a Parzen density consists of the determination of a single parameter. The smoothness parameter gives a trade-off between sensitivity to noise at small h and over-smoothing at large h. The optimal width of the kernel h can be obtained by maximizing the likelihood function. Because only one parameter is estimated the data model is easy to learn.

3.2 Gaussian Mixture Models estimator

A mixture of Gaussians is a linear combination of normal distributions Titterington et al. (1985). The GMM are given by:

$$\widehat{P}_T(x;\theta_T) = \sum_{t=1}^{T} \pi_t G(x;m_t,S_t) \tag{10}$$

where $\theta_T = \{m_1,\ldots,m_T,S_1,\ldots,S_t,\pi_1,\ldots,\pi_T\}$ is the vector parameter of the Gaussian components of a given class, T is the number of components per class, $G(x;m_t,S_t)$ is the d-dimensional gaussian density given by equation (9) and π_t is the mixing weight of the t-th component satisfying:

$$\sum_{t=1}^{T} \pi_t = 1 \quad \text{and} \quad \pi_t \geq 0.$$

When the number of Gaussians T is defined beforehand by the user, the means m_t and covariances S_t of the individual Gaussian components can efficiently be estimated by an Expectation Maximization routine Dempster et al. (1977). The total number of free parameters in the mixture of Gaussians is $T(d + \frac{d(d+1)}{2} + 1)$.

When T is not defined a priori, the task is to estimate the parameters π_t, m_t, S_t and the number T of components that maximize the log-likelihood:

$$\mathcal{L}_T(x_1,\ldots,x_n;\theta_T) = \sum_{p=1}^{n} \log \widehat{P}_T(x_p;\theta_T).$$

The log-likelihood maximization can be carried out by the greedy EM algorithm based on the theoretical results of Li & Barron (1999). In this latter, Li and Barron show that the difference in Kullback-Leibler divergence achievable by T-component mixtures and the Kullback-Leibler distance achievable by any (possibly non-finite) mixture from the same family of components tends to zero with the rate c/T with c a constant dependant from the component family. Furthermore, this bound is reachable by employing the greedy procedure. Therefore, the maximum likelihood of the mixture can be determined by adding iteratively a new component to the mixture. In this chapter, the greedy EM Verbeek et al. (2003); Vlassis & Likas (2002) algorithm for learning GMM is used since it is able to find the global likelihood maxima and to estimate the unknown number of the mixture components. This algorithm can be summarized as follows.

- Starting from a 1-component mixture ($T = 1$), the optimal parameters are obtained by an EM procedure until convergence($| \mathcal{L}^{iteration}(x_1,\ldots,x_n;\theta_T) - \mathcal{L}^{iteration-1}(x_1,\ldots,x_n;\theta_T) | \leq \varepsilon$). Then, a search for a new component $G(x;m^*_{T+1},S^*_{T+1})$ location and a corresponding weight π^*_{T+1} is performed in order to maximize the new log-likelihood:

$$\mathcal{L}_{T+1}(x_1,\ldots,x_n;\theta_{T+1}) = \sum_{p=1}^{n} \log \widehat{P}_{T+1}(x_p;\theta_{T+1})$$

$$= \sum_{p=1}^{n} \log[(1 - \pi^*_{T+1})\widehat{P}_T(x_p;\theta_T) + \pi^*_{T+1}G(x_p;m^*_{T+1},S^*_{T+1})]$$

$$(11)$$

  with $\widehat{P}_T(x;\theta_T)$ remaining unchanged. It is obvious that the crucial step of this algorithm is the search of a new component location. It can be shown that $\mathcal{L}_{T+1}(x_1,\ldots,x_n;\theta_{T+1})$ is concave as function of π_{T+1} but can have multiple maxima as function of m^*_{T+1} and S^*_{T+1}. Hence, a global search is required.
  One way pointed in Vlassis & Likas (2002) proposes to use all the points as initial candidates of the sought component. Every point is the mean of a corresponding candidate ($m_{T+1} = x_p$) with the same covariance matrix $\sigma^2 I$, where σ is set according to Weston & Watkins (1999). For each candidate component, π_{T+1} is set to the mixing weight maximizing the second order Taylor approximation of $\mathcal{L}_{T+1}(x_1,\ldots,x_n;\theta_{T+1})$ around $\pi_{T+1} = 0.5$. The candidate yielding to the highest log-likelihood when added to $\widehat{P}_T(x;\theta_T)$ in (11) is selected and updated using EM until convergence. The new component is added to $\widehat{P}_T(x;\theta_T)$ and the research is repeated until reaching the maximum likelihood on a validation set.

- An improved version of this global search Verbeek et al. (2003) is used in this work. For each insertion problem, the proposed method constructs a fixed number of candidates per existing mixture component. Based on the posterior distributions, we partition the data set in T disjoint subsets A_t. For each set, C candidate components are constructed (for the following experiences $C = 10$ candidates). To generate new candidates from A_t, we pick uniformly random two data points x_l and x_r in A_t. Then, we partition A_t into two disjoint subsets A_{tl} and A_{tr}. For elements of A_{tl} the point x_l is closer than x_r and vice versa for A_{tr}. The mean and covariance of the sets A_{tl} and A_{tr} are used as parameters for two candidate components. The initial mixing weights for candidates generated from A_t are set to $\pi_t/2$. To obtain the next two candidates we draw new x_l and x_r, until the desired number of candidates is reached. After computing the log-likelihood of each of the CT candidates, we set the new component as the candidate that maximizes the log-likelihood $\widehat{P}_{T+1}(x;\theta_{T+1})$ when added to the existing mixture with its corresponding mixing weight.

3.3 Supervised decision rule

In the statistical decision theory framework, the determination of a multiclass rule that satisfies performance constraints consists in finding the optimal Z^* and the optimal Lagrange multipliers μ^* by solving the optimization problem defined in (3). However, in the supervised learning framework, P_j and $P(D_i/w_j)$ are unknown. One strategy to learn a supervised classifier is to estimate these probabilities and determine the corresponding optimal supervised rule $\widehat{Z}^*$ and Lagrange multipliers $\widehat{\mu}^*$. In these experiments, we study the repercussion due to the estimation of $P(x/w_j)$ and we consider that P_j is known. The two estimators introduced above are used. The probability estimates depend on the labeled set and on the density estimators parameters, h of Parzen and T, $(m_t, S_t, \pi_t), t = 1, \ldots, T$ of the GMM. These parameters are determined by maximizing the log-likelihood of a validation set using 10-Cross Validation.

Each estimator produces its own optimal solution $\widehat{Z}^*$ and $\widehat{\mu}^*$ which minimizes the corresponding loss function $\widehat{L}(\widehat{Z}^*, \widehat{\mu}^*) = \widehat{\overline{c}}(\widehat{Z}^*) + \sum_{k=1}^{K} \widehat{\mu}_k^* \left(\widehat{e}^{(k)}(\widehat{Z}^*) - \gamma^{(k)} \right)$. To assess the quality of the supervised rules a criterion, proposed in Grall-Maës et al. (2006b) is used. It is given by $L(\widehat{Z}^*, \mu^*) = \overline{c}(\widehat{Z}^*) + \sum_{k=1}^{K} \mu_k^* \left(e^{(k)}(\widehat{Z}^*) - \gamma^{(k)} \right)$. It has to be estimated on the true optimal lagrange multipliers μ^* and an infinite test set (theoretical densities) in order to get the theoretical performance of the rule. The learning-testing procedures of the GMM and Parzen Windows estimator algorithm are as follow:

1. For each class w_j, estimating the GMM or the Parzen Windows distributions $\widehat{P}(x/w_j)$ using a training set and a validation set.

2. Learning the decision rule by solving the optimization problem (3) with the estimated $\widehat{P}(x/w_j)$, namely, finding the optimal supervised rule $\widehat{Z}^*$ and the optimal $\widehat{\mu}^*$.

3. Assessing the quality of the rule by computing the Lagrangian $\widehat{L}(\widehat{Z}^*, \mu)^*$ of the supervised rule $\widehat{Z}^*$ on an infinite test set using theoretical μ^*.

In a supervised framework, μ^* and the infinite test set are unknown. A supervised procedure to compute this criterion was proposed in Jrad, Grall & Beauseroy (2008) and tested experimentally to show the validity and the relevance of this criterion.

To sum up, we frame the problem of classification with rejection option subject to constraints as a Bayesian inference problem. We formulate a model of how patterns are generated and then derive an algorithm for making optimal inferences under this model.

3.4 Toy problem

To evaluate the performances of the proposed supervised learning approaches, two 2-D problems with three equiprobable classes and performance constraints were considered. For both problems, GMM and PW estimators were used and compared. Synthetic data were constructed and used to investigate different characteristics of the methods. By using artificial data instead of real world data, we avoid focusing on unknown and unsuspected distributions. It gives the opportunity to just focus on some important aspects of data distributions. Experimental results are presented and discussed below.

The first problem is defined by three classes, each one is a 3-gaussian component distribution with unbalanced weights, leading to a trimodal distribution. The aim of this experiment is to study the case where the distributions correspond to the hypothesis of GMM. The second problem is given by three bivariate gamma distributions in order to study the case where

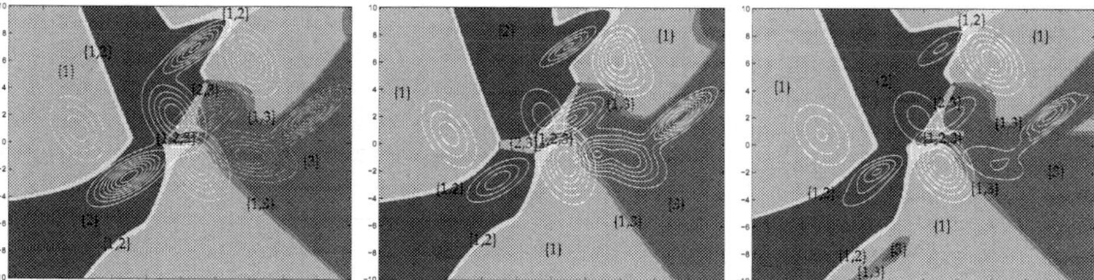

Fig. 1. 3-gaussian component problem: density probabilities and the corresponding partition. From left to right: Theoretical case (left) and an example of estimators in the case of Parzen (middle) and GMM (right)

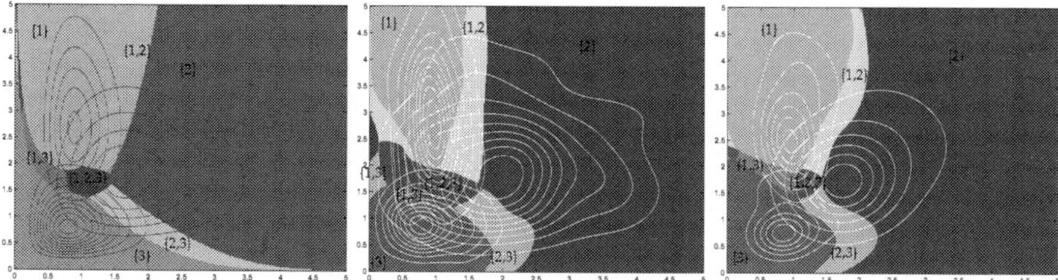

Fig. 2. Bivariate gamma problem: density probabilities and the corresponding partition. From left to right: Theoretical case (left) and an example of estimators in the case of Parzen (middle) and GMM (right)

the hypothesis of GMM is not fulfilled by data distributions. The corresponding theoretical densities are represented using isodensity curves in figures 1 (left) and 2 (left).

For both problems, the decision options are given by: $\psi_1 = \{1\}$, $\psi_2 = \{2\}$, $\psi_3 = \{3\}$, $\psi_4 = \{1,2\}$, $\psi_5 = \{1;3\}$, $\psi_6 = \{2;3\}$ and $\psi_7 = \{1;2;3\}$. The constraints are defined by $P_E \leq 0.05$ and $P_I \leq 0.1$ for the first problem and $P_E \leq 0.1$ and $P_I \leq 0.15$ for the second one. P_E is the probability of error and P_I is the probability of indistinctness, namely, the probability to assign a pattern x of w_j to a subset of classes ψ_i that contains more than one class of which one is w_j. The average loss is defined by $\bar{c}(Z) = P_E + 0.5P_I + P(D_7)$ where $P(D_7)$ corresponds to no decision. Theoretical decision rules are given by the partitions reported in figures 1 (left) and 2 (left).

For both experiments, the influence of the sample size is investigated by proceeding the learning-testing algorithm described above for three sets with different sizes (50, 100 and 200 observations per class). These sets were randomly drawn from the theoretical distributions. Experiments were repeated 40 times for the first set, 20 times for the second and 10 times for the third in order to study the bias and the variance of the results.

3.5 Experimental results and discussions

For both problems, P_E, P_I, $\bar{c}(Z^*)$ and $L(Z^*, \mu^*)$ were computed for the optimal rule. Besides, their estimated values $\widehat{P}_E$, $\widehat{P}_I$, $\widehat{\bar{c}}(\widehat{Z}^*)$ and $\widehat{L}(\widehat{Z}^*, \mu^*)$ were computed on supervised partitions using an infinite test set and the theoretical μ^* as mentioned previously. Their mean and

	GMM			Parzen			Theo.
	50 obs	100 obs	200 obs	50 obs	100 obs	200 obs	
$\widehat{P}_E$	0.084 ± 0.023	0.060 ± 0.011	0.053 ± 0.006	0.033 ± 0.015	0.034 ± 0.010	0.030 ± 0.008	0.050
$\widehat{P}_I$	0.082 ± 0.027	0.094 ± 0.016	0.098 ± 0.006	0.090 ± 0.011	0.087 ± 0.008	0.085 ± 0.006	0.100
$\widehat{\overline{c}}$	0.161 ± 0.040	0.133 ± 0.017	0.136 ± 0.018	0.248 ± 0.039	0.212 ± 0.028	0.207 ± 0.029	0.131
$\widehat{L}$	0.205 ± 0.033	0.147 ± 0.012	0.140 ± 0.011	0.224 ± 0.024	0.189 ± 0.015	0.177 ± 0.017	0.132

Table 1. Values of the theoretical and estimated $\widehat{P}_E$, $\widehat{P}_I$, $\widehat{\overline{c}}(\widehat{Z}^*)$ and $\widehat{L}(\widehat{Z}^*,\mu^*)$ using GMM and Parzen estimators for the 3-gaussian component problem

	GMM			Parzen			Theo.
	50 obs	100 obs	200 obs	50 obs	100 obs	200 obs	
$\widehat{P}_E$	0.114 ± 0.021	0.110 ± 0.010	0.109 ± 0.008	0.083 ± 0.028	0.079 ± 0.018	0.086 ± 0.010	0.100
$\widehat{P}_I$	0.143 ± 0.023	0.143 ± 0.011	0.143 ± 0.012	0.147 ± 0.019	0.148 ± 0.012	0.147 ± 0.010	0.150
$\widehat{\overline{c}}$	0.235 ± 0.022	0.239 ± 0.012	0.234 ± 0.009	0.304 ± 0.044	0.290 ± 0.030	0.268 ± 0.016	0.229
$\widehat{L}$	0.251 ± 0.021	0.249 ± 0.008	0.247 ± 0.006	0.280 ± 0.025	0.260 ± 0.010	0.248 ± 0.003	0.229

Table 2. Values of the theoretical and estimated $\widehat{P}_E$, $\widehat{P}_I$, $\widehat{\overline{c}}(\widehat{Z}^*)$ and $\widehat{L}(\widehat{Z}^*,\mu^*)$ using GMM and Parzen estimators for the gamma distributions problem

their standard deviations are reported in tables 1 and 2. An example of optimal rules built with GMM and Parzen densities using 200 observations per class set are shown in figures 1 (middle) and 1 (right) (for the 3-gaussian component distributions problem) and 2 (middle) and 2 (right) (for the gamma distributions problem).

Results show that decision rules built with GMM and Parzen estimates are relevant. Their accuracy increases as long as the learning set size increases. Furthermore, GMM can be considered as a good family of non-symmetrical density estimators. They achieve results superior to Parzen estimators in term of losses, especially when the learning set size decreases. These results can be explained by several reasons:

    i Parzen estimators converge asymptotically to the real densities.

    ii Parzen density estimates have not a compact form; they are sums of as many local windows as the size of learning set, while the GMM estimates are compact functions parameterized according to a global search over all the learning set. Thus, the local nature of the Parzen estimator can lead to overfitting.

Moreover, for the first problem, the errors, as the function of the number of observations, of the GMM decrease faster than those of Parzen. It is an expected result since the distributions corresponds to the GMM hypothesis and GMM are more accurate fitting a multimodal distribution. Thus the choice of the estimator is a crucial point for class-modeling approaches. The estimator must fit the data pretty well to get good results. The performances of the classification rule are strictly related to those of the density estimator.

To sum up, we can note that when the sample size is sufficiently large and a flexible density model is used, this approach should work very well if the probability density estimator in use is convergent. Unfortunately, as the dimension of the representation space increases, it requires an exponentially increasing number of training samples to overcome the curse of dimensionality Duda & Hart (1973). Finding the right estimator to describe the dataset distribution and the given sample size is a typical incarnation of the bias-variance dilemma.

When a good probability model is assumed (one for which the bias is small) and the sample size is sufficient, this approach has some advantages. Since probability estimates of the patterns are computed explicitly, integration with other potential classes or constraints, not necessarily considered at design time, is facilitated. Besides, progress towards more complicated applications like solving classification problems with time-evolutionary constraints Jrad et al. (2009a) can be also facilitated.

4. Boundary approach

Vapnik argued in Vapnik (1998) that when just a limited amount of data is available, one should avoid solving a more general problem as an intermediate step to solve the original problem. To solve this more general problem more data might be required than for the original problem. In a bayesian framework minimizing the error rate loss, estimating a complete data density for each of the N classes might be too demanding when only the data boundary is required. Therefore, only a boundary between or around the dataset is determined. In the general framework of classe-selective rejection with constraints, a complete data density estimation is also not required. However, one should take into consideration the conditional probabilities estimation in order to evaluate the performance.

In this work, ν-1-SVM will be used. The proposed method is based on the "decomposition-reconstruction" approach. It decomposes the initial problem into N problems and trains one ν-1-SVM Scholkopf et al. (2001); Scholkopf & Smola (2001); Tax (2001) coupled with the regularization path of each class Hastie et al. (2004); Rakotomamonjy & Davy (2007). A reconstruction step is required to decide the winning decision and consequently to derive a decision rule that satisfy the constraints. It uses weighted distance measure between objects and classes.

In the coming subsections we will present the ν-1-SVM concept and explains briefly the derivation of the entire regularization path which enables to get rapidly all ν-1-SVM models for a wide range of values of ν. The proposed method is described and validated on two artificial datasets.

4.1 ν-1-SVM

Considering a set of n vectors $X = \{x_1, x_2, \ldots, x_n\}$ drawn from an input space $\mathcal{X}$, ν-1-SVM computes a function $f_X^\lambda(.)$ and a real number b^λ in order to determine the region $\mathcal{R}^\lambda$ in $\mathcal{X}$ such that:

$$\begin{cases} f_X^\lambda(x) - b^\lambda \geq 0 & \text{if } x \in \mathcal{R}^\lambda \\ f_X^\lambda(x) - b^\lambda < 0 & \text{otherwise} \end{cases}$$

The function $f_X^\lambda(.)$ is designed by minimizing the volume of $\mathcal{R}^\lambda$ under the constraint that all the vectors of X, except a portion λ, must lie in $\mathcal{R}^\lambda$. This portion corresponds to the outliers and parameterizes the function $f_X^\lambda(.)$. An alternative parameter can be refereed to $\nu = \frac{\lambda}{n}$. It corresponds to the fraction of outliers with $0 \leq \nu \leq 1$.

In order to determine $\mathcal{R}^\lambda$, the space of possible functions $f_X^\lambda(.)$ is reduced to a Reproducing Kernel Hilbert Space (RKHS) with kernel function $K(.,.)$. Let $\phi : \mathcal{X} \rightarrow \mathcal{H}$ be the mapping defined over the input space $\mathcal{X}$. Let $< .,. >_{\mathcal{H}}$ be a dot product defined in $\mathcal{H}$. The kernel $K(.,.)$ over $\mathcal{X} \times \mathcal{X}$ is defined by:

$$\forall (x_p, x_q) \in \mathcal{X} \times \mathcal{X} \quad K(x_p, x_q) = < \phi(x_p), \phi(x_q) >_{\mathcal{H}}$$

Without loss of generality, $K(.,.)$ is supposed normalized such that for any $x \in \mathcal{X}$, $K(x,x) = 1$. Thus, all the mapped vectors $\phi(x_p)$, $p = 1, \ldots, n$ are in a subset of a hypersphere with radius

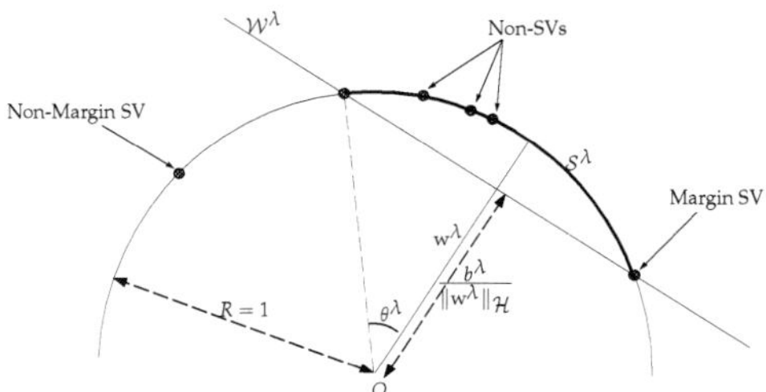

Fig. 3. Training data mapped into the feature space on a portion $\mathcal{S}^\lambda$ of a hypersphere.

one and center O. Provided $K(.,.)$ is always positive, $\phi(X)$ is a subset of the positive orthant of the hypersphere. A common choice of $K(.,.)$ is the Gaussian Radial Basis Function (RBF) kernel $K(x_p, x_q) = \exp[\frac{-1}{2\sigma^2} \parallel x_p - x_q \parallel^2_{\mathcal{X}}]$ with σ the parameter of the Gaussian RBF kernel. ν-1-SVM consists of separating the training vectors in $\mathcal{H}$ from the center O with a hyperplane $\mathcal{W}^\lambda$ while maximizing the margin $\frac{b^\lambda}{\|w^\lambda\|_{\mathcal{H}}}$ with w^λ the normal vector of $\mathcal{W}^\lambda$. The solution will be given by the function $f^\lambda_X(.)$ such that $f^\lambda_X(x) - b^\lambda = < w^\lambda, \phi(x) >_{\mathcal{H}} -b^\lambda \geq 0$ for the $(1-\nu)n$ mapped training vectors.

This yields $f^\lambda_X(.)$ as the solution of the following convex quadratic optimization problem:

$$\min_{w^\lambda, b^\lambda, \xi_p} \sum_{p=1}^{n} \xi_p - \lambda b^\lambda + \frac{\lambda}{2} \parallel w^\lambda \parallel^2_{\mathcal{H}}$$

$$\text{subject to} \quad < w^\lambda, \phi(x_p) >_{\mathcal{H}} \geq b^\lambda - \xi_p$$

$$\text{and} \quad \xi_p \geq 0 \quad \forall p = 1, \dots, n \tag{12}$$

where ξ_p are the slack variables. This optimization problem is solved by introducing Lagrange multipliers α_p. As a consequence to Kuhn-Tucker conditions, w^λ is given by:

$$w^\lambda = \frac{1}{\lambda} \sum_{p=1}^{n} \alpha_p \phi(x_p)$$

which results in:

$$f^\lambda_X(.) - b^\lambda = \frac{1}{\lambda} \sum_{p=1}^{n} \alpha_p K(x_p, .) - b^\lambda.$$

The dual formulation of (12) is obtained by introducing Lagrange multipliers as:

$$\min_{\alpha_1, \dots, \alpha_n} \frac{1}{2\lambda} \sum_{p=1}^{n} \sum_{q=1}^{n} \alpha_p^\lambda \alpha_q^\lambda K(x_p, x_q) \tag{13}$$

$$\text{with} \quad \sum_{p=1}^{n} \alpha_p^\lambda = \lambda \quad \text{and} \quad 0 \leq \alpha_p^\lambda \leq 1 \quad \forall p = 1, \dots, n$$

A geometrical interpretation of the solution in the RKHS is given by figure 3. The function $f^\lambda_X(.)$ and the number b^λ define a hyperplane $\mathcal{W}^\lambda$ orthogonal to w^λ. The hyperplane $\mathcal{W}^\lambda$

separates the $\phi(x_p)$s from the sphere center, while having $\frac{b^\lambda}{\|w^\lambda\|_\mathcal{H}}$ maximum which is equivalent to minimize the portion $\mathcal{S}^\lambda$ of the hypersphere bounded by $\mathcal{W}^\lambda$ that contains the set $\{\phi(x) \quad \text{s.t.} \quad x \in \mathcal{R}^\lambda\}$.

4.2 Regularization Path

Regularization path was first introduced by Hastie et al. (2004) for a binary SVM. Later, Rakotomamonjy & Davy (2007) developed the entire regularization path for a ν-1-SVM. The basic idea of the ν-1-SVM regularization path is that the Lagrange multipliers of a ν-1-SVM is a piecewise linear function of λ. Thus the principle of the method is to start with large λ (ie. $\lambda = n - \epsilon$) and decrease it towards zero, keeping track of breaks that occur as λ varies.

As λ decreases $\| w^\lambda \|_\mathcal{H}$ increases and hence the distance between the sphere center and $\mathcal{W}^\lambda$ decreases. Points move from being outside (Non-Margin SVs with $\alpha_p^\lambda = 1$ in figure 3) to inside the portion $\mathcal{S}^\lambda$ (Non-SVs with $\alpha_p^\lambda = 0$). By continuity, points must linger on the hyperplane $\mathcal{W}^\lambda$ (Margin SVs with $0 < \alpha_p^\lambda < 1$) while their α_p^λs decrease from 1 to 0. Break points occur when a point moves from a position to another one. Since α_p^λ is piecewise-linear in λ, $f^\lambda(.)$ and b^λ are also piecewise-linear in λ. Thus, after initializing the regularization path (computing α_p^λ by solving (13) for $\lambda = n - \epsilon$), almost all the α_p^λs are computed by solving linear systems. Only for some few integer values of λ smaller than n, α_p^λs are computed by solving (13) according to Rakotomamonjy & Davy (2007).

Using simple linear interpolation, this algorithm enables to determine very rapidly the ν-1-SVM corresponding to any value of λ.

4.3 Supervised decision rule

Given N classes and N trained ν-1-SVMs, one should design a supervised decision rule Z that minimizes the loss function (2) and satisfies the constraints (1). The reconstruction step consists of moving from unary to multiclass classifier by assigning samples to a decision option. The assignment condition (6) can not be used since the distributions $P(x/w_j)$ are unknown. The reconstruction step relies on a distance of an unlabelled pattern x to each of the training class set w_j $(j = 1, \ldots, N)$, using the ν-1-SVM parameterized by λ_j, is defined as follows:

$$d^{\lambda_j}(x) = \frac{\cos(\widehat{w^{\lambda_j}, \phi(x)})}{\cos(\theta^{\lambda_j})} = \frac{\| w^{\lambda_j} \|_\mathcal{H}}{b^{\lambda_j}} \cos(\widehat{w^{\lambda_j}, \phi(x)}) \tag{14}$$

where θ^{λ_j} is the angle delimited by w^{λ_j} and the support vector as shown in figure 3, $\cos(\theta^{\lambda_j})$ is a normalizing factor which is used to normalize all the $d_j^\lambda(x)$.

Using $\| \phi(x) \| = 1$ in (14) leads to the following:

$$d^{\lambda_j}(x) = \frac{< w^{\lambda_j}, \phi(x) >_\mathcal{H}}{b^{\lambda_j}} = \frac{\frac{1}{\lambda_j} \sum_{p=1}^{n_j} \alpha_p^{\lambda_j} K(x_p, x)}{b^{\lambda_j}} \tag{15}$$

Since the lagrange multipliers $\alpha_p^{\lambda_j}$ are obtained by the regularization path for any value of λ_j, computing d^{λ_j} is considered as an easy-fast task. The distance measure $d^{\lambda_j}(x)$ is inspired from Davy et al. (2006). When data are distributed in a unimodal form, the $d^{\lambda_j}(x)$ is a decreasing function with respect to the distance between a sample x and the data mean. The probability density function is also a decreasing function with respect to the distance from the mean. Thus, $d^{\lambda_j}(x)$ preserves distribution order relations. In such case, and under optimality of the v-1-SVM classifier, the use of $d^{\lambda_j}(x)$ should reach the same performances as the one obtained using the distribution.

In the simplest case of multiclass problems where the loss function is defined as the error probability, a sample x is assigned to the class maximizing $d^{\lambda_j}(x)$ as follows:

$$x \in \arg\max_{j=1\dots N} \ d^{\lambda_j}(x).$$

To extend the multiclass prediction process to the class-selective scheme, a weighted form of the distance measure is proposed. A weight β_j is associated to the distance d^{λ_j} to pull the location of a pattern toward the class for which a wrong decision costs the most. Thus, introducing weights performs a distance adjustment and helps solving problems with different costs c_{ij} on the classification decisions. The decision rule is defined as:

$$\widehat{Z}(x) = i \quad \text{if} \quad \sum_{j=1}^{N} c_{ij}\widehat{P}_j\beta_j d^{\lambda_j}(x) \leq \sum_{j=1}^{N} c_{lj}\widehat{P}_j\beta_j d^{\lambda_j}(x), \forall i,l = 1,\dots,I, l \neq i.$$

where $\widehat{P}_j$ is the empirical estimators of P_j.

The decision rule depends on the RBF vector parameter $\boldsymbol{\sigma}$, $\boldsymbol{\lambda}$ and $\boldsymbol{\beta}$ vectors of σ_j, λ_j and β_j for $j = 1,\dots,N$. Tuning λ_j is the most time expensive task since changing λ_j leads to solve the optimization problem formulated in (13). Moreover, tuning λ_j is a crucial point, it enables to control the boundary around data. In fact, it was shown in Scholkopf et al. (2001) that this regularization parameter is an upper bound on the fraction of outliers and a lower bound on the fraction of the SVs. In Husband & Lin (2002); Yang et al. (2007) a smooth grid search was supplied in order to choose the optimal values of $\boldsymbol{\lambda}$. The N values λ_js were chosen equal to reduce the computational costs. However, this assumption reduces the search space of parameters too. To avoid this restriction, the proposed approach optimizes all the λ_j with $j = 1,\dots,N$ corresponding to the N v-1-SVMs using regularization path and consequently explores the entire parameters space. Thus the tuned λ_j are most likely to be the optimal ones. The parameter $\boldsymbol{\sigma}$ are set equals $\sigma_1 = \sigma_2 = \dots = \sigma_N$.

In the general framework of class-selective rejection subject to constraints, the decision rule for a given $\boldsymbol{\mu}$ is given by:

$$\widehat{\widehat{Z}}_\mu(x) = i \quad \text{if} \tag{16}$$

$$\sum_{j=1}^{N} \left(c_{i,j} + \sum_{k=1}^{K} \mu_k \alpha_{i,j}^{(k)} \right) \widehat{P}_j\beta_j d^{\lambda_j}(x) \leq \sum_{j=1}^{N} \left(c_{l,j} + \sum_{k=1}^{K} \mu_k \alpha_{l,j}^{(k)} \right) \widehat{P}_j\beta_j d^{\lambda_j}(x), \forall i,l = 1,\dots,I, l \neq i.$$

Since the problem is described by a sample set, an estimate $\widehat{L}(\widehat{Z},\widehat{\mu})$ of $L(Z,\mu)$ given by (1) is used:

$$\widehat{L}(\widehat{Z},\widehat{\mu}) = \sum_{i=1}^{I} \sum_{j=1}^{N} \left(c_{i,j} + \sum_{k=1}^{K} \widehat{\mu}_k \alpha_{i,j}^{(k)} \right) \widehat{P}_j \widehat{P}(D_i/w_j) - \widehat{\mu}^T \gamma \tag{17}$$

where $\widehat{P}(D_i/w_j)$ is the empirical estimators of $P(D_i/w_j)$.

The parameters λ_j, β_j, σ_j and μ_k are optimized so that the estimated Lagrange function $\widehat{L}(\widehat{Z},\widehat{\mu})$ is optimum on a validation set. This is accomplished by employing an iterative search over

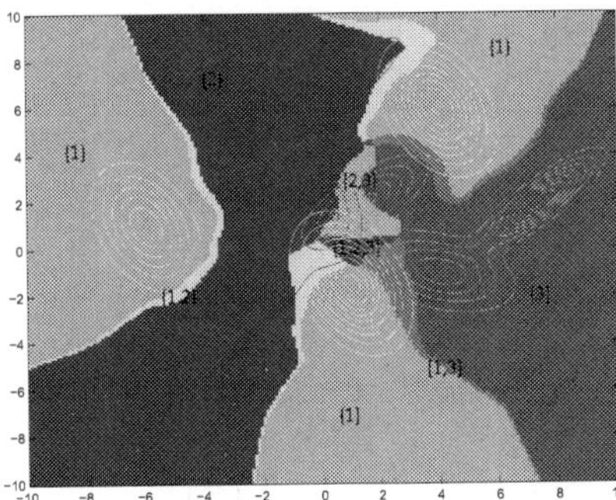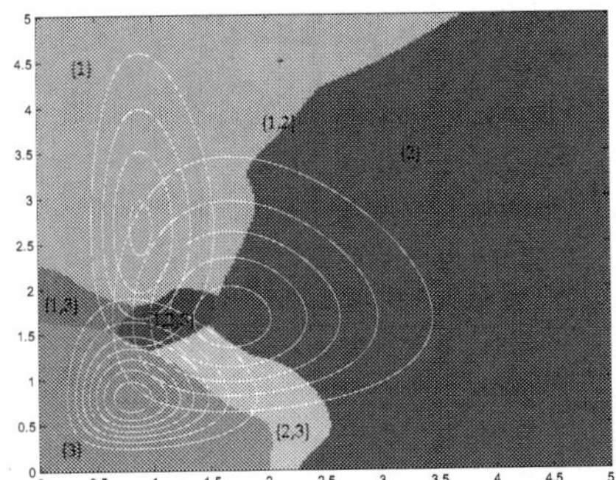

Fig. 4. 3-gaussian component (left) and Bivariate gamma (right) problems: supervised partitions and theoretical density probabilities.

	3-gaussian			Gamma		
	50 obs	100 obs	200 obs	50 obs	100 obs	200 obs
$\widehat{P}_E$	0.076±0.013	0.061±0.008	0.050±0.005	0.101±0.012	0.094±0.014	0.088±0.005
$\widehat{P}_I$	0.138±0.005	0.121±0.002	0.107±0.001	0.176±0.027	0.179±0.033	0.173±0.013
$\widehat{\overline{c}}$	0.163±0.017	0.153±0.008	0.149±0.004	0.267±0.020	0.262±0.018	0.258±0.011
$\widehat{L}$	0.206±0.028	0.165±0.010	0.151±0.006	0.275±0.015	0.271±0.032	0.247±0.006

Table 3. Values of the estimated $\widehat{P}_E$, $\widehat{P}_I$, $\widehat{\overline{c}}(\widehat{Z}^*)$ and $\widehat{L}(\widehat{Z}^*,\mu^*)$ using the boundary method for the 3-gaussian component and the gamma distributions problems

the kernel parameter and a global search over the other ones. More explicitly, the kernel parameters are chosen from a previously defined set of real numbers $[\sigma_0,\ldots,\sigma_s]$ with $s \in \mathbb{N}$. For each given value of σ_j, a decision rule is sought by solving an alternate optimization problem over λ_j, β_j and μ_k. The optimal rule is given by the set of parameters minimizing the Lagrange estimate on a validation set.

4.4 Toy problem

To evaluate the efficiency of the proposed boundary approach and compare it with the class-modeling one, the same bidimensional toy problems considered in section 3 were studied under the same constraints. The same synthetic data with the same number of repetitions were considered. Thus theoretical densities and theoretical decision rules are those illustrated in figures 1 (left) and 2 (left). The theoretical performances are those reported on tables 1 and 2.

Supervised decision rule is optimized according to the supervised learning algorithm defined in the boundary scheme. The estimated values $\widehat{P}_E$, $\widehat{P}_I$, $\widehat{\overline{c}}(\widehat{Z}^*)$ and $\widehat{L}(\widehat{Z}^*,\mu^*)$ were computed on supervised partitions using an infinite test set and the theoretical μ^* as mentioned previously. Their mean and their standard deviations are reported in tables 3. An example of optimal rules learned with 200 observations per class set are shown in figures 4 (left) for the 3-gaussian distribution problem and 4 (right) for the gamma distribution problem.

Experimental results show that the proposed boundary method or MSVM is relevant. It achieves good results on some complex distributions like multimodal and non-symmetrical

Dataset	LEUKEMIA72	OVARIAN	NCI	LUNG CANCER	LYMPHOMA
# Gene	6817	7129	9703	918	4026
# Sample	72	39	60	73	96
# Class	3	3	9	7	9

Table 4. Multiclass gene expression datasets

distributions. For both problems under study, standard deviations are relatively small. The boundary approach is less sensitive to the variation of the dataset representativity. For the 3-gaussian component problem, MSVM performs as good as the GMM based method and better than PW based method. For the gamma distribution problem, MSVM, PW and GMM based methods show similar accuracy for sufficiency large data sets, while GMM based method outperforms PW and MSVM in term of losses for moderated or small amount of data.

5. Cancer diagnosis

To illustrate the proposed approach a biomedical application dealing with cancer tumors is presented using the boundary method. Recently, cancer diagnosis based on gene profiles has received more attention. Since cancer diagnosis problems are usually described by a small set of samples with a large number of genes, feature or gene selection was considered as an important issue in analyzing multiclass microarray data.

In this section, five well-known gene expression datasets are considered. Two experiments based on the boundary approach are presented. The first considers the five cancer diagnosis problems in the classical framework to make results comparable with those of Chen et al. (2005). The second experiment considers the LUNG CANCER problem in the general framework of class-selective rejection and performance constraints.

5.1 Problem description

In this chapter, five multiclass gene expression datasets are studied: LEUKEMIA72 Golub et al. (1999), OVARIAN Welsh et al. (2001), NCI Ross et al. (2000); Scherf et al. (2000), LUNG CANCER Garber et al. (2001) and LYMPHOMA Alizadeh et al. (2000). Table 4 describes the five genes datasets.

Given these microarray datas with N tumor classes, a small amount n of tumor samples and a large number g of genes per sample, one should identify a small subset of d informative genes that contribute most to the prediction task before solving this task. Various feature selection methods exist in literature. One way pointed in Chen et al. (2005) is to use test statistics.

For each dataset, six test statistics are evoked as a first process in a gene-based cancer diagnosis: ANOVA F or F Kutner et al. (2005), Brown-Forsythe test or B Brown & Forsythe (1974), Welch test WELCH (1951) or W, Adjusted Welch test or W^* Hartung & Makambi (2002), Cochran test Cochran (1937) or C and Kruskal-Wallis test or H Daniel (1999). For each test statistics, 50 and 100 informative genes were selected.

The second step is a classification step which is performed, in the classical framework, according to the proposed boundary approach and five existing ones: Naive Bayes, Nearest Neighbor, Linear Perceptron, Multilayer Perceptron Neural Network. The classification step is also studied in the general framework of class-selective rejection and performance constraints according to the proposed boundary approach.

		F	B	W	W*	C	H
LEUKEMIA	Proposed Algorithm	4	3	5	5	3	2
	Mean	3.4	2.4	2.8	2.8	3.2	3.0
	Median	3	2	3	3	3	3
OVARIAN	Proposed Algorithm	0	0	0	0	0	0
	Mean	0.2	0.0	0.0	0.0	0.0	0.0
	Median	0	0	0	0	0	0
NCI	Proposed Algorithm	31	26	27	27	27	33
	Mean	36.0	32.0	27.4	26.0	27.0	35.4
	Median	35	29	27	27	27	35
LUNG CANCER	Proposed Algorithm	14	16	16	16	16	15
	Mean	17.6	17.0	17.6	17.6	18.0	18.0
	Median	17	17	18	18	18	18
LYMPHOMA	Proposed Algorithm	18	16	9	10	9	15
	Mean	23.8	19.8	14.0	14.0	12.8	22.0
	Median	23	19	12	12	13	20

Table 5. Prediction errors of the proposed classifier, mean and median values of the 5 classifiers prediction errors according to Chen et al. (2005) with 50 informative selected genes

5.2 Experimental settings

The cancer diagnosis is accomplished using the classification algorithm introduced in section 4 in both classical and class-selective rejection subject to constraints frameworks. Results are reported in the following sections as a prediction error. Mean and median values of the prediction errors of the five classifiers mentioned above are also reported from Chen et al. (2005). The generalization accuracy of all the classifiers was computed using Leave One Out (LOO) resampling method. LOO divides a gene dataset of n patients into two sets, a set of $n - 1$ patients and a test set of 1 blinded patient. This method involves n separate runs. For each run, the first set of $n - 1$ are used to learn the rule and the test set of 1 blinded sample is used to assess the performance of the rule. The overall prediction error is the sum of the patients misclassified on all n runs. In the following, results are explored and discussed.

5.2.1 Classical framework

First, the cancer diagnosis problem is considered in the traditional Bayesian framework with no constraints. The decisions are given by the possible set of tumor classes and the loss function is defined as the probability of error to make results comparable with those of Chen et al. (2005). In this case, the costs of misclassification $c_{i,j}$ are known, equal and there is no penalty for a correct classification. The decision rule becomes the solution of a minimization problem without constraints (Lagrange multipliers are null). The performance of the proposed method was measured by evaluating its accuracy rate and it was compared to results obtained by the five predictors evoked in Chen et al. (2005): Naive Bayes, Nearest Neighbor, Linear Perceptron, Multilayer Perceptron Neural Network with five nodes in the middle layer, and Support Vector Machines with second order polynomial kernel.

The learning step of the proposed approach consists of finding the minimal value of the loss function estimate. The $n - 1$ samples are divided, using 5-Cross Validation (5-CV), into a

		F	B	W	W*	C	H
LEUKEMIA	Proposed Algorithm	5	2	3	3	4	6
	Mean	3.4	3.0	3.0	3.0	3.2	3.0
	Median	3	3	4	3	3	3
OVARIAN	Proposed Algorithm	0	0	0	0	0	0
	Mean	0.2	0.0	0.0	0.0	0.0	0.0
	Median	0	0	0	0	0	0
NCI	Proposed Algorithm	33	21	26	25	26	36
	Mean	33.0	22.6	23.8	25.2	25.2	31.6
	Median	33	22	25	26	26	31
LUNG CANCER	Proposed Algorithm	11	10	11	11	11	13
	Mean	12.2	12.2	11.4	12.2	12.2	15.8
	Median	12	12	11	11	11	14
LYMPHOMA	Proposed Algorithm	16	16	11	10	11	17
	Mean	21.8	19.2	13.0	13.8	14.4	18.2
	Median	17	16	12	12	12	18

Table 6. Prediction errors of the proposed classifier, mean and median values of the 5 classifiers prediction errors according to Chen et al. (2005) with 100 informative selected genes

training set and a validation set. N ν-1-SVMs are trained using the training set for all values of ν_j. The decision is obtained by tuning the parameters β_j and λ_j for $j = 1, \ldots, N$ for a given kernel parameter σ and by testing different values of σ in the set $[2^{-3}, 2^{-2}, 2^{-1}, 2^0, 2^1, 2^2]$. Finally, the decision rule which minimizes the loss function estimate is selected and used to classify the blinded patient.

Table 5 reports the errors of the proposed algorithm, the average value and the median value of the 5 classifiers prediction errors reported in Chen et al. (2005) when 50 informative genes are used. Table 6 reports values when 100 informative genes are used. F, B, W, W^*, C and H represent the six test statistics.

Experimental results show that, for OVARIAN, NCI, LUNG CANCER and LYMPHOMA multiclass genes problems, the prediction error is data dependent. The proposed boundary approach achieves competitive performances compared to the 5 classifiers reported in Chen et al. (2005). For these datasets, prediction errors of the proposed approach are less than the mean and median values of the 5 classifiers prediction errors reported in Chen et al. (2005). However, for LEUKEMIA72, the proposed algorithm performances are almost in the same range of those provided by the 5 classifiers reported in Chen et al. (2005). The proposed approach prediction error is equal, or in the worst case, slightly higher than the mean and median errors. Focusing on the data nature, the five data under study, described by table 4 show that even though data are all described by a large number of genes and small number of samples they have different nature. Genes number varies from 918 for LUNG CANCER problem to 9703 for NCI. NCI has ten times genes more than LUNG CANCER with less number of patients and more classes. According to the table 4, NCI is the hardest problem since it is described by the largest number of genes with the smallest number of patients per class (60 patients for

		Patient class						
		Normal	SCLC	LCLC	SCC	AC2	AC3	AC1
Predicted decision	Normal	6	0	0	0	0	0	0
	SCLC	0	4	0	0	0	1	0
	LCLC	0	0	3	0	0	4	1
	SCC	0	0	0	16	0	3	0
	AC2	0	0	0	0	4	0	0
	AC3	0	1	1	0	1	4	0
	AC1	0	0	1	0	2	1	20

Table 7. Confusion Matrix of $50W^*$ LUNG CANCER dataset. Total of misclassified is equal to 16.

		Patient class						
		Normal	SCLC	LCLC	SCC	AC2	AC3	AC1
Predicted decision	Normal	5	0	0	0	0	0	0
	SCLC	0	4	0	0	0	0	0
	LCLC	0	0	1	1	0	2	2
	SCC	0	0	2	14	0	1	0
	AC2	0	0	0	0	7	0	0
	AC3	0	0	2	1	0	8	0
	AC1	1	1	0	0	0	2	19

Table 8. Confusion Matrix of $50H$ LUNG CANCER dataset. Total of misclassified is equal to 15.

9 classes). Thus, it is expected that the gene selection task is difficult and consequently the prediction accuracy is not high.

Moreover, it is worthy to note that these data are more or less imbalanced which makes the discrimination step harder. For example, the ratio of the large to the small classes reaches 23 for the LYMPHOMA problem. For this problem, the proposed boundary method results are considerably more accurate than the 5 existing ones. Thus, this approach can be considered as an adapted method solution to solve imbalanced problems: because both minority and majority classes are learned separately, descriptions are not dominated by the majority classes. Finally, we can note that focusing on the test statistics comparison, experimental results confirm those of Chen et al. (2005). B, W and W^* can be the most performing tests under variances heterogeneity assumptions. For the LUNG CANCER dataset where the gene-patient ratio is the smallest, the prediction accuracy is almost the same for all the test statistics.

5.2.2 Class-selective rejection framework

In order to illustrate the interest of considering the multiclass cancer diagnosis in class-selective rejection scheme subject to constraints, one gene dataset is considered and studied.

In the following, we present the study of LUNG CANCER problem in the class selective-rejection scheme subject to two constraints. Let's start by defining the decision options. In fact, LUNG CANCER diagnosis problem is determined by the gene expression profiles of 67 lung tumors and 6 normal lung specimens from patients whose clinical course was followed for up

		Patient class						
		Normal	SCLC	LCLC	SCC	AC2	AC3	AC1
	Normal	6	0	0	0	0	0	0
	SCLC	0	3	0	0	0	0	0
	LCLC	0	0	3	0	0	4	0
	SCC	0	0	0	16	0	2	0
Predicted decision	AC2	0	0	0	0	4	0	0
	AC3	0	0	0	0	1	3	0
	AC1	0	0	1	0	1	1	20
	$\{LCLC,SCC,AC3\}$	0	0	1	0	0	2	0
	All tumors	0	2	0	0	1	1	1
	All classes	0	0	0	0	0	0	0

Table 9. Confusion matrix of the $50W^*$ LUNG CANCER problem with class selective rejection. Total of misclassified is equal to 10, total of partially and totally rejected samples is equal to 8.

to 5 years. The tumors comprised 41 Adenocarcinomas (ACs), 16 squamous cell carcinomas (SCCs); 5 cell lung cancers (LCLCs) and 5 small cell lung cancers (SCLCs). ACs are subdivided into three subgroups 21 AC of group 1 tumors, 7 AC of group 2 tumors and 13 AC of group 3 tumors. Thus, the multiclass diagnosis cancer consists of 7 classes.

Authors in Garber et al. (2001) observed that AC of group 3 tumors shared strong expression of genes with LCLC and SCC tumors. Thus, poorly differentiated AC is difficult to distinguish from LCLC or SCC. Confusion matrices (tables 7 and 8) computed in the classical framework, with $50W^*$ and $50H$ prove well these claims. It can be noticed that 8 of the 16 misclassified $50W^*$ patients and 8 of the 15 misclassified $50H$ patients correspond to confusion between these three subcategories. Therefore, one may define a new decision option as a subset of these three classes to group these errors and set up an additional test to differentiate them.

Moreover, researches affirm that distinction between patients with nonsmall cell lung tumors (SCC, AC and LCLC) and those with small cell tumors or SCLC is extremely important, since they are treated very differently. Thus, a confusion or wrong decision among patients of nonsmall cell lung tumors should cost less than a confusion within nonsmall cells tumors classes or within small cells tumors classes. Besides, one may provide an extra decision option that includes all the subcategories of tumors to avoid this kind of confusion. Finally, another natural decision option can be the set of all classes, which means that the classifier has totally withhold taking a decision.

Given all these information, the classification problem can be defined as follows:

- Ten decision options can be defined. The possible decision options are given by: $\{Normal\}$, $\{SCLC\}$, $\{LCLC\}$, $\{SCC\}$, $\{AC2\}$, $\{AC3\}$, $\{AC1\}$, $\{LCLC,SCC,AC3\}$, $\{SCLC,LCLC,SCC,AC2,AC3,AC1\}$ and $\{Normal,SCLC,LCLC,SCC,AC2,AC3,AC1\}$.

- The chosen comprimised is given by $P_E \leq 0.15$ and $P_I \leq 0.1$ where P_E is the probability of error and P_I is the probability of indistinctness.

- The loss function defined by (2) with the costs $c_{i,j}$ given by:

$$
c_{i,j} = \begin{cases} 1, & w_j \notin \psi_i; \\ \frac{|\psi_i|-1}{N-1}, & w_j \in \psi_i \text{ et } |\psi_i| > 1; \\ 0, & \psi_i = \{w_j\}. \end{cases}
$$

Solving this problem with $50W^*$ LUNG CANCER problem leads to the confusion matrix presented in table 9. As a comparison with table 7, one may mainly note that the number of misclassified patients decreases from 16 to 10 and 8 withhold decisions or rejected patients. The probability of error has decreased from 0.219 to 0.136 with a probability of ambiguity equal to 0.109. This partial rejection contributes to avoid confusion between nonsmall and small lung cells tumors and reduces errors due to indistinctness among LCLC, SCC and AC3. Besides, according to the example under study, no patient is totally rejected. It is an expected result since initially (table 7) there exists no confusion between normal and tumor samples.
To take a decision concerning the rejected patients, we may refer to clinical analysis. It is worth to note that for partially rejected patients, clinical analysis is less expensive in terms of time and money than those on completely blinded patients. Moreover, a supervised solution can be also proposed. It aims to use genes selected from another test statistic in order to assign rejected patients to one of the possible classes Jrad et al. (2009b;d). Many factors play an important role in the cascade classifiers system such as the choice of test statistics, the number of classifiers in a cascade system,... Such concerns are under study.

6. Discussions and conclusion

This chapter presents the multiclass decision problem in a new framework where the performances of the decision rule must satisfy some constraints. A general formulation of the problem with class-selective rejection subject to performance constraints was expounded. The definition of the problem takes into account three kinds of criteria: the label sets, the performance constraints, and the average expected loss. The solution of the stated problem was given within the statistical decision theory framework. Some supervised learning strategies were presented. Two approaches are proposed; a class-modeling approach and a boundary based approach. The first named class-modeling approach is defined within the statistical community. Class-modeling approaches are generally characterized by having an explicit underlying probability model, which provides a probability of being in each class rather than simply a classification. The second is defined in the Support Vector Machines community. It focuses on the boundary of the data. It avoids the estimation of the complete density of the data, which might be difficult using small sample sizes.
Experimental results on artificial datasets show that, on the first hand, class-modeling approaches require big amounts of data because it is based on a complete density estimate. Furthermore, the performances of the classifier is conditioned by the choice of a good convergent estimator. As a comparison between GMM and PW algorithms, it is worthy to note that even though PW is widely used, for some complex distributions like multimodal distributions, GMM fitting can be a better model yielding to an accurate decision rule. GMM produce not only memory and computational advantages, but also superior results in terms of solving the under vs. overfitting compromise. When a large sample of typical data is available, the density method is expected to work well.

On the second hand, MSVM methods based on ν-1-SVM methods is a relatively new approach that avoids the estimation of the complete probability density. This not only gives an advantage when just a limited sample is available, it is even possible to learn from data when the density distribution is difficult to estimate (representation space of high dimension).

Experimental results on real datasets show that, in the particular case where decisions are given by the possible classes and the loss function is set equal to the error rate, the proposed boundary approach, compared with the state of art multiclass algorithms, can be considered as a competitive one. Moreover, this method seems to be an interesting solution to solve imbalanced problems. Because both minority and majority classes are learned separately, descriptions are not dominated by the majority classes. Consequently, the performance of the learning procedure is supposed to outperform multiclass rules learned from imbalanced data sets. In the class-selective rejection scheme with constraints, the proposed classifier ensures higher reliability and reduces time and expense costs by introducing partial and total rejection and restricting the misclassified the ambiguously classified samples.

Finally, we can say that the expounded approaches are a new way to learn accurate multiclass decision rules satisfying users requirements on the global performances of the classification system. To avoid too demanding constrains like $P_E < \epsilon$ and $P_I < \epsilon'$ which lead most of the time to very large total rejection (total rejection should not be subject to constraint otherwise the problem may have no solution), we advocate to choose reasonable constraints as an initial target and then to tune the value of the obtained Lagrange multipliers to select a satisfactory compromise. The main interest of the proposed method is to provide a nice initial starting point for the decision rule design and also to avoid costs adjustments which may be difficult to achieve when the number of decision options and consequently the number of costs is large. In the proposed approach only Lagrangian multipliers need final adjustments. Since the number of the Lagrangian multipliers is equal to the number of monitored performance constraints which is generally limited, the choice of a good trade-off among the performances constraints is not too difficult to achieve.

7. References

Alizadeh, A., Eisen, M. B., Davis, R. E., Ma, C., Lossos, I., Rosenwald, A., Boldrick, J., Sabet, H., Tran, T., Yu, X., Powell, J., Yang, L., Marti, G., Moore, T., Hudson, J., Lu, L., Lewis, D., Tibshirani, R., Sherlock, G., Chan, W., Greiner, T., Weisenburger, D., Armitage, J. O., Warnke, R., Levy, R., Wilson, W., Grever, M., Byrd, J., Botstein, D., Brown, P. & Staudt, L. (2000). Distinct types of diffuse large b-cell lymphoma identified by gene expression profiling, *Nature* **403**(6769): 503–511.

Bishop, C. (2006). *Pattern Recognition and Machine Learning (Information Science and Statistics)*, Springer.

Bottou, L., Cortes, C., Denker, J., Drucker, H., Guyon, I., Jackel, L., LeCun, Y., Muller, U., Sackinger, E., Simard, P. & Vapnik, V. (1994). Comparison of classifier methods: a case study in handwriting digit recognition, *International Conference on Pattern Recognition*, pp. 77–87.

Brown, M. B. & Forsythe, A. B. (1974). The small sample behavior of some statistics which test the equality of several means, *Technometrics* **16**(1): 129–132.

Chen, D., Liu, Z., Ma, X. & Hua, D. (2005). Selecting genes by test statistics, *Journal of Biomedicine and Biotechnology* **2005**(2): 132–138.

Cochran, W. G. (1937). Problems arising in the analysis of a series of similar experiments, *Journal of the Royal Statistical Society* **4**: 102–118.

Daniel, W. W. (1999). *Biostatistics:A Foundation for Analysis in the Health Sciences*, NY: Wiley.

Davy, M., Desobry, F., Gretton, A. & Doncarli, C. (2006). An online support vector machine for abnormal events detection, *Signal Process.* **86**(8): 2009–2025.

Dempster, A., Laird, N. & Rubin, D. (1977). Maximum likelihood from incomplete data via the em algorithm, *J. Roy. Statist* **39**: 1–38.

Duda, R. & Hart, P. (1973). *Pattern Classification and Scene Analysis*, John Wiley and Sons, pp. 98–105.

Emanuel, P. (1962). On estimation of a probability density function and mode, *The Annals of Mathematical Statistics* **33**(3): 1065–1076.

Garber, M., Troyanskaya, O., Schluens, K., Petersen, S., Thaesler, Z., Pacyna-Gengelbach, M., van de Rijn, M., Rosen, G., Perou, C., Whyte, R., Altman, R., Brown, P., Botstein, D. & Petersen, I. (2001). Diversity of gene expression in adenocarcinoma of the lung, *Proc Natl Acad Sci*, Vol. 98, USA, pp. 13784–13789.

Golub, T. R., Slonim, D. K., Tamayo, P., Huard, C., Gaasenbeek, M., Mesirov, J. P., Coller, H., Loh, M. L., Downing, J. R., Caligiuri, M. A., Bloomfield, C. D. & Lander, E. S. (1999). Molecular classification of cancer: class discovery and class prediction by gene expression monitoring, *Science* **286**(5439): 531–537.

Grall-Maës, E. & Beauseroy, P. (2009). Optimal decision rule with class-selective rejection and performance constraints, *IEEE Transactions on Pattern Analysis and Machine Intelligence* **99**(1).

Grall-Maës, E., Beauseroy, P. & Bounsiar, A. (2006a). Multilabel classification rule with performance constraints, *Proceedings of IEEE conference ICASSP'06*, France.

Grall-Maës, E., Beauseroy, P. & Bounsiar, A. (2006b). Quality assessment of a supervised multilabel classification rule with performance constraints, *EUSIPCO'06*, Italy.

Guobin, O. & Lu, M. Y. (2007). Multi-class pattern classification using neural networks, *Pattern Recogn.* **40**(1): 4–18.

Ha, T. M. (1997). The optimum class-selective rejection rule, *IEEE Trans. Pattern Anal. Mach. Intell.* **19**(6): 608–615.

Hao, P. & Lin, Y. (2007). A new multiclass support vector machine with multisphere in the feature space, *IEA/AIE*, pp. 756–765.

Hartung, J. & Makambi, K. H. (2002). Small sample properties of tests on homogeneity in one-way anova and meta-analysis, *Statistical Papers* **43**: 197–235.

Hastie, T., Rosset, S., Tibshirani, R. & Zhu, J. (2004). The entire regularization path for the support vector machine, *J. Mach. Learn. Res.* **5**: 1391–1415.

Horiuchi, T. (1998). Class selective rejection rule to minimize the maximum distance between selected classes, *PR* **31**(10): 1579–1588.

Husband, C. & Lin, C. (2002). A comparison of methods for multiclass support vector machines, *IEEE Transactions on Neural Networks* **13**: 415–425.

Jrad, N., Grall, E. & Beauseroy, P. (2008). Supervised learning rule selection for multiclass decision with performance constraints, *IEEE conference ICPR*, USA.

Jrad, N., Grall-Maës, E. & Beauseroy, P. (2008). A supervised decision rule for multiclass problems minimizing a loss function, *Seventh International Conference on Machine Learning and Applications* pp. 48–53.

Jrad, N., Grall-Maës, E. & Beauseroy, P. (2009a). Apprentissage supervisé de règles de décision multiclasses avec contraintes de performances évolutives, *XXII Colloque Gretsi*.

Jrad, N., Grall-Maës, E. & Beauseroy, P. (2009b). Classification supervisée de tumeurs cancéreuses avec rejet sélectif, *XXII Colloque Gretsi*.

Jrad, N., Grall-Maës, E. & Beauseroy, P. (2009c). Gaussian mixture models for multiclass problems with performance constraints, *ESANN*.

Jrad, N., Grall-Maës, E. & Beauseroy, P. (2009d). Gene-based multiclass cancer diagnosis with class-selective rejections, *Journal of Biomedicine and Biotechnology* .

Kutner, M. H., Nachtsheim, C. J., Neter, J. & Li, W. (2005). *Applied Linear Statistical Models*, 5th edn, McGraw Hill.

Li, J. Q. & Barron, A. R. (1999). Mixture density estimation, *In Advances in Neural Information Processing Systems 12*, MIT Press, pp. 279–285.

Rakotomamonjy, A. & Davy, M. (2007). One-class svm regularization path and comparison with alpha seeding, *ESANN 2007*, Bruge, Belgium, pp. 221–224.

Ross, D., Scherf, U., Eisen, M., Perou, C., Rees, C., Spellman, P., V, V. I., Jeffrey, S., de Rijn, M. V., Waltham, M., Pergamenschikov, A., Lee, J., Lashkari, D., Shalon, D., Myers, T., Weinstein, J., Botstein, D. & Brown, P. (2000). Systematic variation in gene expression patterns in human cancer cell lines, *Nat Genet.*, Vol. 24, USA, pp. 227–235.

Scherf, U., Ross, D. T., Waltham, M., Smith, L. H., Lee, J. K., Tanabe, L., Kohn, K. W., Reinhold, W. C., Myers, T. G., Andrews, D. T., Scudiero, D. A., Eisen, M. B., Sausville, E. A., Pommier, Y., Botstein, D., Brown, P. O. & Weinstein, J. N. (2000). A gene expression database for the molecular pharmacology of cancer, *Nat Genet* **24**(3): 236–244.

Scholkopf, B., Platt, J. C., Shawe-Taylor, J., Smola, A. J. & Williamson, R. C. (2001). Estimating the support of a high-dimensional distribution, *Neural Computation* **13**(7): 1443–1471.

Scholkopf, B. & Smola, A. J. (2001). *Learning with Kernels: Support Vector Machines, Regularization, Optimization, and Beyond*, MIT Press, Cambridge, MA, USA.

Tax, D. (2001). *One-class classification: concept learning in the absence of counter-examples*, PhD thesis, Technische Universiteit Delft.

Titterington, D. M., Smith, A. F. M. & Makov, U. E. (1985). *Statistical Analysis of Finite Mixture Distributions*, John Wiley, New York.

Vapnik, V. N. (1998). *Statistical Learning Theory*, Wiley-Interscience.

Verbeek, J., Vlassis, N. & Krose, B. (2003). Efficient greedy learning of gaussian mixture models, *Neural Computation* **15**(2): 469–485.

Vlassis, N. & Likas, A. (2002). A greedy em algorithm for gaussian mixture learning, *Neural Processing Letters* **15**(1): 77–87.

WELCH, B. L. (1951). On the comparison of several mean values: an alternative approach, *Biometrika* **38**(3-4): 330–336.

Welsh, J., Zarrinkar, P., Sapinoso, L., Kern, S., Behling, C., Monk, B., Lockhart, D., Burger, R. & Hampton, G. (2001). Analysis of gene expression profiles in normal and neoplastic ovarian tissue samples identifies candidate molecular markers of epithelial ovarian cancer, *Proc Natl Acad Sci*, Vol. 98, USA, pp. 1176–1181.

Weston, J. & Watkins, C. (1999). Multiclass support vector machines, *ESANN*.

Yang, X., Liu, J., Zhang, M. & Niu, K. (2007). A new multiclass svm algorithm based on one-class svm, *ICCS 2007*, Beijing, China, pp. 677–684.

## 2

Class-Selective Rejection Rules based on the Aggregation of Pattern Soft Labels

Carl Frélicot and Hoel Le Capitaine
Lab. MIA - Université de La Rochelle
France

1. Introduction

Let $\Omega = \{\omega_1, \cdots, \omega_c\}$ be a set of c classes and let $\mathbf{x}$ be a pattern described by p features, namely a vector $\mathbf{x} = {}^t(x_1 \cdots x_p)$ in a p-dimensional real space $\mathbb{R}^p$. Classifier design aims at defining rules that allow to associate an incoming pattern $\mathbf{x}$ with one class of Ω. Let $\mathcal{L}_{hc}$ be the set of c-dimensional binary vectors whose components sum up to one. Then, such a rule, defined as a mapping D: $\mathbb{R}^p \to \mathcal{L}_{hc}$, $\mathbf{x} \mapsto \mathbf{h}(\mathbf{x})$, is called a *crisp classifier*. In most theoretical approaches to pattern classification, it is convenient to define a classifier as a couple (L, H) where:

- L is a *labeling* function: $\mathbb{R}^p \to \mathcal{L}_{\bullet c}$, $\mathbf{x} \mapsto \mathbf{u}(\mathbf{x})$, $\mathcal{L}_{\bullet c}$ depending on the mathematical framework the classifier relies on, $\mathcal{L}_{pc} = [0,1]^c$ for degrees of typicality or $\mathcal{L}_{fc} = \{\mathbf{u}(\mathbf{x}) \in \mathcal{L}_{pc} | \sum_{i=1}^{c} u_i(\mathbf{x}) = 1\}$ for posterior probabilities and fuzzy membership degrees or even $\mathcal{L}_{hc}$;

- H is a *hardening* function: $\mathcal{L}_{\bullet c} \to \mathcal{L}_{hc}$, $\mathbf{u}(\mathbf{x}) \mapsto \mathbf{h}(\mathbf{x})$, which often reduces to the class of maximum label selection, $\mathcal{L}_{hc} = \{\mathbf{h}(\mathbf{x}) \in \mathcal{L}_{fc} | h_i(\mathbf{x}) \in \{0,1\}\}$.

Thus, the crisp classifier D is a special case of the classifier (L, H). Whenever $\mathcal{L}_{\bullet c} \neq \mathcal{L}_{hc}$, label vectors $\mathbf{u}(\mathbf{x})$ are said to be *soft* and the resulting classifier is called a *soft classifier*. Special cases can be emphasized because of the L-function: the *possibilistic* classifier when $\mathcal{L}_{\bullet c} = \mathcal{L}_{pc}$, the *fuzzy* and the *probabilistic* classifiers when $\mathcal{L}_{\bullet c} = \mathcal{L}_{fc}$. In the probabilistic case, $u_i(\mathbf{x})$ are posterior probabilities $P(\omega_i | \mathbf{x})$ that can be obtained either from (known) class-conditional densities whose parameters are estimated using a learning set $\mathcal{X}$ of patterns, *i.e.* patterns for which the class-assignment is known, or from class-density estimates using the classes of their neighbors in $\mathcal{X}$. Throughout this chapter we shall use these definitions because most statistical pattern classifiers share either the L-function or the H-function, see examples in (Frélicot, 1998). Furthermore, the chapter addresses the problem of aggregating the soft labels issued from the L-function by the design of special H-functions, whatever they have been obtained. However, note that some authors consider the mapping D: $\mathbb{R}^p \to \mathcal{L}_{hc}$, $\mathcal{L}_{fc}$ or $\mathcal{L}_{pc} \backslash \mathbf{0}^1$ to define a crisp, a fuzzy or a possibilistic classifier respectively (Bezdek et al., 1999). Since the L-part is out of the scope of this chapter and there are many ways to compute labels,

---

[1] $\mathbf{0} = {}^t(0 \cdots 0)$ is the p-dimensional null vector

we shall use the degree of typicality defined by:

$$u_i(\mathbf{x}) = \frac{\alpha_i}{\alpha_i + d^2(\mathbf{x}, \mathbf{v}_i)} \tag{1}$$

where α_i is a user-defined parameter, d is a distance in $\mathbb{R}^p$, and $\mathbf{v}_i$ is a prototype of the class ω_i. Among the possible distances, one finds the Mahalanobis distance $d^2(\mathbf{x}, \mathbf{v}_i) = (\mathbf{x} - \mathbf{v}_i)^t \Sigma_i^{-1}(\mathbf{x} - \mathbf{v}_i)$ where $\mathbf{v}_i$ and Σ_i are the mean vector and covariance matrix of ω_i estimated from a learning set $\mathcal{X}$. It has been shown through empirical studies (Zimmermann & Zysno, 1985) that (1) is a good model for membership functions that model vague concepts or classes. Parameters α_i will always all be set to 1 except if mentioned otherwise.

As defined, any H-function results in an exclusive classification rule which is not efficient in practice because it supposes that Ω is exhaustively defined (*closed-world* assumption) and that classes do not ovelap (*separability* assumption). In many real applications, both assumptions are not true and such a classifier can lead to very undesired decisions. It is often more convenient to withhold making a decision and direct the pattern to an exceptional handling than making a wrong assignment, *e.g.* in medical diagnosis where a false negative outcome can be much more costly than a false positive. Reject options have been proposed to overcome these difficulties and to reduce the misclassification risk. The first one, called *distance rejection* (Dubuisson & Masson, 1993) is dedicated to outlying patterns. If $\mathbf{x}$ is far from all the class prototypes, this option allows to assign it to no class. The second one, called *ambiguity rejection*, allows to assign inlying patterns to several or all classes (Chow, 1970), (Ha, 1997). If $\mathbf{x}$ is close to two or more class prototypes, it is associated with the corresponding classes. Including reject options leads to partition the feature space into as many regions as subsets of classes, *i.e.* at most 2^c ones, to which a pattern can be assigned. Formally, it consists in modifying the H-function definition such that $\mathbf{h}(\mathbf{x})$ can take values in the set of vertices $\mathcal{L}_{hc}^c = \{0, 1\}^c$ of the unit hypercube instead of the exclusive subset $\mathcal{L}_{hc} \subset \mathcal{L}_{hc}^c$. Different strategies can be adopted to handle these options at hand, but they all lead to a three types decision system:

- distance rejection when $\mathbf{h}(\mathbf{x})$ is $\mathbf{0}$,

- classification when $\mathbf{h}(\mathbf{x})$ is in $\mathcal{L}_{hc}$,

- ambiguity rejection when $\mathbf{h}(\mathbf{x})$ is in $\mathcal{L}_{hc}^c \backslash \{\mathcal{L}_{hc} \cup \mathbf{0}\}$.

The resulting classification rule is then a matter of selecting, by H, the appropriate number of classes varying from zero (distance rejection) to c (total ambiguity rejection) and which class/es is/are involved, provided its soft label vector $\mathbf{u}$ is available from L. This can be obtained by aggregating the components of $\mathbf{u}$ in a suitable way.

2. Aggregation Operators for Class-Selection

In this section, we first briefly review basic aggregation operators (Calvo et al., 2002), in particular the ones issued from the fuzzy sets theory which have received more attention in the last few decades because of their ability to manage imprecise and/or incomplete data. Then we present some combinations of them that can be used to select the number of classes to which an incoming pattern $\mathbf{x}$ has to be assigned because they allow to define some ambiguity measures.

2.1 Preliminary Definitions

Let us recall basic definitions of aggregation functions or operators that will be used to combine the values of interest, *i.e.* the soft labels of a pattern to be classified. In a broader sense, aggregation functions aim at associating a typical value to a number of several numerical values which are generally defined on a finite real interval on an ordinal scale. They are used in many fields, *e.g.* decision-making and pattern recognition (Grabisch, 1992). Since soft labels $u_i(\mathbf{x})$ are in [0,1], we restrict to functions that aggregate values from the unit interval and we define an aggregation operator as a mapping $\mathcal{A}\colon [0,1]^c \rightarrow [0,1]$, $\mathbf{a} = \{a_1, \cdots, a_c\} \mapsto \mathcal{A}(\mathbf{a})$, satisfying the following conditions:

(A1) $\mathcal{A}(0, \cdots, 0) = 0$ and $\mathcal{A}(1, \cdots, 1) = 1$ (boundaries),

(A2) $\forall c \in \mathbb{N}, a_1 \leq b_1, \cdots, a_c \leq b_c \Rightarrow \mathcal{A}(a_1, \cdots, a_c) \leq \mathcal{A}(b_1, \cdots, b_c)$ (monotonicity).

Adding properties like idempotency, continuity, associativity lead to others definitions but this one is strong enough for our discourse. In the literature, one finds many families of aggregation operators, *e.g.*: triangular norms (Menger, 1942), OWA (Ordered Weighted Averaging) operators (Yager, 1988), γ-operators (Zimmerman & Zysno, 1980), or fuzzy integrals (Sugeno, 1974). They are classified either by some mathematical properties they share or by the way the values are aggregated. An aggregation operator $\mathcal{A}$ is said to be:

(A3) conjunctive if $\mathcal{A}(\mathbf{a}) \leq min\{a_1, a_2, \ldots, a_c\}$,

(A3') disjunctive if $\mathcal{A}(\mathbf{a}) \geq max\{a_1, a_2, \ldots, a_c\}$,

(A3'') compensatory if $min\{a_1, a_2, \ldots, a_c\} \leq \mathcal{A}(\mathbf{a}) \leq max\{a_1, a_2, \ldots, a_c\}$,

refer to (Calvo et al., 2002; Grabisch et al., 2009) for a large survey on aggregation operators.

2.2 Basic Aggregation Operators

Beyond these operators, we choose to use the triangular norms and co-norms because of their ability to generalize the logical AND and OR crisp operators to fuzzy sets, see (Klement & Mesiar, 2005) for a survey. A fuzzy negation (or complement) is defined as a continuous, non increasing function $N\colon [0,1] \rightarrow [0,1]$ satisfying:

(N1) $N(0) = 1$ and $N(1) = 0$ (boundaries),

(N2) $N(N(a)) = a$ (involution).

A triangular norm (or t-norm) is a binary operator $\top\colon [0,1]^2 \rightarrow [0,1]$ satisfying the following four axioms: $\forall a, b, c \in [0,1]$

(T1) $a \top b = b \top a$ (symmetry),

(T2) if $b \leq c \Rightarrow a \top b \leq a \top c$ (monotonicity),

(T3) $a \top (b \top c) = (a \top b) \top c$ (associativity),

(T4) $a \top 1 = a$ (neutral element).

It is easy to see that these axioms make $\top$ satisfy (A1) and (A2), so any t-norm is an aggregation operator.

Given a fuzzy negation N, *e.g.* the strict negation $N(a) = 1 - a$, a triangular conorm (or t-conorm) is the dual operation $\bot$, $[0,1]^2 \rightarrow [0,1]$, defined as:

$$a \bot b = N(N(a) \top N(a)) \tag{2}$$

Therefore, a t-conorm satisfies axioms (T1), (T2), (T3), so any t-conorm is an aggregation operator in the sense of (A1) and (A2), and satisfies:

(S4) $a \perp 0 = 0$ (neutral element).

Axioms (T2), (T4) and (S4) imply additional axioms: $\forall a, b \in [0, 1]$

(T5) $a \top b \leq a$,

(S5) $a \leq a \perp b$,

and it ensues:

(T6) $a \top 0 = 0$ (absorbing element for any t-norm),

(T7) $a \top b \leq min(a, b)$ (min is the largest t-norm),

(S6) $a \perp 1 = 1$ (absorbing element for any t-conorm),

(S7) $max(a, b) \leq a \perp b$ (max is the smallest t-conorm).

Typical examples of dual couples $(\top, \perp)^2$ that will be used in the sequel are given in Table 1, including two parametric ones which generalize other t-norms and t-conorms depending of the parameter value, *e.g.*:

- $(\top_{H_1}, \perp_{H_1}) = (\top_A, \perp_A)$, the *product* and *probabilistic sum*
- $(\top_{D_1}, \perp_{D_1}) = (\top_{H_0}, \perp_{H_0})$, the *Hamacher's product and sum*,
- $(\top_{D_{+\infty}}, \perp_{D_{+\infty}}) = (\top_S, \perp_S)$, the *min* and *max* operators.

Standard	$a \top_S y = \min(a, b)$ $a \perp_S b = \max(a, b)$
Algebraic	$a \top_A b = a\,b$ $a \perp_A b = a + b - a\,b$
Łukasiewicz	$a \top_L b = \max(a + b - 1, 0)$ $a \perp_L b = \min(a + b, 1)$
Hamacher ($\gamma \in [0, +\infty[$)	$a \top_{H_\gamma} b = \dfrac{a\,b}{\gamma + (1-\gamma)\,(a+b-a\,b)}$ $a \perp_{H_\gamma} b = \dfrac{a+b+(\gamma-2)\,a\,b}{1+(\gamma-1)\,a\,b}$
Dombi ($\gamma \in\,]0, +\infty[$)	$a \top_{D_\gamma} b = \left(1 + \left(\left(\frac{1-a}{a}\right)^{\gamma} + \left(\frac{1-b}{b}\right)^{\gamma}\right)^{1/\gamma}\right)^{-1}$ $a \perp_{D_\gamma} b = 1 - \left(1 + \left(\left(\frac{a}{1-a}\right)^{\gamma} + \left(\frac{b}{1-b}\right)^{\gamma}\right)^{1/\gamma}\right)^{-1}$

Table 1. Some triangular norm dual couples.

---

[2] ones also refers to triples $(\top, N, \perp)$

2.3 Ambiguity Measures based on Combination of Basic Operators

An *ambiguity measure* is any aggregation function $\Phi: \mathcal{L}_{\bullet c} \to [0,1]$, $\mathbf{u}(\mathbf{x}) \mapsto \Phi(\mathbf{u})$ that can reveal if an incoming pattern $\mathbf{x}$ could be associated with several classes, hence that can be used to define the H-function of a class-selective rejection classifier. We present hereafter some combinations of basic aggregation operators and the derived ambiguity measures.

Let $\mathcal{P}$ be the powerset of $C = \{1, 2, \cdots, c\}$ and $\mathcal{P}_l = \{A \in \mathcal{P} : card(A) = l\}$. The *fuzzy l-order OR* operator (fOR-*l* for short) is an aggregation function, as defined in subsection 2.1:

$[0,1]^c \to [0,1]$, $\mathbf{u} \mapsto \overset{l}{\perp}(\mathbf{u})$, where

$$\overset{l}{\perp}(\mathbf{u}) = \underset{i=1,\cdots,c}{\overset{l}{\perp}} u_i = \underset{A \in \mathcal{P}_{l-1}}{\top} \left(\underset{j \in C \backslash A}{\perp} u_j \right) \tag{3}$$

Some properties of fOR-*l* result from those of $\top$ and $\perp$, others have been proved in (Mascarilla et. al, 2008). Among these properties, let us recall those that are useful for the context we are interested in:

(L1) $\overset{l}{\perp}(\mathbf{0}) = \mathbf{0}$ and $\overset{l}{\perp}(\mathbf{1}) = \mathbf{1}^3$ (boundaries)

(L2) for $\mathbf{u}$ and $\mathbf{v}$ such as $u_i \leq v_i, \forall i \in C$, $\overset{l}{\perp}(\mathbf{u}) \leq \overset{l}{\perp}(\mathbf{v})$ (monotonicity)

(L3) for any permutation σ of C, $\underset{i=1,\cdots,c}{\overset{l}{\perp}} u_{\sigma(i)} = \underset{i=1,\cdots,c}{\overset{l}{\perp}} u_i$ (symmetry)

(L4) $\overset{1}{\perp}(\mathbf{u}) = \perp(\mathbf{u})$ and $\overset{c}{\perp}(\mathbf{u}) = \top(\mathbf{u})$, whatever c and $(\top, \perp)$,

(L5) if the standard norms are taken, then $\overset{l}{\perp}_S(\mathbf{u}) = u_{(l)}$, the l-th highest value^4 in $\mathbf{u}$; for instance, let us take $C = \{1, 2, 3\}$ and $l = 2$, then $\mathcal{P}_{l-1} = \{\{1\}, \{2\}, \{3\}\}$ and we have
$\overset{2}{\perp}_S(\mathbf{u}) = min(max(u_2, u_3), max(u_1, u_3), max(u_1, u_2))$, so that if $u_2 < u_1 < u_3$, then
$\overset{2}{\perp}_S(\mathbf{u}) = u_1$.

Properties (L1) and (L2) make fOR-*l* be a family (parametrized by $(\top, \perp)$) of aggregation functions in the sense of (A1) and (A2). Axiom (T7) and property (L5) allow us to claim that the fOR-*l* operator measures to what extent the (generalization of the, given by the dual couple) l highest values of $\mathbf{u}$ are all high. So, if $\mathbf{u}$ is the soft label vector of a pattern $\mathbf{x}$ to be classified, it can be used as a family of ambiguity measures to reject it between the l corresponding classes as follows: given a dual couple $(\top, \perp)$, $\forall 2 \leq l \leq c$

$$\Phi_{l,\top}(\mathbf{u}) = \overset{l}{\perp}(\mathbf{u}) \tag{4}$$

Let us illustrate this ability on a simple $c = 3$ classes problem. In this so-called *real line example* ($\mathbf{x} \in \mathbb{R}$), the soft labels degrees $u_i(\mathbf{x})$ are modelized by overlapping triangular functions in

---

^{3} $\mathbf{1} = {}^t(1 \cdots 1)$ is the p-dimensional one vector
^{4} usually $u_{(l)}$ denotes the l-th value in ascending order but reverse order is more convenient in the context of this chapter

order to emphasize them when plotting but similar results would have been obtained using a distance model, *e.g.* by (1). Figures 1 and 2 show these degrees and the values of the ambiguity measure $\Phi_{l,\top}(\mathbf{u})$, with $l = 2$ and $l = 3$ respectively, for the different norm couples of Table 1. Of course, the ambiguity measure values depend on the couple but not in such a way that makes the remarks below not valid. However, it is obvious that some ordering appears because of the basic couples' ordering and/or the asymptotic values of the parametric ones, *e.g.* $\Phi_{l,\top_{D_\gamma}}(\mathbf{u})$ tends to $\Phi_{l,\top_S}(\mathbf{u})$ as γ increases. One can see in both Figures that $\Phi_{l,\top}(\mathbf{u}) = 0$

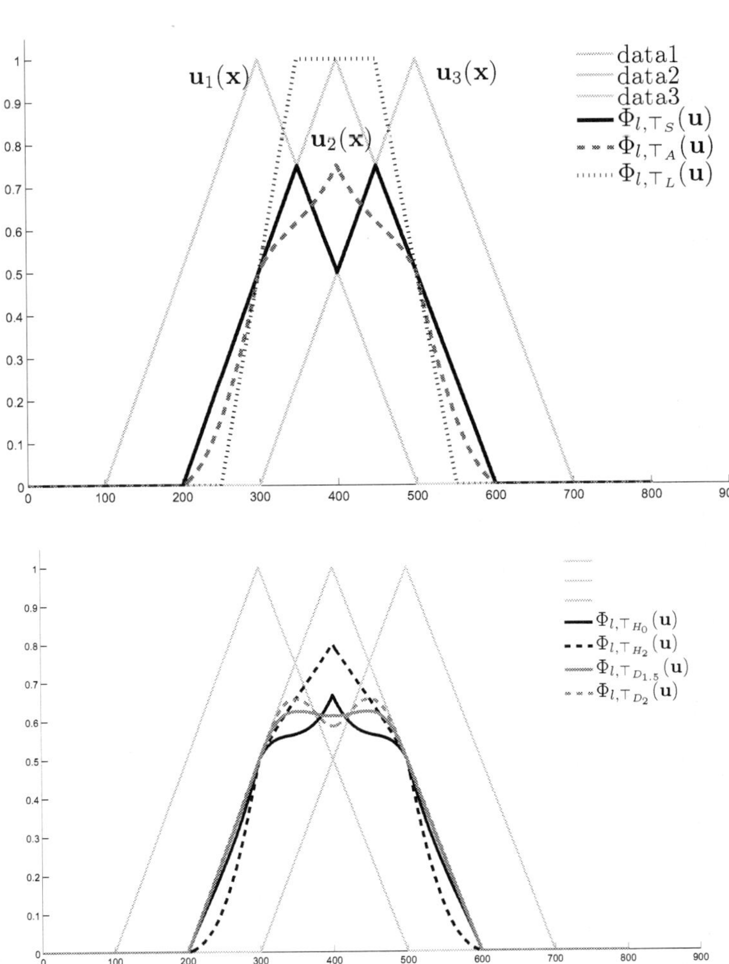

Fig. 1. Soft label degrees $u_{i=1,2,3}(\mathbf{x})$, $\forall \mathbf{x} \in \mathbb{R}$, and ambiguity measures $\Phi_{l=2,\top}(\mathbf{u})$ for different norm couples.

where strictly less than l degrees overlap on the real line, whatever the norm couple $(\top, \bot)$. One can reasonably expect that any pattern $\mathbf{x}$ lying outside these areas should be ambiguity rejected. For instance, if $\Phi_{l,\top}(\mathbf{u}) \geq 0.5$ in Figure 1 (respectively 0 in Figure 2), then all $\mathbf{x} \in [300, 500]$ could be associated with two (respectively three) classes, whatever $(\top, \bot)$. However, a question remains: which order ($l = 2$ or 3) induces more than the other one this ambiguity? This is a matter of selecting the appropriate number of classes which can be processed by the class-selective rule through the $H-$function definition. We address this problem in section 3.

The restriction to $l \geq 2$ in the definition (4) of the family of ambiguity measures $\Phi_{l,\top}(\mathbf{u})$ is motivated by an operational reason. It has been established that class-selective rejection rules that take into account the relationships between the degrees to be aggregated, *e.g.* the historical ones presented in section 3.1, perform better. As the fOR-1 operator reduces to $\bot$ by (L4), there are dual couples for which $\Phi_{1,\top}(\mathbf{u})$ does not depend on such relationships between the u_i values, whenever the soft label vector $\mathbf{u}$ is in $\mathcal{L}_{pc}$, in particular the standard one ($\bot = max$). Of course, whenever $\mathbf{u}$ is in $\mathcal{L}_{fc}$, *i.e.* when it is a collection of posterior probabilities or membership degrees of a pattern $\mathbf{x}$ to be classified, such a relationship holds[5] and $\Phi_{1,\top}(\mathbf{u})$ becomes useful. An alternative in the more general case consists in taking a fuzzy complement of the fOR-1 operator, *e.g.* the strict negation, to define a family of ambiguity measures which has never been proposed: given a t-conorm $\bot$

$$\Phi_{\bar{1},\top}(\mathbf{u}) = 1 - \overset{1}{\bot}(\mathbf{u}) = 1 - \bot(\mathbf{u}) \tag{5}$$

By definition, $\Phi_{\bar{1},\top}(\mathbf{u})$ measures to what extent the (generalization of the, given by fOR-1) highest value in $\mathbf{u}$ is not (by complement) high. Therefore, this family of ambiguity measures is suitable to define a *rejection rule* through a particular $H-$function, but not a *class-selective rejection rule* in a direct way because it does not enable to select the number of classes a pattern has to be associated with, contrarily to the previous family. We will show in the next section that this major difference holds for historical rules that use a single underlying ambiguity measure, so they only allow to reject patterns between at least two classes. This characteristic is well illustrated in Figure 3 where the values of the ambiguity measure $\Phi_{\bar{1},\top}(\mathbf{u})$ on the *real line example* for the different t-conorms of Table 1 are plotted.

Whatever $\top$, the values of $\Phi_{\bar{1},\top}(\mathbf{u})$ can not be used to decide whether two or three classes originate the ambiguity. Note that, once again, the ordering of the different curves is in accordance with that of the basic t-conorms and the parameter values, see for instance that $\Phi_{\bar{1},\top_{D_\gamma}}(\mathbf{u})$ tends to $\Phi_{\bar{1},\top_S}(\mathbf{u})$ as γ increases. Other remarks can be made. First of all, the highest values are obviously obtained with $\top_S$ because of property (S7). Second, even if one can find a threshold on $\Phi_{\bar{1},\top}(\mathbf{u})$ which allows to reject patterns $\mathbf{x}$ lying in areas where two degrees $u_i(\mathbf{x})$ overlap, the threshold would be so small (*e.g.* 0.1 for most of t-conorms) that some patterns lying outside these areas would not reasonably rejected between at least two classes as well. Look for instance all $\mathbf{x} \in [250, 350] \cup [450, 550]$ for which either $u_1(\mathbf{x})$ or $u_2(\mathbf{x})$ is greater than 0.9. Such a drawback could be somewhat avoided by normalizing the degrees. Third, we also have a high value of $\Phi_{\bar{1},\top}(\mathbf{u})$ for all $\mathbf{x} \in]-\infty, 200] \cup [600, +\infty[$ while one can reasonably expect that most of them (the farthest ones) should be distance rejected. This

---

[5] if $\mathbf{u} \in \mathcal{L}_{fc}$, then $\sum_{i=1}^{c} u_i = 1$

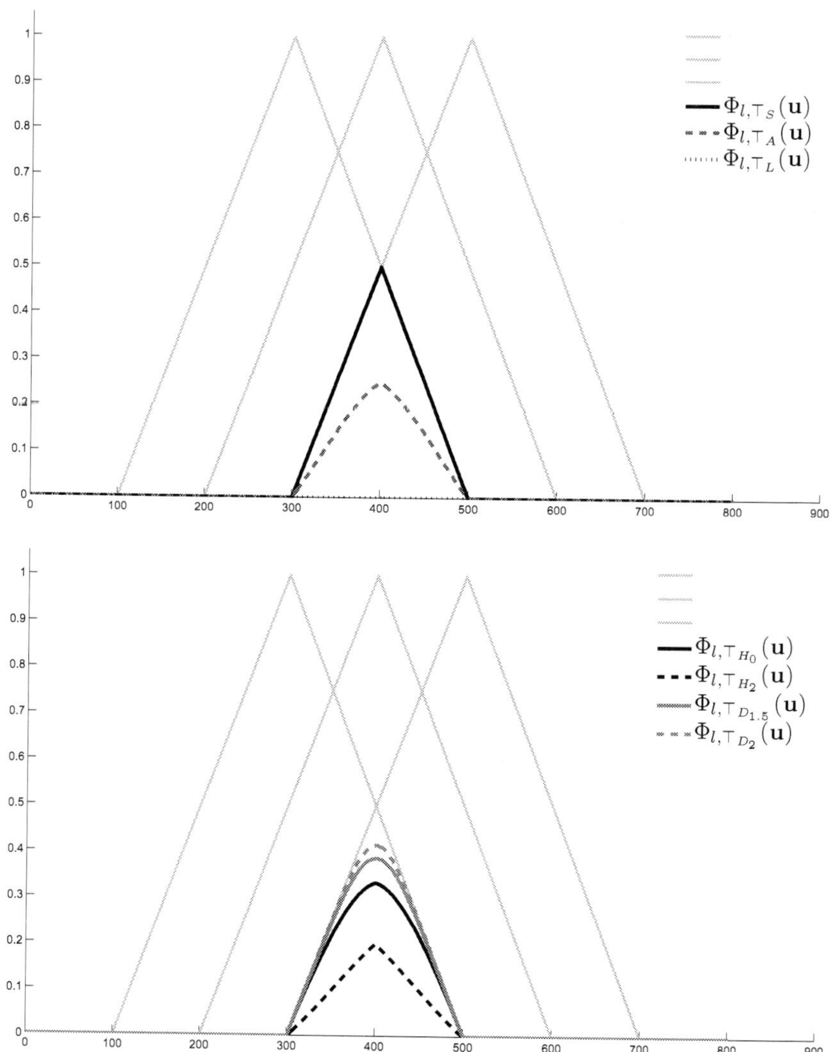

Fig. 2. Soft label degrees $u_{i=1,2,3}(\mathbf{x})$, $\forall \mathbf{x} \in \mathbb{R}$, and ambiguity measures $\Phi_{l=3,\top}(\mathbf{u})$ for different norm couples.

unability to distinguish between both kinds of rejection (distance or ambiguity) is typical of such rejection rules, even if the degrees are normalized.

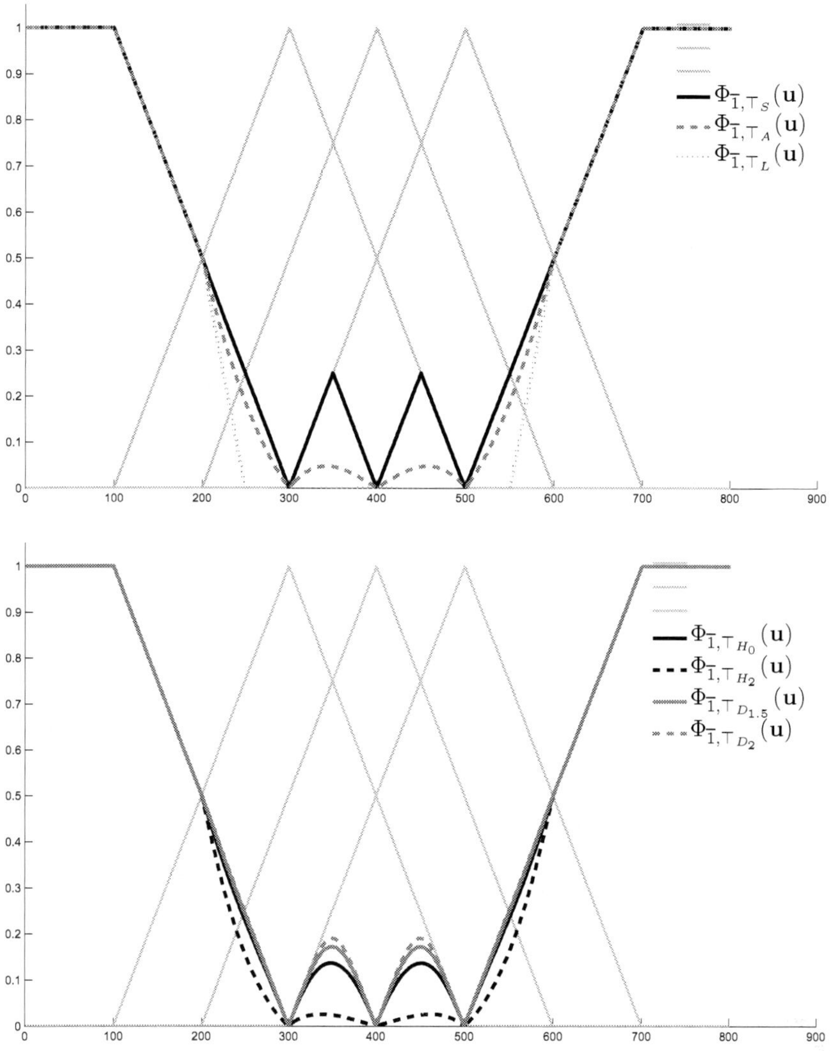

Fig. 3. Soft label degrees $u_{i=1,2,3}(\mathbf{x})$, $\forall \mathbf{x} \in \mathbb{R}$, and ambiguity measures $\Phi_{\bar{1},\top}(\mathbf{u})$ for different norm couples.

Given a fuzzy complement function N, the *fuzzy exclusive OR* operator (fXOR for short) is an aggregation function: $[0,1]^c \to [0,1]$, $\mathbf{u} \mapsto \perp(\mathbf{u})$, where (Mascarilla & Frélicot, 2001):

$$\perp(\mathbf{u}) = \underset{i=1,\cdots,c}{\perp} u_i = \overset{1}{\perp}(\mathbf{u}) \top N\left(\overset{2}{\perp}(\mathbf{u}) \,/\, \overset{1}{\perp}(\mathbf{u})\right) \tag{6}$$

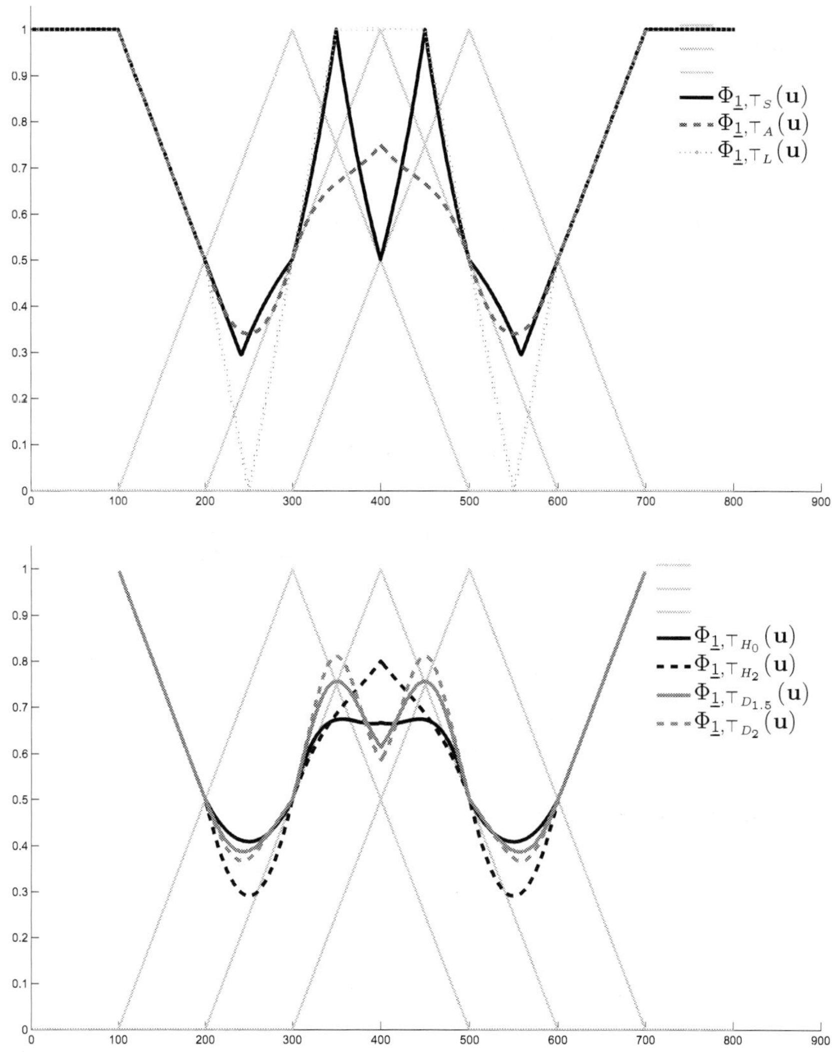

Fig. 4. Soft label degrees $u_{i=1,2,3}(\mathbf{x})$, $\forall \mathbf{x} \in \mathbb{R}$, and ambiguity measures $\Phi_{1,\top}(\mathbf{u})$ for different norm couples.

The term on the right-hand side of $\top$ penalizes the one on the left-hand side, except if $\overset{2}{\perp}(\mathbf{u})$ is significantly lower than $\overset{1}{\perp}(\mathbf{u})$ so that the negation of the ratio becomes high and $\underline{\perp}(\mathbf{u})$ tends to $\overset{1}{\perp}(\mathbf{u}) = \perp(\mathbf{u})$. We can say that the value of $\underline{\perp}(\mathbf{u})$ is high if the (generalization of the, given by fOR-1) highest value is large enough compared to the (generalization of, given by fOR-2) second highest one and therefore to the others. Therefore, fXOR can be used to define another family of ambiguity measures between at least two classes: given a dual triple $(\top, N, \bot)$,

$$\Phi_{1,\top}(\mathbf{u}) = 1 - \underline{\bot}(\mathbf{u}) \tag{7}$$

By property (T5) and definition (4), we have: $\underline{\bot}(\mathbf{u}) \leq \bot(\mathbf{u})$ whatever $(\top, N, \bot)$. As $\bot(\mathbf{u}) = \overset{1}{\underline{\bot}}(\mathbf{u})$ by property (L4), the following property holds:

$$\Phi_{1,\top}(\mathbf{u}) \geq \Phi_{\overline{1},\top}(\mathbf{u}). \tag{8}$$

Therefore, $\Phi_{1,\top}(\mathbf{u})$ is expected to be less sensitive to the choice of the threshold than $\Phi_{\overline{1},\top}(\mathbf{u})$ in order to avoid unexpected rejection, as pointed out on the *real line example*. Figure 4 shows the values of the ambiguity measure $\Phi_{1,\top}(\mathbf{u})$ on the *real line example* for the different norm couples of Table 1. Once again, even if the norm triple $(\top, N, \bot)$ influences the ambiguity measure values, it does not significantly affect the results and the ordering of the different curves is in accordance with that of the basic operators and their parameter values. One can see that this family shares the same major drawbacks with the previous one. In particular, if used in a direct way, it is suitable to define a rejection rule but not a class-selective rule because this measure can not suggest that the number of classes a pattern has to be associated with is in C but in $\{1, c\}$. See, for instance, that we have $\Phi_{1,\top}(\mathbf{u}) \geq 0.5$ whatever the triple $(\top, N, \bot)$ for all $\mathbf{x} \in [300, 500]$, so this measure can be used to ambiguity reject such patterns as expected but without knowing which classes generate this ambiguity. However, contrarily to $\Phi_{\overline{1},\top}(\mathbf{u})$, the threshold to be find is not too small so all $\mathbf{x} \in [250, 350] \cup [450, 550]$ for which either $u_1(\mathbf{x})$ or $u_2(\mathbf{x})$ is greater than 0.9 will be not rejected, as one could expect.

3. Rejection Rules and Class-Selective Rejection Rules based on Soft Labels Aggregation

This section is dedicated to the use of ambiguity measures to define the $H-$function of either a rejection classifier or a class-selective rejection classifier. Historical rejection rules and the ones resulting from the ambiguity measures presented above are unified. This result in a single algorithm aiming at selecting, for an incoming pattern $\mathbf{x}$ to be classified, the appropriate number of classes $n^\star(\mathbf{x})$, given its soft label vector. By convention, we will define mappings

$$H\colon \mathcal{L}_{\bullet c} \to \mathcal{L}_{hc}^c, \ \mathbf{u}(\mathbf{x}) \mapsto \mathbf{h}(\mathbf{x}) \text{ such as } u_{(i)}(\mathbf{x}) \mapsto h_i(\mathbf{x}), \forall i \in C.$$

3.1 Historical Rules and Underlying Ambiguity Measures

The first rejection rule (Chow, 1957) is a probabilistic one which is based on the Bayes decision rule defined by

$$H_B\colon \mathcal{L}_{fc} \to \mathcal{L}_{hc} \subset \mathcal{L}_{hc}^c, \ \mathbf{u}(\mathbf{x}) \mapsto \mathbf{h}(\mathbf{x}) = {}^t(1, 0, \cdots, 0).$$

As $u_i(\mathbf{x})$ are posterior probabilities, this rule assigns the incoming pattern $\mathbf{x}$ to the most probable class and it is known to be optimal with respect to the error probability, *i.e.* no other probabilistic classifier can yeld a lower error probability. Figure 5 - (*left*) illustrates the partition of the feature space into three regions, resulting from H_B, each region corresponding to a single class. The rejection rule introduced by Chow minimizes the error probability for a given reject probability which is specified by a threshold $t \in [0, \frac{c-1}{c}]$, or vice-versa. Thus, this rule yields the optimum error-reject tradeoff (Chow, 1970) and it is defined by

$$H_{Ch}: \mathcal{L}_{fc} \rightarrow \{\mathcal{L}_{hc}, \underline{1}\}, \mathbf{u}(\mathbf{x}) \mapsto \mathbf{h}(\mathbf{x}) = \begin{cases} {}^t(1, 0, \cdots, 0) & \text{if } u_{(1)}(\mathbf{x}) > (1 - t) \\ \underline{1} & \text{otherwise} \end{cases}$$

It means that $\mathbf{x}$ is either exclusively classified or ambiguity rejected between all the classes (*total ambiguity rejection*) if its highest posterior probability $u_{(1)}(\mathbf{x})$ is lower than some given threshold. Therefore, H_{Ch} is not a *class-selective rejection rule* but a simple *rejection rule* because $\mathbf{h}(\mathbf{x})$ can not take any value in $\mathcal{L}_{hc}^c$ but only the ones in $\{\mathcal{L}_{hc}, \underline{1}\}$. Both concepts are illustrated in Figure 5 - (*right*) and - (*center*) respectively. However, Chow's rule uses the complement of the maximum value of the posterior probabilities as an ambiguity measure:

$$\Phi_{Ch}(\mathbf{u}) = 1 - u_{(1)}(\mathbf{x}) \tag{9}$$

and the number of classes $n(\mathbf{x}, t)$ to be selected is in $\{1, c\}$. Since $\mathbf{u}(\mathbf{x}) \in \mathcal{L}_{fc}$, it is easy to show that H_{Ch} is identical to H_B whenever $t > \frac{c-1}{c}$, *i.e.* $\mathbf{x}$ can not be rejected. Note that, as defined, $\Phi_{Ch}(\mathbf{u})$ is a special case of $\Phi_{\bar{1}, \top}(\mathbf{u})$ by definition (5) and property (L4):

$$\Phi_{Ch}(\mathbf{u}) = \Phi_{\bar{1}, \top_s}(\mathbf{u}) \tag{10}$$

Since the work by Chow, most of rejection rules that have been proposed attempt to avoid total ambiguity rejection whenever at least two classes have to be selected. Such a class-selective procedure can be defined, in its general form, as the seek for the optimal number of classes according to:

$$n^{\star}(\mathbf{x}, t) = \min_{k \in C} \{k : \Phi(\mathbf{u}(\mathbf{x})) \leq t\} \tag{11}$$

where Φ is an ambiguity measure on the pattern soft labels, *i.e.* a vector of posterior probabilities or membership degrees in $\mathcal{L}_{fc}$ or even typicality degrees in $\mathcal{L}_{pc}$, $n^{\star}(\mathbf{x}, t)$ is the number of selected classes for the pattern $\mathbf{x}$ to be classified, and t is a user-defined threshold which can be class-order dependent $(t_{(k)})$. This threshold can be set conditionally to cost functions relative to error, reject and correct classification rates instead of error, reject and correct classification probabilities if needed.

Propositions from the literature mainly consist in defining new ambiguity measures Φ suitable for class-selective rejection instead of total ambiguity rejection:

- Ha ranks the posterior probabilities and test their values up to the $(k + 1)$-th to decide if k classes are selected (Ha, 1997):

$$\Phi_{Ha}(\mathbf{u}) = u_{(k+1)}(\mathbf{x}) \tag{12}$$

The corresponding rule H_{Ha} minimizes the error probability for a given average number of classes (Ha, 1996) and the domain of t is $[0, \frac{1}{2}]$. Whenever $t > \frac{1}{2}$, $n^{\star}(\mathbf{x}, t) = 1$

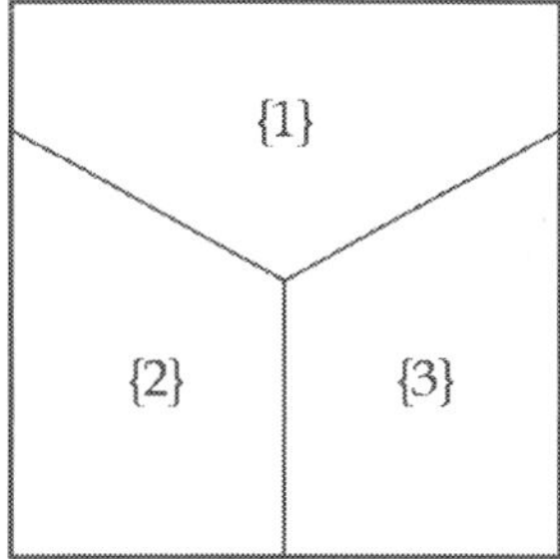

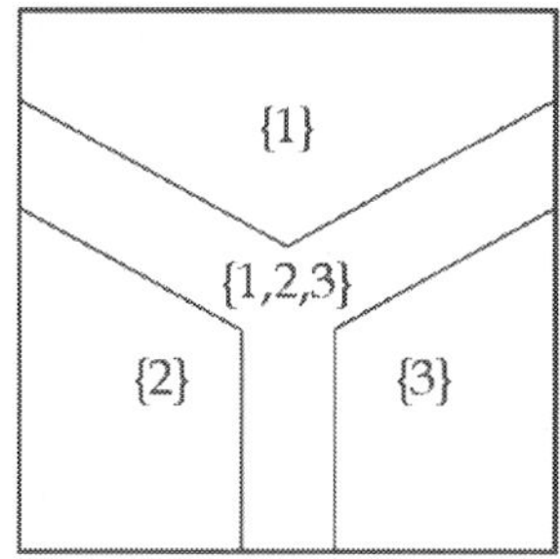

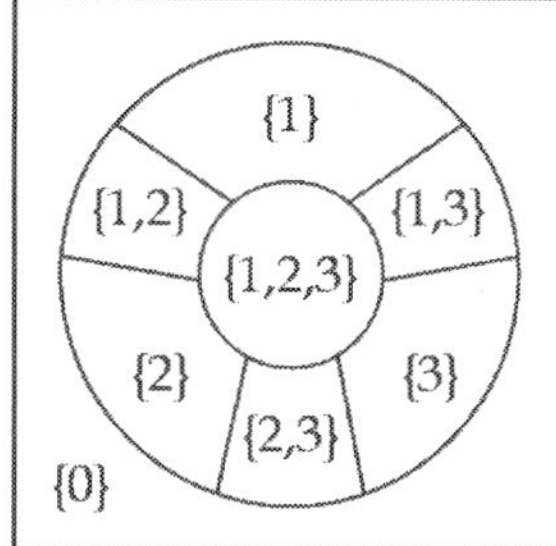

Fig. 5. Feature space partitioning for a three classes problem and reject options – no rejection by H_B (left), rejection rules H_{rej} (center) and class-selective rejection rules H_{sel} (right).

(H_{Ha} reduces to H_B) and can increase up to c as t decreases down to zero. Note that, as defined, $\Phi_{Ha}(\mathbf{u})$ is a special case of $\Phi_{l,\top}(\mathbf{u})$ by definition (4) and property (L4):

$$\Phi_{Ha}(\mathbf{u}) = \Phi_{k+1,\top_s}(\mathbf{u}). \tag{13}$$

- Since this rule is leading to unnatural decisions because of the normalization of $\mathbf{u}(\mathbf{x})$, Horiuchi proposes a new measure defined by the difference of the posterior probabilities (Horiuchi, 1998). This difference is actually a disambiguity measure, so we complement it to derive an ambiguity one:

$$\Phi_{Ho}(\mathbf{u}) = 1 - (u_{(k)}(\mathbf{x}) - u_{(k+1)}(\mathbf{x})) \tag{14}$$

Horuichi's rule H_{Ho} minimizes the maximum distance between selected classes for a given average number of classes which is specified by $t \in [0, 1]$. It is identical to H_B, so $n^\star(\mathbf{x}, t) = 1$ if $t = 0$ and increases up to c as t increases up to 1.

- Before these two works, Frélicot & Dubuisson proposed to use the ratio of typicality degrees (Frélicot & Dubuisson, 1992) in order to relax the summation constraint on $\mathbf{u}(\mathbf{x})$:

$$\Phi_{FD}(\mathbf{u}) = u_{(k+1)}(\mathbf{x})/u_{(k)}(\mathbf{x}) \tag{15}$$

The induced rule H_{FD} allows to select $n^\star(\mathbf{x}, t)$ classes in C, given $t \in [0, 1]$.

As usual, we use the convention that if $\Phi(\mathbf{u}(\mathbf{x})) > t$ for all $k \in C$, then we set $n^\star(\mathbf{x}, t) = c$ which will correspond to total ambiguity rejection.

Even if Chow's, Ha's and Horuichi's rules have been defined within the probabilistic framework ($\mathbf{u}(\mathbf{x}) \in \mathcal{L}_{fc}$), one can intend to use the corresponding ambiguity measures for typicality degrees in $\mathcal{L}_{pc}$. The values of the historical ambiguity measures Φ_{Ch}, Φ_{Ha}, Φ_{Ho} and Φ_{FD} on the *real line example* are shown in Figures 6 and 7 for orders $k + 1 = 2$ and $k + 1 = 3$ respectively. Keeping in mind that Φ_{Ch} will induce a rejection rule and not a class-selective rule, its values are not shown for $k + 1 = 3$, and one can see that Φ_{Ch} has a similar behaviour than $\Phi_{\bar{1},\top}(\mathbf{u})$ and $\Phi_{\underline{1},\top}(\mathbf{u})$, the other families of measures which do not take care of the ambiguity order. A similar discussion to the one we had for $\Phi_{l=k+1,\top}(\mathbf{u})$ in section 2.3 can be done for the other measures. Whatever the ambiguity measure, its lowest values correspond to patterns $\mathbf{x}$ lying in intervals of the real line for which one can reasonably expect that they should not be ambiguity rejected. At the opposite, the higher values correspond to intervals that contain $\mathbf{x}$ for which one can reasonably expect that they should be ambiguity rejected between two (Figure 6) or three classes (Figure 7). The selection of the most appropriate order is still a question of selecting the appropriate number of classes by (11) through the definition of the $H-$function.

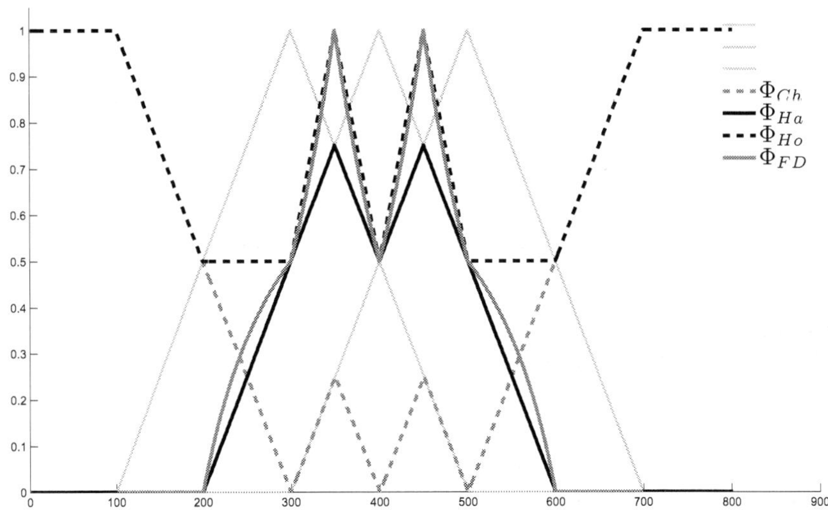

Fig. 6. Ambiguity measures $\Phi_{Ch}(\mathbf{u})$, and for $k + 1 = 2$, $\Phi_{FD}(\mathbf{u})$, $\Phi_{Ho}(\mathbf{u})$ and $\Phi_{Ha}(\mathbf{u})$ on the *real line example*.

Class-selective rule	Ambiguity Measure Φ	
(Ha, 1997)	$\Phi_{Ha}(\mathbf{u}) = u_{(k+1)}(\mathbf{x})$	(12)
	$\quad = \Phi_{k+1,\top_s}(\mathbf{u})$	
(Horiuchi, 1998)	$\Phi_{Ho}(\mathbf{u}) = 1 - (u_{(k)}(\mathbf{x}) - u_{(k+1)}(\mathbf{x}))$	(14)
(Frélicot & Dubuisson, 1992)	$\Phi_{FD}(\mathbf{u}) = u_{(k+1)}(\mathbf{x})/u_{(k)}(\mathbf{x})$	(15)
(Mascarilla *et. al*, 2008)	$\Phi_{k,\top}(\mathbf{u}) = \overset{k}{\bot}(\mathbf{u})$	(4)

Table 2. Class-selective rejection rules and corresponding ambiguity measures.

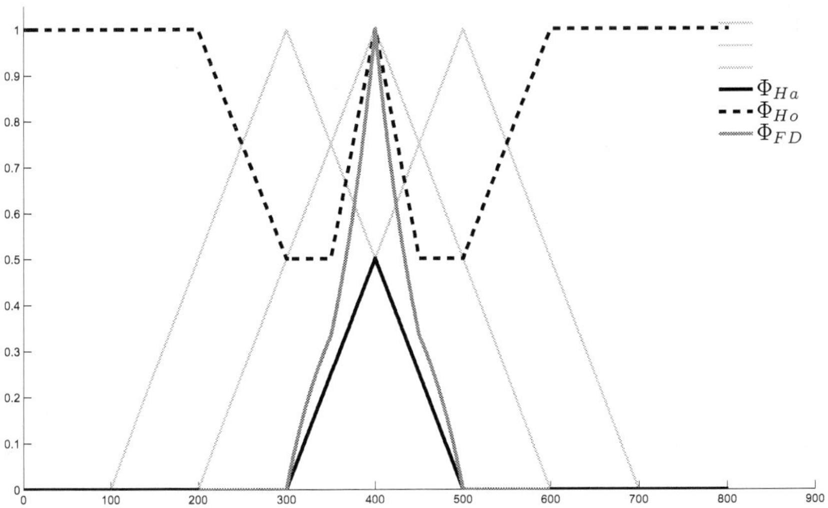

Fig. 7. Ambiguity measures $\Phi_{FD}(\mathbf{u})$, $\Phi_{Ho}(\mathbf{u})$ and $\Phi_{Ha}(\mathbf{u})$ on the *real line example* for $k+1 = 3$.

3.2 Unification of Class-selective Rejection Rules based on Ambiguity Measures

In order to derive $H-$functions that are able to deal with distance rejection using the ambiguity measures that allow it, namely Φ_{Ha}, Φ_{Ho}, Φ_{FD} and $\Phi_{k,\top}(\mathbf{u})$, we only need to replace (11) by:

$$n^\star(\mathbf{x}, t) = \min_{k \in [0,c]} \{k : \Phi(\mathbf{u}(\mathbf{x})) \le t\} \tag{16}$$

with default values $u_0(\mathbf{x}) = 1$ and $u_{c+1}(\mathbf{x}) = 0$. Therefore, the unified $H_{sel}-$function of a class-selective rejesion rule based on any of the ambiguitity measures of Table 2 is given by:

$$H_{sel}: \mathcal{L}_{\bullet c} \to \mathcal{L}_{hc}^c, \ \mathbf{u}(\mathbf{x}) \mapsto \mathbf{h}(\mathbf{x}) \text{ such as } h_i(\mathbf{x}) = 1 \text{ for all } i \in \{0, n^\star(\mathbf{x}, t)\}.$$

and its implementation is shown in Algorithm 1.

Algorithm 1: Class-selective rejection rule ($H-$function implementation).

Data: a vector of soft class-labels $\mathbf{u}(\mathbf{x}) \in \mathcal{L}_{pc}$ and a reject threshold t
Result: a vector of class-selective assignments $\mathbf{h}(\mathbf{x}) \in \mathcal{L}_{hc}^c$
begin
    set $\mathbf{h}(\mathbf{x})$ to 0
    given any ambiguity measure $\Phi(\mathbf{u})$ of Table 2, find $n^\star(\mathbf{x}, t)$ according to (16)
    foreach $j = 1 : n^\star(\mathbf{x}, t)$ **do**
        set $h_j(\mathbf{x}) = 1$ *in decreasing order of* $u_{(j)}(\mathbf{x})'s$
    end
end

Let us see the classification results obtained applying this common implementation of H_{sel} to some typical soft label vectors $\mathbf{u} \in \mathcal{L}_{pc}$, assumed to correspond to patterns $\mathbf{x}$, where $c = 4$:

- $\mathbf{u} = {}^t(0.70\ \ 0.10\ \ 0.85\ \ 0.80)$, so $\mathbf{x}$ is expected to be ambiguity rejected between three classes $\{\omega_1, \omega_3, \omega_4\}$,

- $\mathbf{u} = {}^t(0.20\ \ 0.10\ \ 0.85\ \ 0.80)$, so $\mathbf{x}$ is expected to be ambiguity rejected between two classes $\{\omega_3, \omega_4\}$,

- $\mathbf{u} = {}^t(0.20\ \ 0.10\ \ 0.85\ \ 0.15)$, so $\mathbf{x}$ is expected to be exclusively classified in one class $\{\omega_3\}$, and

- $\mathbf{u} = {}^t(0.20\ \ 0.10\ \ 0.05\ \ 0.15)$, so $\mathbf{x}$ is expected to be distance rejected.

The values of $\Phi(\mathbf{u}(\mathbf{x}))$ for all the values $k \in [0, c]$ are given in Table 3 as well as the interval of the threshold t leading to the (expected) correct classification above. One can see that all rules succeed by setting t to 0.5, except the ones based on $\Phi_{k,\top_H}(\mathbf{u})$ for which a smaller value is needed.

To end this presentation, we also can give the unified H_{rej}−function of a rejection rule based on any of the ambiguity measures summarized in Table 4:

$$H_{rej}: \mathcal{L}_{\bullet c} \to \{\mathcal{L}_{hc}, \underline{1}\}, \ \mathbf{u}(\mathbf{x}) \mapsto \mathbf{h}(\mathbf{x}) = \left\{ \begin{array}{ll} {}^t(1, 0, \cdots, 0) & \text{if } \Phi(\mathbf{u}) \leq t \\ \underline{1} & \text{otherwise} \end{array} \right.$$

As already mentioned, such rules only allow to either exclusively classify an incoming pattern $\mathbf{x}$ or to reject it between all the c classes at hand, and do not allow to select a subset of several classes the patterns have to be associated with or even none (distance rejection), see Figure 5 (*center*). Table 5 reports the classification results obtained applying H_{rej} to the typical soft label vectors $\mathbf{u} \in \mathcal{L}_{pc}$ for which the (unfortunately?) expected results are:

- rejection of the patterns for which $\mathbf{u} = {}^t(0.70\ 0.10\ 0.85\ 0.80)$, $\mathbf{u} = {}^t(0.20\ 0.10\ 0.85\ 0.80)$ and $\mathbf{u} = {}^t(0.20\ 0.10\ 0.05\ 0.15)$,

- exclusive classification of $\mathbf{x}$ in $\{\omega_3\}$ when $\mathbf{u} = {}^t(0.20\ \ 0.10\ \ 0.85\ \ 0.15)$.

One can see that the rules based on the $\Phi_{1,\top}(\mathbf{u})$ family succeed in recovering the expected results, whatever the triple $(\top, N, \bot)$, for any $t > 0.5$. Not surprisingly, the rules based on the $\Phi_{\bar{1},\top}(\mathbf{u})$ family fail most of time. The reasons have been discussed in the previous section, *e.g* the normalization problem. For instance, if you take $\frac{\mathbf{u}}{\sum_{i=1}^{c} u_i(\mathbf{x})}$ instead of $\mathbf{u}$, $\Phi_{\bar{1},\top_s}(\mathbf{u}) = \Phi_{Ch}(\mathbf{u})$ values are respectively: 0.65, 0.56, 0.34 and 0.60, so the expected results are obtained using the corresponding rule with $t > 0.34$.

4. Experimental Results

In this section, we report experiments carried out on both artificial and real benchmark data sets for which it is beneficial to use class-selective rejection rules or rejection rules because the classes overlap in the feature space. The different rules presented in section 3 are compared one to each other.

4.1 Data Sets and Protocol

Table 6 reports the characteristics (number n of patterns, number p of features, number c of classes, degree of overlap) of artificial and real data sets:

- synthetic datasets:

  - D contains 2000 points drawn from a mixture of $c = 2$ normal 7-dimensional distributions of 1000 points each with means $\mathbf{v}_1 = {}^t(1 \quad 0 \quad \cdots \quad 0)$ and $\mathbf{v}_2 = {}^t(-1 \quad 0 \quad \cdots \quad 0)$, and equal covariance matrices $\Sigma_1 = \Sigma_2 = I$,

  - D_H consists of two overlapping gaussian classes with different covariance matrices according to the Highleyman distribution, each composed of 800 observations in $\mathbb{R}^2$ (Highleyman, 1962), see Figure 8.

- real datasets from the UCI Machine Learning Repository (Blake & Merz, 1998).

The classification performance of the different rules are obtained by a 10-fold crossvalidation procedure on the different datasets. Each set of samples is divided at random into 10 approximately equal size and roughly balanced parts, ensuring that the classes are distributed proportionally among each of the 10 parts. The class-parameters are estimated on 90% of the samples (learning set χ) so that the degrees of typicality (1) of the remaining 10% test samples are computed and then their hard label vectors $\mathbf{h}(\mathbf{x})$ are predicted by each rule. This procedure is repeated 10 times, with each part playing the role of the test samples and the errors on all 10 parts added together to compute the overall error and therefore the performance.
In all cases, the threshold t is set to reject 10% of the data, so that 90% is the best achievable correct classification rate and then the error rate is $(90 - correct)\%$. Note that there are no points in the datasets which are identified as outliers even if they lie far from the classes they are assumed to come from, so that some of them can be uncorrectly distance rejected.

4.2 Comparative Performance

Tables 7 and 8 show the classification performance obtained using the presented class-selective rejection rules H_{sel} and rejection rules H_{rej} based on ambiguity measures that aggregate pattern soft labels, namely the $\Phi_{\bar{1},\top}$ and $\Phi_{1,\top}$ families on one hand, and Φ_{Ho}, Φ_{FD} and the $\Phi_{k,\top}$ family on the other hand. For both types, the best score is indicated in bold and the second best score is italicized. One can immediately see that Φ_{FD} is the overall best measure, for all the considered datasets, so it seems more interesting to analyze the results by setting apart it.

Globally, class-selective rules perform better than rejection rules, so the $\Phi_{k,\top}$ family gives better results than the two other families. Also the $\Phi_{1,\top}$ family slightly outperforms the $\Phi_{\bar{1},\top}$ one. However, the $\Phi_{k,\top}$ family appears to be more sensitive to $(\top, \bot)$ than the two others, so its performance variation is higher, especially for some datasets having a number of classes greater than two (e.g. Thyroid and Glass). A positive consequence is its potential good performance compared to other families and the Horiuchi's rule, probably because more than two classes are overlapping so that the interaction between membership degrees is more important. A negative one is the need for the practitioner to carefully choose $(\top, \bot)$. About this choice, the particularly good results obtained using the Dombi norms with $\gamma = 2$ must be emphasized for the $\Phi_{k,\top}$ family compared to Horiuchi's rule and Ha's rule for some datasets (e.g. D, D_H and Thyroid), as well as compared to the other norms within the $\Phi_{\bar{1},\top}$ and $\Phi_{1,\top}$

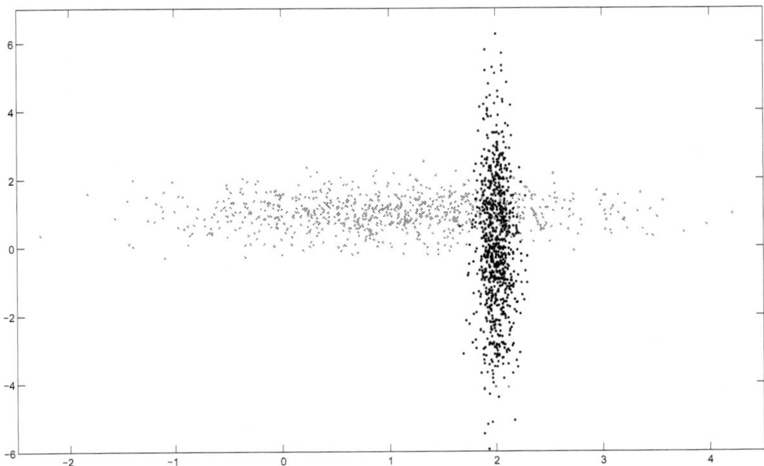

Fig. 8. Highleyman data set D_H.

families. Note finally that, keeping in mind that these two families are less sensitive to $(\top, \bot)$ and the already mentioned asymptotic behaviour of Dombi norms, the Standard norms (so Chow's rule for $\Phi_{\bar{1},\top}$) gives also quite good results for most of the datasets.

5. Conclusion

The problem of aggregating collections of numerical data to obtain a typical value is present in many decision systems. Aggregation operators are used to obtain an overall value for each alternative, which is exploited to establish a final decision. In the context of supervised pattern classification, such a decision consists in assigning objects (or patterns) to one class based on the aggregation of soft labels related to the given classes (posterior probabilities, fuzzy membership degrees, typicality degrees). It is well known that overlapping classes and outliers can significantly decrease a classifier performance and it has been proved that the misclassification risk can significantly be reduced by allowing a classifier to reject extraneous and/or ambiguous patterns (Dubuisson & Masson, 1993), (Tax & Duin, 2008). This results in designing classification rules that allow to assign a pattern to zero (distance rejection), one (exclusive classification) or several (ambiguity rejection) classes, in other words to select a number of classes.

This chapter addressed the problem of designing such rules that use ambiguity measures to aggregate pattern soft labels. The contribution is two-fold. An unified view of the resulting classifiers which can be either class-selective rules or simply rejection rules, depending on the ambiguity measure. Three families of ambiguity measures, based on combination of basic triangular norms and conorms as well as parametric ones, are presented. They allow to derive as many rules as many triangular norms (an infinite number!) and it is shown that they generalize some historical rules, namely Chow's rejection rule (Chow, 1957 & 1970) and Ha's class-selective rule (Ha, 1996 & 1997). An analysis of all ambiguity measures is provided and the classification performance of all the rules on synthetic and real data sets from the public domain of various characteristics (dimensionality, number of classes, degree of overlap) is given.

From the pratitioner's point of view, the choice of a particular triangular couple and/or its parameter value needs further investigation because it influences the behaviour of the ambiguity measure, hence the classification performance. For instance, the threshold on the ambiguity measure is easier to tune using a cautious couple (*e.g.* Standard or Dombi family) than a quite drastic one (*e.g.* Lukaziewicz). A future work will consist in studying more extensively how the mathematical properties of the basic norms affect the behaviour of the families of ambiguity measures and therefore the classification performances, in order to provide guidelines to choose them according to specific operational situations. Another perspective concerns the definition of a family of ambiguity measures based on an new aggregation operator which allows to measure to what extent an exact number of soft labels, but not necessarily the highest ones, are similar . A first proposition can be found in (Le Capitaine & Frélicot, 2008).

$\mathbf{u} = {}^t(0.70\ 0.10\ 0.85\ 0.80)$	$k =$	0	1	2	3	4	$\forall t \in$
	$\Phi_{Ho}(\mathbf{u})$	0.85	0.95	0.90	0.40	0.90	$[0.40, 0.90[$
	$\Phi_{FD}(\mathbf{u})$	0.85	0.94	0.87	0.14	0	$[0.14, 0.87[$
	$\top_S \Rightarrow \Phi_{Ha}(\mathbf{u})$	0.85	0.80	0.70	0.10	0	$[0.10, 0.70[$
	$\top_A$	0.99	0.86	0.39	0.02	0	$[0.02, 0.39[$
	$\top_L$	1	1	0.65	0	0	$[0, 0.65[$
$\Phi_{k,\top}(\mathbf{u})$	$\top_{H_0}$	0.92	0.64	0.37	0.08	0	$[0.08, 0.37[$
	$\top_{H_2}$	0.99	0.92	0.39	0.00	0	$[0, 0.39[$
	$\top_{D_{1.5}}$	0.89	0.70	0.51	0.09	0	$[0.09, 0.51[$
	$\top_{D_2}$	0.87	0.73	0.58	0.09	0	$[0.09, 0.58[$

$\mathbf{u} = {}^t(0.20\ 0.10\ 0.85\ 0.80)$	$k =$	0	1	2	3	4	$\forall t \in$
	$\Phi_{Ho}(\mathbf{u})$	0.85	0.95	0.40	0.90	0.90	$[0.40, 0.85[$
	$\Phi_{FD}(\mathbf{u})$	0.85	0.94	0.25	0.50	0	$[0.25, 0.85[$
	$\top_S \Rightarrow \Phi_{Ha}(\mathbf{u})$	0.85	0.80	0.20	0.10	0	$[0.20, 0.80[$
	$\top_A$	0.97	0.70	0.10	0.00	0	$[0.10, 0.70[$
	$\top_L$	1	1	0.15	0	0	$[0.15, 1[$
$\Phi_{k,\top}(\mathbf{u})$	$\top_{H_0}$	0.90	0.58	0.18	0.05	0	$[0.18, 0.58[$
	$\top_{H_2}$	0.99	0.76	0.07	0.00	0	$[0.07, 0.76[$
	$\top_{D_{1.5}}$	0.88	0.67	0.21	0.07	0	$[0.21, 0.67[$
	$\top_{D_2}$	0.87	0.71	0.21	0.08	0	$[0.21, 0.71[$

$\mathbf{u} = {}^t(0.20\ 0.10\ 0.85\ 0.15)$	$k =$	0	1	2	3	4	$\forall t \in$
	$\Phi_{Ho}(\mathbf{u})$	0.85	0.35	0.95	0.95	0.90	$[0.35, 0.85[$
	$\Phi_{FD}(\mathbf{u})$	0.85	0.23	0.75	0.67	0	$[0.23, 0.85[$
	$\top_S \Rightarrow \Phi_{Ha}(\mathbf{u})$	0.85	0.20	0.15	0.10	0	$[0.20, 0.85[$
	$\top_A$	0.90	0.24	0.00	0.00	0	$[0.24, 0.90[$
	$\top_L$	1	0.45	0	0	0	$[0.45, 1[$
$\Phi_{k,\top}(\mathbf{u})$	$\top_{H_0}$	0.86	0.28	0.08	0.03	0	$[0.28, 0.86[$
	$\top_{H_2}$	0.93	0.25	0.00	0.00	0	$[0.25, 0.93[$
	$\top_{D_{1.5}}$	0.85	0.26	0.10	0.05	0	$[0.26, 0.85[$
	$\top_{D_2}$	0.85	0.24	0.11	0.07	0	$[0.24, 0.85[$

$\mathbf{u} = {}^t(0.20\ 0.10\ 0.05\ 0.15)$	$k =$	0	1	2	3	4	$\forall t \in$
	$\Phi_{Ho}(\mathbf{u})$	0.20	0.95	0.95	0.95	0	$[0.20, 1[$
	$\Phi_{FD}(\mathbf{u})$	0.20	0.75	0.67	0.5	0	$[0.20, 1[$
	$\top_S \Rightarrow \Phi_{Ha}(\mathbf{u})$	0.20	0.15	0.10	0.05	0	$[0.20, 1[$
	$\top_A$	0.41	0.00	0.00	0.00	0	$[0.41, 1[$
	$\top_L$	0.50	0	0	0	0	$[0.50, 1[$
$\Phi_{k,\top}(\mathbf{u})$	$\top_{H_0}$	0.37	0.08	0.03	0.01	0	$[0.37, 1[$
	$\top_{H_2}$	0.46	0.00	0.00	0.00	0	$[0.46, 1[$
	$\top_{D_{1.5}}$	0.28	0.10	0.05	0.02	0	$[0.28, 1[$
	$\top_{D_2}$	0.24	0.11	0.06	0.03	0	$[0.24, 1[$

Table 3. Ambiguity measures derived from class-selective rules for different $\mathbf{u}$ for which $n^\star(\mathbf{x}, t) = 3, 2, 1, 0$ respectively (from top to bottom), $\forall t$ in the specified interval.

Rejection rule	Ambiguity Measure Φ	
(Chow, 1970)	$\Phi_{Ch}(\mathbf{u}) = 1 - u_{(1)}(\mathbf{x})$	(9)
	$= \Phi_{\overline{1},\top_S}(\mathbf{u})$	
(Mascarilla & Frélicot, 2001)	$\Phi_{\underline{1},\top}(\mathbf{u}) = 1 - \underline{\perp}(\mathbf{u})$	(7)
(Frélicot & Le Capitaine, 2009, this book)	$\Phi_{\overline{1},\top}(\mathbf{u}) = 1 - \perp(\mathbf{u})$	(5)

Table 4. Rejection rules and corresponding ambiguity measures.

$\mathbf{u} = {}^{t}(0.70\ 0.10\ 0.85\ 0.80)$		
$\Phi_{\overline{1},\top}(\mathbf{u})$	$\top_S \Rightarrow \Phi_{Ch}(\mathbf{u})$	0.15
	$\top_A$	0.00
	$\top_L$	0
	$\top_{H_0}$	0.07
	$\top_{H_2}$	0.00
	$\top_{D_{1.5}}$	0.10
	$\top_{D_2}$	0.12
$\Phi_{\underline{1},\top}(\mathbf{u})$	$\top_S$	0.94
	$\top_A$	0.89
	$\top_L$	1
	$\top_{H_0}$	0.75
	$\top_{H_2}$	0.94
	$\top_{D_{1.5}}$	0.81
	$\top_{D_2}$	0.86

$\mathbf{u} = {}^{t}(0.20\ 0.10\ 0.85\ 0.80)$		
$\Phi_{\overline{1},\top}(\mathbf{u})$	$\top_S \Rightarrow \Phi_{Ch}(\mathbf{u})$	0.15
	$\top_A$	0.02
	$\top_L$	0
	$\top_{H_0}$	0.09
	$\top_{H_2}$	0.01
	$\top_{D_{1.5}}$	0.11
	$\top_{D_2}$	0.13
$\Phi_{\underline{1},\top}(\mathbf{u})$	$\top_S$	0.94
	$\top_A$	0.75
	$\top_L$	1
	$\top_{H_0}$	0.70
	$\top_{H_2}$	0.79
	$\top_{D_{1.5}}$	0.78
	$\top_{D_2}$	0.84

$\mathbf{u} = {}^{t}(0.20\ 0.10\ 0.85\ 0.15)$		
$\Phi_{\overline{1},\top}(\mathbf{u})$	$\top_S \Rightarrow \Phi_{Ch}(\mathbf{u})$	0.15
	$\top_A$	0.09
	$\top_L$	0
	$\top_{H_0}$	0.13
	$\top_{H_2}$	0.06
	$\top_{D_{1.5}}$	0.15
	$\top_{D_2}$	0.15
$\Phi_{\underline{1},\top}(\mathbf{u})$	$\top_S$	0.24
	$\top_A$	0.37
	$\top_L$	0.45
	$\top_{H_0}$	0.41
	$\top_{H_2}$	0.36
	$\top_{D_{1.5}}$	0.34
	$\top_{D_2}$	0.31

$\mathbf{u} = {}^{t}(0.20\ 0.10\ 0.05\ 0.15)$		
$\Phi_{\overline{1},\top}(\mathbf{u})$	$\top_S \Rightarrow \Phi_{Ch}(\mathbf{u})$	0.80
	$\top_A$	0.58
	$\top_L$	0.5
	$\top_{H_0}$	0.62
	$\top_{H_2}$	0.53
	$\top_{D_{1.5}}$	0.71
	$\top_{D_2}$	0.75
$\Phi_{\underline{1},\top}(\mathbf{u})$	$\top_S$	0.80
	$\top_A$	0.60
	$\top_L$	0.50
	$\top_{H_0}$	0.68
	$\top_{H_2}$	0.55
	$\top_{D_{1.5}}$	0.73
	$\top_{D_2}$	0.77

Table 5. Ambiguity measures derived from rejection rules for different $\mathbf{u}$.

Data set	n	p	c	overlap
D	2000	7	2	slight
D_H	1600	2	2	very slight
$Digits$	10992	16	10	very slight
$Thyroid$	215	5	3	very slight
$Pima$	768	9	2	strong
$Statlog$	6435	36	6	slight
$Glass$	214	9	6	moderate

Table 6. Datasets and their characteristics.

(%)		D	D_H	$Digits$	$Thyroid$	$Pima$	$Statlog$	$Glass$
$\Phi_{Ho}(\mathbf{u})$		77.95	83.88	88.76	86.98	62.89	**77.68**	68.22
$\Phi_{FD}(\mathbf{u})$		**79.05**	**86.75**	89.13	**87.91**	**63.28**	77.48	**71.03**
$\Phi_{k,\mathsf{T}}(\mathbf{u})$	$\mathsf{T}_S \Rightarrow \Phi_{Ha}(\mathbf{u})$	78.15	86.63	87.38	86.98	60.55	75.56	69.63
	T_A	77.55	86.19	86.21	84.19	60.16	75.23	67.76
	T_L	77.55	86.50	86.60	84.38	60.16	75.29	67.76
	T_{Ho}	77.75	86.50	86.60	86.98	60.68	75.29	68.22
	T_{H_2}	77.55	86.06	86.21	84.19	60.16	75.23	67.76
	$\mathsf{T}_{D_{1.5}}$	78.10	86.56	86.82	86.98	60.55	75.23	68.69
	T_{D_2}	78.20	86.63	86.96	87.44	60.55	75.15	68.69

Table 7. Classification performance of class-selective rejection rules on datasets.

(%)		D	D_H	$Digits$	$Thyroid$	$Pima$	$Statlog$	$Glass$
$\Phi_{\bar{1},\mathsf{T}}(\mathbf{u})$	$\mathsf{T}_S \Rightarrow \Phi_{Ch}(\mathbf{u})$	75.15	**83.75**	88.03	84.19	59.51	**75.66**	**66.82**
	T_A	75.55	83.13	87.55	**85.12**	60.81	74.73	65.89
	T_L	75.55	83.13	87.55	**85.12**	60.81	74.73	65.89
	T_{Ho}	75.55	83.13	87.55	**85.12**	60.81	74.73	65.89
	T_{H_2}	75.55	83.13	87.55	**85.12**	60.81	74.73	65.89
	$\mathsf{T}_{D_{1.5}}$	75.65	83.13	87.76	**85.12**	61.07	74.97	66.36
	T_{D_2}	75.75	83.19	87.84	**85.12**	61.33	75.12	65.82
$\Phi_{1,\mathsf{T}}(\mathbf{u})$	T_S	75.90	83.44	**88.04**	**85.12**	**61.59**	**75.66**	**66.82**
	T_A	77.55	83.13	87.55	**85.12**	60.81	74.73	65.89
	T_L	77.55	83.13	87.55	**85.12**	60.81	74.73	65.89
	T_{Ho}	77.55	83.13	87.55	**85.12**	60.81	74.73	65.89
	T_{H_2}	77.55	83.13	87.55	**85.12**	60.81	74.73	65.89
	$\mathsf{T}_{D_{1.5}}$	77.65	83.13	87.76	**85.12**	60.55	74.97	66.36
	T_{D_2}	**77.75**	83.19	87.84	**85.12**	61.33	75.12	**66.82**

Table 8. Classification performance of rejection rules on datasets.

6. References

Bezdek, J.C & Keller, J.M. & Krishnapuram, R. & Pal, N.R. (1999). Fuzzy Models and Algorithms for Pattern Recognition and Image Processing, Kluwer Academic

Blake, C. & Merz, C. (1998). UCI repository of machine learning databases, http://www.ics.uci.edu/mlearn/ MLRepository.html

Calvo, C. & Mayor, G. & Mesiar, R. (2002). Aggregation Operators: New Trends and Applications, Physica-Verlag

Chow, C.K. (1957). An optimum character recognition system using decision functions. IRE Transactions on Electronic Computers, Vol. 6, No 4, 247-254

Chow, C.K. (1970). On optimum error and reject tradeoff. IEEE Transactions on Information Theory, Vol. 16, No 1, 41-46

Dubuisson, B. & Masson, M. (1993). A statistical decision rule with incomplete knowledge about classes. Pattern Recognition, Vol. 26, No 1, 155-165

Frélicot, C. (1998). On unifying probabilistic/fuzzy and possibilistic rejection-based classifiers, In Lecture Notes in Computer Science 1451: Advances in Pattern Recognition, A. Amin & D. Dori & P. Pudil & H. Freeman (Eds), 736-745, Springer

Frélicot, C. & Dubuisson, B. (1992). A multi-step predictor of membership function as an ambiguity reject solver in pattern recognition, Proceedings of 4th International Conference on Information Processing and Management of Uncertainty in Knowledge-based Systems, pp. 709-715, Palma de Mallorca, Spain

Frélicot, C. & Mascarilla, L. (2002). Reject strategies driven combination of pattern classifiers. Pattern Analysis and Applications, Vol. 5, No 2, 234-243

Grabisch, M. (1992). Fuzzy pattern recognition by fuzzy integrals and fuzzy rules, In: Pattern Recognition - From Classical to Modern Approaches, S. Pal and P. Pal (Eds), 257-280, World Scientific

Grabisch, M. & Marichal, J. & Mesiar, R. & Pap, E. (2009). Aggregation Functions, Cambridge University Press, No 127 in Encyclopedia of Mathematics and its Applications

Ha, T. (1996). An optimum class-selective rejection rule for pattern recognition, Proceedings of 13th International Conference on Pattern Recognition, Vol. 2, pp. 75-80, Vienna, Austria

Ha, T. (1997). The optimum class-selective rejection rule. IEEE Transactions on Pattern Analysis and Machine Intelligence, Vol. 19, No. 6, 608-615

Highleyman, W. (1962). Linear decision functions, with application to pattern recognition, Proceedings of the IRE, Vol. 50, No 6, 1501-1514

Horiuchi, T. (1998). Class-selective rejection rule to minimize the maximum distance between selected classes. Pattern Recognition, Vol. 31, No 10, 1579-1588

Klement, E. & Mesiar, R. (2005). Algebraic, Analytic, and Probabilistic Aspects of Triangular Norms, Elsevier

Le Capitaine, H. & Frélicot, C. (2008). A class-selective rejection scheme based on blockwise similarity of typicality degrees, Proceedings of 19th IAPR International Conference on Pattern Recognition, Tampa, Florida

Mascarilla, L. & Berthier, M. & Frélicot, C. (2008). A k-order fuzzy or operator for pattern classification with k-order ambiguity rejection. Fuzzy Sets and Systems, Vol. 159, No 15, 2011-2029

Mascarilla, L. & Frélicot, C. (2001). A class of reject-first possibilistic classifiers based on dual triples, Proceedings of 9th International Fuzzy Systems Association Worldcongress, pp. 743-747, Vancouver, Canada

Menger, K (1942). Statistical metrics, Proceedings of the National Academy of Science USA, Vol. 28, No 12, pp. 535-537

Sugeno, M. (1974). Theory of fuzzy integrals and its applications, PhD thesis of the Tokyo Institute of Technology

Tax, D. & Duin, R. (2008). Growing a multi-class classifier with a reject option. Pattern Recognition Letters, Vol. 29, No 10, 1565-1570

Yager, R.R. (1988). Ordered weighted averaging aggregation operators in multi-criteria decision making. IEEE Transactions on Systems, Man, and Cybernetics, Vol. 18, No 1, 183-186

Zimmermann, H.J. & Zysno, P. (1985). Quantifying vagueness in decision models. European Journal of Operational Research, Vol. 22, No 2, 148-158

## 3

A Model-Based Approach for Building Optimum Classification Cascades

Ezzat El-Sherif and Sherif Abdelazeem,
Electronics Engineering Department, American University in Cairo
ezzatali@aucegypt.edu, shazeem@aucegypt.edu

For a long time, the main concern of the pattern recognition research community has been to achieve high accuracy. For example, in the area of Multi-Classifier Systems (MCS), researchers have developed very powerful techniques that combine large number of classifiers through complex combination schemes to achieve satisfactory accuracies. However, this was at the expense of complexity. Even powerful single classifiers (e.g. SVM) have very high complexity. This might give the impression that high accuracies could not be achieved without sacrificing recognition time.

Classification cascades are relatively neglected because speed is usually considered a secondary issue by researchers in pattern recognition field. This fact is going to change in the near future because as the world relies more and more on the Internet, web applications are going to include very complex pattern recognition and data mining tasks that are required to be done online.

Classification cascades are usually created manually using domain knowledge and are composed in most cases of two or three stages. In this chapter, a model-based algorithm of automatic generation of optimum classification cascades is devised. Given a large pool of classifiers (of size N), it builds a cascade that achieves the lowest possible recognition time while preserving the accuracy of the most powerful classifier in the pool. The proposed algorithm has a low complexity of $O(N^2)$ where N is the number of classifiers in the pool. This gives us the freedom of using a large pool of classifiers which leads to more efficient cascades. Other cascade design techniques devised in the literature have very high complexity which hinders using large pool of classifiers.

In this chapter we also analyze the performance of the devised algorithm showing its powerfulness and limitations. Also we present an algorithm for building a classification cascade of a given fixed length. This helps building cascades with space complexity constraints and helps in analyzing the performance of the devised algorithm for building optimum classification cascades.

1. Introduction

Suppose we have a classification task on which we have already found a complex classification technique that achieves a satisfactory accuracy. Suppose also while such classification technique is very powerful, its time complexity is unacceptably high. This scenario happens frequently in real life as many powerful but very time-consuming techniques have been devised in recent years (e.g. SVM and multi-classifier systems). Our goal would be to build a system that preserves the accuracy of that complex classifier while having much better timing performance.

The high complexity of powerful classifiers might give the impression that high accuracies could not be achieved without sacrificing recognition time. In fact, this is not true. The high recognition time of a classifier in many cases is due to improper resource allocation. To achieve a high recognition rate, the classifier is built to recognize the hardest of patterns; though most of the patterns are 'regular' patterns and could be classified using a simple classification technique. This observation led to the development of cascade systems which is the main concern of this paper. In such a system, all the patterns to be classified first go through a first stage; those patterns that are classified with confidence score higher than a certain threshold leave the system with the labels given to them by the first stage. The patterns that are classified with confidence scores lower than the threshold are rejected to the second stage. In the same manner, the patterns pass through different stages until they reach the powerful last stage that does not reject any patterns. Figure 1 illustrates this idea.

The idea of classification cascades has been well-known for long time but has not attracted much attention in spite of its practical importance [Kuncheva 2004]. Recently, and since the prominent work of Viola and Jones [VIOLA & JONES 2001], the idea of cascade has been attracting considerable attention in the context of object detection which is a rare-event classification problem [VIOLA & JONES 2001, LUO 2005, CHEN, X. & YUILLE 2005, YUANN ET AL. 2005, Brubaker et al. 2006, SUN ET AL. 2004, WU ET AL. 2008].

To avoid any confusion, we will call the cascades used in the context of object detection "detection cascades" while we will call the cascades used in regular classification problems "classification cascades" in which we are interested in this chapter.

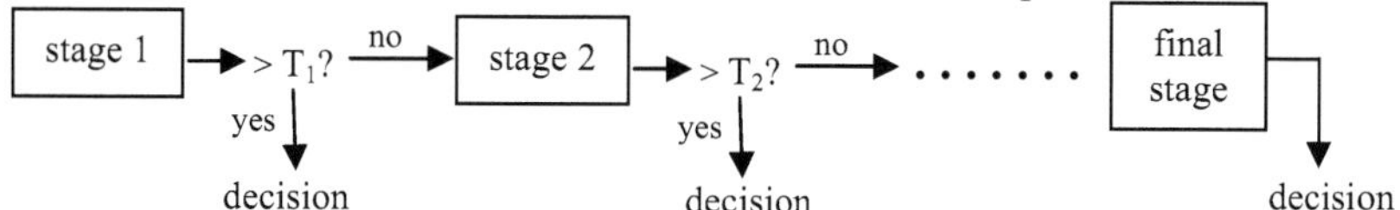

Fig 1 Typical classification cascade system.

The remaining of the chapter is organized as follows. Section 2 presents an algorithm for automatically generating optimum classification cascades. In section 3, we present an algorithm for generating optimum classification cascades of specific number of stages. Section 4 presents an experimental validation of our proposed algorithms. In section 5 we review previous works on classification cascades and in section 6 we conclude.

2. Model-Based Algorithm for Automatically Generating Optimum Classification Cascades

In this section a novel algorithm for automatically generating optimum classification cascades is proposed that achieves as high accuracy as we can get with the lowest complexity possible. The proposed algorithm is built according to a model of how classification cascade works; thus we named it 'model-based' approach. Assume that we have a pool of N classifiers: S_1, S_2, ..., S_N, and a powerful classifier S_F that achieves an accuracy higher than any classifier in the pool. However, S_F has a very high complexity. The proposed algorithm automatically builds a cascade that achieves accuracy not less than that of S_F with the lowest complexity possible. Classifiers of the pool are assumed to be trained independently before applying the proposed algorithm, and no further training is done for any of them after applying the algorithm.

2.1 Problem statement

We first present our notation. We denote an unordered set by boldface character surrounded by curly braces, and its elements by the same character but in italics and subscripted by numbers (e.g. $A_1, A_2, A_3,... \in \{\mathbf{A}\}$). Note that the subscripts of the unordered set are arbitrary and hold no ordering significance. An ordered set (or an array) is denoted by just a boldface character and its elements by the same character but in italics and subscripted by numbers according to their order in the array (e.g. $A_1, A_2, A_3,... \in \mathbf{A}$, where A_1 is the first element in $\mathbf{A}$, and A_2 is the second element, etc.). $\mathbf{B} \subset \mathbf{A}$ means that all the elements of the ordered set $\mathbf{B}$ exists in the ordered set $\mathbf{A}$ with the same order. $\mathbf{B} \subset \{\mathbf{A}\}$ means that all the elements of the ordered set $\mathbf{B}$ exist in the unordered set {A}. $\mathbf{B} \equiv \{\mathbf{A}\}$ means that the elements of $\mathbf{B}$ are the same as that of $\mathbf{A}$ but with order, i.e. $\mathbf{B}$ is an ordered version of $\mathbf{A}$. We enumerate the elements of an unordered set {A} as follows $\{\mathbf{A}\} = \{A_1, A_2,...\}$ and the elements of an ordered set $\mathbf{A}$ as follows $\mathbf{A} = [A_1\ A_2\ ...]$. C=[A B] means that the ordered set $\mathbf{C}$ is a concatenation of the two ordered sets $\mathbf{A}$ and $\mathbf{B}$. In this chapter we will represent a cascade by an ordered set whose elements are the classification stages ordered in the set from left to right.

Here we state our problem. Given a set of N classifiers $\{\mathbf{S}\} = \{S_1, S_2, S_3,..., S_N\}$ and a powerful classifier $S_F \notin \{\mathbf{S}\}$ that achieves a satisfactory accuracy. The problem is to select an ordered set $\mathbf{S}^{opt} \subset \{\mathbf{S}\}$ and a corresponding ordered set of thresholds $\mathbf{T}^{opt}$ that makes $[\mathbf{S}^{opt}\ S_F]$ if put in a cascade structure give the optimal cascade. We mean by 'optimal cascade' the one that gives the least possible complexity with accuracy not less than that of S_F.

2.2 The Algorithm

In this section, an algorithm that automatically generates optimal classification cascades will be presented. The algorithm is composed of three major steps:

i.   Find the set of thresholds {T}. Each element of {T} is a threshold for the corresponding classifier in {S} such that $\mathbf{T}^{opt} \subset \{\mathbf{T}\}$.

ii.   Sort the set {S} to form $\mathbf{S}^{ord} \equiv \{\mathbf{S}\}$ such that $\mathbf{S}^{opt} \subset \mathbf{S}^{ord}$. With the same ordering pattern of $\mathbf{S}^{ord}$, sort {T} to form $\mathbf{T}^{ord}$.

iii.   From $\mathbf{S}^{ord}$, select $\mathbf{S}^{opt} \subset \mathbf{S}^{ord}$ $_t$ and the corresponding $\mathbf{T}^{opt} \subset \mathbf{T}^{ord}$.

These three steps is illustrated in Figure 2 and described in the following subsections. But we want here to give a note about how {S} and S_F were generated. The dataset available for training and testing the system was first partitioned into 3 parts: training set, validation set, and test set. Then, many classifiers were generated with different accuracies and complexities and were trained using the training set. The most powerful of these classifiers was found and denoted by S_F, and the rest were grouped in the set {S}. The validation set is used to find the best cascade. The test set is used for testing the overall system. The algorithm proposed in this chapter for generating classification cascade trains the classifiers only once and uses different performance measurements (specifically, their rejection rates and complexities, as will be discussed soon) of these classifiers using the validation set to build the cascade. No retraining of classifiers is held.

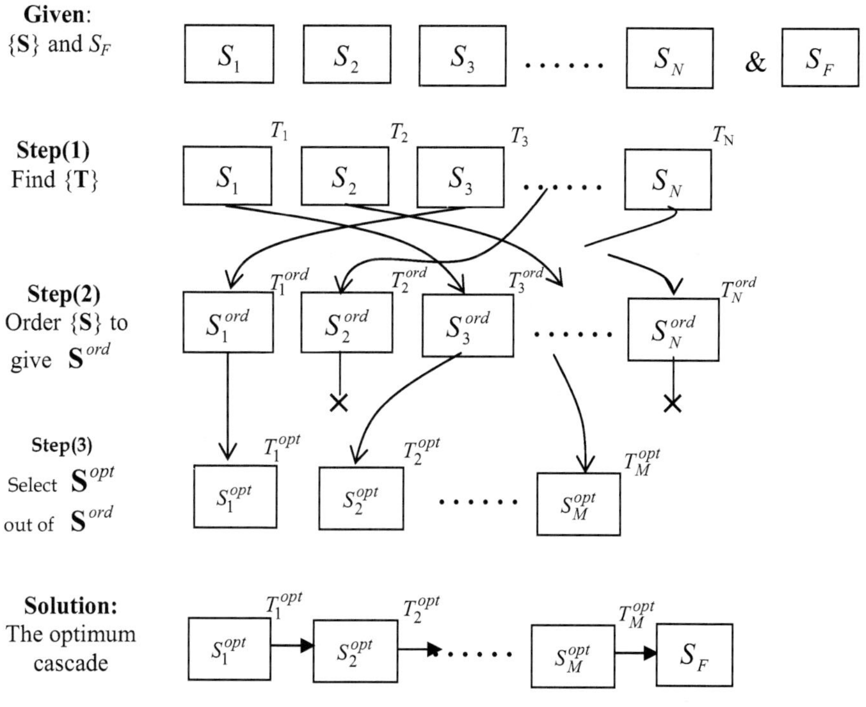

Fig. 2. An example to show how the proposed algorithm works.

2.2.1 Step1: Find {T} for {S}

Our procedure for finding {T} of {S} will be as follows. Using every classifier $S_i \in \{\mathbf{S}\}$, classify the patterns of the validations set and order them according to the confidence scores they are given by S_i. Traverse these ordered patterns from the one that has been classified by the highest confidence score to the lowest. While traversing the patterns, monitor whether the patterns are correctly or falsely classified. Once you hit a pattern that is falsely classified, check whether this same pattern is falsely classified by S_F or not. If yes, then this pattern would not contribute to the errors of the overall cascade and can be safely ignored, and we continue traversing the patterns. We stop when we hit a pattern that is falsely classified by the classifier under consideration S_i but correctly classified by S_F. Then we set the threshold T_i of the classifier S_i to be the confidence score of the pattern we stopped at. We do the same for all the classifiers in the set {S} to form the corresponding set of thresholds {T}. This procedure is illustrated in Figure 3.

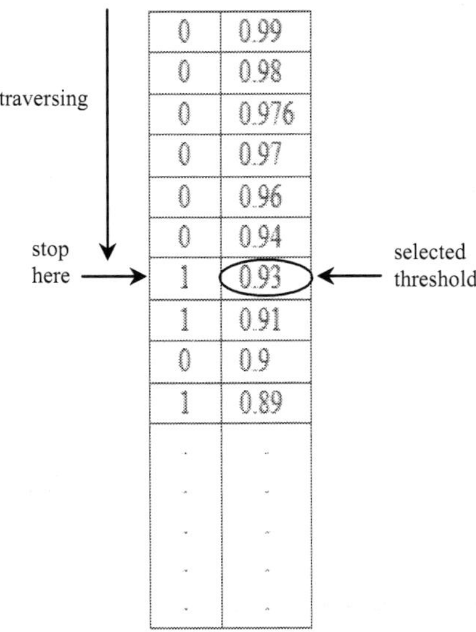

Fig. 3. A hypothetical example illustrating threshold selection process for some classifier S_i belongs to the pool $\{S\}$. Each row represents a different pattern of the validation set classified by S_i. The right entry of each record is labeled '1' if a classification error is committed by S_i while the pattern is correctly classified by the most powerful classifier S_F. The second entry of each record is the top decision score of the corresponding pattern given to it by S_i. The patterns are ordered according to the decision score. This process is done for every classifier in $\{S\}$ to get the corresponding set of thresholds $\{T\}$.

2.2.2 Step 2: Sort {S} to form $S^{ord} = \{S\}$

The criterion by which we sort $\{S\}$ is based on the following assumption:

Assumption 1 Using sufficiently tough thresholds T_i and T_j for the two classifiers S_i and S_j, respectively, if the classifier S_j has a lower rejection rate than S_i, then it is said that S_j is more powerful than S_i; and S_i would reject all the patterns that S_j would reject.

The "rejection rate" of a certain classifier S_i using threshold T_i is the number of rejected patterns divided by the number of validation set patterns if the threshold T_i is applied on its output.

This assumption, while not perfectly realistic, is reasonable. Since S_j is more powerful than S_i, then it will be of little possibility for S_i to *confidently* classify some pattern that was hard for S_j to classify. To what extent this assumption is valid will be discussed in section 4.2.

Assumption 1 leads to a great simplification of the system design. Suppose that while designing a cascade system we put a classifier S_2 that has high rejection rate after a classifier S_1 that has lower rejection rate. According to Assumption 1, S_1 is more powerful than S_2, and S_2 would be then useless. This is because S_2 would reject all the patterns that are rejected from S_1. In this case, S_2 would do nothing except increasing the complexity of the cascade.

This means that the only reasonable criterion of sorting the classifiers in the cascade is to sort them by decreasing rejection rates. By this principle, {S} is sorted to give $\mathbf{S}^{ord}$. The corresponding set of thresholds for $\mathbf{S}^{ord}$ will be $\mathbf{T}^{ord}$. Now we are guaranteed that $\mathbf{S}^{opt} \subset \mathbf{S}^{ord}$, because any other order would give more complex cascade.

2.2.3 Step 3: Select $\mathbf{S}^{opt}$ out of $\mathbf{S}^{ord}$

Now we want to select $\mathbf{S}^{opt} \subset \mathbf{S}^{ord}$. This selection process, if done exhaustively, is of complexity $O(2^N)$. Hence, exhaustive search would not be feasible for large values of N. In this section an algorithm is suggested for finding $\mathbf{S}^{opt} \subset \mathbf{S}^{ord}$ of complexity $O(N^2)$.

Now, a formula will be introduced to have an estimate for the average complexity of a cascade given the complexities and rejection rates of the constituent classifiers. This formula will be used to find the best cascade in a sequential manner without doing an exhaustive search. How this formula is deduced can be shown through an example. Let $\mathbf{S}' = [S_1'\ S_2'\ S_3'\ ....S_M'] \subset \mathbf{S}^{ord}$ have thresholds $\mathbf{T}' = [T_1'\ T_2'\ T_3'\ ...T_M']$, complexities $\mathbf{C}' = [C_1'\ C_2'\ C_3'\ ....C_M']$, and rejection rates $\mathbf{R}' = [R_1'\ R_2'\ R_3'\ ....R_M']$. Let C_F be the complexity of S_F. Figure 4 represents each stage in the cascade by a rectangular representing the validation set. The hashed portion of the rectangular is the portion that is not rejected from the validation set. Assumption 1 is evident in Figure 4 as each stage rejections include the rejections of preceding stage. It is obvious from Figure4 that the cascade $[\mathbf{S}'\ C_F]$ has an overall complexity C_{tot}, where,

$$C_{tot} = C_1' + R_1'C_2' + R_2'C_3' + ...+ R_{M-1}'C_M' + R_M'C_F \qquad (1)$$

We note here that Equation (1) validity is dependent on a hypothetical model of how the classification cascades works which is represented by Figure 4. This model in its turn is dependent on the validity Assumption 1.

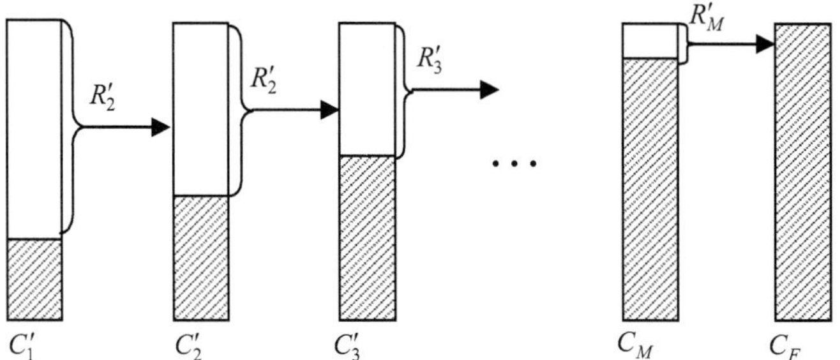

Fig. 4. A cascade represented by accepted and rejected patterns. The shaded region represents the accepted patterns.

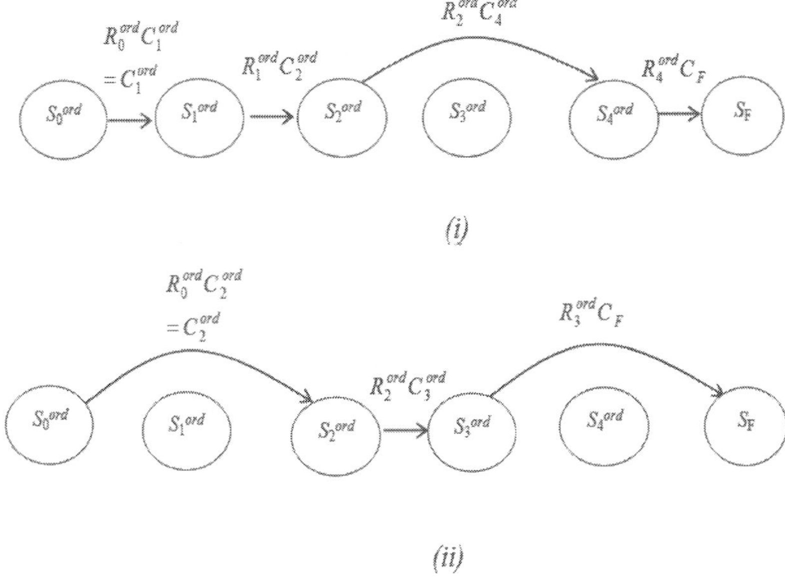

Fig. 5. Two examples to illustrate how $\mathbf{S}^{opt}$ is selected from $\mathbf{S}^{ord}$

Equation (1) suggests a very simple algorithm to find $\mathbf{S}^{opt} \subset \mathbf{S}^{ord}$. The algorithm is going to be described through an example. Assume that $\mathbf{S}^{ord}$ is composed of four stages: S_1^{ord}, S_2^{ord}, S_3^{ord}, S_4^{ord}, and the last stage S_F. We can represent such scheme by successive nodes in a digraph as shown in Figure 5. For convenience, we added a dummy node S_0^{ord} before S_1^{ord}. Node S_0^{ord} is the source of all the patterns to be classified and has zero complexity and a rejection rate of 1 (i.e. $C_0^{ord} = 0$, and $R_0^{ord} = 1$). The problem now is to get the path from S_0^{ord} to S_F that leads to the least complex cascade. Now, define the distance from node S_i^{ord} to node S_j^{ord} for $j>i$ to be equal to $R_i^{ord}C_j^{ord}$. Hence, each cascade can be represented by some path in $\mathbf{S}^{ord}$. For example, the path indicated in Figure 3(i) has a distance of $C_1^{ord} + R_1^{ord}C_2^{ord} + R_2^{ord}C_4^{ord} + R_4^{ord}C_F$ which is equal to the cascade complexity. Another possible path of complexity $C_2^{ord} + R_2^{ord}C_3^{ord} + R_3^{ord}C_F$ is shown in Figure 3(ii). The problem of finding the least complex cascade can be seen then as finding the shortest path in a directed acyclic graph (DAG) which is a well-known problem. However, for completeness, we will present its solution in the context of our problem.

Assume that each node tries to find the shortest path from itself to S_F as well as the distance of this path. All the nodes can easily collect this information if we started by last stage and proceeded backwardly to the first. For example, in Figure 5 we start by S_4^{ord}. The shortest path from S_4^{ord} to S_F is obviously [S_4^{ord} S_F] as this is the only possible path. The distance of this path is $R_4^{ord}C_F$. For node S_3^{ord}, we have two possible paths: [S_3^{ord} S_4^{ord} S_F] and [S_3^{ord} S_F]. Hence, we compare the two paths distances: $R_3^{ord}C_4^{ord} + R_4^{ord}C_F$ and $R_3^{ord}C_F$, respectively. The shortest path as well as its distance are found and saved at node S_3^{ord}. Then, we proceed to S_2^{ord}. Node S_2^{ord} has just 3 options: to jump to S_3^{ord}, to jump to S_4^{ord}, or to jump to S_F. If we jumped form S_2^{ord} to S_3^{ord}, and if we are interested in just shortest paths, the path from S_3^{ord} to S_F would be previously decided by S_3^{ord} and need not to be recalculated; and the complexity of the path in this case is $R_2^{ord}C_3^{ord}$ + the distance of shortest path from S_3^{ord} to S_F. The remaining two options for S_2^{ord} (to jump to S_4^{ord} and to jump to S_F.) are also examined and the option of the least distance is saved at node S_2^{ord}. The same procedure is done for S_1^{ord} and S_0^{ord}. Finally, the shortest path from S_0^{ord} to S_F is the cascade of least complexity.

To present the algorithm more formally, it would be of much help to introduce some simple definitions. Define 'single-hop distance' $d_h(S_i^{ord}, S_j^{ord})$ between stages S_i^{ord} and S_j^{ord}, $j \geq i$, $S_i^{ord}, S_j^{ord} \in \mathbf{S}^{ord} \forall i, j$,

$$d_h(S_i^{ord}, S_j^{ord}) = \begin{cases} R_i^{ord} C_j^{ord} & , j > i \\ 0 & , i = j \\ \text{undefined} & , j < i \end{cases} \qquad (2)$$

Define also the shortest distance $D(S_i^{ord}, S_j^{ord})$ between stages S_i^{ord} and S_j^{ord}, $j \geq i$ as the minimum distance between stages S_i^{ord} and S_j^{ord}. Note that as in the case of single-hop distance, for $i=j$, the distance will be 0 and undefined for $i>j$. Clearly the shortest path is a succession of single hops, whose distances are calculated as given in Equation (2).

Finally, define the shortest path $\mathbf{P}(S_i^{ord}, S_j^{ord})$ between stages S_i^{ord} and S_j^{ord}, $j \geq i$ as the path of shortest distance (that is of $D(S_i^{ord}, S_j^{ord})$) between stages S_i^{ord} and S_j^{ord} represented as an ordered set starting with S_i^{ord} and ending with S_j^{ord}. If $i=j$, then $\mathbf{P}(S_i^{ord}, S_j^{ord}) = [S_i^{ord}]$; and $\mathbf{P}(S_i^{ord}, S_j^{ord})$ is undefined for $i>j$.

Algorithm 1 shows the three steps of the proposed algorithm for automatic generation of optimum classification cascades. Step 3 uses the definitions given above to show how to Select $\mathbf{S}^{opt} \subset \mathbf{S}^{ord}$.

Algorithm 1 The three steps of the proposed algorithm to find optimum classification cascade

---

Step 1. Use the validation set to get a set of thresholds $\{T\}$ for $\{S\}$ that ensures that none of the classifiers in $\{S\}$ commits any error that is not committed by S_F.

Step 2. Sort $\{S\}$ in a descending order of rejection rates to form $\mathbf{S}^{ord}$.

Step 3. Select $\mathbf{S}^{opt} \subset \mathbf{S}^{ord}$ as follows,

$$D(S_N^{ord}, S_F) = d_h(S_N^{ord}, S_F) = R_N^{ord} C_F$$
$$P(S_N^{ord}, S_F) = [S_F]$$

for $i = N - 1$ down to 0

$$k = \underset{j=i+1,i+2,\ldots,N}{\arg\min} (d_h(S_i^{ord}, S_j^{ord}) + D(S_j^{ord}, S_F))$$
$$D(S_i^{ord}, S_F) = d_h(S_i^{ord}, S_k^{ord}) + D(S_k^{ord}, S_F)$$
$$\mathbf{P}(S_i^{ord}, S_F) = [S_i^{ord}\ P(S_k^{ord}, S_F)]$$

end

// $\mathbf{P}(S_0^{ord}, S_F)$ is the optimum cascade, where

// $\mathbf{P}(S_0^{ord}, S_F) = [\mathbf{S}^{opt}\ S_F]$

// and $D(S_0^{ord}, S_F)$ is its complexity

---

3. An Algorithm for Generating the Optimum Classification Cascade of a Given Length

In the previous section, we introduced an algorithm that finds the least complex cascade that achieves an accuracy not less than that of S_F. The found cascade in this case would be of any length $\leq N$ (for convenience, the cascade length would be used to mean the number of stages of the cascade excluding S_F). In some cases, due to memory limitation, we would like to use a cascade of smaller length. In this section, an algorithm will be introduced that builds the best cascade of any preferred length. This will also help in studying the effect of increasing the number of stages in a cascade on its performance (refer to section 4.3).

To introduce the algorithm, we will first add two more definitions. Define the shortest path of length n, $\mathbf{P}_n(S_i^{ord}, S_j^{ord})$, between stages $S_i^{\;ord}$ and $S_j^{\;ord}$ as the shortest path of n hops between nodes $S_i^{\;ord}$ and $S_j^{\;ord}$. Define also shortest distance of length n, $D_n(S_i^{ord}, S_j^{ord})$, between nodes $S_i^{\;ord}$ and $S_j^{\;ord}$ as the distance (complexity) of $\mathbf{P}_n(S_i^{ord}, S_j^{ord})$.

The algorithm for finding the best cascades of different lengths is presented in Algorithm 2. Step 1 and 2 of the algorithm is the same as that of Algorithm 1. Step 3 is a modified version of Step 3 of Algorithm 1. Instead of saving only the information of best path, each node saves the best path of every possible length.

4. Experiments and Discussion

In this section we present some experiments that validate the proposed approach and shed light on its strengths and limitations.

4.1 Model-Based Approach versus DFS

The problem of finding optimal classification cascades has other possible solutions than that proposed (e.g. using stochastic search techniques [Chellapilla et al. 2006a]). But we will compare the proposed technique with the most elegant solution, that is the one using depth-first search (DFS) devised by Chellapella et al. [Chellapilla et al. 2006b] (refer to section 5.6 for more details on this technique). Given a set of N ordered classifiers, the DFS algorithm searches systematically all possible cascade structures with Q permissible threshold values to find the optimum cascade. Using some heuristics, all the search space need not be visited and extensive pruning of search space is possible. The goal of the DFS algorithm is more general than ours. Given a certain permissible margin of error, it finds the least complex cascade. The proposed model-based system design procedure on the other hand finds least complex cascade that commits *no more error* than the last stage in the cascade. Actually, The DFS algorithm could be used to solve the problem if we adjusted the margin of error to be that of the final stage.

Algorithm 2. Generating optimum cascades of different lengths

---

Step 1. Use the validation set to get a set of thresholds $\{T\}$ for $\{S\}$ that ensures that none of the classifiers in $\{S\}$ commits any error that is not committed by S_F.

Step 2. Sort $\{S\}$ in a descending order of rejection rates to form $\mathbf{S}^{ord}$.

Step 3. Select cascades of different lengths,

$$D_1(S_N^{ord}, S_F) = d_h(S_N^{ord}, S_F) = R_N^{ord} C_F$$
$$\mathbf{P}_1(S_N^{ord}, S_F) = [S_F]$$

for $i = N-1$ down to 0

$$D_1(S_i^{ord}, S_F) = d_h(S_i^{ord}, S_F) = R_i^{ord} C_F$$
$$\mathbf{P}_1(S_i^{ord}, S_F) = [S_i^{ord}\ S_F]$$

    for $n = 2$ to $N - i + 1$

$$k = \underset{j=i+1,i+2,\dots,N-n+2}{\arg\min}\ (d_h(S_i^{ord}, S_j^{ord}) + D_{n-1}(S_j^{ord}, S_F))$$
$$D_n(S_i^{ord}, S_F) = d_h(S_i^{ord}, S_k^{ord}) + D_{n-1}(S_k^{ord}, S_F)$$
$$\mathbf{P}_n(S_i^{ord}, S_F) = [S_i^{ord}\ \mathbf{P}_{n-1}(S_k^{ord}, S_F)]$$

    end n

end i

// $\mathbf{P}_n(S_0^{ord}, S_F)$ is the least complex cascade

//of length n, $n = 1, 2, \dots, N$

// and its complexity is $D_n(S_0^{ord}, S_F)$

The proposed algorithm has a number of advantages over the DFS algorithm:

i.   DFS algorithm has a training complexity of $O(Q^N)$, where Q is the number of thresholds quantization levels which equals 32 as suggested by [Chellapilla et al. 2006b]. While extensive pruning of search space is possible, the algorithm takes very long training times especially for large N. On the other hand, the proposed algorithm is of only a complexity of $O(N^2)$. This means that the proposed procedure is faster in training.

ii.   Besides being faster, the proposed algorithm is scalable to large numbers of N. While the actual number of stages selected for the optimum cascade is only around 6 or 7 stages, making a large number of classifiers N available for the algorithm gives it more flexibility to *select* the most suitable stages for the cascade. In case of DFS, and to make the algorithm terminates with reasonable time, we should select by hand around 8 stages for the algorithm as done by [Chellapilla et al. 2006b]. This makes the proposed algorithm a means for system design and for classifier selection at the same time. This means also that the proposed system is more automatic than DFS.

In this section, we will compare the performance of the proposed system design procedure with the DFS algorithm on the digit recognition problem. The dataset used in the experiments is the MNIST [LECUN ET AL. 1998]. The MNIST has a total of 70,000 digits which partitioned into 3 parts: *i*) a training set, which includes 50,000 digits and used for training the classifiers, *ii*) a validation set, which contains 10,000 digits used for optimizing the cascade system, and *iii*) a test set, which is used for final testing of the cascade. Each digit image of all sets was transformed into 200-element feature vector using the gradient feature extraction technique [LIU ET AL. 2003].

Forty-eight different classifiers were trained with different complexities and accuracies on the training set. Three different types of classifiers are used: one-layer neural network (1-NN or linear classifier), two-layer neural network (2-NN), and RBF SVM [WEBB 2002]. For each classifier type, a number of classifiers of different structures were generated. First all 200 gradient feature elements were ranked according to their importance using ReliefF feature ranking technique [KONONENKO 1994]. Then, for 1-NN, a classifier was generated that has as the most important 25 feature elements as input, and then another one with the most important 50 feature elements, then 75, and so on, till finally a classifier with all the 200 feature elements was generated. Hence, we have 8 different 1-NN classifiers. The same was done for SVM; hence, we have additional 8 different classifiers. This also was done for 2-NN, but for each number of inputs, a classifier was generated with different number of hidden units: 50, 100 150, and 200 (i.e. 2-layer neural network of structures: 25-50-10, 25-100-10, ..., 25-200-10, 50-50-10, 50-100-10, ..., 200-200-10). Hence, we have 8 1-NN classifiers, 8 SVMs, and 8×4 2-NN classifier; hence we have a total of 48 classifiers of different structure and accuracies. Table 1 shows the performance of the most powerful classifier (that is, the SVM classifier with 200 feature elements): its number of errors and its complexity on the test set. The complexity of a certain classifier is measured as the number of floating point operations (flops) [RIDDER ET AL. 2002] it needs to classify one pattern divided by the number of flops the least complex classifier generated (that is, the 1-NN with 25 inputs) needs to classify one pattern.

Test set errors	Complexity
66	5638.2

Table 1 The performance of the most powerful classifier (SVM with 200 features as input)

	Complexity	Errors	Number of Stages
Model-Based on 5 randomly selected stages from {S}	376.9	67.3	3.5
DFS on 5 randomly selected stages from {S}	358.7	66.5	4.9

Table 2 Average complexity, average errors, and average number of stages when applying both model-based approach and DFS on 5 randomly selected stages from the pool of classifiers

	Complexity	Errors	Number of Stages
Model-Based applied to the whole {S}	187.8	70	6

Table 3 Complexity and errors of model-based approach on the entire pool of classifiers

Now, all the generated 48 classifiers can be handed to the proposed algorithm to generate the best cascade out of them. However, this would not be possible for the DFS algorithm due to its large complexity. In order to compare the proposed algorithm with DFS, the most powerful classifier (that is, the SVM with 200 features) was used as the last stage and then randomly selected 5 classifiers from the remaining 47 classifiers. The same was done 15 times; each time with different randomly selected 5 classifiers. For each of these selections, both model-based algorithm and DFS was used to select the optimum cascade. The averages of the 15 trials of both cases are calculated and summarized in Table 2. The average cascade length (number of stages excluding S_F) is also indicated for both cases. Table 2 shows that DFS got slightly better results.

However, the main advantage of the proposed approach is that we can use classifiers pools of large sizes N which is impossible for DFS. The entire set of 48 classifiers was given to the proposed algorithm to build the optimum cascade out of them. The results are shown in Table 3. We see that the cascade built when the proposed algorithm is given all the 48 has a complexity of 187.8 which is lower than that of both model-approach and DFS when applied to 5 randomly selected stages. This clarifies the importance of using large number of classifiers N, and hence, the importance of the low complexity of our proposed algorithm.

4.2 The Validity of Assumption 1

The optimality of Algorithm 1 is guaranteed if Equation (1) is valid. Equation (1) on its turn is based on the validity of Assumption 1. In this section we are going to explore the condition under which Assumption 1 is valid.

Assumption 1 states that the weaker classifier rejects all the patterns that the stronger classifier rejects. In fact, this is true only when the stronger classifier is *much* stronger than the weaker. Classifiers of near degree of strength reject overlapping sets of patterns; but never totally conform to Assumption 1; this phenomenon is called 'diversity' and is exploited in building classifiers ensembles [Kuncheva 2000]. Figure 6 is a scatter plot showing the dependency of the invalidity of Assumption 1 for different classifier pairs (taken from the pool of 48 classifiers mentioned above) on the difference in strength between them. The invalidity of Assumption 1 is measured by the number of cases that violated it and put on the vertical axis. The difference in strength between two classifiers is represented by the difference in rejection rates between them. As clear from Figure 6, the more the difference in rejection rates between two classifiers is, the less the number of violations of Assumption 1 is found.

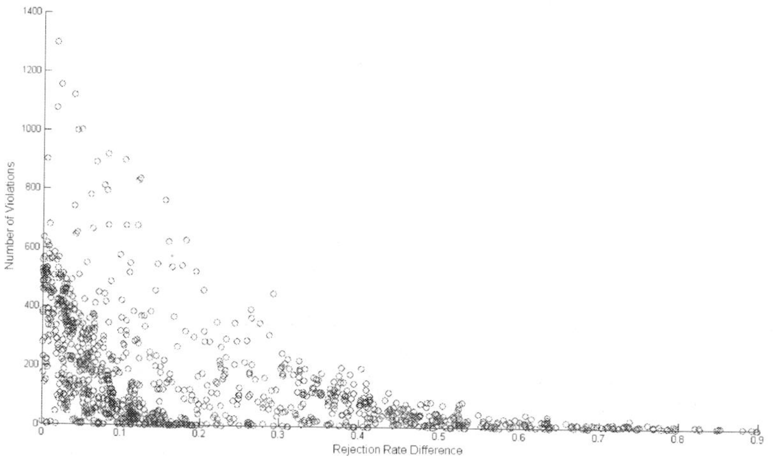

Fig. 6. A scatter plot that showing the dependency of the validity of Assumption 1 on the difference in strength between the two classifiers.

But how could the inaccuracy of Assumption 1 affect the structure of cascades built by the model-based approach? In fact, Assumption 1 leads us to believe that putting two classifiers of near degree of strength one after the other is of no use. This is because the second classifiers will not confidently recognize much of the patterns rejected from the first classifier, and hence would not do but just increasing the complexity of the cascade. This leads the model-based approach selects classifiers of very distant rejection rates from each other to build the cascade. Because the rejection rate domain is finite (from 0 to 1), this makes the model-based approach tends to build cascades of small lengths. This is clear if we refer to Table 2 and compared the average cascades lengths built by model-based approach and DFS.

Now, would this lead us to miss an opportunity for building less complex cascades? The answer is yes. Putting a classifier of near strength to some classifiers increases its complexity indeed *but* might result in a drop in rejection rate. Consider the following hypothetical example. Suppose that there are two classifiers; both have rejection rate of 0.5. According to Assumption 1, there is no point of putting one after the other in a cascade as this will lead to more complex system of the same rejection rate of 0.5. But according to the concept of diversity, there is. To take the extreme case of Assumption 1 violation, assume that the sets of patterns rejected from the two classifiers are exclusive. This will make the overall rejection rate of both classifiers when put one after the other in a cascade drop to 0. Of course, this extreme case does not occur in reality, but this shows how two classifiers of near strength could lead to rejection rates enhancements, and hence to more efficient classification cascades. This is clear from Table 2, as the DFS (which is an exhaustive procedure) finds cascades of better performance than model-based approach. However, DFS is of very high complexity and does not scale to large pool sizes and this leads us to select classifiers for it by hand which leads to inferior results to model-based approach as clear from Table 3.

4.3 The Effect of Number of Stages on the Cascade Performance

In section 3 we presented an algorithm that builds the best cascade of specific length. Besides being useful for memory-limited applications, it is very helpful in studying the effect of increasing the number of cascade stages on its performance. Figure 7 shows the complexities of best cascades with i stages, where i = 2, 3, 4, ..., 48. It is clear from the figure that the complexity decreases as we add more stages until certain limit, after which the complexity starts to increase. Note that the complexities are calculated using the test set.

It would be interesting if we compared the theoretical cascade complexities anticipated by Equation (1) with the actual cascade complexities. Because the theoretical complexities were calculated using the validation set while building the cascade; hence, we will compare them to the actual complexities calculated using the validation set, not the test set. This is to clarify the difference between the theoretical and actual complexity setting aside the differences between the validation and test sets. Figure 8 compares the theoretical and actual complexities of best cascades with i stages, where i = 2, 3, 4, ..., 48. From Figure 8, we note that the theoretical complexity decreases with adding more stages until we reach the cascade with 5 stages, then the complexity starts to increase again. On the other hand, the actual complexities continue to decrease with adding more stages till reaching the cascade with 22 stages. The actual complexity difference between best 5 stages and best 22 stages cascade is not substantial; however, it sheds the light on the concept of diversity discussed in section 4.2. In the point of view of Assumption 1, adding more stages after 5 stages limit does nothing but increasing the complexity; however, in reality, the diversity continues to enhance the performance and the cascade complexity continues to drop. We also note that with adding more and more stages, the difference between the theoretical and actual complexities increases since the effect of diversity increases between more classifiers.

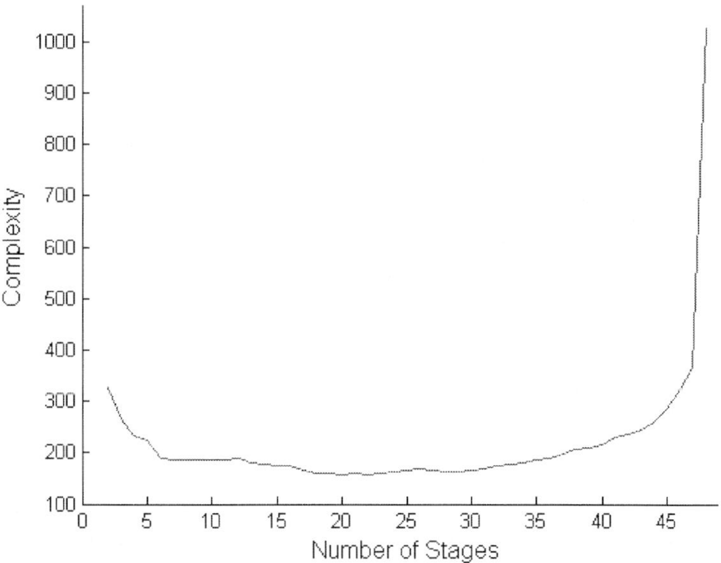

Fig. 7. The cascade actual complexity as the number of stages increases (calculated using the test set)

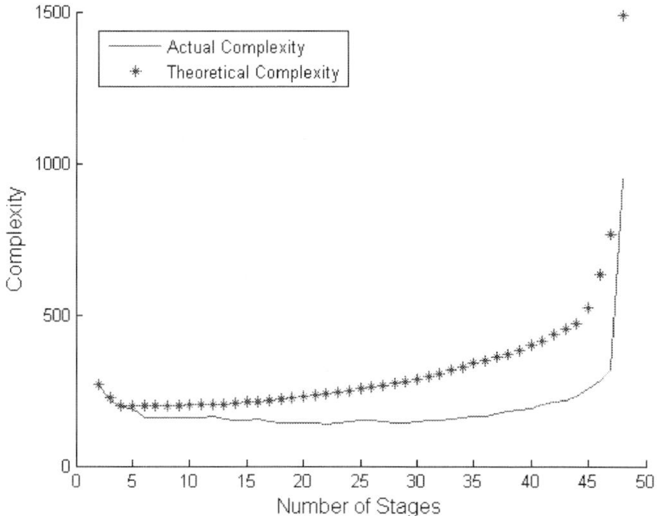

Fig. 8. The cascade actual as well as theoretical complexities as the number of stages increases (calculated using the validation set)

5. Related Works

In this section, we first present a taxonomy for the classification cascade research and then review some related works.

Classification cascades could be categorized according to four different aspects:
1- <u>Accuracy versus speed oriented cascades.</u>
One could build a cascade to increase the accuracy [RAHMAN & FAIRHURST 1999], or to increase the speed of the classification system [KAYNAK & ALPAYDIN 1997, PUDIL et al. 1992, GIUSTI ET AL. 2002, GORGEVIK & CAKMAKOV 2004, ,FERRI et al. 2004, Chellapilla et al. 2006a, Chellapilla et al. 2006b].

2- <u>Reevaluation-based versus information-passing cascades.</u>
In reevaluation-based cascades, the pattern to be classified is presented to the first classifier to give a decision with a confidence score. If the confidence score is higher than some threshold, the classification process terminates and the decision taken by the first classifier is declared to be the final decision. If the confidence score is lower than the threshold, the pattern is passed to the next classifier to re-classify it, and the process continues in the same manner. There is no information passed from one stage to the next. Each stage, if evoked, starts the classification process from scratch. In information passing cascades, each stage passes some information to the next stage. The most important of this category is the class reduction cascade, in which each stage passes a list of the most probable classes the pattern could belong to. Each stage focuses only on this list neglecting other classes [TSAY ET AL. 2004].

3- <u>Dependent versus independent training of classifiers.</u>
Each stage in the cascade could be trained independently using all the training set patterns [Chellapilla et al. 2006a, Chellapilla et al. 2006b This is called 'independent training of stages'. On the other hand, each stage could be trained using only the patterns rejected from the previous stage [FERRI ET AL. 2004]. This is called 'dependent training of stages'.

4- <u>Manual versus automatic building of cascades.</u>
A cascade could be manually built [GORGEVIK & CAKMAKOV 2004,], or automatically built [Chellapilla et al. 2006a, Chellapilla et al. 2006b]. The degree of cascade building automation differs. For example, in some cascade design technique, the structure of the cascade is automated but some other parameters (e.g. thresholds) are not.

According to this categorization scheme, the proposed model-based approach for building classification cascades is: speed-oriented, re-evaluation based, with independent training of classifiers, and entirely automatic.

There are many cascade design techniques in the literature. However, they have common themes. In the following some works on classification cascades will be presented, each representing some theme, mentioning similar works.

5.1 Risk analysis of multistage pattern recognition with reject option by Pudil et al.

One way to build a multistage system is to generate different systems with different structures and then to asses each of them using some criterion. Then the best cascade in terms of this criterion is selected. One problem with this method is that there are two conflicting requirements of a cascade system: high accuracy and low complexity. Any reasonable criterion should consider both requirements. Pudil et al. [PUDIL ET AL. 1992] suggested a criterion to assess the performance of multistage systems using a modified version of average risk analysis [DUDA et al. 2000].

Pudil's et al. technique is then considered according to the proposed categorization of cascades: speed-oriented, reevaluation-based, independent learning of stages, and automatic if we are ready to generate very large set of cascades and select the best; and partly-manual if we used our experience of the problem to select some reasonable set of cascades.

5.2 Kaynak-Alpaydin cascade

Kanyak and Alpaydin [KAYNAK & ALPAYDIN 1997] suggested a technique for building classification cascades that achieves high accuracy with low complexity. In this technique, a sequence of learners S_j's is used, where S_{j+1} learner is more complex than S_j. Associated with each learner is a confidence score $conf_j$ such that we say S_j is confident of its output and can be used if $conf_j > t_j$ where $0 < t_j \le t_{j+1} < 1$ is the confidence threshold. Learner S_j is used if all the preceding learners are not confident. Starting with $j = 1$, given a training set, S_j is trained. All the patterns on which S_j's performance is not acceptable are found and used to train S_{j+1}. This means that Kaynak-Alpaydin cascade falls in the category of dependent-training cascades.

This technique is to some degree similar to AdaBoost learning [DUDA et al. 2000, CHEVA (2004)]. Both techniques build a sequence of classifiers, each specializes in recognizing the pattern not recognized (or not confidently recognized) by the previous stage. However, there are some important differences between the two techniques. In AdaBoost classification, all the stages should be evoked in order to get the final classification decision. In Kaynak-Alpaydin cascade, the decision could be made at any stage according to the decision confidence of that stage. This property is behind the low complexity of the cascade classifier. AdaBoost uses weak learners of the same type. Kaynak-Alpaydin cascade uses different learner of increasing powerfulness and complexity.

Experiments show good performance of Kaynak-Alpaydin cascade. However, Kaynak-Alpaydin technique is not fully automatic, and relies of the users' experience to select the classifiers constituting the cascade as well as their rejection thresholds by hand.

Kaynak-Alpaydin cascade is considered according to the proposed categorization of classification cascades: speed-oriented, reevaluation-based, dependent training of stages, and manual.

5.3 Delegating classifier

Delegating classifier is another name coined by Ferri et al. [FERRI ET AL. 2004] for cascade classifier. Ferri et al. first suggest a two-stage system in which the first stage has a threshold at its output to reject the uncertain classifications to the second stage. This threshold is found such that the first stage would reject a certain percentage of the examples to the second stage. Here the first stage is trained using all the available examples and the second stage is trained using only the samples rejected by the first stage. This idea is also generalized to the case of more than two stages.

Ferri et al. suggest an interesting modification to the two-stage system. They put another threshold on the second stage output of the two-stage system. If the confidence score of the second stage falls below this threshold, the decision of the second stage is ignored and the final decision would be of the first stage. This approach is verified by the fact that the second stage inclines to overfit as it is trained using the noisy patterns rejected by the first stage. This technique was called 'Round Rebound' and was shown to slightly improve the results of the two-stage system.

Delegating classifier is considered according to the proposed categorization of classification cascades: speed-oriented, reevaluation-based, dependent training of stages. Ferri et al. suggested an automatic way of building cascade, though it is not theoretically verified and needs some manual calibration.

5.4 Two-stage system of Giusti et al.

Kaynak et al. [KAYNAK & ALPAYDIN 1997] studied one implementation of Kaynak-Alpaydin Cascade in which there is only two stages: the first stage is a global classifier like ANN, and the second stage is a local classifier like KNN. Giusti et al. [GIUSTI ET AL. 2002] studied a similar system theoretically with the addition to one time-saving technique. That is, if the first stage rejects some patterns, it indicates the h top most probable classes that the pattern belongs to. The KNN does not need then to search in its whole database, only within patterns belonging to the h top classes.

Giusti's two-stage system is considered according to the proposed categorization of classification cascades: speed-oriented, information-passing-based, dependent training of stages, and manual. Similar works to Giusti's system are [TSAY ET AL. 2004, GORGEVIK & CAKMAKOV 2004,].

5.5 Sequential combination of classifiers by Rahman and Fairhurst

'Sequential classifier' is another name for cascade classifier. Rahman and Fairhurst [RAHMAN & FAIRHURST 1999] presented two versions of the cascade classifiers: one is reevaluation-based and the other is information-passing-based. The information-passing-version passes a subset of most probable classes from one stage to the next narrowing down the scope of classes we search in. The first version resembles Kaynak-Alpaydin cascade but the stages are trained independently. The second version resembles the work of Giusti et al. but the role of successive stages is only to narrow down the list of possible classes more and more; an intermediate stage cannot classify a pattern; just the last stage can.

The major difference between Rahman and Fairhurst's cascade and other cascades is that it is accuracy-oriented. However, it is remarked that it has much less complexity than other accuracy-oriented classifiers combination scheme. Also, while they optimized the cascade accuracy, they could optimize its speed as well or they could optimize a cost function that considers both accuracy and speed.

It is understood how could a cascade enhance the speed; but how could it enhance the accuracy? The answer is different for each of the two versions of Rahman and Fairhurst's cascade. For the reevaluation version, the cause is as follows. If all stage before the last rejects or misclassify the patterns of the last stage, there will be no gain in accuracy. But actually what happens is that some stages correctly and confidently classify some patterns that are not correctly classified by the last stage (the concept of diversity discussed earlier). This is why the accuracy increases. For the information-passing version of the cascade, the cause behind the increase in accuracy is as follows. It happens that the last stage confuses between the true class of some pattern and other class. If this other class has been omitted from the list of considered classes passed through the cascade, this will lead the last stage make the correct classification as the rival class is omitted beforehand. This could increase the overall accuracy of the system.

Rahman and Fairhurst's cascade is considered according to the proposed categorization of classification cascades: accuracy-oriented but can easily modified to speed-oriented, reevaluation-based for the first version and information-passing-based for the second version, independent training of stages, and manual.

5.6 Searching in the space of thresholds by Chellapilla et al.

The most elegant work on classification cascade design is that of Chellapilla et al. [Chellapilla et al. 2006a, Chellapilla et al. 2006b]. They first presented a framework for the cascade design problem as an optimization problem that can be solved using any combinatorial optimization technique. Their cascade is speed-oriented, reevaluation-based, with independent training of stages, and is automatic to a large extent.

They start with a cascade of N classifier S_1, S_2, . . ., S_N; each has a complexity C_i and a threshold t_i, $i=1, 2, . . ., N$. The stages are ordered in the cascade in an ascending order of complexities (i.e. $C_1<C_2< . . . <C_N$). The pattern to be classified goes initially through the first stage. If it is classified with confidence score higher than t_1, then it is absorbed (i.e. the classification process terminates taking the decision of S_1 to be the final decision). If the confidence score is below t_1, the pattern is rejected to the next stage S_2, and the process continues. The last stage has a threshold $t_N=0$ (i.e. it absorbs all the patterns it receives and rejects nothing).

The problem of cascade design now reduces to the setting of the set of N thresholds t_1, t_2, . . ., t_N. Note that a stage could be excluded from the cascade by setting its threshold to 1 (i.e. it rejects everything). The problem is then formulated into an optimization problem. There are actually two optimization problems reflecting the goal from building the cascade. The first goal is to minimize the overall system complexity given some error constraint. The second goal is to minimize the error given some complexity constraint. The search space of solutions is then $V=\{t_1\}\times\{t_2\}\times \ldots \times\{t_N\}$, where $\{t_i\}$ is the set of all thresholds of stage i. The goal is then to find the optimal threshold vector $T^* = [t_1^*, t_2^*, ..., t_N^*]$ that solves one of the following two optimization problems,

i) minimizing the complexity,

$$T^* = \arg\min\{C(T) \mid T \in V, e(T) \le e_{\max}\} \qquad (3)$$

or ii) minimizing the error,

$$T^* = \arg\min\{e(T) \mid T \in V, C(T) \le C_{\max}\} \qquad (4)$$

where $C(T)$ is the complexity of the cascade with threshold vector $T=[t_1, t_2,..., t_N]$, $e(T)$ is the error rate of the cascade with threshold vector T, e_{max} is the error constraint, and C_{max} is the complexity constraint.

Left is the procedure by which the set of possible threshold $\{t_i\}$ for the stage S_i for each i, i=1, 2, …, N is prepared. First, each stage S_i is used to classify all the examples of a validation set. The examples are then sorted in a descending order according to the confidence scores they are given by S_i. The examples are partitioned into Q-2 subset. The thresholds $\{t_i\}$ are then the confidence score of the first example of each subset, plus the two thresholds: 0 (means S_i absorbs all the examples) and 1 (means S_i rejects all the examples). Here then we have Q thresholds in the set $\{t_i\}$. This is equivalent to quantizing t_i to Q quantization levels. Then the size of the space of thresholds V is Q^N. The optimization problem is then to search through the space V of threshold to satisfy either Equation (3) or Equation (4).

This problem can be solved using any combinatorial optimization technique. Cellapilla et al. tried solving the problem using steepest descent, dynamic programming, simulated annealing, depth first search (DFS). All these algorithms are suboptimal except DFS. The DFS [Chellapilla et al. 2006b] is a simple search algorithm that searches through the space of solution intelligently. It prunes large sections of the search space that are guaranteed not to give the best solution.

This framework is elegant and fully automatic except that the procedure of ordering the stages by increasing complexity is not verified theoretically. The DFS solution is elegant and optimal but it has an exponential complexity in N (that is, $O(Q^N)$) which means that using large value number of stages is computationally prohibitive. This made Chellapilla et al. do manual selection of the N classifiers to be used with algorithm. Hence, though DFS could be fully automatic, its high computational complexity hinders it to be.

6. Conclusion

In this chapter, we presented a model-based approach for automatically building classification cascades. The experiments showed that the algorithm is efficient and scalable. The algorithm was also analyzed and its strengths and limitations were clarified. In addition, we presented an algorithm that builds cascades with given lengths which is useful in memory-limited systems helped in studying the effect of increasing the number of stages in a cascade on its performance.

7. References

Brubaker, S., Mullin, M., and Rehg J., (2006), "Towards optimal training of cascaded detectors," ECCV06, vol. 1, pp. 325-337, Graz, Austria, May.

Chellapilla, K., M. Shilman, P. Simard, (2006a) "Combining Multiple Classifiers for Faster Optical Character Recognition", DAS, pp. 358-367.

Chellapilla, K.; Shilman, M. , Simard, P., (2006b), "Optimally Combining a Cascade of Classifiers", SPIE Document Recognition and Retrieval (DRR).

Chen, X. & Yuille, A., (2005), "A time-efficient cascade for real-time object detection: with application for the visually impaired," IEEE CVPR-05, vol. 3, pp. 28, San Diego, CA, USA, June 20-25.

Duda, R., Hart, P., Stork, D., (2000), Pattern Classification, 2nd Edition, Wiley, New York.

Ferri, C.; Flach, P. ,and Hernandez-Orallo, J., (2004) "Delegating classifiers," Proceedings of 21st International Conference on Machine Learning, pp. 37.

Giusti, N.; Masulli, F. and Sperduti, A. (2002), "Theoretical and experimental analysis of a two-stage system for classification," IEEE TPAMI, vol. 24, no. 7, pp. 893-904.

Gorgevik, D.& Cakmakov, D. (2004), "An efficient three-stage classifier for handwritten digit recognition", ICPR'04, pp. 1051-4651.

Kaynak, C. & Alpaydin, E. (1997), "Multistage classification by cascaded classifiers," Proceedings of 1997 IEEE international symposium on Intelligent Control, pp. 95-100.

I. Kononenko,(1994) "Estimating attributes: analysis and extensions of Relief," ECML-94, pp. 171–182.

Kuncheva, L., (2004), *Combining Pattern Classifiers*, Wiley-Interscience.

LeCun, Y.; Bottou, L. Bengio, Y. and Haffner, P. (1998), "Gradient-Based Learning Applied to Document Recognition", Proceedings of the IEEE, vol. 86 no. 11, pp. 2278-2324.

Liu, C.; Nakashima, K. Sako, Fujisawa, H. H., (2003), "Handwritten digit recognition: benchmarking of state-of-the-art techniques," Pattern Recognition, vol. 36, pp. 2271 – 2285.

Luo, H. , (2005), "Optimization design of cascades classifiers," IEEE CVPR-05, vol. 1, pp. 480- 485, San Diego, CA, USA, June 20-25.

Pudil, P. ; Novovicova, J. , Blaha, S., Kittler, J., (1992), "Multistage pattern recognition with reject option," 11th IAPR, pp. 92-95.

Rahman, A. & Fairhurst, M,. (1999), "Serial combination of multiple experts: a unified evaluation," Pattern Analysis and Applications, vol. 2, no. 4, pp. 292-311.

Ridder, D.; Pekalska, E., Duin, R. (2002), "The economics of classification: error vs. complexity", The 16th International Conference on Pattern Recognition, pp. 244-247.

Sun, J., Regh, J., Bobick, A. ,(2004), "Automatic cascade training with perturbation bias," IEEE CVPR-04, vol. 2, pp. 276-283, Washington, DC, June 27 – July 2.

Tsay, J., Lin, C. ,Hung, C. ,and Lin, C. , 2004 ,"Cascaded class reduction for time-efficient multi-class classification," 18th Annual ACM International Conference on Supercomputing (ICS'04), pp. 189-194, Saint-Malo, France, June 26-July 1.

Viola, P. & M. Jones, (2001), "Rapid object detection using a boosted cascade of simple features", ICPR, vol 1., pp. 511-518.

Webb, (2002), Statistical pattern recognition, 2nd Edition, Wiley.

Wu, J., Brubaker, S., Mullin, M., and Regh, J. ,(2008), "Fast asymmetric learning for cascade face detection," IEEE PAMI, vol. 30, no. 3, pp. 369-382.

Yuann, Q. Thangali, A. . Sclaroff, S,(2005) ,"Face identification by a cascade of rejection classifiers," IEEE CVPR-05, vol. 3, p. 152, San Diego, CA, USA, June 20-25.

4

Efficient Feature Subset Selection and Subset Size Optimization

Petr Somol, Jana Novovičová and Pavel Pudil
*Institute of Information Theory and Automation
of the Academy of Sciences of the Czech Republic*

1. Introduction

A broad class of decision-making problems can be solved by *learning approach*. This can be a feasible alternative when neither an analytical solution exists nor the mathematical model can be constructed. In these cases the required knowledge can be gained from the past data which form the so-called learning or training set. Then the formal apparatus of statistical pattern recognition can be used to learn the decision-making. The first and essential step of statistical pattern recognition is to solve the problem of feature selection (FS) or more generally dimensionality reduction (DR).

The problem of feature selection in statistical pattern recognition will be of primary focus in this chapter. The problem fits in the wider context of dimensionality reduction (Section 2) which can be accomplished either by a linear or nonlinear mapping from the measurement space to a lower dimensional feature space, or by measurement subset selection. This chapter will focus on the latter (Section 3). The main aspects of the problem as well as the choice of the right feature selection tools will be discussed (Sections 3.1 to 3.3). Several optimization techniques will be reviewed, with emphasis put to the framework of sequential selection methods (Section 4). Related topics of recent interest will be also addressed, including the problem of subset size determination (Section 4.7), search acceleration through hybrid algorithms (Section 5), and the problem of feature selection stability and feature over-selection (Section 6).

2. Dimensionality Reduction

The following elementary notation will be followed throughout the chapter. We shall use the term "pattern" to denote the D-dimensional data vector $\mathbf{x} \in \mathcal{X} \subseteq \mathbb{R}^D$, the components of which are the measurements of the features characterizing an object. We also refer to $\mathbf{x}$ as the feature vector. Let $Y = \{f_1, \cdots, f_{|Y|}\}$ be the set of $D = |Y|$ features, where $|\cdot|$ denotes the size (cardinality). The features are the variables specified by the investigator. Following the statistical approach to pattern recognition, we assume that a pattern $\mathbf{x}$ is to be classified into one of a finite set Ω of C different classes. A pattern $\mathbf{x}$ belonging to class $\omega \in \Omega$ is viewed as an observation of a random vector drawn randomly according to the class-conditional probability density function and the respective *a priori* probability of class ω.

One of the fundamental problems in pattern recognition is representing patterns in the reduced number of dimensions. In most of practical cases the pattern descriptor space dimensionality is rather high. It follows from the fact that in the design phase it is too difficult or impossible to evaluate directly the "usefulness" of particular input. Thus it is important to initially include all the "reasonable" descriptors the designer can think of and to reduce the set later on. Obviously, information missing in the original measurement set cannot be later substituted. Dimensionality reduction refers to the task of finding low dimensional representations for high-dimensional data. Dimensionality reduction is an important step in data preprocessing in pattern recognition and machine learning applications. It is sometimes the case that such tasks as classification or approximation of the data represented by so called feature vectors, can be carried out in the reduced space more accurately than in the original space.

2.1 DR Categorization According to Nature of the Resulting Features

There are two main distinct ways of viewing DR according to the nature of the resulting features:

- DR by *feature selection* (FS)
- DR by *feature extraction* (FE).

The FS approach does not attempt to generate new features, but to select the "best" ones from the original set of features. (Note: In some research fields, e.g., in image analysis, the term feature selection may be interpreted as feature extraction. It will not be the case in this chapter.) Depending on the outcome of a FS procedure, the result can be either a set of weighting-scoring, a ranking or a subset of features. The FE approach defines a new feature vector space in which each new feature is obtained by combinations or transformations of the original features. FS leads to savings in measurements cost since some of the features are discarded and the selected features retain their original physical interpretation. In addition, the retained features may be important for understanding the physical process that generates the feature vectors. On the other hand, transformed features generated by feature extraction may provide a better discriminative ability than the best subset of given features, but these new features may not have a clear physical meaning.

2.2 DR Categorization According to the Aim

DR can be alternatively divided according to the aim of the reduction:

- DR *for optimal data representation*
- DR *for classification*.

The first aims to preserve the topological structure of data in a lower-dimensional space as much as possible, the second one aims to enhance the subset discriminatory power. Although the same tools may be often used for both purposes, caution is needed. An example is PCA, one of the primary tools for representing data in lower-dimensional space, which may easily discard important information if used for DR for classification. In the sequel we shall concentrate on the feature subset selection problem only, with classification being the primary aim. For a broader overview of the subject see, e.g., Duda et al. (2000), McLachlan (2004), Ripley (2005), Theodoridis et al. (2006), Webb (2002).

3. Feature Subset Selection

Given a set Y of $|Y|$ features, let us denote $\mathcal{X}_d$ the set of all possible subsets of size d, where d represents the desired number of features. Let $J(X)$ be a criterion function that evaluates feature subset $X \in \mathcal{X}_d$. Without any loss of generality, let us consider a higher value of J

to indicate a better feature subset. Then the feature selection problem can be formulated as follows: Find the subset $\tilde{X}_d$ for which

$$J(\tilde{X}_d) = \max_{X \in \mathcal{X}_d} J(X). \tag{1}$$

Assuming that a suitable criterion function has been chosen to evaluate the effectiveness of feature subsets, feature selection is reduced to a search problem that detects an optimal feature subset based on the selected measure. Note that the choice of d may be a complex issue depending on problem characteristics, unless the d value can be optimized as part of the search process.

One particular property of feature selection criterion, the monotonicity property, is required specifically in certain optimal FS methods. Assuming we have two subsets S_1 and S_2 of feature set Y and a criterion J that evaluates each subset S_i. The *monotonicity condition* requires the following:

$$S_1 \subset S_2 \Rightarrow J(S_1) \leq J(S_2). \tag{2}$$

That is, evaluating the feature selection criterion on a subset of features of a given set yields a smaller value of the feature selection criterion.

3.1 FS Categorization With Respect to Optimality

Feature subset selection methods can be split into basic families:

- *Optimal methods*: These include, e.g., *exhaustive search* methods which are feasible for only small size problems and accelerated methods, mostly built upon the Branch & Bound principle (Somol et al. (2004)). All optimal methods can be expected considerably slow for problems of high dimensionality.

- *Sub-optimal methods*: They essentially trade the optimality of the selected subset for computational efficiency. They include, e.g., Best Individual Features, Random (Las Vegas) methods, Sequential Forward and Backward Selection, Plus-l-Take Away-r, their generalized versions, genetic algorithms, and particularly the Floating and Oscillating algorithms (Devijver et al. (1982), Pudil et al. (1994), Somol et al. (2000), Somol et al. (2008b)).

Although the exhaustive search guarantees the optimality of a solution, in many realistic problems it is computationally prohibitive. The well known Branch and Bound (B&B) algorithm guarantees to select an optimal feature subset of size d without involving explicit evaluation of all the possible combinations of d measurements. However, the algorithm is applicable only under the assumption that the feature selection criterion used satisfies the monotonicity condition (2). This assumption precludes the use of classifier error rate as the criterion (cf. wrappers, Kohavi et al. (1997b)). This is an important drawback as the error rate can be considered superior to other criteria, Siedlecki et al. (1993), Kohavi et al. (1997b), Tsamardinos et al. (2003). Moreover, all optimal algorithms become computationally prohibitive for problems of high dimensionality. In practice, therefore, one has to rely on computationally feasible procedures which perform the search quickly but may yield sub-optimal results. A comprehensive list of sub-optimal procedures can be found, e.g., in books Devijver et al. (1982), Fukunaga (1990), Webb (2002), Theodoridis et al. (2006). A comparative taxonomy can be found, e.g., in Blum et al. (1997), Ferri et al. (1994), Guyon et al. (2003), Jain et al. (1997), Jain et al. (2000), Yusta (2009), Kudo et al. (2000), Liu et al. (2005), Salappa et al. (2007), Vafaie et al. (1994) or Yang et al. (1998). Our own research and experience with FS has led us to the conclusion that *there exists no unique generally applicable approach* to the problem. Some approaches are more suitable under certain conditions, others are more appropriate under other conditions, depending on our *knowledge of the problem*. Hence continuing effort is invested in developing new methods to cover the majority of situations which can be encountered in practice.

3.2 FS Categorization With Respect to Selection Criteria

Based on the *selection criterion* choice, feature selection methods may roughly be divided into:

- *Filter methods* (Yu et al. (2003), Dash et al. (2002)) are based on performance evaluation functions calculated directly from the training data such as *distance, information, dependency, and consistency,* and select feature subsets without involving any learning algorithm.

- *Wrapper methods* (Kohavi et al. (1997a)) require one predetermined learning algorithm and use its estimated performance as the evaluation criterion. They attempt to find features better suited to the learning algorithm aiming to improve performance. Generally, the wrapper method achieves better performance than the filter method, but tends to be more computationally expensive than the filter approach. Also, the wrappers yield feature subsets optimized for the given learning algorithm only - the same subset may thus be bad in another context.

- *Embedded methods* (Guyon et al. (2003), but also Kononenko (1994) or Pudil et al. (1995), Novovičová et al. (1996)) integrate the feature selection process into the model estimation process. Devising model and selecting features is thus one inseparable learning process, that may be looked upon as a special form of wrappers. Embedded methods thus offer performance competitive to wrappers, enable faster learning process, but produce results tightly coupled with particular model.

- *Hybrid approach* (Das (2001), Sebban et al. (2002), Somol et al. (2006)) combines the advantages of more than one of the listed approaches. Hybrid algorithms have recently been proposed to deal with high dimensional data. These algorithms mainly focus on combining filter and wrapper algorithms to achieve best possible performance with a particular learning algorithm with the time complexity comparable to that of the filter algorithms.

3.3 FS Categorization With Respect to Problem Knowledge

From another point of view there are perhaps two basic classes of situations with respect to *a priori* knowledge of the underlying probability structures:

- *Some a priori knowledge is available*: It is at least known that probability density functions are unimodal. In these cases, one of probabilistic distance measures (Mahalanobis, Bhattacharyya, etc., see Devijver et al. (1982)) may be appropriate as the evaluation criterion. For this type of situations we recommend either the recent prediction-based B&B algorithms for optimal search Somol et al. (2004), or sub-optimal search methods in appropriate filter or wrapper setting (Sect. 4).

- *No a priori knowledge is available*: We cannot even assume that probability density functions are unimodal. For these situations either a wrapper-based solution using sub-optimal search methods (Sect. 4) can be found suitable, or, provided the size of training data is sufficient, it is possible to apply one of the embedded mixture-based methods that are based on approximating unknown class-conditional probability density functions by finite mixtures of a special type (Pudil et al. (1995), Novovičová et al. (1996)).

4. Sub-optimal Search Methods

Provided a suitable FS criterion function (cf. Devijver et al. (1982)) is available, the only tool needed is the search algorithm that generates a sequence of subsets to be tested. Despite the advances in optimal search (Somol et al. (2004), Nakariyakul et al. (2007)), for larger than moderate-sized problems we have to resort to sub-optimal methods. Very large number of various methods exists. The FS framework includes approaches that take use of evolutionary (genetic) algorithms (Hussein et al. (2001)), tabu search (Zhang et al. (2002)), or ant colony (Jensen (2006)). In the following we present a basic overview over several tools that are useful for problems of varying complexity, based mostly on the idea of sequential search (Section 4.2). An integral part of any FS process is the decision about the number of features to be selected. Determining the correct subspace dimensionality is a difficult problem beyond the scope of this chapter. Nevertheless, in the following we will distinguish two types of FS methods: d-parametrized and d-optimizing. Most of the available methods are d-parametrized, i.e., they require the user to decide what cardinality should the resulting feature subset have. In Section 4.7 a d-optimizing procedure will be described, that optimizes both the feature subset size and its contents at once.

4.1 Best Individual Features

The Best Individual Features (BIF) approach is the simplest approach to FS. Each feature is first evaluated individually using the chosen criterion. Subsets are then selected simply by choosing the best individual features. This approach is the fastest but weakest option. It is often the only applicable approach to FS in problems of very high dimensionality. BIF is standard in text categorization (Yang et al. (1997), Sebastiani (2002)), genetics (Xing (2003), Saeys et al. (2007)), etc. BIF may be preferable in other types of problems to overcome FS stability problems (see Sect. 6.1). However, more advanced methods that take into account relations among features are likely to produce better results. Several of such methods are discussed in the following.

4.2 Sequential Search Framework

To simplify further discussion let us focus only on the family of sequential search methods. Most of the known sequential FS algorithms share the same "core mechanism" of adding and removing features to/from a current subset. The respective algorithm steps can be described as follows (for the sake of simplicity we consider only non-generalized algorithms that process one feature at a time only):

Definition 1. *For a given current feature set* X_d, *let* f^+ *be the feature such that*

$$f^+ = \arg\max_{f \in Y \setminus X_d} J^+(X_d, f), \tag{3}$$

where $J^+(X_d, f)$ *denotes the criterion function used to evaluate the subset obtained by adding* f ($f \in Y \setminus X_d$) *to* X_d. *Then we shall say that* $ADD(X_d)$ *is an operation of adding feature* f^+ *to the current set* X_d *to obtain set* X_{d+1} *if*

$$ADD(X_d) \equiv X_d \cup \{f^+\} = X_{d+1}, \quad X_d, X_{d+1} \subset Y. \tag{4}$$

Definition 2. *For a given current feature set* X_d, *let* f^- *be the feature such that*

$$f^- = \arg\max_{f \in X_d} J^-(X_d, f), \tag{5}$$

where $J^-(X_d, f)$ denotes the criterion function used to evaluate the subset obtained by removing f ($f \in X_d$) from X_d. Then we shall say that $REMOVE(X_d)$ is an operation of removing feature f^- from the current set X_d to obtain set X_{d-1} if

$$REMOVE(X_d) \equiv X_d \setminus \{f^-\} = X_{d-1}, \quad X_d, X_{d-1} \subset Y. \tag{6}$$

In order to simplify the notation for a repeated application of FS operations we introduce the following useful notation

$$X_{d+2} = ADD(X_{d+1}) = ADD(ADD(X_d)) = ADD^2(X_d), \tag{7}$$
$$X_{d-2} = REMOVE(REMOVE(X_d)) = REMOVE^2(X_d),$$

and more generally

$$X_{d+\delta} = ADD^\delta(X_d), \quad X_{d-\delta} = REMOVE^\delta(X_d). \tag{8}$$

Note that in standard sequential FS methods $J^+(\cdot)$ and $J^-(\cdot)$ stand for

$$J^+(X_d, f) = J(X_d \cup \{f\}), \quad J^-(X_d, f) = J(X_d \setminus \{f\}), \tag{9}$$

where $J(\cdot)$ is either a filter- or wrapper-based criterion function (Kohavi et al. (1997b)) to be evaluated on the subspace defined by the tested feature subset.

4.3 Simplest Sequential Selection

The basic feature selection approach is to build up a subset of required number of features incrementally starting with the empty set (*bottom-up* approach) or to start with the complete set of features and remove redundant features until d features remain (*top-down* approach). The simplest (among recommendable choices) yet widely used *sequential forward (or backward) selection* methods, SFS and SBS (Whitney (1971), Devijver et al. (1982)), iteratively add (remove) one feature at a time so as to maximize the intermediate criterion value until the required dimensionality is achieved.

SFS (*Sequential Forward Selection*) yielding a subset of d features:

1. $X_d = ADD^d(\emptyset)$.

SBS (*Sequential Backward Selection*) yielding a subset of d features:

1. $X_d = REMOVE^{|Y|-d}(Y)$.

As many other of the earlier sequential methods both SFS and SBS suffer from the so-called nesting of feature subsets which significantly deteriorates optimization ability. The first attempt to overcome this problem was to employ either the Plus-l-Take away-r (also known as (l, r)) or generalized (l, r) algorithms (Devijver et al. (1982)) which involve successive augmentation and depletion process. The same idea in a principally extended and refined form constitutes the basis of Floating Search.

4.4 Sequential Floating Search

The Sequential Forward Floating Selection (SFFS) (Pudil et al. (1994)) procedure consists of applying after each forward step a number of backward steps as long as the resulting subsets are better than previously evaluated ones at that level. Consequently, there are no backward steps at all if intermediate result at actual level (of corresponding dimensionality) cannot be improved. The same applies for the backward version of the procedure. Both algorithms allow a 'self-controlled backtracking' so they can eventually find good solutions by adjusting the trade-off between forward and backward steps dynamically. In a certain way, they compute only what they need without any parameter setting.

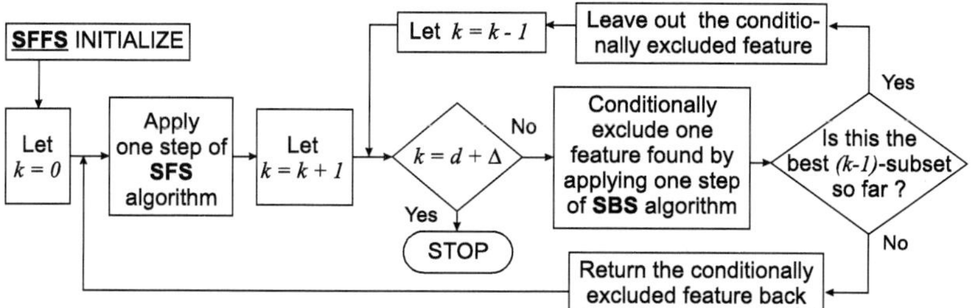

Fig. 1. Sequential Forward Floating Selection Algorithm

SFFS (*Sequential Forward Floating Selection*) yielding a subset of d features, with optional search-restricting parameter $\Delta \in [0, D - d]$:

1. Start with $X_0 = \emptyset$, $k = 0$.

2. $X_{k+1} = ADD(X_k)$, $k = k + 1$.

3. Repeat $X_{k-1} = REMOVE(X_k)$, $k = k - 1$ as long as it improves solutions already known for the lower k.

4. If $k < d + \Delta$ go to 2.

A detailed formal description of this now classical procedure can be found in Pudil et al. (1994). Nevertheless, the idea behind it is simple enough and can be illustrated sufficiently in Fig. 1. (Condition $k = d + \Delta$ terminates the algorithm after the target subset of d features has been found and possibly refined by means of backtracking from dimensionalities greater than d.) The backward counterpart to SFFS is the Sequential Backward Floating Selection (SBFS). Its principle is analogous.

Floating search algorithms can be considered universal tools not only outperforming all predecessors, but also keeping advantages not met by more sophisticated algorithms. They find good solutions in all problem dimensions in one run. The overall search speed is high enough for most of practical problems.

SBFS (*Sequential Backward Floating Selection*) yielding a subset of d features, with optional search-restricting parameter $\Delta \in [0, d]$:

1. Start with $X_0 = Y$, $k = |Y|$.

2. $X_{k-1} = REMOVE(X_k)$, $k = k - 1$.

3. Repeat $X_{k+1} = ADD(X_k)$, $k = k+1$ as long as it improves solutions already known for the higher k.

4. If $k > d - \Delta$ go to 2.

4.4.1 Further Developments of the Floating Search Idea

As the Floating Search algorithms have been found successful and generally accepted to be an efficient universal tool, their idea was further investigated. The so-called Adaptive Floating Search has been proposed in Somol et al. (1999). The ASFFS and ASBFS algorithms are able to outperform the classical SFFS and SBFS algorithms in certain cases, but at a cost of considerable increase of search time and the necessity to deal with unclear parameters. Our experience shows that ASFFS/ASBFS is usually inferior to newer algorithms, which we focus on in the following. An improved version of Floating Search has been published recently in Nakariyakul et al. (2009).

4.5 Oscillating Search

The more recent Oscillating Search (OS) (Somol et al. (2000)) can be considered a "meta" procedure, that takes use of other feature selection methods as sub-procedures in its own search. The concept is highly flexible and enables modifications for different purposes. It has shown to be very powerful and capable of over-performing standard sequential procedures, including Floating Search algorithms. Unlike other methods, the OS is based on repeated modification of the current subset X_d of d features. In this sense the OS is independent of the predominant search direction. This is achieved by alternating so-called *down-* and *up-swings*. Both *swings* attempt to improve the current set X_d by replacing some of the features by better ones. The *down-swing* first removes, then adds back, while the *up-swing* first adds, then removes. Two successive opposite swings form an *oscillation cycle*. The OS can thus be looked upon as a controlled sequence of oscillation cycles. The value of o denoted *oscillation cycle depth* determines the number of features to be replaced in one swing. o is increased after unsuccessful oscillation cycles and reset to 1 after each X_d improvement. The algorithm terminates when o exceeds a user-specified *limit* Δ. The course of Oscillating Search is illustrated in comparison to SFS and SFFS in Fig. 2. Every OS algorithm requires some initial set of d features. The initial set may be obtained randomly or in any other way, e.g., using some of the traditional sequential selection procedures. Furthermore, almost any feature selection procedure can be used in *up-* and *down-swings* to accomplish the replacements of feature o-tuples. For OS flow-chart see Fig. 3.

OS (*Oscillating Search*) yielding a subset of d features, with optional search-restricting parameter $\Delta \geq 1$):

1. Start with initial set X_d of d features. Set cycle depth to $o = 1$.

2. Let $X_d^{\downarrow} = ADD^o(REMOVE^o(X_d))$.

3. If $X_d^{\downarrow}$ better than X_d, let $X_d = X_d^{\downarrow}$, let $o = 1$ and go to 2.

4. Let $X_d^{\uparrow} = REMOVE^o(ADD^o(X_d))$.

5. If $X_d^{\uparrow}$ better than X_d, let $X_d = X_d^{\uparrow}$, let $o = 1$ and go to 2.

6. If $o < \Delta$ let $o = o + 1$ and go to 2.

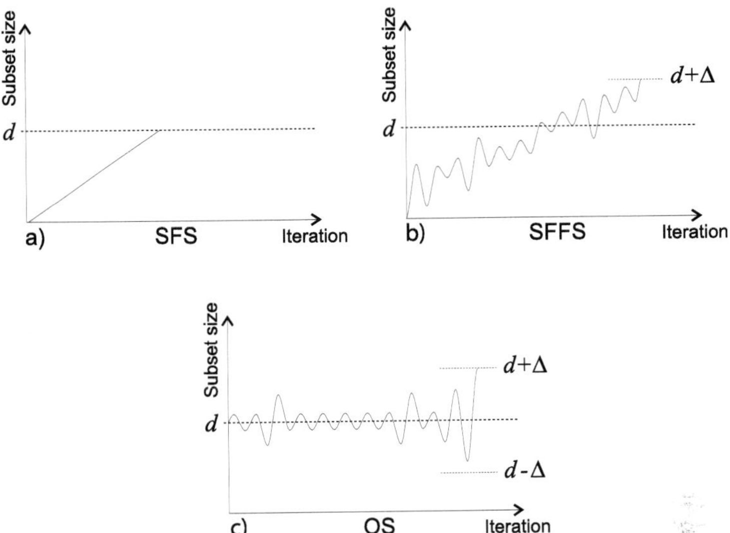

Fig. 2. Graphs demonstrate the course of d-parametrized search algorithms: a) Sequential Forward Selection, b) Sequential Forward Floating Selection, c) Oscillating Search.

The generality of OS search concept allows to adjust the search for better speed or better accuracy (by adjusting Δ, redefining the initialization procedure or redefining ADD / REMOVE). As opposed to all sequential search procedures, OS does not waste time evaluating subsets of cardinalities too different from the target one. This "focus" improves the OS ability to find good solutions for subsets of given cardinality. The fastest improvement of the target subset may be expected in initial phases of the algorithm, because of the low initial cycle depth. Later, when the current feature subset evolves closer to optimum, low-depth cycles fail to improve and therefore the algorithm broadens the search ($o = o + 1$). Though this improves the chance to get closer to the optimum, the trade-off between finding a better solution and computational time becomes more apparent. Consequently, OS tends to improve the solution most considerably during the fastest initial search stages. This behavior is advantageous, because it gives the option of stopping the search after a while without serious result-degrading consequences. Let us summarize the key OS advantages:

- It may be looked upon as a universal tuning mechanism, being able to improve solutions obtained in other way.

- The randomly initialized OS is very fast, in case of very high-dimensional problems may become the only applicable alternative to BIF. For example, in document analysis (Novovičová et al. (2006)) for search of the best 1000 words out of a vocabulary of 10000 all other sequential methods prove to be too slow.

- Because the OS processes subsets of target cardinality from the very beginning, it may find solutions even in cases, where the sequential procedures fail due to numerical problems.

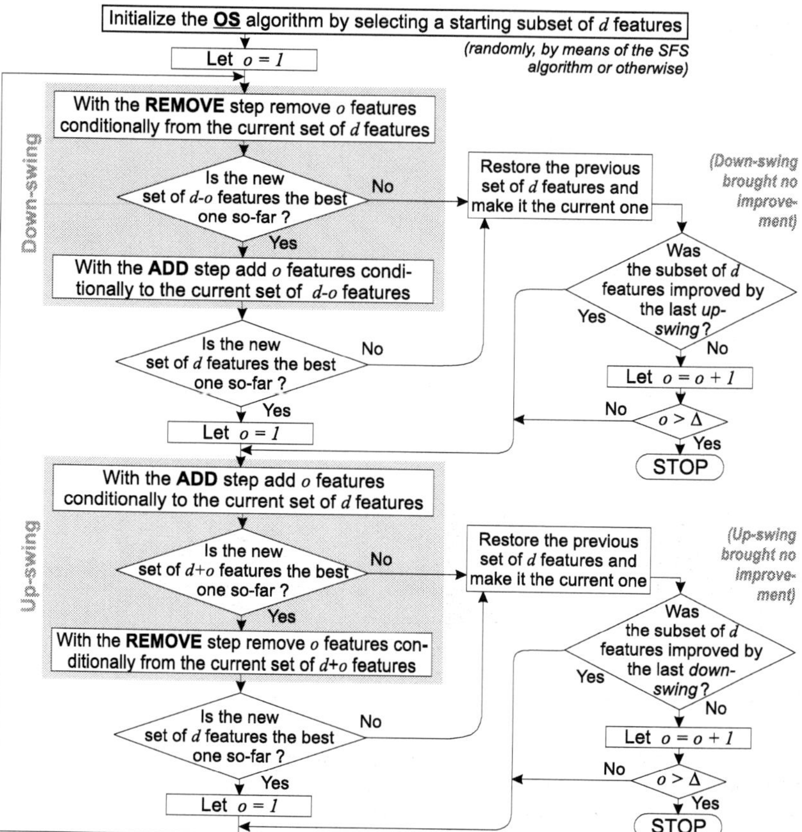

Fig. 3. Simplified Oscillating Search algorithm flowchart.

- Because the solution improves gradually after each oscillation cycle, with the most notable improvements at the beginning, it is possible to terminate the algorithm prematurely after a specified amount of time to obtain a usable solution. The OS is thus suitable for use in real-time systems.

- In some cases the sequential search methods tend to uniformly get caught in certain local extremes. Running the OS from several different random initial points gives better chances to avoid that local extreme.

4.6 Experimental Comparison of d-Parametrized Methods

The d-parametrized sub-optimal FS methods as discussed in preceding sections 4.1 to 4.5 have been listed in the order of their speed-vs-performance characteristics. The BIF is the fastest but worst performing method, OS offers the strongest optimization ability at the cost of slowest computation (although it can be adjusted differently). To illustrate this behavior we compare the output of BIF, SFS, SFFS and OS on a FS task in wrapper (Kohavi et al. (1997a)) setting.

The methods have been used to find best feature subsets for each subset size $d = 1,\ldots,34$ on the *ionosphere* data (34 dim., 2 classes: 225 and 126 samples) from the UCI Repository (Asuncion et al. (2007)). The dataset had been split to 80% train and 20% test part. FS has been performed on the training part using 10-fold cross-validation, in which 3-Nearest Neighbor classifier was used as FS criterion. BIF, SFS and SFFS require no parameters, OS had been set to repeat each search 15× from different random initial subsets of given size, with $\Delta = 15$. This set-up is highly time consuming but enables to avoid many local extremes that would not be avoided by other algorithms.

Figure 4 shows the maximal criterion value obtained by each method for each subset size. It can be seen that the strongest optimizer in most of cases is OS, although SFFS falls behind just negligibly. SFS optimization ability is shown to be markedly lower, but still higher than that of BIF.

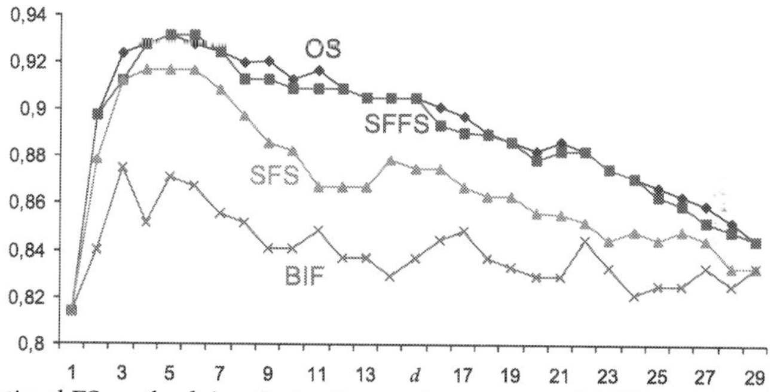

Fig. 4. Sub-optimal FS methods' optimization performance on 3-NN wrapper

Figure 5 shows how the optimized feature subsets perform on independent test data. From this perspective the differences between methods largely diminish. The effects of feature over-selection (over-fitting) affect the strongest optimizer – OS – the most. SFFS seems to be the most reliable method in this respect. SFS yields the best independent performance in this example. Note that although the highest optimized criterion values have been achieved for subsets of roughly 6 features, the best independent performance can be observed for subsets of roughly 7 to 13 features. The example thus illustrates well one of the key problems in FS – the difficulty to find subsets that generalize well, related to the problem of feature over-selection (Raudys (2006)).

The speed of each tested method decreases with its complexity. BIF runs in linear time. Other methods run in polynomial time. SFFS runs roughly 10× slower than SFS. OS in the slow test setting runs roughly 10 to 100× slower than SFFS.

4.7 Dynamic Oscillating Search – Optimizing Subset Size

The idea of Oscillating Search (Sect. 4.5) has been further extended in form of the Dynamic Oscillating Search (DOS) (Somol et al. (2008b)). The DOS algorithm can start from any initial subset of features (including empty set). Similarly to OS it repeatedly attempts to improve the current set by means of repeating oscillation cycles. However, the current subset size is allowed to change, whenever a new globally best solution is found at any stage of the oscillation cycle. Unlike other methods discussed in this chapter the DOS is thus a d-optimizing procedure.

of differently sized subsets. We will refer to this problem as to "the problem of subset-size bias". Note that most of available stability measures are affected by the same problem. For this reason we introduce another measure, to be called the *relative weighted consistency*, which suppresses the influence of the sizes of subsets in system on the final value.

Definition 6. *The* relative weighted consistency $CW_{rel}(\mathcal{S}, Y)$ *of system $\mathcal{S}$ characterized by N, n and for given Y is defined as*

$$CW_{rel}(\mathcal{S}, Y) = \frac{CW(\mathcal{S}) - CW_{min}(N, n, Y)}{CW_{max}(N, n) - CW_{min}(N, n, Y)}, \tag{22}$$

where $CW_{rel}(\mathcal{S}, Y) = CW(\mathcal{S})$ for $CW_{max}(N, n) = CW_{min}(N, n, Y)$.
Denoting $D = N \bmod |Y|$ and $H = N \bmod n$ for simplicity, it has been shown in Somol et al. (2008a) that

$$CW_{min}(N, n, Y) = \frac{N^2 - |Y|(N - D) - D^2}{|Y|N(n - 1)} \tag{23}$$

and

$$CW_{max}(N, n) = \frac{H^2 + N(n - 1) - Hn}{N(n - 1)}. \tag{24}$$

The relative weighted consistency then becomes:

$$CW_{rel}(\mathcal{S}, Y) = \frac{|Y| \left(N - D + \sum_{f \in Y} F_f(F_f - 1) \right) - N^2 + D^2}{|Y| \left(H^2 + n(N - H) - D \right) - N^2 + D^2}. \tag{25}$$

The weighted consistency bounds $CW_{max}(N, n)$ and $CW_{min}(N, n, Y)$ are illustrated in Fig. 8.

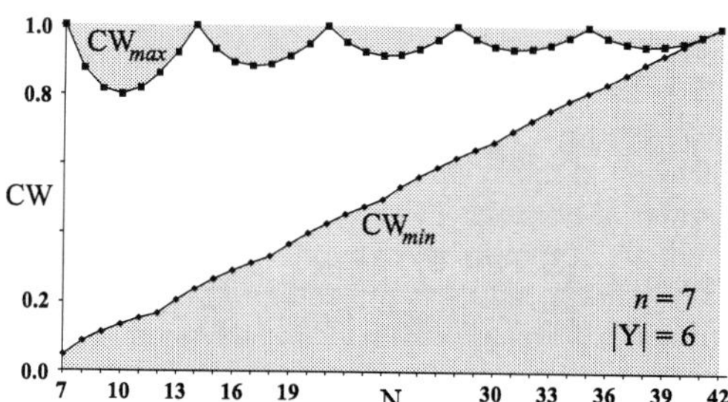

Fig. 8. Illustration of CW measure bounds

Note that CW_{rel} may be sensitive to small system changes if N approaches maximum (for given $|Y|$ and n).
It can be seen that for any N, n representing some system of subsets $\mathcal{S}$ and for given Y it is true that $0 \le CW_{rel}(\mathcal{S}, Y) \le 1$ and for the corresponding systems $\mathcal{S}_{min}$ and $\mathcal{S}_{max}$ it is true that $CW_{rel}(\mathcal{S}_{min}) = 0$ and $CW_{rel}(\mathcal{S}_{max}) = 1$.
The measure (22) does not exhibit the unwanted behavior of yielding higher values for systems with subset sizes closer to $|Y|$, i.e., is independent of the size of feature subsets selected by the examined FS methods under fixed Y. We can say that this measure characterizes for given $\mathcal{S}, Y$ the relative degree of randomness of the system of feature subsets on the scale between the maximum and minimum values of the weighted consistency (20).

Next, following the idea of Kalousis et al. (2007) we define a conceptually different measure. It is derived from the *Tanimoto index (coefficient)* defined as the size of the intersection divided by the size of union of the subsets S_i and S_j, Duda et al. (2000):

$$S_K(S_i, S_j) = \frac{|S_i \cap S_j|}{|S_i \cup S_j|} .$$ (26)

Definition 7. *The* Average Tanimoto Index *of system $\mathcal{S}$ is defined as follows:*

$$ATI(\mathcal{S}) = \frac{2}{n(n-1)} \sum_{i=1}^{n-1} \sum_{j=i+1}^{n} S_K(S_i, S_j) .$$ (27)

$ATI(\mathcal{S})$ is the average similarity measure over all pairs of feature subsets in $\mathcal{S}$. It takes values from $[0, 1]$ with 0 indicating empty intersection between all pairs of subsets S_i, S_j and 1 indicating that all subsets of the system $\mathcal{S}$ are identical.

Wrap.	FS Meth.	Classif. rate		Subset size		CW	CW rel	ATI	FS time h:m:s
		Mean	S.Dv.	Mean	S.Dv.				
Gauss.	rand	.908	.059	14.90	8.39	.500	.008	.296	00:00:14
	BIF*	.948	.004	27.15	4.09	.927	.244	.862	00:04:57
	SFS*	.963	.003	11.95	5.30	.506	.181	.332	01:02:04
	SFFS*	.969	.003	12.17	4.66	.556	.259	.387	09:13:03
	DOS	.973	.002	8.85	2.36	.584	.419	.429	12:49:59
3NN	rand	.935	.061	14.9	8.30	.501	.009	.297	00:00:45
	BIF*	.970	.002	24.78	3.70	.912	.513	.840	00:38:39
	SFS*	.976	.002	15.45	5.74	.584	.148	.401	07:27:39
	SFFS*	.979	.002	17.96	5.67	.658	.149	.481	33:53:55
	DOS	.980	.001	13.27	4.25	.565	.227	.393	116:47:
SVM	rand	.942	.059	14.94	8.58	.502	.008	.295	00:00:50
	BIF*	.974	.003	21.67	2.71	.929	.774	.875	01:01:48
	SFS*	.982	.002	9.32	4.12	.433	.185	.283	07:13:02
	SFFS*	.983	.002	10.82	4.58	.472	.179	.310	30:28:02
	DOS	.985	.001	8.70	3.42	.442	.222	.295	74:28:51

Table 3. Stability of wrapper FS methods evaluated on *wdbc* data, 30-dim., 2-class.

6.1.2 Experiments With Stability Measures

To illustrate the discussed stability measures we have conducted several experiments on *wdbc* data (30 dim., 2 classes: 357 benign and 212 malignant samples) from UCI Repository (Asuncion et al. (2007)). The results are collected in Table 3. We focused on comparing the stability of principally different FS methods discussed in this chapter: BIF, SFS and SFFS and DOS in d-optimizing setting; d-parametrized methods are run for each possible subset size to eventually select the subset size that yields the highest criterion value. To mark the difference from standard d-parametrized course of search we denote these methods BIF*, SFS*and SFFS*. We used the classification accuracy of three conceptually different classifiers as FS criteria: Gaussian classifier, 3-Nearest Neighbor (majority voting) and SVM with RBF kernel (Chang et al. (2001)). In each setup FS was repeated $1000\times$ on randomly sampled 80% of the data (class size ratios preserved). In each FS run the criterion was evaluated using 10-fold cross-validation, with 2/3 of available data randomly sampled for training and the remaining 1/3 used for testing.

The results are collected in Table 3. All measures, CW, CW_{rel} and ATI indicate BIF* as the most stable FS method, what confirms the conclusions in Kuncheva (2007). Note that CW_{rel} is the only measure to correctly detect random feature selection (values close to 0). Note that apart from BIF*, with 3-NN and SVM the most stable FS method appears to be SFFS*, with Gaussian classifier it is *DOS*. Very low CW_{rel} values may indicate some pitfall in the FS process - either there are no clearly preferable features in the set, or the methods overfit, etc. Note that low stability measure values are often accompanied by higher deviations in subset size.

7. Summary

The current state of art in feature selection based dimensionality reduction for decision problems of classification type has been overviewed. A number of recent feature subset search strategies have been reviewed and compared. Following the analysis of their respective advantages and shortcomings, the conditions under which certain strategies are more pertinent than others have been suggested.

Concerning our current experience, we can give the following recommendations. Floating Search can be considered the first tool to try for many FS tasks. It is reasonably fast and yields generally very good results in all dimensions at once, often succeeding in finding the global optimum. The Oscillating Search becomes better choice whenever: 1) the highest quality of solution must be achieved but optimal methods are not applicable, or 2) a reasonable solution is to be found as quickly as possible, or 3) numerical problems hinder the use of sequential methods, or 4) extreme problem dimensionality prevents any use of sequential methods, or 5) the search is to be performed in real-time systems. Especially when repeated with different random initial sets the Oscillating Search shows outstanding potential to overcome local extremes in favor of global optimum. Dynamic Oscillating Search adds to Oscillating Search the ability to optimize both the subset size and subset contents at once.

No FS method, however, can be claimed the best for all problems. Moreover, any FS method should be applied cautiously to prevent the negative effects of feature over-selection (over-training) and to prevent stability issues.

Remark: Source codes can be partly found at `http://ro.utia.cas.cz/dem.html`.

7.1 Does It Make Sense to Develop New FS Methods?

Our answer is undoubtedly yes. Our current experience shows that no clear and unambiguous qualitative hierarchy can be established within the existing framework of methods, i.e., although some methods perform better then others more often, this is not the case always and any method can show to be the best tool for some particular problem. Adding to this pool of methods may thus bring improvement, although it is more and more difficult to come up with new ideas that have not been utilized before. Regarding the performance of search algorithms as such, developing methods that yield results closer to optimum with respect to any given criterion may bring considerably more advantage in future, when better criteria may have been found to better express the relation between feature subsets and classifier generalization ability.

8. Acknowledgements

The work has been supported by projects AV0Z1075050506 of the GAAV CR, GAČR 102/08/0593, 102/07/1594 and CR MŠMT grants 2C06019 ZIMOLEZ and 1M0572 DAR.

9. References

Asuncion, A. & Newman, D. (2007). UCI machine learning repository, http://www.ics.uci.edu/ ~mlearn/ mlrepository.html.

Blum, A. & Langley, P. (1997). Selection of relevant features and examples in machine learning. *Artificial Intelligence*, 97(1-2), 245–271.

Chang, C.-C. & Lin, C.-J. (2001). *LIBSVM: a library for SVM*. http://www.csie.ntu.edu.tw/~cjlin/libsvm.

Das, S. (2001). Filters, wrappers and a boosting-based hybrid for feature selection. In *Proc. of the 18th International Conference on Machine Learning* pp. 74–81.

Dash, M.; Choi, K.; P., S., & Liu, H. (2002). Feature selection for clustering - a filter solution. In *Proceedings of the Second International Conference on Data Mining* pp. 115–122.

Devijver, P. A. & Kittler, J. (1982). *Pattern Recognition: A Statistical Approach*. Englewood Cliffs, London, UK: Prentice Hall.

Duda, R. O.; Hart, P. E., & Stork, D. G. (2000). *Pattern Classification (2nd Edition)*. Wiley-Interscience.

Dunne, K.; Cunningham, P., & Azuaje, F. (2002). *Solutions to Instability Problems with Sequential Wrapper-based Approaches to Feature Selection*. Technical Report TCD-CS-2002-28, Trinity College Dublin, Department of Computer Science.

Ferri, F. J.; Pudil, P.; Hatef, M., & Kittler, J. (1994). Comparative study of techniques for large-scale feature selection. *Machine Intelligence and Pattern Recognition*, 16.

Fukunaga, K. (1990). *Introduction to Statistical Pattern Recognition (2nd ed.)*. San Diego, CA, USA: Academic Press Professional, Inc.

Guyon, I. & Elisseeff, A. (2003). An introduction to variable and feature selection. *J. Mach. Learn. Res.*, 3, 1157–1182.

Hussein, F.; Ward, R., & Kharma, N. (2001). Genetic algorithms for feature selection and weighting, a review and study. *icdar*, 00, 1240.

Jain, A. & Zongker, D. (1997). Feature selection: Evaluation, application, and small sample performance. *IEEE Trans. Pattern Anal. Mach. Intell.*, 19(2), 153–158.

Jain, A. K.; Duin, R. P. W., & Mao, J. (2000). Statistical pattern recognition: A review. *IEEE Trans. Pattern Anal. Mach. Intell.*, 22(1), 4–37.

Jensen, R. (2006). *Performing Feature Selection with ACO*, volume 34 of *Studies in Computational Intelligence*, pp. 45–73. Springer Berlin / Heidelberg.

Kalousis, A.; Prados, J., & Hilario, M. (2007). Stability of feature selection algorithms: A study on high-dimensional spaces. *Knowledge and Information Systems*, 12(1), 95–116.

Kohavi, R. & John, G. (1997a). Wrappers for feature subset selection. *Artificial Intelligence*, 97, 273–324.

Kohavi, R. & John, G. H. (1997b). Wrappers for feature subset selection. *Artif. Intell.*, 97(1-2), 273–324.

Kononenko, I. (1994). Estimating attributes: Analysis and extensions of relief. In *ECML-94: Proc. European Conf. on Machine Learning* pp. 171–182. Secaucus, NJ, USA: Springer-Verlag New York, Inc.

Křížek, P.; Kittler, J., & Hlaváč, V. (2007). Improving stability of feature selection methods. In *Proc. 12th Int. Conf. on Computer Analysis of Images and Patterns*, volume LNCS 4673 pp. 929–936. Berlin / Heidelberg, Germany: Springer-Verlag.

Kudo, M. & Sklansky, J. (2000). Comparison of algorithms that select features for pattern classifiers. *Pattern Recognition*, 33(1), 25–41.

Kuncheva, L. I. (2007). A stability index for feature selection. In *Proc. 25th IASTED International Multi-Conference AIAP'07* pp. 390–395. Anaheim, CA, USA: ACTA Press.

Liu, H. & Yu, L. (2005). Toward integrating feature selection algorithms for classification and clustering. *IEEE Transactions on Knowledge and Data Engineering*, 17(4), 491–502.

McLachlan, G. J. (2004). *Discriminant analysis and statistical pattern recognition*. Wiley-IEEE.

Nakariyakul, S. & Casasent, D. P. (2007). Adaptive branch and bound algorithm for selecting optimal features. *Pattern Recogn. Lett.*, 28(12), 1415–1427.

Nakariyakul, S. & Casasent, D. P. (2009). An improvement on floating search algorithms for feature subset selection. *Pattern Recognition*, 42(9), 1932–1940.

Novovičová, J.; Pudil, P., & Kittler, J. (1996). Divergence based feature selection for multimodal class densities. *IEEE Trans. Pattern Anal. Mach. Intell.*, 18(2), 218–223.

Novovičová, J.; Somol, P., & Pudil, P. (2006). Oscillating feature subset search algorithm for text categorization. In *Structural, Syntactic, and Statistical Pattern Recognition*, volume LNCS 4109 pp. 578–587. Berlin / Heidelberg, Germany: Springer-Verlag.

Pudil, P.; Novovičová, J., & Kittler, J. (1994). Floating search methods in feature selection. *Pattern Recogn. Lett.*, 15(11), 1119–1125.

Pudil, P.; Novovičová, J.; Choakjarernwanit, N., & Kittler, J. (1995). Feature selection based on approximation of class densities by finite mixtures of special type. *Pattern Recognition*, 28, 1389–1398.

Raudys, Š. J. (2006). Feature over-selection. In *Structural, Syntactic, and Statistical Pattern Recognition*, volume LNCS 4109 pp. 622–631. Berlin / Heidelberg, Germany: Springer-Verlag.

Reunanen, J. (2003). Overfitting in making comparisons between variable selection methods. *J. Mach. Learn. Res.*, 3, 1371–1382.

Ripley, B. D., Ed. (2005). *Pattern Recognition and Neural Networks*. Cambridge University Press, 8 edition.

Saeys, Y.; naki Inza, I., & naga, P. L. (2007). A review of feature selection techniques in bioinformatics. *Bioinformatics*, 23(19), 2507–2517.

Salappa, A.; Doumpos, M., & Zopounidis, C. (2007). Feature selection algorithms in classification problems: An experimental evaluation. *Optimization Methods and Software*, 22(1), 199–212.

Sebastiani, F. (2002). Machine learning in automated text categorization. *ACM Computing Surveys*, 34(1), 1–47.

Sebban, M. & Nock, R. (2002). A hybrid filter/wrapper approach of feature selection using information theory. *Pattern Recognition*, 35, 835–846.

Siedlecki, W. & Sklansky, J. (1993). *On automatic feature selection*, pp. 63–87. World Scientific Publishing Co., Inc.: River Edge, NJ, USA.

Skurichina, M. (2001). *Stabilizing Weak Classifiers*. PhD thesis, Pattern Recognition Group, Delft University of Technology, Netherlands.

Somol, P.; Novovičová, J., & Pudil, P. (2006). Flexible-hybrid sequential floating search in statistical feature selection. In *Structural, Syntactic, and Statistical Pattern Recognition*, volume LNCS 4109 pp. 632–639. Berlin / Heidelberg, Germany: Springer-Verlag.

Somol, P. & Novovičová, J. (2008a). Evaluating the stability of feature selectors that optimize feature subset cardinality. In *Structural, Syntactic, and Statistical Pattern Recognition*, volume LNCS 5342 pp. 956–966.

Somol, P.; Novovičová, J.; Grim, J., & Pudil, P. (2008b). Dynamic oscillating search algorithms for feature selection. In *ICPR 2008* Los Alamitos, CA, USA: IEEE Computer Society.

Somol, P. & Pudil, P. (2000). Oscillating search algorithms for feature selection. In *ICPR 2000*, volume 02 pp. 406–409. Los Alamitos, CA, USA: IEEE Computer Society.

Somol, P.; Pudil, P., & Kittler, J. (2004). Fast branch & bound algorithms for optimal feature selection. *IEEE Transactions on Pattern Analysis and Machine Intelligence*, 26(7), 900–912.

Somol, P.; Pudil, P.; Novovičová, J., & Paclík, P. (1999). Adaptive floating search methods in feature selection. *Pattern Recogn. Lett.*, 20(11-13), 1157–1163.

Theodoridis, S. & Koutroumbas, K. (2006). *Pattern Recognition*. USA: Academic Press, 3rd edition.

Tsamardinos, I. & Aliferis, C. F. (2003). Towards principled feature selection: Relevancy, filters, and wrappers. In *9th Int. Workshop on Artificial Intelligence and Statistics (AI&Stats 2003)* Key West, FL.

Vafaie, H. & Imam, I. F. (1994). Feature selection methods: Genetic algorithms vs. greedy-like search. In *Proc. Int. Conf. on Fuzzy and Intelligent Control Systems*.

Webb, A. R. (2002). *Statistical Pattern Recognition (2nd Edition)*. John Wiley and Sons Ltd.

Whitney, A. W. (1971). A direct method of nonparametric measurement selection. *IEEE Trans. Comput.*, 20(9), 1100–1103.

Xing, E. P. (2003). *Feature Selection in Microarray Analysis*, pp. 110–129. Springer.

Yang, J. & Honavar, V. G. (1998). Feature subset selection using a genetic algorithm. *IEEE Intelligent Systems*, 13(2), 44–49.

Yang, Y. & Pedersen, J. O. (1997). A comparative study on feature selection in text categorization. In *ICML '97: Proc. 14th Int. Conf. on Machine Learning* pp. 412–420. San Francisco, CA, USA: Morgan Kaufmann Publishers Inc.

Yu, L. & Liu, H. (2003). Feature selection for high-dimensional data: A fast correlation-based filter solution. In *Proceedings of the 20th International Conference on Machine Learning* pp. 56–63.

Yusta, S. C. (2009). Different metaheuristic strategies to solve the feature selection problem. *Pattern Recogn. Lett.*, 30(5), 525–534.

Zhang, H. & Sun, G. (2002). Feature selection using tabu search method. *Pattern Recognition*, 35, 701–711.

5

Non-Linear Feature Extraction by Linear Principal Component Analysis Using Local Kernel

Kazuhiro Hotta
The University of Electro-Communications
Japan

1. Introduction

In the last decade, the effectiveness of kernel-based methods for object detection and recognition have been reported Fukui et al. (2006); Hotta (2008c); Kim et al. (2002); Pontil & Verri (1998); Shawe-Taylor & Cristianini (2004); Yang (2002). In particular, Kernel Principal Component Analysis (KPCA) took the place of traditional linear PCA as the first feature extraction step in various researches and applications. KPCA can cope with non-linear variations well. However, KPCA must solve the eigen value problem with the number of samples × the number of samples. In addition, the computation of kernel functions with all training samples are required to map a test sample to the subspace obtained by KPCA. Therefore, the computational cost is the main drawback. To reduce the computational cost of KPCA, sparse KPCA Tipping (2001) and the use of clustering Ichino et al. (2007 (in Japanese) were proposed. Ichino et al. Ichino et al. (2007 (in Japanese) reported that KPCA of cluster centers is more effective than sparse KPCA. However, the computational cost becomes a big problem again when the number of classes is large and each class has one subspace. For example, KPCA of visual words (cluster centers of local features) Hotta (2008b) was effective for object categorization but the computational cost is high. In this method, each category of 101 categories has one subspace constructed by 400 visual words. Namely, $40,400 (= 101$ categorizes $\times 400$ visual words) kernel computations are required to map a local feature to all subspaces.

On the other hand, traditional linear PCA is independent of the number of samples when the dimension of a feature is smaller than the number of samples. This is because the size of eigen value problem depends on the minimum number of the feature dimension and the number of samples. To map a test sample to a subspace, only inner products between basis vectors and the test sample are required. Therefore, in general, the computational cost of linear PCA is much lower than KPCA. In this paper, we propose how to use non-linearity of KPCA and computational cost of linear PCA simultaneously Hotta (2008a).

Kernel-based methods map training samples to high dimensional space as $x \rightarrow \phi(x)$. Non-linearity is realized by linear method in high dimensional space. The dimension of mapped feature space of the Radial Basis Function (RBF) kernel becomes infinity, and we can not describe the mapped feature explicitly. However, the mapped feature $\phi(x)$ of the polynomial kernel can be described explicitly. This means that KPCA with the polynomial kernel can be solved directly by linear PCA of mapped features. Unfortunately, in general, the dimension of mapped features is too high to solve by linear PCA even if the polynomial kernel with 2nd degrees $K(x,y) = (1 + x^T y)^2$ is used. The dimension of mapped features of the polynomial kernel with 2nd degrees becomes $_{nd+2}C_2 = (nd + 2)!/(nd!\ 2!)$ where nd is the number of dimension of input features. For example, the dimension of mapped feature becomes $20,301$ even when the dimension of an input feature is 200. However, if the polynomial kernel with 2nd degrees is applied to local features not a whole feature, the dimension of mapped features is not so high. For example, when the polynomial kernel with 2nd degrees is applied to each local 10 dimensional feature of 200 dimensional input feature without overlap, each local feature x_{li} is mapped to 66 dimensional feature $\phi(x_{li})$ independently. Namely, the 200 dimensional input feature is mapped to $1,320$ (= 66 dimensions × 20 local features) dimensional feature as $\left(\phi(x_{l1})^T, \ldots, \phi(x_{l20})^T\right)^T$. In fact, this corresponds to the local summation kernel (the summation of local kernels) Hotta (2008c) because the inner product between $1,320$ dimensional features is the summation of the outputs of inner product between 66 dimensional features as $\sum_{i}^{20} \phi(x_{li})^T \phi(y_{li}) = \sum_{i}^{20} K(x_{li}, y_{li})$. This shows that KPCA with the local summation kernel can be solved by linear PCA. This approach is independent of the number of training samples. Subspace is obtained by solving the eigen value problem of mapped features (e.g. $1,320$ dimensions). To map a test sample to a subspace, only the inner products with basis vectors with $1,320$ dimensions are required. In addition, it can represent non-linear distribution while the computational cost is low. Furthermore, it is reported that the local summation kernel outperforms standard RBF kernel and polynomial kernel under partial occlusion Hotta (2008c).

We evaluate the proposed approach in object categorization problem which has many categories and requires much computational cost. We demonstrate that the proposed approach gives much higher recognition rate than linear PCA. The computational cost is lower than KPCA while the accuracy is slightly worse than KPCA. We also demonstrate that the proposed method can be used for large number of training samples to which KPCA can not be applied. Although our method uses only linear PCA and Support Vector Machine (SVM) with linear kernel, the accuracy is comparable with conventional object categorization methods Fei-Fei et al. (2006); Grauman & Darrell (2005); Holub et al. (2005); Mutch & Lowe (2006); Serre et al. (2005); Wang et al. (2006).

In section 2, KPCA and its drawback are described. Section 3 explains the details of the proposed method. Object categorization method using the proposed approach is explained in section 4. Experimental results using the Caltech 101 database are shown in section 5. Finally, conclusion and future works are described in section 6.

2. KPCA and its drawback

This section explains KPCA Müller et al. (2001); Schölkopf et al. (1998) and its drawback briefly. When data $\{x_1 \ldots, x_L\}$ is given, x is mapped into high dimensional space by non-linear mapping $\phi(x)$. By applying linear PCA in high dimensional space, non-linear principal components are obtained. Covariance matrix in high dimensional space is computed by

$$C = \frac{1}{l} \sum_{i=1}^{L} \phi(x_i)\phi(x_i)^T. \tag{1}$$

Eigen value problem for KPCA is defined by $\lambda V = CV$ where λ is eigen value and V are eigenvectors. Eigenvectors lie in the span of $\phi(x_1), \ldots, \phi(x_L)$. Therefore, eigenvectors are represented by

$$V = \sum_{i=1}^{L} \alpha_i \phi(x_i), \tag{2}$$

where α_i is the coefficient.

The equation does not change when $\phi(x_k)$ is multiplied to both sides. Then the eigen value problem is changed as

$$\lambda \phi(x_k)^T V = \phi(x_k)^T C V \quad \text{for all } k = 1, \ldots, L. \tag{3}$$

By substituting eigenvectors shown in equation (2) into equation (3) and using the kernel matrix K where $K_{ij} = \phi(x_i)^T \phi(x_j)$, we obtain the following eigen value problem

$$L\lambda\alpha = K\alpha. \tag{4}$$

The size of matrix K depends on the number of training samples. Namely, the computational cost also depends on the number of samples. Thus, the computational cost becomes high when the number of samples is large. There is the case that we can not use KPCA due to the size of eigen value problem. This is the drawback of KPCA. By solving the eigen value problem, α is obtained. We have to normalize the obtained α^p for satisfying $(V^p)^T V^p = 1$ for all $p = 1, \ldots, L$.

An input sample x is mapped into p-th principal component axis by

$$(V^p)^T \phi(x) = \sum_{i=1}^{L} \alpha_i^p K(x_i, x). \tag{5}$$

This equation means that the computation of kernel functions with all training samples is required to map the input to the subspace. Thus, in the test phase not only the training phase of KPCA, the computational cost becomes a big problem. Due to this problem, KPCA is not appropriate for on-line processing. Since non-linearity of KPCA is effective for various applications, we must overcome this drawback. In next section, we show a solution using local kernel.

3. KPCA with local summation kernel by linear PCA

This section explains how to solve KPCA with the local summation kernel by linear PCA. At first, an input feature is divided into N local features as $x = \left(x_{l1}^T, x_{l2}^T, \ldots, x_{lN}^T\right)^T$. In the following experiments, the division is carried out without overlap[1]. Each local feature x_{li} is mapped to high dimensional space as $\phi(x_{li})$. All mapped local features $\phi(x_{l1}), \ldots, \phi(x_{lN})$ are connected and used as a new feature vector $x' = (\phi(x_{l1})^T, \ldots, \phi(x_{lN})^T)^T$. The inner product of new feature vectors corresponds to the summation of local kernels.

$$\begin{aligned}
x'^T y' &= (\phi(x_{l1})^T, \ldots, \phi(x_{lN})^T)(\phi(y_{l1})^T, \ldots, \phi(y_{lN})^T)^T, \\
&= \sum_{i}^{N} \phi(x_{li})^T \phi(y_{li}), \\
&= \sum_{i}^{N} K(x_{li}, y_{li}) \tag{6}
\end{aligned}$$

---

[1] We consider that local features with structure (e.g. local region of an image) are more effective than meaningless local features selected randomly

This means that KPCA with the local summation kernel can be solved by linear PCA of new features x' if local mapped features $\phi(x_{li})$ can be described explicitly. Basis vectors are obtained by solving the eigen value problem of the covariance matrix $C = XX^T$ where $X = (x'_1, \ldots, x'_L)$. The dimension of basis vectors is the same as x'.

Note that mapped features of the polynomial kernel can be described explicitly. In the case of the polynomial kernel with 2nd degrees, the dimension of a mapped feature $\phi(x)$ becomes $_{nd+2}C_2$ where nd is the number of dimension of an input feature x. For example, an input feature with 2 dimensions $x = (x_1, x_2)^T$ is mapped to 6 dimensional feature as $\phi(x) = (x_1^2, x_2^2, \sqrt{2}x_1x_2, \sqrt{2}x_1, \sqrt{2}x_2, 1)^T$. Thus, when the dimension of local feature (x_{li}) is not large, KPCA with the local summation kernel can be solved by linear PCA. Of course, if the dimension of local features is large, the dimension of mapped features becomes large. However, the size of covariance matrix in linear PCA depends on the minimum value of the dimension of features and the number of samples. When the number of samples is smaller than the dimension of features, we solve the eigen value problem of $D - X^TX$ where $X - (x'_1, \ldots, x'_L)$. Then the eigen vectors A that we want to obtain can be computed from the eigen vectors B of D as $A = XB\Lambda^{-1/2}$ where diagonal elements of Λ is the eigen values.

In recent years, it is reported that the normalized polynomial kernel outperforms standard polynomial kernel and the RBF kernel after setting optimal parameters Debnath & Takahashi (2004). Therefore, in the following experiments, we use the normalized polynomial kernel with 2nd degrees as local kernel function. The dimension of mapped feature $\phi(x)$ is the same as the standard polynomial kernel. The difference is the norm of mapped feature. In the standard polynomial kernel, the norm of mapped feature $||\phi(x)||$ is not normalized. However, the normalized polynomial kernel normalizes the norm of a mapped feature is normalized as $\phi(x)/||\phi(x)||$. By the norm normalization, the maximum value of the kernel is bounded to 1. In this paper, KPCA with the summation kernel of local normalized polynomial kernels is solved by linear PCA of new feature $(\phi(x_{l1})^T/||\phi(x_{l1})||, \ldots, \phi(x_{lN})^T/||\phi(x_{lN}))^T$. This approach can treat many samples easily in which KPCA can not treat by the computational cost and memory required. In addition, it can represent non-linear distribution while linear PCA can not. Furthermore, the computational cost for mapping a test sample to a subspace is much lower than KPCA because kernel computations with all training samples are not required in the proposed approach. The test sample is mapped to a subspace by inner products with basis vectors whose dimension is the same as the new feature. Therefore, it is effective for multi-class classification problem such as object categorization. In this paper, the proposed approach is evaluated in object categorization problem using the Caltech 101 database. We compare it with KPCA and linear PCA of visual words Hotta (2008b).

4. Object categorization method

In object categorization problem, we can not know the position of objects in advance. Therefore, characteristic local features (regions) are selected automatically from training images of each category. In Hotta (2008b), visual words of each category are made by applying clustering to the ensemble of local features of each category, and KPCA with the normalized polynomial kernel with 5 degrees is used to represent the category specific visual words. After extracting features specialized for each category, SVM with linear kernel is used. In this paper, KPCA with the local summation kernel which is solved by linear PCA is used, and we evaluate whether our approach can represent non-linear variations with low computational cost.

For fair comparison with conventional KPCA of visual words Hotta (2008b), the same descriptor and experimental settings are used. We explain the descriptor briefly[2]. First, the characteristic local regions are selected automatically by using Harris operator Harris & Stephens (1998). The orientation histogram of multi-resolution Gabor features is used to describe each local region. Figure 1 shows how to make the orientation histogram. Concretely, Gabor filters of 8 different orientations with 3 scales are used. Gabor features of 9 (height) $\times$ 9 (width) $\times$ 3 (scales) $\times$ 8 (orientations) dimensions are extracted from a local region. Orientation histogram is computed in a non-overlap region of 3×3 pixels of each scale independently. As a result, we obtain 216 (= 3 (height) $\times$ 3 (width) $\times$ 3 (scales) $\times$ 8 (orientations)) dimensional features. These are used as the descriptor of a local region.

In the proposed approach, local kernel is applied to each 8 dimensional orientation histogram. Since the normalized polynomial kernel with 2nd degrees is used, each 8 dimensional orientation histogram x_{li} is mapped to 45 dimensional feature $\phi(x_{li})/||\phi(x_{li})||$. Thus, the dimension of new features x' becomes $1,215$ dimensions (= 3 (height) $\times$ 3 (width) $\times$ 3 (scales) $\times$ 45 dimensions).

After describing the local regions, k-means is adopted to obtain visual words of each category. Since the visual words include various kinds of local regions, the distribution becomes non-linear. To represent the ensemble of visual words of each category well, non-linearity of KPCA is required. Therefore, linear PCA can not represent the distribution, and the accuracy of the proposed method shows whether our method represents the non-linear distribution well or not. In the proposed approach, non-linearity is realized by local summation kernel.

In our object categorization method, each category has one subspace. In standard KPCA, kernel computations with all visual words in certain category is required to compute the covariance matrix. On the other hand, the proposed approach can compute the covariance matrix by the inner product of $1,215$ dimensional visual words. The maximum benefit of our approach is obtained in mapping a test sample to subspaces. In standard KPCA, when the number of visual words is 400, $40,400$ (= 101 categorizes $\times$ 400 visual words) kernel computations is required to map a local region to all subspaces. However, our approach does not need to compute $40,400$ kernel computations. Only inner products with basis vectors of $1,215$ dimensions are required to map a local region to all subspaces. Therefore, the computational cost is much lower than KPCA of visual words. This is the merit of our approach.

After mapping local regions into the subspaces specialized for each category, SVM with linear kernel is used to classify object categories. Since non-linear feature is extracted by KPCA, SVM with linear kernel is sufficient. In this paper, the projection length to the subspace is used as the features for SVM. However, the projection values to the principal component axes with lower rank become small. To compensate it, the projection value to each axis is normalized by standard deviation of training samples at the axis. The normalized projection length of q-th local region to the p-th axis of the subspace of category k is defined as

$$z'^{p}_{kq} = \left(A_{kp}^{T} x'_{q} / \sqrt{\sigma_{kp}^2} \right)^2$$

where σ_{kp}^2 is the variance of p-th principal component axis of category k. Since M local regions are obtained from a test image, we must integrate M projection length to be robust to the shift, the order, and the number of local regions. We use the mean projection length to integrate all

---

[2] Please refer to Hotta (2008b) for details

Fig. 1. How to describe a local feature

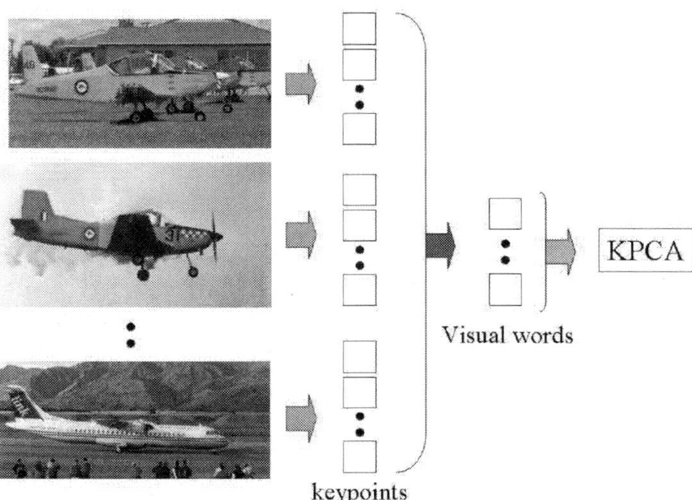

Fig. 2. How to model the visual words

local regions. Namely, the p-th feature in the subspace of category k is computed as

$$z'^{p}_{k} = \frac{1}{M}\sum_{q}^{M} z'^{p}_{kq}.$$

This is the same as the case in which the similarities of M local regions are combined by summation when the similarity between each axis of the subspace and a local region is defined as projection length. Of course, the mean projection length is invariant to the shift, the number, and the order of local regions. These features are used in SVM. We use one-against-all SVM Heisele et al. (2003); Schölkopf et al. (1995) to treat multi-categories. A feature vector of a test image is fed into all NC SVMs, and it is classified to the category given maximum output.

5. Evaluation using the Caltech 101 database

The proposed approach is evaluated using the Caltech 101 database Fei-Fei et al. (2004) which is used in recent papers Fei-Fei et al. (2006); Grauman & Darrell (2005); Holub et al. (2005); Lazebnik et al. (2006); Mutch & Lowe (2006); Serre et al. (2005); Wang et al. (2006); Zhang et al. (2006). The number of images in each category is different. The minimum is 31 and the maximum is 800. Many conventional methods evaluate the accuracy when 15 and 30 images are used in training. Thus, we also use 15 and 30 images selected randomly in training. All remaining images of all categories are used for evaluation. To reduce the bias of the different number of test images in each category, the mean of the classification rate of each category is used. This evaluation is repeated 3 times with different initial seeds of a random function, and the mean classification rate of 3 runs is used as a final result.

In this paper, all images are transformed to gray-level images. The image size is normalized so that all images have nearly same area. Serre et al. Serre et al. (2005) and Mutch et al. Mutch & Lowe (2006) also normalize the image size because the parameters of Gabor filters are fixed. The number of local regions M cropped from an image is set to 500 empirically. When the number of visual words becomes large, the computational cost and memory required by standard KPCA is very large. Therefore, at first, the number of visual words is set to 400 which was used in Hotta (2008b). Although the proposed approach is independent of the number of visual words, the same number of visual words is used for fair comparison.

The results of KPCA (the normalized polynomial kernel with 5 degrees of input features x in Hotta (2008b)) of visual words, linear PCA of visual words, and the proposed method are shown in Table 1. The second column of the table shows the mean classification rates of 3 runs when 15 images per category are used in training. The third column shows the classification rates with 30 training images. The accuracy of linear PCA of visual words is very low. This means that non-linearity of visual words of each category is high, and linear PCA can not represent it well. The proposed method gives much higher accuracy than linear PCA. This shows that the proposed method can represent non-linear distribution though each subspace is constructed by linear PCA. However, the accuracy is worse than that of KPCA of visual words while the computational cost is lower than KPCA[3]. The one reason is that KPCA of visual words Hotta (2008b) uses the normalized polynomial kernel with 5 degrees. The non-linearity of the proposed method based on the normalized polynomial kernel with 2nd degrees may not be slightly enough.

In the upper experiment, the number of visual words is set to 400 because of the computational cost and memory required by KPCA of visual words. However, the proposed method is independent of the number of visual words. When the number of samples per category is 30, the number of local parts in a category is $15,000$ (= 500 local parts per image $\times$ 30 images per category). Here, we set the number of visual words to $1,500$ which is the 10% of the number of local parts. In the case of KPCA with $1,500$ visual words, $151,500$ kernel computations (101 categories $\times$ $1,500$ visual words) are required to map a local part to all subspaces. This is too much computational cost to do. However, the proposed method can construct subspaces by solving the eigen value problem with $1,215 \times 1,215$ dimensions. In addition, only inner products with basis vectors are required to map local parts to subspaces. In our approach, the difference between $1,500$ and 400 visual words is only the dimension of subspaces. This is also the advantage of our approach. Of course, the subspace can be constructed by all local parts of each category. In this case, only inner products with basis vectors are also required to map local parts to subspaces.

Table 2 shows the results with $1,500$ visual words and all local parts. Note that KPCA of local parts can not evaluate because of the computational cost. By using the $1,500$ visual words, the accuracy of the proposed method and linear PCA is improved slightly. The accuracy is

---

[3] The computational time of Hotta (2008b) and the proposed method for classifying one test image is 80 and 20 seconds respectively on a standard PC with Xeon 2.0 GHz CPU.

Method	15	30
Proposed method (K=400)	48.7%	54.8%
Linear PCA of visual words (K=400)	30.5%	36.2%
KPCA of visual words (K=400) Hotta (2008b)	51.8%	60.0%

Table 1. Performance with 400 visual words

Method	15	30
Proposed method (K=400)	48.7%	54.8%
Proposed method (K=1500)	49.5%	56.8%
Proposed method (K=All)	49.3%	56.7%
Linear PCA of visual words (K=400)	30.5%	36.2%
Linear PCA of visual words (K=1500)	32.1%	38.0%
Linear PCA of visual words (K=All)	31.7%	37.6%
KPCA of visual words (K=400) Hotta (2008b)	51.8%	60.0%

Table 2. Performance with different number of visual words

not changed even when all local parts are used to construct subspace. This means that about 10% visual words of all local parts are sufficient to represent all local parts. The accuracy of the proposed method is worse slightly than the KPCA of visual words. However, it is not so important because the purpose of this paper is not to improve the accuracy. The purpose is to show that our method can represent non-linear distribution by linear PCA with low computational cost. Another purpose is to demonstrate that the proposed approach can be used for the large number of samples to which KPCA can not be applied. These are the contributions of this paper. Our approach will contribute to many applications which requires non-linearity and large number of samples.

Finally, the accuracy of our method is compared with conventional methods. However, the direct comparison can not be done though the features, classifiers, and experimental settings are different. This comparison is just one measure. Table 3 shows the comparison result when the number of training images is 15 and 30. The proposed method is superior to SVM with linear kernel of biological inspired features Serre et al. (2005) and SVM with Fisher kernel Holub et al. (2005). It is comparable with Grauman & Darrell (2005); Mutch & Lowe (2006) though it is worse than Wang's approach Wang et al. (2006). It is surprised that our method uses only linear PCA and SVM with linear kernel. These results demonstrate the possibility of our approach.

6. Conclusions and future works

We propose how to solve KPCA with the local summation kernel by linear PCA. In the classification process, KPCA must compute kernel functions with all training samples, and the computational cost and memory required are high. This is the drawback. In this paper, an input feature is divided into some local features, and local feature x_{li} is mapped to high dimensional space by $\phi(x_{li})$. In this formulation, the dimension of new feature vector $\left(\phi(x_{l1})^T, \ldots, \phi(x_{lN})^T\right)^T$ is not so high. Thus, we can use linear PCA of new features directly.

Method	15	30
Proposed method (K=1500)	49.5%	56.8%
Linear PCA of visual words (K=1500)	32.1%	38.0%
KPCA of visual words (K=400) Hotta (2008b)	51.8%	60.0%
Wang et al. (CVPR06) Wang et al. (2006)	49%	63%
Grauman et al. (ICCV05) Grauman & Darrell (2005)	49.5%	58.23%
Mutch et al. (CVPR06) Mutch & Lowe (2006)	51%	56%
Serre et al. (CVPR05) Serre et al. (2005)	35%	42%
Holub et al. (ICCV05) Holub et al. (2005)	37%	not evaluate
Fei-Fei et al. (PAMI06) Fei-Fei et al. (2006)	17.7%	not evaluate

Table 3. Comparison result

We show that linear PCA of new features corresponds to the KPCA with the local summation kernel.

Effectiveness of the proposed method is shown in object categorization problem. In the first experiment, the number of visual words is set to 400 for fair comparison with KPCA of visual words. The proposed method is much better than linear PCA of visual words though both methods use linear PCA. The computational time of our method is $1/4$ of KPCA of visual words while its performance is worse slightly than KPCA. The computational cost and memory required are the advantages of our approach. Since the proposed method is independent of the number of visual words, it can be used for the large number of samples to which KPCA can not be applied. The experiments demonstrate that the proposed method is effective for the large number of training samples. Only inner products with basis vectors of $1,215$ dimensions is required to map a local part to subspaces even when all parts per category is used in training. The applicability to large number of samples is also the advantage.

Of course, the proposed method is not universal. It does not work for the case in which linear PCA does not work. Concretely, when dimension of input feature and the number of samples is high, the size of eigen value problem of linear PCA becomes high, and our method does not work well. However, the proposed method works well when the feature dimension is small and the number of samples is large. In general, many training samples are required to achieve high generalization ability. Thus, the proposed approach will be useful in various applications.

The proposed method is a general framework which is independent of recognition tasks. It can be applied to other recognition problem. In addition, the proposed idea is also applicable to SVM and Kernel Fisher Discriminant Analysis Mika et al. (1999) without any changes. This means that kernel-based methods with local summation kernel can be solved by linear method. Our approach will contribute to many applications which have problems about non-linearity, computational cost and large number of samples.

Acknowledgements

This work is supported in part by the Grant-in-Aid for Scientific Research (No.18700170) from the Ministry of Education, Culture, Sports, Science and Technology of Japan.

7. References

Debnath, R. & Takahashi, H. (2004). Kernel selection for the support vector machine, *IEICE Trans. Info. & Syst.* **E87-D**(12): 2903–2904.

Fei-Fei, L., Fergus, R. & Perona, P. (2004). Learning generative visual models from few training examples: An incremental baysian approach tested on 101 object categories, *Proc. CVPR Workshop of Generative Model Based Vision*.

Fei-Fei, L., Fergus, R. & Perona, P. (2006). One-shot learning of object categories, *IEEE Trans. Pattern Analysis and Machine Intelligence* **28**(4): 594–611.

Fukui, K., Stenger, B. & Yamaguchi, O. (2006). A framework for 3d object recognition using the kernel constrained mutual subspace method, *Proc. Asian Conference on Computer Vision*, Vol. I, pp. 315–324.

Grauman, K. & Darrell, T. (2005). Discriminative classification with sets of image features, *Proc. International Conference on Computer Vision*, pp. 1458–1465.

Harris, C. & Stephens, M. (1998). A combined corner and edge detector, *Proc. Alvey Vision Conference*, pp. 147–151.

Heisele, B., Ho, P., Wu, J. & Poggio, T. (2003). Face recognition: component-based versus global approaches, *Computer Vision and Image Understanding* **91**(1/2): 6–21.

Holub, A., Welling, M. & Perona, P. (2005). Combining generative models and fisher kernels for object recogntion, *Proc. International Conference on Computer Vision*, pp. 136–143.

Hotta, K. (2008a). Non-linear feature extraction by linear pca using local kernel, *Proc. IEEE International Conference on Pattern Recognition*.

Hotta, K. (2008b). Object categorization based on kernel principal component analysis of visual words, *Proc. IEEE Workshop on Applications of Computer Vision*.

Hotta, K. (2008c). Robust face recognition under partial occlusion based on support vector machine with local gaussian summation kernel, *Image and Vision Computing* **26**(11): 1490–1498.

Ichino, M., Sakano, H. & Komatsu, N. (2007 (in Japanese)). Reducing the complexity of kernel mutual subspace method using clustering, *Trans. of IEICE D* **J90-D**: 2168–2181.

Kim, K.-I., Jung, K. & Kim, H.-J. (2002). Face recognition using kernel principal component analysis, *IEEE Siginal Processing Letters* **9**(2): 40–42.

Lazebnik, S., Schmid, C. & Ponce, J. (2006). Beyond bags of features: Spatial pyramid matching for recognizing natural scene categories, *Proc. IEEE Computer Society Conference on Computer Vision and Pattern Recognition*, pp. 2169–2178.

Mika, S., Rätsch, G., Weston, J., Schölkopf, B. & Müller, K.-R. (1999). Fisher discriminant analysis with kernels, *Proc. IEEE International Workshop on Neural Networks for Signal Processing*, pp. 41–48.

Müller, K.-R., Mika, S., Rätsch, G., Tsuda, K. & Schölkopf, B. (2001). An introduction to kernel-based learning algorithms, *IEEE Trans. Neural Networks* **12**(2): 181–201.

Mutch, J. & Lowe, D. (2006). Multiclass object recognition using sparse, localized features, *Proc. IEEE Computer Society Conference on Computer Vision and Pattern Recognition*, pp. 11–18.

Pontil, M. & Verri, A. (1998). Support vector machines for 3d object recognition, *IEEE Trans. Pattern Analysis and Machine Intelligence* **20**(6): 637–646.

Schölkopf, B., Burges, C. & Smola, A. (1998). *Advances in kernel methods: support vector learning*, MIT Press.

Schölkopf, B., Burges, C. & Vapnik, V. (1995). Extracting support data for a given task, *Proc. first International Conference on Knowledge Discovery and Data Mining*, pp. 252–257.

Serre, T., Wolf, L. & Poggio, T. (2005). Object recognition with features inspired by visual cortex, *Proc. IEEE Computer Society Conference on Computer Vision and Pattern Recognition*, pp. 994–1000.

Shawe-Taylor, J. & Cristianini, N. (2004). *Kernel Methods for Pattern Analysis*, Cambridge University Press.

Tipping, M. (2001). Sparse kernel principal component analysis, *Advances in Neural Information Processing Systems 13*, pp. 633–639.

Wang, G., Zhang, Y. & Fei-Fei, L. (2006). Using dependent regions for object categorization in a generative framework, *Proc. IEEE Computer Society Conference on Computer Vision and Pattern Recognition*, pp. 1597–1604.

Yang, M.-H. (2002). Face recognition using kernel methods, *Advances in Neural Information Processing Systems 14*, pp. 215–220.

Zhang, H., Berg, A., Maire, M. & Malik, J. (2006). Svm-knn: Discriminative nearest neighbor classification for visual category recognition, *Proc. IEEE Computer Society Conference on Computer Vision and Pattern Recognition*, pp. 2126–2136.

## 6

Low-Level Image Features
for Real-Time Object Detection

Adam Herout, Pavel Zemčík, Michal Hradiš, Roman Juránek,
Jiří Havel, Radovan Jošth and Lukáš Polok
Graph@FIT, Brno University of Technology, Faculty of Information Technology
Czech Republic

1. Introduction

Object detection in still images and in video sequences has a wide range of applications and while it is a very costly task from the computational resources point of view, very high demand exists for efficient object detection methods and implementations. One of the frequently used techniques of fast object detection is usage of classifiers to scan the image and attempt classification of every potential object position or even every potential position in the image being searched. The classifiers can be implemented as statistical classifiers based on supervised machine learning and can take as their input *low-level features* (sometimes called weak classifiers) extracted from the window being classified. In principle, such features can be immediately the image pixels, but by using more complex feature extractors, the classifiers can achieve better performance – both in the detection rate and in the speed.

This chapter describes several image feature extractors used in real-time object detection and in detail discusses the novel features based on local ranks. The features have been designed so that they have equal descriptive and generalization power as their state-of-the-art alternatives, but at the same time to be efficiently implementable in hardware. These features prove to be efficient, not only in the hardware implementations (tested in FPGA chips), but also when implemented using the SSE instruction set of the contemporary CPU's and implemented in the graphics processors (GPU's).

The classification background and specification of requirements on the low-level image feature extractors is given in section 2. Formal definition of the features based on local ranks is given in section 3. The performance of the LRP image feature extractors was evaluated from the point of view of the classifier construction and the results are also given in section 3. Section 4 describes efficient implementations of the feature extractor on different hardware platforms, namely the SSE instruction set; FPGA (Field-Programmable Gate Arrays) defined in the hardware definition language VHDL; and GPU implementations, using both the shading language GLSL and the CUDA programming environment. Section 4 also contains performance evaluation of the different implementations of the low-level feature extractors.

$$LRF : Z^n \rightarrow Z . \tag{6}$$

One of the possible variants of LRF is the *Local Rank Pattern* image feature (LRP) (Hradiš et al., 2008), which selects two specific ranks and encodes their values. The LRP is defined as

$$LRP(a,b) = R_a \cdot n + R_b, \quad a,b \in \{1,\ldots,n\}. \tag{7}$$

Note that n is the number of samples taken in the neighborhood and therefore the result of LRP is unique for each combination of values of the two ranks R_a and R_b. This fact suggests an alternative definition of the LRP when we allow the results of LRP to be pairs of values instead of a single value

$$LRP(a,b) = [R_a\ R_b]. \tag{8}$$

The LRP have some interesting properties which make them promising for image pattern recognition. Mainly, LRP are invariant to monotonous gray-scale changes such as changes of illumination intensity. This invariance results from using ranks instead of absolute values to compute the value of the feature. In fact, using the ranks has the same effect as locally equalizing the histogram of the convolved image $f * g$.

Further, LRP are strictly local – their results are not influenced by image values outside the neighborhood defined by **U**. This is a clear advantage over wavelet features (e.g. Haar-like features) which, in the way they are commonly used, need global information to normalize their results. This locality makes the LRP highly independent, for example, on changes of background and on changes of intensity of directional light.

The meaning of the values produced by the LRP can be understood in two ways. First and most naturally, the results give information about the image at the locations of the two ranks $\mathbf{x}+\mathbf{u}_a$ and $\mathbf{x}+\mathbf{u}_b$ and information about their mutual relation. On the other hand, the results also carry information about the rest of the neighborhood, especially if the neighborhood is small. In such cases the results of LRP carry good information about the local pattern in the image.

In the previous text, the LRP have been defined for two-dimensional images. However, the notation allows very a simple generalization for higher-dimensional images by changing the dimensionality of $\mathbf{x}$, $\mathbf{u}$ and of the relative coordinates in **U** to Z^3 for 3D or Z^k for general dimensionality. Furthermore, it is possible to use more than two ranks to compute the results of the LRP. For example:

$$LRP(a,b,c) = R_a \cdot n^2 + R_b \cdot n + R_c \tag{9}$$

The LRP from their nature produce a large set of possible results, which can in the context of recognition/detection cause problems when only small training datasets are available and when the memory available on the target computational platform is limited. One way to deal with this issue – and to shrink the output set of the image features – are the Local Rank Differences (Polok et al., 2008), which can be defined as

$$LRD(a,b) = R_a - R_b . \tag{10}$$

The LRD computes the difference of two ranks which is very similar to the Haar-like features (Fig. 3) with added local image contrast normalization.

The definition of the LRP (and LRD) which was given in the previous text is very general. It allows arbitrary sizes and shapes of the neighborhoods and arbitrary convolution kernels. However, we can define a set of LRP which is suitable for creating classifiers for detecting objects in images – which is both informative and efficient to compute. This particular version is used in the reported experiments.

First, let us define a suitable set of neighborhoods. The number of samples taken in the neighborhood should be high enough for the features to have good discriminative power. However, the number of samples must not be unreasonably high because the computational complexity of the LRP grows linearly with the number of samples. A good first choice is local rectangular sub-sampling which takes nine samples arranged in a regular 3×3 grid. Such neighborhoods can be defined by a base neighborhood $\mathbf{U}^{base}$ which is then scaled to generate all the required sizes, e.g. for 3×3, $\mathbf{U}^{base} = [[0\,0][1\,0][2\,0][0\,1][1\,1][2\,1][0\,2][1\,2][2\,2]]$.

In the further text, $\mathbf{U}^{(mn)}$ will refer to a neighborhood which is created from $\mathbf{U}^{base}$ by scaling the x-coordinates by m and scaling the y-coordinates by n.

The type and purpose of the convolution kernel g in the LRP can differ. It could be a derivation filter or a wavelet, but the most basic purpose of g is to avoid aliasing when scaling the neighborhood. Aliasing could be avoided by using any low-pass filter such as the Gaussian filter. For efficiency reasons, we use rectangular averaging convolution kernels. In the following text, $g^{(kl)}$ will stand for a rectangular averaging filter of dimensions k by l:

$$g^{(kl)}(\mathbf{x}) = \begin{cases} 1, \text{if } 0 \le \mathbf{x}_1 < k \text{ and } 0 \le \mathbf{x}_2 < l \\ 0, \text{otherwise} \end{cases}. \tag{11}$$

When scaling the neighborhood, it is reasonable to keep the size of the averaging filter the same as the distance between the samples. In such a case, m in $\mathbf{U}^{(mn)}$ is equal to k in $g^{(kl)}$ and n is equal to l. In (Polok et al., 2008), a set of LRD with only four neighborhoods $\mathbf{U}^{(11)}$, $\mathbf{U}^{(12)}$, $\mathbf{U}^{(21)}$ and $\mathbf{U}^{(22)}$ for samples of dimension 24×24 pixels is used with success.

3.3 Detection Performance

In the context of real-time object detection, the main measurable criterion which should be used to compare individual types of features is how much useful information they can extract in a certain amount of time. The second criterion is how much are they invariant to irrelevant information. Both of these criteria have to be evaluated with respect to a certain learning algorithm. The first criterion can be directly evaluated on a training set and the second corresponds to generalization on a test set. When using some focus-of-attention mechanism, the amount of extracted useful information determines the speed of the classifier which can be then related to the precision of detection on a testing set.

We have used WaldBoost (Šochman & Matas 2005) as the learning algorithm and tested the features on two detection tasks – face detection and eye detection. We have compared the Haar-like features, LBP, LRD and LRP (all neighborhoods $\mathbf{U}^{(mn)}$ which completely fit into the samples are used). For each type of the features, classifiers for five different target error rates (1%, 2%, 5%, 10% and 20%) were created. The five target error rates resulted in five gradually faster classifiers which allowed us to explore the speed/precision tradeoff provided by the features on the particular detection task. Ideally, the speed of the classifiers should be measured using some efficient implementation of the features. However, such an approach distorts the results with a different level of optimality of the individual feature implementations. To remove these, we report here the speed in average number of evaluated features per classified position.

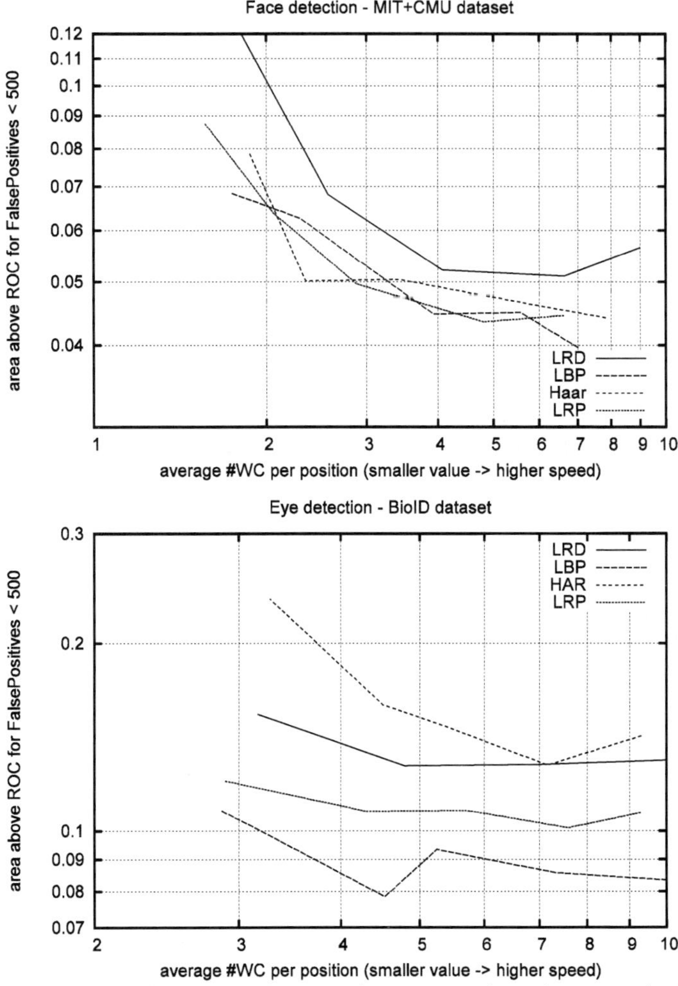

Fig. 7. Comparison of performance of image features on face detection (top) and eye detection (bottom) tasks. The graphs show the area above ROC (integrating miss-rate over false positives) as a function of average classifier speed (lower is more precise and to the left is faster). The classifiers were created by the WaldBoost algorithm for five different target error rates (1%, 2%, 5%, 10% and 20%) for each type of feature-set. The five target error rates resulted in five gradually faster classifiers – shown as a single line. The graphs can be also used to evaluate the precision/speed tradeoff for each type of feature-set for the particular task.

As can be seen in Fig. 7, Haar-like features, LBP and LRP all perform very similarly on the face detection task followed by the LRD. On the other hand, clear differences can be seen on the eye detection task where LBP are the best, second are the LRP which are followed by the LRD, while the Haar-like features are the worst. These results show that it is not possible to select a single best feature set for a variety of detection tasks. The performance of the features can be influenced by the number of the training samples, the type of distinguishing information and by the amount of intra-class variance. However, the experiments show that LRP and LRD provide in general similar detection performance as Haar-like features and LBP. Also, LRP should perform better than LRD on most tasks.

4. Fast Implementations of Selected Feature Sets

The image classification and detection tasks, as discussed in section 2, can be used as a base for various image processing and computer vision applications. Inevitably, this fact causes a situation (and it happens in many applications), where the classification and detection tasks become time critical and possibly their performance also becomes an enabling factor of various applications. Therefore, fast implementation of the classifiers is very important.

Obviously, computation of the image features is the most time-consuming part of the detectors derived from the Viola & Jones (2001) face detector. While its complexity varies with the type of the features, it is at least an order of a magnitude more demanding than the actual classifier itself (consisting of merely the sum of the feature responses). Therefore, the extraction of features seems to be the most critical part of the detection applications.

4.1 Object Detection Using the SSE Instruction Set

This section presents a high performance implementation of the LRP feature extraction on today's standard CPU's. The implementation uses pre-convolved images to obtain values of the sampling function and SIMD instruction set (of Intel CPU and compatible) for actual response computation.

The implementation must address two crucial issues: memory accesses performed by the algorithm (minimizing the number of memory accesses and ensuring their speed by aligning the operands) and the actual computation of the local ranks. Current CPUs provide SIMD capabilities that are interesting for efficient LRP evaluation. The SSE instruction set (and SSE2 in particular) has extensive support of instructions working with sixteen 8bit values in a single 128bit register.

Compared to naive LRP implementation the described implementation benefits from parallel processing when calculating the ranks. Its disadvantage is the limited number of convolution kernels $g^{(kl)}$ and neighborhoods $\mathbf{U}^{(mn)}$ (see section 3.1), because for each grid size a separate pre-calculated image is required. Minimizing the number of these images thus reduces computational cost of the preprocessing stage. In this work we use four sizes – $\mathbf{U}^{(11)}$, $\mathbf{U}^{(12)}$, $\mathbf{U}^{(21)}$ and $\mathbf{U}^{(22)}$, so four convolution images need to be calculated during the preprocessing stage.

Storing of the Image Convolutions

To simplify the feature evaluation as much as possible the convolution of the input image with a rectangular kernel (corresponding to feature block shape) is pre-computed and stored in the memory so that all the results of the LRP grid can be fetched into CPU registers by two 64-bit loads.

The convolved image is divided into separate blocks which correspond to different modulo shifts of the convolution kernel in the image – e.g. for 4×2px convolution kernel eight possible shifts exist: 0,0; 0,1; … 0,3; 1,0; … 1,3. This structure of the image is important for loading adjacent convolution values with the same modulo shift of the kernel. Fig. 8 shows the situation where the 2×2px kernel is used and four blocks are formed in the convolved image.

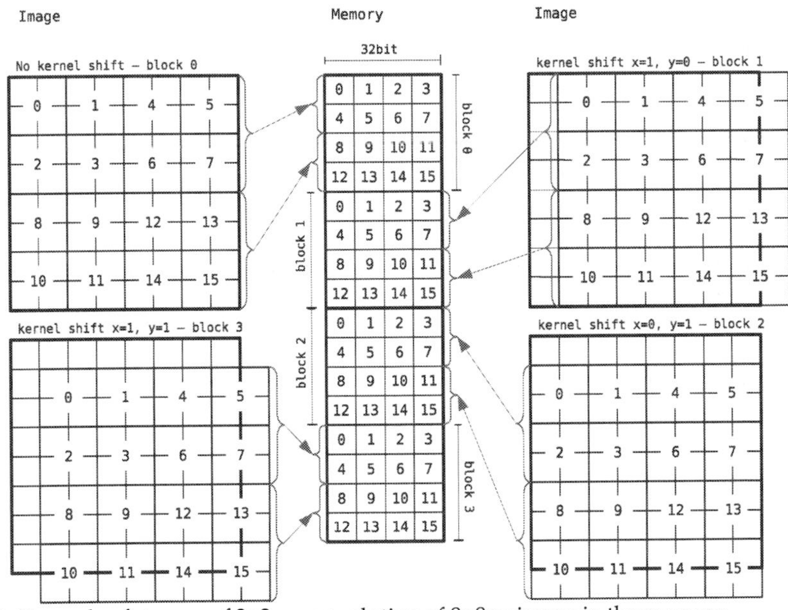

Fig. 8. Example of storage of 2×2px convolution of 8×8px image in the memory.

The convolution image $I^{(k,l)}$ represents pre-calculated sampling function $S^{(g)}$ with $g^{(k,l)}$. I is divided into a set of blocks B, where each block corresponds to an image convolved with a differently shifted convolution kernel.

$$I^{(k,l)} = \left\{ B_{0,0}, B_{1,0} \ldots B_{k-1,l-1} \right\}. \tag{12}$$

Each block is divided into stripes P representing two rows of pixels and each stripe is further divided into 32-bit words corresponding to four adjacent results of the sampling function. $P_{u,v}$ refers to the v-th word of the u-th stripe (Fig. 9).

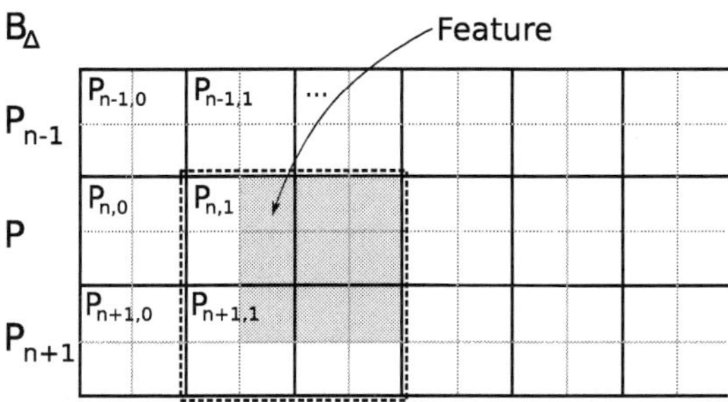

Fig. 9. Stripes in a convolution image in block B_Δ.

The LRP feature is always located in two consecutive stripes and in two consecutive words in each of them which allows them to be read by a small number of read operations.

LRP Evaluation

For evaluation of feature $F_{x,y,w,h}$ with position (x, y) and size of sampling function (w, h), we use convolved image $I^{(w,h)}$. The feature is then located in block B_Δ corresponding to the shift of the feature sampling function in the image:

$$\Delta = (x \bmod w, y \bmod h) .\tag{13}$$

The first word in which the feature's values are placed in the block is $P_{u,v}$.

$$u = \frac{y}{2h}, v = \frac{x}{2w} .\tag{14}$$

By loading words $P_{u,v}$, $P_{u,v+1}$, $P_{u+1,v}$ and $P_{u+1,v+1}$ we obtain 16 responses of the sampling function in a 4×4 grid. The sub-grid of 3×3 values aligned to Δ_M corresponds to the actual feature data.

$$\Delta_M = \left(\frac{x}{w} \bmod 2, n = \frac{y}{h} \bmod 2 \right) .\tag{15}$$

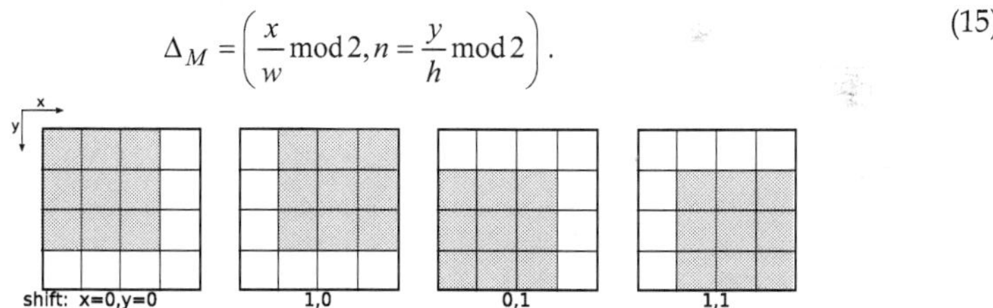

Fig. 10. Four masks used for a 4×4 grid.

Note that the previous equations stand only when the width and height of the sampling function are powers of 2. In that case, the computations are reduced to simple bit manipulations which can be very efficiently optimized. The block and mask indexing can be pre-calculated in look-up tables to further reduce the computations in the run-time to simple table indexing.

The code of the evaluation using SIMD instructions (by using Intel's intrinsic functions in C language) is shown in Fig. 11 and the block diagram of the evaluation is in Fig. 12. The LRP are parameterized by the feature's position within the classified image *fx,fy*, the block size *fw,fh* which determines the convolution image to use, and indexes of the rank pixels *idxA* and *idxB*.

```c
// Inputs:
//    fx,fy,fw,fh,idxA,idxB - feature parameters
//    conv - two dimensional array of four convolution images
//    mask - array with masks stored linearly
///////////// PREPARATORY PHASE /////////////////////
// Pointers to image convolved with kernel corresponding to the size of
feature blocks
Convolution & c = conv[fx][fy];
signed char * base = c.block[fx % fw][fy % fh]; // Ptr to block data
// get ptr to proper stripe and word in it
signed char * data0 = base + c.row_step * (fy / (2 * fh)) + 4 * (fx / (2 *
fw));
signed char * data1 = data0 + c.row_step;
// Position dependent mask
int mask_shift_x = (fx / fw) % 2;
int mask_shift_y = (fy / fh) % ?;
// Get values of rank pixels
char valA = (idxA < 8) ? data0[idxA] : data1[idxA-8];
char valB = (idxB < 8) ? data0[idxB] : data1[idxB-8];
///////////// LRP EVALUATION /////////////////////
// Load the LRP grid to register
__m128i data = _mm_set_epi64(*(__m64*)(data0), *(__m64*)(data1));
// Zero register
__m128i zero = _mm_setzero_si128();
// Expansion of values of rank pixels
__m128i A = _mm_set1_epi8(valA);
__m128i B = _mm_set1_epi8(valB);
// Count values greater or equal to A
union {
    __m128i q;
    signed short ss[8];
} P1 = { _mm_sad_epu8( // Sum the results
            _mm_and_si128( // Mask the comparison result
             _mm_cmpgt_epi8(A, data), // compare the data to value A
             masks[mask_shift_x][mask_shift_y]),
            zero)
};
// Count values greater or equal to B
union {
    __m128i q;
    signed short ss[8];
} P2 = { _mm_sad_epu8( // Sum the results
            _mm_and_si128( // Mask the comparison result
             _mm_cmpgt_epi8(B, data), // compare the data to value B
             masks[mask_shift_x][mask_shift_y]),
            zero)
};
// calc the LRP results as sum of top and bottom part of SAD result.
int pattern1 = P1.ss[0] + P1.ss[4];
int pattern2 = P2.ss[0] + P2.ss[4];
// LRD is then pattern1 - pattern2
```

Fig. 11.   LRP feature evaluation code

The basic step of the evaluation is to compare all data to the values in the rank positions. The comparison of two registers results in -1 (`0xFF`) when the condition is satisfied. The masking discards values that are not in the feature mask and also converts `0xFF` values to `0x01` so the sum of all items of the register corresponds to the number of positive comparisons. The results are summed together by an instruction which calculates the sum of absolute differences (SAD) of two registers. The instruction operates over the higher and lower 64 bits separately, so the results need to be summed together to obtain the actual sum.

The sums for A and B rank values are then subtracted to obtain the LRD response or used as a 2D vector – LRP.

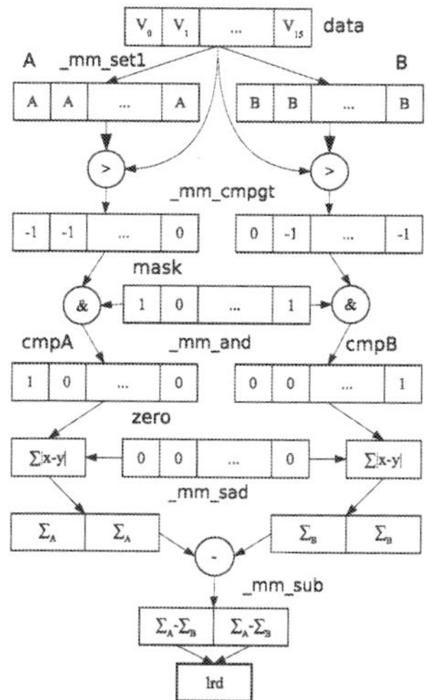

Fig. 12. Block scheme of the code from the previous figure (evaluation part only).

The LRD evaluation is described in Fig. 12. First, the data are compared to A and B vectors and masked (temporary results *cmpA, cmpB*). The sums of absolute differences of *cmpA* and *cmpB* are subtracted and the results for high and low parts are summed together producing the LRD value.

The evaluation is much more efficient compared to CPU code without SSE since all the values are processed in parallel. The slowest step of the evaluation is the expansion of an 8-bit value to a full 128-bit SSE register. Since the instruction set lacks a single instruction to do this, the expansion must be done by a sequence of *shift-left* and *or* instructions.

4.2 Object Detection Using GP-GPU (CUDA)

Today's GPUs provide a large amount of brute-force computational power and can be used for General Purpose usage of GPU (GP-GPU), among others for image processing and pattern recognition. CUDA is an architecture which allows one to easily use the GPU for GP-GPU algorithms with high parallelization capabilities. The programming is done in a language that strongly resembles the C language and is therefore easily understandable. The CUDA code is closely coupled with the host computer C/C++ code and their mutual communication is straightforward.

Various image-processing tasks execute large numbers of identical operations on different pieces of data that makes the highly parallel CUDA suitable for them. In the context of object detection by statistical classifiers, different positions of the sliding window are the mutually parallel tasks which perform an identical operation: the statistical classifier. In cases of the classification cascade or WaldBoost (mentioned above), the evaluation of the classifier at various locations is identical, but can be interrupted by the focus-of-attention mechanism used.

The CUDA implementation is structured to several separate operational blocks:

- First, the constant data is prepared which is mainly the data of the classifiers for object detection. Two possibilities exist for their location: the texture memory or the constant memory. The texture memory is very fast, but as a resource is shared with other parts of the algorithm, so the constant memory (cached in CUDA) was finally preferred.
- To detect in multiple scales, an image pyramid is constructed from the input image (see Fig. 13). The pyramid is constructed using OpenGL and uses the hardware-accelerated texturing available in today's graphics hardware. Thus constructed OpenGL frame-buffer is converted into a CUDA texture.
- The CUDA part of the program is executed in *kernels*, which are divided into *blocks* and further into *threads*, which are organized into *warps*. To use the execution environment most efficiently, the implementation is structured to totally use the shared memory (memory shared among threads within a block) and hardware registers. Each scanning window position is evaluated independently of the others; the positions, therefore, can be evaluated in different threads. To use the resources efficiently, at least 128 threads should be used. Our solution executes one thread for one scan-line within a rectangular part of the input image; the length of the scan-line is limited by the size of the shared memory. This arrangement is the result of a set of experiments – it organizes the threads into a sufficient number of blocks (to use all multiprocessors on contemporary GPU's), the number of threads is suitable, the shared memory is maximally used. See Fig. 13 for illustrations of arrangement into blocks and threads.
  Because of the nature of the WaldBoost evaluation which terminates the evaluation of weak classifiers at different stages of the classifier, a significant fraction of threads (grouped into warps in CUDA platform) can be idle at various times of the execution. The tasks assigned to the threads are rearranged repeatedly – the strategy of rearrangement of threads exceeds the scope of this text.

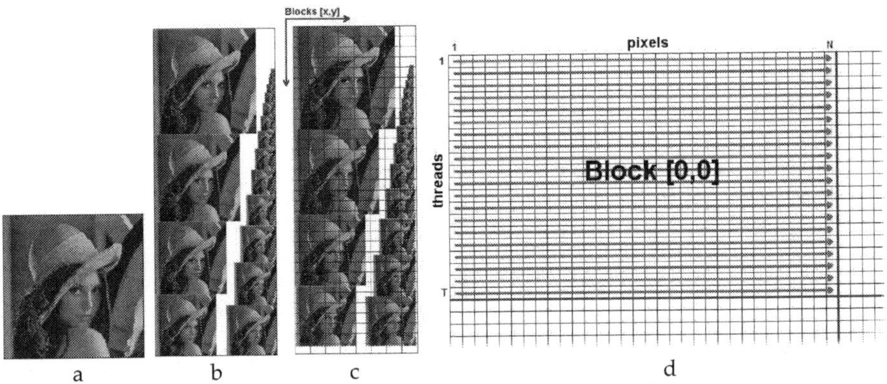

a   b   c   d

Fig. 13.   Image pyramid (b); assignment to blocks (c) and threads (d) for an input image (a)

- The output data is stored in the global memory and is retrieved by device-to-host memory copying. Memory mapped pointers could be used instead which would provide the advantages of automatic asynchronous copy between the device and the host memory, thread/stream synchronize would have to be performed in that case.

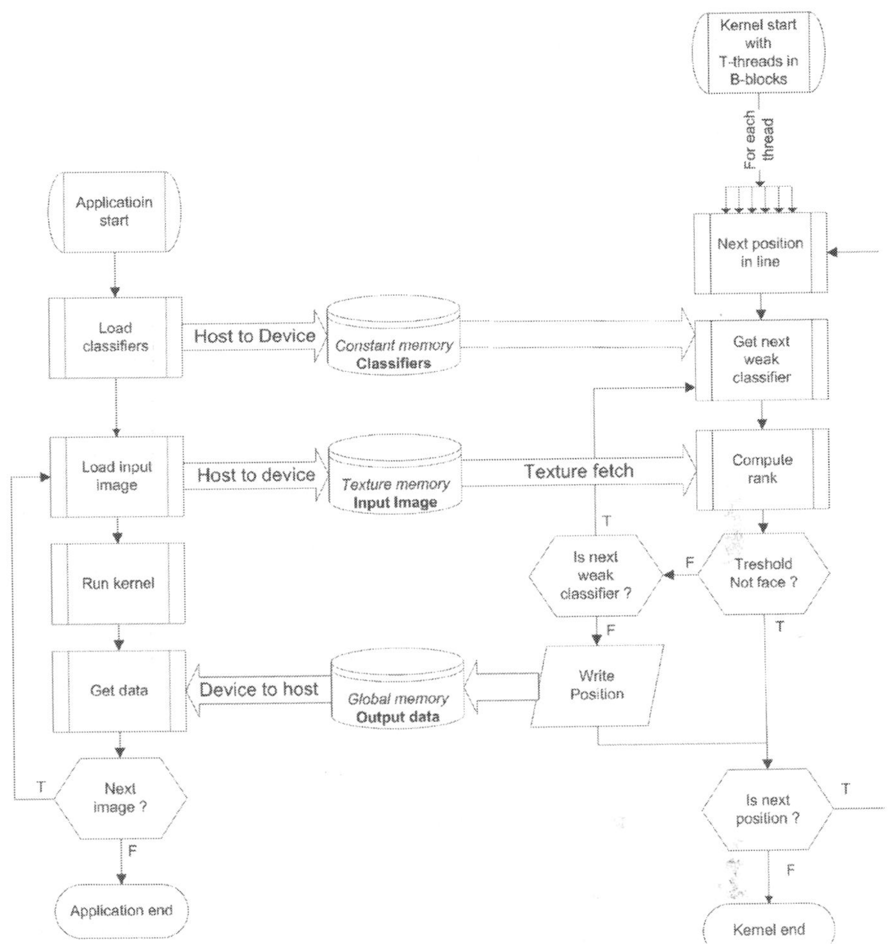

Fig. 14.   Overall CUDA implementation structure

4.3 Object Detection Using GPU (GLSL)

This section presents our experiments with an OpenGL implementation of the LRD detector, consisting of the *convolution precalc* module and a *feature extractor*. It can work on most of today's common GPU's which support OpenGL 2.0. To achieve better compatibility and portability, our implementation prefers the frame-buffer objects (FBO) above platform-dependent P-buffers and GLSL shading language above the Cg language.

The implementation takes a raster image in the system memory as input, then it needs to upload it to an OpenGL texture in the GPU memory, feature evaluation shaders get executed and a raster with detector responses is downloaded back to the system memory.

There was no attempt for asynchronous data transfers to hide transport delay, but earlier work proved that such transfers are possible on GPU.

One implementation is already described in (Polok et al. 2008) which relies on complex, optimized image data storage. The implementation measured here is more straightforward because it is limited to sampling function dimensions 1x1, 1x2, 2x1 and 2x2. Such a limitation does not notably harm the information content extracted by the features, but significantly improves the performance. The bilinear filter (implemented in the texturing hardware of GPU) samples four pixels and assigns them weights, based on fractional texture coordinates. It is possible to simulate 1x1, 1x2, 2x1 and 2x2 pixel sums just by a texture coordinate offset:

$$\left(s_f, t_f\right) = \left(s - \lfloor s \rfloor, t - \lfloor t \rfloor\right)$$
$$w_{0,0} = \left(1 - s_f\right)\left(1 - t_f\right)$$
$$w_{1,0} = s_f\left(1 - t_f\right)$$
$$w_{0,1} = \left(1 - s_f\right)t_f$$
$$w_{1,1} = s_f t_f$$

where s, t are texture coordinates (in pixel scale, not OpenGL normalized coordinates), s_f and t_f are fractional texture coordinates and finally $w_{i,j}$ is the weight for texel with offset (i, j). It is now possible to illustrate the creation of some simple convolution kernels. In case that the texture coordinates are integers, fractional coordinates are zero and all weights are zero, except $w_{0,0}$ which is one, a 1x1 kernel is created. Adding offset ½ to s yields s_f = ½ and therefore $w_{0,0}$ and $w_{1,0}$ are ½ while $w_{0,1}$ and $w_{1,1}$ remain zero, acting as a 1×2 convolution kernel. Other kernels can be achieved analogously, as illustrated in Fig. 15.

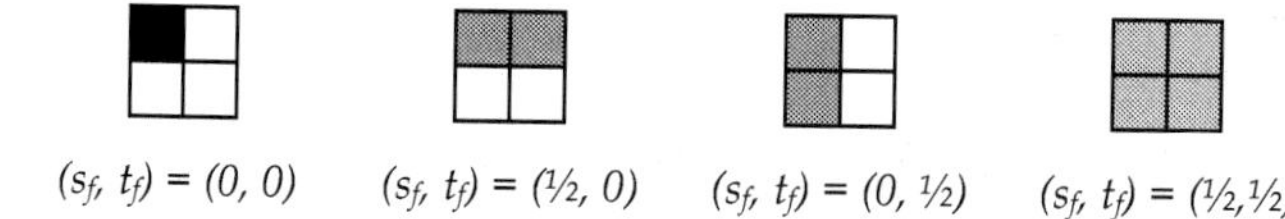

Fig. 15.   Simple equal-weights convolution kernels using bilinear filtering

This introduces some interesting consequences. There is no need for a pre-calculation phase; also, we just need a single texture to evaluate all weak classifiers in the WaldBoost classifier, which is important for two reasons:

First – there is no need for branching in the classifier to select the proper convolution texture for a particular weak classifier and, therefore, there is no need to split the classifier evaluation into multiple rendering passes as in (Polok et al. 2008).

And second – all textures required to evaluate the WaldBoost classifier can be bound simultaneously to available texturing units. This issue could be actually solved using 3D textures to contain more convolution images, which can be indexed by a texture coordinate; that however severely limits the maximal image resolution (to 512×512 on nVidia cards). Another similar approach could be using custom-generated mipmap levels, where the third texture coordinate would be the texture LOD bias, which somewhat decreases the precision but could be used in practical implementations. Finally, the proper solution is using a texture array object, which contains multiple convolution images, occupies a single texturing unit and can be indexed from within the shader; but this increases the hardware requirements as this extension is not implemented in all common graphic cards today.

As we can now evaluate all the weak classifiers in a loop in a single pass, we need a way to store the classifier properties. These are the sampling function parameters – the origin of the sampling x and convolution kernel g (represented by fractional texture coordinate offset - which is added to x and stored with it, and the kernel dimensions). Next, there are positions of blocks a and b, and finally, WaldBoost thresholds (negative and positive). These values can be fit into two RGBA pixels in a floating-point texture, as illustrated in Fig. 16.

$$\begin{bmatrix} x.x + g.s_f \\ x.y + g.t_f \\ g.width \\ g.height \end{bmatrix} \begin{bmatrix} a \\ b \\ negThresh \\ posThresh \end{bmatrix}$$

Fig. 16. Weak classifier properties, stored in two pixels of a RGBA texture

We chose to store the classifier alphas in one texture and the rest of the classifier properties in another. This separation of otherwise related data is justified by their different formats and different access patterns into these textures. While the alpha texture needs a single channel (LUMINANCE) and is sampled rather randomly, the classifier properties need four channels (RGBA) and they all are read in a sequential manner.

Once the textures described above are generated, it is possible to evaluate the features in the fragment shader. The shader requires the data textures and the image texture as its input. For each weak classifier, the properties texture is read first so the mask can be read from the source image texture. Then it is necessary to get values of blocks a and b from the mask. In the fragment shader it is not possible to use an array referencing operator to select values from the matrix, so these need to be masked-out using dot products. Once the values of blocks a and b are known it is straightforward to evaluate their ranks R_a and R_b. All that remains is to read the alpha texture, accumulate the classifier response and compare it with the WaldBoost thresholds. The complete shader code is in Fig. 17.

```glsl
#extension ARB_texture_rectangle : enable

uniform sampler2DRect n_alphas, n_cl_data, n_src_image;
// texture samplers: alphas, classifier properties and source image

uniform float f_final_thresh;
// final threshold

void main()
{
    float f_accum = 0.0;
    // classifier response accumulator

    for(int i = 0; i < classifier_count; ++ i) {
        vec4 v_data_a = texture2DRect(n_cl_data, vec2(i, 0.0)); // off.x, off.y, step.x, step.y
        vec3 v_data_b = texture2DRect(n_cl_data, vec2(i, 1.0)).xyz; // a, b, negThreshold
        // get classifier properties (as described in Fig. 16, positive threshold not implemented)

        vec3 lrd0, lrd1, lrd2;
        {
            vec4 v_tc01 = gl_TexCoord[0].xyxy + v_data_a.xyxy;
            v_tc01.z += v_data_a.z;
            vec2 v_tc2 = v_tc01.zw;
            v_tc2.x += v_data_a.z;
            // get texcoords for first three pixels of LRD grid

            lrd0.x = texture2DRect(n_src_image, v_tc01.xy).x;
            lrd1.x = texture2DRect(n_src_image, v_tc01.zw).x;
            lrd2.x = texture2DRect(n_src_image, v_tc2).x;

            v_tc01.yw += v_data_a.ww;
            v_tc2.y += v_data_a.w;
```



```glsl
        // shift texcoords to the next pixels of LRD grid

        lrd0.y = texture2DRect(n_src_image, v_tc01.xy).x;
        lrd1.y = texture2DRect(n_src_image, v_tc01.zw).x;
        lrd2.y = texture2DRect(n_src_image, v_tc2).x;

        v_tc01.yw += v_data_a.ww;
        v_tc2.y += v_data_a.w;
        // shift texcoords to the next pixels of LRD grid

        lrd0.z = texture2DRect(n_src_image, v_tc01.xy).x;
        lrd1.z = texture2DRect(n_src_image, v_tc01.zw).x;
        lrd2.z = texture2DRect(n_src_image, v_tc2).x;
    }
    // read LRD grid 3x3 pixels (convolutions hidden inside texture sampling units)

    float a, b;
    {
        vec4 ax_ay_bx_by;
        ax_ay_bx_by.xz = mod(v_data_b.xy, 3.0); // get x-coords of a, b
        ax_ay_bx_by.yw = v_data_b.xy / 3.0; // get y-coords of a, b

        vec4 v_first_col = vec4(lessThan(ax_ay_bx_by, vec4(1.0)));
        vec4 v_third_col = vec4(greaterThanEqual(ax_ay_bx_by, vec4(2.0)));
        vec4 v_second_col = vec4(1.0) - v_first_col - v_third_col;
        // compare coords to < 1, >= 1 && < 2, >= 2
        // (index to x-y conversion and multiplexing, using fp arithmetic)

        vec3 v_a_row = vec3(v_first_col.y, v_second_col.y, v_third_col.y);
        vec3 v_b_row = vec3(v_first_col.w, v_second_col.w, v_third_col.w);
        a = dot(lrd0 * v_first_col.x + lrd1 * v_second_col.x + lrd2 * v_third_col.x, v_a_row);
        b = dot(lrd0 * v_first_col.z + lrd1 * v_second_col.z + lrd2 * v_third_col.z, v_b_row);
        // mask-out values of blocks a and b
    }
    // demultiplex values of a and b blocks

    vec3 lrd_vec = vec3(greaterThan(vec3(a), lrd0));
    lrd_vec += vec3(greaterThan(vec3(a), lrd1));
    lrd_vec += vec3(greaterThan(vec3(a), lrd2));
    lrd_vec -= vec3(greaterThan(vec3(b), lrd0));
    lrd_vec -= vec3(greaterThan(vec3(b), lrd1));
    lrd_vec -= vec3(greaterThan(vec3(b), lrd2)); // three comparisons in parallel
    float lrd = dot(vec3(1.0), lrd_vec); // sum-up lrd vector components
    // calculate rank difference

    f_accum += texture2DRect(n_alphas, vec2(8.0 + lrd, i)).x;
    // fetch response from alpha texture, accumulate

    if(f_accum < v_data_b.z) // compare with WaldBoost negative threshold
        discard; // framebuffer is pre-filled with zeros (using glClear())
    // early cutoff, as simple as that
}
// loop trough all classifiers

gl_FragColor.xyz = vec3(f_accum > f_final_thresh);
// perform threshold here, write result
}
```

Fig. 17.   LRD detector shader in GLSL

Note that the shader actually evaluates the LRD. An axtension to LRP is rather simple, rank differences for *a* and *b* are calculated separately and are then combined to be used as an index to the alphas texture. The other approach could be using a 3D texture for alphas and using both rank differences as texture coordinates, the third coordinate being the classifier index.

There is one more issue to mention: loops in the fragment shaders are limited to 255 iterations (at least in nVidia implementations), after that they are interrupted (as if a break instruction was called). WaldBoost classifiers used in the performance evaluation were about 1,000 weak classifiers long, so the shader needs to contain four identical loops of 250 iterations each. The only modification then is using the classifier index instead of the loop counter to address the classifier properties texture and the alphas texture.

Even though branching on GPU is not very efficient because the program-flow control is shared between multiple processor cores, this implementation is faster than the previous attempts to control the shader execution using occlusion queries and tile-based rendering. The implementation is now, thanks to bilinear filter convolutions, very simple and can be executed without modifications on as old hardware as GeForce 6600.

4.4 Object Detection Using FPGA

The primary criteria of the FPGA design considered were high speed and using also a small consumption of resources. An additional design criterion was an adaptability to various modifications of the detectors based on AdaBoost. As a result, the proposed architecture is similar to a specialized processor. The program of the processor is composed of a feature description calculation field and a feature result processing field to enable implementation of the feature evaluation and feature result processing part of the AdaBoost classifier. Note that the number of the evaluated weak classifiers is especially in the case of early termination modifications of AdaBoost (e.g. WaldBoost in Šochman, Matas, 2005), very small (typically below 20) and variable as the early termination is based on the intermediate result of the first weak classifiers.

The maximum classification window size of 31×31 pixels was chosen while the size of the scanned image is not explicitly limited. The actual processing is performed in 128×31 image stripes that should be selected from the image of interest.

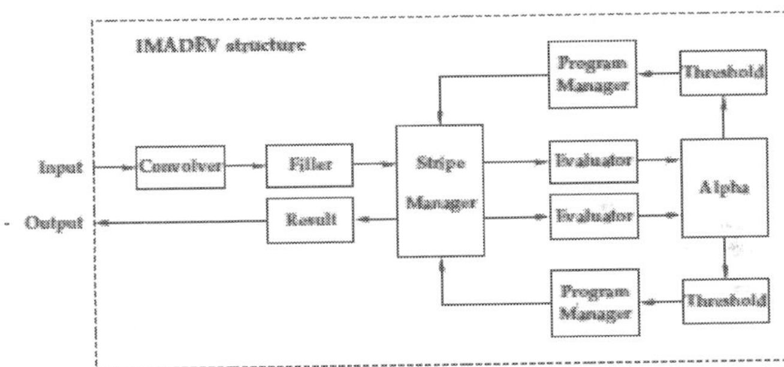

Fig. 18.   The overall structure of the FPGA classifier

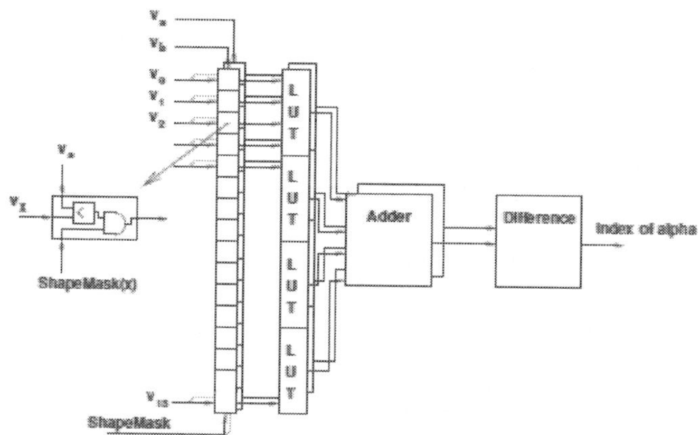

Fig. 19. The block diagram of the implementation of the LRD/LRP features implementation.

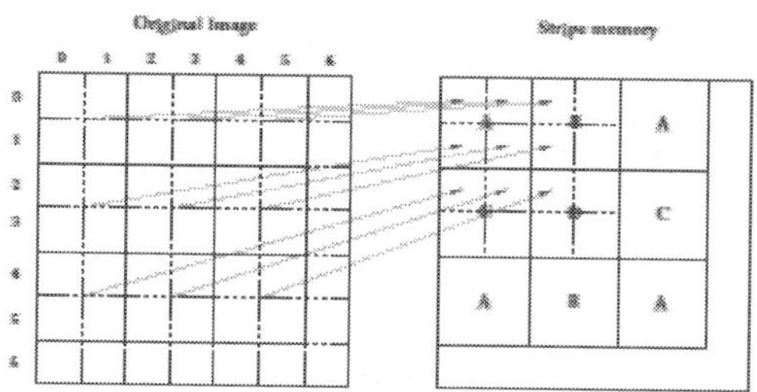

Fig. 20. Organization of the data in the BlockRAM.

It is efficient to use the pipeline in such a manner that several virtual instances of the classifier (for several locations of the window within the image stripe) are allocated. An attempt to speculatively calculate future terms in the sum is much less efficient, because if early termination is performed in this case, all the pipeline content is rendered useless and must be flushed – having an adverse effect on performance. Efficiency of the implementation can also be improved by building more instances of the engine around the memory that stores the convolved picture elements while the memory can sufficiently supply more engines with data. This approach increases the efficiency of exploitation of the hardware resources (in the case of, for example, Xilinx Virtex FPGA series it is efficient to use two ports of the BlockRAMs to supply the two engines with data).

The engine (see block structure in Fig. 18) is designed to process stream of incoming data using a FIFO-like interface. While the input part keeps filling the memory of Stripe Manager by the data, the processing part performs the classification using valid data in the Stripe Manager. If the classification is successful (the result is evaluated to 1 - current position contains the object of interest) then the position is returned as a result. If the evaluation is -1, no output is performed. Pixels of the original image are pre-processed by the convolution unit (Convolver). The concept of the processing pipeline is based on an efficient hardware resource utilization by several virtual instances of the AdaBoost classifier (time multithreading). The total number of virtual instances is equal to the number of stages in the processing pipeline. In our case, five virtual instances circulate through the pipeline to overlap the execution time of the features (i.e., there is always one virtual instance in every stage of the pipeline). The engine exploits the parallelism at the level of the sliding windows used for object detection; each instance corresponds to one position of the sliding window in the image stripe. It means that in the beginning the instance acquires its sliding window and then evaluates all the features till program termination. Finally, it again acquires a new sliding window position if available in the stripe. Additional parallelism is gained using a memory technology which allows connecting two independent processing pipelines to one dual-port memory. The pipeline starts in Program Manager which stores the program common to all virtual instances. The program consists of 64-bit instructions, each defining one weak classifier. The most important fields of the instruction are: convolution index, X and Y position of the 3x3 grid in the window, and threshold. The instruction is sent to the Stripe Manager, which stores the valid stripe of the image in four individually addressable banks/BlockRAMs. Each bank has two reading ports, each one allocated for one of the pipelines.

The evaluator block shown in Fig. 19 is designed to compute the feature in a parallel manner. Note that the mask is applied on the results of the comparators using logic ANDs, thus invalid picture elements are not included in the ranking, although they are compared. The result of LRD is transformed with an arbitrary normalization function (based on LUT) into an index to the memory containing the desired coefficients based on machine learning. The Threshold module that calculates the sums of such coefficients holds a separate sum for each virtual instance, which is compared with a threshold (stored in the instruction). The result of the comparison determines how the evaluation of the classifier should continue. It can either continue with the next feature or end the evaluation of current position with a result (detected, not detected). The result is sent to the Program Manager and the pipeline is closed.

The engine was synthesized in a small FPGA Virtex-II 250 which is placed on the PCI board together with a DSP. The DSP uses DMA transfers to move data in and out of FPGA using the EMIF. Face detection was chosen for performance evaluation as it is considered to be a hard and widely known detection problem in machine vision community. A dataset containing 5,396 faces and 70,820 non-faces with resolution of 26x26 pixels was used to train and evaluate the classifier. The engine is able to evaluate two classifiers in one clock cycle (10ns) due to two processing pipelines. The AdaBoost with twenty weak classifiers was chosen for its acceptable error rate and still low computational demands. The performance comparison is done using the number of evaluated windows per second or frames per second. In our case, eight million evaluated windows per second have been achieved. The design is written in VHDL and synthesized for Xilinx Virtex-II technology. It takes about 1,490 Slices and 14 BlockRAMs.

4.5 Performance evaluation

Comparing the performance of these diverse implementations is not trivial. The most significant performance metric is probably the detector throughput in frames per second for a sufficiently long video. The processing time for one frame does not reflect the case where more frames are processed in parallel or pipelined. This is the case of FPGA implementation, for example. There, processing is divided into two pipeline stages - transfer to/from the card and detection. Also with four detection engines on the Uni1p card, up to eight frames can be processed in one moment; this situation also occurs on the GPU implementation. On the other hand, the time for one frame is an important metric in situations where separate frames are processed.

The processing time can be split into several phases. The crudest division is on preprocessing and scanning. The preprocessing can be further divided into contruction of the image pyramid and calculation of the convolutions. In some implementations, some of these phases do not exist at all or are interleaved. In that case, the time is measured for all interleaved phases together, since separate measurement would seriously affect the performance.

The tests were performed on a computer with CPU Intel Core2 Duo E8200 at 2.66 GHz, 3 GB DDR3 RAM and ASUS NVidia ENGTX280/HTDP graphics card. The table shows all three partial times for one frame, together with the total frame processing time. These times are in milliseconds. The times for missing or interleaved phases are left blank, meaning the time is equal to zero. The last column shows the theoretical throughput in frames per second (only the detection phases were measured, no video reading/decoding, waiting for the camera or image displaying were counted in).

A recording of television news was used as the test data. Three experiments with differently sized video were executed: low resolution video (640×350px, Table 1), broadcasting quality video (720×576px, Table 2) and high resolution HD video (1920×1080px, Table 3). *Simple* refers to straightforward implementation of LRD evaluation with no special optimizations, *Haar* is the same case as *Simple* but Haar-like features are used in the classifiers. The *SSE*, *CUDA* and *GPU* correspond to the implementations described in section 4. Note that the percentage of participation of the preprocessing and scanning phases do not have to sum up to 100 %; the rest small amount of time is overhead spent in the auxiliary parts of the program.

	Preprocessing		Scanning		Total	Throughput
	[ms]	%	[ms]	%	[ms]	[fps]
Simple	3.2	1.6	191.2	98.0	195.0	5.2
SSE	0.5	1.4	31.3	96.8	32.3	31.1
CUDA	0.2	1.1	12.1	94.5	12.8	78.7
GPU	0.1	1.0	10.0	87.3	11.5	86.9
Haar	7.6	3.9	187.7	95.8	195.9	5.1

Table 1. Results for low resolution video (640×350px)

	Preprocessing		Scanning		Total	Throughput
	[ms]	%	[ms]	%	[ms]	[fps]
Simple	8.5	1.8	448.0	97.8	458.0	2.2
SSE	1.4	1.7	78.4	96.5	81.2	12.3
CUDA	0.5	2.8	17.2	89.7	19.2	52.1
GPU	0.3	1.4	20.4	85.0	24.0	41.6
Haar	20.4	3.5	551.8	96.2	573.8	1.7

Table 2. Results for broadcasting quality video (720×576px)

	Preprocessing		Scanning		Total	Throughput
	[ms]	%	[ms]	%	[ms]	[fps]
Simple	20.2	2.5	764.3	97.0	787.9	1.3
SSE	3.2	2.0	153.1	96.0	159.6	6.3
CUDA	1.1	3.4	28.2	86.2	32.7	30.6
GPU	0.5	1.4	25.4	77.3	32.8	30.4
Haar	48.2	4.3	1059.9	95.3	1111.4	0.9

Table 3. Results for full HD video (1920×1080px)

The FPGA implementation was measured separately, because it significantly differs from the other implementations. Most importantly, it does not support classifiers longer than 256 stages, because of limited on chip memory. Therefore, direct comparison would be misleading.

Each of the four DX64 modules on the Uni1p board is able to process 21 frames 320×240 px or 6 frames 640×480 per second. In both cases, the image pyramid has 15 levels. Because of the FPGA size, only one evaluator and one convolving unit was employed and a part of the data-filling functionality is done by the DSP instead of the FPGA.

5. Conclusions

This contribution presents the Local Rank Differences/Patterns low-level image feature extractor and its efficient implementations on several hardware architectures. This image feature set was not only developed to provide equal classification performance as its state-of-the-art alternatives, but to be executed much more efficiently in hardware implementations – either programmable hardware (FPGA) or custom specialized chips (ASIC). However, the feature set performs well also on more conventional platforms based on processors.

The measurements given in section 4 show that the speed achieved by using Local Rank Functions – namely Local Rank Differences (the special case) – is interesting. The baseline implementation outperformed the state-of-the-art Haar wavelets (especially in case of higher resolutions), and the hardware-accelerated implementations speeded-up the baseline LRD implementations more than by order of magnitude. Measurements show that the performance on the GPU's is equal for CUDA and GLSL programming. Considering that CUDA is much more intuitive and compatible to standard C language programming, the conclusion can be drawn that CUDA (or possibly OpenCL in near future) is a good selection for exploiting graphics hardware for non-rendering tasks, such as object detection.

Future work should include exploiting more general Local Rank Functions and conducting further investigation of the combinations of the features with more traditional ones.

6. References

Acharya, T. & Ray, A. (2005) *Image Processing: Principles and Applications*, Wiley-Interscience ISBN 0-471-71998-6

Brubaker, S. C.; Mullin, M. D. & Rehg, J. M. (2006) Towards Optimal Training of Cascaded Detectors, *In ECCV06,pp.* 325-337

Freund, Y. & Schapire, R. E. (1995). A decision-theoretic generalization of on-line learning and an application to boosting, EuroCOLT '95: *Proceedings of the Second European Conference on Computational Learning Theory, Springer-Verlag*, pp. 23-37

Freund, Y. & Schapire, R. (1999). A short introduction to boosting, *Japonese Society for Artificial Intelligence, 14*, pp. 771-780

Hradiš, M.; Herout, A. & Zemčík, P (2008) Local Rank Patterns - Novel Features for Rapid Object Detection, *Proceedings of International Conference on Computer Vision and Graphics 2008*, pp. 1-12

Lienhart, R., Maydt, J. (2002). *An Extended Set of Haar-Like Features for Rapid Object Detection*, IEEE ICIP 2002, pp. 900-903

Ojala, T., Pietikäinen, M., Mäenpää, T. (2000). *Multiresolution Gray-Scale and Rotation Invariant Texture Classification with Local Binary Patterns*, pp. 971-987, IEEE Trans. Pattern Anal. Mach. Intell., Vol. 24., ISSN 0162-8828

Papageorgiou, C. P.; Oren, M. & Poggio, T. (1998). A General Framework For Object Detection, *Proceedings of the Sixth International Conference on Computer Vision*, ISBN 81-7319-221-9, Washington, DC, USA, 1998

Polok, L.; Herout, A.; Zemčík, P.; Hradiš, M.; Juránek, R. & Jošth, R. (2008). "Local Rank Differences" Image Feature Implemented on GPU, *Proceedings of the 10th International Conference on Advanced Concepts for Intelligent Vision Systems*, pp. 170-181, ISBN 978-3-540-88457-6, Juan-les-Pins, France, Springer, Berlin, Heidelberg, DE

Schapire, R.E. & Singer, Y. (1999) Improved boosting algorithms using confidence-rated predictions. *Machine Learning*, 37: pp. 297–336

Šochman, J. & Matas, J. (2004) Inter-Stage Feature Propagation in Cascade Building with AdaBoost, *ICPR '04: Proceedings of the Pattern Recognition, 17th International Conference on (ICPR'04) Volume 1, IEEE Computer Society*, pp. 236-239

Šochman, J. & Matas, J. (2005). WaldBoost – Learning for Time Constrained Sequential Detection, *CVPR '05: Proceedings of the 2005 IEEE Computer Society Conference on Computer Vision and Pattern Recognition (CVPR'05) - Volume 2, IEEE Computer Society*, pp. 150-156

Viola, P. & Jones, M. (2001) Rapid Object Detection using a Boosted Cascade of Simple Features, *Computer Vision and Pattern Recognition, IEEE Computer Society Conference on, IEEE Computer Society, 1*, pp. 511

Wald, A. (1945), Sequential Tests of Statistical Hypotheses, *The Annals of Mathematical Statistics*, 16, 117-186

Windridge, D & Kittler, J. (2003) A Morphologically Optimal Strategy for Classifier Combination: Multiple Expert Fusion as a Tomographic Process, *IEEE Transactions on Pattern Analysis and Machine Intelligence*, Volume 25 , Issue 3 (March 2003), pp. 343 – 353, ISSN:0162-8828

Xiao, R.; Zhu, L. & Zhang, H.-J. (2003) Boosting Chain Learning for Object Detection. ICCV '03: *Proceedings of the Ninth IEEE International Conference on Computer Vision*, IEEE Computer Society, 2003, pp. 709

Zhang, L.; Chu, R.; Xiang, S.; Liao, S. & Li, S. Z. (2007) Face Detection Based on Multi-Block LBP Representation, *ICB*,11-18 Xiao, R.; Zhu, L. & Zhang, H.-J. (2003) Boosting Chain Learning for Object Detection. ICCV '03: *Proceedings of the Ninth IEEE International Conference on Computer Vision*, IEEE Computer Society, 709

π-SIFT: A Photometric and Scale Invariant Feature Transform

Jae-Han Park, Kyung-Wook Park,
Seung-Ho Baeg and Moon-Hong Baeg
Korea Institute of Industrial Technology (KITECH)
South Korea

1. Introduction

For many years, various local descriptors that are insensitive to geometric changes such as viewpoint, rotation, and scale changes, have been attracting attention due to their promising performance. However, most existing local descriptors including the SIFT are based on luminance information rather than colour information thereby resulting in instability to photometric variations such as shadows, highlights, and illumination changes. In this paper, we propose a novel local descriptor, PI-SIFT, that are invariant to both geometric and photometric variations. In order to achieve photometric invariance, we adopt photometric quasi-invariant features based on the dichromatic reflection model and for geometric invariance, the Scale Invariant Feature Transform (SIFT) is used. The performance of the proposed descriptor is evaluated with other local descriptors. Experimental results show that our descriptor gives similar performance or outperforms them with respect to imaging conditions including photometric and geometric variations.

In computer vision, the need for a stable local descriptor that is robust to geometric variations such as viewpoint, scaling, and affine transformation has captured the attention of researchers for years. Intensive research efforts have resulted in many robust local descriptors that provide distinctiveness as well as robustness (D. G. Lowe, 2004; Y. Ke & R. Sukthankar, 2004; H. Bay et al., 2006; S. Lazebnik et al., 2003; C. Harris & M. Stephens, 1988). However, most of the existing local descriptors are based on gray-level images paying little attention to Colour information.

Colour has been investigated for a long time because of its excellent discriminating capability compared to gray-level images and various Colour models have been introduced. For instance, opponent Colour space has the characteristic which is invariant to changes in illumination intensity and shadows in addition to isolates the brightness information from RGB Colour space. Besides, HSV Colour space is often employed to obtain photometric invariance since the hue is invariant under the orientation of the object with respect to the light source and viewing directions. In order to get more reliable features, a local descriptor needs to deal with the invariance with respect to imaging conditions including geometric and photometric variations.

In this paper, we propose a novel Photometric quasi-Invariant SIFT (PI-SIFT) describing features that are both invariant to geometric and photometric variations. In order to induce photometric quasi-invariant features, we first use the dichromatic reflection model (S. A. Shafer, 1985) which describes the light reflected at the material surface and the light reflected from the material body. The spatial derivative of this model, which gives the photometric derivative structure of the image, links differential-based features such as edge and corner to the theory of photometric invariance. Next, in order to obtain the features that are invariant to geometric variations such as translation, rotation, and scaling, we build scale-spaces based on the photometric quasi-invariant features. Finally, The same strategy of SIFT (D. G. Lowe, 2004) is used to build key-point descriptors.

2. Related Work

In recent years, some researchers have been attempted to combine geometric and photometric invariance. A. E. Abdel-Hakim & A. A. Farag proposed a novel method (called CSIFT) that aims at not only embedding the colour information in the descriptor, but also giving the robustness with respect to both photometric and geometrical changes. Especially, they used colour invariance approach, proposed by J. M. Geusebroek et al., to achieve photometric invariance. Even though colour invariance method provides a set of photometric invariant derivative filters, the nonlinear transformations for computing photometric invariants have several drawbacks such as instability and loss of discriminative power. J. van de Weijer & C. Schmid had been detected photometric invariant features using a strategy similar to our method. However, in their method, colour invariant features are independently formed regardless of what the SIFT generates and concatenated to the chosen descriptor only after the initial detection of key-points from gray-level images. Therefore, this method increases the dimension of the descriptor, and may cause 'the curse of dimensionality' problem. As a result, the quality of image matching will be degraded because the descriptor becomes sparse and distance measures become undesirable.
Considering these issues, we focus on describing the robust features without additional dimensions as building scale-spaces using photometric quasi-invariant features.

3. The Overview of SIFT

In order to describe interest points which are invariant for image scaling, rotation, and illumination changes, the SIFT is proposed by D. G. Lowe. Empirically, an extensive study by K. Mikolajczyk & C. Schmid has shown that the SIFT acquires superior performance compared to most local descriptors. In addition, since the SIFT detects interest points at different scales and resolutions, it generates a greater number of interest points compared to other point detectors.
The SIFT mainly consists of four stages: In the first stage, potential interest points that are invariant to scale are identified through the convolution of the image with Gaussian filters at different scales and the generation of Difference-of-Gaussian (DoG) pyramid. In the second stage, candidate keypoints are localized by the Taylor expansion of the scale-space function. Besides, unstable keypoints are eliminated in this stage. In the third stage, one or more dominant orientations are identified for each keypoint based on its local image gradient directions. A local image descriptor for each keypoint is built based on a patch of

pixels around it in the final stage. Eventually the created keypoint descriptor becomes distinctive and partially robust to changes in illumination and camera viewpoint.

The rest of this paper is organized as follows: In Section 4, we introduce photometric quasi-invariant features based on the dichromatic reflection model and the PI-SIFT descriptor robust to geometric and photometric variations. The performance of the PI-SIFT is evaluated and compared with other descriptors (i.e., the SIFT and the CSIFT) in Section 5. Finally, we conclude our work in Section 6.

4. Photometric Quasi-Invariant Features

We use photometric quasi-invariant features, which are proposed by Joost van de Weijer et al., to detect interest points that are invariant to photometric variations.

In this section, we describe how to detect features robust to photometric and geometric variations by using photo-metric quasi-invariant features and the SIFT.

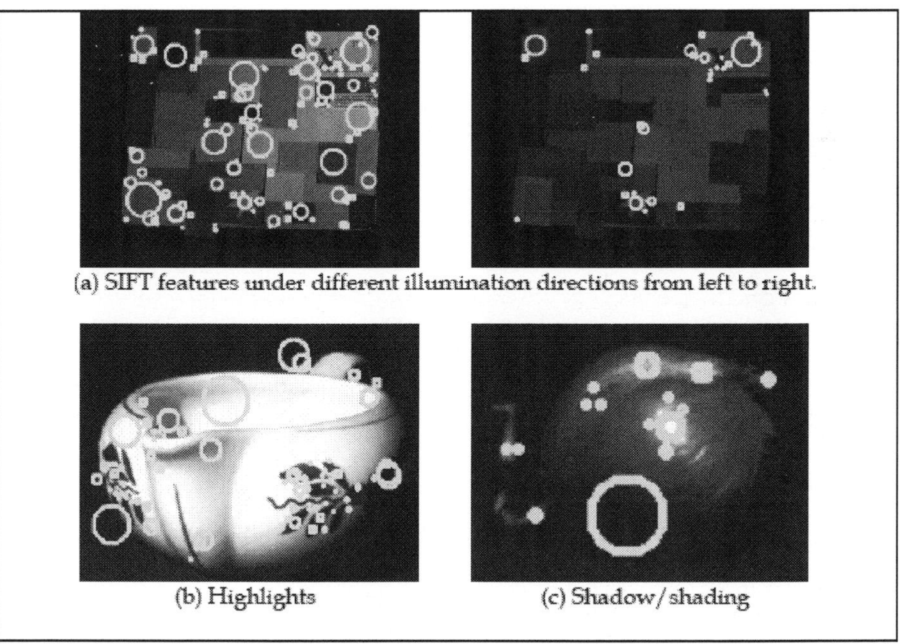

Fig. 1. Undesirable local features caused by photometric variations. Above images can be obtained from image database collected by J. M. Geusebroek et al.

4.1 Problem Statement

In real-world applications, the existing local descriptors may suffer from undesirable interest points as they do not take account of colour information that is an important component for distinction between objects.

Fig. 1 shows the effects of photometric variations on SIFT descriptor. In Figure 1(a), we can easily see that the number of SIFT features increase or decreases depending on different illumination directions. The blue rectangle areas in Figure 1(b) and 1(c) represent the interest points extracted by highlights (or specularities) and shadow/shading reflected from object's surface. Particularly, since these effects may be continuously changed according to surface geometry variations such as the light source direction and viewing angle, the existing local descriptors may have the poor interest points for the stability and distinctiveness. Therefore, we need to employ colour information to describe the more reliable interest points under different imaging conditions.

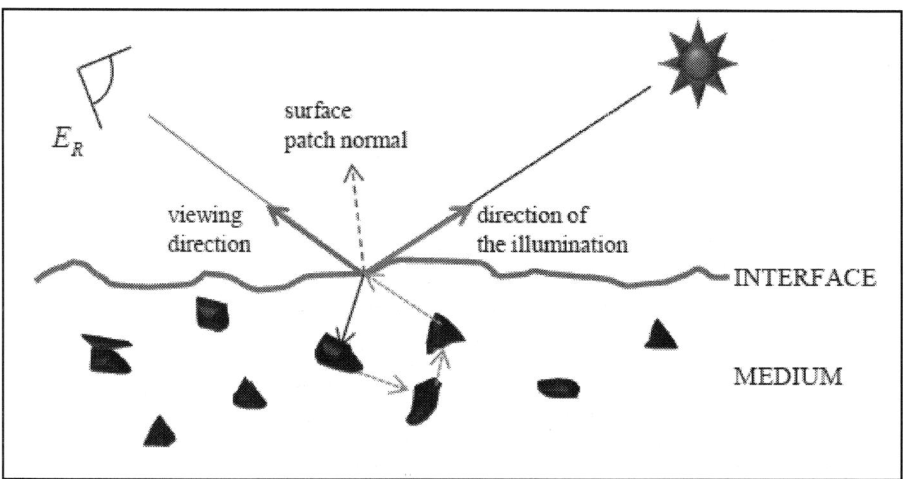

Fig. 2. The illustration of the light reflection of inhomogeneous materials.

4.2 The Dichromatic Reflection Model

Before we describe photometric quasi-invariant features, we give a brief description of Shafer's dichromatic reflection model.

The dichromatic reflection model decomposes the reflected spectrum from a point in viewing direction, $E_R(\lambda)$, into two additive components (i.e., the light $L_s(\lambda,\vec{n},\vec{s},\vec{v})$ reflected at the material surface (so called *surface reflection component*) and the light $L_b(\lambda,\vec{n},\vec{s},\vec{v})$ reflected from the material body (so called *body reflection component*) for inhomogeneous materials such as papers and plastics as follows:

$$E_R(\lambda) = L_s(\lambda,\vec{n},\vec{s},\vec{v}) + L_b(\lambda,\vec{n},\vec{s},\vec{v}) \tag{0}$$

Where the parameters $\vec{n},\vec{s}$, and $\vec{v}$ denote the surface patch normal, the direction of the illumination, and the viewing direction respectively; λ is the wavelength. The surface reflection component has approximately the same spectral power distribution as the illumination and appears as highlights on object. On the other hand, the body reflection component provides the characteristic object colour and indicates the properties of object shading.

Furthermore, the model separates the spectral reflection properties of L_s and L_b from their geometric reflection properties as follows:

$$E_R(\lambda) = m^s(\vec{n},\vec{s},\vec{v})c^s(\lambda) + m^b(\vec{n},\vec{s},\vec{v})c^b(\lambda) \qquad (2)$$

$c^s(\lambda)$ and $c^b(\lambda)$ are products of spectral power distributions (S.P.D.), and geometric terms m^b and m^s model the effect of the illuminant geometry (incident angle, viewing direction, and surface orientation) on the body and surface reflectance, respectively. That is, the model mixes two distinct SPDs, each of which is scaled according to the geometric reflection properties of surface and body reflection, to describe the light that reflected from a surface patch.

The infinite-dimensional vector space of spectral color distributions is reduced to a three-dimensional colour space by spectral integration.

4.3 Photometric Quasi-Invariants

We have given a brief description of the dichromatic reflection model, in section 2.2. In this section, we explain photometric quasi-invariant features based on the dichromatic reflection model.

Consider the image of an infinitesimal surface patch. We assume that the scene consists of inhomogeneous materials such as paper and Fresnel reflectance coefficient has a constant value over the spectrum (i.e., the neutral interface reflection model). In addition, for multiple light sources, we assume that the combination can be approximated as a single light source for the local feature. Then, using the spectral sensitivity of i-th sensor $s_i(\lambda)$, $i \in \{1, 2, 3\}$, the measured sensor values at location $\vec{x}$ can be given by Shafer's dichromatic reflection model:

$$E^i(\vec{x}) = m^b(\vec{x})\int_\omega b(\lambda,\vec{x})e(\lambda)s_i(\lambda)d\lambda + m^s(\vec{x})\int_\omega \rho_f(\lambda)e(\lambda)s_i(\lambda)d\lambda \qquad (3)$$

for $E = \{R,G,B\}$ giving the i-th sensor response. Furthermore, $b(\lambda,\vec{x})$ and $\rho_f(\lambda)$ denote the albedo and Fresnel reflectance respectively. $e(\lambda)$ is the spectral profile of the illuminant; ω denotes the visible spectrum.

However, the diffuse light that occurs in outdoor/indoor scene (e.g., diffuse light coming from the sky or causing by reflectance from walls) cannot be modeled by Eq. (3). So, Shafer [6] expands Eq. (3) by introducing the diffuse light, a , by third term.

$$E^i(\vec{x}) = m^b(\vec{x})\int_\omega b(\lambda,\vec{x})e(\lambda)s_i(\lambda)d\lambda + m^s(\vec{x})\int_\omega \rho_f(\lambda)e(\lambda)s_i(\lambda)d\lambda + \int_\omega a(\lambda)s_i(\lambda)d\lambda \qquad (4)$$

If the sensors $s_i(\lambda)$ are narrowband with spectral response and are approximated by delta functions $s_i(\lambda) = \delta(\lambda - \lambda_i)$, then the reflection function can be simplified to

$$E^i(\vec{x}) = e^i\left(m^b(\vec{x})b^i(\vec{x}) + m^s(\vec{x})\rho_f{}^i\right) + a^i \tag{5}$$

Here, the photometric derivative structure of the image can be computed by calculating the spatial derivative of Eq. (5):

$$E_x^i(\vec{x}) = e^i(\ \underbrace{m_x^b(\vec{x})b^i(\vec{x})}_{\text{shading-shadow}} + \underbrace{m^b(\vec{x})b_x^i(\vec{x})}_{\text{body reflectance}} + \underbrace{m_x^s(\vec{x})}_{\text{specular}}\ ) = G^n\left(\mathbf{x};\sigma^2\right) * E^i(\mathbf{x}) \tag{6}$$

where the subscript, x, indicates spatial differentiation and spatial differential quotients can be obtained by convolution $E^i(\vec{x})$ with n-order Gaussian derivative filters $G^n\left(\mathbf{x};\sigma^2\right)$ at any scale σ. Since we assume neutral interface reflection model, $\rho_f{}^i$ has a constant value and is independent of $\vec{x}$. Note that the spatial derivative is composed of shading-shadow, body reflectance, and specular change.

For a given image $f(x,y)$, its linear scale-space is a family of derived signals $L\left(x,y;\sigma^2\right)$ as follows:

$$L\left(x,y;\sigma^2\right) = G\left(x,y;\sigma^2\right) * f(x,y) \tag{7}$$

At any scale in scale-space, it is possible to apply local derivative operators to the scale-space. That is,

$$L_{x^m y^n}\left(x,y;\sigma^2\right) = \partial_{x^m y^n}\left(L\left(x,y;\sigma^2\right)\right) = \left(\partial_{x^m y^n}G\left(x,y;\sigma^2\right)\right) * f(x,y) \tag{8}$$

Here, such scale-space derivatives can be computed by convolving $f(x,y)$ with Gaussian derivative operators due to the commutative property between the derivative operator and the Gaussian smoothing operator. Therefore, the photometric derivative structure $E_x^i(\vec{x})$, can be built in scale-space at any scale. And then, in order to accomplish photometric quasi-invariance, the derivatives need to be transformed to the underlying colour space which is uncorrelated with respect to photometric variations. For this purpose, we use the opponent colour space and hue (for more details see the method proposed by J. van de Weijer et al.).

In the case of a white illuminant (i.e., smooth spectrum of nearly equal energy at all wavelength), the opponent colour space, $OC = \{O^1,O^2,O^3\}$, is known as the orthonormal transformation invariant with respect to specularities, m^s. The colour derivatives are rotated to the opponent colour space as follows:

$$O_x^1 = \frac{R_x - G_x}{\sqrt{2}} = \frac{e\left(m_x^b(\vec{x})\left(b^R(\vec{x}) - b^G(\vec{x})\right) + m^b(\vec{x})\left(b_x^R - b_x^G\right)\right)}{\sqrt{2}}$$

$$O_x^2 = \frac{(R_x + G_x - 2B_x)}{\sqrt{6}} = \frac{e\left(m_x^b(\vec{x})\left(b^R(\vec{x}) + b^G(\vec{x}) - 2b^B(\vec{x})\right) + m^b(\vec{x})\left(b_x^R + b_x^G - 2b_x^B\right)\right)}{\sqrt{6}} \tag{9}$$

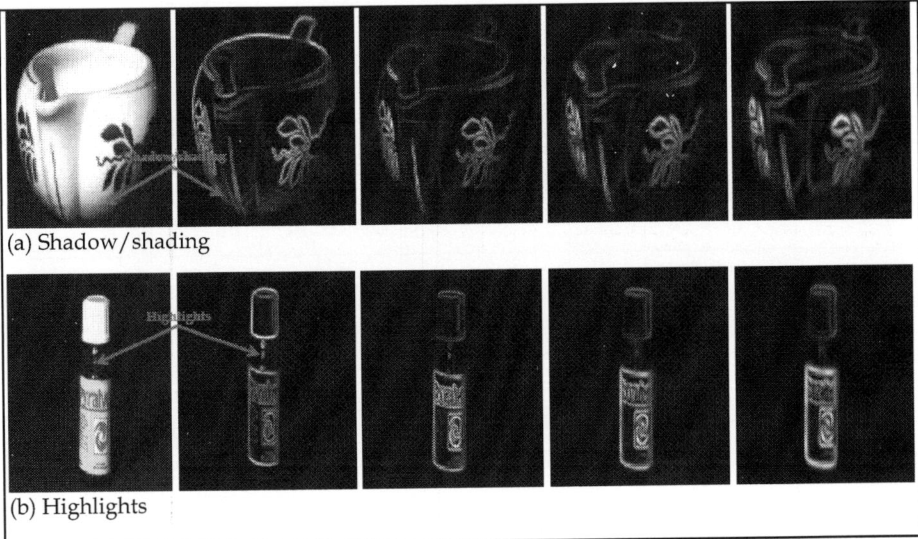

(a) Shadow/shading

(b) Highlights

Fig. 3. First-order derivatives and photometric quasi-invariant features at scale σ=1.2, 1.6, and 2.4 in order.

Now the opponent colour space becomes invariant to m^s. However, since these transformations are still variant to lighting geometry, m^b, these need to be transformed to hue for obtaining invariance to both the specularities and lighting geometry as follows:

$$hue_x = \arctan\left(\frac{O_x^1}{O_x^2}\right) = \arctan\left(\frac{\sqrt{3}\left(\left(b^R(\vec{x}) - b^G(\vec{x})\right) + \left(b_x^R(\vec{x}) - b_x^G(\vec{x})\right)\right)}{\left(\left(b^R(\vec{x}) + b^G(\vec{x}) - 2b^B(\vec{x})\right) + \left(b_x^R + b_x^G - 2b_x^B\right)\right)}\right) \qquad (10)$$

Even though these photometric quasi-invariants do not inherit the instabilities of existing photometric invariants, they can only be applied to feature detection. However, since we focus on detecting the photometric quasi-invariant points, this problem is not considered. A more detailed description and discussion can be found in [13].

4.4 PI-SIFT Descriptor

The local descriptors have to deal with significant geometric transformations as well as photometric variations. In order to detect the interest points that are robust to both changes, we substitute photometric quasi-invariant features into scale spaces. We thus can extract photometric quasi-invariant features at different scales by using Gaussian derivative with a scaling factor σ, to build scale spaces. And then, we detect candidate points at the extrema of scale spaces. Finally, after eliminating unstable candidate points, the maximum geometrical stability of the stable candidate points is achieved by interpolation.

In this paper, we follow the same strategy of the SIFT in building our PI-SIFT descriptor.

5. Experimental Results

We evaluated the PI-SIFT descriptor with respect to various image deformations such as illumination direction, light source, viewpoint, scale, imaging blur, JPEG compression, and material surface changes along with the SIFT and the CSIFT for performance comparison.

5.1 Experimental Setup

Dataset	Variation	Image size	Image No.	Obj. Name	Material	Surface Properties
ALOI	Illumination direction	384x288	26	Optic lampbox	Paper	
	View point		36	Child cup	Plastic	
	Material surface		92	Autan stick	Plastic	
			122	Silvo spicebox	Plastic, paper	Shiny
			124	Pyralvex	Paper, metals, plastic	Composite
			132	Yellow cat	Wood	Smooth
			209	Dog	Glass	Shiny
			264	Droste box	Metal	
			277	Selderie jar	Glass, paper, metal	Composite
			290	Lionking cup	Pottery	Shiny
			406	Snowman	Candle	Smooth
SFU	Light			Mondrian		
Leuven	Zoom + rotation		Boat			
	Blur		Trees			
	JPEG compression		Ubc			

Table 1. The image sets used for our experiments.

To evaluate our PI-SIFT method, we used three image libraries: Amsterdam Library of Object Images (ALOI) [10] from the University of Amsterdam, a data set for color research from Simon Fraser University [11], and Katholieke Universiteit Leuven [15]. Due to the lack of space, instead of showing detail test images, we represent briefly the description of the test images in Table 1.

We carried out experiments and evaluated our PI-SIFT descriptor based on the following criteria: (i) robustness to the direction of illumination; (ii) robustness to a change in the illumination; (iii) robustness to a change in viewpoint; (iv) robustness to changes in scale, image blur and JPEG compression; (v) robustness to a change in material surfaces.

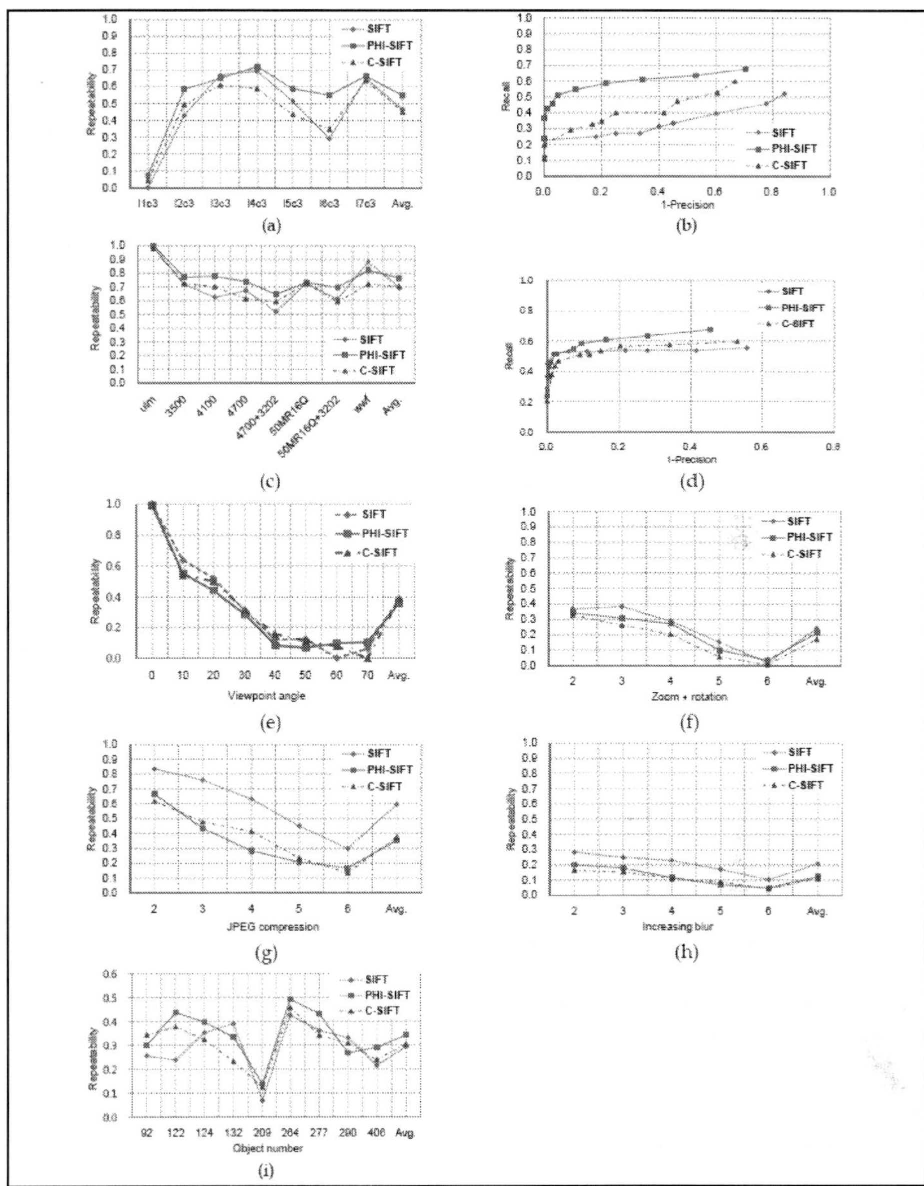

Fig. 4. (a) and (b) represent the results for varying illumination directions (*i.e.*, form l1c3 to l8c3). Here, l8c3 is used as a reference image. (c) and (d) show the experimental results for each algorithm under different illuminant. The reference image is ph-ulm. (e) and (f) denotes the repeatability according to the viewpoint and scale changes respectively. (g) and

(h) indicate the results according to increasing amounts of image blur and JPEG compression respectively. (i) shows the repeatability for different materials with various surfaces under different illumination directions (*i.e.*, l2c3 and l8c3).

Evaluation criterion: The results are presented in terms of both repeatability as described in [14], and recall vs. 1-precision as described in [2]. The repeatability is computed as the number of points repeated between two images with respect to the lowest total number of detected points. Especially, the invariance of the detector under varying transformation is reflected in the slope of the curve, *i.e.*, how much a given curve degrades with increasing transformations. Recall-precision is usually known to be effective for evaluating detectors so we adopt this as an evaluation criterion. Besides, since we want to know the number of false detections relative to the total number of detections, we use *1-precision* rather than *precision* as shown in the literature.

Matching strategy: We use the nearest neighbor-based ratio matching [12]. In this strategy, two regions are matched if the $||D_P - D_Q|| / ||D_R - D_Q|| < t$, where D_P is the first nearest neighbor to D_Q, D_R the second nearest neighbor to D_Q and t is a threshold. The recall-precision curves are formed as the value of t varies.

When calculating repeatability, the threshold for matching is set to 0.4. For recall-precision, the thresholds for matching vary from 0.1 to 0.99 inclusively. We set σ to 1.2 for the SIFT, the CSIFT and our PI-SIFT for the fair comparison.

5.2 Discussion

Figure 4 shows the results for the PI-SIFT with the image dataset. Performance is compared against the original SIFT and the CSIFT.

In light of repeatability when the illuminant direction changes, the PI-SIFT shows relatively the best performance among variants of the SIFT as in Figure 4(a). The average repeatability for the SIFT, the CSIFT, and the PI-SIFT are 0.464, 0.450 and 0.547. Figure 4 shows the interest points detected by the PI-SIFT and the SIFT under different illumination directions respectively.

In figure 4(b), PI-SIFT outperforms both the SIFT and the CSIFT. A good descriptor would give a recall close to 1 for any precision and the PI-SIFT shows the best performance among others. Figure 4(c) shows the average number of matched points and the number of consistent points under varying illumination directions. The average number of matched points for the SIFT, the CSIFT, and the PI-SIFT are 84, 221, and 343 respectively. The average number of constant matches under varying illuminant directions is 14, 31 and 71. Since the PI-SIFT gives the highest in both cases, it leads to the conclusion that the PI-SIFT is most robust under variations of illuminant directions.

In Figure 4(d), all curves are nearly horizontal, showing good robustness to illumination changes, although the PI-SIFT shows the relatively good performance. The average repeatability values for the SIFT, the CSIFT, and the PI-SIFT are 0.695, 0.705, and 0.777 respectively. Still, in terms of recall-precision, the PI-SIFT is better than the SIFT and the CSIFT. The average number of matched points for the SIFT, the CSIFT, and the PI-SIFT are 177, 341, and 441. In addition, the average number of consistent points across illumination changes for the SIFT, the CSIFT, and the PI-SIFT are 38, 101, and 196. The PI-SIFT gives the biggest number of matched points and of the consistent points under variations on illumination directions.

Figure 4(g) and (h) represent the results for the effects of viewpoint and scale changes. Here, although the best results are obtained with the SIFT, other descriptors shows the results similar to the SIFT as well. Besides, as shown in Figure 4(i) and (j), the SIFT well outperforms other descriptors for the transformation which is outside the range for which the descriptor is designed.

Although we assumed that the material is inhomogeneous to induce photometric quasi-invariant features using the dichromatic reflection model, the PHI-SIFT shows better performance for various materials than other descriptors, except for object number 92, 132, and 290 as shown in Figure 4(i).

6. Conclusion

In this chapter, we presented a novel photometric quasi-invariant SIFT descriptor, PHI-SIFT, which is insensitive to photometric variations in addition to geometric invariance. The dichromatic reflection model is used for extracting photometric quasi-invariant features and the similar approach to the SIFT is used for obtaining geometric invariance. For performance evaluation, we compared this descriptor with the SIFT and the CSIFT descriptors. Experiments show that our method gives similar performance or outperforms them with respect to stability and distinctiveness. This method may be applicable to image retrieval, object detection and recognition.

7. References

Y. Ke and R. Sukthankar. (2004). PCA-SIFT: A more distinctive representation for local image descriptors, *Proceedings of Computer Vision and Pattern Recognition*, pp. 511-517

H. Bay; T. Tuytelaars & L. V. Gool. (2006). SURF: Speeded up robust features. *Proceedings of European Conference on Computer Vision*

D. G. Lowe (2004). Distinctive image features from scale-invariant keypoints. *International Journal of Computer Vision*, Vol.60, No.2, 91-110

S. Lazebnik; C. Schmid & J. Ponce. (2003). Sparse texture representation using affine-invariant neighborhoods. *Proceedings of Computer Vision and Pattern Recognition*, pp. 319-324

C. Harris and M. Stephens. (1988). A combined corner and edge detector. *Proceedings of Alvey Vision Conference*, pp. 147-151

S. A. Shafer. (1985). Using color to separate reflection components. *Color Res. Appl.*, Vol.10, No.4, 210-218

A. E. Abdel-Hakim and A. A. Farag. (2006). CSIFT: A SIFT descriptor with color invariant characteristics. *Proceedings of Computer Vision and Pattern Recognition*, pp. 1978-1983

J. M. Geusebroek; R. van den Boomgaard, A. W. M. Smeulders, and H. Geerts. (2001). Color invariance. *IEEE Transaction on Pattern Analysis and Machine Intelligence*, Vol. 23, No.12, 1338-1350

J. van de Weijer and C. Schmid. (2006). Coloring local feature extraction. *Proceedings of European Conference on Computer Vision*

J. M. Geusebroek; G. J. Burghouts & A. W. M. Smeulders. (2005). The Amsterdam library of object images. *International Journal of Computer Vision*, Vol.61, No.1, 103-112

K. Barnard; L. Martin, B. Funt, and A. Coath. (2002). A data set for colour research. *Color Research and Application*. Vol.27, No.3, 147-151

K. Mikolajczyk and C. Schmid. (2003). A performance evaluation of local descriptors. *Proceedings of Computer Vision and Pattern Recognition*, pp. 257-263

J. van de Weijer; T. Gevers & J. M. Geusebroek. (2005). Edge and corner detection by photometric quasi-invariants, *IEEE Transaction on Pattern Analysis and Machine Intelligence*, Vol.27, No.4, 625-630

K. Mikolajczyk; T. Tuytelaars, C. Schmid, A. Zisserman, J. Matas, F. Schaffalitzky, T. Kadir, and L. V. Gool. (2005). A comparison of affine region detectors. *International Journal of Computer Vision*, Vol.65, No.1, 43-72

http://www.robots.ox.ac.uk/~vgg/research/affine/index.html

8. Appendix

Fig. 5. SIFT vs. PI-SIFT on varying illumination direction.

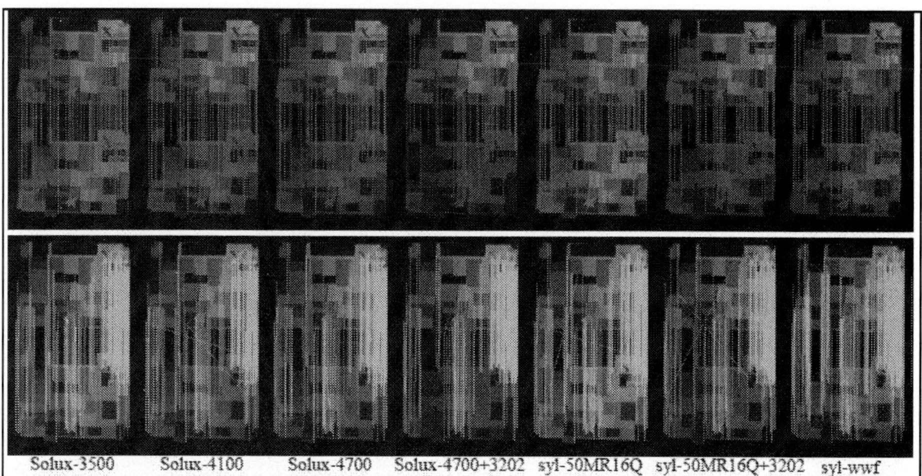

Fig. 6. SIFT vs. PI-SIFT on different light sources.

Fig. 7. SIFT vs. PI-SIFT on varying zoom + rotation.

 Pattern Recognition, Recent Advances

Fig. 8. SIFT vs. PI-SIFT on blurring.

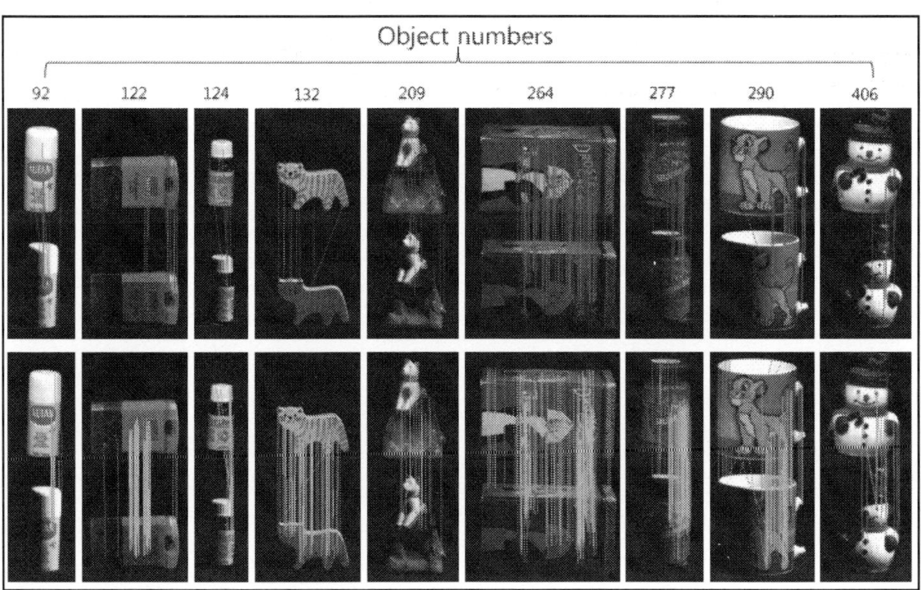

Fig. 9. SIFT vs. PI-SIFT according to the surface materials.

## 8

Wavelet-based Moving Object Segmentation
From Scalar Wavelets to Dual-tree Complex Filter Banks

Aryaz Baradarani and Q.M. Jonathan Wu
University of Windsor
CANADA

1. Introduction

In this chapter we explain wavelet based moving object detection and segmentation in video frames. Starting from discrete wavelet transform (DWT), we show the recent developments employing multi-wavelets (MW), and later on we switch to the use of dual-tree complex wavelet transform (DT-CWT). Working on a video instead of an image requires more attention, and at the same time, proposes novel approaches such as the so-called non-separable 3D oriented dual-tree complex wavelet transform. A comprehensive comparison shows the advantages and disadvantages of current wavelet based techniques used in image/video segmentation.

The segmentation and tracking of moving objects in video are important tasks in many applications. These tasks make it possible for video coding standards such as MPEG4 Sikora (1997), which provides content based functionalities through the concept of video object plane while employing ideas like content based scalability, as well as separate and flexible reconstruction and manipulation of contents Kim & Hwang (2002). The video surveillance systems designed for security applications need to track and furthermore distinguish intruding objects. All these applications require algorithms to detect, segment and track moving objects so that further high level processing can be performed. The approaches for moving object segmentation can be categorized into several groups. In fact, video segmentation algorithms can be categorized into four general subgroups; segmentation based on motion information only, segmentation based on motion and spatial information, segmentation based on change detection, and segmentation based on edge detection Kim & Hwang (2002).

Due to the lack of spatial information motion segmentation techniques, which are closely related to motion estimation, suffer from occlusion and aperture problem. This limits the accuracy of the boundaries of segmented objects. The algorithms in the second group are suggested to improve some of the weak points of the first group. Spatial information is blended with motion information to make algorithms more stable in extraction of object boundaries. However, these techniques are not suitable for content based applications as they are not necessarily characterized by similar intensity, color, or motion. The algorithms in the third group start with the gray value difference image between two consecutive frames, and then a decision rule is applied on the absolute difference in order to identify moving areas. If the moving objects are not sufficiently textured, only the occlusion areas are marked as changed and interior of the objects remain unchanged. Therefore, the objects that stop moving for a certain period of time will be lost. The algorithms in the last category address video sequences as the sequence of edge maps rather than gray-level images. The method is less sensitive to illumination changes and since binary information is used fewer computations are required. Several relevant references are given in Baradarani et al. (2006) for details.

Change detection for inter-frame differences is one of the most feasible solutions Kim & Hwang (2002), since it enables automatic detection of new appearance. Huang and Hsieh proposed a wavelet based technique for moving object detection Huang & Hsieh (2003). Using the single change detection (SCD) method in the wavelet domain they showed that their method gives better results than Kim's method Kim & Hwang (2002). SCD is typically based on considering two consecutive frames in a video sequence. Huang and Hsieh refined their method in a more recent paper Huang et al. (2004) by introducing a double change detection (DCD) approach which improves the number of detected edge points. Double change detection overcomes the double edge problem inherent in change detection techniques. The problem of moving object segmentation resembles that of a denoising problem where multi-wavelets Strela et al. (1999) and DT-CWT Sendur & Selesnick (2002a), Sendur & Selesnick (2002b), Baradarani & Yu (2007) have been shown to offer a good solution to the denoising problems Strela et al. (1999). One can consider the moving part of a video frame as the desired image and the background as noise (almost). Thus, denoising techniques can be employed to aid the successful extraction of moving object edges from noisy backgrounds in video frames. The work of Strela et al. (1999) has revealed that multi-wavelets, which introduce redundancy through the repeated row pre-processing, offer a better solution to denoising problems whenever compared with the scalar wavelet transform. Sendur and Selesnick proposed a bivariate shrinkage function and introduced an important denoising algorithm based on DT-CWT in Sendur & Selesnick (2002a), Sendur & Selesnick (2002b).

Motivated by these facts, in Baradarani et al. (2006), we developed a multi-wavelet based method for moving object detection and segmentation. It is well known that over sampled representation is a useful tool for feature extraction Strela et al. (1999) where the repeated row pre-processing technique in multi-wavelet transform is an over sampled data representation. The method is based on determining the change detection mask in the multi-wavelet domain. In view of the success of the mentioned techniques and the celebrated achievements of DT-CWT in signal/image processing, we proposed a DT-CWT based method for moving object detection and segmentation Baradarani & Wu (2008). The method is based on determining the change detection mask in the complex wavelet domain. The approach is enriched by using DCD and bivariate shrinkage denoising.

2. Preliminaries

2.1 Structure of a Two-channel Wavelet Filter Bank

A typical two-channel filter bank with the decomposition (analysis) and reconstruction (synthesis) stages is shown in Fig. 1. Let $H_0(\omega) = \sum_n h_0[n]e^{-jn\omega}$ be the lowpass and $H_1(\omega) = \sum_n h_1[n]e^{-jn\omega}$ the highpass discrete-time filters in the analysis and synthesis side of the filter bank, respectively. The scaling and wavelet functions associated with the analysis side of the filter bank are defined by the two-scale iterative equations

$$\phi_h(t) = 2\sum_n h_0[n]\phi_h(2t - n) \tag{1}$$

$$\psi_h(t) = 2\sum_n h_1[n]\phi_h(2t - n) \tag{2}$$

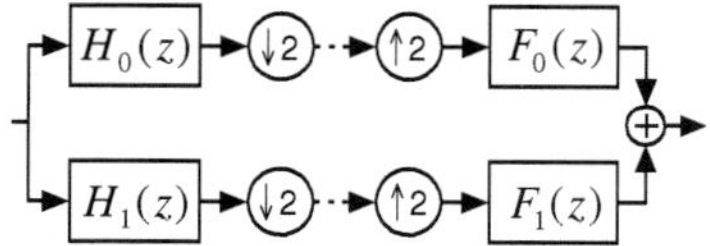

Fig. 1. Two-channel analysis/synthesis filter bank.

where n is an integer. The lowpass and highpass filters, $F_0(\omega)$ and $F_1(\omega)$, in the synthesis side define the scaling and wavelet functions similarly in terms of the filter coefficients $f_0[n]$ and $f_1[n]$, respectively. Recall that the scaling function ϕ_f and wavelet function ψ_f in the synthesis side of the filter bank are similarly defined via f_0, f_1, ϕ_f, and ψ_f.

A 'biorthogonal' filter bank constitutes a perfect reconstruction filter bank if and only if its filters satisfy the no-distortion condition

$$H_0(z)F_0(z) + H_1(z)F_1(z) = z^{-n_d} \tag{3}$$

for some integer $n_d \geq 0$, and the no-aliasing condition

$$H_0(-z)F_0(z) + H_1(-z)F_1(z) = 0. \tag{4}$$

The above no-aliasing condition is automatically satisfied if

$$H_1(z) = F_0(-z) \text{ and } F_1(z) = -H_0(-z). \tag{5}$$

Note that in an 'orthogonal' design, the conjugate quadrature filter, e.g., $G(z)$, can be obtained from the spectral factorization of a product filter $P(z)$, where $P(z) = G(z)G(z^{-1})$ and the product filter satisfies the halfband condition $P(z) + P(-z) = 1$, and the nonnegativity of the frequency response $P(e^{j\omega}) \geq 0$ for all $\omega \in \mathbb{R}$. Thus, $H_0(z) = G(z)$, $H_1(z) = z^{-1}G(-z^{-1})$, $F_0(z) = G(z^{-1})$, and $F_1(z) = zG(-z)$ and an orthogonal wavelet with the specified number of vanishing moments can then be obtained from the CQF Daubechies (1992).

2.2 The 9/7-10/8 Dual-tree Complex Filter Bank

In this Section we introduce our recently designed dual-tree complex filter bank Yu & Baradarani (2008). Consider the two-channel dual-tree complex implementation of the DT-CWT. The primal filter bank $\mathbf{B}$ in each level defines the real part of the wavelet transform. The dual filter bank $\widetilde{\mathbf{B}}$ defines the imaginary part. Recall that the scaling and wavelet functions associated with the analysis side of $\mathbf{B}$ are defined by the two-scale equations as in (1) and (2), respectively. The scaling function ϕ_f and wavelet function ψ_f in the synthesis side of $\mathbf{B}$ are similarly defined via f_0 and f_1. The same is true for the scaling functions ($\widetilde{\phi}_h$ and $\widetilde{\phi}_f$) and wavelet functions ($\widetilde{\psi}_h$ and $\widetilde{\psi}_f$) of the dual filter bank $\widetilde{\mathbf{B}}$.

The dual-tree filter bank defines *analytic* complex wavelets $\psi_h + j\widetilde{\psi}_h$ and $\widetilde{\psi}_f + j\psi_f$, if the wavelet functions of the two filter banks form Hilbert transform pairs. Specifically, the analysis wavelet $\widetilde{\psi}_h(t)$ of $\widetilde{\mathbf{B}}$ is the Hilbert transform of the analysis wavelet $\psi_h(t)$ of $\mathbf{B}$, and the synthesis wavelet $\psi_f(t)$ of $\mathbf{B}$ is the Hilbert transform of $\widetilde{\psi}_f(t)$. That is, $\widetilde{\Psi}_h(\omega) = -j\text{sign}(\omega)\Psi_h(\omega)$ and $\Psi_f(\omega) = -j\text{sign}(\omega)\widetilde{\Psi}_f(\omega)$, where $\Psi_h(\omega)$, $\Psi_f(\omega)$, $\widetilde{\Psi}_h(\omega)$, and $\widetilde{\Psi}_f(\omega)$ are the Fourier transforms of wavelet functions $\psi_h(t)$, $\psi_f(t)$, $\widetilde{\psi}_h(t)$, and $\widetilde{\psi}_f(t)$ respectively, and sign represents the signum function. This introduces limited redundancy and allows the

n	$h_0[n]$	$f_0[n]$	$\widetilde{h}_0[n]$	$\widetilde{f}_0[n]$
0	-0.06453888262894	0.03782845550700	0.007907138780809	0.007907138780809
1	-0.04068941760956	-0.02384946501938	0.024551288858761	0.024551288858761
2	0.41809227322221	-0.11062440441842	-0.034625448075824	-0.034625448075824
3	0.78848561640566	0.37740285561265	0.034326519849208	0.034326519849208
4	0.41809227322221	0.85269867900940	0.426623278407580	0.426623278407580
5	-0.04068941760956	0.37740285561265	0.534215466311194	0.534215466311194
6	-0.06453888262894	-0.11062440441842	0.132844641161696	0.132844641161696
7		-0.02384946501938	-0.103642547077988	-0.103642547077988
8		0.03782845550700		-0.032744815205268
9				0.010539924856555

Table 1. The scaling filters of the primal and dual filter banks of 9/7–10/8

transform to provide approximate shift-invariance and more directionality of filters Kingsbury (2006), Selesnick et al. (2005), preserving the usual properties of perfect reconstruction and computational efficiency with good frequency responses. It should be noted that these properties are missing in the discrete wavelet transform.

Theorem Yu & Ozkaramanli (2005): *Consider filter banks* $\mathbf{B}$ *and* $\widetilde{\mathbf{B}}$. *Suppose their wavelet filters are defined as above. Then, the dual-tree complex wavelets* $\psi_h + j\widetilde{\psi}_h$ *and* $\widetilde{\psi}_f + j\psi_f$ *are analytic, if and only if the scaling filters are related as*

$$\widetilde{H}_0(z) = z^{-\frac{1}{2}} H_0(z) \text{ and } \widetilde{F}_0(z) = z^{\frac{1}{2}} F_0(z). \tag{6}$$

The theorem states that in order to form the two Hilbert pairs, the scaling filters of the dual filter bank $\widetilde{\mathbf{B}}$ must be a *half-delayed* or a *half-advanced* version of the corresponding scaling filter of the primal filter bank $\mathbf{B}$. For orthogonal filter banks, condition (6) becomes the well-known half-sample delay requirement Selesnick (2001). It is pointed out that when the dual tree complex wavelets are analytic, the two filter banks $\mathbf{B}$ and $\widetilde{\mathbf{B}}$ share common properties including vanishing moments of the wavelet functions, symmetry, and orthogonality or biorthogonality. In other words, properties of one filter bank can be inherited from the other via the Hilbert transform pair requirement.

This suggests that we can design dual filter banks from a given primal filter bank. This is the approach we used in Yu & Baradarani (2008) to design the 9/7-10/8 complex filter bank. In this chapter, we have employed the *modified* version of our recently designed complex filter banks in Yu & Baradarani (2008). The modification procedure is twofold. A recent and important SDP based work of Dumitrescu Dumitrescu (2008) has improved the orthogonality error of our dual-tree wavelet filters significantly. Following the procedure in Dumitrescu (2008) we first obtain an enhanced version of our earlier filter bank. Then we align and tune the obtained filters to be usable in a dual-tree structure with suitable time-shift to preserve orthogonality. Table 1 shows the respective scaling filters in analysis side of the primal filter bank.

It should be noted that the magnitude spectra plot of the complex wavelets $\psi_h(t) + j\widetilde{\psi}_h(t)$ and $\psi_f(t) + j\widetilde{\psi}_f(t)$ are essentially one-sided Selesnick et al. (2005). This implies that the wavelet bases form (approximate) Hilbert transform pairs. This is shown in Fig. 2 both for the analysis and synthesis sides of the *modified* 9/7-10/8.

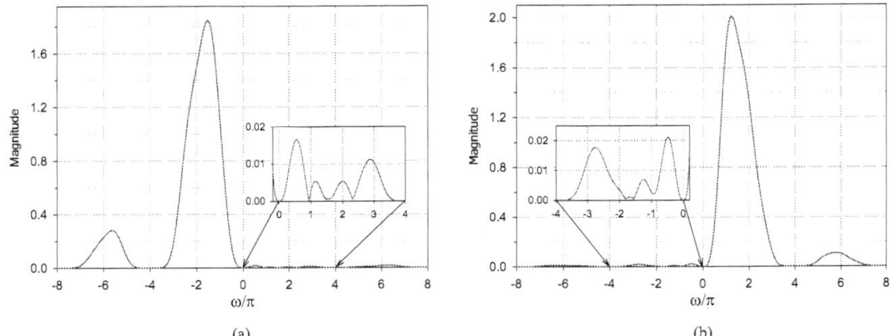

Fig. 2. Magnitude spectra of the complex wavelets of the *modified* 9/7-10/8: (a) $|\Psi_h(\omega) + j\widetilde{\Psi}_h(\omega)|$; (b) $|\Psi_f(\omega) + j\widetilde{\Psi}_f(\omega)|$. Insets show magnification of spectrum portions that need to be suppressed.

3. Detection Algorithms

3.1 Scalar Wavelet-based Method

The application of wavelet transform in segmentation of moving objects in video frames is motivated by the fact that background removal part of this problem can be cast as a denoising problem. The background in video sequences is far from being constant. It is affected by camera noise and non-uniform illumination. The difference frame in the wavelet domain is comprised of the moving object edges and noise. The aim here is to detect as many moving object edges as possible and at the same time suppress the noise. The block diagram of wavelet based moving object detection using single change detection (SCD) approach, proposed by Huang & Hsieh (2003), is shown in Fig. 3. This approach uses two consecutive frames, namely f_{n-1} and f_n. Fig. 4 presents the same technique but employing double change detection (DCD) instead of SCD Huang et al. (2004). The concept of DCD is straightforward. To extract the moving objects without the double edge problem, three successive frames, i.e., f_{n-1}, f_n and f_{n+1} are used. Therefore, the moving objects in frame n can be obtained by detecting the common regions of the difference frames between f_{n-1} and f_n, and between f_n and f_{n+1}, i.e., the moving object in frame n can be determined by the intersection of the two obtained frame differences (see Fig. 4). We focus on DCD as it has been shown that DCD can simply outperform the SCD based techniques Huang et al. (2004).

The three spatial domain frames are transformed into the wavelet domain resulting in three images I_{n-1}, I_n and I_{n+1} with respective subbands. The two frame differences in the wavelet domain are obtained by

$$FD_n = |I_n - I_{n-1}| \tag{7}$$

$$FD_{n+1} = |I_{n+1} - I_n|. \tag{8}$$

The observed frame differences FD_n and FD_{n+1} are corrupted by camera noise and non-uniform illumination. This is expressed as

$$FD_n = FD_n^* + \eta_1 \tag{9}$$

$$FD_{n+1} = FD_{n+1}^* + \eta_2 \tag{10}$$

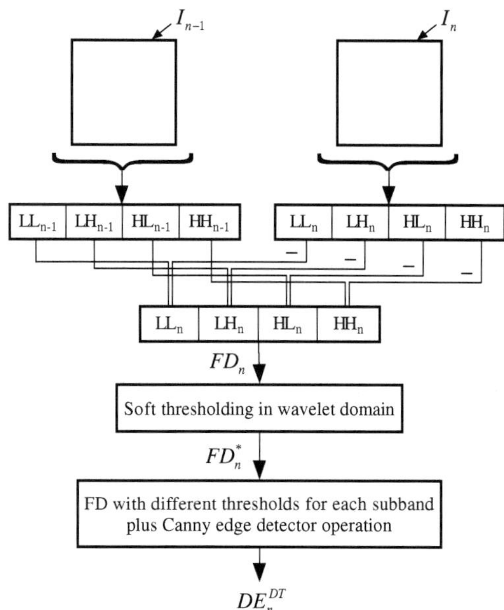

Fig. 3. Block diagram of the DWT based algorithm using SCD method.

where FD_n^* and FD_{n+1}^* are the desired frame differences and η_1 and η_2 represent the noise. It can be shown that the distribution of noise in the observed difference frames follows approximately a Gaussian Donoho (1995). A univariate soft thresholding technique Donoho (1995), Strela et al. (1999) is used to estimate the desired frame differences FD_n^* and FD_{n+1}^*. Finally, Canny edge detector is applied on FD_n^* and FD_{n+1}^* in order to extract DE_n and DE_{n+1}, and the edge maps of the two difference frames are then obtained by

$$DE_n^W = \Phi(FD_n^*) \tag{11}$$
$$DE_{n+1}^W = \Phi(FD_{n+1}^*) \tag{12}$$

where Φ denotes the Canny edge detector and the superscript W indicates that the edge maps are in the wavelet domain. The union operation is applied to obtain the edge maps DE_n and DE_{n+1} of the significant difference pixels in the spatial domain. Finally the intersect operator is used to obtain the moving object edge map (ME_n) of frame n

$$ME_n = DE_n \cap DE_{n+1}. \tag{13}$$

This is the main idea behind all the wavelet based moving object *detection* techniques. It should be noted that the algorithms and results in Huang & Hsieh (2003) and Huang et al. (2004) do not cover *segmentation*, and the given results are only detection and extraction of the moving object edge maps.

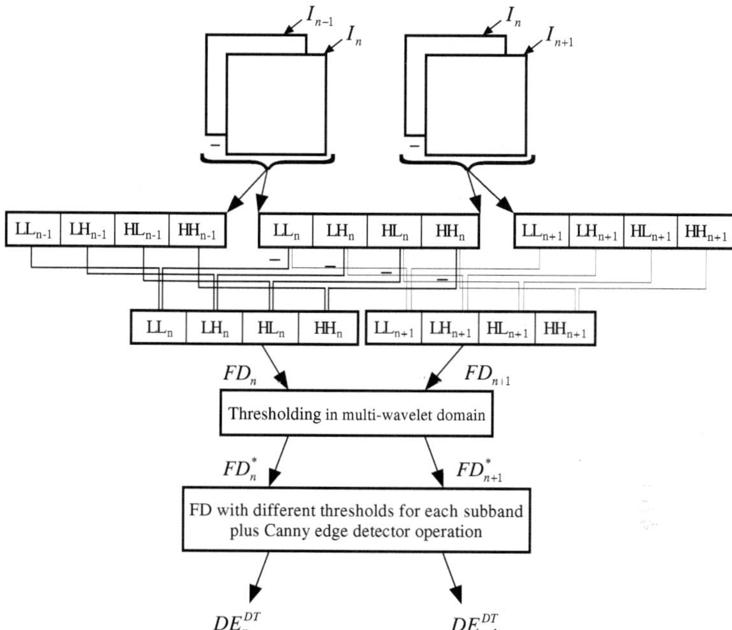

Fig. 4. Block diagram of the DWT based algorithm using DCD method.

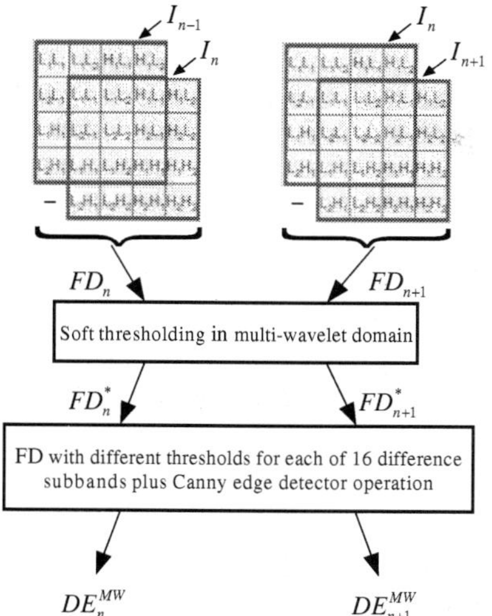

Fig. 5. Block diagram of the MW based algorithm using DCD method.

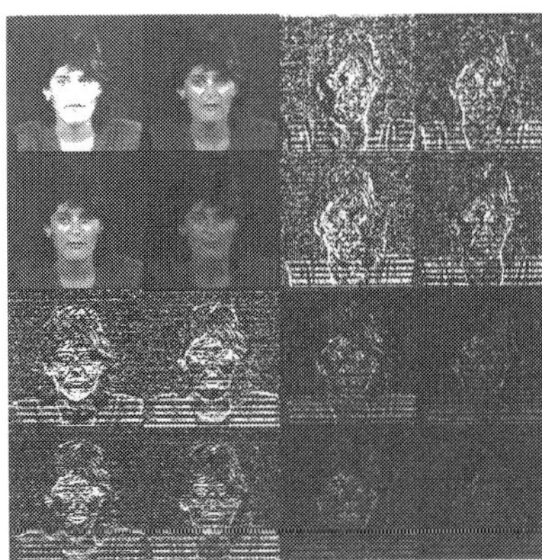

Fig. 6. Decomposition of frame 26 of the Missa video using one-level GHM_p3_rr multi-wavelets.

3.2 Multi-wavelets and Moving Object Detection

Although the structure of a multi-wavelet based method is almost the same as the above mentioned scalar wavelet based algorithm, followings are the main differences:

1) Two pairs of scaling functions and wavelets are used in each level (stage) of the analysis and synthesis sides of the filter bank. Recall that a single scaling function and wavelet is employed in scalar wavelet based structure. That is, in fact, the definition of multi-wavelets (see Fig. 5 for L_1L_1, L_1L_2, H_1L_1, L_1H_2,...).

2) Multi-wavelets have shown a high performance in denoising issues. We imposed a soft-thresholding step in MW domain as is seen in Fig. 5 to improve the raw data of subbands before reconstruction.

3) Even if a one-level multi-wavelet structure is selected, sixteen subbands are generated. More frequency subbands with different directionality leads to more information in a raw dataset.

4) Multi-wavelets are well known for their edge preserving property. The main performance increment in multi-wavelet based approachs is due to this fundamental property.

The MW-based method, shown in Fig. 5, is applied to the Missa and Trevor sequences which are typical 256×256 gray level videos. To have a better understanding about the steps and observations, for instance, we have shown the decomposition of frame 33 of the Trevor video in Fig. 6 using one-level GHM_p3_rr multi-wavelets. Fig. 7 shows further steps, moving object edge map between frames 1, 2, and 3 of the Trevor video, for instance. Moving object edge points of frame 33[1] are extracted using frames 32, 33, and 34. We use "GHM" Geronimo et al. (1994), "GHM_p3" Ozkaramanli (2003) and "Alpert" Alpert (1993) multi-wavelets with repeated row (MW_rr) and approximation order (MW_ap) pre-processing to obtain the edge maps. The performance of these multi-wavelets employing the DCD technique is depicted in

---

[1] Recall that we always need three consecutive frames due to the use of DCD.

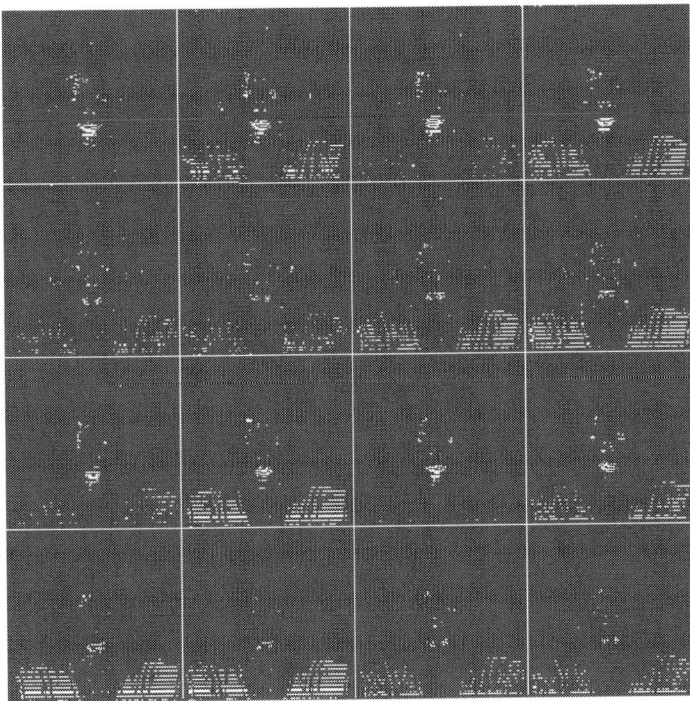

Fig. 7. Moving object edge map for frame 26 is obtained using the frames 25, 26, and 27 of the Missa video.

Fig. 11. Scalar wavelet base methods, presented in Huang et al. (2004) with SCD and DCD, are also shown for reference. The proposed method in Huang et al. (2004) gives better performance than previous studies in literature Kim & Hwang (2002), Huang & Hsieh (2003). The presented MW_{rr} method in Baradarani et al. (2006) provides better results when compared with the scalar wavelets given in Huang & Hsieh (2003), Huang et al. (2004). Furthermore, MW_{rr} outperforms MW_{ap} approach approximately by 34 percent on the average. This confirms the usefulness of repeated row pre-processing in detecting moving object edges in Strela et al. (1999) due to the similarity of this problem to that of denoising.
It is pointed out that in case of using multi-wavelets, two wavelets and two scaling functions are used in the structure, i.e., there are 4, 16, 64,... subbands at the first, second,... stages in the respective filter bank structure (see Fig. 5).

3.3 DT-CWT in Moving object Detection

Motivated by our MW-based approach, we are interested in investigating the application of DT-CWT to segmentation of moving objects in video employing the *modified* 9/7-10/8 filter bank. In the first application, we demonstrated the application of 9/7–10/8 in image denoising. Our motivation here is twofold. Firstly, DT-CWT has been shown to be a useful tool for image denoising. Sendur and Selesnick have shown that DT-CWT is more effective than

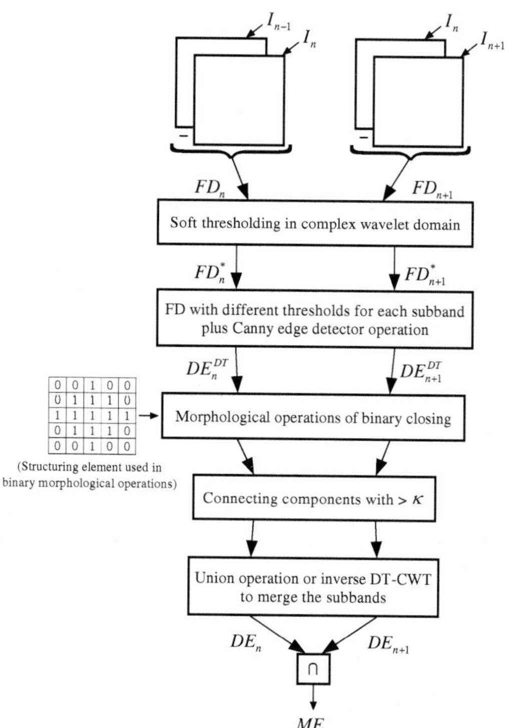

Fig. 8. Block diagram of the DT-CWT based algorithm using DCD method.

DWT for denoising purposes Sendur & Selesnick (2002a). Secondly, we already showed that the 9/7–10/8 filter bank has promising results in image denoising Baradarani & Yu (2007). Thus, DT-CWT is expected to be a good candidate for moving object edge map detection algorithms. The block diagram of the proposed technique is shown in Fig. 8. This approach, which is based on DCD, uses three consecutive frames, namely f_{n-1}, f_n, and f_{n+1}.

The method is applied to the Missa and Trevor sequences, which are typical gray level videos. Figure 11 shows the performance of six MW-based implementations along with the results obtained by *modified* 9/7-10/8 DT-CWT filter bank for Trevor video, all with DCD enrichment. Scalar wavelet based methods, presented in Huang et al. (2004) with SCD and DCD, are also shown for reference. As is shown in Figure 11, it stands somewhere in between the results of MW_{rr} and MW_{ap}. Although it is better than the 9/7-10/8, it cannot outperform MW_rr. Our earlier experiments show that DT-CWT performs better for frame and single image segmentation, and multi-wavelets are preferred for video and moving object segmentation. In general, the performance of multi-wavelets with repeated row is better than multi-wavelets with approximation order with pre-processing. The *modified* 9/7-10/8 is also competitive to MW_{rr} in the sense of the number of edges they extract. Not only the number of detected edge points has been increased significantly when the *modified* 9/7–10/8 filter bank is used, also the accuracy of the detected moving object edges is greatly improved. The term accuracy here is reflected in the sharpness of fine features, e.g., mouth, nose, eyes, and eyeglasses. This is attributed to the edge preserving property of MW_{rr} and the good directionality and shift invariance of the DT-CWT approach.

4. Moving Object Segmentation

After moving object edge extraction, the moving objects formed by the edges can be segmented from the rest of the frame. Because of non-ideal segmentation of moving object edges, there are some disconnected edges which make it impossible to extract the whole object. Therefore, post-processing is applied using morphological operations in order to generate connected edges representing a connected moving object. Morphological operations of binary closing Gonzales & Woods (2005) are used with the structuring element shown in Figure 8. The structuring element is a binary 5×5 matrix whose size can be changed with respect to the frame size. The connected components with a pixel count less than κ (a threshold) are assumed as noise. These components are not accepted as moving objects. The ones with a pixel count greater than κ segmented as moving objects. The value of κ is determined with respect to the image size. For example, it is not reasonable to choose a large value of threshold, e.g., $\kappa = 2000$, as it looks like an object rather than noise in a 256×256 frame. Moving object segmentation in Missa and Trevor videos, in 256×256 gray format, are shown in Figs. 9 and 10. In these figures, (a), (b), and (c) show the frames 25 (32), 26 (33), 27 (34), from left to right, for the Missa (and for the Trevor with the frame numbers inside parenthesis) respectively. In Fig. 9, (d), (h), and (l) represent ME_n for frame 26; (e), (i), and (m) refer to ME_n after binary closing; (f), (j), and (n) show connected components; (g), (k), and (o) present segmented moving object. Also, in this figure, the second row corresponds to the use of GHM_p3_rr multi-wavelets; the third row shows the results obtained by using 9/7–10/8 DT-CWT; and the last row shows the results if DWT is employed. Figs. 10 (d), (e), and (f) illustrate the segmented moving object in Trevor video for frame 33 using GHM_p3_rr multi-wavelets, *modified* 9/7–10/8 DT-CWT, and DWT with DCD (DWT_DCD) respectively.

5. Conclusions and Future Work

In this Chapter we briefly discussed the most famous current wavelet based moving object detection and segmentation algorithms, and the main concepts behind them. By the term wavelet here, we refer to DWT, multi-wavelets, and DT-CWT. DWT is very good for compression, it has the perfect reconstruction property, and contains low computation. However, DWT is a shift-dependent approach, poor in directional selectivity, and sensitive for edges. Multi-wavelets are very good for denoising problems, preserve edges better, but computationally expensive. DT-CWT has the perfect reconstruction property, the transformation is shift-invariance, it has good directionality, and preserves edges better. However, the method is computationally expensive. The simulation results show that the performance improvement of DT-CWT based technique is on the average over the scalar wavelets. Furthermore, the results indicate that *modified* 9/7–10/8 DT-CWT outperforms multi-wavelets with approximation order pre-processing considerably and performs slightly less than multi-wavelets with repeated row pre-processing. The former is probably due to the good directionality and shift-invariance of DT-CWT, while the later is obtained because of the better edge preserving property of multi-wavelets with repeated row pre-processing.

Another open topic, which can reduce the computational complexities, is the use of concept of new 3D transformations such as non-separable oriented 3D–DT-CWT which deals with whole video as a single box of 3D data.

In view of the success of the 9/7 filter bank in JPEG2000 standard, as well as the improved shift-invariance and better directionality of the dual-tree complex wavelet transform, it is reasonable to hope that dual-tree complex filter banks may also give better results in image (video) compression.

Aknowledgement

The work is supported in part by the Canada Research Chair program, the NSERC Discovery Grant, and AUTO21.

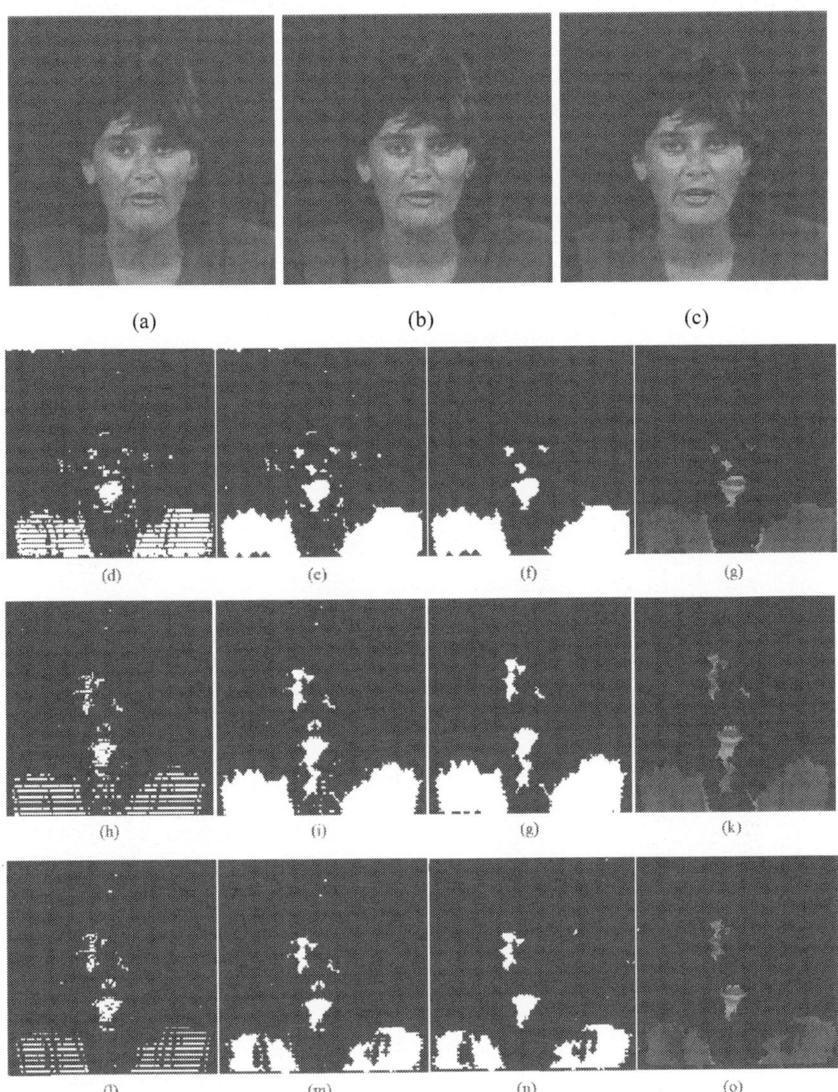

Fig. 9. Moving object segmentation for frame 26 in Missa. (a), (b), and (c) Frames 25, 26, and 27 respectively; (d), (h), (l) ME_n for frame 26; (e), (i), (m) ME_n after binary closing; (f), (j), (n) Connected components; (g), (k), (o) Segmented moving object. Second row: using GHM_p3_rr multi-wavelets; Third row: using the *modified* 9/7-10/8 DT-CWT; Last row: using DWT_DCD.

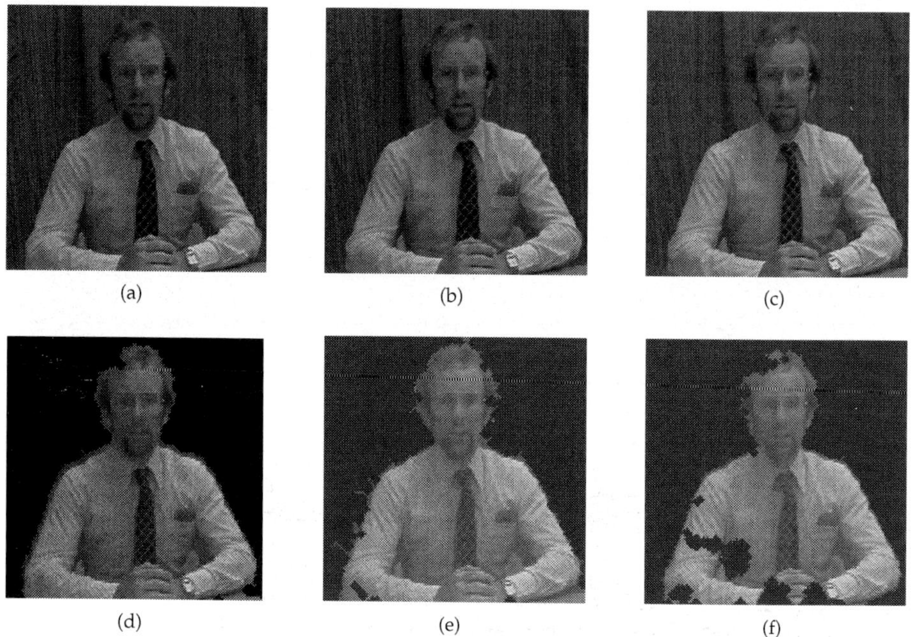

Fig. 10. Moving object segmentation for frame 33 in Trevor video. (a), (b), and (c) frames 32, 33, and 34, respectively; (d), (e), and (f) segmented moving object using GHM_p3_rr multi-wavelets, *modified* 9/7-10/8 DT-CWT, and DWT_DCD respectively.

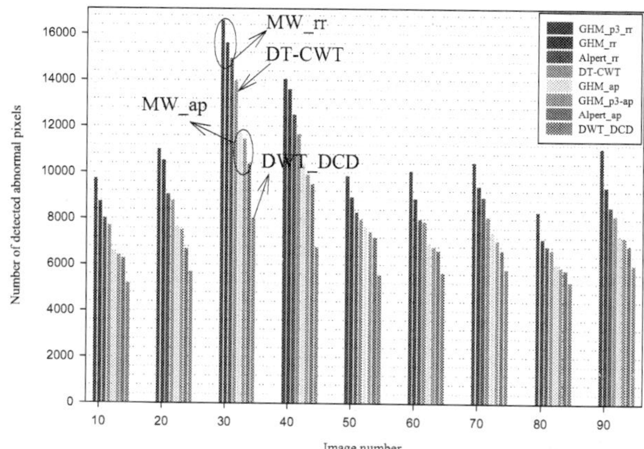

Fig. 11. Number of edge points of ME_n with different methods.

6. References

Alpert, B. (1993). A class of bases in L2 for the sparse representation of integral operators, *SIAM Jour. of Math. Analysis*, **24**: 246–262.

Baradarani, A., Ozkaramanli, H., Ozmen, B., Demirel, H. & Celik, T. (2006). Multi-wavelet based moving object detection and segmentation, *Global Confs., Int. Conf. on Signal Process.*, pp. 112–116.

Baradarani, A. & Wu, J. (2008). Moving object segmentation using the 9/7–10/8 dual-tree complex filter bank, *IEEE 19th Int. Conf. on Pattern Recognition*, pp. 1–4.

Baradarani, A. & Yu, R. (2007). A dual-tree complex wavelet with application in image denoising, *IEEE Int. conf. on Signal Process. and Communication*, pp. 1203–1206.

Daubechies, I. (1992). *Ten Lectures on Wavelets*, SIAM.

Donoho, D. L. (1995). De-noising by soft-thresholding, *IEEE Trans. on Information Theory*, **41**: 613–627.

Dumitrescu, B. (2008). SDP approximation of a fractional delay and the design of dual-tree complex wavelet transform, *IEEE Trans. on Signal Process.*, **56**: 4255–4262.

Geronimo, J. S., Hardin, D. P. & Massopust, P. R. (1994). Fractal functions and wavelet expansions based on several scaling functions, *Jour. Approx. Theory*, **78**: 373–401.

Gonzales, R. C. & Woods, R. E. (2005). *Digital Image Processing*, Prentice Hall, New Jersey.

Huang, J. C. & Hsieh, W.-S. (2003). Wavelet-based moving object segmentation, *Electronic Letters*, **39**: 1380–1382.

Huang, J. C., Su, T. S., Wang, L.-J. & Hsieh, W.-S. (2004). Double change detection method for wavelet-based moving object segmentation, *Electronic Letters*, **40**: 798–799.

Kim, C. & Hwang, J.-N. (2002). Fast and automatic video object segmentation and tracking for content based applications, *IEEE Trans. on Circuits Syst. and Video Tech.*, **12**: 122–129.

Kingsbury, N. G. (2006). The dual-tree complex wavelet transform: A new technique for shift invariance and directional filters, *IEEE 8th DSP Workshop*, .

Ozkaramanli, H. (2003). A unified approach for constructing multi-wavelet with approximation order using refinable super functions, *IEE Proc.-Vis. Image Signal Processing*, **150**: 143–152.

Selesnick, I. W. (2001). Hilbert transform pairs of wavelet bases, *IEEE Signal Processing Letters*, **8**: 170–173.

Selesnick, I. W., Baraniuk, R. G. & Kingsbury, N. G. (2005). The dual-tree complex wavelet transform – A coherent framework for multiscale signal and image processing, *IEEE Signal Processing Mag.*, **6**: 123–151.

Sendur, L. & Selesnick, I. W. (2002a). Bivariate shrinkage functions for wavelet-based denoising exploiting inter scale dependency, *IEEE Trans. on Signal Process.*, **50**: 2744–2756.

Sendur, L. & Selesnick, I. W. (2002b). Bivariate shrinkage with local variance estimation, *IEEE Signal Processing Letters*, **9**: 438–441.

Sikora, T. (1997). The MPEG-4 video standard verification model, *IEEE Trans. on Circuits Syst. and Video Tech.*, **7**: 19–31.

Strela, V., Heller, P. N., Strang, G., Topiwala, P. & Heil, C. (1999). The application of multi-wavelet filterbanks to image processing, *IEEE Trans. on Image Process.*, **4**: 548–563.

Yu, R. & Baradarani, A. (2008). Sampled-data design of FIR dual filter banks for dual-tree complex wavelet transforms, *IEEE Trans. on Signal Process.*, **56**: 3369–3375.

Yu, R. & Ozkaramanli, H. (2005). Hilbert transform pairs of orthogonal wavelet bases: necessary and sufficient conditions, *IEEE Trans. on Signal Process.*, **53**: 4723–4725.

## 9

Pattern Recognition Based on Straight Line Segments

João Henrique Burckas Ribeiro and Ronaldo Fumio Hashimoto
Universidade de São Paulo - Instituto de Matemática e Estatística
Rua do Matão, 1001, São Paulo, SP - Brasil

1. Introduction

A very common way to represent objects in Pattern Recognition is to extract their features and normalize them into vectors in the space $\mathbb{R}^d$. With the objects being represented by points in the space $\mathbb{R}^d$, the distance among them is an intuitive way to compare their similarities and differences and it is used in the most methods in Pattern Recognition. For instance, one of the first and intuitive method in Pattern Recognition that uses this idea is the k-Nearest Neighbor (k-NN). After that, many other methods have emerged using distances, such as Condensed Nearest Neighbor (CNN) (Hart, 1968), Learning Vector Quantization (LVQ) (Kohonen et al., 1988), Nearest Feature Line (NFL) (Li & Lu, 1999), and a new method called Straight Line Segments (SLS) which takes advantage of some good caracteriscs of LVQ and NFL with low computational complexity (lower than Support Vector Machines) (Ribeiro & Hashimoto, 2006; 2008). This chapter gives a brief discussion about the mentioned methods and details about the SLS method. The next section discusses about the k-NN, CNN, LVQ and NFL methods which are related to the SLS method; Section 3 shows in details the SLS method; Section 4 presents the experimental results using the SLS method; and finally, Section 5 gives the conclusions about the SLS method and presents some future perspectives.

2. Pattern Recognition Based on Distances

This chapter deals only with supervised Pattern Recognition, that is, given a set of labeled objects whose labels were assigned by a tutor. It is desirable that a machine learns how to assign labels to new objects as the tutor does. For simplicity, this work is concentrated on binary classification meaning that there are just two possible values for the labels. For instance, in a system that needs to recognize whether a tumor is malign or benign, a set of examples (that is, a set of labeled objects) could be a set of tomographic images where a doctor has already assigned a label (malign or benign) to each one. The Pattern Recognition system needs to learn how to recognize and classify whether a new input image corresponds to a malign or benign cancer by observing the sample (that is, the set of examples) given by the doctor. To design a system like this, the designer must choose what machine learning is needed to be used in order to have a good classification performance for new objects. A set of machines learning can be represented by a parameterized set of functions $\mathcal{F}_\Lambda = \{f_\alpha : \mathbb{R}^d \mapsto \{0,1\}, \alpha \in \Lambda\}$. Typically, a training algorithm will select the function (or equivalently, the parameter $\alpha \in \Lambda$)

which best classifies new objects (points $x \in \mathbb{R}^d$) by observing the set of examples. Formally a supervised Pattern Recogniton system can be defined in the following way (Vapnik, 1999):

1. let $\mathcal{F}_\Lambda = \{f_\alpha : \mathbb{R}^d \mapsto \{0,1\}, \alpha \in \Lambda\}$ be a set of parameterized functions, where Λ is a set of parameter vectors;

2. let $S_N = \{(x_i, y_i) \in \mathbb{R}^d \times \{0,1\}, i = 1,2,\ldots,N\}$ be a set of N examples (x_i, y_i), such that each vector $x_i \in \mathbb{R}^d$ is drawn independently from a fixed but unknown probability distribution $P(x)$; for each input vector x_i, a supervisor returns an output value (label) $y_i \in \{0,1\}$ according to a conditional probability distribution $P(y \mid x)$, also fixed but unknown;

3. it is desired to find the parameter $\alpha^* \in \Lambda$ such that the function $f_{\alpha^*} \in \mathcal{F}$ minimizes a certain error or risk function in order to classify (that is, to give labels $y \in \{0, 1\}$ to) new query points $x \in \mathbb{R}^d$.

To evaluate any supervised Pattern Recognition system is necessary to define a *loss function* $l_\alpha : \mathbb{R}^d \times \{0, 1\} \mapsto \mathbb{R}$, which represents the penalty given to the machine learning (that is, the function f_α) in case of misclassifying the labeled point (x, y). The most used loss functions are the absolute and square errors described respectively by Eqs. 1 and 2:

$$l_\alpha(x, y) = |f_\alpha(x) - y|, \tag{1}$$
$$l_\alpha(x, y) = (f_\alpha(x) - y)^2. \tag{2}$$

The loss function gives the penalty for just one misclassification. To obtain the overall behavior of the machine learning it is necessary to compute the *functional risk*. In case of binary classification the functional risk can be the probability of the machine learning making a misclassification. Eq. 3 describes the functional risk.

$$R(\alpha) = \int l_\alpha(x,y) \cdot dP(x,y) \tag{3}$$

However, in most Pattern Recognition problems, the probability $P(x,y)$ is usually unknown and the functional risk is estimated by the *empirical risk*. Let $S_N = \{(x_i, y_i) : x_i \in \mathbb{R}^d$ and $y_i \in \{0, 1\}, i \in \{0, 1, \cdots , N\}\}$ be a set of N examples, the empirical risk of the machine learning with parameter $\alpha \in \Lambda$ with respect to S_N is defined by:

$$R_{S_N}(\alpha) = \frac{1}{N} \sum_{i=1}^{N} l_\alpha(x_i, y_i). \tag{4}$$

Since in this chapter we only deal with binary classification, the probability of correct classification can be computed by $1 - R(\alpha)$ and estimated by $1 - R_{S_N}(\alpha)$. After these formal definitions, we give a brief introduction of some supervised Pattern Recognition methods based on distances (or metrics).

2.1 The k-Nearest Neighbor Method

The simplicity and intuitive interpretation are the main qualities of the k-Nearest Neighbor (k-NN) method. According to Devroye et al. (1996), Fix and Hodges presented the k-NN for the first time in 1951. As the name of the method suggests, the k-NN classifies a point $x \in \mathbb{R}^d$ with the class of the majority among the k nearest examples. Usually, k is an odd number to avoid ties in classification. Interesting fact is that Cover & Hart (1967) proved that the asymptotic error rate of k-NN is not greater than twice the Bayes error.

For the most simple implementation of k-NN, the computational complexity is $O(N)$ in both memory use and execution time. Devroye et al. cited several works that reduce the computational time complexity, normally by preprocessing the set of examples (Devroye et al., 1996). For instance, the method proposed in (Friedman et al., 1977) reduces the time complexity to $O(log(N))$; in another work (Bandyopadhyay & Maulik, 2002) the sample is sorted according to the distance with respect to some reference point. These methods reduces the time complexity and maintain the same precision of the original k-NN, but they still maintain the same memory complexity.

Although the biggest problem of k-NN is the overfitting (that is, the empirical risk can be much lower than the functional risk), the k-NN method is very often used as a reference for other methods, because it does not depend on a lot of parameters and, in many cases, does not depend on the implementation (Jain et al., 2000).

2.2 The Condensed Nearest Neighbor Method

The *Condensed Nearest Neighbor* (CNN) method (Hart, 1968) aims at keeping in the sample just the examples that are relevant for classification in order to achieve a reduction on the computational complexity for both memory use and execution time. The training algorithm for CNN consists in taking out the examples that are not relevant for the classification. Following this idea, many other authors proposed similar methods to reduce the number of examples without loss accuracy. Wilson & Martinez (2000) wrote a good review of these methods and also proposed six more variants.

Although the CNN method tries to reduce the computational time when it is applied to the test phase, as for k-NN, the overfitting issue is still the biggest problem for CNN and derivative methods.

2.3 The Learning Vector Quantization Method

Kohonen et al. (1988) proposed a method based on 1-NN, called *Learning Vector Quantization* (LVQ), in which (i) a predetermined number of processing units, where each processing unit is a reference vector in $\mathbb{R}^d$ that is associated to one class; (ii) an input vector x is classified with the nearest reference vector class. Differently from 1-NN, the reference vectors are not the examples; they are determined by a training algorithm. There are many variants of LVQ, but basically, their training algorithm consists of two main components: (i) a clustering algorithm determines the initial position of the reference vectors, and (ii) an iterative algorithm tries to find the best position for all reference vectors.

After Kohonen's work, many other variations of LVQ have emerged. For instance, Geva & Sitte (1991) proposed a new training algorithm for LVQ called *Decision Surface Mapping*; Hammer & Villmann (2002) presented the *Generalized Relevance Learning Vector Quantization* method which is a training and a feature selection algorithm at the same time. Hammer & Villmann (2002) also compared LVQ to *Support Vector Machines* (SVM). They emphasize two advantages of LVQ over SVM: (i) LVQ is more intuitive and easy to implement; and (ii) the computational complexity od LVQ (on test phase) does not increase with the number of examples as occurs with SVM (Burges, 1998; Hammer et al., 2004).

The computational complexity of LVQ on test phase are directly proportional to the number of reference vectors. Therefore, if N_v is the number of the reference vectors chosen by the user, the computational complexity of LVQ is $O(N_v)$.

2.4 The Nearest Feature Line Method

Li & Lu (1999) presented a method for face recognition called *Nearest Feature Line* (NFL). the main idea behind this method is to define a feature line for each pair of examples of the same class. A new point $x \in \mathbb{R}^d$ is classified as the same class of the nearest feature line. This is a way to virtually increase the information of the sample, interpolating and extrapolating it from a pair of examples. Therefore, each class with N_C examples has $N_C(N_C - 1)/2$ feature lines. If (x_i, y_i) and (x_j, y_j) are two examples in the same class, then $y_i = y_j$. The feature line defined by this pair of examples is denoted by $\overleftrightarrow{x_i x_j}$. The distance from a point x to the feature line $\overleftrightarrow{x_i x_j}$ is defined as (Li & Lu, 1999):

$$d(x, \overleftrightarrow{x_i x_j}) = \|x - p\| \tag{5}$$

where

$$p = x_i + \frac{\left\langle (x - x_i), (x_j - x_i) \right\rangle}{\left\langle (x_j - x_i), (x_j - x_i) \right\rangle} (x_j - x_i). \tag{6}$$

where $\|a\|$ is the Euclidean norm of $a \in \mathbb{R}^d$ and $\langle a, b \rangle$ is the scalar product between $a \in \mathbb{R}^d$ and $b \in \mathbb{R}^d$.

It was shown that this method has a good classification performance when the number of examples is small and the feature space has a high dimension (Li & Lu, 1999). The disadvantage of this method is its high computational complexity and, depending on the dataset, it could make many misclassifications simply because it exaggerates on interpolation and extrapolation.

Based on NFL, other methods have emerged, for instance, the *Extended Nearest Feature Line* method (Zhou et al., 2004); *Center-based Nearest Neighbor* (Gao & Wang, 2007) and *Rectified Nearest Feature Line* (Du & Chen, 2007). Those methods improved the idea behind the NFL, however they still have a high computational complexity.

3. Pattern Recognition Method Based on Straight Line Segments

Although the Pattern Recognition method based on *Straight Line Segments* (SLS) presented in this section was not designed based on any of the methods described in the previous section, it uses similar ideas. For example, the SLS method uses straight line segments instead of reference vectors of LVQ; and the extremities of the straight line segments do not need to be examples like in NFL and derivatives. Thus, SLS obtains the low computational time complexity of LVQ and uses the interpolation capacity of NFL. So, the SLS method could be considered as an extension of LVQ with some ideas of NFL.

Let $p, q \in \mathbb{R}^{d+1}$. The straight line segment with extremities at p and q, denoted $\overline{pq}$, is the closed segment of a line in $\mathbb{R}^{d+1}$ with endpoints p and q. More formally,

$$\overline{pq} = \{x \in \mathbb{R}^{d+1} : x = p + \lambda \cdot (q - p), \ 0 \leq \lambda \leq 1\}. \tag{7}$$

The set of all possible straight line segments is denoted by $\overline{PQ} = \{\overline{pq} : p, q \in \mathbb{R}^{d+1}\}$.

Given a point $x \in \mathbb{R}^d$, the extension of x to $\mathbb{R}^{d+1}$, denoted by $x_e \in \mathbb{R}^{d+1}$, is the point $x_e = (x, 0)$, that is, the point x is extended to $\mathbb{R}^{d+1}$ by adding one more coordinate with zero value. Given a point $x \in \mathbb{R}^d$ and a straight line segment $\overline{pq}$, with $p, q \in \mathbb{R}^{d+1}$, the pseudo-distance between x and $\overline{pq}$ is the function $pdist : \mathbb{R}^d \times \overline{PQ} \mapsto \mathbb{R}$ defined as:

$$pdist(x,\overline{pq}) = \frac{dist(x_e,p) + dist(x_e,q) - dist(p,q)}{2}, \tag{8}$$

where $dist(a,b)$ denotes the Euclidean distance between points $a \in \mathbb{R}^{d+1}$ and $b \in \mathbb{R}^{d+1}$. Note that $pdist$ is not the Euclidean distance between a point $x \in \mathbb{R}^d$ and a straight line segment $\overline{pq}$, but it satisfies the following reasonable axioms:

1. If $p = q$, then $pdist(x,\overline{pq}) = dist(x,p)$.

2. If $x \in \overline{pq}$, then $pdist(x,\overline{pq}) = 0$.

3. If $x \notin \overline{pq}$, then $pdist(x,\overline{pq}) > 0$.

Let $\mathbb{L}$ be the collection of all possible sets of straight line segments, that is, $\mathbb{L} = \{L : L \subseteq \overline{PQ}\}$. Given two sets the straight line segments, L_0 and L_1, (that is, $L_0, L_1 \in \mathbb{L}$), if $\mathcal{L} = (L_0, L_1) \in \mathbb{L}^2$, then we define the *discriminant function* $T : \mathbb{R}^d \times \mathbb{L}^2 \mapsto \mathbb{R}$ as

$$T(x, \mathcal{L}) = \lim_{\epsilon \to 0} \left(\sum_{\overline{pq} \in L_1} \frac{1}{pdist(x,\overline{pq}) + \epsilon} - \sum_{\overline{pq} \in L_0} \frac{1}{pdist(x,\overline{pq}) + \epsilon} \right). \tag{9}$$

Finally, given a pair of sets of straight line segments $\mathcal{L} = (L_0, L_1) \in \mathbb{L}^2$, we define the *classification function* $y_{\mathcal{L}} : \mathbb{R}^d \mapsto [0,1]$ as

$$y_{\mathcal{L}}(x) = \frac{1}{1 + e^{-g \cdot T(x,\mathcal{L})}}, \tag{10}$$

where g is a positive real constant. Note that, if $\exists \overline{p_a q_a} \in L_1$ such that $pdist(x,\overline{p_a q_a}) \to 0$ and $pdist(x,\overline{p_b q_b}) \gg 0$ such that $\forall \overline{p_b q_b} \in L_0$, then the first term in Eq. 9 tends to $+\infty$. Consequently $T(x, \mathcal{L}) \to +\infty$ and, therefore, $y_{\mathcal{L}}(x) \to 1$. On the other hand, if $\exists \overline{p_b q_b} \in L_0$ such that $pdist(x,\overline{p_b q_b}) \to 0$ and $pdist(x,\overline{p_a q_a}) \gg 0$ such that $\forall \overline{p_a q_a} \in L_1$, then the second term in Eq. 9 tends to $-\infty$. Consequently $T(x, \mathcal{L}) \to -\infty$ and, therefore, $y_{\mathcal{L}}(x) \to 0$. Furthermore, when both terms in Eq. 9 are equal, $T(x, \mathcal{L}) \to 0$ and $y_{\mathcal{L}}(x) \to 0.5$. Thus, in the case of binary classification, the class of a point $x \in \mathbb{R}^d$ can be obtained by thresholding the function $y_{\mathcal{L}}(x)$ at level 0.5 in the following way: the class of point x is 0 if and only if $y_{\mathcal{L}}(x) \leq 0.5$. Therefore, the decision boundary that separates classes 0 from 1 depends on the choice of pair of sets of straight line segments $\mathcal{L} = (L_0, L_1) \in \mathbb{L}^2$. Observe that the SLS method has a difference of all other methods mentioned in previous section: while points $x \in \mathbb{R}^d$, the straight line segments are in $\mathbb{R}^{d+1}$. It gives more flexibility for the decision boundary.

Although this chapter does not deal with regression, in order to show how the classification function $y_{\mathcal{L}}(x)$ can be versatile, we illustrate that $y_{\mathcal{L}}(x)$ can be used to approximate four different functions $f_i : [0,1] \mapsto [0,1]$, $i \in \{1,2,3,4\}$, with only a few straight line segments. The four functions are the following:

$$f_1(x) = \frac{1}{4} + \frac{x}{2}; 0 \leq x \leq 1; \tag{11}$$

$$f_2(x) = \begin{cases} 1 & 0 \leq x < 0.25 \\ 0 & 0.25 \leq x < 0,5 \\ 1 & 0.5 \leq x < 0.75 \\ 0 & 0.75 \leq x \leq 1; \end{cases} \tag{12}$$

$$f_3(x) = 0.5 + 0.4 \sin(2 \cdot \pi \cdot x); 0 \leq x \leq 1; \tag{13}$$

$$f_4(x) = \begin{cases} 0.5 + 1.8\,x & 0 \le x < 0.25 \\ 1.4 - 1.8\,x & 0.25 \le x < 0.75 \\ -1.3 + 1.8\,x & 0.75 \le x \le 1; \end{cases} \qquad (14)$$

In Figure 1, we show the plots of the approximation of f_i using the function $y^i_{\mathcal{L}}(x)$. The functions $f_i(x)$, $i \in \{1,2,3,4\}$, are represented by red lines; while the corresponding approximation functions $y^i_{\mathcal{L}}(x)$ are represented by blue lines; the straight line segments in L_0 are represented with circles at the extremities, and the straight line segments in L_1 with $\times$ at the extremities. Note that the four functions are quite different and the approximations are very good (in the domain $[0,1]$). Observe that, for only function $f_4(x)$, it is necessary to use two straight line segments for each class, where one of them is degenerated into a point; in all other functions, just one straight line segment for each class is sufficient to make a good approximation. In Table 1, we provide the obtained empirical risk of these approximations.

Function	absolute error	squared error
$f_1(x)$	0.002011	0.000005
$f_2(x)$	0.000367	0.000011
$f_3(x)$	0.008240	0.000090
$f_4(x)$	0.009094	0.000120

Table 1. Empirical risk of the approximations of the functions f_i.

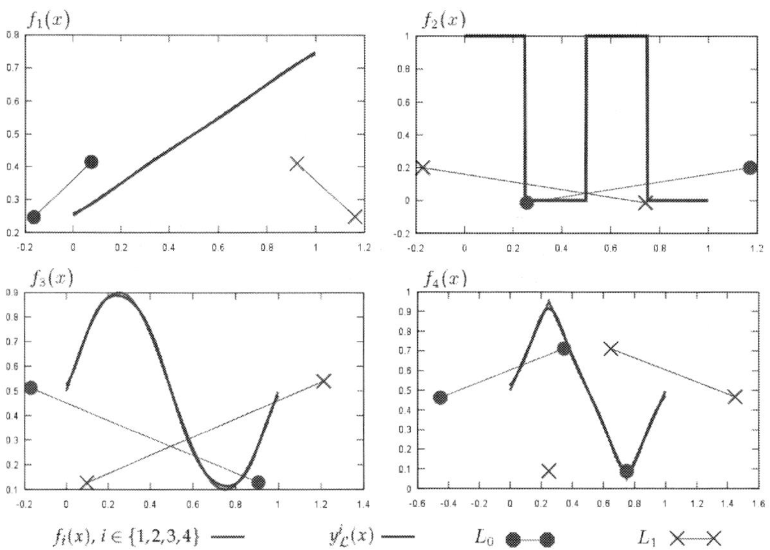

Fig. 1. Plots of the functions $f_i(x)$ and the corresponding approximations $y^i_{\mathcal{L}}(x)$, $i = 1,2,3,4$, with the respectives straight line segments.

3.1 Training Algorithm

The objective of the training algorithm is to find two sets of straight line segments that minimize the functional risk (Eq. 3). However, usually it is impossible to compute the functional risk, since the probability distribution is unknown in many situations. Therefore, the functional risk must be estimated by the empirical risk (Eq. 4). In this way, the training algorithm is based on the empirical risk minimization principle (Vapnik, 1999). More formally, given a sample S_N, the training algorithm must find two sets of straight line segments, L_0 and L_1, that minimize the empirical risk $R_{S_N}(\alpha)$, where the parameter vector α is defined by the positions of the straight line segments in both L_0 and L_1. The training algorithm is divided into two phases:

1. **Placing Algorithm**: In this phase, a heuristic pre-allocates (initializes) the straight line segments.

2. **Tuning Process**: In this phase, the straight line segments are moved from the initial position driven by an optimization algorithm thats tries to minimize the empirical risk.

3.2 Placing Algorithm

The first phase of the training algorithm consists of pre-allocating (that is, finding the initial positions of) the straight line segments which will be tuned later. The **Placing Algorithm** (see below) is based on the fact that the points in the region of the feature space that are near to the straight line segments belonging to L_0 (respectively, L_1) make the function $y_\mathcal{L}(x)$ tend to 0 (respectively, 1). Thus the first step of the Placing algorithm is to split the sample S_N into two groups of point sets X_0 and X_1 (see Lines 4 and 5 of the Placing algorithm). Group $X_0 \subseteq \mathbb{R}^d$ will initialize the straight line segments of L_0; while group $X_1 \subseteq \mathbb{R}^d$ will initialize the straight line segments of L_1. At Line 9, the k-means clustering algorithm(Duda et al., 2001; Jain et al., 1999) is applied to each group X_j ($j = 0, 1$) in order to find k clusters $C_0, C_1, \ldots, C_{k-1} \subseteq X_j$, with their corresponding centers $c_0, c_1, \ldots, c_{k-1} \in \mathbb{R}^d$. After that, the k-means clustering is applied again to each cluster in C_i ($i = 0, 1, \ldots, k-1$) using $k = 2$ (Line 11 of the Placing algorithm). The two centers d_0 and d_1 returned by 2-means determines the extremities of a straight line segment for each cluster C_i. Since we have k clusters C_i for each class, we have in total k straight line segments for each class. After that, each extremity of the straight line segments is extended in one extra dimension and the value of the corresponding extra coordinate is initially set to 1 for all extremities (see Lines 12 to 14). This value will be adjusted in the tuning process. Although any other clustering algorithm could be used in the Placing algorithm, the k-means was chosen as clustering algorithm because it is simple to implement and has fast convergence (Duda et al., 2001; Jain et al., 1999).

```
 1: PLACING(S_N, nSLS)
 2: Input: A sample S_N = {(x_i, y_i) : x_i ∈ R^d, y_i ∈ {0,1}, i = 1,2,...,N} and nSLS
           (number of straight line segments for each set L_0 and L_1).
 3: Output: Two sets of straight line segments L_0 and L_1 (with nSLS elements in each one).
 4: X_0 ← {x_i ∈ R^d : (x_i, y_i) ∈ S_N and y_i = 0};
 5: X_1 ← {x_i ∈ R^d : (x_i, y_i) ∈ S and y_i = 1};
 6: for j ← 0 to 1 do
 7:     L_j ← ∅;
 8:     k ← nSLS;
 9:     [(c_0, C_0),...,(c_{k-1}, C_{k-1})] ← k-means(X_j);
10:     for i ← 0 to k − 1 do
```

11:     $[(d_0, D_0), (d_1, D_1)] \leftarrow$ 2-means(C_i);

12:     $\ell \leftarrow 1$;

13:     $p \leftarrow (d_0, \ell)$;

14:     $q \leftarrow (d_1, \ell)$;

15:     $L_j \leftarrow L_j \cup \overline{pq}$;

16: **end for**

17: **end for**

18: **return** L_0, L_1;

The computational complexity of k-means is $O(N \cdot d \cdot k \cdot i)$, where i is the number of inter-actions, typically less than N. As k-means is applied twice to the sample, the computational complexity for placing is $O(N \cdot d \cdot k \cdot i)$. Considering $i \ll N$, with $k = nSLS$ at Line 9 and $k = 2$ at Line 11, it is possible to conclude that the computational complexity of Placing Algorithm is $O(N \cdot d \cdot nSLS)$ (Lingras & Yao, 2002).

3.3 Tuning the Straight Line Segments

The natural way to find the positions of the straight line segments that minimize the empirical risk (Eq. 4) is to find a point where its derivative is equal to zero. Since this calculation is not analytically feasible, we opted to use the gradient descent method. Since the gradient descent does not guarantee the global minimum, the final positions of the straight line segments will depend on the their initial position computed previouly by the Placing algorithm. In this way, the Placing algorithm is very important, because it can make the second part of the training algorithm to converge to a "good" local solution.

3.4 Gradient Descent

The optimization gradient descent method consists of moving in small steps the parameters (the vector α) in same direction of the gradient of the objective function in order to minimize (or maximize) its value (Michie et al., 1973).

Each displacement of vector α is proportional to γ which is a real positive number. If γ is too big, the displacement can be exaggerated and the empirical risk can increase instead of decrease. On the order hand, if γ was too small, the minimization process of the empirical risk can be too slow. It is possible to implement the gradient descent using a constant value for γ, but in this case, it is necessary to chose small values for γ to avoid exaggerate moves. Because of that, we use a dynamic γ. For each iteration, if the empirical risk decreases, γ increases proportionally to $1 + \gamma_{inc}$ (Line 11 of the GradDesc algorithm). On the other hand, if the iteration increases the empirical risk, the value of γ decreases proportionally to γ_{dec} (Line 15 of the GradDesc algorithm). Although the value of γ is updated dynamically during the training process, it must not be exaggerated in order to avoid the instability of the initial steps of tuning process. Empirically, we observed that γ stabilizes around 0.1, so this value is adopted for the initial γ. To compute the γ value dynamically it is interesting not to change the value of γ too much when the empirical risk is decreasing, and it is also interesting to decrease the value of γ quickly when the iteration increases the empirical risk. Therefore we set $\gamma_{inc} = 0.1$ and $\gamma_{dec} = 0.5$.

1: GRADDESC $(\alpha, I_{max}, I_{min}, \gamma_{ini}, \gamma_{inc}, \gamma_{dec}, Disp_{min}, R_{min})$;

2: **Input**: The vector α that must be optimized; the maximum number I_{max} of iterations; the minimum number I_{min} of iterations; the initial value γ_{ini} for γ; the increasing rate γ_{inc} for γ; the decreasing rate γ_{dec} for γ; the minimum displacement $Disp_{min}$; and finally the minimum empirical risk R_{min}.

3: **Output**: the vector α with optimized values.
4: $\alpha_{best} \leftarrow \alpha; \gamma \leftarrow \gamma_{init}; R0 \leftarrow R_{S_N}(\alpha); I \leftarrow 0;$
5: **repeat**
6:    $dR \leftarrow \nabla_\alpha R_{S_N}(\alpha);$
7:    $\alpha \leftarrow \alpha - \gamma \cdot dR;$
8:    $Disp \leftarrow |\gamma \cdot dR| / \sqrt{dim(\alpha)};$
9:    $R1 \leftarrow R_{S_N}(\alpha);$
10:    **if** $R0 \geq R1$ **then**
11:      $\gamma \leftarrow \gamma \cdot (1 + \gamma_{inc})$;
12:      $\alpha_{best} \leftarrow \alpha;$
13:      $R0 \leftarrow R1;$
14:    **else**
15:      $\gamma \leftarrow \gamma \cdot \gamma_{dec}$;
16:      $\alpha \leftarrow \alpha_{best};$
17:    **end if**
18:    $I \leftarrow I + 1;$
19: **until** $((I > I_{min})$ and $((I > I_{max})$ or $(Disp < Disp_{min})$ or $(R1 < R_{min})));$
20: **return** $\alpha_{best};$

Four conditions are used to stop the gradient descent process. First, the condition $I > I_{min}$ guaranties a minimum number I_{min} of iterations. Secondly, the number of iterations can not exceed I_{max} to guarantee that the algorithm will stop; thirdly, if the displacement of the parameters is smaller than $Disp_{min}$, it may mean that the parameter vector has achieved a local minimum; and the fourth criterion is useful when it is known what is the minimal empirical risk in order to avoid overfitting.

Note that the value of displacement $Disp$ is computed using $|\gamma \cdot dR|$ and is divided by the square root of the dimension of vector α (see Line 8). This division normalizes the displacement with respect to the number of parameters. Thus, the value for $Disp_{min}$ is normalized for all optimization problem. Empirically we observed that with $Disp_{min} = 0.001$ the empirical risk is stabilized.

3.5 The Proposed Training Algorithm

Before tuning of the extremities of the initial straight line segments (that is, adjusting their positions), it is necessary to determine the best initial value ℓ for the last coordinate of all extremities of the straight line segments (the value of the variable ℓ which was initialized with 1 in the Placing algorithm) and for the constant g (see Eq. 10).

In previous versions of the training algorithm, the initial value of ℓ was determined by the standard deviation of the examples in the sample (Ribeiro & Hashimoto, 2006; 2008). This heuristic aims at making the initial displacement of the last coordinate proportional to the examples dispersion. Also, in a previous version, the value of g was also chosen by a heuristic that makes the values of $y_L(x)$ have a uniform distribution (Ribeiro & Hashimoto, 2008). This way, low and high values of g is prevented, which make $y_L(x)$ tend to 0.5 and to 0 or 1, respectively. Although those heuristics work well, they do not consider the empirical risk. So, here, we have applied the gradient descent to find better values for both ℓ and g.

In our case we desire to minimize the empirical risk. The training algorithm applies the gradient descent twice: first to find the best values for ℓ and g; and, secondly to find the best position for all extremities of all straight line segments (of course, including all their last coordinates).

1: TRAINING (S_N, $nSLS$, I_{max}, I_{min}, γ_{ini}, γ_{inc}, γ_{dec}, $Disp_{min}$, R_{min});
2: **Input**: A sample $S_N = \{(x_i, y_i) : x_i \in \mathbb{R}^d; y_i \in \{0,1\}, i = 1, 2, \ldots, N\}$ and $nSLS$ (number of straight line segments for each set L_0 and L_1). The other inputs are: the maximum number I_{max} of iterations; the minimum number I_{min} of iterations; the initial value γ_{ini} for γ; the increasing rate γ_{inc} for γ; the decreasing rate γ_{dec} for γ; the minimum displacement $Disp_{min}$; and finally the minimum empirical risk R_{min}.
3: **Output**: two sets of straight line segments L_0 and L_1.
4: $[L_0, L_1] \leftarrow$ Placing(S_N, $nSLS$);
5: $g \leftarrow 1$;
6: $\alpha_1 \leftarrow$ Vectorize(g, ℓ);
7: $(g, \ell) \leftarrow$ GradDesc (α_1, I_{max}, I_{min}, γ_{ini}, γ_{inc}, γ_{dec}, $Disp_{min}$, R_{min});
8: $\alpha_2 \leftarrow$ Vectorize(L_0, L_1);
9: $(L_0, L_1) \leftarrow$ GradDesc (α_2, I_{max}, I_{min}, γ_{ini}, γ_{inc}, γ_{dec}, $Disp_{min}$, R_{min});
10: **return** L_0, L_1 and g;

The parameters g and ℓ define the vector α_1, where g is a positive real number that defines how "smooth" the sigmoid $y_{\mathcal{L}}(x)$ will be with respect to $T(x, \mathcal{L})$; and ℓ is the value for the last coordinate of all straight line segments that is initially equal to 1 for all segments.
The function Vectorize(g, ℓ) returns the following parameter vector α_1:

$$\alpha_1 = \left[\begin{array}{c} g \\ \ell \end{array} \right]. \tag{15}$$

The function Vectorize(L_0, L_1) returns the parameter vector α_2 for the second gradient descent whose coordinates are the extremities of each straight line segment (including all their last coordinates):

$$\alpha_2 = \left[\begin{array}{c} p_h^{j,k} \\ \vdots \\ q_h^{j,k} \\ \vdots \end{array} \right], \ j \in \{0,1\}, \ k \in \{1, \ldots, |L|\}, \ h \in \{1, \ldots, d+1\}, \tag{16}$$

where $L = |L_0|$ (assuming that $|L_0| = |L_1|$) and $p_h^{j,k}$ is the value of the h-th coordinate of the extremity p of the k-th straight line segment $\overline{p_k q_k}$ of L_j. The other extremity q of $\overline{p_k q_k} \in L_j$ is represented in analogous way. The function vectorize(L_0, L_1) returns the vector α_2 as described in Eq. 16. We should remark that after the application of the second gradient descent, the last coordinates of all straight line segments are not equal anymore.
We use the square error (Eq. 2) as the loss function. Thus, the empirical risk is defined by Eqs. 17 and 18. To simplify the notation, we will omit the parameters of some functions such as: $T_i = T(x_i, \mathcal{L})$, $y_{\mathcal{L}} = y_{\mathcal{L}}(x_i)$ and $pdist_{i,k}^j = pdist(x_i, L_k^j)$. In the following, we present the calculations for the gradient of $R_{S_N}(\alpha)$, where $\alpha = \alpha_2$, that is, $\nabla_{\alpha_2} R_{S_N}$. Let

$$err_i(y_{\mathcal{L}}) = y_{\mathcal{L}}(x_i) - y_i \ \text{ and} \tag{17}$$

$$R_{S_N}(\alpha) = \frac{1}{N} \sum_{i=1}^{N} [err_i(y_{\mathcal{L}})]^2. \tag{18}$$

The gradient $\nabla_{\alpha_2} R_{S_N}$ is defined for $j = \{0,1\}$, $k = \{1, \ldots, |L|\}$ and $h = \{1, \ldots, d+1\}$ as:

$$\nabla_{\alpha_2} R_{S_N}(\alpha_2) = \begin{bmatrix} \frac{\partial R_{S_N}}{\partial p_h^{j,k}} \\ \vdots \\ \frac{\partial R_{S_N}}{\partial q_h^{j,k}} \\ \vdots \end{bmatrix}, \tag{19}$$

where

$$\frac{\partial R_{S_N}}{\partial p_h^{j,k}} = \frac{1}{N} \sum_{i=1}^{n} 2 \cdot err_i \frac{g}{e^{g \cdot T_i} + e^{-g \cdot T_i} + 2} \frac{(-1)^j}{(pdist_{i,k}^j + \epsilon)^2} \cdot \tag{20}$$

$$\left(\frac{p_h^{j,k} - x_{i,h}}{2 \cdot dist(x_i, p^{j,k})} - \frac{p_h^{j,k} - q_h^{j,k}}{2 \cdot dist(p^{j,k}, q^{j,k})} \right). \tag{21}$$

The calculations of the parameters for the first gradient are g and ℓ. The value for the last coordinate of all straight line segments is set $p_{d+1}^{j,k} = q_{d+1}^{j,k} = \ell$ (that is, $p_{d+1}^{j,k}$ and $q_{d+1}^{j,k}$ are replaced with ℓ in the empirical risk R_{S_N} making it as a function of g and ℓ). Then, we have:

$$\nabla_{\alpha_1} R_{S_N}(\alpha_1) = \begin{bmatrix} \frac{\partial R_{S_N}}{\partial g} \\ \frac{\partial R_{S_N}}{\partial \ell} \end{bmatrix}, \tag{22}$$

$$\frac{\partial R_{S_N}}{\partial g} = \sum_{i=1}^{N} \frac{2\, err_i\, T_i\, e^{g\, T_i}}{e^{2g\, T_i} + 2\, e^{g\, T_i} + 1} \quad \text{and} \tag{23}$$

$$\frac{\partial R_{S_N}}{\partial \ell} = \sum_{j=0}^{1} \sum_{k=1}^{|L_j|} \left(\frac{\partial R_{S_N}}{\partial p_{d+1}^{j,k}} + \frac{\partial R_{S_N}}{\partial q_{d+1}^{j,k}} \right). \tag{24}$$

By the beginning of the first gradient, the last coordinates $p_{d+1}^{j,k} = q_{d+1}^{j,k} = 1$. Between the first gradient and the beginning of the second gradient, the last coordinates $p_{d+1}^{j,k} = q_{d+1}^{j,k} = \ell$ for all straight line segments. Finally, after the second gradient each last coordinate can have different values among them.

The time complexity for the *Training* algorithm is the sum of the complexity of *Placing* Algorithm plus twice the complexity of *GradDesc* Algorithm, that is $O(N \cdot d \cdot nSLS) + 2\,O(N \cdot d \cdot nSLS \cdot I_{max})$, which is equal to $O(N \cdot d \cdot nSLS \cdot I_{max})$.

To avoid overfitting and unnecessary increasing of computational time complexity, the best choice is to use a minimum number of straight line segments (for each class) for which the SLS method still has a good classification performance.

4. Experimental Results

In this section we describe the experiments we performed in order to evaluate the SLS method and compare it with other methods. For that, the experiments were divided into two parts: the first one uses artificial data to evaluate the behavior of the SLS method; while the second one uses public datasets to analyse the SLS method with real applications and compare our results with the results obtained by other methods.

4.1 Artificial Data

The artificial data for each class $C \in \{0, 1\}$ were generated using probability distributions associated to the density function defined by the sum of M two dimensional normal density functions as shown in Eq. 25:

$$p(\boldsymbol{x}, y = C) = \sum_{i=1}^{M} P_i^C \cdot Normal(\boldsymbol{x}, \mu_i^C, \Sigma_i^C), \tag{25}$$

where $\mu_i^C \in \mathbb{R}^2$ is the center of the normal density function, Σ_i^C is the 2×2 covariance matrix and P_i^C is a real number such that $\sum_{i=1}^{M} P_i^C = 1$. In general, each covariance matrix Σ^C is positive semidefinite matrix and has the following form:

$$\begin{pmatrix} (\sigma_1)^2 & \rho\sigma_1\sigma_2 \\ \rho\sigma_1\sigma_2 & (\sigma_2)^2 \end{pmatrix}, \tag{26}$$

where ρ is the correlation between the two random variables x_1 and x_2, and υ_j, for $j = 1, 2$, is the standard deviation of x_j. We designed four probability density functions called *Simple*, *distX*, *distS* and *DistF*. Each probability density function (pdf) is defined as follows:

***Simple* pdf:**

$$\begin{aligned} P_1^0 &= 1.0 & P_1^1 &= 1.0 \\ \mu_1^0 &= (0.6,\, 0.6) & \mu_1^1 &= (0.4,\, 0.4) \\ \Sigma_1^0 &= \begin{pmatrix} 0.010 & -0.009 \\ -0.009 & 0.010 \end{pmatrix} & \Sigma_1^1 &= \begin{pmatrix} 0.010 & 0.009 \\ 0.009 & 0.010 \end{pmatrix} \end{aligned} \tag{27}$$

***DistX* pdf:**

$$\begin{aligned} P_1^0 &= P_2^0 = 0.5 & P_1^1 &= P_2^1 = 0.5 \\ \mu_1^0 &= (0.25,\, 0.25) & \mu_1^1 &= (0.25,\, 0.75) \\ \mu_2^0 &= (0.75,\, 0.75) & \mu_2^1 &= (0.75,\, 0.25) \\ \Sigma_i^C &= \begin{pmatrix} 0.04 & 0.00 \\ 0.00 & 0.04 \end{pmatrix}, & C &\in \{0,\, 1\} \text{ and } i \in \{1,\, 2\} \end{aligned} \tag{28}$$

***DistS* pdf:**

$$\begin{aligned} P_1^0 &= P_2^0 = 0.5 & P_1^1 &= P_2^1 = 0.5 \\ \mu_1^0 &= (0.4,\, 0.4) & \mu_1^1 &= (0.6,\, 0.2) \\ \mu_2^0 &= (0.4,\, 0.8) & \mu_2^1 &= (0.6,\, 0.6) \\ \Sigma_i^C &= \begin{pmatrix} 0.02 & 0.00 \\ 0.00 & 0.01 \end{pmatrix}, & C &\in \{0, 1\} \text{ and } i \in \{1,\, 2\} \end{aligned} \tag{29}$$

***DistF* pdf:**

$$P_1^0 = 0.574 \qquad\qquad P_1^1 = 0.574$$
$$P_2^0 = P_3^0 = 0.213 \qquad\qquad P_2^1 = P_3^1 = 0.213$$
$$\mu_1^0 = (0.125,\ 0.5) \qquad\qquad \mu_1^1 = (0.875,\ 0.5)$$
$$\mu_2^0 = (0.5,\ 0.375) \qquad\qquad \mu_2^1 = (0.5,\ 0.125)$$
$$\mu_3^0 = (0.5,\ 0.875) \qquad\qquad \mu_3^1 = (0.5,\ 0.625)$$
$$\Sigma_1^C = \begin{pmatrix} 0.010 & 0.000 \\ 0.000 & 0.040 \end{pmatrix} \quad \Sigma_2^C = \begin{pmatrix} 0.012 & 0.000 \\ 0.000 & 0.010 \end{pmatrix}$$
$$\Sigma_3^C = \begin{pmatrix} 0.012 & 0.000 \\ 0.000 & 0.010 \end{pmatrix},\ \ C \in \{0,\ 1\}.$$

(30)

Figure 2 shows four graphics, each one representing one of the probability density functions. In Figure 3, there are four samples with 800 examples, each one drawn from one of the probability distributions associated with the 4 probability density functions.

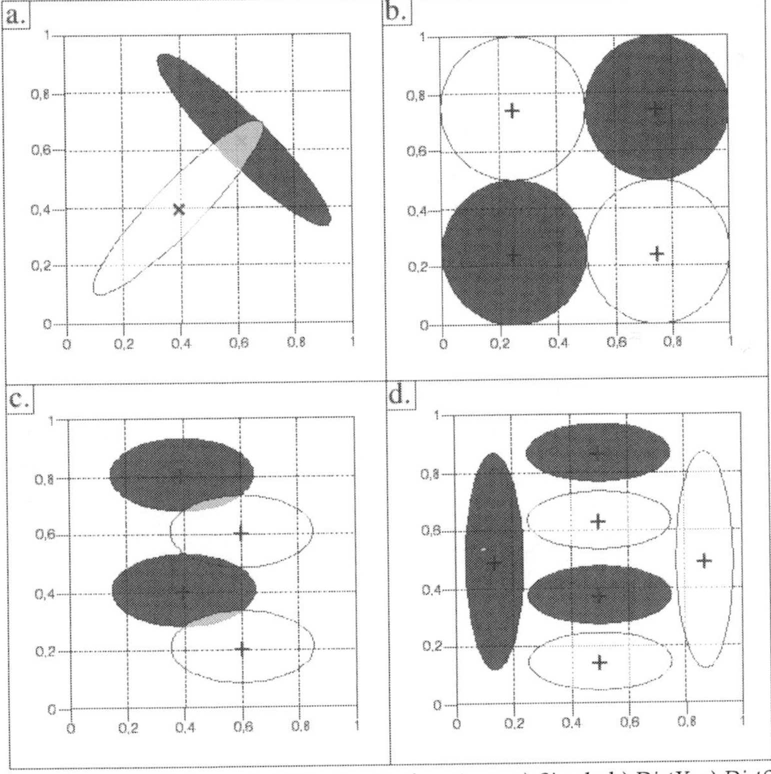

Fig. 2. Representation of the probability density functions: a) *Simple*, b) *DistX*, c) *DistS* and d) *DistF*.

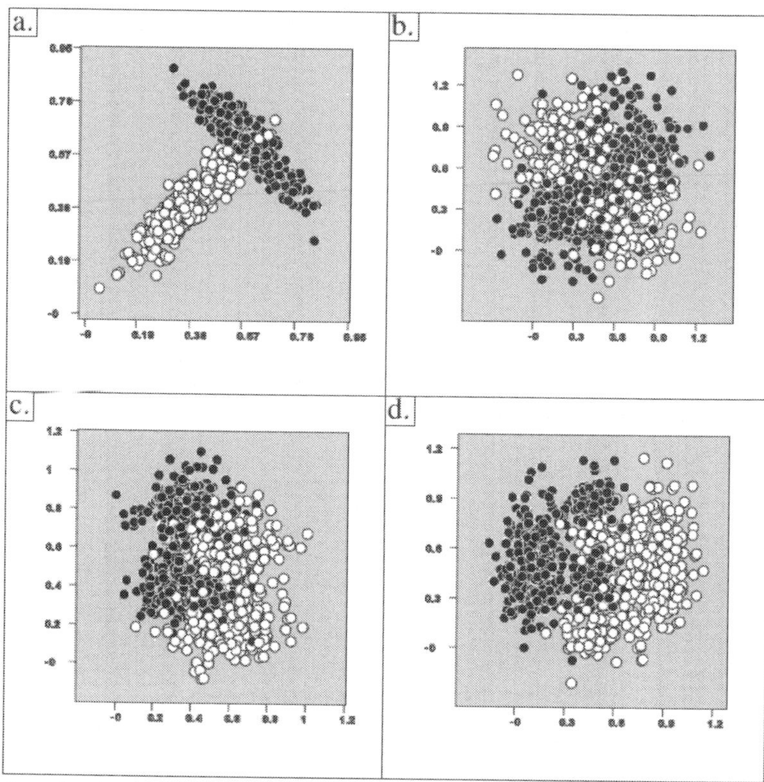

Fig. 3. Samples drawn from the probability distributions with 800 examples: a) *Simple*, b) *DistX*, c) *DistS* and d) *DistF*.

Since the probability density function is known, it is possible to compute the functional risk $R(\alpha)$ (see Eq. 3) of the SLS and Bayes classifiers (Duda et al., 2001). Consequently, it is possible to compute the actual probability of correct classification, that is $1 - R(\alpha)$, for both classifiers. For that, we used the numerical integration considering the values for $x \in \mathbb{R}^2$ inside the rectangle defined by the corners $(-0.5, -0.5)$ and $(1.5, 1.5)$. Inside this rectangle, there are more than 99% of examples for all probability density functions. The numerical integration was done using 160 000 points. The probability of correct classification for Bayes classifier for each probability density function is shown in Table 2.

Probability Density Function	Bayes (%)
Simple	96.95
DistX	81.11
DistS	84.39
DistF	91.43

Table 2. Probability of Correct Classification using Bayes Classifier.

For each probability density function (*Simple, DistX, DistS and DistF*), $4 \times 3 = 12$ samples (3 for each quantity of examples) with 100, 200, 400 and 800 examples were generated. The SLS training algorithm using 1, 2, 3, and 4 straight line segments for each class was applied to each sample, totalling 192 applications of the training algorithm. The parameters used for training algorithm are shown in Table 3.

Parameter	Value
I_{max}	10 000
min	20
γ_{init}	0.1
γ_{inc}	0.1
γ_{dec}	0.5
$Desl_{min}$	0.001
R_{min}	0.0001

Table 3. Training parameters for the SLS Training Algorithm.

The obtained results for the probability density functions *Simple, DistX, DistS* and *DistF* are respectively shown in Tables 4, 5, 6 and 7. The rows of these tables present the results using the same number of examples; while the columns show the results with the same number of straight line segments for each class. On left part of each column, it is presented the best result among the three performed tests with the same number of examples and de same number of straight line segments for each class. On right part of each column, it is shown the average of probability of correct classification for the three tests. The results shown in bold have the difference from the respective Bayes correct classification less than 1%.

In Figure 4, there are four response maps, one for each probability density function. In these maps, the gray scale is proportional to $y_{\mathcal{L}}(x) \in [0, 1]$ value, where black represents 0 and white represents 1. In these maps, the straight line segments are projected to a bidimensional plane. For these projections of the straight line segments, white represents class 0 and black class 1.

Since the probability density functions are known, we can compute and compare the probability of correct classification of SLS and Bayes classifiers. The results show that the SLS method achieved good performace. For all cases, we obtained a difference that is less than 1% comparing to Bayes classifier.

For distributions *DistS* and *DistF* (that have a more complex decision boundary), it was necessary to add more straight line segments for each class to obtain a good performace. For distributions *Simple* and *DistX*, just one straight line segment for each class was enough for a good performace. As expected, the more training examples, the better performace of the classifier.

4.2 Experiments with Public Datasets

To compare the performance of SLS with other methods, we did experiments using 8 public datasets. These datasets were chosen from (Van Gestel et al., 2004) in which a benchmarking for SVM and other methods can be found. In this way, it is possible to compare our results with theirs (Van Gestel et al., 2004). The datasets taken from (Van Gestel et al., 2004) correspond only to binary classification. All datasets are available in UCI Machine Learning Repository (Asuncion & Newman, 2007) and they are *Australian Credit Approval* (**australian**), *Breast Cancer Wisconsin* (**breast-cancer**), *Pima Indians Diabetes* (**diabetes**), *German Credit Data* (**german**), *Heart* (**heart**), *Ionosphere* (**ionosphere**), *Liver Disorders* (**liver-disorders**) and *Sonar,*

Simple (Bayes = 96.951 %)							
# of SLS/class	1		2		3		4	
	Max.	Avg.	Max.	Avg.	Max.	Avg.	Max.	Avg.
100	**96.40**	95.93	**96.69**	**96.07**	**96.41**	**96.17**	**96.32**	**95.97**
200	**96.43**	**96.37**	**96.51**	**96.47**	**96.45**	**96.40**	**96.44**	**96.39**
400	**96.64**	**96.60**	**96.65**	**96.54**	**96.63**	**96.55**	**96.56**	**96.47**
800	**96.80**	**96.52**	**96.55**	**96.48**	**96.79**	**96.57**	**96.58**	**96.48**

Table 4. Results for **Simple** pdf.

DistX (Bayes = 81.105 %)							
# of SLS/class	1		2		3		4	
	Max.	Avg.	Max.	Avg.	Max.	Avg.	Max.	Avg.
100	78.86	78.45	78.37	77.68	76.46	76.36	78.39	77.65
200	**80.49**	**80.33**	79.98	79.75	79.61	79.29	79.70	79.32
400	**80.90**	**80.63**	**80.76**	**80.41**	**80.73**	**80.45**	**80.74**	79.86
800	**81.03**	**80.86**	**80.98**	**80.77**	**81.06**	**80.84**	**80.86**	**80.75**

Table 5. Results for **DistX** pdf.

DistS (Bayes = 84.386 %)							
# of SLS/class	1		2		3		4	
	Max.	Avg.	Max.	Avg.	Max.	Avg.	Max.	Avg.
100	82.85	80.67	82.94	81.12	**83.76**	82.23	**83.58**	82.21
200	81.88	80.80	**83.54**	82.92	**83.77**	83.11	**83.66**	81.94
400	81.17	80.29	**83.94**	**83.64**	84.03	83.78	**83.99**	81.50
800	80.83	80.61	**83.90**	**83.78**	83.98	83.80	**83.98**	**83.88**

Table 6. Results for **DistS** pdf.

DistF (Bayes = 91.435 %)							
# of SLS/class	1		2		3		4	
	Max.	Avg.	Max.	Avg.	Max.	Avg.	Max.	Avg.
100	85.25	84.72	89.12	88.94	**90.46**	88.68	89.84	87.91
200	83.56	83.46	90.27	89.64	89.79	89.72	89.86	89.57
400	85.60	84.61	**90.47**	90.25	**90.45**	90.22	**90.84**	**90.63**
800	83.61	83.53	90.12	89.80	**90.53**	90.05	**90.68**	90.41

Table 7. Results for **DistF** pdf.

Mines vs. Rocks (**sonar**). The number of attributes in each dataset is shown in Table 8. For more detailed information, we recommend to visit the UCI Machine Learning Repository (Asuncion & Newman, 2007).

We performed the experiment using the same methodology described in (Van Gestel et al., 2004), that is, for each training, the sample is randomly split into two sets: one for training containing 2/3 of examples; and other for the test phase with 1/3 of examples. This spliting process is repeated ten times for each dataset. Besides, the training parameters used for training the SLS method were the same values used for artificial data (see Table 3).

Table 8 shows the average and the standard deviation (presented between parenthesis) of correct classification. The results for the SLS method using 1, 2, 3, 4, 6, 8, and 10 straight line segments for each class, respectively, are shown at Rows from 1 to 7. The results obtained by Van Gestel et al. (2004) using SVM and k-NN are presented at Rows from 8 to 17. Finally,

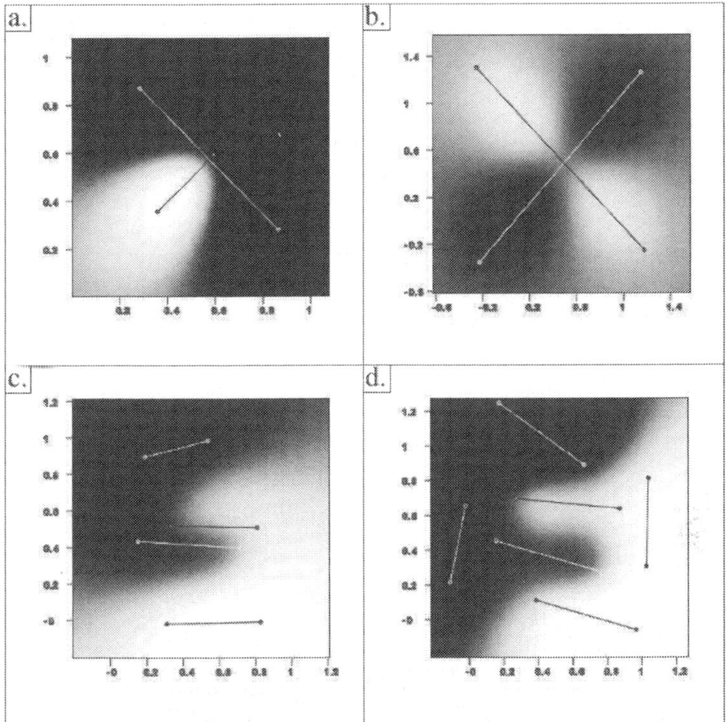

Fig. 4. Response maps for each probability density function:
a) *Simple*, sample with 800 examples and using 1 straight line segment for each class;
b) *DistX*, sample with 800 examples and using 1 straight line segment for each class;
c) *DistS*, sample with 800 examples and using 2 straight line segments for each class;
d) *DistF*, sample with 400 examples and using 3 straight line segments for each class.

the results using SVM with RBF and polynomial kernels (Eqs. 31 and 32 - in these equations, δ and ϱ are kernel parameters and C controls how the errors are penalized) are shown at Rows 18 and 22. In particular, the last two results were obtained using the LibSVM software developed by Chang & Lin (2001) with parameters δ, C and ϱ (shown at Rows 20, 21, 24, 25 and 26) chosen by an exhaustive search for the best combination using the values presented in Table 9.

		australian	breast-cancer	diabetes	german	heart	ionosphere	liver-disorders	sonar
	N_{test}	690	683	768	1000	270	351	345	208
	d	14	9	8	20	13	33	6	60
1	$SLS\,1$	86.7 (1.5)	97.7 (0.6)	**76.4** (1.8)	76.4 (1.0)	81.7 (4.6)	94.1 (1.7)	59.9 (17.5)	84.1 (4.1)
2	$SLS\,2$	86.3 (1.9)	97.8 (0.7)	74.8 (2.5)	**76.7** (2.2)	80.6 (3.9)	94.6 (1.4)	67.6 (3.3)	84.1 (4.7)
3	$SLS\,3$	86.5 (1.7)	98.1 (0.8)	74.2 (2.0)	75.9 (2.1)	81.7 (3.6)	94.4 (2.1)	**70.1** (2.8)	85.9 (4.1)
4	$SLS\,4$	86.3 (1.8)	**98.1** (0.7)	73.7 (1.7)	76.3 (1.4)	81.9 (3.3)	93.4 (3.1)	70.0 (3.8)	**86.3** (4.1)
5	$SLS\,6$	86.1 (1.6)	98.0 (0.7)	72.4 (2.9)	76.5 (1.6)	81.0 (2.8)	94.9 (1.3)	65.3 (11.7)	85.3 (4.8)
6	$SLS\,8$	**87.0** (1.8)	97.9 (0.8)	72.4 (2.4)	76.2 (1.6)	81.4 (3.4)	94.8 (1.6)	65.8 (9.6)	86.1 (3.6)
7	$SLS\,10$	86.8 (1.8)	97.8 (0.7)	72.2 (3.2)	76.4 (1.6)	**82.2** (3.3)	**95.2** (2.6)	63.4 (9.1)	85.4 (4.4)
8	$RBFLS-SVM$	87.0 (2.1)	96.4 (1.0)	76.8 (1.7)	76.3 (1.4)	84.7 (4.8)	**96.0** (2.1)	70.2 (4.1)	73.1 (4.2)
9	$RBFLS-SVM_F$	86.4 (1.9)	96.8 (0.7)	72.9 (2.0)	70.8 (2.4)	83.2 (5.0)	93.4 (2.7)	65.1 (2.9)	73.6 (4.6)
10	$LinLS-SVM$	86.8 (2.2)	95.8 (1.0)	76.8 (1.8)	75.4 (2.3)	84.9 (4.5)	87.9 (2.0)	65.6 (3.2)	72.6 (3.7)
11	$LinLS-SVM_F$	86.5 (2.1)	96.9 (0.7)	73.1 (1.7)	68.6 (2.3)	82.8 (4.4)	85.0 (3.5)	61.8 (3.3)	73.3 (3.4)
12	$PolLS-SVM$	86.5 (2.2)	96.4 (0.9)	77.0 (1.8)	76.3 (1.4)	83.7 (3.9)	91.0 (2.5)	70.4 (3.7)	76.9 (4.7)
13	$PolLS-SVM_F$	86.6 (2.2)	96.9 (0.7)	73.0 (1.8)	70.3 (2.3)	82.4 (4.6)	91.7 (2.6)	65.3 (2.9)	77.3 (2.6)
14	$RBFSVM$	86.3 (1.8)	96.4 (1.0)	77.3 (2.2)	75.9 (1.4)	84.7 (4.8)	95.4 (1.7)	70.4 (3.2)	75.0 (6.6)
15	$LinSVM$	86.7 (2.4)	96.3 (1.0)	77.0 (2.4)	75.4 (1.7)	83.2 (4.2)	87.1 (3.4)	67.7 (2.6)	74.1 (4.2)
16	$1-NN$	81.1 (1.9)	95.3 (1.1)	69.6 (2.4)	69.3 (2.6)	74.3 (4.2)	87.2 (2.8)	61.3 (6.2)	77.7 (4.4)
17	$10-NN$	86.4 (1.3)	96.4 (1.2)	73.6 (2.4)	72.6 (1.7)	80.0 (4.3)	85.9 (2.5)	60.5 (4.4)	69.4 (4.3)
18	$libSVMRBF$	**87.4** (1.6)	97.8 (0.5)	**77.8** (1.8)	**77.3** (0.5)	**85.1** (3.3)	95.4 (1.9)	**72.7** (2.7)	**88.4** (4.2)
19	$\#SV$	407.7	46	277.9	371.9	145.8	65.6	166.1	99.3
20	γ	0.01	0.01	0.01	0.01	0.1	0.1	0.1	0.1
21	C	0.1	10	50	20	0.1	10	50	10
22	$libSVMPol$	87.3 (1.7)	**97.9** (0.9)	77.3 (2.2)	76.4 (1.4)	82.4 (4.0)	92.8 (2.6)	71.5 (3.2)	87.1 (4.0)
23	$\#SV$	158.9	52.8	277.2	386.5	143.2	78.3	165.6	88.8
24	δ	2	0.01	5	0.01	0.01	2	0.1	0.1
25	C	0.01	200	0.01	50	20	0.01	200	10
26	ϱ	2	2	2	2	2	2	2	4

The results presented in this table are the average of correct classification for 10 tests. The number in parenthesis corresponds to the standart deviation. For each column there are two values in bold: the first one is the best result using SLS method and second one is the best result among the others. The underlined numbers for the SLS method are statistically equal to the best results among the other methods by t-test with 95% of confidence.

Table 8. Average of Correct classification for public datasets.

$$K(x_i, x_j) = e^{-\delta \|x_i - x_j\|^2} \tag{31}$$

$$K(x_i, x_j) = \left(\delta \left\langle x_i, x_j \right\rangle\right)^{\varrho}. \tag{32}$$

C	0.01, 0.1, 10, 20, 50, 100, 200
δ	0.01, 0.1, 0.5, 1.0, 2.0, 5.0, 10.0
ϱ	2, 4, 6, 8, 10

Table 9. Parameters for RFB and Polynomial Kernels (Eqs. 31 and 32).

In order to have a good view of the results, the average of correct classification for each dataset can also be viewed in the plots presented in Figure 5.

By observing the plots in Figure 5, we can see that the good performance of SLS method with respect to the others is well-posted on the graphic of the breast-cancer dataset. More details about the results can be viewed on Table 8. In particular, this table is divided in two blocks: the first one presents the results of the SLS method (Rows from 1 to 7); while the second one shows the results using SVM and k-NN taken from(Van Gestel et al., 2004). The best results in each block are in bold. We also applied the t-test with 95% of confidence (Dietterich, 1998) to the results of the SLS method and the best result of SVM and k-NN. The underlined values in the table indicate that the results obtained by SLS method are statistically equal to the best result among the others. By observing Table 8, it is possible to notice that by t-test the SLS method has always the performance significantly equal to the performance of SVM. In the case of **breast-cancer** dataset, the performance of SLS method was better than SVM.

On one hand, the computational time complexity of SVM on test phase is $\Theta(N_{SV} \cdot K)$, where N_{SV} is the number of support vectors and K is the computational complexity for computing the kernel (Burges, 1998). The time complexity for both polynomial and RBF kernel computations is proportional to distance computations. On the other hand, the computational time complexity of the SLS method on test phase is $\Theta(|L_0| + |L_1|)$. Note that, for each straight line segment, there are two distance computations. Then, with respect to the computational complexity, one straight line segment in SLS is equivalent to two support vectors in SVM.

In the experiments presented in this chapter, for the SLS method, we used no more than 10 straight line segments for each class meaning the maximum of 20 straight line segments. This is equivalent to 40 support vectors in SVM. Note that, at Rows 19 and 23 in Table 8, the lowest average of support vectors is 46 in breast-cancer dataset with RBF kernel. However, in general, the number of support vectors is commonly higher than it. Therefore, comparing the computational complexity of both methods, we can conclude that the SLS method is computationally more efficient than SVM for similar classification performance.

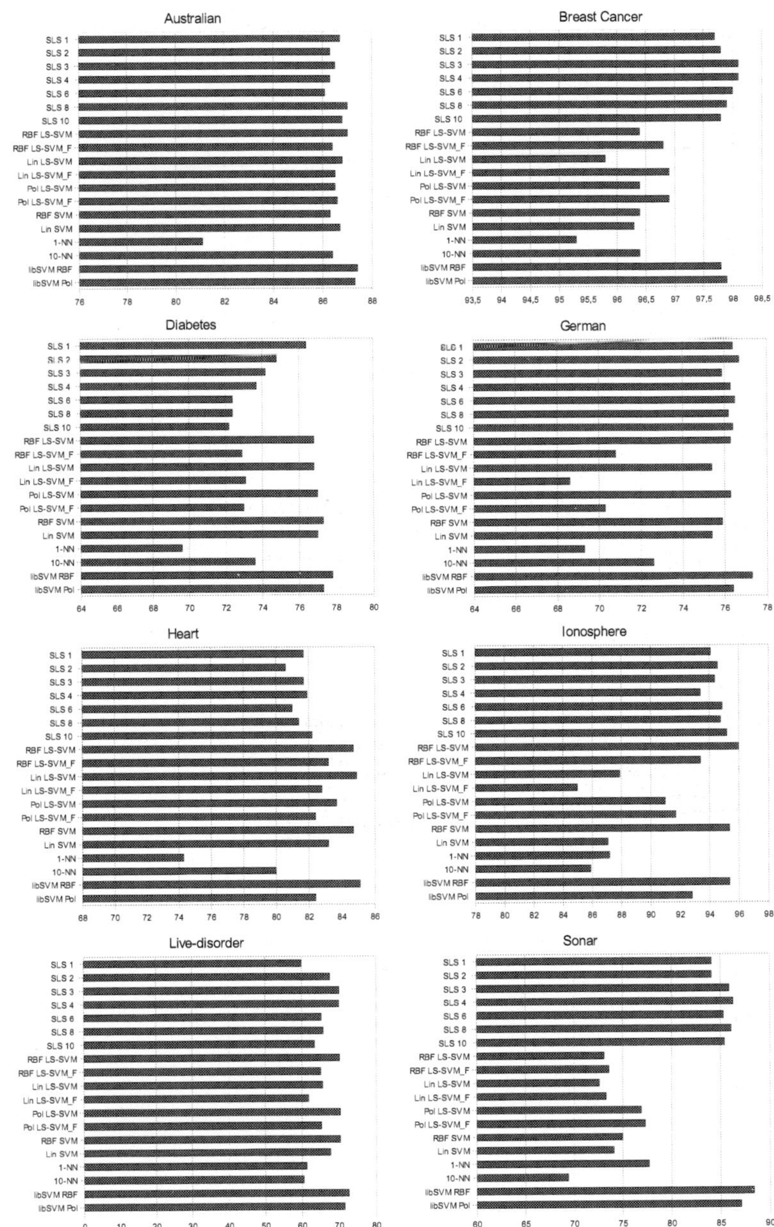

Fig. 5. Graphics showing the average of correct classification for public datasets.

5. Conclusion

In this chapter we presented a new method for Pattern Recognition based on distance between points and straight line segments called SLS method. Although the design of the SLS method was not initially based on any other method, it has some similarities to the Learning Vector Quantization (LVQ) and the Nearest Feature Line (NFL) methods so that SLS can take the advantages of both methods. For instance, SLS has the low computational complexity of LVQ and the interpolation capacity of straight lines of NFL. The experiments presented here confirm these advantages showing that the SLS method has lower computational complexity than SVM on the test phase with similar classification performance. By observing these results, we can conclude that the SLS method is a new and good option for supervised pattern recognition systems.

The SLS method also opens new perspectives for future research on Pattern Recognition. One of the main interest is to improve the training algorithm (which outputs a local optimal solution) by solving the underlying nonlinear optimization problem using other methods than gradient descent (for example, genetic algorithms). Other topics of interest are to extend the method for multiclassification and regression problems.

6. Acknowledgment

We would like to thank the financial support of CAPES (www.capes.gov.br), CNPq (www.cnpq.br), FAPESP (www.fapesp.br) and UOL (www.uol.com.br). And a special thanks to Manuel do Santos Fernandes Ribeiro for the support and incentive to this work.

7. References

Asuncion, A. & Newman, D. J. (2007). UCI Machine Learning Repository, [http://archive.ics.uci.edu/ml/]. Irvine, CA: University of California, School of Information and Computer Science.
URL: *http://www.ics.uci.edu/~mlearn/MLRepository.html*

Bandyopadhyay, S. & Maulik, U. (2002). Efficient prototype reordering in nearest neighbor classification, *Pattern Recognition* 35(12): 2791–2799.

Burges, C. J. C. (1998). A Tutorial on Support Vector Machines for Pattern Recognition, *Data Mining and Knowledge Discovery* 2(2): 121–167.
URL: *http://citeseer.ist.psu.edu/397919.html*

Chang, C.-C. & Lin, C.-J. (2001). *LIBSVM: a library for support vector machines*. Software available at http://www.csie.ntu.edu.tw/~cjlin/libsvm.

Cover, T. & Hart, P. (1967). Nearest neighbor pattern classification, *Information Theory, IEEE Transactions on* 13(1): 21–27.
URL: *http://ieeexplore.ieee.org/xpls/abs_all.jsp?arnumber=1053964*

Devroye, L., Gyorfi, L. & Lugosi, G. (1996). *A Probabilistic Theory of Pattern Recognition*, Springer-Verlag, New York.

Dietterich, T. G. (1998). Approximate statistical tests for comparing supervised classification learning algorithms, *Neural Computation* 10: 1895–1923.

Du, H. & Chen, Y. Q. (2007). Rectified nearest feature line segment for pattern classification, *Pattern Recognition* 40: 1486–1497.

Duda, R. O., Hart, P. E. & Stork, D. G. (2001). *Pattern Classification*, John Wiley and Sons.

Friedman, J. H., Bentley, J. L. & Finkel, R. A. (1977). An algorithm for finding best matches in logarithmic expected time, *ACM Trans. Math. Softw.* 3(3): 209–226.

Gao, Q. & Wang, Z.-Z. (2007). Center-based nearest neighbor classifier, *Pattern Recognition* **40**: 346–349.

Geva, S. & Sitte, J. (1991). Adaptive nearest neighbor pattern classification, *Neural Networks, IEEE International Conference on* pp. 318–322.
  URL: *http://ieeexplore.ieee.org/xpls/abs_all.jsp?arnumber=80344*

Hammer, B., Strickert, M. & Villmann, T. (2004). Relevance lvq versus svm, *Artificial Intelligence and Soft computing, volume 3070 of Springer Lecture Notes in Artificial Intelligence*, Springer, pp. 592–597.

Hammer, B. & Villmann, T. (2002). Generalized relevance learning vector quantization, *Neural Networks* **15**: 1059–1068.
  URL: *http://dx.doi.org/10.1016/S0893-6080(02)00079-5*

Hart, P. (1968). The condensed nearest neighbor rule, *Information Theory, IEEE Transactions on* **14**(3): 515–516.

Jain, A. K., Duin, R. P. W. & Mao, J. (2000). Statistical Pattern Recognition: A Review, *IEEE Transactions on Pattern Analysis and Machine Intelligence* **22**(1): 4–37.
  URL: *citeseer.ist.psu.edu/article/jain00statistical.html*

Jain, A. K., Murty, M. N. & Flynn, P. J. (1999). Data Clustering: a Review, *ACM Comput. Surv.* **31**(3): 264–323.

Kohonen, T., Barna, G. & Chrisley, R. (1988). Statistical pattern recognition with neural networks: benchmarking studies, *Neural Networks, 1988., IEEE International Conference on*, pp. 61–68 vol.1.
  URL: *http://dx.doi.org/10.1109/ICNN.1988.23829*

Li, S. & Lu, J. (1999). Face recognition using the nearest feature line method, *IEEE Transactions on Neural Networks* **10**(2): 439–443.

Lingras, P. & Yao, Y. Y. (2002). Time Complexity of Rough Clustering: GAs versus K-Means, *Rough Sets and Current Trends in Computing*, Springer Berlin / Heidelberg, pp. 263–270.

Michie, D., Spiegelhalter, D. J. & Taylor, C. C. (1973). *Introdution to Optimization Theory*, Prentince-Hall.

Ribeiro, J. H. B. & Hashimoto, R. F. (2006). A New Machine Learning Technique Based on Straight Line Segments, *ICMLA '06: Proceedings of the 5th International Conference on Machine Learning and Applications*, IEEE Computer Society, Washington, DC, USA, pp. 10–16.

Ribeiro, J. H. B. & Hashimoto, R. F. (2008). A New Training Algorithm for Pattern Recognition Technique Based on Straight Line Segments, *SIBGRAPI '08: Proceedings of the 2008 XXI Brazilian Symposium on Computer Graphics and Image Processing*, IEEE Computer Society, Washington, DC, USA, pp. 19–26.

Van Gestel, T., Suykens, J. A. K., Baesens, B., Viaene, S., Vanthienen, J., Dedene, G., De Moor, B. & Vandewalle, J. (2004). Benchmarking least squares support vector machine classifiers, *Mach. Learn.* **54**(1): 5–32.

Vapnik, V. N. (1999). An Overview of Statistical Learning Theory, *IEEE Transactions on Neural Networks* **10**(5): 988–999.
  URL: *http://ieeexplore.ieee.org/xpls/abs_all.jsp?arnumber=788640*

Wilson, D. R. & Martinez, T. R. (2000). Reduction Techniques for Instance-Based Learning Algorithms, *Machine Learning*, pp. 257–286.

Zhou, Y., Zhang, C. & Wang, J. (2004). Extended Nearest Feature Line Classifier, *PRICAI 2004: Trends in Artificial Intelligence*, Springer Berlin / Heidelberg, pp. 183–190.

From Conformal Geometric Algebra to Spherical Harmonics for a Correlation with Lines

Luis Falcón-Morales and Eduardo Bayro-Corrochano
Tecnológico de Monterrey Campus Guadalajara; CINVESTAV Unidad Guadalajara
México

1. Introduction

In this chapter we will apply the classic theory of Harmonic Analysis and the Conformal Geometric Algebra to evaluate the Radon transform on the unit sphere S^2 and on the rotation group $SO(3)$ to recover the 3D camera rotation. Since the images taken by omnidirectional sensors can be mapped to the sphere, the problem of attitude estimation of a 3D camera rotation can be treated as a problem of estimating rotations between spherical images.

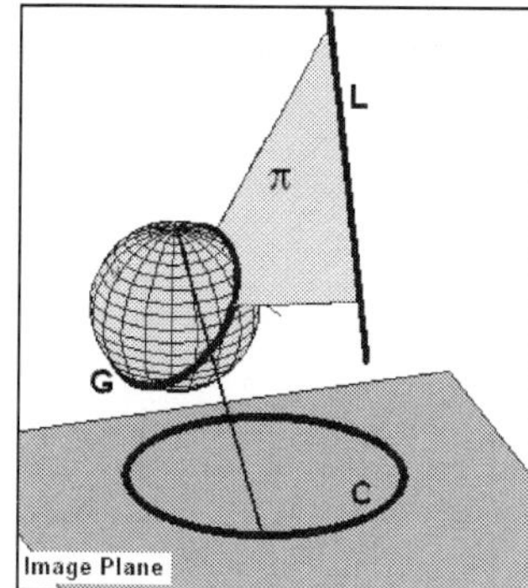

Fig. 1. A 3D line L as a circle C in the image plane.

From [Geyer & Daniilidis, 2000], we know that the parabolic, hyperbolic and elliptic mirrors are equivalent to the equivalent sphere, that is, a 3D-point P is projected to the sphere in a point η which is the intersection of the sphere and the line from the origin to P. Then, if the mirror is parabolic, η is stereographically projected from the north pole to the image plane

$z = 0$. See Figure 1. This is the reason to study harmonic analysis on S^2 and $SO(3)$. In recent years harmonic analysis has been used in computer vision to obtain 3D rotations with the Radon and Hough transforms. In [Geyer et al., 2004] harmonic analysis is used to obtain the *essential matrix* of two omnidirectional images. In [Makadia et al., 2005] and [Makadia & Daniilidis, 2003] the Euler angles are obtained with the Radon transform as a correlation of points on S^2 and $SO(3)$. In [Falcon-Morales & Bayro-Corrochano, 2007] the Radon transform is defined as a correspondence of lines to obtain a 3D rotation. In reference to the notation and theory about spherical harmonics we are following [Arfken & Weber, 1966] and [Chirikjian & Kyatkin, 2001]. The objective is to combine the almost forgotten mathematical framework conformal geometric algebra with the classical analysis theory, to obtain a different approximation, focus on geometric entities, to a well know omnidirectional vision problem.

2. Geometric Algebra

The algebras of Clifford and Grassmann are well known to pure mathematicians, but since the beginning were abandoned by physicists in favor of the vector algebra of Gibbs, the commonly algebra used today in most areas of physics. The approach to Clifford algebra that we adopt here has been developed since the 1960's by David Hestenes. See [Hestenes & Sobczyk, 1984] and [Li et al., 2001].

2.1 Basic definitions

Let V_n be a vector space of dimension n. We are going to define and generate an algebra G_n, called *geometric algebra*. Let $\{e_1, e_2, \ldots, e_n\}$ be a set of basis vectors of V_n. The *scalar multiplication* and *sum* in G_n are defined in the usual way of a vector space. The *product* or *geometric product* of elements of the basis of G_n will be simply denoted by juxtaposition. In this way, from any two basis vectors e_j and e_k, a new element of the algebra is obtained and denoted as $e_j e_k \equiv e_{jk}$. The product of basis vectors is anticommutative, that is,

$$e_j e_k \equiv -e_k e_j, \quad \forall j \neq k. \tag{1}$$

The basis vectors must *square* in $+1, -1$ or 0, this means that there are no-negative integers p, q and r such that $n = p + q + r$ and

$$e_i e_i = e_i^2 = \begin{cases} +1 & \text{for} & i = 1, \ldots, p \\ -1 & \text{for} & i = p+1, \ldots, p+q \\ 0 & \text{for} & i = p+q+1, \ldots, n \end{cases} \tag{2}$$

This *product* will be called the *geometric product* of G_n. With these operations G_n is an associative linear algebra with identity and it is called the *geometric algebra* or *Clifford algebra* of dimension $n = p + q + r$, generated by the vector space V_n. It is usual to write $G_{p,q,r}$ instead of G_n. The elements of this geometric algebra are called *multivectors*, because they are entities generated by the sum of elements of *mixed grade* of the basis set of G_n, such as

$$A = \langle A \rangle_0 + \langle A \rangle_1 + \cdots + \langle A \rangle_n \tag{3}$$

where the multivector $A \in G_n$ is expressed by the addition of its 0-*vector* part (or scalar part) $\langle A \rangle_0$, its 1-*vector* part (or vector part) $\langle A \rangle_1$, its 2-*vector* part (or bivector part) $\langle A \rangle_2$, its 3-*vector* part (or trivector part) $\langle A \rangle_3$, and in general its *n-vector* part $\langle A \rangle_n$. A multivector $A \in G_n$ is called *homogeneous* of grade r if $A = \langle A \rangle_r$.

It will be convenient to define other products between the elements of this algebra which will allow us to set up several geometric relations (unions, intersections, projections, etc.) between different geometric entities (points, lines, planes, spheres, etc.) in a very simple way.

Firstly, we define the *inner product* $a \cdot b$, and the *exterior or wedge product* $a \wedge b$, of any two 1-*vectors* a and b, as the *symmetric* and *antisymmetric* parts of the geometric product ab, respectively. That is, using the expression

$$ab = \frac{1}{2}(ab + ba) + \frac{1}{2}(ab - ba) \tag{4}$$

we can define the inner product

$$a \cdot b = \frac{1}{2}(ab + ba) \tag{5}$$

and the outer or wedge product

$$a \wedge b = \frac{1}{2}(ab - ba). \tag{6}$$

Now, from (4), (5) and (6) we can express the geometric product of two vectors as

$$ab = a \cdot b + a \wedge b. \tag{7}$$

From (5) and (6), $a \cdot b = b \cdot a$, and $a \wedge b = -b \wedge a$.

Now we can define the inner and outer products for more general elements. For any two homogeneous multivectors A_r and B_s of grades r and s, we define the *inner product*

$$A_r \cdot B_s = \begin{cases} \langle A_r B_s \rangle_{|r-s|} & \text{if } r > 0 \text{ and } s > 0 \\ 0 & \text{if } r = 0 \text{ or } s = 0 \end{cases} \tag{8}$$

and the *outer or wedge product*

$$A_r \wedge B_s = \langle A_r B_s \rangle_{r+s}. \tag{9}$$

By definition, for a scalar α and a homogeneous multivector A, $\alpha \cdot A = 0$ and $\alpha \wedge A = \alpha A$. The *dual*, A^*, of the multivector A is defined as $A^* = AI_n^{-1}$ where $I_n \equiv e_{12\cdots n}$ is the *unit pseudoscalar* of G_n. And the inverse of a multivector A, if it exists, is defined by the equation $A^{-1}A = 1$.

We say that an homogeneous vector A_r is an r-*blade* or a *blade of grade* r if $A_r = a_1 \wedge a_2 \wedge \cdots \wedge a_r$, for 1-vectors a_1, a_2,..., a_r and $A_r \neq 0$.

From (8) it can be said that the inner product $A_r \cdot B_s$ *lowers the grade of* A_r *by s units* when $r \geq s > 0$, and from equation (9) that the outer product $A_r \wedge B_s$ *raises the grade of* A_r *by s units* for every $r, s \geq 0$.

The manipulation of multivectors is easier with the use of the next recursively equality of two blades $A_r = a_1 \wedge a_2 \wedge \cdots \wedge a_r$, and $B_s = b_1 \wedge b_2 \wedge \cdots \wedge b_s$,

$$A_r \cdot B_s = \begin{cases} \left((a_1 \wedge a_2 \wedge \cdots \wedge a_r) \cdot b_1 \right) \cdot (b_2 \wedge b_3 \wedge \cdots \wedge b_s) & \text{if } r \geq s \\ (a_1 \wedge a_2 \wedge \cdots \wedge a_{r-1}) \cdot \left(a_r \cdot (b_1 \wedge b_2 \wedge \cdots \wedge b_s) \right) & \text{if } r < s \end{cases} \tag{10}$$

where

$$(a_1 \wedge a_2 \wedge \cdots \wedge a_r) \cdot b_1 = \sum_{i=1}^{r} (-1)^{r-i} a_1 \wedge \cdots \wedge a_{i-1} \wedge (a_i \cdot b_1) \wedge a_{i+1} \wedge \cdots \wedge a_r , \tag{11}$$

and

$$a_r \cdot (b_1 \wedge b_2 \wedge \cdots \wedge b_s) = \sum_{i=1}^{s} (-1)^{i-1} b_1 \wedge \cdots \wedge b_{i-1} \wedge (a_r \cdot b_i) \wedge b_{i+1} \wedge \cdots \wedge b_s . \tag{12}$$

2.2 Conformal Geometric Algebra

The geometric algebra of a 3D Euclidean space $G_{3,0,0}$ has a point basis and the motor algebra $G_{3,0,1}$ a line basis. In the latter the lines expressed in terms of Plücker coordinates can be used to represent points and planes as well, [Bayro-Corrochano et al., 2000]. In the conformal geometric algebra the unit element is the sphere, which will allow us to represent other entities. We begin giving an introduction in conformal geometric algebra following the same formulation presented in [Li et al., 2001] and [Bayro-Corrochano, 2001] and showing how the Euclidean vector space R^n is represented in $R^{n+1,1}$.

Let $R^{n+1,1}$ be the vector space with an orthonormal vector basis given by $\{e_1,...,e_n,e_+,e_-\}$, with the property (1) expressed as:

$$e_i^2 = 1, \; e_+^2 = 1, \; e_-^2 = -1, \tag{13}$$

$$e_i \cdot e_+ = e_i \cdot e_- = e_+ \cdot e_- = 0 \tag{14}$$

for $i = 1, \ldots, n$. Now, we define the *null basis* $\{e_0, e_\infty\}$ as

$$e_0 = \frac{1}{2}(e_- - e_+),\tag{15}$$

$$e_\infty = e_- + e_+\tag{16}$$

where from (4) and (5) we have the properties

$$e_0^2 = e_\infty^2 = 0, \ e_\infty \cdot e_0 = -1.\tag{17}$$

A unit pseudoscalar $E \in R^{1,1}$, representing the Minkowski plane, is defined by

$$E = e_\infty \wedge e_0,\tag{18}$$

and from (10), (11), (12), (17) and (18) we have that

$$E^2 = (e_\infty \wedge e_0) \cdot (e_\infty \wedge e_0) = ((e_\infty \wedge e_0) \cdot e_\infty) \cdot e_0 = (e_\infty \wedge (e_0 \cdot e_\infty) - (e_\infty \cdot e_\infty) \wedge e_0) \cdot e_0,\tag{19}$$

$$= (e_\infty \wedge (-1) - (0) \wedge e_0) \cdot e_0 = -e_\infty \cdot e_0 = 1,\tag{20}$$

that is, for the Minkowski plane E, $E^2 = 1$.

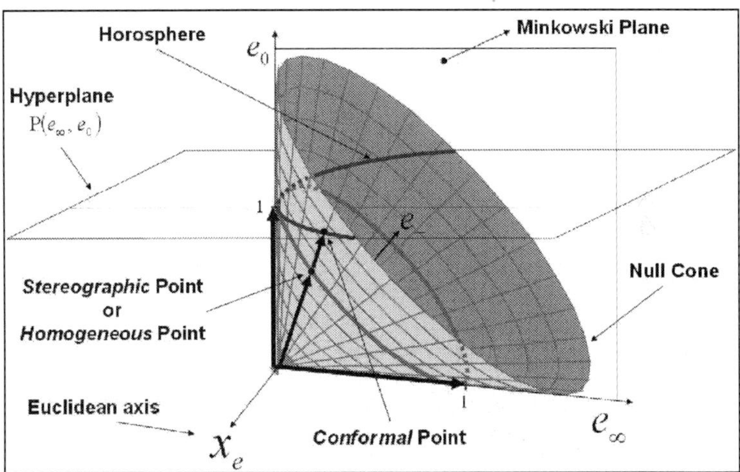

Fig. 2. The one dimensional null cone.

One of the results of the non-Euclidean geometry demonstrated by Nikolai Lobachevsky in the XIX century is that in spaces with hyperbolic structure we can find subsets which are isomorphic to a Euclidean space. In order to do this, Lobachevsky introduced two constraints to the now so-called *conformal point* $x_c \in R^{n+1,1}$. See Figure 2. The first constraint is the *homogeneous* representation of the conformal point x_c, which is obtained by the *normalization*

$$x_c \cdot e_\infty = -1 , \tag{21}$$

and the second constraint is to made the conformal point a *null vector*, that is,

$$x_c^2 = 0 . \tag{22}$$

Thus, conformal points are required to lie in the intersection space, denoted N_e^n, between the *null cone* N^{n+1} and the *hyperplane* $P(e_\infty, e_0)$, that is

$$N_e^n = N^{n+1} \cap P(e_\infty, e_0) = \left\{ x_c \in R^{n+1,1} \mid \; x_c^2 = 0, \; x_c \cdot e_\infty = -1 \right\}. \tag{23}$$

The constraints (21) and (22) define an isomorphic mapping between the Euclidean and the conformal space. Thus, for each conformal point $x_c \in R^{n+1,1}$ there is a unique Euclidean point $x_e \in R^n$ and unique scalars α, β such that the mapping $x_e \mapsto x_c = x_e + \alpha\, e_\infty + \beta\, e_0$ is bijective. From (21) and (22) we can now obtain the values of the scalars, $\alpha = \frac{1}{2} x_e^2$ and $\beta = 1$. Then, the *standard form* of a conformal point x_c is

$$x_c = x_e + \frac{1}{2} x_e^2 \, e_\infty + e_0 . \tag{24}$$

3. Orthogonal Expansion in Spherical Coordinates

We use the spherical coordinates as a parameterization of S^2. Let θ be the meridian angle measure from the north pole which is called colatitude or polar angle. Let ϕ the angle measure on the equator in a counter-clockwise direction, and where $\phi = 0$ correspond to the x-axis. ϕ is called azimuth or longitude. By definition $\theta \in [0, \pi]$ and $\phi \in [0, 2\pi)$. See Figure 3. Thus, any point $u = u(\theta, \phi) \in S^2$ has a unique representation on the unit sphere as $u = (\cos\phi \sin\theta, \sin\phi \sin\theta, \cos\theta)$. The unit sphere in the Euclidean space R^3 is a two dimensional surface denoted as S^2 defined by the constraint $x_1^2 + x_2^2 + x_3^2 = 1$. If f is a real-valued function on S^2, its integral is performed as

$$\int_{S^2} f\, ds = \int_{\phi=0}^{2\pi} \int_{\theta=0}^{\pi} f(\theta, \phi) \sin(\theta)\, d\theta\, d\phi . \tag{25}$$

Since sine function is defined only for μ, the volume element in (25) can be viewed as the product of the volume elements $[0, \pi]$ and S^2, with the weighting factor $\sin(\theta)$.

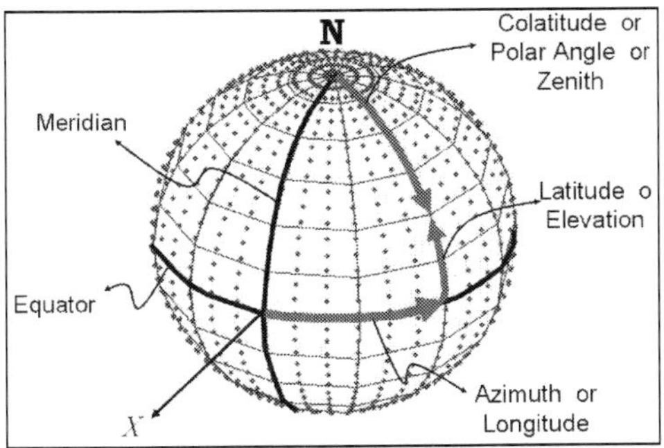

Fig. 3. Parametrization of S^2 with band-limit bw.

This allows us to use the Sturm-Liouville theory to generate orthogonal functions in these two domains separately. From classical theory an orthogonal basis for $L^2(S^1)$ is the set $\{e^{im\phi}\}_{m \in Z}$ where S^1 is the unit circle and L^2 the Hilbert space of square integrable functions. Likewise, an orthogonal basis for $L^2([-1,1], dx)$ is given by the Legendre polynomials $P_l(x)$. Using the change of variable $x = \cos(\theta)$, the functions

$$\sqrt{\frac{2l+1}{2}}\, P_l(\theta) \tag{26}$$

are an orthogonal basis of the space $L^2([0, \pi], \sin(\theta)d\theta)$, and the set of functions

$$\sqrt{\frac{2l+1}{4\pi}}\, P_l(\theta) e^{im\phi} \tag{27}$$

where $l = 0,1,2,\ldots$, and $m \in Z$, form a complete orthonormal set of functions on the sphere S^2. It is much more common to choose the associated Legendre functions $\{P_l^m(\theta)\}$, where each integer $m \in Z$ satisfy $|m| \le l$. Thus, the elements of the orthogonal basis that we need to expand functions on the sphere are of the form

$$Y_l^m(\theta, \phi) = \sqrt{\frac{(2l+1)(l-m)!}{4\pi(l+m)!}}\, P_l^m(\cos\theta) e^{im\phi}, \tag{28}$$

and they are called *spherical harmonics*. Then, given any function $f \in L^2\!\left(S^2\right)$, its spherical Fourier series is given as

$$f(\theta,\phi) = \sum_{l=0}^{\infty} \sum_{m=-l}^{l} \hat{f}(l,m)\, Y_l^m(\theta,\phi),$$
(29)

where

$$\hat{f}(l,m) = \int_{S^2} f\, \overline{Y_l^m}\, ds .$$
(30)

Each coefficient $\hat{f}(l,m)$ will be called the *spherical Fourier transform* of $f(\theta,\phi)$, and the set $\{\hat{f}(l,m)\}$ is called the *spectrum on the sphere* of $f(\theta,\phi)$. The spherical harmonics $Y_l^m(\theta,\phi)$ are the usual common functions used to expand functions on the sphere because they are eigenfunctions of the Laplacian operator. Indeed, for a constant radius $r = 1$ the Laplacian of a smooth function f in spherical coordinates is given as

$$\nabla^2(f) = \frac{1}{\sin(\theta)}\frac{\partial}{\partial\theta}\left(\sin(\theta)\frac{\partial f}{\partial\theta}\right) + \frac{1}{\sin^2(\theta)}\frac{\partial^2 f}{\partial\phi^2} .$$
(31)

In analogy with the Sturm-Liouville theory, an eigenfunction of the Laplacian operator is defined as

$$\nabla^2(f) = \lambda f$$
(32)

for some eigenvalues λ. Moreover, in spherical coordinates the boundary conditions are periodic in the variable ϕ, that is, $f(\theta,\phi+2\pi) = f(\theta,\phi)$, and a solution set of eigenfunctions of the Laplacian (32) is the set of spherical harmonics (28) with eigenvalue $\lambda = -l(l+1)$.

4. Representation Theory on SO(3)

From a classical result of linear algebra a matrix $\dot{R}$ is a *rotation matrix* or a *special orthogonal matrix* if and only if $RR^T = I$, where I is the identity matrix, and the determinant satisfies $\det(R) = +1$. Let $SO(3)$ be the *special orthogonal group* or *rotation group* for three dimensional space.

In the same way that with the square integrable functions on the unit circle or on the line, we can say that a function is square integrable on the space $L^2(SO(3))$ if

$$\int_{SO(3)} |f(R)|^2 d(R) < \infty .$$
(33)

$L^2(SO(3))$ is a vector space with the usual addition and scalar multiplication, that is, $(f+g)(R)=f(R)+g(R)$ and $(\alpha f)(R)=\alpha f(R)$.

We can now define the convolution of two functions f and $g \in L^2(SO(3))$ as

$$(f*g)(R)=\int_{SO(3)} f(Q)g(Q^{-1}R)d(R).$$

(34)

See [Chirikjian & Kyatkin, 2001]. On the contrary to the classical case, the convolution on $L^2(SO(3))$ is not a
commutative product.
With the Euler parameterization ZYZ now we can state one of the most important properties of the spherical harmonics

$$Y_l^n(R^T\eta)=\sum_{|k|\le l} U_{kn}^l(R)Y_l^k(\eta)$$

(35)

where $\eta \in S^2$, $R \in SO(3)$ and the $(2l+1)\times(2l+1)$ unitary matrices U^l are the irreducible representation of $SO(3)$, where their components are given as

$$U_{mn}^l(R(\alpha,\beta,\gamma))=i^{m-n}e^{-im\alpha}P_{mn}^l(\cos\beta)e^{-in\gamma},$$

(36)

and P_{mn}^l are the generalized associated Legendre functions . In fact, the unitary matrices U^l are the representation group of $SO(3)$ and they constitute a basis which can be used to obtain a Fourier transform on the rotation group, that is

$$f(R)=\sum_l \sum_{|m|\le l} \sum_{|k|\le l} \hat{f}_{mk}^l U_{mk}^l(R)$$

(37)

where the Fourier coefficients of f on the rotation group $SO(3)$ are

$$\hat{f}_{mk}^l = \int_{R\in SO(3)} f(R)\overline{U_{mk}^l(R)}\,dR.$$

(38)

Now, from (35) we can obtain a *shift theorem*, relating the coefficients of the rotation functions

$$h(\eta)=f(R^{-1}\eta) \quad \Leftrightarrow \quad \hat{h}_m^l = \sum_{|k|\le l}\hat{f}_k^l U_{mk}^l(R).$$

(39)

This *shift theorem* is telling us that the effect caused by a rotation R on a spherical function f, is equivalent in the Fourier space to the effect of the Fourier coefficients $\hat{f}_k^l$ by the unitary matrices U_{mk}^l of the irreducible representation of $SO(3)$. More explicitly, while the spherical functions are rotated by orthogonal matrices, the Fourier coefficients of longitude $(2l+1)$ are affected by the unitary matrices U^l.

As expected, this theory can be extended to the direct product group $SO(3) \times SO(3)$ acting on the homogenous space $S^2 \times S^2$. Thus, the expansion of functions on $S^2 \times S^2$ is given as

$$f(\omega_1,\omega_2) = \sum_{l \in N} \sum_{|m| \leq l} \sum_{n \in N} \sum_{|p| \leq n} \hat{f}_{np}^{ln} Y_l^m(\omega_1) Y_n^p(\omega_2) \tag{40}$$

where the Fourier transform on $S^2 \times S^2$ is

$$\hat{f}_{mp}^{ln} = \int_{\omega_1 \in S^2} \int_{\omega_2 \in S^2} f(\omega_1,\omega_2) \overline{Y_l^m(\omega_1) Y_n^p(\omega_2)} d\omega_1 d\omega_2 . \tag{41}$$

Also, a *shift theorem* exists for functions on $S^2 \times S^2$ given as

$$h(\omega_1,\omega_2) = f\left(R_1^T \omega_1, R_2^T \omega_2\right) \quad \Leftrightarrow \quad \hat{h}_{mp}^{ln} = \sum_{|r| \leq l} \sum_{|q| \leq n} U_{rm}^l(R_1) U_{qp}^n(R_2) \hat{f}_{rq}^{ln} . \tag{42}$$

These expressions have been used in [Makadia et al., 2005] and [Makadia & Daniilidis, 2003] to obtain the Euler angles of a 3D rotation, using the *point correlation* of two given images without correspondences.

5. Radon Transform with Lines

In this section we will extend the way of obtain the Euler angles of a 3D rotation as presented in [Makadia et al., 2005]. As these authors used correlation between *points* of two images, we will use *lines* instead of points. Note that lines are less noise sensitive. From [Makadia et al., 2005] the Radon transform on points is defined as

$$G(R,t) = \int_{p \in S^2} \int_{q \in S^2} g(p,q) \Delta(Rp,q,t) \, dp \, dq \tag{43}$$

where the *similarity* function g is based on the SIFT points. See [Lowe, 2004] for details of the SIFT algorithm. For sake of simplicity from now on we will call *sift points* to the sift descriptors returned by the SIFT algorithm. The Δ function is the Kronecker delta function relating the points of two images with the epipolar constraint of a stereo camera system. Now, to extend the Radon transform to a correlation of lines to estimate pure rotations, we need to define analogue *similarity* and *delta* functions for lines, instead of points, as well as a *constraint* for lines instead of the epipolar constraint for points.

Let $R \in SO(3)$ be a 3D rotation relating two 3D lines, l and l' which were projected to two omnidirectional images $Im1$ and $Im2$. Then we can write $l' = R\,l$ or $l = R^T l'$. The three dimensional line l is associated to a great circle C on the sphere S^2. Let $\eta \in S^2$ be an orthogonal vector to the plane containing the great circle C, then η and $R^T l'$ are orthogonal, that is, $\eta^T R^T l' = 0$. We will use this constraint as the delta function to define our desired integral, that is, as the constraint for lines. Thus, the integral of the *Radon transform on lines* would be

$$G(R) = \int_{l' \in S^2} \int_{\eta \in S^2} g(\eta, l')\, \Delta\!\left(\eta^T R^T l'\right) d\eta\, dl' \tag{44}$$

where g is a *similarity function* between the lines of both images and Δ the delta Kronecker function over the constraint with lines. So, (44) can be used as a correlation function between g and Δ, where g , $\Delta : S^2 \times S^2 \rightarrow \{0,1\}$.

Although we know how to calculate the analytical expressions of the continuous Fourier and Radon transforms in spherical coordinates, it is necessary a discretization process for their applications with real omnidirectional images. Thus, given a function on the space $L^2\!\left(S^2\right)$ with band-limit bw, its spherical Fourier transform SFT can be obtained with the FFT algorithm of order $O\!\left((bw)^2 \log^2(bw)\right)$ on S^2, see [Driscoll & Healy, 1994] for details. Similarly, we can use the FFT algorithm of order $O\!\left((bw)^3 \log^2(bw)\right)$ in the case of the rotation space $SO(3)$, see [Kostelec & Rockmore, 2003] for details.

Then, applying the spherical Fourier expansion (40) to the similarity function g of (44), we have that

$$g(\omega_1, \omega_2) = \sum_{l_1=0}^{bw-1} \sum_{|m_1| \le l_1} \sum_{l_2=0}^{bw-1} \sum_{|m_2| \le l_2} \hat{g}^{\,l_1 l_2}_{m_1 m_2}\, Y^{m_1}_{l_1}(\omega_1)\, Y^{m_2}_{l_2}(\omega_2), \tag{45}$$

where we used $g(\omega_1, \omega_2)$ instead of $g(\eta, l')$ to simplify notation. Likewise, we get $\Delta(\omega_1, R\omega_2)$, the expansion of the Δ function for each $(\omega_1, \omega_2) \in S^2 \times S^2$ and $R \in SO(3)$ as

$$\Delta(\omega_1, R\omega_2) = \sum_{p_1=0}^{bw-1} \sum_{|k_1| \le p_1} \sum_{p_2=0}^{bw-1} \sum_{|k_2| \le p_2} \hat{\Delta}^{\,p_1 p_2}_{k_1 k_2}(R)\, Y^{k_1}_{p_1}(\omega_1)\, Y^{k_2}_{p_2}(\omega_2). \tag{46}$$

Now, because $0 = \omega_1^T R \omega_2 = \left(\omega_1^T R \omega_2\right)^T = \omega_2^T R^T \omega_1$, we can write $\hat{\Delta}_{k_1 k_2}^{p_1 p_2}\left(\omega_1, R^T \omega_2\right)$ instead of $\hat{\Delta}_{k_1 k_2}^{p_1 p_2}(R)$ in (46), and by the shift theorem

$$\Delta_{k_1 k_2}^{p_1 p_2}\left(\omega_1, R^T \omega_2\right) = \sum_{|b| \leq p_2} U_{bk_2}^{p_2}(R) \hat{\Delta}_{k_1 b}^{p_1 p_2} , \tag{47}$$

where $\hat{\Delta}_{k_1 b}^{p_1 p_2} \equiv \hat{\Delta}_{k_1 b}^{p_1 p_2}\left(\omega_1, \omega_2\right)$.

Substituting (45), (46) and (47) in the Radon transform on lines (44) we get

$$G(R) = \int_{\omega_1 \in S^2} \int_{\omega_2 \in S^2} \left(B_1\right)\left(B_2\right) d\omega_1 \, d\omega_2 \tag{48}$$

where

$$B_1 = \sum_{l_1} \sum_{|m_1| \leq l_1} \sum_{l_2} \sum_{|m_2| \leq l_2} g_{m_1 m_2}^{l_1 l_2} \, Y_{l_1}^{m_1}\left(\omega_1\right) Y_{l_2}^{m_2}\left(\omega_2\right), \tag{49}$$

$$B_2 = \sum_{p_1} \sum_{|k_1| \leq p_1} \sum_{p_2} \sum_{|k_2| \leq p_2} \left(B_3\right) \overline{Y_{p_1}^{k_1}\left(\omega_1\right) Y_{p_2}^{k_2}\left(\omega_2\right)} \tag{50}$$

and

$$B_3 = \sum_{|b| \leq p_2} \overline{U_{bk_2}^{p_2}(R) \hat{\Delta}_{k_1 b}^{p_1 p_2}} . \tag{51}$$

Interchanging integrals and summation in (48) we can write it now as

$$G(R) = \sum_{l_1} \sum_{|m_1| \leq l_1} \sum_{l_2} \sum_{|m_2| \leq l_2} \sum_{p_1} \sum_{|k_1| \leq p_1} \sum_{p_2} \sum_{|k_2| \leq p_2} \left(D_1\right)\left(D_2\right)\left(D_3\right), \tag{52}$$

where

$$D_1 = \sum_{|b| \leq p_2} g_{m_1 m_2}^{l_1 l_2} \, \overline{U_{bk_2}^{p_2}(R) \hat{\Delta}_{k_1 b}^{p_1 p_2}} , \tag{53}$$

$$D_2 = \int_{\omega_1 \in S^2} Y_{l_1}^{m_1}\left(\omega_1\right) \overline{Y_{p_1}^{k_1}\left(\omega_1\right)} \, d\omega_1 \tag{54}$$

and

$$D_3 = \int_{\omega_2 \in S^2} Y_{l_2}^{m_2}(\omega_2)\, \overline{Y_{p_2}^{k_2}(\omega_2)}\, d\omega_2 . \tag{55}$$

Now, applying the orthonormal property

$$\int_{\omega \in S^2} Y_l^m(\omega)\overline{Y_{l'}^{m'}(\omega)}\, d\omega = \delta_{ll'}\delta_{mm'} , \tag{56}$$

to (54) and (55), the expression (48) for the Radon transform $G(R)$ is reduced now to

$$G(R) = \sum_{l_1} \sum_{|m_1| \le l_1} \sum_{l_2} \sum_{|m_2| \le l_2} \sum_{b \le p_2} g_{m_1 m_2}^{l_1 l_2}\, \overline{\hat{A}_{m_1 b}^{l_1 l_2}}\, U_{b m_2}^{l_2}(R). \tag{57}$$

We know that in $SO(3)$ the unitary elements U's are an orthonormal set too, that is,

$$\int_{R \in SO(3)} U_{mk}^l(R)\overline{U_{m'k'}^{l'}(R)}\, dR = \delta_{ll'}\delta_{mm'}\delta_{kk'} . \tag{58}$$

Then, for each $l_2' = 0,1,\ldots,(bw-1)$ and b', $m_2' \in \{-l_2',\ldots,-1,0,1,\ldots,l_2'\}$ we can multiply (57) by $U_{b'm_2'}^{l_2'}(R)$, and take the integration on $SO(3)$ to obtain

$$\int_{R \in SO(3)} G(R) U_{b'm_2'}^{l_2'}\, dR = \sum_{l_1} \sum_{|m_1| \le l_1} \sum_{l_2} \sum_{|m_2| \le l_2} \sum_{b \le p_2} g_{m_1 m_2}^{l_1 l_2}\, \overline{\hat{A}_{m_1 b}^{l_1 l_2}} \int_{R \in SO(3)} U_{b'm_2'}^{l_2'}(R)\overline{U_{b m_2}^{l_2}(R)}\, dR \tag{59}$$

and from (58)

$$\int_{R \in SO(3)} G(R) U_{b'm_2'}^{l_2'}\, dR = \sum_{l_1} \sum_{|m_1| \le l_1} g_{m_1 m_2'}^{l_1 l_2'}\, \overline{\hat{A}_{m_1 b'}^{l_1 l_2'}} . \tag{60}$$

From (60) we can have now the 3D Fourier transform $\hat{G}$ of G on $SO(3)$. Indeed, rewriting indices without primes in (60), the Fourier transform $\hat{G}$ of G on the rotation group $SO(3)$ is given as

$$\hat{G} = \left(\hat{G}_{b m_2}^{l_2} \right) \tag{61}$$

where $l_2 = 0,1,\ldots,(bw-1)$ and b, $m_2 \in \{-l_2,\ldots,-1,0,1,\ldots,l_2\}$, and

$$\hat{G}_{b m_2}^{l_2} = \sum_{l_1} \sum_{|m_1| \le l_1} g_{m_1 m_2}^{l_1 l_2}\, \overline{\hat{A}_{m_1 b}^{l_1 l_2}} . \tag{62}$$

The expressions (61) and (62) obtained for lines and a pure rotation is consistent with the formula for points obtained in [Makadia et al., 2005].

6. Radon Transform with Lines using Conformal Geometric Algebra

The conformal geometric algebra is a mathematical framework that helps to unify matrices, vectors, transformations, complex numbers in one unique theory using the geometric product, with its inner and wedge products, to generate the former mathematical concepts. Let $R \in SO(3)$ be a rotation relating two 3D lines, L_1 and L_2, which were projected to two omnidirectional images Im1 and Im2 using the equivalent sphere as depicted in Figure 1 . In conformal geometric algebra the 3D rotation can be expressed as $R = e^{-\frac{\varphi}{2}\hat{n}}$, where $\hat{n}$ is unit bivector which represents the dual of the rotation axis, and the φ angle, which represents the amount of the rotation. Then, these lines satisfy $L_2 = RL_1 R^{-1}$, where the lines are expressed in conformal form too, that is, the dual form is $L_j^* = x_{j1} \wedge x_{j2} \wedge e_\infty$, $j \in \{1,2\}$ for two points $x_{j1}, x_{j2} \in L_j^*$. Using the origin e_0 of the conformal space, we can obtain the planes Π_j generated by the 3D line L_j and the origin e_0, that is, the dual planes are

$$\Pi_j^* = L_j^* \wedge e_0 = x_{j1} \wedge x_{j2} \wedge e_\infty \wedge e_0 = x_{j1} \wedge x_{j2} \wedge E , \tag{63}$$

where E represents the Minkowski plane. The intersection these planes and the unit sphere S^2 are two great circles, expressed by the multivector $\eta_j^* = z_{j1} \wedge z_{j2} \wedge z_{j3}$, with dual orthogonal axis η_j, where z_j are conformal points on the great circle. Thus, if $L_2 = RL_1 R^{-1}$, then the dual plane $\Pi_1^* = L_1^* \wedge e_0$ is orthogonal to the dual orthogonal axis η_2 of the dual plane $\Pi_2^* = L_2^* \wedge e_0$, and

$$\Pi_1^* \cdot \eta_2^* = 0 , \tag{64}$$

that is

$$(x_{11} \wedge x_{12} \wedge E) \cdot (z_{21} \wedge z_{22} \wedge z_{23}) / I = 0 , \tag{65}$$

where I is the unit pseudoscalar of the five dimensional conformal space. Thus, we have a correspondence between 3D points obtained from x_{11} and $x_{12} \in L_1$ and points η_2 on the unit sphere S^2. Then the characteristic function Δ must obey the constraint for lines

$$\Delta(R\eta_1, \eta_2) = \delta\left((R\eta_1 R^{-1}) \cdot \eta_2\right) = \begin{cases} 1 & if & \left|(R\eta_1 R^{-1}) \cdot \eta_2\right| < \varepsilon \\ 0 & other\ case \end{cases} , \tag{66}$$

for $\varepsilon > 0$ depending of the band-limit used in the discretization process. Thus, the characteristic function (66) is measuring how close the two lines L_1 and L_2 are.

Finally, following the work in [Makadia & Daniilidis, 2003] and [Makadia et al., 2005], we take the similarity function as

$$g\left(l_1, l_2\right) = e^{-\left| l_1 - l_2 \right|}, \tag{67}$$

where $\left| \cdot \right|$ is the Euclidean norm and l_1 and l_2 are the 128-dimensional sift vectors of the sift algorithm applied to each omnidirectional image. See Figure 4.

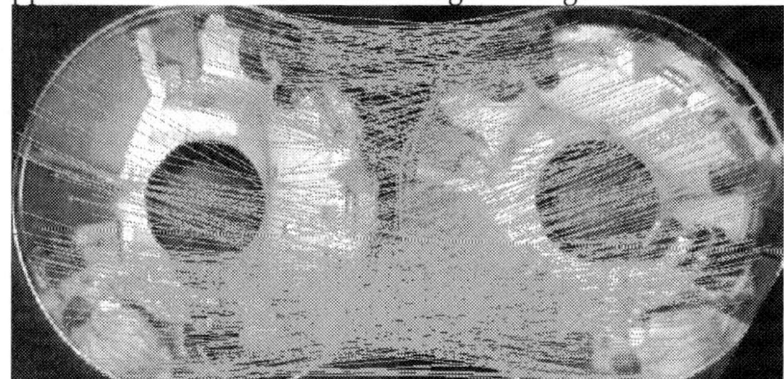

Fig. 4. SIFT descriptors between two omnidirectional images related by a rotation.

Notice that in the Radon transform with lines (44) the domain of the integral is now on the unit sphere but in conformal representation.
Future implementations with real and simulated images will be used to verify and compare the efficiency of the theory with respect to the works in [Makadia et al., 2005] and [Falcon & Bayro-Corrochano, 2007].

7. Conclusions

This chapter can give us an idea about how conformal geometric algebra can be used with traditional mathematical theory in order to expand the applications of this almost forgotten framework. The authors believe that this theoretical framework can be used to obtain different approximations to old and new computer vision problems. The author believe the use of harmonic analysis based on Radon transform using lines and conformal geometric algebra on incidence algebra is promising for omnidirectional image processing.

8. References

Arfken, G. & Weber, H. (1966). *Mathematical methods for physicists,4th Edition*, Academic Press, ISBN 0-12-059816-7, San Diego, CA.
Bayro-Corrochano, E. (2001). *Computing for perception action systems*, Springer, ISBN 0387951911, Boston.
Bayro-Corrochano, E.; Daniilidis, K. & Sommer, G. (2000). Motor algebra for 3D kinematics: The case of the hand-eye calibration. *Journal of Mathematical Imaging and Vision*, Vol. 13, No. 2, October 2000, 79-100, ISSN 0924-9907.

Chirikjian, G. & Kyatkin, A. (2001). *Engineering Applications of Noncommutative Harmonic Analysis, with emphasis on rotation and motion groups*, CRC Press, ISBN 0-8493-0748-1, Boca Raton, Florida.

Driscoll, J. R. & Healy, D. M. (1994). Computing Fourier transform and convolutions on the 2-sphere. *Advances in Applied Mathematics*, Vol. 15, No. 2, June 1994, 202-250, ISSN 0196-8858.

Falcon-Morales, L. & Bayro-Corrochano, E. (2007). Radon transform and harmonical analysis using lines for 3D rotation estimation without correspondences for omnidirectional vision. *Proceedings of IEEE International Conference on Computer Vision*, pp. , ISBN, Rio de Janeiro, October 2007, Rio de Janeiro, Brazil.

Geyer, Ch. ; Sastry, S. & Bajcsy, R. (2004). Euclid meets Fourier : Applying harmonic analysis to essential matrix estimation in omnidirectional cameras, *Proceedings of workshop on omnidirectional vision, camera networks and non-classical cameras*, Prague, Czech Republic, May 2004.

Geyer, Ch. & Daniilidis, K. (2000). A unifying theory for central panoramic systems and practical applications, *Proceedings Part II, 6th European Conference on Computer Vision, ECCV'00*, Vol. 1843, pp. 445-461, ISBN 3-540-67686-4, Dublin, Ireland, June 2000, Springer.

Hestenes, D. & Sobczyk, G. (1984). *Clifford algebra to geometric calculus: a unified language for mathematics and physics*, D. Reidel Publishing Company, ISBN 90-277-2561-6, Dordrecht, Holland.

Kostelec, P. & Rockmore, D. (2008). FFTs on the Rotation Group. *Journal of Fourier and Applications*, Vol. 14, No. 2, April 2008, 145-179, ISSN 1069-5869.

Li, H. ; Hestenes, D. & Rockwood, A. (2001). Generalized homogeneous coordinates for computational geometry, In: *Geometric computing with Clifford Algebras, theoretical foundations and applications in computer vision and robotics*, Sommer, G. (Ed.), 27-59, Springer, ISBN 3-540-41198-4, Berlin.

Lowe, D. (2004). Sift (scale invariant feature transform): Distinctive image features from scale-invariant keypoints. *International Journal of Computer Vision*, Vol. 60, No. 2, November 2004, 91-110, ISSN 0920-5691.

Makadia, A ; Geyer, Ch. ; Sastry, S. & Daniilidis, K. (2005). Radon-based structure from motion without correspondences, *Proceedings of Computer Vision and Pattern Recognition*, Vol. 1, pp. 796-803, San Diego, CA, June 2005.

Makadia, A.; & Daniilidis, K. (2003). Direct 3D-rotation estimation from spherical images via a generalized shift theorem, *Proceedings of IEEEConference on Computer Vision and Pattern Recognition*, Vol. 2, pp. 217-224, Madison, 2003.

## 11

Block-Diagonal Forms of Distance Matrices for Partition Based Image Retrieval

Dmitry Kinoshenko, Vladimir Mashtalir and Elena Yegorova
Kharkov National University of Radio Electronics
Ukraine

1. Introduction

Rapid expanding of the multimedia data collections volume brings forward the need for visual data efficient organization, storing and search methods. It stipulated diversity of investigations directed to creating efficient image retrieval methods satisfying performance speed and validity requirements. The indexing efficiency is generally evaluated by parameters of storage access number, computational expenses of the index structure search and number of operations for the distance computation between query representation and objects in the database. As image processing requires a lot of time and resources the most efficient practical way to reduce search time expenses is creation of indexing structure on the preliminary processing stage. Unfortunately, existing indexing methods are not applicable to a wide range of problem-oriented fields due to their operating time limitations and strong dependency on the traditional descriptors extracted from the image.

One of the most promising perspective in multimedia data search, storing and interpretation is to represent images as segmentation results and define metrics for their comparison such as Minkowski-type metric (including Euclidean and Manhattan distances), Mahalanobis metric, EMD, histogram metric, metric for probability density functions, sets of entropy metrics, pseudo metrics for semantic image classification (Rubner et al., 2000; Cheng et al., 2005; Wang et al., 2005). Yet, because of their limitations these metrics cannot give the desirable results, so a new metric was introduced and extended for considering the embedded partitions and it was effectively used for the content image retrieval (Kinoshenko et al., 2007). Due to the nested structure it becomes possible to perform the search with different level of refinement or roughening.

Using the region based image retrieval methods allows to make a step towards overcoming the semantic gap between law-level image description and high level conception. But from the other hand it definitely leads to increase of the computation complexity of image processing and distance calculation operations methods. Thus when creating an efficient indexing structure for image database one should first consider the methods providing minimal number of matching operations.

Many of multidimensional indexing methods used in the field of text retrieval were modified and improved in order to index high-dimensional image content descriptors. Among them X-trees, VA-file and I-Distance approaches are the most promising (Bohm et al., 2001). However, in case of comparing images as nested partitions there is no features to describe complex objects and only information about distances between them is available, and so-called 'distance-based' indexing methods come to the aid (Chavez et al., 2001; Hjaltason, Samet, 2003). In this work existing 'distance-based' indexing methods are analyzed and improved and their possible application for the region-based image retrieval is considered.

Often on the pre-processing analysis stage we have only information of the mutual distance between the database objects. In this case such indexing methods as X-trees, VA-file, i-Distance, cannot be used as there is not enough information about objects coordinates. One of the possible solutions of this problem is to create an indexing structure based on the triangular inequality axiom. This principle lays in the base of metrical indexing methods. Here a distance matrix is formed and analysed for some selection of special objects subset (these objects are called pivots). Forming different data structures allows to eliminate from the consideration whole families of images situated far from the query at the search stage.

Clustering methods are often used for the image database preliminary processing. Thus we consider a possible hierarchical mechanism of the query processing: one can seek suitable clusters in nested partitions with an arbitrary indexing scheme. This way the amount of matches can be greatly reduced, but traditional clustering methods do not guarantee the optimal result.

Thus in order to optimize this Content-based image retrieval (CBIR) scheme it is necessary to minimize a total number of matches at the retrieval stage. We propose a new hierarchical clustering method which allows to construct images partitions into disjoint subsets so that firstly one can seek suitable class, then the most similar to the query subclass is chosen and so on. The exhaustive search is fulfilled only on the lowest level of hierarchy.

In this chapter we shall consider theoretical premises and methods of database images metrical indexing and find the tools providing guaranteed number of matching operations between a query and database objects.

2. Theoretical background for the CBIR distance matrix based indexing

Let $X = \{x_1, x_2, ..., x_n\}$ be a set characterising images which constitute a database. Each element of this set can be:

- image itself $B(z)$, $z \in D \subset \mathbb{R}^2$, where D is a sensor's field of view, $B(z)$ is a brightness distribution function;

- feature vector $p \in \mathbb{R}^k$ ($\mathbb{Z}^k$);

- some combination of the image processing results and features, for example segmentation results, contour preparations or regions shape features.

Then we consider $X \subseteq U$, where U is some universum which corresponds to an object-oriented field and provides introduction of the distance functional (metric in particular). Under such X we shall understand a database.

The task is to search the best suiting element (or elements) $x_i \in X$, under given query $y \in U$, which is represented (or can be brought to) by one of the listed above types. When we say "best suiting" we mean the minimal distance $\rho(y, x)$, $y \in U$.

It should be reminded that a non-negative function $\rho(y, x) \in \mathbb{R}^+$ is a metric on set U if

$\forall x, y, z \in U$ next axioms are fulfilled:

a) $\rho(x, y) = 0 \Leftrightarrow x = y$ – reflexivity;

b) $\rho(x, x) = 0$ – symmetry;

c) $\rho(x, z) \le \rho(x, y) + \rho(y, z)$ – triangular inequality.

Talking about variety of image representations we need to emphasize that if there is a set of metrics $\rho_j(x, y)$, then their non-negative linear combination $\forall \alpha_j \ge 0$ $\sum_j \alpha_j \rho_j(x, y)$ is a metric. Moreover if some nonnegative function $f : \mathbb{R}^+ \to \mathbb{R}^+$ such that $f(0) = 0$ and $f(z)$ is convex $\forall z \ge 0$, then $f(\rho(x, y))$ is a metric.

Using a metric for similarity criteria firstly provides adequacy of the search result to the query (if the choice of metric corresponding to the domain was correct), and secondly takes into account the triangular inequality, what creates premises for elimination from the consideration whole image sets without calculating distances to them. We shall note that search with limited matches number can be performed in two ways: using preliminary clustering in image or feature spaces, or considering methods which analyse values of pre-calculated distance matrix of all image collection elements. From the other hand all search algorithms can be divided into 3 groups:

- search of k most similar images ordered according to the similarity extent,
- search of the images which differ from the query on not more than given threshold δ,
- combination of these approaches.

Definition 1. (δ)- search result for the query $y \in U$ is any element (all elements) $x_i \in X$ if $\rho(y, x_i) \le \delta$ for given $\delta \ge 0$, which is called a search radius.

It is obvious that choice of δ threshold is a non trivial task. Moreover, choice of rational δ value essentially depends on configuration (mutual location in regard to the chosen metric) of the database objects. Still often the choice of this value is defined by the application, i.e. by the required similarity of the images. Note that under $\delta = 0$ we get a special case of searching the duplicates in the database.

Definition 2. Result of (k)- search for the query $y \in U$ are elements of the set $X^k = \{x_{i_1}, x_{i_2}, ..., x_{i_k}\} \subseteq X$, for which

$$\forall x_{i_j} \in X^k, \forall x \in X \setminus X^k, \forall y \in U \ \ \rho(y, x_{i_j}) \le \rho(y, x), \ \ \rho(y, x_{i_j}) \le \rho(y, x_{i_{j+1}}), j = \overline{1, k-1}.$$

There is an important special case of $y \in X, k = 1$. The exact match of the query should be found among the database elements, in other words the query should be identified and its corresponding image characteristics should be extracted. It is like identifying a person according to his finger prints.

Definition 3. The result of (δ, k)- search of query $y \in U$ are elements of the set $X^m = \{x_{i_1}, x_{i_2}, ..., x_{i_m}\} \subseteq X$, $m \le n$, for which

$$\forall x_{i_j} \in X^m, \ \forall x \in X \setminus X^m, \ \forall y \in U \ \ \rho(y, x_{i_j}) \le \delta, \ \delta \ge 0,$$

$$\rho(y, x_{i_j}) \le \rho(y, x), \ \rho(y, x_{i_j}) \le \rho(y, x_{i_{j+1}}), j = \overline{1, m-1}.$$

The search is considered as successful one if there are elements satisfying definitions 1, 2 and 3. In other case a feedback is required to refine the query object, search parameters (for example radius δ), which is closely connected to the problem of representing images as features description and matching. It should be emphasised that formally (k)- search is always successful: decision as for query refining should be made on base of obtained distances analysis and the application requirements.

Calculation of N $\rho(y, x_i)$ values can be rather expensive, especially in the image space. Let us analyse the ways to reduce the operations number. For that a symmetric pair-distances matrix of database elements can be pre-calculated

$$d(X) = \begin{pmatrix} 0 & \rho(x_1, x_2) & \rho(x_1, x_3) & \dots & \dots & \rho(x_1, x_n) \\ & 0 & \rho(x_2, x_3) & \dots & \dots & \rho(x_2, x_n) \\ & & 0 & \dots & \dots & \dots \\ & & & \dots & \dots & \dots \\ & & & & 0 & \rho(x_{n-1}, x_n) \\ & & & & & 0 \end{pmatrix}. \tag{1}$$

Let $y \in U$ be a query image. We shall fix some image $x^* \in X$, called as a pivot object (point), and consider a triangular inequality picking out one more image $x_i \in X, \ i \in \{1, 2, ..., n\}$ (the distance $\rho(x^*, x_i)$ is known)

$$\rho(y, x_i) \le \rho(y, x^*) + \rho(x^*, x_i), \tag{2}$$

$$\rho(x_i, x^*) \le \rho(y, x^*) + \rho(y, x_i), \tag{3}$$

$$\rho(y, x^*) \le \rho(y, x_i) + \rho(x_i, x^*). \tag{4}$$

From equations (1) – (3) it follows that when knowing two distances, namely: $\rho(y, x^*)$ and $\rho(x^*, x_i)$, it is not hard to obtain upper and lower distance bounds

$$\rho(x_i, x^*) - \rho(y, x^*) \mid \le \rho(y, x_i) \le \rho(y, x^*) + \rho(x_i, x^*). \tag{5}$$

Thus the implication takes place

$$\forall y \in U, \ \forall x_i, x^* \in X \ : \ \rho(x_i, x^*) \ge 2\rho(y, x^*) \Rightarrow \rho(y, x_i) \ge \rho(y, x^*). \tag{6}$$

Let us consider the case when exact value of distance $\rho(x^*, x_i)$ is unknown but can be evaluated

$$\varepsilon_{min} \le \rho(x^*, x_i) \le \varepsilon_{max}. \tag{7}$$

Then for x_i the following evaluation of the upper and lower bound of distance to y is obtained:

$$max\{\rho(y, x^*) - \varepsilon_{max}, \varepsilon_{min} - \rho(y, x^*), 0\} \le \rho(y, x_i) \le \rho(y, x^*) + \varepsilon_{max}. \qquad (8)$$

Indeed, according to the triangular inequality and (7) we get

$$\rho(y, x^*) \le \rho(y, x_i) + \rho(x_i, x^*) \le \rho(y, x_i) + \varepsilon_{max},$$

then

$$\rho(y, x^*) - \varepsilon_{max} \le \rho(y, x_i). \qquad (9)$$

From the other hand for objects x_i and x^* it is true that

$$\varepsilon_{min} \le \rho(x_i, x^*) \le \rho(y, x^*) + \rho(y, x_i),$$

from where

$$\varepsilon_{min} - \rho(y, x^*) \le \rho(y, x_i). \qquad (10)$$

Expressions (9) and (10) are the lower bounds of $\rho(x, x_i)$, and to narrow the equation condition we chose the maximal value. Also both values can be negative simultaneously, what is shown in (8). Finally, evaluation of upper bound $\rho(y, x^*)$ directly follows from the triangular inequality (2) and condition $\rho(x^*, x_i) \le \varepsilon_{max}$.

It is easy to show that if the exact value $\rho(y, x^*)$ is unknown and within the limits

$$\sigma_{min} \le \rho(y, x^*) \le \sigma_{max}, \qquad (11)$$

then the next evaluation of the lower and upper distance bound takes place:

$$max\{\sigma_{min} - \varepsilon_{max}, \varepsilon_{min} - \sigma_{max}, 0\} \le \rho(y, x_i) \le \sigma_{max} + \varepsilon_{max}. \qquad (12)$$

From (8) and inequality $\sigma_{min} - \varepsilon_{max} \le \rho(y, x^*) - \varepsilon_{max}$, $\varepsilon_{min} - \sigma_{max} \le \le \varepsilon_{min} - \rho(y, x^*)$ the left part of (12) is obvious. The left part follows from $\rho(y, x^*) + \varepsilon_{max} \le \sigma_{max} + \varepsilon_{max}$ and right part of inequality (8).

Till now for evaluating $\rho(y, x_i)$ the distance from the target object x_i to pivot point x^* and distance from x^* to the search object y were considered. It is obvious that introducing to the analysis additional pivot point $\overset{*}{x}_j$ in some cases will allow to narrow the ranking interval $\rho(x_i, y)$.

Let the object x_i be situated «closer» to the pivot point $\overset{*}{x}_1$, than to $\overset{*}{x}_2$, i.e.

$$\rho(x_i, \overset{*}{x}_1) \le \rho(x_i, \overset{*}{x}_2). \qquad (13)$$

Then the equation takes place

$$max\left\{\frac{\rho(y,x_1^*)-\rho(y,x_2^*)}{2},0\right\}\leq\rho(y,x_i). \qquad (14)$$

Indeed according to the triangular inequality axiom we have

$$\rho(y,x_1^*)\leq\rho(y,x_i)+\rho(x_i,x_1^*),$$

then

$$\rho(y,x_1^*)-\rho(y,x_i)\leq\rho(x_i,x_1^*). \qquad (15)$$

Further the following takes place

$$\rho(x_i,x_2^*)\leq\rho(y,x_2^*)+\rho(y,x_i). \qquad (16)$$

Using condition (13), from equations (15) and (16) we get

$$\rho(y,x_1^*)-\rho(y,x_i)\leq\rho(y,x_2^*)+\rho(y,x_i)$$

what under possible negativity of expression $\dfrac{\rho(y,x_1^*)-\rho(y,x_2^*)}{2}$ gives evaluation (14).

3. Metrical search models

We shall consider some approaches to (δ)- search, which create the premises for creating an efficient indexing system to reduce a number of distance calculations on the search stage.

We shall agree that distance matrix $d(\mathrm{X})$ is calculated in the result of preliminary processing. The most simple but at the same time often most practically effective (in terms of matching operations number) indexing method is based on the full distance matrix calculation. Let us briefly describe this method. Suppose on iteration i there is a set of $\mathrm{X}^{(i-1)}\subseteq\mathrm{X}$ objects for which decision is not made if they are inside the search radius or not. It should be pointed out that $\mathrm{X}_0=\mathrm{X}$. Then some element $x^{(i-1)}\in\mathrm{X}^{(i-1)}$ is being chosen randomly or according to some criteria, $\rho(y,x^{(i-1)})$ is calculated and the next set is produced

$$\mathrm{X}^{(i)}=\{x_j^{(i-1)}\in\mathrm{X}^{(i-1)}\bigcap\{x^{(i-1)}\}:|\rho(x^{(i-1)},x_j^{(i-1)})-\rho(y,x^{(i-1)})|\leq\delta\}. \qquad (17)$$

It is obvious that $\forall x_j'^{(i-1)}\in X^{(i-1)}\bigcap X^{(i)}\Rightarrow|\rho(x^{(i-1)},x_j^{(i-1)})-\rho(y,x^{(i-1)})|>\delta$ and all such elements can be eliminated from the consideration. Figure 1 illustrates forming of set $\mathrm{X}^{(1)}$ on first iteration: all elements $x_i\in\mathrm{X}^{(0)}$ situated in the crosshatched region are eliminated from consideration and the rest of elements will form set $\mathrm{X}^{(1)}$.

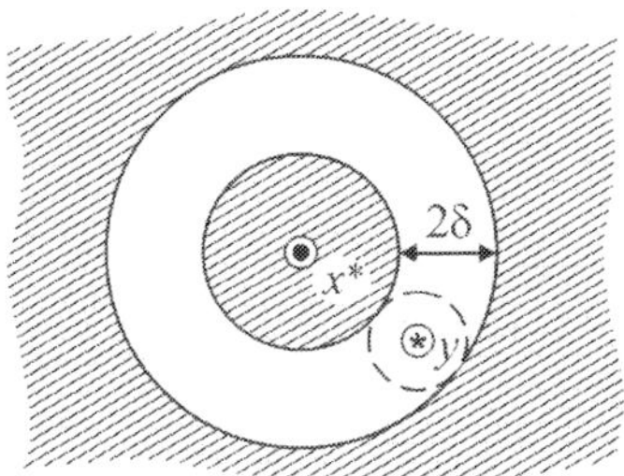

Fig. 1. Geometrical interpretation of eliminating the elements based on the lower distance evaluation

Let Y be a goal set of elements X, situated inside of the search radius, which is empty on the initial stage. Then on i iteration we get $Y = Y \bigcup x^{(i-1)}$, if $\rho(y, x^{(i-1)}) \leq \delta$. The procedure is carried out recursively till step l, when

$$\forall k = \{l - m, l - m + 1, \dots, l\} \quad card(X^{(k-1)}) - 1 = card(X^{(k)}), \quad X^{(k)} \subseteq X^{(k-1)},$$

i.e. exactly one element is eliminated from consideration during m iterations. In this case $\rho(x_j^{(l)}, y)$, $x_j^{(l)} \in X^{(l)}$, $j = \overline{1, card(X^{(l)})}$ are calculated and evaluated directly completing the Y forming. Total number of matching operations will be equal to

$$N(\delta) = l + card(X^{(l)}) . \tag{18}$$

In practice storing full distance matrix $d(X)$ is expensive due to the quadratic dependency of the required memory on database dimensionality. To solve this problem which is extremely acute on big data sets, a 'sparse' view $d(X)$ is used or special data structures are formed which in some way approximate the distance matrix considering correlation of its elements. Obviously a natural requirement for such methods would be a compromise between cost of resources storage and distance matching operations number at the search stage which should tend to $N(\delta)$ in (18). At the same time it should be noted that value $N(\delta)$ is random in sense that it depends on the objects space configuration, mutual location and order of choosing objects $x^{(1)}, x^{(2)}, \dots, x^{(l)}$, as well as location of query object y. For example, $N(\delta)$ value can be decreased if object $x^{(2)}$ is chosen at first iteration, and $x^{(1)}$ is chosen at the second one. Thus indexing methods which operate on not complete information comparing with method on complete distance matrix theoretically can perform less matching operation then the last one.

Let us introduce a set of fixed image database elements $X^* = \{x_1^*, x_2^*, \dots, x_k^*\}$. From (5) the lower distance bound follows

$$\rho(y, x_i) \geq \rho_{X^*}(y, x_i) \tag{19}$$

where $\rho_{X^*}(y, x_i) \triangleq \max_{x^* \in X^*} |\rho(y, x^*) - \rho(x^*, x_i)|$. It is the simplest indexing method based on

a 'sparse' distance matrix where $d(X)$ after corresponding re-ordering of indexes takes the

form

$$d(X)_k^* = \begin{pmatrix} 0 & 0 & 0 & \cdots & \rho(x_1,x_{k+1}) & \cdots & \rho(x_1,x_n) \\ & 0 & 0 & \cdots & \rho(x_2,x_{k+1}) & \cdots & \rho(x_2,x_n) \\ & & 0 & \cdots & & \cdots & \cdots \\ & & 0 & \rho(x_k,x_{k+1}) & \cdots & \rho(x_k,x_n) \end{pmatrix} \Rightarrow$$

$$\Rightarrow \begin{pmatrix} \rho(x_1,x_{k+1}) & \cdots & \rho(x_1,x_n) \\ \rho(x_2,x_{k+1}) & \cdots & \rho(x_2,x_n) \\ \cdots & \cdots & \cdots \\ \rho(x_k,x_{k+1}) & \cdots & \rho(x_k,x_n) \end{pmatrix}. \tag{2.20}$$

It should be noted that this approach can be interpreted as mapping $(X, \rho) \to (\mathbb{R}^k, \rho_\infty)$ and

fulfilling the search in k-arity space.

Lower distance bounds (8), (12), (14) can be obtained without information about exact

$\rho(y, x^*)$ or $\rho(x^*, x_i)$ values. For example, m columns of some rows of the sparse distance

matrix can be defined by interval (7). If $\varepsilon_{max} - \varepsilon_{min} \to 0$, lower bound (8) will tend to the

lower bound (5). Thus, the greater is m value, the greater is the volume of released

memory, which can be used for the additional pivot objects choice what should potentially

increase indexing algorithms efficiency, for example will increase the $\rho_{X^*}(y, x_i)$ value for

the sparse distance matrix. Further let for each non-pivot object x_i be defined the closest in

terms of chosen metric pivot object x^*, what allows to form a membership matrix. Then on

the search stage for obtaining the lower distance bound $\rho(y, x_i)$ one can use (14) and there

is no necessity for storing exact values $\rho(x_i, x^*)$. It can be noted that produced membership

matrix is few times more compact (depending on programming realization) as for the

resources used for its storing comparing with the distance matrix. All that also allows to

allocate greater number of pivot objects.

The described approaches allow to construct different variants of data structures, including

hierarchical ones for the indexing organization. We will consider several of them.

We shall chose a random point x^* and calculate the distance $\rho(x^*, x_i), x_i \in X$. We shall

introduce the equivalence relation φ_ρ such that $x_i \underset{\varphi_\rho}{\sim} x_j$, if $\rho(x^*, x_i) = \rho(x^*, x_j)$. Given

relation allows to partite X into equivalence classes $\{X_d\}$, where

$X_d = \{x_i \in X : \rho(x^*, x_i) = d\}$ for $d > 0$, $X_0 = \{x^*\}$. The partition process can be continued

recursively inside of each class. On the search stage all X_d, for which $|\rho(y, x^*) - d| > \delta$ is

fulfilled are eliminated from consideration.

Let us consider another method of X partition. We shall call it a binary tree method. On the starting stage a pivot object x_j^*, which has index j in the matrix $d(X)$ is singled out, and row j of the given matrix is calculated. This way we shall define distances to all other objects $d(X)_{j,1}, d(X)_{j,2}, \ldots, d(X)_{j,n}$. We shall sort values of row j ascending, having re-labelled indices $d^*(X)_{j,1}, d^*(X)_{j,2}, \ldots, d^*(X)_{j,n}$, and define $M = \rho\left(x_j^*, d^*(X)_{j,\left\lceil \frac{n}{2} \right\rceil}\right)$ – the distance to the median object. We produce partition of X into two classes $X_\leq = \{ x_i \in X : \rho(x_j^*, x_i) \leq M \}$ and $X_> = \{ x_i \in X : \rho(x_j^*, x_i) > M \}$ (Figure 2).

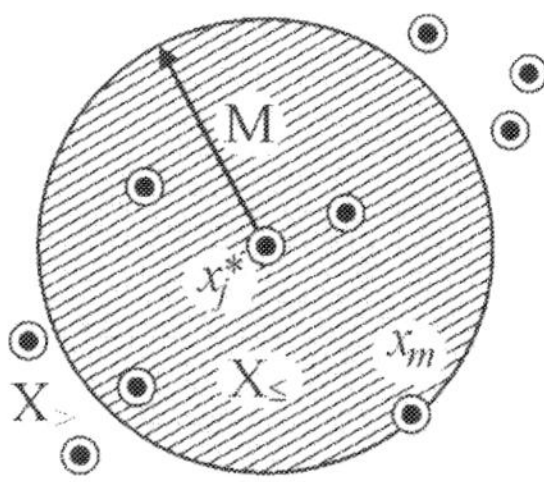

Fig. 2. Geometrical interpretation of the indexation method structure forming by binary tree

On the search stage it is necessary to search only class $X_\leq$ under $\rho(x_j^*, y) \leq M - \delta$, and class $X_>$ under $\rho(x_j^*, y) > M + \delta$. On figure 3-a is shown that when the first equation is fulfilled $X_>$ contains the hypersphere formed around the query object. Figure 3-b illustrates fulfilment of the second equation.

Thus when one of two mentioned equations is fulfilled a half of the elements in set X can be eliminated from the consideration. If not, i.e. when $M + \delta \leq \rho(x_j^*, y) \leq M - \delta$, hypersphere with centre in x_j^* and radius M intersects hypersphere of the query object, analysis of each of the $X_\leq$ and $X_>$ sets is required (figure 3-c).

One possible way to solve the problem is to introduce into consideration an additional equivalence class $X_{M,\lambda} = \{ x_i \in X : M - \lambda < \rho(x_j^*, x_i) \leq M + \lambda \}$ and redefine existing classes $X_\leq = \{ x_i \in X : \rho(x_j^*, x_i) \leq M - \lambda \}$ and $X_> = \{ x_i \in X : \rho(x_j^*, x_i) > M + \lambda \}$, where $\lambda > \delta$.

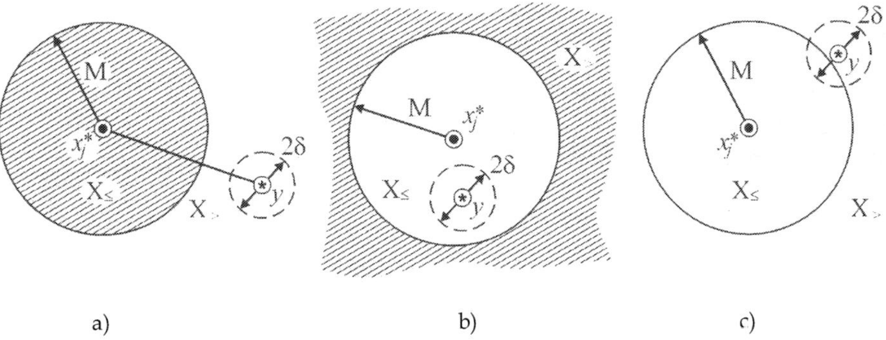

a)   b)   c)

Fig. 3. Three possible variants of considering sets $X_>$, $X_\le$ under different location of the query object

In this case on the search stage (depending on the data configuration and query object location) consideration of the following classes will be required (see figure 4 where all elements situated in the crosshatched region are eliminated from the consideration):

- $X_>$ under $\rho(y, x_j^*) > M + \lambda + \delta$ (figure 4-a);

- $X_>$ and $X_{M,\lambda}$ under $M + \lambda - \delta < \rho(y, x_j^*) \le M + \lambda + \delta$ (figure 4-b);

- $X_{M,\lambda}$ under $M - \lambda + \delta < \rho(y, x_j^*) \le M + \lambda - \delta$ (figure 4-c);

- $X_{M,\lambda}$ and $X_\le$ under $M - \lambda - \delta < \rho(y, x_j^*) \le M - \lambda + \delta$ (figure 4-d);

- $X_\le$ under $\rho(y, x_j^*) \le M - \lambda - \delta$ (figure 4-e).

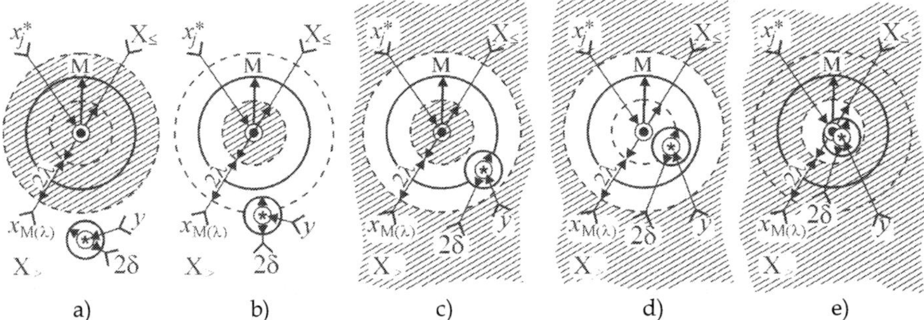

a)   b)   c)   d)   e)

Fig. 4. Possible variants of considering sets $X_>$, $X_{M,\lambda}$, $X_\le$ under different location of the query object

Obtained partition has both advantages and disadvantages. Obviously regardless of the location of y one of sets $X_\leq$, $X_>$ will be eliminated from the consideration. From the other hand cardinalities of $X_\leq$ and $X_>$ can differ and thus the search tree will not be balanced.

Partition of set X should be «granulated» recursively under $card(X) > b$, where b is maximally allowed cardinality of «leaf» set, $b \geq 3$.

Let us consider method of indexing by partitions. We shall fix a set of pivot objects $X^* = \{ x_1^*, x_2^*, ..., x_k^* \}$. If elements x_s^*, $s = \overline{1,k}$ form regions X_s^* based on the following

$$X_s^* = \{ x_i \in X : \forall t = \overline{1,k}, t \neq s \; \rho(x_i, x_s^*) < \rho(x_i, x_t^*) \}, \tag{21}$$

then $\{X_s^*\}$ is a partition of X. Notice that in case when metrical space is a $\mathbb{R}^2$, partition elements are cells of the Voronoi diagram. Voronoi diagram for the finite points set S on plane is a partition of this plane in such way that each region of this partition forms a set of points which are more close to one of the elements of set S, than to any other element of the set.

Introduced in this way partition allows to obtain several lower bounds of distance $\rho(y, x_i)$.

We shall denote them as $\rho_{min}^{(p)}$, where p is a number of evaluation.

Condition (13) is fulfilled in consequence of (21), as $\rho(x_i, x_s^*) \leq \rho(x_i, x_t^*) \; \forall x_i \in X_s^*$, $t \neq s$. Then from (14) for k pivot points we get evaluation of lower bound of distance $\rho(y, x_i)$ $\forall x_i \in X_s^*$:

$$\rho_{min}^{(1)}(s) = max \left\{ \max_{t=1,k,t \neq s} \left\{ \frac{\rho(y, x_s^*) - \rho(y, x_t^*)}{2} \right\}, 0 \right\}. \tag{22}$$

Let $\varepsilon_{max}(s) = \max_{x_i \in X_s^*} \rho(x_s^*, x_i)$ be a radius of partition X_s^* cover. Then according to (8) we get second lower distance evaluation:

$$\rho_{min}^{(2)}(s) = \rho(y, x_s^*) - \varepsilon_{max}(s). \tag{23}$$

On the preliminary processing stage minimal and maximal distances between partitions should be calculated:

$$\varepsilon_{min}(s,t) = \min_{x_i \in X_t^*} \rho(x_s^*, x_i), \tag{24}$$

$$\varepsilon_{max}(s,t) = \max_{x_i \in X_t^*} \rho(x_s^*, x_i), \tag{25}$$

where $s,t = \overline{1,k}$.

Then $\varepsilon_{min}(s,t)$ and $\varepsilon_{max}(s,t)$ under $s \neq t$ are corresponding evaluations of ε_{min} and ε_{max} distances $\rho(x_s^*, x_i) \; \forall x_i \in X_t^*$ in (8). It should be noted that under $s = t$ $\varepsilon_{min}(s,s) = 0$

and $\varepsilon_{max}(s,s) = \max\limits_{x_i \in X_s^*} \rho(x_s^*, x_i) = \varepsilon_{max}(s)$. From here it can be stated that evaluation

$\rho_{min}^{(2)}(s)$ in (23) is a special case of evaluation

$$\rho_{min}^{(3)}(s) = max\,\{\,\max\limits_{t=1,k}\{\rho_{min}^{(3)}(s,t)\},0\}\,,\tag{26}$$

$$\rho_{min}^{(3)}(s,t) = max\,\{\rho(y,x_s^*) - \varepsilon_{max}(s,t), \varepsilon_{min}(s,t) - \rho(y,\rho(y,x_s^*))\}\,.\tag{27}$$

Evaluation $\rho_{min}^{(1)}(s)$ allows to eliminate from the consideration all elements of class X_s^*, while evaluation $\rho_{min}^{(3)}(s,t)$ allows to obtain lower distance bound for class (and all its objects) X_t^* with no necessity for calculating the distance $\rho(y,x_t^*)$.

Finally, the maximal lower bound of distance $\rho(y,x_i)$, $x_i \in X_s^*$ is defined as

$$\rho_{min}(s) = max\,\{\rho_{min}^{(1)}(s),\rho_{min}^{(3)}(s)\}\,.\tag{28}$$

One way to use the obtained distance lower bounds on the search stage is to calculate k distances to pivot objects and eliminate those classes X_s^*, for which $\rho_{min}(s) > \delta$ is fulfilled. This task can be solved more optimally by defining the distance from y to not all of elements x_s^*. Let E contain a set of pivot objects producing the partitions which cannot be eliminated. On the initial stage $E = \{x_s^*\}_{s=1}^k$. Then we chose random $x_s^* \in E$, for which $\rho(y,x_s^*)$ is not calculated, compute this distance and fix lower bound $\rho_{min}^{(3)}(s,t)$ on (2.27) for all $x_t^* \in E$, performing $E = E \bigcap \{x_t^*\}$ in case of $\rho_{min}^{(3)}(s,t) > \delta$. The procedure is repeated till E becomes an empty set or till distances to all $x_s^* \in E$ are calculated. As interval $(\varepsilon_{min}(s,t),\varepsilon_{max}(s,t))$ can be large, the refinement of the lower bound of the regions still contained in E can be done via (22).

The algorithms described above do not exhaust all the potentialities of the distance matrix analysis. The matrix factorization provides a certain perspective for pivot points choice and the search itself. This factorization in fact correspons to object clustering in the given metrical space. Let us consider such a method.

4. Block-diagonal forms of distance matrix

We shall denote $\rho_{i,j} = \rho(x_i, x_j)$ as elements of distance matrix $d(X)$ and consider a random subset of the database objects for which $\rho_{i,j} \le \delta$. These objects can be used as the result of (δ)- search, although for that the formalization of search of all such groupings under given criteria is needed. Here a number of matching operations between query and database objects will be taken as a main criteria. In other words the task lies in preliminary clustering of the database with the search strategy of finding the closest cluster and if necessary continue the search inside of the chosen cluster. The goal of the clustering here is minimization of the matching operations number (under given precision of search).

Definition 4. We shall name a quadratic symmetric matrix of l-th order as Δ_l^k-block of a distance matrix $d(X)$

$$\Delta_l^k[d(X)] = \begin{pmatrix} 0 & \rho_{k,k+1} & \rho_{k,k+2} & \cdots & \rho_{k,k+l-1} \\ \rho_{k+1,k} & 0 & \rho_{k+1,k+2} & & \rho_{k+1,k+l-1} \\ \cdots & \cdots & \cdots & \cdots & \cdots \\ \cdots & \cdots & \cdots & \cdots & \cdots \\ \rho_{k+l-1,k} & \rho_{k+l-1,k+1} & \cdots & \rho_{k+l-1,k+l-2} & 0 \end{pmatrix}$$

which is the result of rearranging of rows and columns with numbers $\{i_1, i_2, ..., i_l\}$ such that $\forall i', i'' \in \{i_1, i_2, ..., i_l\} \Rightarrow \rho_{i'i''} \leq \delta$.

We shall call a Δ_l^k-block of matrix $d(X)$ maximal if

$$\nexists r \in \{1, 2, ..., n\} \setminus \{i_1, i_2, ..., i_l\} : \rho_{r,i'} \leq \delta \ \ \forall i' \in \{i_1, i_2, ..., i_l\}.$$

It should be emphasised that some elements can belong to two or more Δ_l^k-blocks of matrix $d(X)$ simultaneously. Obviously there are two possible variants in this case: they are included into all possible blocks, or they are included into blocks where sums of elements are minimal, what meets the maximal clusters compactness criterion. Generally in the first case we deal with a cover (weak clustering) of database elements set, in the second case – with partition. In result the means of Δ_l^k-blocks forming influences the search algorithms implementation, especially if more detailed result is required, for instance for (k)- or (δ, k)- search.

We shall call a Δ-representation a block-diagonal shape of matrix $d(X)$

$$\Delta[d(X)] = \begin{pmatrix} \Delta_{l_1}^{k_1} & & 0 & \\ & \Delta_{l_2}^{k_2} & & 0 \\ 0 & & \cdots & 0 \\ & 0 & 0 & \Delta_{l_m}^{k_m} \end{pmatrix},$$

where $k_1 = 1$, $k_i = \sum_{j=1}^{i-1} l_j + 1$, $\sum_{j=1}^{m} l_j \geq n$.

It is clear that the best Δ-representation (in sense of matching operations number) at (δ)- search, is the one with minimal number of blocks. In other words forming of matrix Δ-representation under given δ should provide

$$\min_{\Delta_l^k \in d(X)} m. \tag{29}$$

In the situation mentioned above the criterion can be considered

$$\min_{\Delta^k_l \in d(X)} \sum_{i,j \in \{i_1, i_2,..., i_l\}} p_{i,j} \qquad (30)$$

which does not change the value of goal function (29), but allows to obtain more adequate clustering of the database.

We shall consider the procedure of forming the maximal Δ^i_j-block of distance matrix $d(X)$ on set $\{p_1, p_2,..., p_r\} \subseteq \{1, 2,..., n\}$. We shall find a new row α^* such that

$$\alpha^* = \arg \max_{\alpha \in \{p_1, p_2,..., p_r\}} \{card\{\rho_{\alpha,q}\} : \rho_{\alpha,q} \leq \delta, \; q \in \{p_1, p_2,..., p_r\}\} . \qquad (31)$$

Let us discuss the choice of one of them (under equality α^* for some rows). We denote found in (31) indices $q \in \{p_1, p_2,..., p_r\}$ as $\{\alpha_1,...,\alpha^*_i,..., \alpha_\beta\}$. There also can be few of such sets: let us chose any of them. Two cases are possible:

$$\forall \alpha', \alpha'' \in \{\alpha_1,...,\alpha^*_i,..., \alpha_\beta\} \Rightarrow \rho_{\alpha',\alpha''} \leq \delta , \qquad (32)$$

$$\exists \alpha', \alpha'' \in \{\alpha_1,...,\alpha^*_i,..., \alpha_\beta\} \text{ such that } \rho_{\alpha',\alpha''} > \delta . \qquad (33)$$

Implication (32) means that a choice of α^* guarantees forming of maximal $\Delta^i_{\beta+1}$-block of distance matrix $d(X)$ on set $\{p_1, p_2,..., p_r\}$. So, having redefined the search field

$$\{p_1, p_2,..., p_r\} \leftarrow \{p_1, p_2,..., p_r\} \setminus \{\alpha_1, \alpha_2 ,..., \alpha_\beta\} , \qquad (34)$$

if $\{p_1, p_2,..., p_r\} \neq \varnothing$, we can move to the construction of maximal Δ^i_j-block, starting with (31). This case is illustrated in figure 5.

Situation described in (33) is more complicated, but it can be brought to (32) by sequential elimination of far situated elements. Here 2 situations are possible as well: equality of the eliminated and remained elements and their discrepancy.

In case of the elements count discrepancy, till fulfilment of (32) every element α'_γ, ($\gamma = 1, 2,..., \Gamma$, $\{\alpha'_0\}=\varnothing$, Γ: $\exists \alpha', \alpha'' \in \{\alpha_1,...,\alpha_\beta\} \Rightarrow \rho_{\alpha',\alpha''} > \delta$, are sequentially eliminated $\{\alpha_1,..., \alpha_\beta\} \leftarrow \{\alpha_1,..., \alpha_\beta\} \setminus \{\alpha'_{\gamma-1}\}$) such that

$$\alpha'_\gamma = \arg \max_{s \in \{\alpha_1,..., \alpha_\beta\}} \{card\{\rho_{q,s}\} : \rho_{q,s} > \delta, \; q \in \{\alpha_1,..., \alpha_\beta\}\} . \qquad (35)$$

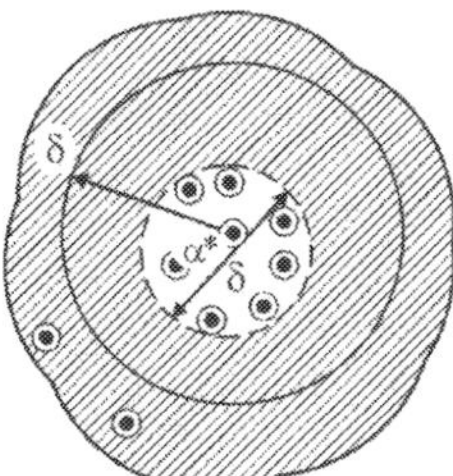

Fig. 5. Geometrical interpretation of Δ^i_j -block under (32)

If cardinality of reduced indexing set exceeds the number of close elements of the next biggest on (31) value distance matrix row it means that the next block is obtained. Otherwise, having temporarily eliminated α'_γ from $\{p_1, p_2, ..., p_r\}$, we repeat the considered steps till the next Δ^i_j -block is obtained, after that all eliminated rows are brought back for further analysis. Figure 6-a illustrates geometrical interpretation of this case, figure 6-b illustrates the result of Δ^i_j -blocks forming.

If at any step of the procedure there is an equal number of the eliminated and remained elements (figure 7) element α^* , as was mentioned above, can be included into all blocks (on the given step we get a few maximal blocks and reduction (34) is fulfilled multiple times) or using (30), we chose a maximal compact block, and after that start the formation of the next block.

Now we can discuss the choice of α^* when having multiple rows in (31). First of all we shall emphasise that for (32) we have exactly β rows and choice of α^* does is of no importance, as all elements will be simultaneously put into one Δ^i_j -block (see figure 5), or there are few blocks of the same cardinality, and all of them are obtained sequentially. If the (33) takes place, then

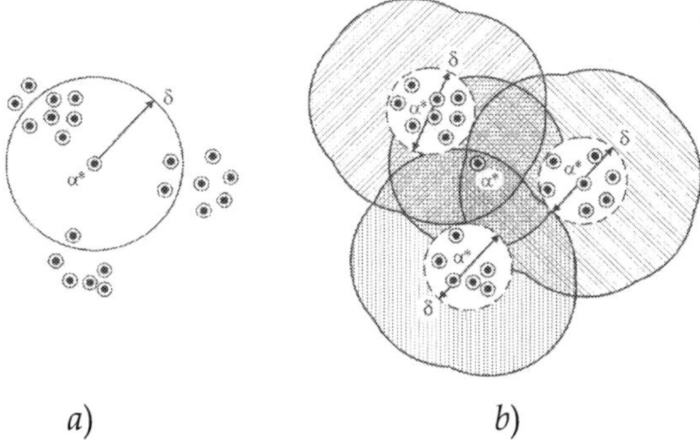

$a)$ $b)$

Fig. 6. Geometrical interpretation of -blocks forming for (33)

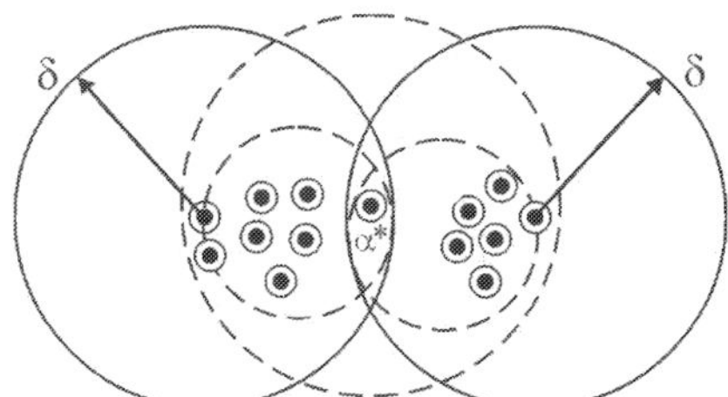

Fig. 7. Forming of Δ^i_j-blocks when the number of eliminated and remained elements are equal

the choice of α^* is also random, as accurate within the numeration all maximal blocks will be sequentially reduction formed till cases (32).

Thus, we have considered forming of some Δ^i_j-block on index set $\{p_1, p_2,..., p_r\} \subseteq \{1, 2,..., n\}$. After search and renumbering on set $\{1, 2,..., n\}$ of first maximal block in Δ-representation of distance matrix we get

$$
\begin{pmatrix}
0 & \rho_{1,2} & \rho_{1,3} & \cdots & \rho_{1,k_1} & & & & & & \\
\rho_{2,1} & 0 & \rho_{2,3} & \cdots & \rho_{2,k_1} & & & & & & \\
\cdots & \cdots & \cdots & \cdots & \cdots & & & 0 & & & \\
\rho_{k_1,1} & \rho_{k_1,1} & \cdots & \rho_{k_1,k_1-1} & 0 & & & & & & \\
 & & & & & 0 & \rho_{k_1+1,k_1+2} & \rho_{k_1+1,k_1+3} & \cdots & \cdots & \rho_{k_1+1,n} \\
 & & & & & \rho_{k_1+2,k_1+1} & 0 & \rho_{k_1+2,k_1+1} & \cdots & \cdots & \rho_{k_1+2,n} \\
 & & 0 & & & \cdots & \cdots & \cdots & \cdots & \cdots & \cdots \\
 & & & & & \cdots & \cdots & \cdots & \cdots & \cdots & \cdots \\
 & & & & & \rho_{k_1+n-1,k_1+1} & \rho_{k_1+n-1,k_1+2} & \cdots & \cdots & 0 & \rho_{k_1+n-1,n} \\
 & & & & & \rho_{n,k_1+1} & \rho_{n,k_1+2} & \cdots & \cdots & \rho_{n,n-1} & 0
\end{pmatrix}
$$

Further elimination of indices set $\{1, 2,..., k_1\}$, we get distance matrix of dimension $(n-k_1) \times (n-k_1)$. Repeating the procedure for every new distance matrix we at first get the required representation, at second due to maximality of blocks on each steps fulfil (29).

Some notes should be made. First of all, it is not necessary to eliminate elements α'_γ, as the next element α^* can be temporary omitted. Maximal Δ^i_j-block will still be found, but possibly it will take more iterations to execute. It can be emphasised that efficiency of computational models of forming Δ-representations will improve a lot if rows of matrix $d(X)$ is ordered descending accordingly to (31) criterion. Firstly reduction (34) will be simplified due to sequential elimination of the distance matrix rows. Secondly, in many cases we will not need renumbering of Δ^i_j-block elements under including it into the Δ-representation.

5. Computational models optimization.

In practice depending on data configurations used in the metric space fulfilment of (29) may not provide sufficient search efficiency. It will happen if for example value δ was not chosen rationally, or dimensionalities of blocks in Δ-representations are still too large to be used as a result of the (δ)- search. Then, one way is to keep searching inside of the best block (best in terms of closeness to the query), another way is to expand (extend) the preliminary processing. Particularly within distance matrix preprocessing Δ-representations can be formed in each of the found Δ^i_j-blocks. Though the task becomes more complicated as it is not known which of the Δ-representations will be used on the second search stage. In other words the guaranteed search operations number is determined by number of Δ^i_j-blocks, obtained on the first stage, maximal number of nested $\Delta^{i'}_{j'}$-blocks in each of Δ^i_j-blocks and maximal number of their elements. At that as Δ-representation with closeness parameter δ is already found, we can confine ourselves to splitting on nested Δ^i_j-blocks of possibly same dimension, maximising intra-cluster distances.

We shall order obtained Δ^i_j-blocks ascending their dimensions. Let us have s_0 elements not included into any of the blocks, s_1 blocks of dimension l_1, s_2 – of dimension $l_2,...,s_t$ s_2 – of dimension l_t, i.e. $1=l_0 \le l_1 < l_2 < l_t \le n$. Then, assuming that we need to split blocks starting with dimension l_i, and denoting the maximal dimension of the resulting blocks as $M \in [l_{i-1}, l_i] \cap \mathbb{N}$ (figure 8), we get two possible search realization strategies. The first one is searching the best block of nested Δ-representation, then the nested block of Δ-representation and exhaustive search in the closest Δ^i_j-blocks. The second one consists in choosing the block among union of all blocks of two-level Δ- representation of the distance matrix. The first strategy is a special case of the stratified analysis and is out of our research field. Let us stop on the second one: maximal matching operation number is equal to the sum of blocks number and their maximal dimensionality, i.e.

$$f(M) = M + \sum_{j=1}^{i-1} s_j + \sum_{j=i}^{t} \lceil l_j/M \rceil s_j , \; i = \overline{1, t} \tag{36}$$

where $\lceil \circ \rceil$ is minimal integer number exceeding the given one.

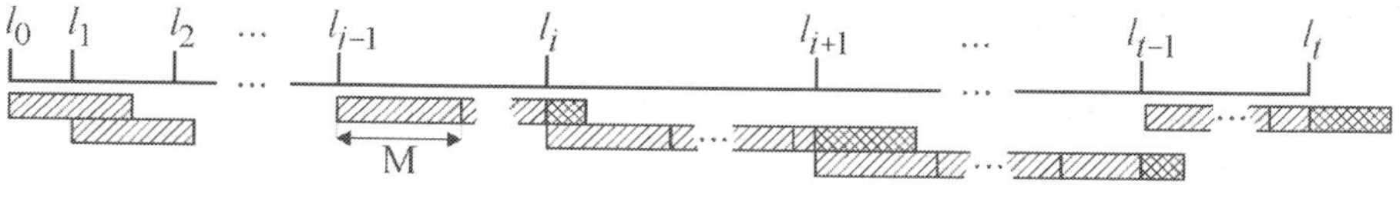

Fig. 8. Splitting of Δ^i_j-blocks

Thus it is necessary to find value M, providing minimum (36). Searching of minimum $f(M)$ we shall sequentially perform on each $[l_0, l_1]$, $[l_1, l_2]$,...,$[l_{t-1}, l_t]$. Among the best obtained results we shall chose the minimal one which provides nested splitting of given Δ- representation blocks. Let us analyse the local minimum $f(M)$ search procedure.

Let us chose a partial interval $[l_{i-1}, l_i] \cap \mathbb{N}$. If it is small enough ($l_i - l_{i-1} \in \{1, 2, 3\}$), then solution can be found by exhaustive search. In other case we shall change discrete function $f(M)$ with continuous on $[l_{i-1}, l_i]$ function $\varphi(x) = x + u/x + v$, where $u = \sum_{j=i}^{t} l_j s_j > 0$, $v = \sum_{j=1}^{i-1} s_j > 0$. It is easy to see that $\forall x \in [l_{i-1}, l_i], \forall M \in [l_{i-1}, l_i] \cap \mathbb{N} \Rightarrow \varphi(x) \le f(M)$. Error of transition to continuous function has the upper bound

$$\max_{[l_{i-1}, l_i]} f(M) - \varphi(x) \le \sum_{j=i}^{t} s_j = C.$$

Stationary point of function $\varphi(x) = x + u/x + v$ according to condition $x > 0$ is

$$x^* = \sqrt{\sum_{j=i}^{t} l_j s_j}.$$

As function $\varphi(x)$ is monotonic on intervals $(0, x^*]$ and $[x^*, \infty)$, its optimum on integer interval $[l_{i-1}, l_i] \cap \mathbb{N}$ should be searched for either on its ends or if $x^* \in (l_{i-1}, l_i)$, in points $M_1^* = \lfloor x^* \rfloor$, $M_2^* = \lceil x^* \rceil$, where «$\lfloor \circ \rfloor$» is a maximal integer not exceeding the given one. Therefore,

$$\varphi^* = \min_{[l_{i-1}, l_i] \cap \mathbb{N}} \varphi(x) = \min \{\varphi(l_{i-1}), \varphi(l_i),$$
$$\varphi(\max \{\min \{M_1^*, l_i\}, l_{i-1}\}), \varphi(\max \{\min \{M_2^*, l_i\}, l_{i-1}\})\}.$$

In the same way we shall find

$$f^* = \min_{[l_{i-1}, l_i] \cap \mathbb{N}} f(x) = \min \{f(l_{i-1}), f(l_i),$$
$$f(\max \{\min \{M_1^*, l_i\}, l_{i-1}\}), f(\max \{\min \{M_2^*, l_i\}, l_{i-1}\})\}.$$

If $f^* = \varphi^*$, than according to condition $\varphi(x) \le f(M)$ optimal value on $[l_{i-1}, l_i]$ is found. If no $f^* - \varphi^* \le C > 0$ is an error of optimal value definition. If the error is small (for example, $f^* - \varphi^* < 1$), the optimization process is finished. In other case the field of search should be narrowed for what we shall find solutions x' and x'' of the equation

$$x + u/x + v = m^* + u/m^* + v + f^* - \varphi^*, \tag{37}$$

where $m^* \in \{l_{i-1}, l_i, M_1^*, M_2^*\}$ such that $f(m^*) = f^*$.

From here

$$x'(x'') = \frac{m^* + u - (f^* - \varphi^*)m^* \pm \sqrt{((m^*)^2 + u - (f^* - \varphi^*)m^*)^2 - 4(m^*)^2 u}}{2(m^*)^2}.$$

It is obvious that equation (37) always has solution because

$$((m^*)^2 + u - (f^* - \varphi^*)m^*))^2 - 4u(m^*)^2 =$$
$$= (u - (m^*)^2)^2 + (f^* - \varphi^*)m^* ((f^* - \varphi^*)m^* + 2u + 2(m^*)^2) > 0.$$

Taking into consideration that $m^* > 0$ and

$$(m^*)^2 + u - (f^* - \varphi^*)m^* \geq \sqrt{((m^*)^2 + u - (f^* - \varphi^*)m^*)^2 - 4(m^*)^2 u} \ ,$$

i.e. $x' \geq x'' \geq 0$, we shall form the interval $[l', l''] \subset [l_{i-1}, l_i]$ as following

$$[l', l''] = \begin{cases} [\lfloor x' \rfloor, \lceil x'' \rceil], & m^* \in \{M_1^*, M_2^*\}; \\ [l_{i-1}, \lfloor x' \rfloor], & m^* = l_{i-1}; \\ [\lceil x'' \rceil, l_i], & m^* = l_i \end{cases}$$

And repeating the suggested procedure necessary number times we shall be solving the task of finding optimal maximal possible dimension of nested Δ_j^i-blocks on shortened intervals, namely

$$f(M) \to \min_{[l', l''] \cap \mathbb{N}}.$$

Under high enough dimensionality of task the number of analysed partial intervals can become very big. The proposed procedure of nested Δ_j^i-blocks maximal dimensionality search can be applied for reducing the number of analysed intervals on the admitted region, i.e. interval $[1, l_t]$. Considering that $\forall M \in [l_{i-1}, l_i]$ (2.36) is fulfilled, then $\forall M \in [l_1, l_t]$ we get

$$f(M) = M + \sum_{j=1}^{t} \lceil l_j / M \rceil s_j,$$

Therefore the continuous function $\Phi(x)$, which does not exceed discrete function $f(M)$ on all interval $[1, l_t]$, has a form

$$\Phi(x) = x + \frac{\sum_{j=1}^{t} l_j s_j}{x}.$$

We shall note that the limitation evaluation at that has form

$$f(M) - \Phi(M) \le \sum_{j=1}^{t} s_j \ge C.$$

Acting the same way as described above we find on interval $[1, l_i] \cap \mathbb{N}$ values Φ^* and f^*.
Then we define $[l', l'']$, and intersection $([l', l''] \cap [l_{i-1}, l_i]) \cap \mathbb{N} \ne \varnothing$ $(i = \overline{1,t})$ defines reduced set of partial intervals $[l_{i'-1}, l_{i'}]$, $\{i'\} \subseteq \{1, 2, ..., t\}$.

Found in result partition parameter M only defines optimal maximal dimension of nested blocks or, what is equivalent, their quantity. As it is possible that cases $M > l_i$ $(i = \overline{1,t})$ and $mod_M \, l_i \ne 0$ (see figure 8) may arise, elements should be redistributed among sub-blocks aiming to minimise sum of inter-block distances and maximize intra-blocks distances, what should provide search reliability increase.

So, to provide the guaranteed maximum of matching operations number it is necessary to independently split each of the Δ_j^i-blocks if its dimension exceeds found M value. We shall fix some Δ_j^i-block, which needs to be split, and corresponding cardinality denote as N. The number of nested blocks under that is equal to L, $L = \lceil N/M \rceil$. It can be noted that we should obtain not less than L^* blocks of dimension M

$$L^* = \begin{cases} N/M, & mod_M \, N = 0, \\ \lceil N/M \rceil - M + mod_M \, N, & M - mod_M \, N > \lceil N/M \rceil, \\ 0, & M - mod_M \, N \le \lceil N/M \rceil. \end{cases}$$

We can point out conditions for defining potential dimensions and orders of nested blocks

$$mod_M \, N \le p_r \le M, \quad \sum_{r=1}^{L} p_r = N$$

where p_r are dimensions of nested blocks.
In other words we get the Diophantine equation

$$\alpha_1 M + \alpha_2 (M-1) + ... + \alpha_S (M-S+1) = N, \tag{38}$$

where $\alpha_s \in \mathbb{N} \cup \{0\}$,

$$s = \overline{1, S}, \quad S = \begin{cases} M - mod_M \, N + 1, & mod_M \, N \ne 0, \\ 1, & mod_M \, N = 0. \end{cases}$$

Solutions of the linear equation (38) on subset of positive integers induce all possible redistributions of elements into subclusters, invariant regarding main criterion – minimum of comparative recognition operations. Let $\{\alpha_1^q, \alpha_2^q, ..., \alpha_S^q\}_{q=1}^{Q}$ be solutions of equation (38), then under $S = 1$, obviously the single case is considered, yet if at least two elements are not equal to 0, then taking into account that we are operating with blocks where distanced do not exceed threshold δ, under forming the nested blocks one should chose the best variant in the sense of maximization of intra-blocks distances among V possible situations

$$V = \sum_{q=1}^{Q} \frac{(\alpha_1^q + \alpha_2^q + \ldots + \alpha_S^q)!}{(\alpha_1^q! \, \alpha_2^q! \ldots \alpha_S^q!)} = L! \, Q \sum_{q=1}^{Q} (\alpha_1^q! \, \alpha_2^q! \ldots \alpha_S^q!)^{-1} \, .$$

6. Experimental comparative analysis of search models

A number of tests have been performed on set of points in $\mathbb{R}^2$ space with L_2 metric. We used two configurations of data distribution: uniform and with formed clusters. We implemented the following index structures to preprocess the initial data set:

Table 1. Indexing methods used for the experiments.

i)	Full matrix	Random choice of key objects. Maximal number of iterations under which not a single element is eliminated from the consideration $m = 3$.
ii)	«Sparse» matrix	64 pivot points chosen randomly.
iii)	Binary tree	Random choice of pivot points on the tree construction stage. Maximal allowed cardinality of «leaf» set $b = 3$.
iv)	Partitions	64 randomly chosen pivot points. On the search stage one eliminate regions using criteria (27) iterative procedure which exploits (28).

The purpose was to calculate the matches number during the search on uniform and clusters distribution of objects and its dependency on the query object position and data set configuration.

Data for uniform distribution consisted of 1024 points, for the clusters one there were 16 clusters, with cluster cardinality mean equal to $\mu = 64$ and variance equal to $\sigma = 10$ of (1024 elements in total). Both sets of points coordinated were within the range [0;256] (data square here and after). The example of these configuration is presented on Figure 9.

Variance of single cluster points location was set to 6 for both coordinates. It was allowed that clusters could overlap. We used $k = \sqrt{n}$ parameters for indexation ii), and created one-level partition with $k = \sqrt{n}$ number of pivots in indexation iv).

First experiment examined dependency of the index structure on the position of the query object. We generated uniform and cluster data structures, created all index structures and randomly chose query object from the data square 500 times, tracking the number of matches of each data structures for all queries. We then calculated the mean and variance of matches count for each index structure (Table 1).

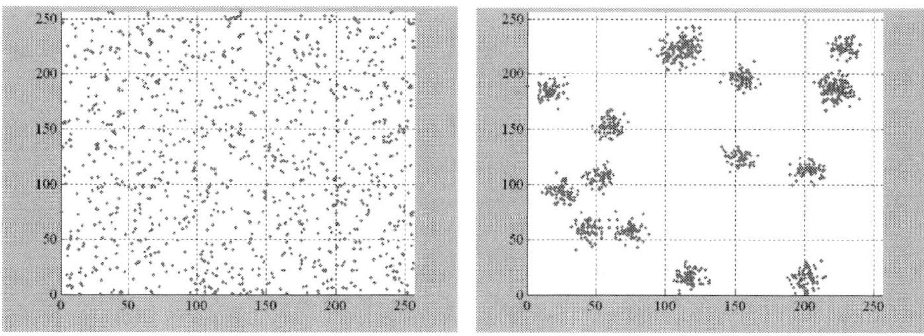

Fig. 9. Example of points configuration for cluster (left side) and uniform (right side) data configuration.

As it was expected indexation which exploits a full distance matrix i) outperforms the other ones while indexation on sparse matrix ii) keeps the second place. Indexations iii) and iv) have approximately equal efficiency.

We can claim that when objects of database tend to form clusters the number of matches does not vary dramatically for all indexing methods, they only differ notably on variance and therefore in some cases performance of methods iii) and iv) can take much more time than it was expected. On the other hand, when distribution of objects is uniform then indexation i) perform 4 times better results than iii) and iv) while indexation ii) performs 2 times better results.

In the second experiment we tried to track dependency of index structures efficiency on different data configurations.

We created 50 random configurations of uniform and cluster data distributions and ran routines of the first experiment changing query object position 20 times. We found out that statistics of the indexations efficiency was almost the same compared to first experiment results, only variance grew a bit.

On figures 10 and 11 an average number of distance computations on 50 iterations for indexation algorithms i) – iv) is given for uniform and cluster data configuration.

Data configuration	Full matrix		Sparse matrix		Partition search		Binary search	
	μ	σ	μ	σ	μ	σ	μ	σ
uniform	23.56	4.82	50.98	4.58	107.78	36.18	90.08	23.7
clusters	30.63	29.73	55.19	26.27	71.2	71.39	74.362	48.49

Table 2. Dependency of the matches number on different data configurations

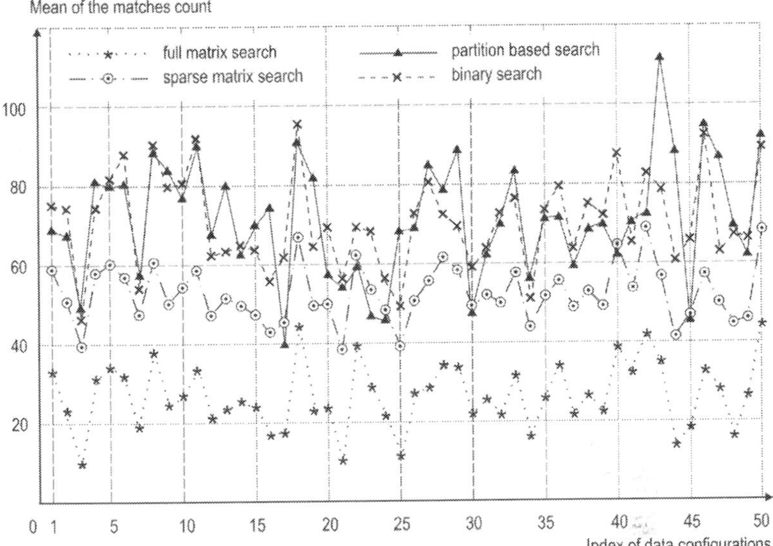

Fig. 10. Results of matches count dependency on change of cluster data configuration

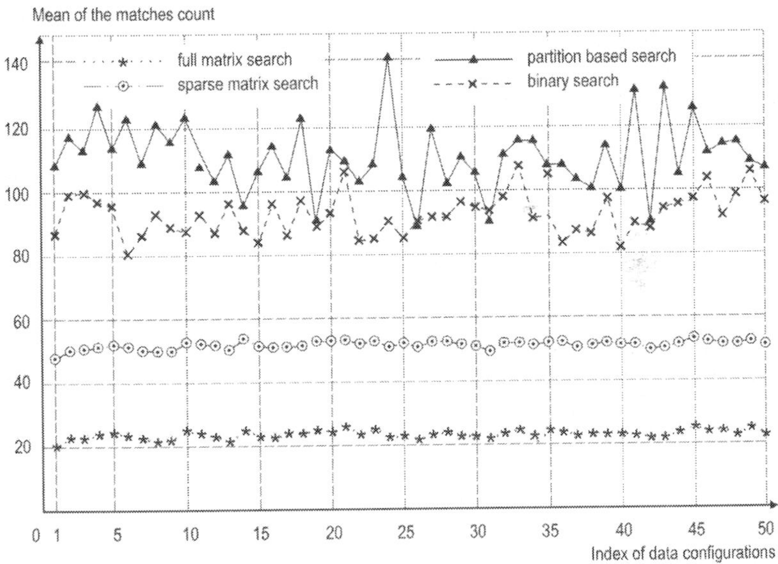

Fig. 11. Results of matches count dependency on change of uniform data configuration

6. More experiments, conclusions and future work

It was shown that index methods efficiency depends on the data configuration. If objects location is uniform, methods on full and sparse matrix outperform binary tree and partition methods. Though if objects form clusters the difference of the methods efficiency becomes less. Asit was assumed full matrix method outperforms all the others on every search stage regardless the data configurations.

Yet considering square dependency of $card(X)$ storing resources this method becomes inefficient for database of large dimensionality. Sparse matrix method in general requires less matching operations number than binary trees and partition methods. Efficiency of the last ones is almost the same, still the partition method has larger variance of matching operations number. First of all it in connected to the fact that partition method results are more depending on the pivot points location. If points are located close to each other partition method search performance becomes less efficient.

We can conclude that only index structures i) and ii) can guarantee rather constant low bound of matches count on uniformly distributed data set solely.

We have proposed a novel indexing structure using sparse distance matrices for the image search with queries 'ad exemplum' which considering embedded partitions of the images. The experimental exploration of the method has proved it to be fast and efficient. The future work will be directed for investigation of the pivots choice method and possibility to use clustering methods for distance matrices analysis which would provide effective using of the partition metric for content image retrieval.

Offered here method for block-diagonal distance matrix synthesis allows to get a special case of sparse matrix. Optimal detalization of resulting blocks cardinality increase speed of search and reduce recourses needed for indexing structures storing. Let us see some results of this approach research.

We used data from Berkley University collection which contains 1000 images and their ground-truth representations (figures 12 and 13).

Method of forming block-diagonal matrix is based on matching results of image segmentations and so there are few parameters which influence the result: segmentation algorithm, method of segmentations matching and δ value.

For segmenting database images we use a wide known color-textured algorithm JSEG, what is shown on figure 14. Having the corresponding ground-truth representations we have opportunity to define level of dependency of the distance matrix block-diagonal structure distances from the segmentation algorithm. Further we shall denote partition extracted from the ground-truth representation as gt-partition, and the one obtained from the JSEG segmentation results as jseg-partition.

To compare segmentation results we shall use the partition metric (Mashtalir et al., 2006). Measure $\mu(A)$ will be defined as regions area and we shall carry out normalization in limits $[0;1]$ as

$$\rho^*(\alpha,\beta) = \frac{\sum\limits_{i=1}^{n}\sum\limits_{j=1}^{m} \mu(A_i \Delta B_j)\mu(A_i \cap B_j)}{(n \cdot m)^2}. \tag{39}$$

Fig. 12. Example of image set from database. 72 items from Berkley collection

Fig.13. Example of ground-truth representations for 72 images from figure 12

Fig.14. Example of JSEG segmentation results for 72 images from figure 12

On figure 15 you can see dependency of number of Δ-blocks of block-diagonal distance matrix representation on value δ, changing from 0,1 to 0,5 with step 0,05 for gt-partitions and jseg-partitions. With increasing of δ number of blocks does not increase. It confirms the stated here optimality of Δ-blocks forming strategy.

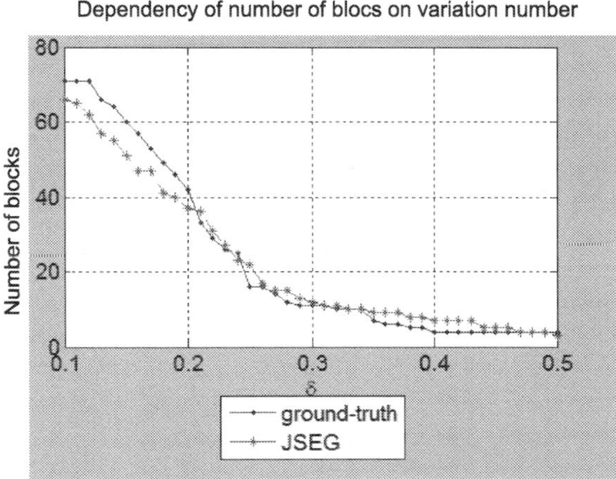

Fig.15. dependency of number of Δ-blocks of block-diagonal distance matrix representation from value δ

It also should be noted that character of Δ-blocks changing for gt-partitions and jseg-partitions is quite similar, what proves the comparative independency of block-diagonal distance matrix representation forming method from algorithms of segmentation.

So the metric indexing provides synthesis of effective two-stages search procedures. At first all images not satisfying query image are eliminated, at second search is fulfilled on a limited set. Image segmentation inducing quotient sets can be a tool for obtaining sufficient enough feature descriptions of images in metric space, which provides indexed search of images according to its content.

8. References

Berchtold, S., Keim, D. (2001) Searching in High-Dimensional Spaces: Index Structures for Improving the Performance of Multimedia Databases. *ACM Computing Surveys*. Vol. 33, No. 3, 2001, pp. 322–373.

Bohm C., Berchtold S., Keim D.A. (2001) Searching in high-dimensional spaces: Index structures for improving the performance of multimedia databases. *ACM Computing Surveys (CSUR)*. Vol. 33, No. 3, 2001, pp. 322–373.

Chavez, E., Navarro, G., Baeza-Yates, R., Marroquin, J.L. (2001) Searching in Metric Spaces. *ACM Computing Surveys*. Vol. 3, No. 3, 2001, pp. 273–321.

Cheng, W., Xu, D., Jiang, Y., Lang C. (2005) Information Theoretic Metrics in Shot Boundary Detection. In: Knowledge-Based Intelligent Information and Engineering

Systems. Khosla R., et al. (eds.). *Lecture Notes in Computer Science, Springer-Verlag, Berlin Heidelberg.* Vol. 3683, 2005, pp. 388-394.

Greenspan,H., Dvir, G., Rubner, Y. (2004) Context-Dependent Segmentation and Matching in Image Database. *Computer Vision and Image Understanding.* Vol. 93, No. 1, 2004, pp. 86-109.

Hjaltason, G., Samet, H. (2003) Index-driven Similarity Search in Metric Spaces. *ACM Transactions on Database Systems.* Vol. 8, No. 4, 2003, pp. 517-580.

Kinoshenko, D., Mashtalir, V., Shlyakhov V. (2007) A Partition Metric for Clustering Features Analysis. *International Journal 'Information Theories and Applications.* Vol. 14, No 3, 2007, pp. 230-236.

Mashtalir, V., Mikhnova, E., Shlyakhov, V., Yegorova E. (2006). A Novel Metric on Partitions for Image Segmentation. *In Proceedings of IEEE International Conference on Video and Signal Based Surveillance,* P. 18.

Rubner, Y., Tomasi, C., Guibas, L.J. (2000) The Earth Mover's Distance as a Metric for Image Retrieval. *International Journal of Computer Vision.* Vol. 40, No 2, 2000, pp. 99-121.

Wang, D., Ma, X., Kim, Y. (2005) Learning Pseudo Metric for Intelligent Multimedia Data Classification and Retrieval. *Journal of Intelligent Manufacturing.* Vol. 16, No 6, 2005, pp. 575–586.

Yokoyama, T., Watanabe, T. (2007) DR Image and Fractal Correlogram: A New Image Feature Representation Based on Fractal Codes and Its Application to Image Retrieval. *In: Lecture Notes in Computer Science.* Vol. 4351, 2007, pp. 428-439.Berlin Heidelberg: Springer-Verlag.

## 12

Tile-based Image Visual Codewords Extraction for Efficient Indexing and Retrieval

Zhiyong Zhang and Olfa Nasraoui
University of Louisville
US

1. Introduction

Inspired by the success of inverted-file indexing in text search engines, content based image retrieval (CBIR) researchers have begin to consider using inverted indexing for image content search Squire et al. (1999) Jing et al. (2004). For inverted indexing to be effective in image content search, two issues need to be addressed. First, the image content features need to follow a power-law distribution the same way as textual document terms do. Second, a mechanism is needed to *textualize* the low-level image content features. We addressed these two constraints. First of all, we tested the sparseness of image content features and our results confirmed the sparseness assumption. This makes the inverted file indexing on image content well grounded. However, to translate to image content feature into texts, a vector quantization (VQ) scheme is needed. K-means (or Generalized Lloyd Algorithm) clustering is usually used for vector quantization. But for sparse data, K-means algorithm may generate cluster centers overcrowded in high density area. To solve this problem, we developed a cluster-merge algorithm to guarantee the quality of cluster centers. Based on these preliminary efforts, we are able to *textualize* the image content features. More specifically, we developed the *textualization* procedures for image content features, which include both codebook generation and codewords extraction process. To better describe image textures and image shapes, we defined three types of tiles: *inner tiles*, *bordering tiles*, and *crossing tiles*. Furthermore, to reduce the dependence on accurate image segmentation for shape-based retrieval, we propose to use more basic elements, *boundary angles*, to represent the shape feature. With these efforts and methods, we are able to enjoy high level visual codewords representation of low-level image features, thus making efficient and scalable image content search realizable.

This chapter is organized as follows: in section 2, we discuss related work. In section 3 and section 4, we discuss the sparseness of image content features and the cluster-merge algorithm respectively. We focus on image content codewords representation in section 5. After that, we present our experimental results in section 6, and finally we draw conclusions and give future works in section 7.

2. Related Works

QBIC Flickner et al. (1995), Blobworld Carson et al. (1999), WALRUS Natsev et al. (2004), and WBIIS Wang et al. (1997), which uses the QBIC system, all use *R*-trees* Beckmann et al. (1990) for indexing. The *R*-tree* is a variant of the *R-tree* by Guttman Guttman (1984). These tree-based method claim to have good performance for nearest neighbor search. However, *curse of dimensionality* spells potential trouble for these tree-based methods. In Weber et al. (1998), Weber et al showed that the performance of these tree-based methods degrade significantly as the number of dimensions increases and is even outperformed by a sequential scan whenever the dimensionality is above 10. Weber et al then proposed a scheme named *vector approximation file* (or 'VA-file') and demonstrated that *VA-file* can offer better performance for high dimensional similarity search. An *OVA-file* (*Ordered VA-file*) structure, which places *approximations* that are close to each other in close positions for later fast access, was later used in Lu et al. (2006) for video retrieval. The *VA-file* structure adopts a signature-file like filtering method, thus trying to build a mechanism for fast scanning for nearest neighbors search. However, in Witten et al. (1999) Zobel et al. (1998), Zobel et al showed that signature files are distinctly inferior to inverted files as data structure methods for indexing. At the same time, the success of inverted files in texts search engine and scalability concerns have drawn attention to the potential of using inverted files for multimedia indexing. Viper Squire et al. (1999) had attempted to use inverted files for indexing image databases and their experiment results showed their inverted indexing scheme had better performance than the vector space system used before by the same authors. In Jing et al. (2004), Jing et al tried to use a modified inverted file for image indexing and showed through experiments that inverted file indexing is much more efficient than sequential search without much loss of accuracy. In Rahman et al. (2006), Rahman et al also used inverted files for image indexing and observed comparable accuracy results for inverted file indexing and sequential search method. In order to build an inverted index, image content features need to be transformed into textual words. Vector Quantization (VQ) is usually used to achieve such goal. A Uniform Quantizer has been used in a image indexing and search system Zhang et al. (2006). However, since there are several advantages of using Nonuniform Quantization such as an improved Signal to Noise Ratio (SNR) (see Gersho & Gray (1992)) over Uniform Quantization, Nonuniform quantization are more widely used. Among the Nonuniform Quantization methods, the Generalized Lloyd Algorithm (GLA), also known as k-means or LBG algorithm, is widely used for generating image codebooks for indexing or retrieval. See Ma & Manjunath (1998) Sivic & Zisserman (2003) Jegou et al. (2007) Mojsilovic et al. (2000) and Malik et al. (1999).

As image segmentation technology develops from theoretical Ncut Shi & Malik (2000) to practical efficient Kruskal style realization Felzenszwalb & Huttenlocher (2004), people can expect the successful landing of shape-based image retrieval in real life in the near future. Shape based image retrieval are divided into two categories: *boundary-based* and *region-based* Safar et al. (2000). Among several different approaches, the grid-based method Lu & Sajjanhar (1999), which belongs to region-based methods, was later used by Prasad et al. (2004). There are several factors that make shape-based image retrieval very challenging and that have limited development of shape-based image retrieval. First, shape-based retrieval relies too much on an accurate image segmentation, which is not a solved problem yet. Second, it is very hard to build a shape-based retrieval system which is invariant to transformation, rotation, and scaling. A few systems like Lu & Sajjanhar (1999) have considered these factors, however they paid high computation costs to solve these problems. Third, humans don't have a uniform definition of the shapes of different objects other than some very common and simple shapes such as triangle, rectangle, and circle, etc. Several working system of query by shape include CIRES Iqbal & Aggarwal (2002), which used perceptual grouping and several image structural boundary types like "L" junctions, "U" junctions, "polygons", etc to differentiate manmade objects from outdoor images. No image segmentation was used in their methods. Another work is *query by sketch* such as Retrievr Jacobs et al. (1995).

3. Sparseness of Image Features

One assumption and reason behind the success of the inverted file structure for indexing text and documents is the sparseness of terms in documents. The total number of terms in a large document collection is very high with dimensionality $O(10^4)$ Squire et al. (1999) Westerveld (2000), while the number of terms that occur in a single document is comparatively low $O(10^2)$. In other words, human have accumulated a big enough vocabulary to cover each field of our everyday life, yet for a specific topic or article, a small portion suffices. However for the case of images, since "a picture is worth a thousand words" and since pictures tend to be self-explanatory, it can be hard to develop a complete thesaurus for images. The result is that a *sparse* dictionary comparable to documents does not exist. However, an analysis of images based on its color, texture, and shape, shows that although a term-document like high sparseness is not achieved, a slightly lower sparseness could be reached with an appropriate content to codeword mapping. For instance, a picture may contain only a few dominant colors when using a color histogram containing hundreds of bins. The sparseness also depends on the visual word representation.

Figure 1 gives the log-log distribution of the resulting colorwords (mapped from original colors) using different methods to represent 10,000 actual images randomly selected from flickr.com. For equal color quantization, we use $4 \times 4 \times 4$ quantization on the RGB color channels to get 64 bins. For the clustering-merge based method, we use 1000 images as the training set to obtain the global color or texture codebook, then use the global codebook to represent these 10,000 images.

We can see that these representations roughly follow a power law distribution. In Jurie & Triggs (2005), Frederic et al showed that texture features followed a power law distribution. Their results match our experimental results, and lay the foundation for our inverted indexing scheme. In the following, we will discuss our clustering-merge method to compute the global codebook.

4. GLA and Cluster-Merge Algorithm

There are two reasons for us to use GLA (Generalized Lloyd Algorithm) vector quantization instead of uniform quantization. The first reason is that the latter is not feasible for high-dimensional features, whereas GLA can be used in such cases. The second reason is that the latter does not take the actual feature distribution into account and can lose some accuracy in representing the images, while GLA does better.

One issue with most K-mean-based clustering algorithm such as GLA for codebook generation is that for power law distributed data, more cluster centers are generated around high density areas Jurie & Triggs (2005). Our experiments also confirmed such phenomenon, see figure 3. This can cause the codewords to be overpopulated in the high density area while the sparse area not properly represented. To solve this problem, we propose to merge these very close cluster centers after obtaining the K-means clustering result. We first use K-means to generate more centers than what we expect, then we merge these centers into the number of centers we desire. Through merging close centers, we can avoid cluster centers to crowd into high density areas. At the same time, we fully take advantage of the efficiency of K-means.

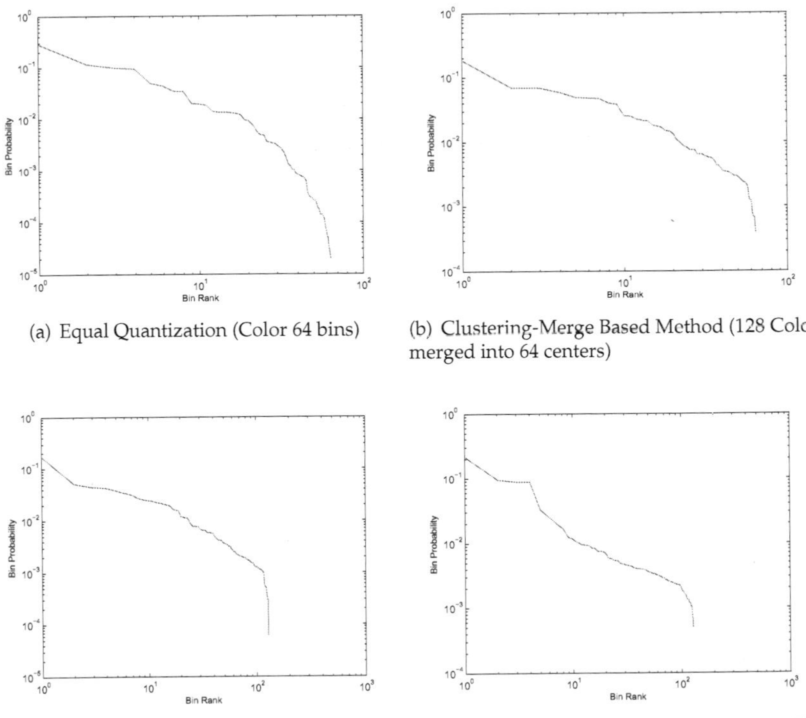

(a) Equal Quantization (Color 64 bins)

(b) Clustering-Merge Based Method (128 Colors merged into 64 centers)

(c) Clustering-Merge Based Method (256 Colors merged into 128 centers)

(d) Clustering-Merge Based Method (256 Textures merge into 128 centers

Fig. 1. Log-log plots of different quantization methods.

Thus, our clustering merge algorithm will be much more efficient than purely hierarchical clustering algorithm.

The pseudocode for merging clusters is shown in pseudocode 2. In pseudocode 2, we check two constraints, the number of clusters and the distance between two closest clusters. Once we obtain the desired number of clusters or if the distance between two closest clusters becomes greater than a preset threshold value, we terminate the merging and return the results.

Figure 3 gives a two-dimension visualization of how our cluster-merge algorithm works. For Figure 3, we use 2,541 manually synthesized 2D data points for K-means clustering test. We manipulate these data points to make it roughly follow certain degree of sparseness. The two big clusters on the left are used to simulate the high-density area, while the three small clusters in the right are used to simulate the sparse area. For visualization purpose, we scale the red circle proportionally smaller to cover only a portion of the clusters while the center of the red circles show the real cluster centers. The left figure shows the k-means clustering result by setting k equals to 10, we can see more cluster centers are crowded into the high density area. After our cluster-merge algorithm, the resulting 6 clusters are satisfactory to our demand.

```
Input: n clusters
Output: k clusters
MergeCluster(n,k,r)
if(k>=n)
    return n; //already <= k clusters
while(k<n)
    do
        find two closest centers c1, c2 among n clusters
        if(dist(c1,c2) > r)  //radius limit
            break;
        merge c1, c2 into c
        insert c into the list of cluster centers
        delete c1 and c2 from the list of cluster centers
    n = n - 1
return n
```

Fig. 2. Pseudocode for merging clusters.

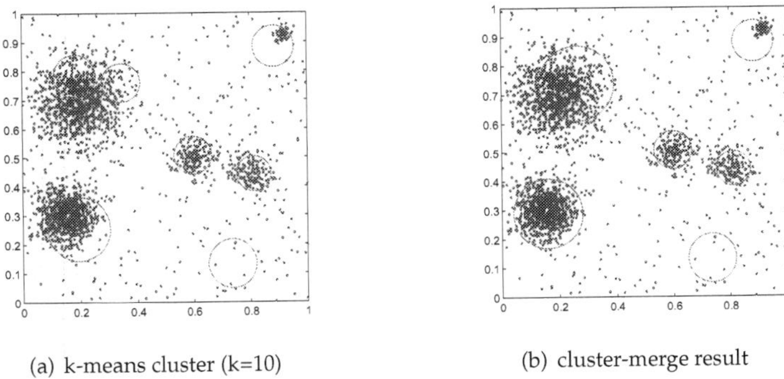

(a) k-means cluster (k=10)   (b) cluster-merge result

Fig. 3. Merge close clusters (setting radius < 0.1732).

5. Codebook Design and Feature Extraction

In this section, we are going to use the clustering-merge algorithm discussed in seciton 4 in image codebook design. As image color codebook design is very straightforward, we are not going to include it in this chapter due to page limit. We only discuss image texture and shape codebooks.

5.1 Inner, Bordering and Crossing Tiles

Before we discuss texture words and shape words, we will define several relevant tile types that will support extracting such features. Figure 4 shows how we divide an actual image from into small (64 × 64) tiles for further feature extraction. Notice that if we divide the original image into small grids (as in the top right image), some small tiles (tile 4, 5, and 6, etc) will have uniform texture patterns since they are totally inside one object or inside the background. We will name these tiles *inner tiles* as they lay totally inside an object or the background. On the other side, tiles such as tile 1, 2, and 3 don't have uniform texture patterns as they

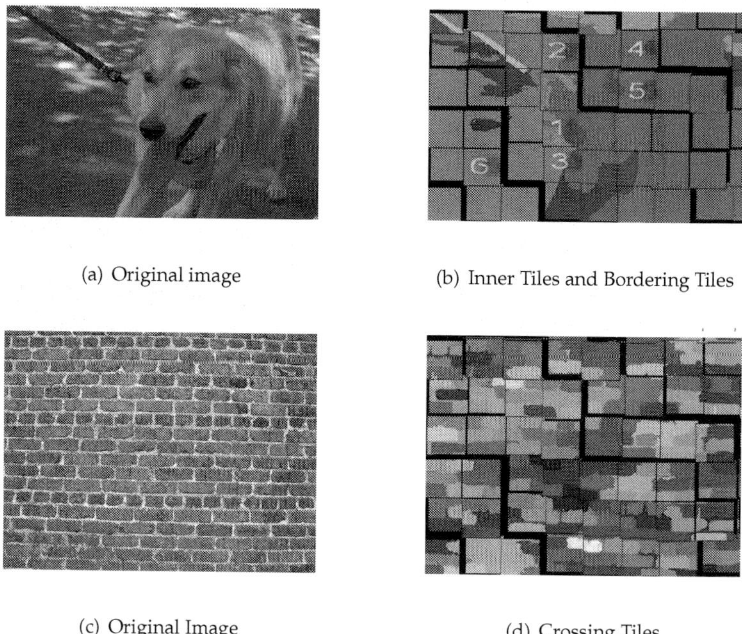

(a) Original image   (b) Inner Tiles and Bordering Tiles

(c) Original Image   (d) Crossing Tiles

Fig. 4. Inner tiles (4, 5, 6), Bordering tiles (1, 2, 3), and Crossing tile (right bottom image).

contain multiple conceptual areas (the dog fur and the road). We name these tiles *bordering tiles* as they tend to border a big block and some other small blocks. *Inner tiles* are very helpful in identifying the texture pattern of an object, while *bordering tiles* are useful for identifying shapes or contours of objects. *Inner tiles* and *bordering tiles* are not sufficient to characterize image tiles. For instance, when we segment and divide the brick wall image (in Figure 4), we cannot get even one tile (right figure) which purely belongs to one big block or borders one big block. To deal with such case, we define another type of tile: *crossing tile*. By definition, it contains many small blocks without any pixel belonging to any big block. Such segmentation results often mean that the image is a texture image. *Crossing tiles* will be very meaningful in identifying texture patterns. For the above three types of tiles, we will select *inner tiles* and *crossing tiles* for image texture extraction and select *only bordering tiles* for shape analysis.

In order to take advantage of tiling, we need to be able to decide whether an image tile is an inner tile, bordering tile, or crossing tile. To differentiate between these three kinds of tiles, we train a simple decision tree classifier (C4.5) to learn how to automatically classify a tile into the correct type. We use three features: number of components (*len*), number of pixels of the maximum component (*max*), and standard deviation (*std*) of the number of pixels of each component in the segmented tile, and three class labels: inner tile (0), bordering tile (1), and crossing tile (2). We first use 1000 tiles as a training set. For these 1000 color segmented tiles, we manually label each segmented tile as inner tile, bordering tile, or crossing tile. After training and 10-fold cross-validation, we get the following classification model (with 93.8596

```
max <= 972
|   max <= 552
|   |   max <= 494: 2 (163.0/2.0)
|   |   max > 494
|   |   |   len <= 3: 1 (38.0/8.0)
|   |   |   len > 3: 2 (56.0/9.0)
|   max > 552
|   |   len <= 4: 1 (489.0/10.0)
|   |   len > 4
|   |   |   std <= 223.637
|   |   |   |   len <= 5
|   |   |   |   |   max <= 593: 2 (8.0/2.0)
|   |   |   |   |   max > 593: 1 (8.0/1.0)
|   |   |   |   len > 5
|   |   |   |   |   std <= 198.513: 2 (6.0)
|   |   |   |   |   std > 198.513
|   |   |   |   |   |   max <= 635: 1 (3.0)
|   |   |   |   |   |   max > 635: 2 (4.0)
|   |   |   std > 223.637: 1 (49.0/5.0)
max > 972: 0 (316.0/3.0)
```

Fig. 5. Decision Tree Model for Classifying Tiles.

% Correctly Classified Instances). For image segmentation, we use the graph based method proposed by Felzenszwalb & Huttenlocher (2004).

5.2 Image Texture Codebook

We use Gabor texture feature extraction to generate the image texture codebook. However, because we first need to get the global image texture dictionary from a set of training texture images, instead of clustering the filtered image output *pixel-wise* for only one image as in Malik et al. (1999), we will perform clustering *tile-wise* on an entire *set* of training images. This way, each texture image can be subdivided into small *tiles* which corresponds to certain *texture words*. We analyze texture tile-wise instead of textel-wise because this corresponds to our visual understanding of images: textures can make sense to us only when they are displayed in a *region* and thus form a pattern.

Furthermore, we do not use all the segmented components for texture analysis. Instead we use only the inner tiles and crossing tiles. This is because first of all, image segmentation is not very accurate especially in the bordering part separating two components or blocks. Another reason is that sampling inner tiles instead of all the segmented blocks can help reduce the computational cost and raises the possibility of saving even more computations by only computing the texture features of those tiles that are not similar to any other analyzed tiles. For instance, before we compute one tile's texture feature, we can check whether most of its pixel values are similar to the previous neighboring tile in the same block by taking the pixel value difference. If we find that the tiles are very similar, then we can simply classify this tile into the same pattern as the previous tile and avoid computing its texture features.

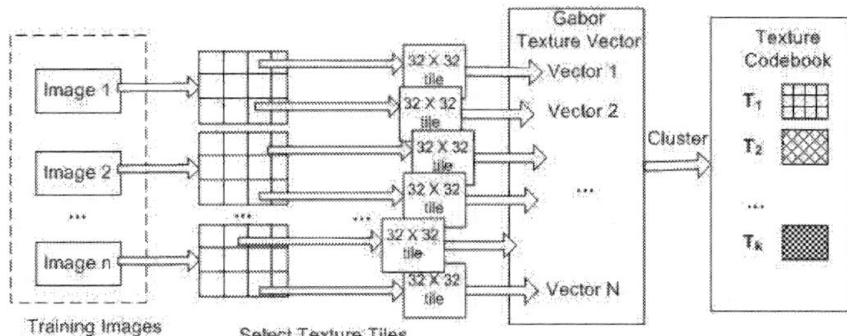

Fig. 6. Process of Generating Image Texture Codebook.

To compute the texture codebook, we divide each image into 32×32 pixel blocks or tiles, select texture tiles (inner tiles and crossing tiles) according to image segmentation results, then apply Gabor filters to each texture tile, and finally record the corresponding texture features. The process for generating the image texture codebook is summarized in Figure 6. We use 1000 texture pictures for training (each picture roughly contains 160 (32×32 pixel) tiles with more than half of the tiles are selected as texture tiles). This process yield 128 texture words (compared to Ma & Manjunath (1998) which yields 950 codewords).

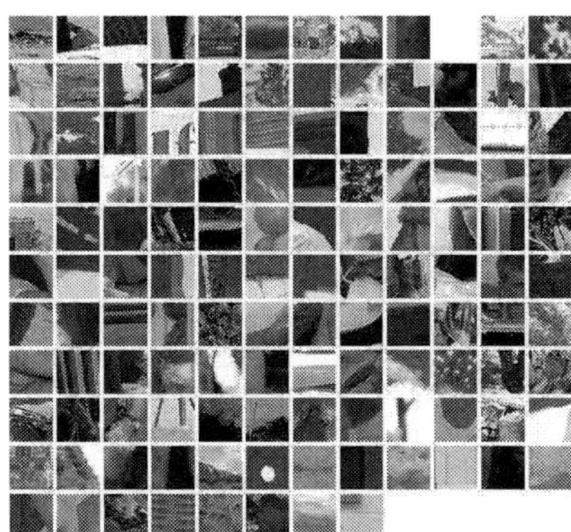

Fig. 7. Example Texture Codebook.

The clustering method used is GLA followed by the cluster-merge algorithm, as discussed above. Figure 7 shows an example texture book generated using the above procedure.

5.3 Extracting and Indexing Texture Features

When we try to extract image texture words, we apply Gabor filters to small 32×32 image texture tiles. After extracting the image texture feature vector, we use Nearest Neighbor (accelerated by a Kd-tree structure) to determine the corresponding texture codeword from the texture codebook.

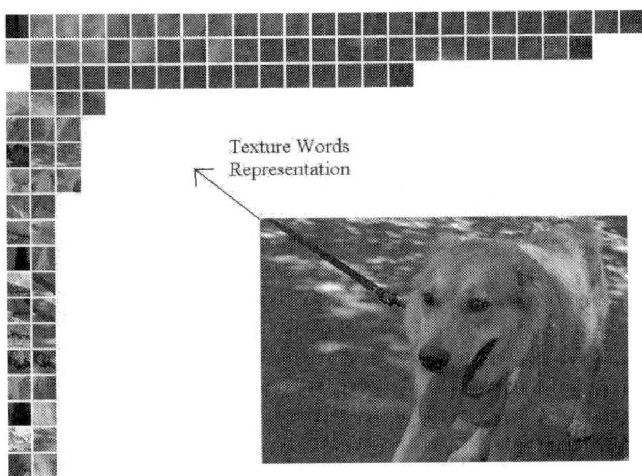

Fig. 8. Extracting Texturewords from An Image.

Figure 8 gives an example of extracting texture words from an actual image. The leftmost column contains the representative tiles selected from the codebook in Figure 7, while the remaining tiles are the corresponding image tiles extracted from the actual image. In the process of extracting texturewords from an actual image, we adopt a similar procedure, where we segment the image and select texture tiles (inner tiles and crossing tiles) according to the segmentation results using the decision tree model show in model 5. We use nearest neighbor search method to find the representative texture word in the texture codebook to represent each texture tile.

5.4 Image Boundary Angle Codebook

In this section, we propose a novel method of image retrieval that is very similar to shape-based image retrieval. We name this new type of retrieval *boundary angle-based image retrieval* or *BABIR*. In section 2, we have reviewed several shape-base image retrieval systems, and their limitations. Considering all of the drawbacks, we propose to use an important part of the shape boundaries, *boundary angles*, to represent a shape. For instance, we can use two 90 degree angles or even four straight lines to represent a rectangle. These boundary angles seem to agree with human's atomic understanding of shapes, and constitute the basic elements in drawing a picture. This simplification has important consequences. First, while it can be hard for an image segmentation system to identify the accurate shape, most image segmentation systems would easily identify the boundary lines or angles. Second, boundary-angle-based retrieval relies on basic elements like straight lines or turning angles or arcs which are actually scale and rotation invariant. As discussed in section 5.3, we will use *bordering tiles*, for boundary-angle-based retrieval. Figure 9 gives another example showing these tiles, where we can see that it is very hard for an image segmentation scheme to render the whole bird shape as one component. However, we are able to segment image for the boundary-angle contours to extract boundary-angle words.

(a) Original image

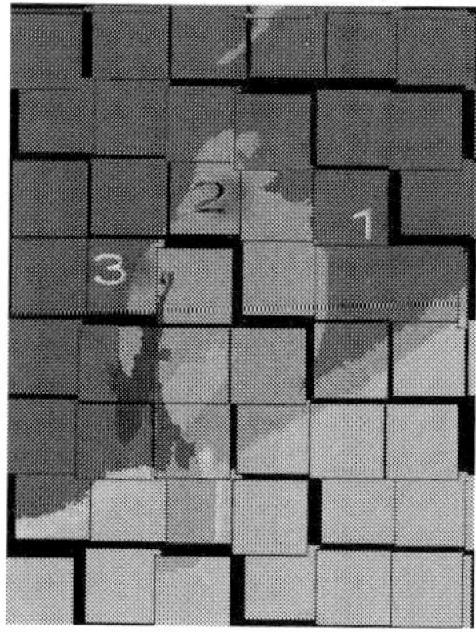

(b) Segmented Tiles

Fig. 9. sample boundary angles tiles (1, 2, 3).

For shape feature, we will adopt the region-based shape representation proposed in Lu & Sajjanhar (1999) and Prasad et al. (2004) with slight modification. The region based method

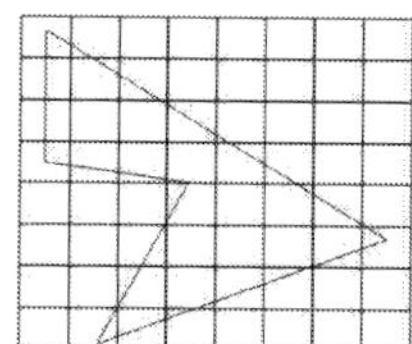

Fig. 10. Region based shape representation.

can be illustrated in Figure 10, where a grid with fixed-size square cells was used to cover the shape region. "1" and "0" are assigned to the small cells in which the shape covers above or below 25% of the cell respectively. This allows representing the shape using the binary sequence: 00000000 11000000 11110000 01111000 00011110 00011110 00111000 00100000. To adapt the grid-based method to our application, we further grid each image tile into $8 \times 8 = 64$ small pixel cells. Instead of using "0" and "1" to represent each cell, we use integer value ranging from "0" to "16" to represent each cell, where the value of the cell is a count of image pixels belonging to the dominant component of the image tile. This sequence of 64 counts will represent the shape of each boundary angle tile, and is called the *shape vector* of the image tile. Then we perform clustering and cluster-merging in the same way as we did for image

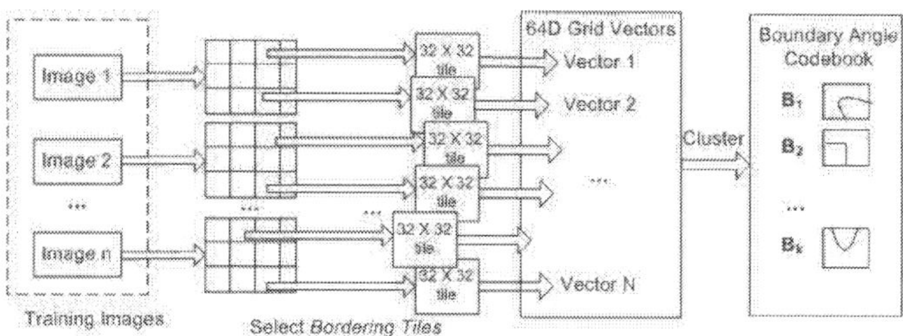

Fig. 11. Process of Generating the Boundary-Angle Codebook.

textures. Here, as well, we use a training set (e.g., 1000 shape images) and use tile selection, GLA method and the cluster-merging algorithm to generate a shape codebook. This process is summarized in Figure 11, while Figure 12 shows an example of a boundary angle codebook generated using our method.

Once we have obtained the boundary angle codebook, during the image crawling phase, we adopt a procedure that is similar to extracting texture codewords (Kd-tree-based Nearest Neighbor mapping) to extract image-boundary-angle code words. Figure 13 shows an example of extracting boundary angle words from an image.

6. Experimental Results

6.1 Effectiveness of Texture Word Representation

To demonstrate the effectiveness of our tile-based image representation, we will compare the retrieval precision of using image texture tiles with that of using the whole image texture vectors. Our assumption is that although we use a much faster boolean query consisting of several representative image texture words, we can get a comparable retrieval precision to that of using the whole image texture vectors for similarity search, which the general CBIR systems would use. To evaluate the precision, we adopt a similar strategy as was used in SIMPLIcity Wang et al. (2001). We use a subset of COREL database with 10 categories shown in table 1, where each category contains 100 semantically coherent images. Altogether, there are 1000 images in total for testing. In the codebook generation stage, we collect 100 images

Africa	Beach	Buildings	Buses	Dinosaurs
Horses	Flowers	Elephants	Food	Mountains

Table 1. COREL Categories of Images Tested

by randomly selecting 10 images from each category. We use these 100 images to generate a global image texture codebook. After we build the image search by implementing Nutch[1]

---

[1] http://lucene.apache.org/nutch/

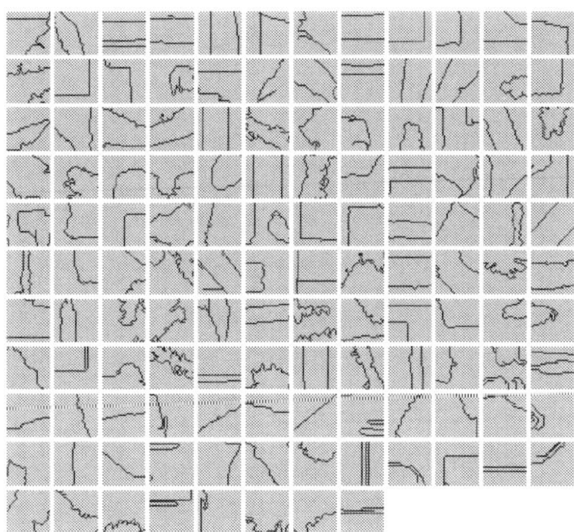

Fig. 12. Example Boundary Angle Codebook.

on image texture feature, we conduct our testing by randomly selecting three images from each category as query images (30 queries for each case). To form the actual queries, for the texture words representation case, we select top-N (N ranges from 1 to 10) texture words for the query image to form the boolean query and we use Nutch's default $TF \times IDF$ ranking. For the texture vector query case, we take the whole 48 dimension texture vector for the query image to form the query and use Euclidean distance measure for ranking. We show 10 results in each page and examine the number of category matches in the first page. In case the total number of results is less than 10, we show all the results in the first page. We then calculate the precision as the number of category matches in the first page divided by the number of results in the same page. We then average the precision of the 30 result-sets and compare the two types of methods. The results is shown in Figure 14.

As shown in Figure 14, the precision for Texture words boolean query case increases as the number of query terms increases. As the number of query terms approaches 5 or 6, the average precision of boolean query comes close to the vector similarity query case. On the other hand, the number of returned results drops dramatically as the number of query terms increases as shown in Figure 15. For instance, the average number of returned results drops from 13.5 to 6.6 as the number of terms in the query increases from 5 to 6. Although the average precision is high as we include much more terms (say 9 or 10), the very few number of results returned should prevent us from using too many terms. Combining Figure 14 and Figure 15, we can see that selecting around 5 query terms would give us a balanced results of desirable precision and total number of results.

On the other end, the retrieval efficiency benefit of using boolean query over vector similarity query is obvious, as shown in Figure 16 and the experiments are with the Linux server (with

Fig. 13. Extract Boundary-Angle Words.

Intel(R) Xeon(TM) CPU 2.80GHz, 2cpu, and 2G memory). We also can see that as the number of terms contained in the boolean query increases, the retrieval speed does not fluctuate much. This is guaranteed by the inverted indexing structure.

6.2 Effectiveness of on Boundary-angle Based Retrieval

Since we have argued for using boundary-angle instead of whole shape for image retrieval, we need to empirically justify this choice. For this experiment, we use the Columbia image testing set, which contains 7200 images of 100 objects traditionally used to evaluate shape-based retrieval, and measure the precision of retrieval. We adopt a similar procedure to get the global boundary-angle codebooks. We first randomly select 7 images for each object and get 700 images in total for training the boundary-angle codebook. Then we use Nutch to build the inverted index and conduct the testing by two types of search. For each object, we randomly choose 2 images to form the query images and altogether we get 200 query images. To form the boundary-angle boolean query, we use top-N (N ranges from 1 to 5) boundary-angle words and to form the shape vector query, we use the 64D shape grid vector. Again, we consider the returned results that correspond to the same object as accurate matches. We compare the precision of using the two methods. We can see from Figure 17 and Figure 18 that when we choose a boolean query that contains 3 or 4 terms, we can get very close precision as the vector nearest-neighbor query case without losing too much recall. Note the average number of returned results is 29.2 for 3-term boolean query and 6.6 for 4-term boolean query. Also, we can see the obvious efficiency benefit of using boolean queries from Figure 19.

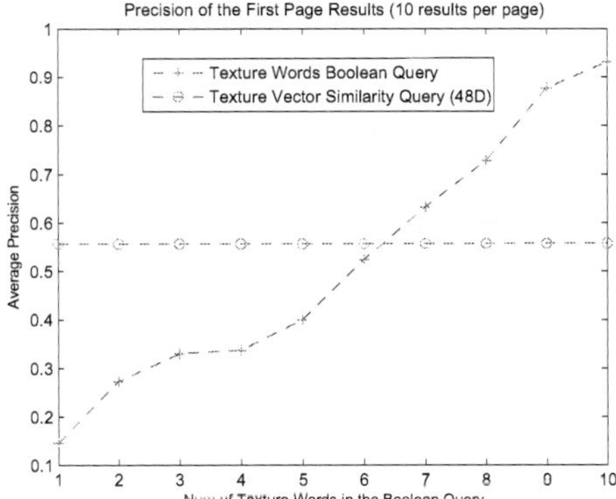

Fig. 14. Texture Query Precision Comparison.

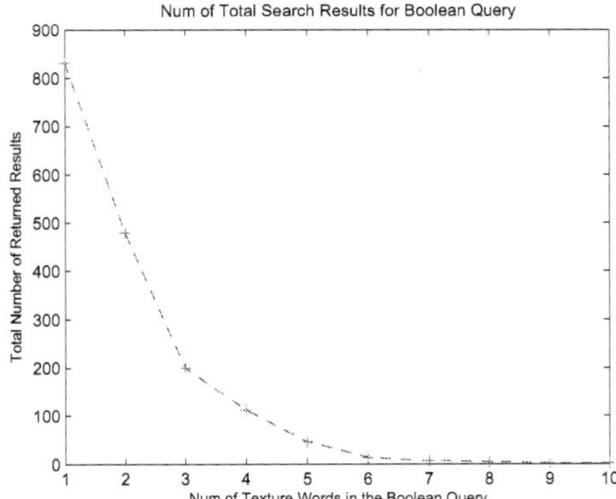

Fig. 15. Number of Results Returned (Texture).

7. Conclusions and Future Works

We have shown through our experiments that image content features follow the power-law spare distribution. Then we take advantage of such sparseness for inverted file indexing. Our clustering-merge algorithm gave us better cluster center representations over GLA clustering, which generated cluster centers over-crowdedness in high density area for sparse data. Our experimental results shows our tile-based image *textualization* process for image texture and shape features are effective. Such techniques can be used for scalable and efficient content-based image retrieval and search systems.

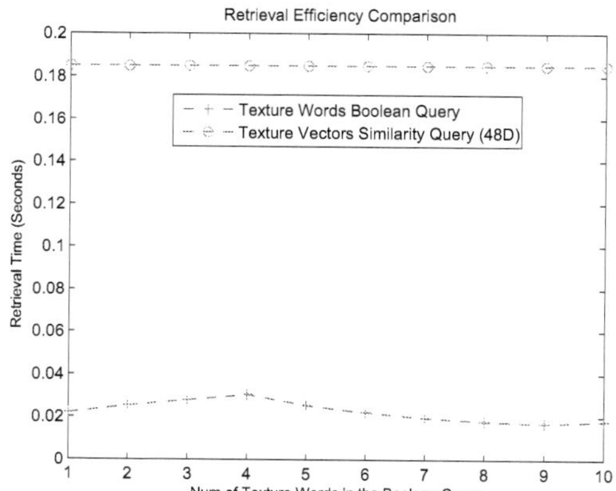

Fig. 16. Texture Retrieval Efficiency Comparison.

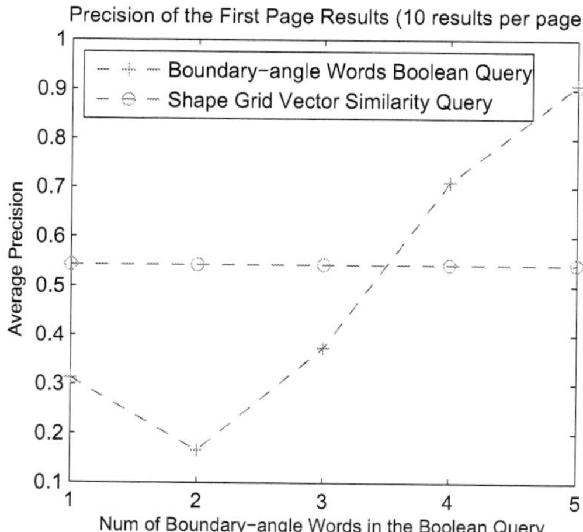

Fig. 17. Shape Query Precision Comparison.

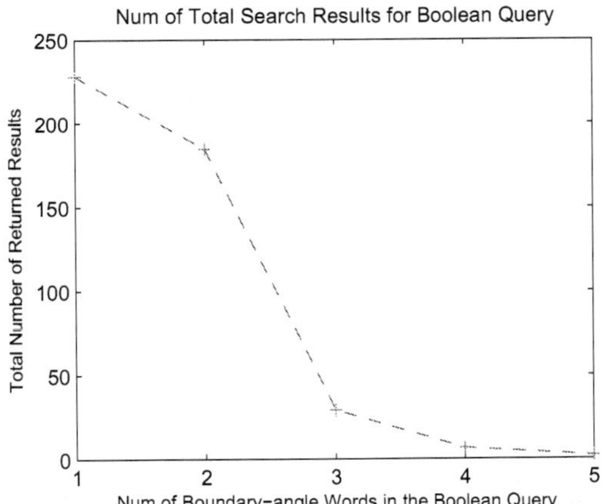

Fig. 18. Number of Results Returned (Shape).

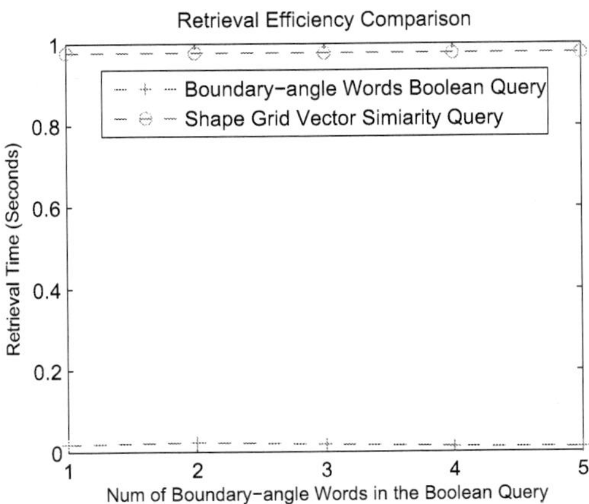

Fig. 19. Shape Retrieval Efficiency Comparison.

8. References

Beckmann, N., Kriegel, H. P., Schneider, R. & Seeger:, B. (1990). The r*-tree: An efficient and robust access method for points and rectangles, *SIGMOD Conference*, pp. 322–331.

Carson, C., Thomas, M., Belongie, S., Hellerstein, J. & Malik, J. (1999). Blobworld: A system for region-based image indexing and retrieval, *Proc. Third International Conf. Visual Information Systems*, pp. 509–516.

Felzenszwalb, P. F. & Huttenlocher, D. P. (2004). Efficient graph-based image segmentation, *Int. J. Comput. Vision* **59**(2): 167–181.

Flickner, M., Sawhney, H., Niblack, W., Ashley, J. & et al (1995). Query by image and video content: the qbic system, *IEEE computer* **28**(9): 23–32.

Gersho, A. & Gray, R. M. (1992). Kluwer Academic Publishers.

Guttman, A. (1984). R-trees: A dynamic index structure for spatial searching, *ACM SIGMOD International Conference on Management of Data*, pp. 47–57.

Iqbal, Q. & Aggarwal, J. (2002). Retrieval by classification of images containing large man-made objects using perceptual grouping, *Pattern Recognition* **35**: 1463–1479.

Jacobs, C. E., Finkelstein, A. & Salesin, D. H. (1995). Fast multiresolution image querying, *Computer Graphics* **29**(Annual Conference Series): 277–286.

Jegou, H., Harzallah, H. & Schmid, C. (2007). A contextual dissimilarity measure for accurate and efficient image search, *IEEE Conference on Computer Vision & Pattern Recognition*.

Jing, F., Li, M., Zhang, H. & Zhang, B. (2004). An efficient and effective region-based image retrieval framework, *IEEE TRANSACTIONS ON IMAGE PROCESSING* **13**(5).

Jurie, F. & Triggs, B. (2005). Creating efficient codebooks for visual recognition, *ICCV '05: Proceedings of the Tenth IEEE International Conference on Computer Vision (ICCV'05) Volume 1*, IEEE Computer Society, Washington, DC, USA, pp. 604–610.

Lu, G. & Sajjanhar, A. (1999). Region-based shape representation and similarity measure suitable for content-based image retrieval, *Multimedia Syst.* **7**(2): 165–174.

Lu, H., Ooi, B. C., Shen, H. T. & Xue, X. (2006). Hierarchical indexing structure for efficient similarity search in video retrieval, *IEEE TRANSACTIONS ON KNOWLEDGE AND DATA ENGINEERING*, **18**(11): 1544–1559.

Ma, W.-Y. & Manjunath, B. S. (1998). A texture thesaurus for browsing large aerial photographs, *Journal of the American Society for Information Science* **49**(7): 633–48.

Malik, J., Belongie, S., Shi, J. & Leung, T. K. (1999). Textons, contours and regions: Cue integration in image segmentation, *ICCV (2)*, pp. 918–925.

Mojsilovic, A., Kovacevic, J., Hu, J., Safranek, R. J. & Ganapathy, K. (2000). Matching and retrieval based on the vocabulary and grammar of color patterns, *IEEE Trans. on Image Processing* **9**(1): 38–54.

Natsev, A., Rastogi, R. & Shim, K. (2004). Walrus: A similarity retrieval algorithm for image databases, *IEEE TRANSACTIONS ON KNOWLEDGE AND DATA ENGINEERING* **16**(3): 301–316.

Prasad, B. G., Biswas, K. K. & Gupta, S. K. (2004). Region-based image retrieval using integrated color, shape, and location index, *Comput. Vis. Image Underst.* **94**(1-3): 193–233.

Rahman, M. M., Desai, B. C. & Bhattacharya, P. (2006). Visual keyword-based image retrieval using latent semantic indexing, correlation-enhanced similarity matching and query expansion in inverted index, *10th International Database Engineering and Applications Symposium (IDEAS'06)*, pp. 201–208.

Safar, M., Shahabi, C. & Sun, X. (2000). Image retrieval by shape: A comparative study, *IEEE International Conference on Multimedia and Expo (I)*, pp. 141–144.

Shi, J. & Malik, J. (2000). Normalized cuts and image segmentation, *IEEE Transactions on Pattern Analysis and Machine Intelligence* **22**(8): 888–905.

Sivic, J. & Zisserman, A. (2003). Video Google: A text retrieval approach to object matching in videos, *Proceedings of the International Conference on Computer Vision*, Vol. 2, pp. 1470–1477.

Squire, D., Muller, W., Muller, H. & Raki, J. (1999). Content-based query of image databases, inspirations from text retrieval: inverted files, frequency-based weights and relevance feedback.

Wang, J. Z., Li, J. & Wiederhold, G. (2001). SIMPLIcity: Semantics-sensitive integrated matching for picture LIbraries, *IEEE Transactions on Pattern Analysis and Machine Intelligence* **23**(9): 947–963.

Wang, J. Z., Wiederhold, G., Firschein, O. & Wei, S. X. (1997). Content-based image indexing and searching using daubechies' wavelets, *International Journal on Digital Libraries* 1: 311–328.

Weber, R., Schek, H.-J. & Blott, S. (1998). A quantitative analysis and performance study for similarity-search methods in high-dimensional spaces, *Proc. 24th Int. Conf. Very Large Data Bases, VLDB*, pp. 194–205.

Westerveld, T. (2000). Image retrieval: Content versus context, *Content-Based Multimedia Information Access, RIAO*, p. 276ÍC284.

Witten, I. H., Moffat, A. & Bell, T. C. (1999). *Managing gigabytes (2nd ed.): compressing and indexing documents and images*, Morgan Kaufmann Publishers Inc., San Francisco, CA, USA.

Zhang, Z., Rojas, C., Nasraoui, O. & Frigui, H. (2006). Show and tell: A seamlessly integrated tool for searching with image content and text, *In Proceedings of the ACM-SIGIR Open Source Information Retrieval workshop*.

Zobel, J., Moffat, A. & Ramamohanarao, K. (1998). Inverted files versus signature files for text indexing, *ACM Transactions on Database Systems* **23**(4): 453–490.

13

Illumination Invariants Based on Markov Random Fields

Pavel Vácha and Michal Haindl
Institute of Information Theory and Automation of the ASCR
Czech Republic

1. Introduction

Ongoing expansion of digital images requires new methods for sorting, browsing, and searching through huge image databases. Content-based image retrieval (CBIR) systems, which are database search engines for images, typically takes a user selected image or series of images and tries to retrieve similar images from a large image database. Although image retrieval has been an active research area for many years (Smeulders et al., 2000) this difficult problem is still far from being solved. One of the reasons is that common image features do not provide required discriminability and invariance. Optimal robust features should be geometry and illumination invariant and still remain highly discriminative, which are often contradictory requirements.

Simpler CBIR methods are based only on colour features and achieve illumination invariance by normalising colour bands or using the colour ratio histogram (Gevers & Smeulders, 2001). However, colour based methods rarely perform sufficiently well in natural visual scenes because they cannot detect similar objects in different locations, backgrounds or illuminations.

Textures are important clues to specify objects present in a visual scene. Unfortunately, the visual appearance of natural prevailing textures is highly illumination and view direction dependent. As a consequence, most recent natural texture based classification or segmentation methods require multiple training images captured under a full variety of possible illumination and viewing conditions for each class (Suen & Healey, 2000; Varma & Zisserman, 2005). Such learning is obviously clumsy and very often even impossible if required measurements are not available. Drbohlav & Chantler (2005) allow a single training image per class, but they require surfaces of uniform albedo, smooth and shallow relief, the illumination sufficiently far from the texture macro-normal and most seriously the knowledge of illumination direction for all involved (trained as well as tested) textures. It was demonstrated by Chen et al. (2000); Jacobs et al. (1998) that for grey image of an object with Lambertian reflectance there are no discriminative functions that are invariant to change of illumination direction. However, multispectral images can also rely on relations of spectral planes and therefore overcome this theoretical property.

Colour constancy algorithms, represented by Finlayson (1995), attempt to recover the image illuminated by some standard illumination, which is an unnecessarily complex task and it induces additional assumptions on a recognised scene. The normalisation of an image before the recognition proposed in Finlyason & Xu (2002) is able to cancel changes of illumination colour, lighting changes caused by the object geometry and even a power (gamma) function, which is usually applied to image data during the coding process. However, since the method normalises lighting changes caused by the geometry it completely wipes out the structure of rough textures and therefore it destroys the possibility to recognise such textures. Simultaneously, the invariants to geometry introduced lighting changes tend to be unstable because of nonlinear transformations usually involved. An interesting approach of quasi-invariants (Weijer et al., 2005) relieves the condition of full invariance and therefore it is less sensitive to noise. Parameters of Weibull-distribution of image edges (Geusebroek & Smeulders, 2005) are proposed as insensitive to illumination brightness. Healey & Wang (1995), Yang & Al-Rawi (2005) employ properties of correlation functions between different spectral channels to achieve invariance to illumination spectrum changes. Hoang & Geausebroek (2005), Geusebroek et al. (2003) introduced a method based on the logarithm of Gabor filter responses together with a new Gaussian colour model. However, the Gaussian colour model of RGB texture is implemented as a simple matrix multiplication and invariance to any linear transformation of texture values is inherent part of the illumination invariant features proposed in the rest of this article.

Local Binary Patterns (Ojala, Pietikäinen & Mäenpää, 2002) (LBP) are popular illumination invariant features, which we use for comparison. The texton representation (Varma & Zisserman, 2005) based on MR8 filter responses have been extended to incorporate colour information and to be illumination invariant (Burghouts & Geusebroek, 2009). Another approach (Targhi et al., 2008) generates unseen training images using the photometric stereo approach. Although, it improves classification accuracy, this algorithm has strong requirements of three mutually registered images with different illumination direction for each material.

We present textural features, which are invariant to illumination brightness and spectrum changes and which do not require any knowledge of illumination spectrum. The features are robust to illumination direction changes and do not require knowledge of illumination direction or mutual texture registration. They can be applied for textured object retrieval if only a single illumination training image is available for each class.

These properties are verified on Outex database (Ojala, Mäenpää, Pietikäinen, Viertola, Kyllönen & Huovinen, 2002), where texture images are illuminated under three different spectra, and University of Bonn BTF texture measurements (Meseth et al., 2003), where illumination sources are spanned over 75% of possible illumination direction above material samples. Preliminary experiments were published in Vacha & Haindl (2008), Vacha & Haindl (2007).

The chapter is organised as follows: The illumination model assumptions are reviewed in Section 2. Texture model description and derivation of illumination invariant features follow in Section 3. Experimental results are presented in Section 5 and Section 6 concludes this chapter.

2. Illumination Model

Illumination conditions can change due to various reasons. In our approach we allow changes of brightness and spectrum of illumination sources. We assume that positions of viewpoint and illumination sources remain unchanged and that the illumination sources are far enough to produce uniform illumination. Furthermore, we assume planar textured Lambertian surfaces with varying albedo and surface texture normal.

The previous assumptions are quite strong and they are required to theoretically derive the illumination invariance of features. However, our experiments with natural surfaces show that the derived features are very robust even in the setup, which is in contradiction with previous assumptions (test with eighty different illumination positions).

Let us denote a multiindex $r = (r_1, r_2)$ where r_1 is the row and r_2 the column index, respectively. Value acquired by the j−th sensor at the location r can be expressed as

$$Y_{r,j} = \int_\omega E(\lambda)\, S(r,\lambda)\, R_j(\lambda)\, d\lambda \ ,$$

where $E(\lambda)$ is the spectral power distribution of a single illumination, $S(r,\lambda)$ is a Lambertian reflectance coefficient at the position r, $R_j(\lambda)$ is the j−th sensor response function, and the integral is taken over the visible spectrum ω. The Lambertian reflectance term $S(r,\lambda)$ depends on surface normal, illumination direction, and surface albedo.

Following the work of Finlayson (1995), we approximate the surface reflectance $S(r,\lambda)$ by a linear combination of a fixed basis $S(r,\lambda) = \sum_{c=1}^{C} d_c\, s_c(\lambda)$, where functions s_c are optimal basis functions that represent the data. The method for finding suitable basis was introduced by Marimont & Wandell (1992), they also conclude that, given the human receptive cones, a 3-dimensional basis set is sufficient to model colour observations. However, finding such basis set is not necessary our method, because the key assumption is its existence.

Provided that $j = 1,\ldots,C$ sensor measurements are available and the illumination and view point positions are the same, the images acquired with different illumination spectra can be transformed to each other by the linear transformation:

$$\tilde{Y}_r = B\, Y_r \quad \forall r \ , \tag{1}$$

where $\tilde{Y}, Y$ are texture images with different illuminations, and B is a $C \times C$ transformation matrix. The formula (1) is valid even for several illumination sources with variable spectra provided that the spectra of all sources are the same and the positions of the illumination sources remain fixed.

More importantly, it can be proved that formula (1) is valid not only for Lambertian surfaces, but also for surface model with specular reflectance component (e.g. dichromatic reflection model (Shafer, 1985), which comprise also the well-known Phong reflection model).

If we assume further diagonal transformation (1), then the invariance to illumination colour change can be achieved by the spectral planes normalisation:

$$Y'_{r,j} = \frac{Y_{r,j}}{\sum_s Y_{s,j}} \quad \forall j = 1,\ldots,C \ . \tag{2}$$

Since neither of our methods requires this type of normalisation, it is applied to Gabor features, which are further used for comparison purposes, only.

No method that guarantee an illumination invariance to surface geometry effects have been used. The primary reason is that the invariance to this geometry effects is not desirable because a surface structure is the inherent part of a surface texture appearance. Moreover, many images are extremely dark and the normalisation of RGB triplets $\frac{z}{r+g+b}, z \in \{r, g, b\}$ produces not only a huge amount of noise, but it is also undefined for black pixels ($r + g + b = 0$). On the other hand, invariants based on pixel hues are ambiguous on the black-white axis and again they are not suitable for rough textures with uniform colours.

3. Texture Representation

Let us assume each texture to be composed of C spectral planes measured by the corresponding sensors. Texture analysis starts with the factorisation of a texture into K levels of the Gaussian pyramid. All C spectral planes are factorised using the same pyramid thus the corresponding multispectral pixels for every pyramid level have C components $Y_r = [Y_{r,1}, \ldots, Y_{r,C}]^T$. Each pyramid level is either modelled by 3-dimensional Markov random field (MRF) model or mutually decorrelated by the Karhunen-Loeve transformation (Principal Component Analysis) and subsequently modelled using a set of C 2-dimensional MRF models. The MRF model parameters are estimated and finally illumination invariants are computed from these parameters.

3.1 CAR Model

The CAR representation assumes that the multispectral texture pixel Y_r at the k-th Gaussian pyramid level can be locally modelled by an adaptive simultaneous Causal Autoregressive Random (CAR) field model. We denote the $C\eta \times 1$ data vector

$$Z_r = [Y_{r-s}^T : \forall s \in I_r]^T \tag{3}$$

where $r = (r_1, r_2), s, t$ are multiindices, Z_r consists of neighbour pixel values for given r. The multiindex changes according to the chosen direction of movement on the image plane e.g. $t - 1 = (t_1, t_2 - 1)$, $t - 2 = (t_1, t_2 - 2), \ldots$. Some selected contextual causal or unilateral neighbour index shift set is denoted I_r and $\eta = cardinality(I_r)$. The matrix form of an adaptive CAR model is:

$$Y_r = \gamma Z_r + \epsilon_r \ , \tag{4}$$

where $\gamma = [A_1, \ldots, A_\eta]$ is the $C \times C\eta$ unknown parameter matrix with matrices A_s. In the case of C 2D CAR models stacked into the model equation (4) the parameter matrices A_s are diagonal otherwise they are full matrices for general 3D CAR models. The white noise vector ϵ_r has zero mean and constant but unknown covariance matrix Σ. Moreover, we assume the probability density of ϵ_r to have the normal distribution independent of previous data and being the same for every position r. Additionally for 2D CAR model, we assume uncorrelated noise vector components, i.e.,

$$E\{\epsilon_{r,i}\epsilon_{r,j}\} = 0 \qquad \forall r, i, j, \ i \neq j \ .$$

The task consists in finding the parameter conditional density $p(\gamma \,|\, Y^{(t-1)})$ given the known process history $Y^{(t-1)} = \{Y_{t-1}, Y_{t-2}, \ldots, Y_1, Z_t, Z_{t-1}, \ldots, Z_1\}$ and taking its conditional mean as the textural feature representation. Assuming normality of the white noise component ϵ_t, conditional independence between pixels and the normal-Wishart parameter prior, we have shown (Haindl & Šimberová, 1992) that the conditional mean value is:

$$E[\gamma \,|\, Y^{(t-1)}] = \hat{\gamma}_{t-1} \ . \tag{5}$$

The following notation is used in (5):

$$
\begin{aligned}
\hat{\gamma}_{t-1}^T &= V_{zz(t-1)}^{-1} V_{zy(t-1)} \ , \\
V_{t-1} &= \tilde{V}_{t-1} + V_0 \ , \\
\tilde{V}_{t-1} &= \begin{pmatrix} \sum_{u=1}^{t-1} Y_u Y_u^T & \sum_{u=1}^{t-1} Y_u Z_u^T \\ \sum_{u=1}^{t-1} Z_u Y_u^T & \sum_{u=1}^{t-1} Z_u Z_u^T \end{pmatrix} \\
&= \begin{pmatrix} \tilde{V}_{yy(t-1)} & \tilde{V}_{zy(t-1)}^T \\ \tilde{V}_{zy(t-1)} & \tilde{V}_{zz(t-1)} \end{pmatrix} \ , \\
\lambda_{t-1} &= V_{yy(t-1)} - V_{zy(t-1)}^T V_{zz(t-1)}^{-1}
\end{aligned}
\tag{6}
$$

and V_0 is a positive definite matrix. It is easy to check (see Haindl & Šimberová (1992)) also the validity of the following recursive parameter estimator:

$$\hat{\gamma}_t^T = \hat{\gamma}_{t-1}^T + \frac{V_{zz(t-1)}^{-1} Z_t (Y_t - \hat{\gamma}_{t-1} Z_t)^T}{(1 + Z_t^T V_{zz(t-1)}^{-1} Z_t)} , \tag{7}$$

and λ_t can be evaluated recursively too. For numerical realisation of the model statistics (5)-(7) see discussion in Haindl & Šimberová (1992).

Textural features for each Gaussian pyramid level k is represented by the parametric matrix $\hat{\gamma}^{(k)}$, $k = 1, \ldots, K$. These parametric estimates are combined into the resulting parametric matrix:

$$\Theta = [\hat{\gamma}^{(k)} \ \forall k] . \tag{8}$$

This matrix contains estimations of the multiresolution CAR model (a set of either 2D or 3D CAR models) parameters. Illumination invariants are subsequently derived from these parameters.

3.2 GMRF Factor Model

The alternative representation assumes that spectral planes of the $k-$th pyramid level are locally modelled using a 2D Gaussian Markov Random Field model (GMRF). This model is obtained if the local conditional density of the MRF model is Gaussian:

$$p(Y_{r,j}|Y_{s,j} \ \forall s \in I_r) = \frac{1}{\sigma_j \sqrt{2\pi}} \exp\left\{ -\frac{(Y_{r,j} - \gamma_j Z_{r,j})^2}{2\sigma_j^2} \right\}, \tag{9}$$

where $Y_{r,j}$ are mean centred values and j is the spectral plane index $j = 1 \ldots C$. The data vector is redefined as $Z_{r,j} = [Y_{r+s,j} \ \ \forall s \in I_r]^T$ and the parameter vector is $\gamma_j = [a_{s,j} \ \ \forall s \in I_r]$. The contextual neighbourhood I_r is non-causal and symmetrical. The GMRF model for centred values $Y_{r,j}$ can be expressed also in the matrix form (4), but the driving noise ϵ_r and its correlation structure is now more complex:

$$E\{\epsilon_{r,i}\epsilon_{r-s,j}\} = \begin{cases} \sigma_j^2 & \text{if } (s) = (0,0) \text{ and } i = j, \\ -\sigma_j^2 a_{s,j} & \text{if } (s) \in I_r \text{ and } i = j, \\ 0 & \text{otherwise,} \end{cases} \tag{10}$$

where $\sigma_j, a_{s,j} \ \forall s \in I_r$ are unknown parameters. The parameter estimation of the GMRF model is complicated because either Bayesian or Maximum likelihood estimate requires an iterative minimisation of a nonlinear function. Therefore we use the pseudo-likelihood estimator which is computationally simple although not efficient. The pseudo-likelihood estimate for $a_{s,j}$ parameters has the form

$$\hat{\gamma}_j^T = [a_{s,j} \ \ \forall s \in I_r]^T$$

$$= \left[\sum_{\forall r \in I} Z_{r,j} Z_{r,j}^T \right]^{-1} \sum_{\forall s \in I} Z_{r,j} Y_{r,j} , \tag{11}$$

$$\hat{\sigma}_j^2 = \frac{1}{|I|} \sum_{\forall r \in I} (Y_{r,j} - \hat{\gamma}_j Z_{r,j})^2 , \tag{12}$$

where $j = 1 \ldots C$, I is an image lattice. Single spectral plane parameters are set up using the direct sum

$$\hat{\gamma}^{(k)} = diag(\hat{\gamma}_1, \ldots, \hat{\gamma}_C) = \oplus_{j=1}^{C} \hat{\gamma}_j \tag{13}$$

and the resulting parametric matrix is again (8).

3.3 MRF Illumination Invariant Features

Illumination invariant feature vectors can be derived from the estimated MRF statistics such as (8), which is composed of the model parameter matrices A_m. On the condition that two images Y, $\tilde{Y}$ under different illumination are related by $\tilde{Y}_r = B Y_r$ (see (1)), the model data vectors are also related by the linear transformation $\tilde{Z}_r = \Delta Z_r$, where Δ is the $C\eta \times C\eta$ block diagonal matrix with blocks B on the diagonal. By substituting $\tilde{Y}_r, \tilde{Z}_r$ into the parameter estimate of the CAR model (4), (6), (7) we can derive that

$$\tilde{A}_m = B A_m B^{-1}, \quad \tilde{\lambda}_r = B \lambda_r B^T . \tag{14}$$

The matrices $\tilde{A}_m, \tilde{Z}_r, \tilde{\lambda}_r$ are related to the model of the same texture, but with different illumination. The similar substitution into the GMRF parameter estimate (4), (11), (12) produces equations

$$\tilde{A}_m = B A_m B^{-1}, \quad \hat{\tilde{\Sigma}} = B \hat{\Sigma} B^T , \tag{15}$$

where $\hat{\Sigma} = diag(\hat{\sigma}_1, \ldots, \hat{\sigma}_C)$. It is easy to prove that the following features are illumination invariant for both models:

1. trace: $\operatorname{tr} A_m$, $m = 1, \ldots, \eta K$

2. eigenvalues: $v_{m,j}$ of A_m, $m = 1, \ldots, \eta K$, $j = 1, \ldots, C$

for each CAR model (for 2D CAR models the invariants $\alpha_1, \alpha_2, \alpha_3$ are computed for each spectral plane separately):

3. α_1: $1 + Z_r^T V_{zz}^{-1} Z_r$,

4. α_2: $\sqrt{\sum_r (Y_r - \hat{\gamma} Z_r)^T \lambda^{-1} (Y_r - \hat{\gamma} Z_r)}$,

5. α_3: $\sqrt{\sum_r (Y_r - \mu)^T \lambda^{-1} (Y_r - \mu)}$,
   μ is the mean value of vector Y_r,

and for each GMRF model with centred $Y_{r,j}$:

6. α_4: $\sqrt{\sum_r \hat{\sigma}_j^{-2} \left(Y_{r,j} - \hat{\gamma}_j Z_{r,j} \right)^2}$,

7. α_5: $\sqrt{\sum_r \hat{\sigma}_j^{-2} \left(Y_{r,j} \right)^2}$.

The feature vector is formed from these illumination invariants. For CAR models we use traces, eigenvalues, α_1, α_2, and α_3 features because they can be easily evaluated during the parameters estimation process. For GMRF models we use trace, eigenvalues, α_4, and α_5 features, respectively.

3.4 Feature Comparison Distances

The distance between illumination invariant feature vectors of two textures T, S is computed using the Minkowski norms L_1, $L_{0.2}$, or alternatively with fuzzy contrast FC_3 proposed by Santini & Jain (1999). The Minkowski norm and its σ normalised variant $L_{p\sigma}$, which is used for comparison of alternative texture features, is defined as follows

$$L_p(T,S) = \left(\sum_{i=0}^{M} \left| f_i^{(T)} - f_i^{(S)} \right|^p \right)^{\frac{1}{p}} \, , \tag{16}$$

$$L_{p\sigma}(T,S) = \left(\sum_{i=0}^{M} \left| \frac{f_i^{(T)} - f_i^{(S)}}{\sigma(f_i)} \right|^p \right)^{\frac{1}{p}} \, , \tag{17}$$

$$\tag{18}$$

where M is the feature vector size and $\mu(f_i)$ and $\sigma(f_i)$ are average and standard deviation of the feature f_i computed over all image database, respectively.

Fuzzy contrast $FC_{\alpha\beta}$ models features as predicates in fuzzy logic using sigmoid truth function τ. Subsequently, the feature vector dissimilarity is defined as

$$FC_{\alpha\beta}(T,S) = M - \left\{ \sum_{i=1}^{m} \min \left\{ \tau(f_i^{(T)}), \tau(f_i^{(S)}) \right\} \right. \tag{19}$$

$$- \alpha \sum_{i=1}^{p} \max \left\{ \tau(f_i^{(T)}) - \tau(f_i^{(S)}), 0 \right\}$$

$$\left. - \beta \sum_{i=1}^{p} \max \left\{ \tau(f_i^{(S)}) - \tau(f_i^{(T)}), 0 \right\} \right\} \, ,$$

$$\tau(f_i) = \left(1 + \exp \left(-\frac{f_i - \mu(f_i)}{\sigma(f_i)} \right) \right)^{-1} \, ,$$

It is worth to note that $FC_{\alpha\beta}$ is not a metric, because it does not hold $FC_{\alpha\beta}(T,S) = 0$ and it is not necessary symmetrical. However, we use only its symmetrical form FC_3, where $\alpha = \beta = 3$.

4. Alternative Features

Our proposed illumination invariant features are compared with the most frequently used features in image retrieval applications such as the Gabor features, steerable pyramid features and Local Binary Patterns (LBP).

4.1 Gabor Features

The Gabor filters (Bovik, 1991; Randen & Husøy, 1999) can be considered as orientation and scale tunable edge and line detectors. The statistics of Gabor filter responses in a given region are used to characterise the underlying texture information. A two dimensional Gabor function $g(r) : \mathbb{R}^2 \to \mathbb{C}$ and its Fourier transform can be specified as

$$g(r) = \frac{1}{2\pi\sigma_{r_1}\sigma_{r_2}} \exp\left[-\frac{1}{2}\left(\frac{r_1^2}{\sigma_{r_1}^2} + \frac{r_2^2}{\sigma_{r_2}^2}\right) + 2\pi iVr_1\right] ,$$

$$G(r) = \exp\left\{-\frac{1}{2}\left[\frac{(r_1 - V)^2}{\sigma_{r_1}^2} + \frac{r_2^2}{\sigma_{r_2}^2}\right]\right\} ,$$

where $\sigma_{r_1}, \sigma_{r_2}, V$ are filter parameters. The convolution of the Gabor filter and a texture image extracts edges of given frequency and orientation range. The whole filter set was obtained by four dilatations and six rotations of the function $g(r)$, the filter set is designed so that Fourier transformations of filters cover most of image spectrum, see Manjunath & Ma (1996) for details. The Gabor features (Manjunath & Ma, 1996) are defined as the mean μ_l and the standard deviation σ_l of the magnitude of filter responses computed separately for each spectral plane and concatenated into the feature vector. The suggested distance between feature vectors of textures T, S is $L_{1\sigma}(T, S)$ normalised Minkowski norm (18).

The Opponent Gabor features (Jain & Healey, 1998) are the extension to colour textures, which analyses also relations between spectral channels. The monochrome part of these features is:

$$\eta_{i,m,n} = \sqrt{\sum_r W_{i,m,n}^2(r)} ,$$

where $W_{i,m,n}$ is the response to Gabor filter of orientation m and scale n, i is i−th spectral band of the colour texture T, while the opponent part of features is:

$$\psi_{i,j,m,m',n} = \sqrt{\sum_r \left(\frac{W_{i,m,n}(r)}{\eta_{i,m,n}} - \frac{W_{j,m',n}(r)}{\eta_{j,m',n}}\right)^2} ,$$

for all i,j with $i \neq j$ and $|m - m'| \leq 1$. The previous formula could be also expressed as correlation between spectral planes responses. The distance between textures T, S using the Opponent Gabor features is measured with $L_{2\sigma}(T, S)$ normalised Minkowski norm (18), as suggested by Jain & Healey (1998).

In order to achieve illumination invariance, it is possible to normalise spectral channels using (2) normalisation prior to computation of features. We have tested Gabor features and Opponent Gabor features, the both options with and without the normalisation.

4.2 Steerable Pyramid Features

The steerable pyramid (Portilla & Simoncelli, 2000) is an over complete wavelet decomposition similar to the Gabor decomposition. The pyramid is built up of responses to steerable filters, where level of pyramid extracts certain frequency range. All pyramid levels (except the highest and the lowest one) are further decomposed to different orientations. The transformation is implemented using the set of oriented complex analytic filters B_l that are polar separable in the Fourier domain (see details in Simoncelli & Portilla (1998), Portilla & Simoncelli (2000)):

$$
\begin{aligned}
B_l(R,\theta) &= H(R)G_l(\theta), & l \in [0, L-1], \\[2mm]
H(R) &= \begin{cases} \cos\left(\frac{\pi}{2}\log_2\left(\frac{2R}{\pi}\right)\right), & \frac{\pi}{4} < R < \frac{\pi}{2} \\ 1, & R \geq \frac{\pi}{2} \\ 0, & R \leq \frac{\pi}{4} \end{cases} \\[2mm]
G_l(\theta) &= \begin{cases} \alpha_l\left[\cos\left(\theta - \frac{\pi l}{L}\right)\right]^{L-1}, & \left|\theta - \frac{\pi l}{L}\right| < \frac{\pi}{2}, \\ 0, & \text{otherwise,} \end{cases}
\end{aligned}
$$

where $\alpha_l = 2^{l-1}\frac{(L-1)!}{\sqrt{L[2(L-1)!]}}$, R, θ are polar frequency coordinates, $L = 4$ is the number of orientation bands, and $K = 4$ is the number of pyramid levels. The used steerable pyramid features was skewness, kurtosis, mean, variance, minimum and maximum values of image function, and scale-based auto-correlations and subband cross-correlations of filter responses, respectively, which were proposed for texture synthesis in Portilla & Simoncelli (2000). The feature vectors are compared using the $L_{1\sigma}$ norm (18). Again, we have tested steerable pyramid features with and without the channel normalisation.

4.3 Local Binary Patterns

Local Binary Patterns (LBP) (Ojala, Pietikäinen & Mäenpää, 2002) are histograms of texture micro patterns. For each pixel, a circular neighbourhood around the pixel is sampled, then sampled points values are thresholded by the central pixel value and the pattern number is formed as follows:

$$
LBP_{P,R} = \sum_{q=0}^{P-1} \text{sign}\left(Y_q - Y_c\right)2^q, \quad \text{sign}\left(x\right) = \begin{cases} 1, & x \geq 0 \\ 0, & x < 0, \end{cases} \tag{20}
$$

where P is the number of samples and R is the radius of the circle, *sign* is the signum function, Y_q is a grey value of the sampled pixel, and Y_c is a grey value of the central pixel. Subsequently, the histogram of patterns is computed. Because of thresholding, the features are invariant to any monotonic grey scale change. The multiresolution analysis is done by growing the circular neighbourhood size. However, complex patterns do not have enough occurrences in a texture, therefore uniform LBP features denoted as LBP^{u2} distinguish only among patterns that include only 2 or less transitions between 0 and 1 at neighbouring bits (20), all other patterns are considered to be the same. Moreover, the features can be also made rotation invariant (Ojala, Pietikäinen & Mäenpää, 2002). All LBP histograms were normalised to have a unit L_1 norm. The similarity between texture feature vectors T, S is defined as

$$
L_G(T,S) = \sum_{i=1}^{M} f_i^{(T)} \log \frac{f_i^{(T)}}{f_i^{(S)}}. \tag{21}
$$

We have tested features: $LBP_{8,1+8,3}$ and $LBP^{u2}_{16,2}$ which demonstrated the best performance in the test with illumination changes (Maenpaa et al., 2002; Pietikainen et al., 2002) (test set Outex 14). We have also comprised rotation invariant feature $LBP^{riu2}_{16,2}$. The features were computed either on grey-scale images or on each spectral plane separately and concatenated to form the feature vector. A normalisation to change of illumination brightness or spectrum change is not necessary.

| | experiment | | |
method	1	2	3
Gabor features	144	144	144
Gabor features, grey img.	48	48	48
Opponent Gabor features	**252**	**252**	**252**
Steerable pyramid	2904	2904	2904
Gabor features, norm.	144	144	144
Gabor features, grey img., norm.	48	48	48
Opponent Gabor features, norm.	**252**	**252**	**252**
$LBP_{8,1+8,3}$	1536	1536	1536
$LBP^{u2}_{16,2}$	729	729	729
$LBP^{riu2}_{16,2}$	54	54	54
$LBP_{8,1+8,3}$, grey img.	512	512	512
$LBP^{u2}_{16,2}$, grey img.	243	243	243
$LBP^{riu2}_{16,2}$, grey img.	18	18	18
2D CAR-KL	**260**	**132**	**325**
2D CAR	**260**	**132**	**325**
GMRF-KL	248	120	310
3D CAR	236	108	295

Table 1. The size of feature vectors.

5. Experiments

We demonstrate the performance of the proposed illumination invariant MRF features on two image databases, each with different variations in illumination conditions. The first, BTF database is acquired with a fixed illumination spectrum and with 91 different illumination directions, which drastically violates our restrictive assumption of fixed illumination position. On the other hand, the Outex texture database is acquired with three illuminations with different spectra and only with slight differences in illumination positions, which complies with our assumptions.

We tested three proposed MRF models: 2D CAR (2-dimensional), 3D CAR (3-dimensional) and GMRF. The models were computed over K levels of the Gaussian pyramids, which were built either directly on C spectral planes or on spectral planes decorrelated by the Karhunen-Loeve transformation (indicated with '-KL' suffix).

The proposed features were compared with the following alternatives: Gabor features, Opponent Gabor features, Steerable pyramid features, all with and without spectral channels normalisations (2), and also the LBP features (see details in Section 4). The grey value based features as Gabor features and LBP were computed not only on grey images, but also separately on each spectral plane of colour images and concatenated subsequently. Tab. 1 compares the sizes of feature vectors used in our experiments.

5.1 Experiment 1

We have designed the first experiment to test the feature robustness against illumination direction changes, which is in contradiction with our theoretical assumptions. The experiment is performed on three different sets of BTF texture images. These BTF data are from the University of Bonn database (Meseth et al., 2003) and consists of fifteen BTF colour measurements

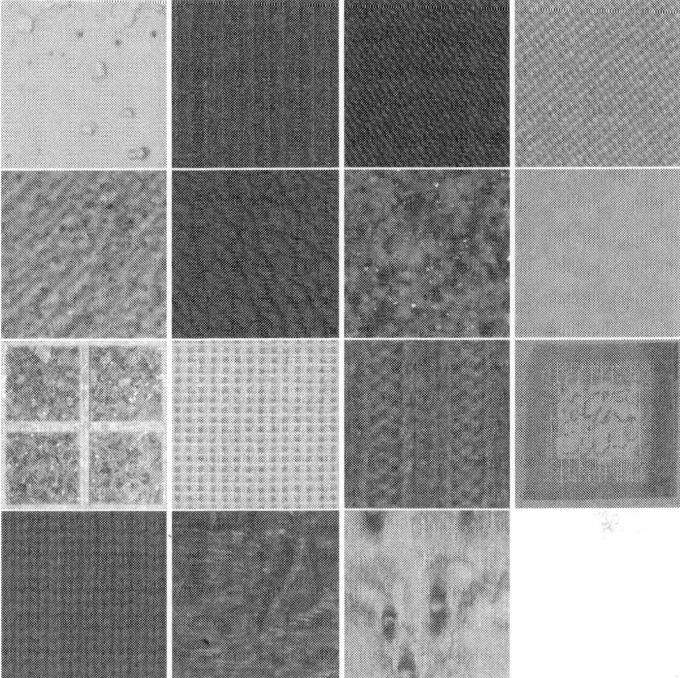

Fig. 1. BTF material measurements, row-wise from left to right: ceiling, corduroy, fabric1, fabric2; walk way, foil, floor tile, pink tile; impalla, proposte, pulli, wallpaper; wool, and two lacquered wood textures.

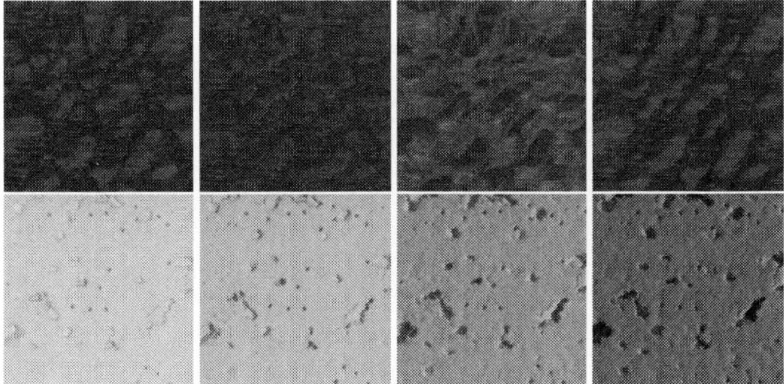

Fig. 2. Illumination variance of BTF materials, the top row is wood with different azimuth of illumination, bottom is ceiling with changing declination of illumination.

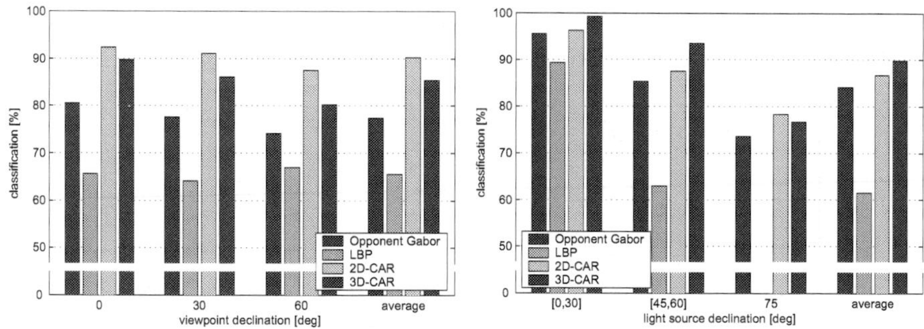

Fig. 3. Correct classification [%], in the left picture for random training samples, in the right picture for training image fixed to top illumination.

(Fig. 1), ten of these measurements are now publicly available[1]. Each BTF material is measured in 81 illumination angles as a RGB image ($C = 3$). Fig. 2 shows examples of material appearance under varying illumination direction. We have three image test sets, which differs in viewpoint direction. The declination angles of viewing direction from surface normal are $0°$, $30°$, and $60°$, in plane rotation is not included. Each test set consists in 1215 images, all cropped to the same size 256×256.

In this experiment, single training image per each material was randomly chosen and the remaining images were classified using the nearest neighbour approach. The MRF models were computed with the sixth order hierarchical neighbourhood and four levels of the Gaussian pyramid, the size of feature vectors is listed in Tab. 1. The results of correct classification are in Tab. 2, all averaged over 10^5 random choices of training images. Bold typeset rows from Tab. 2 are shown in Fig. 3. We can see that the far best performance (90.3%) was achieved with 2D CAR-KL model and L_1 distance. The best alternative features were Opponent Gabor features with average performance 77.4%, the best of LBP features achieved 65.6%. Standard deviation is bellow 4% for Gabor features and LBP features, and below 3% for CAR and GMRF models. Although the LBP features are invariant to brightness changes, these results demonstrate their inefficiency to handle illumination direction variations. Rotation invariant LBP features are more capable, however rotating illumination cannot be modeled as a simple image rotation. For the MRF features, the worst classification result were for ceiling and fabric2 materials. Ceiling material was misclassified as floor tile (for illumination near surface), and fabric2 was sometimes misclassified as fabric1, because they have very similar structures.

We have also explored, how the performance of features depends on light source declination from surface normal. The test set with viewpoint fixed at $0°$ declination was used and single training sample per each material was selected. All selected training samples were illuminated under $0°$ declination angle, other 1200 images were classified. Tab. 3 depicts how correct classification decreases as the illumination position of test sample move away from training sample position. Again, bold typeset rows from Tab. 3 are shown in Fig. 3. The best result were achieved by 3D CAR model and FC_3 dissimilarity with average accuracy 89.8%, similar results 88.7% were achieved by 2D CAR model with FC_3.

---

[1] http://btf.cs.uni-bonn.de/

method	viewpoint declination angle			
	0°	30°	60°	avg.
Gabor features	71.7	64.6	60.1	65.5
Gabor features, grey img.	69.8	62.9	55.6	62.8
Opponent Gabor features	**82.5**	**77.7**	**71.7**	**77.3**
Steerable pyramid	72.3	65.5	60.4	63.1
Gabor features, norm.	60.1	58.1	57.9	58.7
Gabor features, grey img., norm.	50.8	50.1	51.3	50.7
Opponent Gabor features, norm.	**80.5**	**77.6**	**74.2**	**77.4**
$LBP_{8,1+8,3}$	**65.7**	**64.2**	**67.0**	**65.6**
$LBP_{16,2}^{u2}$	62.5	61.6	64.6	62.9
$LBP_{16,2}^{riu2}$	**68.4**	60.7	57.4	62.2
$LBP_{8,1+8,3}$, grey img.	61.2	61.1	65.4	62.6
$LBP_{16,2}^{u2}$, grey img.	55.7	56.3	60.7	57.6
$LBP_{16,2}^{riu2}$, grey img.	58.6	52.1	52.5	54.4
2D CAR-KL, L_1	**92.4**	**91.1**	**87.5**	**90.3**
3D CAR, L_1	87.4	84.3	78.9	83.5
GMRF-KL, L_1	89.6	86.3	81.0	85.6
2D CAR, FC_3	**88.7**	**87.3**	**82.9**	**86.3**
GMRF-KL, FC_3	86.5	82.6	78.7	82.6
GMRF-KL, $L_{0.2}$	87.1	83.7	79.6	83.5
2D CAR-KL, FC_3	92.3	89.6	85.7	89.2
2D CAR-KL, $L_{0.2}$	91.8	89.5	85.8	89.0
3D CAR, FC_3	**89.8**	**86.1**	**80.2**	**85.4**
3D CAR, $L_{0.2}$	89.2	85.7	81.0	85.3

Table 2. Correct classification [%], using single training image per texture. The results are averages over 10^5 random choices of training images, the last column consists in averages of previous columns.

5.2 Experiment 2

In the second experiment, we demonstrate the performance of the proposed illumination invariant MRF features on the Outex database (Ojala, Mäenpää, Pietikäinen, Viertola, Kyllönen & Huovinen, 2002), which consists of natural material images acquired, under three different illuminations. The illumination sources were 2856K incandescent CIE A light source, 2300K horizon sunlight, and 4000K fluorescent TL84, the illumination positions are very close. All the images were acquired with a fixed camera position.

The experiment was performed on the Outex classification test set number 14 (Ojala, Mäenpää, Pietikäinen, Viertola, Kyllönen & Huovinen, 2002). In this test set, 68 materials selected from the Outex database were treated in the following manner. Twenty subsamples with size 128×128 were extracted from each material image. The train set consists of 10 samples per material, all illuminated with the 2586K incandescent CIE A light source. The test set consists of 10 remaining subsamples for each material, all of them illuminated with other two illuminants. Consequently, the train set consists of 680 images, while the test set is composed of 1360 images. The classification was performed using 3 nearest neighbours as in Maenpaa et al. (2002), Pietikainen et al. (2002).

method	light source declination			
	$0{:}30°$	$45{:}65°$	$75°$	avg.
Gabor features	96.3	71.4	28.9	64.2
Gabor features, grey img.	95.2	64.7	34.7	62.6
Opponent Gabor features	95.6	83.9	50.0	76.4
Steerable pyramid	90.7	69.5	36.1	64.3
Gabor features, norm.	81.9	49.1	19.4	47.6
Gabor features, grey img., norm.	81.9	38.8	13.9	41.0
Opponent Gabor features, norm.	**95.6**	**85.3**	**73.6**	**84.1**
$LBP_{8,1+8,3}$	**89.3**	**63.0**	**38.6**	**61.6**
$LBP_{16,2}^{u2}$	84.4	51.4	35.6	54.1
$LBP_{16,2}^{riu2}$	84.4	44.6	31.9	49.8
$LBP_{8,1+8,3}$, grey img.	86.3	57.4	38.3	58.2
$LBP_{16,2}^{u2}$, grey img.	79.3	50.7	34.7	52.3
$LBP_{16,2}^{riu2}$. grey img.	74.1	36.8	16.7	39.2
2D CAR-KL, L_1	**96.3**	**87.5**	**78.3**	**86.7**
3D CAR, L_1	97.8	89.6	75.6	87.2
GMRF-KL	95.9	82.6	65.3	80.4
2D CAR, FC_3	**96.7**	**91.6**	**78.1**	**88.7**
GMRF-KL, FC_3	93.3	86.5	72.2	83.7
GMRF-KL, $L_{0.2}$	94.4	82.3	68.3	80.8
2D CAR-KL, FC_3	97.8	90.5	79.4	88.8
2D CAR-KL, $L_{0.2}$	96.7	85.4	78.3	85.8
3D CAR, FC_3	**99.3**	**93.6**	**76.7**	**89.8**
3D CAR, $L_{0.2}$	97.8	91.2	72.8	87.2

Table 3. Correct classification [%] with traning image fixed to top illumination. The performance is grouped for different intervals of illumination declination angles of test images, the last column is average for all test images. Viewpoint declination angle was $0°$ all images.

The highest reported classification accuracy on the test set (Maenpaa et al., 2002) was 69% for $LBP_{16,2}^{u2}$ features, which outperformed Gabor features with 66% of accuracy (unfortunately our implementation of Gabor features reached only 54.5% in Tab. 4), both features were computed on grey-scale images. Moreover, Pietikainen et al. (2002) reported 68.4% accuracy for $LBP_{8,1+8,3}$ also on grey-scale images, and 53.3% of accuracy achieved by Opponent Gabor features on colour images preceded by comprehensive colour normalisation.

In addition to the previously described experiment, we have also degraded test set images with an additive Gaussian noise. The experiment was performed directly on noisy images, without any noise removal method. The application of such method might increase classification accuracy, but only on condition that it would not introduce any artificial micro structures into the images.

Because of small image size, the neighbourhood of MRF models have to be restricted to the third order hierarchical neighbourhood. As a consequence the feature vector of 2D CAR, is about four times smaller than the vector of $LBP_{8,1+8,3}$ features. The best result on the original test set was achieved with $LBP_{8,1+8,3}$ on grey images with 71.6% followed by the best of MRF features with 67.5% classification accuracy. However, the results change dramatically

method	added noise σ			
	0	2	4	8
Gabor features	37.5	37.0	36.2	35.6
Gabor features, grey img.	44.3	43.3	43.2	41.3
Opponent Gabor features	50.7	49.3	45.3	37.3
Steerable pyramid	37.5	35.9	34.9	32.6
Gabor features, norm.	57.0	59.9	60.3	57.1
Gabor features, grey img., norm.	**54.5**	**61.3**	**63.3**	**62.9**
Opponent Gabor features, norm.	**56.7**	**55.8**	**54.3**	**47.9**
$\text{LBP}_{8,1+8,3}$	66.8	56.6	48.8	36.7
$\text{LBP}^{u2}_{16,2}$	62.0	52.9	41.2	28.7
$\text{LBP}^{riu2}_{16,2}$	44.6	30.8	22.6	15.3
$\text{LBP}_{8,1+8,3}$, grey img.	**71.6**	**62.2**	**54.6**	**38.6**
$\text{LBP}^{u2}_{16,2}$, grey img.	67.6	60.4	49.8	33.0
$\text{LBP}^{riu2}_{16,2}$, grey img.	56.9	45.2	34.2	19.7
2D CAR-KL, L_1	**67.6**	**60.8**	**55.7**	**52.3**
GMRF-KL, L_1	61.5	57.0	51.1	46.1
3D CAR, L_1	63.6	61.3	60.6	54.9
2D CAR, FC_3	**67.5**	**62.2**	**61.0**	**56.6**
2D CAR-KL, FC_3	67.5	63.3	55.8	51.0
2D CAR-KL, $L_{0.2}$	66.3	60.5	55.2	51.0
3D CAR, FC_3	65.3	60.4	58.0	51.3
3D CAR, $L_{0.2}$	63.5	59.7	55.4	47.4

Table 4. Results [%] of the Outex classification test set number 14. The classification was performed using three nearest neighbours.

with added noise, the $\text{LBP}_{8,1+8,3}$ features drop down to 38.6% showing their vulnerability to noise degradation. The MRF based features are not so noise sensitive, because Gaussian noise is inherent part of the model and the Gaussian pyramid suppresses noise at its higher levels. The MRF features without KL transform performed better on noisy images than features with KL transform, which was deflected by uncorrelated noise. In this experiment, Gabor features performed better than Opponent Gabor Features, especially on noisy images.

5.3 Experiment 3

The last test is an illumination invariant image retrieval from the Outex texture database. In this task, a CBIR system tries to retrieve images similar with a given query image, it differs from the previous experiment in two major points. At first, all 318 materials were used and at second, the task of image retrieval do not allow more training samples per material (previous experiment used 20 training samples per each of 68 materials).

The test set consists of 3 different illuminations for each material, without any rotation and with 100 dpi resolution, which is 954 images in total. All images were cropped to size 512×512 pixels. We have tested image retrieval using every image from the test set. The relevant images were defined as images of the same material with the other two illuminations. Therefore there were 2 relevant images present in the test set for each query image, a total amount of 3 images were retrieved. Furthermore, images were again corrupted with an additive Gaussian noise to test the noise robustness of the features. The retrieval performance was measured using the

	added noise σ	
method	0	8
Gabor features	14.0	13.4
Gabor features, grey img.	42.8	42.4
Opponent Gabor features	38.8	30.5
Steerable pyramid	19.4	18.9
Gabor features, norm.	40.4	27.5
Gabor features, grey img, norm.	**53.4**	**56.1**
Opponent Gabor features, norm.	**46.9**	**37.8**
$LBP_{8,1+8,3}$	51.5	20.0
$LBP^{u2}_{16,2}$	47.3	11.7
$LBP^{riu2}_{16,2}$	24.3	3.1
$LBP_{8,1+8,3}$, grey img.	**83.1**	**50.3**
$LBP^{u2}_{16,2}$, grey img.	80.6	40.8
$LBP^{riu2}_{16,2}$, grey img.	61.5	21.3
2D CAR-KL L_1	**83.4**	**60.8**
GMRF-KL, L_1	73.4	50.4
3D CAR, L_1	79.6	61.5
2D CAR, FC_3	**94.0**	**83.0**
GMRF-KL, FC_3	81.3	55.9
GMRF-KL, $L_{0.2}$	80.7	60.2
2D CAR-KL, FC_3	90.2	68.0
2D CAR-KL, $L_{0.2}$	87.8	69.4
3D CAR, FC_3	82.7	63.0
3D CAR, $L_{0.2}$	79.1	58.8

Table 5. Illumination invariant retrieval from the Outex texture database. The performance is measured as recall rate [%] of 3 retrieved images.

recall rate

$$\mathrm{rr} = \frac{\text{retrieved and relevant}}{\text{all retrieved}},$$

the results are summarised in Tab. 5.

In this test, the proposed illumination invariant MRF features achieved retrieval recall rate 94%, which clearly present their insensitivity to illumination spectrum variations. The MRF models were computed with the sixth order hierarchical neighbourhood and five levels of the Gaussian pyramid, since the images are large enough. This experiment also confirms that MRF features without Karhunen-Loeve transform are more robust to noise degradation. The LBP features also show their illumination invariance property with 83% recall rate. However, their performance drops with added Gaussian noise increase. This results also demonstrate that the spectral channel normalisation is essential for Gabor and steerable pyramid features, nevertheless, any variant of Gabor or steerable pyramid features did not performed satisfactory in this test.

Some examples of retrieved textures are presented in Fig. 4. The first two retrieved images are both correct, however, more interesting are images retrieved at the further positions. We can observe that the proposed features managed to recognise visual similarity of various canvas materials, and at the bottom, it is obvious that MRF features with pyramids prefer over-

Query image:

canvas034-inca

Retrieval result (Outex - proposed 2DCAR):

Retrieval result (Outex - LBP):

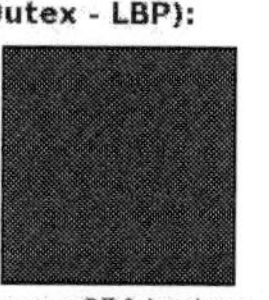

canvas034-horizon   canvas034-tl84   canvas035-horizon   canvas034-tl84   canvas034-horizon   gravel005-tl84

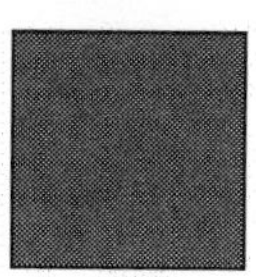

canvas035-inca   canvas037-horizon   canvas035-tl84   gravel005-inca   gravel005-horizon   flour013-inca

Query image:

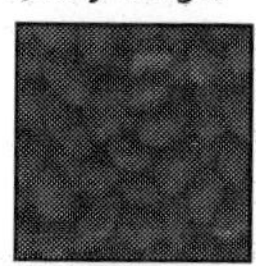

seeds013-horizon

Retrieval result (Outex - proposed 2DCAR):

Retrieval result (Outex - LBP):

seeds013-tl84   seeds013-inca   plastic031-horizon   seeds013-tl84   seeds013-inca   pasta006-horizon

plastic029-horizon   plastic030-horizon   plastic031-tl84   pasta004-inca   pasta006-tl84   pasta004-horizon

Fig. 4. Illumination invariant image retrieval from Outex database for materials canvas034 (top), seed013 (bottom). Screenshots are from our online demonstration at `http://cbir.utia.cas.cz` or `http://ro.utia.cz/dem.html`.

all structure contrary to micro patterns (such as lines) preferred by the LBP features. These screenshots were taken from our online demonstration,[2] where it is possible to try performance of the proposed features on images from Outex database.

6. Conclusions

We have proposed new illumination invariant features, which are suitable for content based image retrieval systems and other analysis of natural scene images. These features are derived from the underlying Markov random field texture representation and they are invariant to brightness and illumination spectrum variations. We have experimentally verified that introduced MRF features are considerably robust to illumination direction changes and they are simultaneously robust to image degradation by an additive Gaussian noise. Moreover, the MRF features are also fast to compute and the feature vector has low dimension. The disadvantage is that reliable estimation of MRF parameters requires sufficient size of training data.
The proposed methods were compared with Gabor features, Opponent Gabor features, steerable pyramid and LBP features, respectively. Although the LBP features confirmed their illumination spectrum invariance, they had significant difficulties with natural materials illuminated with different directions and images degraded by an additive noise. The best results were achieved with invariants based on the 2-dimensional CAR model with Fuzzy contrast dissimilarity.

7. Acknowledgements

This research was supported by grants GAČR 102/08/0593 and partially by the MŠMT grants 1M0572 DAR, 2C06019.

8. References

Bovik, A. (1991). Analysis of multichannel narrow-band filters for image texture segmentation, *IEEE Trans. on Signal Processing* **39**(9): 2025–2043.

Burghouts, G. J. & Geusebroek, J. M. (2009). Material-specific adaptation of color invariant features, *Pattern Recognition Letters* **30**: 306–313. `www.science.uva.nl/research/publications/2009/BurghoutsPRL2009`.

Chen, H. F., Belhumeur, P. N. & Jacobs, D. W. (2000). In search of illumination invariants, *IEEE Computer Vision and Pattern Recognition or CVPR*, pp. I: 254–261.

Drbohlav, O. & Chantler, M. (2005). Illumination-invariant texture classification using single training images, *Texture 2005: Proceedings of the 4th international workshop on texture analysis and synthesis*, pp. 31–36.

Finlayson, G. D. (1995). *Coefficient color constancy*, PhD thesis, Simon Fraser University.

Finlyason, G. & Xu, R. (2002). Illuminant and gamma comprehensive normalisation in log rgb space, *Patterm Recognition Letters* **24**: 1679–1690.

Geusebroek, J.-M., Boomgaard, R. v. d., Smeulders, A. W. & Gevers, T. (2003). Colour constancy from physical principes, *Pattern Recognition Letters* **24**: 1653–1662.

Geusebroek, J. M. & Smeulders, A. W. (2005). A six-stimulus theory for stochastic texture, *International Journal of Computer Cision* **62**: 7–16.

---

[2] `http://cbir.utia.cas.cz` or `http://ro.utia.cz/dem.html`

Gevers, T. & Smeulders, A. W. M. (2001). Color constant ratio gradients for image segmentation and similarity of texture objects, *CVPR*, IEEE Computer Society, pp. 18–25.

Haindl, M. & Šimberová, S. (1992). *Theory & Applications of Image Analysis*, World Scientific Publishing Co., Singapore, chapter A Multispectral Image Line Reconstruction Method, pp. 306–315.

Healey, G. & Wang, L. (1995). The illumination-invariant recognition of texture in color texture, *ICCV*, pp. 128–133. computer.org/proceedings/iccv/7042/70420128abs.htm.

Hoang, M. A. & Geausebroek, Jan-Mark Smeulders, A. W. (2005). Color texture measurement and segmentation, *Signal Processing* **85**: 295–275.

Jacobs, D., Belhumeur, P. & Basri, R. (1998). Comparing images under variable illumination, *Proceedings IEEE Conference on Computer Vision and Pattern Re cognition, 2000*, Vol. 1, IEEE, IEEE, pp. 610 – 617.

Jain, A. & Healey, G. (1998). A multiscale representation including opponent colour features for texture recognition, *IEEE Transactions on Image Processing* **7**(1): 125–128.

Maenpaa, T., Pietikainen, M. & Viertola, J. (2002). Separating color and pattern information for color texture discrimination, *International Conference on Pattern Recognition*, pp. I: 668–671.

Manjunath, B. S. & Ma, W. Y. (1996). Texture features for browsing and retrieval of image data, *IEEE Transactions on Pattern Analysis and Machine Intelligence* **18**(8): 837–842.

Marimont, D. H. & Wandell, B. A. (1992). Linear models of surface and illuminant spectra, *Journal of the Optical Society of America* **9**: 1905–1913.

Meseth, J., Müller, G. & Klein, R. (2003). Preserving realism in real-time rendering of bidirectional texture functions, *OpenSG Symposium 2003*, Eurographics Association, Switzerland, pp. 89–96.

Ojala, T., Mäenpää, T., Pietikäinen, M., Viertola, J., Kyllönen, J. & Huovinen, S. (2002). Outex - new framework for empirical evaluation of texture analysis algorithms, *16th International Conference on Pattern Recognition*, pp. 701–706.

Ojala, T., Pietikäinen, M. & Mäenpää, T. (2002). Multiresolution gray-scale and rotation invariant texture classification with local binary patterns, *IEEE Trans. Pattern Anal. Mach. Intell* **24**(7): 971–987.

Pietikainen, M., Maenpaa, T. & Viertola, J. (2002). Color texture classification with color histograms and local binary patterns, *Workshop on Texture Analysis in Machine Vision*, pp. 109–112.

Portilla, J. & Simoncelli, E. P. (2000). A parametric texture model based on joint statistics of complex wavelet coefficients, *International Journal of Computer Vision* **40**(1): 49–71.

Randen, T. & Husøy, J. H. (1999). Filtering for texture classification: A comparative study, *IEEE Transactions on Pattern Analysis and Machine Intelligence* **21**(4): 291–310.

Santini, S. & Jain, R. (1999). Similarity measures, *IEEE Trans. Pattern Anal. Mach. Intell* **21**(9): 871–883. www.computer.org/tpami/tp1999/i0871abs.htm.

Shafer, S. A. (1985). Using color to seperate reflection components, *COLOR research and application* **10**(4): 210–218.

Simoncelli, E. P. & Portilla, J. (1998). Texture characterization via joint statistics of wavelet coefficient magnitudes, *Proceedings of Fifth International Conference on Image Processing*, IEEE Computer Society, pp. I: 62–66.

Smeulders, A. W., Worring, M., Santini, S., Gupta, A. & Jain, R. (2000). Content-based image retrieval at the end of the early years, *IEEE Transactions on Pattern Analysis and Machine Intelligence* **22**(12): 1349–1380.

Suen, P. H. & Healey, G. (2000). The analysis and reconstruction of real-world textures in three dimensions, *IEEE Transactions on Pattern Analysis and Machine Intelligence* **22**(5): 491–503.

Targhi, A. T., Geusebroek, J.-M. & Zisserman, A. (2008). Texture classification with minimal training images, *Proceedings of the 19th International Conference on Pattern Recognition*.

Vacha, P. & Haindl, M. (2007). Image retrieval measures based on illumination invariant textural MRF features, *in* N. Sebe & M. Worring (eds), *CIVR*, ACM, pp. 448–454. `doi.acm.org/10.1145/1282280.1282346`.

Vacha, P. & Haindl, M. (2008). Illumination invariants based on markov random fields, *Proceedings of the 19th International Conference on Pattern Recognition*.

Varma, M. & Zisserman, A. (2005). A statistical approach to texture classification from single images, *International Journal of Computer Vision* **62**(1-2): 61–81. `dx.doi.org/10.1007/s11263-005-4635-4`.

Weijer, J., Gevers, T. & Geusebroek, J. (2005). Edge and corner detection by photometric quasi-invariants, *IEEE Transactions Pattern Analysis and Machine Intelligence* **27**(4): 625–630.

Yang, J. & Al-Rawi, M. (2005). Illumination invariant recognition of three-dimensional texture in color images, *J. Comput. Sci. Technol* **20**(3): 378–388.

## 14

Study of the effect of lighting technology in texture classification systems

Rubén Muñiz, José Antonio Corrales, Manuel Rico-Secades
and Juan Ángel Martínez-Esteban
University of Oviedo
Spain

1. Introduction

Traditionally, the most commonly used lighting technology in computer vision applications has been the halogen one. In some cases, fluorescent lamps are used due to intrinsic restrictions of the site where the application is running (e.g.: car parks).

A few years ago, new improvements in LED technology started to appear, giving birth to a totally new range of products for domestic and industrial use. These new high efficiency diodes offer many advantages over older technologies, such as longer life span, less heat radiated and less power consumption.

On the other hand, with the introduction of low cost colour cameras for computer vision applications, the effect of the technology of the lamps used is even more noticeable. In previous papers we have studied how variations in the intensity of the illumination affect the quality of the descriptors measured from texture samples. For that work we used a halogen projector and a mainstream digital video camera.

This time we are going to use an industrial IEEE colour camera from Pixelink and a custom-built RGB LED projector. We seek to validate the results we have from former studies on a new image set using the LED lamp and a halogen one.

2. Introduction to texture classification

Texture classification is a key field in many computer vision applications, ranging from quality control to remote sensing. Briefly described, there are a finite number of texture classes we have to learn to recognize. In the first stage of the development of such kind of systems, we extract useful information (features) from a set of digital images, known as the training set, containing the textures we are studying. Once this task has been done, we proceed to classify any unknown texture into one of the known classes. This process can be summarised in the following steps:

1. Image (texture) acquisition and preprocessing

2. Feature extraction

3. Feature selection

4. Classification

Since earlier approaches to the problem greyscale images have been widely used, primarily due to acquisition hardware limitations and/or limited processing power. In the recent past, much effort has been made to develop new feature extraction algorithms (also known as texture analysis algorithms) to take advantage of the extra information contained in colour images. On the other hand, many classical greyscale algorithms have been extended to process colour textures (de Wouver, 1998; Jain & Healy, 1998; Palm, Keysers, Lehmann & Spitzer, 2000).

Texture analysis algorithms can be divided into statistical and spectral ones. The former methods extract a set of statistical properties from the spatial distribution of intensities of a texture. Common examples of this approach are the histogram method and the family of algorithms based on cooccurrence matrices (Conners & McMillin, 1983; Haralick et al., 1973). The latter techniques, on the other hand, compute a number of features obtained from the analysis of the local spectrum of the texture. In the following sections we will give an overview of two spectral methods (Gabor filters and Wavelets) and a statistical one (Cooccurrence matrices).

3. Gabor filters

Gabor filters have been extensively used for texture classification and segmentation of greyscale and colour textures (Bovik & Clark, 1990; Dunn et al., 1994; Jain & Healy, 1998; Kruizinga et al., 1999; Palm, Keysers, Lehmann & Spitzer, 2000). These filters are optimally localized in both space and spatial frequency and allow us to get a set of filtered images which correspond to a specific scale and orientation component of the original texture. There are two major approaches to texture analysis using Gabor filters. First, one can look for specific narrowband filters to describe a given texture class, while the other option is to apply a bank of Gabor filters over the image and process its outputs to obtain the features that describe the texture class.

3.1 2D Gabor filterbank

The Gabor filter bank used in this work is defined in the spatial domain as follows:

$$
\begin{aligned}
f_{mn}(x,y) &= \frac{1}{2\pi\sigma_m^2} \exp^{-\frac{x^2+y^2}{2\sigma_m^2}} \times \\
&\times \quad \cos 2\pi(u_m x \cos\theta + u_m y \sin\theta)
\end{aligned}
\tag{1}
$$

where m and n are the indexes for the scale and the orientation, respectively, for a given Gabor filter. Depending on these parameters, the texture will be analyzed (filtered) at a specific detail level and direction. The half peak radial and orientation bandwidths (Bovik & Clark, 1990) are defined as follows:

$$
B_r = \log_2\left(\frac{2\pi\sigma_m u_m + \sqrt{2\ln 2}}{2\pi\sigma_m u_m - 2\sqrt{2\ln 2}}\right)
\tag{2}
$$

$$
B_\theta = 2\tan^{-1}\left(\frac{\sqrt{2\ln 2}}{2\pi\sigma_m u_m}\right)
\tag{3}
$$

As in (Jain & Healy, 1998), we define a filterbank with three scales and four orientations. The bandwidth B_θ is taken to be $40°$ in order to maximize the coverage of the frequency domain and minimize the overlap between the filters.

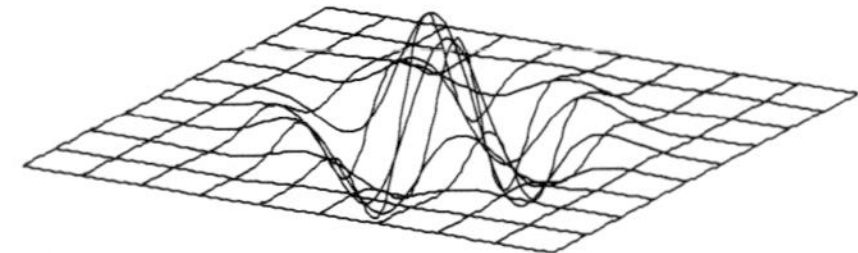

Fig. 1. Gabor filter computed by $f_{1,45°}$

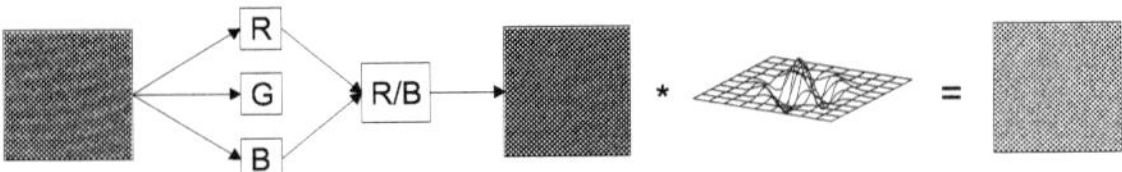

Fig. 2. Gabor filtering of rationed images

3.2 Gabor features

To obtain texture features we must filter the texture images using the generated filters. This is achieved by convolution on the frequency domain (4), due to the size of the filters used. For each filtered image, we extract a single feature μ_{mn} which represents its energy, as shown below.

$$G_{mn}(x,y) = I(x,y) * f_{mn} \tag{4}$$

$$\mu_{mn}(x,y) = \sqrt{\sum_{x,y}(G_{mn}(x,y))^2} \tag{5}$$

This approach is only valid when greyscale images are used. If we want to filter a colour image, we have to preprocess it before this method can be applied. The more obvious solution to this problem is to transform the image by a weighted average of the three colour bands.

$$I(x,y) = aR(x,y) + bG(x,y) + cB(x,y) \tag{6}$$

The coefficients a, b, c from equation (6), can be selected to properly model the human eye's perception model of colour, since the number of cones sensitive to red, green and blue light is not equal (Hecht, 1987). For this reason, an adequate choice of these weights can be $a = 0.65, b = 0.33, c = 0.02$, but this is only needed for human visualization and does not necessary provide a good representation for texture feature extraction. In this paper, we will use the simplest choice of coefficients given by $a = b = c = \frac{1}{3}$.
Using this transformation, different colours can give the same greyscale intensity, so colour information is lost. To overcome this obstacle, (4) can be applied on each of the RGB colour bands of the image to obtain unichrome features (Jain & Healy, 1998). With this approach, we obtain a set of energies from each spectral band, so the information extracted from textures, grows by a factor of three. Another disadvantage of this technique is that colour information is not correlated because it is simply concatenated. A good idea to solve this independency was proposed by Palm et al. in (Palm, Keysers, Lehmann & Spitzer, 2000). They converted the RGB image to HSV, discarding the intensity value, and taking the Hue and Saturation to form a complex number, which can be used to compute the convolution between the image and the gabor filter by means of a complex FFT.

4. Wavelets

4.1 Introduction

The name "Wavelets" was first introduced by Morlet, a French geophysicists, in the early 80's. The kind of data he was studying could not be properly analysed by Fourier analysis, due to the fast change of their frequency contents. For this reason, he looked for a family of functions suitable for the analysis of that kind of signals and he found the wavelets.

A wavelet family is a set of functions derived from a single function with special features, named the *mother* wavelet, by means of two parameters a and b:

$$\psi_{a,b}(t) = \frac{1}{\sqrt{a}} \psi \left(\frac{t-b}{a} \right) \tag{7}$$

The parameter a represents the dilation (which is inversely proportional to frequency) and b the displacement (time localization).

Wavelets are rather complex and we would require a complete book (Mallat, 1999) to deal with them. In the following lines we will show only the basics of this kind of analysis, focused on texture feature extraction.

4.2 2D Discrete Wavelet Transform and multiscale analysis

Wavelets allow us to study a signal at different levels of detail. In the case of 2D signals, this can be interpreted as analysing the images at different resolutions or scales. For instance, if we take a image of 512×512 pixels, we can study its frequency content at $256 \times 256, 128 \times 128, 64 \times 64$ and so on. In the special case of images containing textures, this is of vital importance since a texture varies significantly depending on the distance from which we are looking at it.

If we take a such as $a = 2^m$, the transform is known as dyadic DWT and relies on a specific form of Wavelet derived from a smoothing or scaling function represented by $\theta(t)$. From both the scaling function and the Wavelet, we can derive two FIR filters that can be used to compute the DWT. These filters are commonly named h and g and are, respectively, a low-pass and a high-pass filter. The 2D transform can be represented as shown in Fig. 3, where $*$ denotes the convolution operator and the subscript for each filter represents if it is applied over the rows or the columns of the image. Finally $\downarrow 2$ denotes downsampling of the rows or columns by a factor of two.

Looking at Fig. 3, we can see that the DWT in 2D produces four images as output. In each filtering step, a *low resolution* image L_{j+1} and three *detail images* are produced. The detail images $D_j^{1..3}$ contain the details (high frequency components) extracted from D_j that are not present in $D_j + 1$. This scheme can be applied recursively until a given depth is reached.

4.3 Wavelet features

Detail images obtained by applying 2D DWT can be used as a source for extracting texture features. Since those images contain essentially edge information at a specific direction (horizontal, vertical and diagonal), their energy is a very good texture feature. It is defined as follows:

$$E_{ij}(x,y) = \sqrt{\sum_{x,y} \left(D_{ij}(x,y) \right)^2} \tag{8}$$

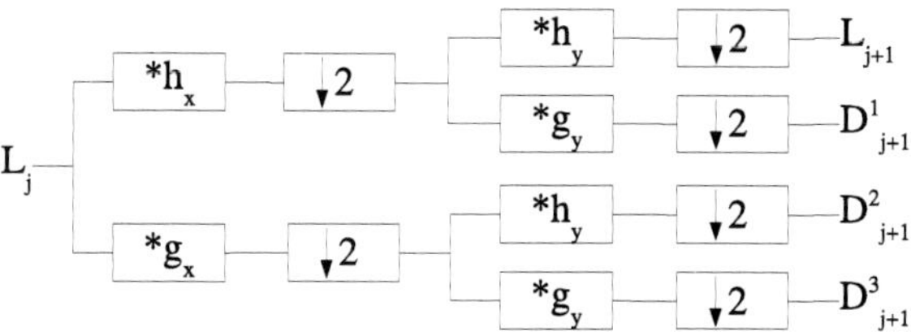

Fig. 3. 2D DWT using FIR filters

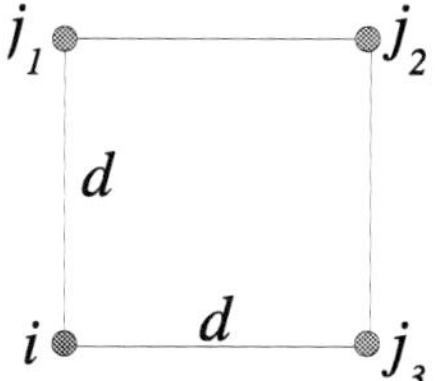

Fig. 4. Neighbourhood of a given pixel.

where $i = 1 \ldots 3$ and $j = 0 \ldots depth - 1$.

As in the case of Gabor filters, we need some mechanism to be able to process colour images, such as greyscale conversion (6) and independent colour band feature extraction. In this particular case we can use a correlation measure (de Wouver, 1998). This feature is named the *wavelet covariance signature* and is defined as follows:

$$C_{ij}^{B_k B_l}(x,y) = \sum_{x,y} D_{ij}^{B_l} D_{ij}^{B_k} \tag{9}$$

where B_k and B_l represent a colour band, and $k, l = 1, 2, 3, k \leq l$.

5. Grey level cooccurrence matrices

5.1 Introduction

Grey level cooccurrence matrices (GLCM) were introduced for the first time by Haralick (Haralick et al., 1973) in the early 70's. A GLCM is a matrix where each cell i, j contains the number of times a point having intensity i occurs in a position j located at an angle θ and a distance d. If we want to make this approach non sensible to orientation variations, we can use the neighbourhood located at a distance d from the pixel with intensity i. Only the first quadrant of that neighbourhood need to be explored, which is equivalent to taking $\theta = 0, 45, 90$ simultaneously for the same matrix (Fig. 4).

A final topic concerns the size of the GLCM. If we directly use the 256 grey levels available in a image, the resulting matrix will be huge, so a mechanism to reduce its dimensions is needed. There are some options to do this. In this paper, we have used two different preprocessing tasks:

Preprocessing algorithm	Feature #	Hits
greyscale	12	87.86%
Red band	12	89.52%
Green band	12	90.24%
Blue band	12	87.38%
R+G+B	12×3	93.57%
Ratio R/G	12	86.67%
Ratio R/B	12	90.24%
Ratio G/B	12	85.48%
Ratios R/G & R/B	12×2	95.24%
Ratios R/G, R/B & G/B	12×3	95.24%
Complex colour features	31	92%
PCA	12	90.71%

Table 1. Classification rates for Gabor data.

Preprocessing algorithm	Feature #	Hits
greyscale	12	86.19%
Red band	12	90.48%
Green band	12	85.24%
Blue band	12	86.19%
R+G+B	12×3	91.19%
Ratio R/G	12	83.33%
Ratio R/B	12	87.62%
Ratio G/B	12	80.95%
Ratios R/G & R/B	12×2	93.57%
Ratios R/G, R/B & G/B	12×3	93.81%
Covariance signatures	72	95.24%
PCA	12	87.14%

Table 2. Classification rates for Wavelet data.

8.1.2 Wavelet results

For Wavelet features we have set the analysis depth at 4, which produces a total number of 12 features for each texture sample. The wavelet functions used for this analysis were the biorthogonal Wavelets *Bior6.8* available in MatLAB. In this case the performance of the concatenation of two band ratios is not the best at all, but the classification success is only 1.67% less than the case when covariance signatures are used, computing three times less features.

8.1.3 Cooccurrence matrices results

GLCM features were obtained by computing two coocurrence matrices at distances 2 and 4. For each matrix, we have calculated Haralick features, $f_1 \ldots f_{12}$, that give us a total number of 24 texture measures for each sample. The overall performance in this case is worse than for the case where spectral methods are used, but we still see a performance increase when band

Preprocessing algorithm	Feature #	Hits CGM	Hits SGLDM
greyscale	24	78.81%	82.14%
Red band	24	78.57%	83.10%
Green band	24	79.29%	84.05%
Blue band	24	79.05%	85.24%
R+G+B	24 × 3	84.76%	93.1%
Ratio R/G	24	72.38%	74.76%
Ratio R/B	24	70.24%	76.43%
Ratio G/B	24	64.29%	70%
Ratios R/G & R/B	24 × 2	85.24%	91.67%
Ratios R/G, R/B & G/B	24 × 3	85.71%	91.67%
Cross-coocurrence	24 × 3	81.19%	90.24%
PCA	24	74.29%	77.14%

Table 3. Classification rates for CGM and SGLDM data.

ratios are involved. It is remarkable to notice how the concatenation of two band ratios still provides the best results while keeping the number of used features low.

8.2 Conclusions of the Vistex problem

In the previous sections, by means of the band ratioing technique we have combined RGB colour bands to produce monochromatic images suitable to use as input to any feature extraction algorithm currently available. From an implementation point of view, feature extraction algorithms that can use real images are preferred since no information is lost from band ratios. The most important conclusion is the fact that this technique allows us to compress textural colour information which leads to higher classification performance while keeping the number of features low. It is interesting to see how the use of three band ratios does not lead to better performance (or very little) than the case where only two ratios are involved. This is obvious since the third one is a linear combination of the two other, so the extra features do not contain additional information.

A final consideration concerns the use of the Hotelling transform. This process improves the performance of the simpler greyscale transform in the case where spectral methods (Gabor and Wavelets) are used, which leads us to think that the colour compression performed is better, as expected. For coocurrence matrices this is not true, since the grey levels reduction performed for the computation of those matrices seems to be affected by the use of this transform.

9. LED lighting

LED lighting is an emerging technology these days. It has evolved from the typical signaling diodes present on many different electronic devices to the more sophisticated lamps which are aimed at replacing conventional ones. It has applications for many different aspects of our lives, such as cars, traffic lights, show lighting and lamps at home.

Computer vision is not an exception here, the application of high power LEDs to almost any application is straightforward as it only requires replacing an "old" lamp with another one with a sufficient number of high power LEDs.

Fig. 8. LED module

During recent years we have been working with colour textures and we have developed a technique for compensating the performance loss when the illumination on the scene varies significantly. In this paper we want to reproduce those experiments with our custom-built LED projector and compare the results with the ones obtained when a conventional lamp is used.

9.1 Modern LED technology
As we have already mentioned, LED technology has been vastly improved during this decade. Nowadays it is very easy to find a product that fits our needs from many of the different manufacturers that have LEDs in their catalogues. However, in order to build our custom projector we have to perform minor research to find out which is the best one for our purposes. The first question to answer is if we need a colour or a monochrome LED. If we just need to replace a conventional lamp with a LED-based one, probably the monochrome choice is the best bet as we will have less issues to solve (driver choice, power supply, etc.). On the other hand, if we are looking for a more refined product and we want to try different spectral choices for the light source, we might be interested in getting RGB LEDs instead.
For our work we have decided to go for a power LED from OSRAM (LRTB-G6T6), shown in Fig. 8. This product includes the 3 RGB LEDs required in a single package and it has been optimised for additive mixture of colour stimuli by independent driving of the individual LEDs.
In order to control both the LED-based and the halogen light source, we are going to need a dimming technology. We have to keep in mind that we have a twin goal: on the one hand we want to compare the two technologies from a performance point of view but, on the other hand, we are looking forward to evaluating our formerly introduced algorithms [1][2][3] with the new LED projector. In the following chapter we will give a brief description of the most popular control technologies we have available in the market.

9.2 Dimming technologies
If we intend to simulate different lighting scenarios, one of the best approaches is choosing a light control system. There are a number of different choices on the market. Some of them are closed developments which means they are made ad hoc by a manufacturer and they are usually operated by an infrared remote or some kind of potentiometer / push button interface. On the other hand, we have a number of standard technologies which might serve to our purposes while allowing us the access to a full range of devices from different manufacturers.

9.2.1 1-10 V Interface
The 1-10 V interface is the oldest of the three approaches shown here. It is a fully analogue system and it allows us to control the attached ballast or transformer by means of two wires.

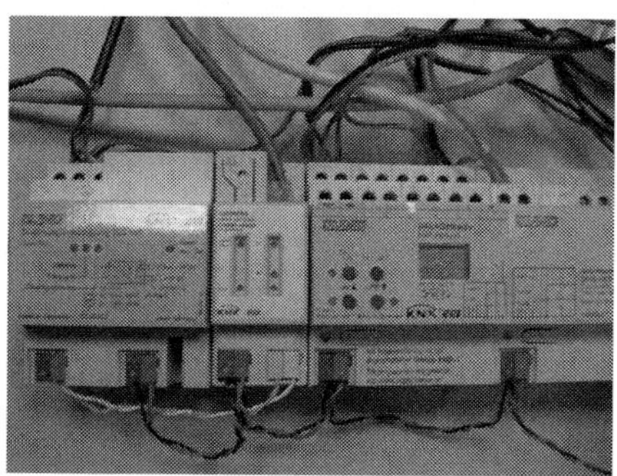

Fig. 9. KNX devices

On the other side of the connection we usually find a potentiometer as the only device required to operate the dimmed light. Its main advantage is that it is very cheap as opposed to other technologies but it is not very accurate and it is very slow in operation.

9.2.2 DALI

DALI stands for Digital Addressable Lighting Interface. As its name indicates, it is digital technology as opposed to the 1-10 V interface. As in the previous case, only two wires are required but the main difference is that up to 64 ballasts can be attached to a single controller. It is very common to find this technology in offices and buildings as it provides a high degree of control while keeping the cost reasonably low.

9.2.3 DMX512

DMX (Digital MultipleX) is also a digital protocol like DALI, but it focuses on the speed of the dimming which allows us to create special effects and smooth colour changes. The cost of the lamps and the required controller is usually higher than its DALI counterpart.

9.2.4 KNX

KNX or Konnex is not dimming technology. Instead, we are talking about a standard bus commonly used in Europe for connecting different systems in a house (heating, blinds, lights, etc.). Why we have decided to mention it here is because many different KNX (formerly known as EIB) manufacturers offer interfaces and controllers of the three systems described before in their catalogues. In addition, it is very simple to control a KNX-based installation from a PC, using one of the different interfaces available (RS-232, USB and Ethernet).

As we will describe later, we have decided to use this technology in combination with a DALI controller to perform all the tests required to compute the comparison charts.

10. Illumination-independent texture analysis

If we suppose that a spectral band b_1 from an image $f_{b1}(x, y)$ has been formed according to Lambert's reflectivity model (Lambert., 1760) then we can say that:

$$f_{b_1}(x, y) = I_{b_1} * R_{b_1} * \cos \Theta \ . \tag{13}$$

a.   Bright texture   b.   Dark texture

Fig. 10. Bright and dark textures

where I_{b1} represents the intensity of the light source on the surface of the texture for the spectral band b_1 and R_{b1} the reflectivity coefficient of that surface.

For another band b_2, the previous equation would be rewritten as:

$$f_{b_2}(x,y) = I_{b_2} * R_{b_2} * \cos \Theta \ . \tag{14}$$

The band ratio of bands b_1 and b_2 is defined as:

$$BR_1 = \frac{f_{b_1}}{f_{b_2}} = \frac{I_{b_1}}{I_{b_2}} \frac{R_{b_1}}{R_{b_2}} \frac{\cos \Theta}{\cos \Theta} = k \frac{R_{b_1}}{R_{b_2}} \ . \tag{15}$$

If the lighting components I_{b1} and I_{b2} are modified we will get new ones, I'_{b1} and I'_{b2}. Then, the equation (15) would be rewritten as follows:

$$BR_2 = \frac{f'_{b_1}}{f'_{b_2}} = \frac{I'_{b_1}}{I'_{b_2}} \frac{R_{b_1}}{R_{b_2}} \frac{\cos \Theta}{\cos \Theta} = k' \frac{R_{b_1}}{R_{b_2}} \ . \tag{16}$$

If we want to calculate the difference between the rationed images BR_1 and BR_2, we only have to subtract equation (15) from equation (16):

$$BR_1 - BR_2 = k \frac{R_{b_1}}{R_{b_2}} - k' \frac{R_{b_1}}{R_{b_2}} = (k - k') \frac{R_{b_1}}{R_{b_2}} \ . \tag{17}$$

If the variations from the light source are proportional to both bands we can state that $k = k'$, then equation (17) could be rewritten as:

$$BR_1 - BR_2 = k \frac{R_{b_1}}{R_{b_2}} - k \frac{R_{b_1}}{R_{b_2}} = (k - k) \frac{R_{b_1}}{R_{b_2}} = 0 \ . \tag{18}$$

From the previous result we can state that if a surface can be expressed or modelled according to Lambert's reflectivity model and if the lighting variations are proportional between bands, then the rationed images do not change.

Obviously, the assumptions made before are not always true in real-world applications, but our experiments have shown us that this approach performs very well if we compare it with regular texture analysis.

Fig. 11. Real-world textures (darkest ones) taken under different lighting conditions with a halogen projector

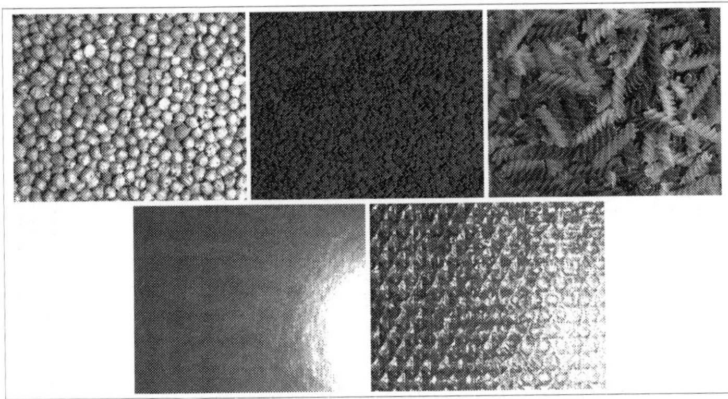

Fig. 12. Real-world textures (darkest ones) taken under different lighting conditions with a LED projector

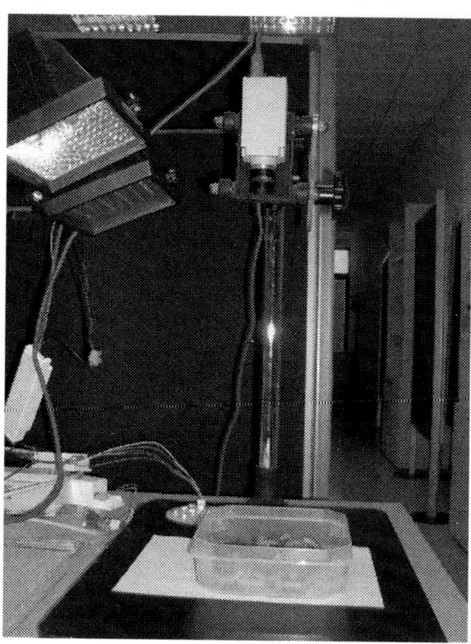

Fig. 13. Pixelink camera

10.1 Experiments

To analyse the performance of our technique we have taken shots from 5 real world textures (Fig. 11 and 12), food and fabrics. We have used an industrial colour camera from Pixelink, model PL-B742F (Fig. 13). We have changed the lighting conditions of the whole scene by means of a KNX DALI controller and a universal dimmer. We have used a standard 150 watt halogen projector and a custom-built LED projector (Fig. 14). The images have a resolution of 1280x1024 pixels each, and they are organised in 5 different sets representing 5 different illumination conditions, numbered from 0 (brightest) to 4 (darkest). We have performed two major tests:

1. For this experiment, we have built a training set from the textures from lighting level 0 and we have used the remaining images for testing (levels 1..4)

2. In this case, the training set is composed of the textures from lighting level 4 and the remaining images are used for testing (levels 0..3)

These tests allow us to evaluate the performance of the system using images from the left end and the right end for training, i.e, the brightest and the darkest ones. We have computed Gabor features from the training and testing sets. For this purpose the images were divided into 320 disjunct images of 64x64 pixels.

We have performed a number of experiments, applying different preprocessing techniques to be able to process colour images. The charts showed in the next section gather the classifier performance in all cases.

Fig. 14. Halogen and LED projectors

Preprocessing algorithm	0-1	0-2	0-3	0-4
Greyscale	88.25%	87.13%	82.69%	38.93%
R+G+B	95.81%	95.69%	90.31%	33.81%
Ratios R/G & R/B	96.87%	96.69%	95.19%	68.31%

Table 4. Halogen projector results (I)

10.2 Results

For evaluating the performance of the feature sets obtained in each case, we have used a Knn classifier, taking $K = 5$. To measure the distance between two feature vectors in $\Re^n$, the 1-norm is used.

We have performed a number of experiments, applying different preprocessing techniques in order to process colour images. These algorithms can be summarised as follows:

1. Greyscale conversion.- We convert the colour image to greyscale and we compute the features.

2. RGB concatenation.- We extract the texture features from each colour band and we build a single feature vector.

3. Band ratioing.- This technique, previously introduced in (Muñiz & Corrales, 2003), consists in getting a monochrome image, which is the result of dividing two spectral bands of the image, such as R/G. The rationed image can be used as an input to virtually any feature extraction algorithm, as in the previous cases.

Gabor features were extracted by filtering the textures at 3 scales and 4 different orientations. This gives us a total of 12 gabor energies for each texture sample.

In tables 4 and 5 we have summarised the results of the halogen tests. It is very noticeable how band ratios perform very well when compared to the greyscale and RGB features. The numbers shown tell us that these features are very stable in terms of performance when the illumination changes. It is also interesting the overall bad performance of the system when we use the dark images as the training set. Even in this case, the behaviour of the R/G and R/B features is very stable.

Preprocessing algorithm	4-3	4-2	4-1	4-0
Greyscale	39.56%	37.00%	34.06%	34.19%
R+G+B	42.88%	39.18%	35.94%	33.25%
Ratios R/G & R/B	63.81%	64.50%	64.63%	65.38%

Table 5. Halogen projector results (II)

Preprocessing algorithm	0-1	0-2	0-3	0-4
Greyscale	86.31%	84.25%	76.63%	73.19%
R+G+B	95.69%	93.81%	90.43%	85.06%
Ratios R/G & R/B	86.19%	84.43%	83.19%	80.13%

Table 6. LED projector results (I)

The results of the LED projector create a totally new scenario. In this case the performance of the classifier is always reasonably high. The most interesting fact is that the behaviour of the LED lamp seems to be more stable when the intensity of the light varies. This phenomena can be explained as a more consistent colour spectrum when we change the intensity of the LEDs. The light produced by a halogen lamp, on the other hand, tends to be more yellowish, which is something that obviously has an effect on the images we get from the camera.

10.3 Conclusions of the lighting problem

In this section we have shown the result of applying modern LED technology to texture analysis and classification. We have built a custom projector using high power LEDs from Osram and we have used a standard enclosure to fit the PCB. The results obtained with the Gabor features show that the images captured when the LED projector was used are more resistant to changes in the intensity of the light and, in addition, the visual quality of the images seems to be better than the halogen ones.

11. Conclusions

In this chapter we have started to explore the possibilities of modern LED lighting for computer vision. The results obtained are very promising but further research has to be conducted. The first drawback was the LED module used and the number of them mounted on the PCB. For future work we are going to look for a more powerful module and we should consider fitting an increased number of them on the projector. Nevertheless, the low power consumption and the uniformity of the colour spectrum when the lamp ages show us where we should be directing our attention.

Preprocessing algorithm	4-3	4-2	4-1	4-0
Greyscale	84.25%	81.50%	74.75%	79.25%
R+G+B	97.81%	94.63%	91.06%	86.88%
Ratios R/G & R/B	98.06%	98.38%	96.63%	83.31%

Table 7. LED projector results (II)

12. Acknoledgements

This work has been performed under support of the Spanish MEC project reference DPI2007-63129.

13. References

Bovik, A. & Clark, M. (1990). Multichannel texture analysis using localized spatial filters, *IEEE Transactions on Pattern Analysis and Machine Inteligence* **12(1)**: 55–73.

Conners, R. & McMillin, C. (1983). Identifying and locating surface defects in wood: Part of an automated lumber processing system, *IEEE Transactions on Pattern Analysis and Machine Intelligence* 5(6): 573–584.

de Wouver, G. V. (1998). *Wavelets for Multiscale Texture Analysis*, PhD thesis, University of Antwerp (Belgium).

Dunn, D., Higgings, W. & Wakeley, J. (1994). Texture segmentation using 2-d gabor elementary functions, *IEEE Transactions on Pattern Analysis and Machine Intelligence* 16(2): 130–149.

Haralick, R., Shanmugam, K. & Dinstein, I. (1973). Textural features for image classification, *IEEE Transactions on Systems, Man, and Cybernetics* 3(6): 610–621.

Hecht, E. (1987). *Optics*, Addison Wesley.

Jain, A. & Healy, G. (1998). A multiscale representation including opponent color features for texture recognition, *IEEE Transactions on Image Processing* **7(1)**: 124–128.

Kruizinga, P., Petkov, N. & Grigorescu, S. (1999). Comparison of texture features based on gabor filters, *Proceedings of the 10th International Conference on Image Analysis and Processing, Venice, Italy*, pp. 142–147.

Lambert., J. H. (1760). Photometria sive de mensure de gratibus luminis, colorum umbrae., Eberhard Klett.

Mallat, S. (1999). *A Wavelet Tour of Signal Processing*, Academic Press.

Muñiz, R. & Corrales, J. A. (2003). Use of band ratioing for color texture classification., *in* F. J. P. López, A. C. Campilho, N. P. de la Blanca & A. Sanfeliu (eds), *IbPRIA*, Vol. 2652 of *Lecture Notes in Computer Science*, Springer, pp. 606–615.

Palm, C., Keysers, D., Lehmann, T. & Spitzer, K. (2000). Gabor filtering of complex hue/saturation images for color texture classification, *Proceedings of 5th Joint Conference on Information Science (JCIS2000), Atlantic City, USA*, Vol. 2, pp. 45–49.

Palm, C., Metzler, V., Lehmann, T. & Spitzer, K. (2000). Color texture classification by within and cross-cooccurence matrices, *Proceedings of 15th International Conference on Pattern Recognition, Barcelona, Spain*.

Smith, L. I. (2002). A tutorial on principal components analysis.

## 15

Generic scale-space architecture for handwriting documents analysis

Joutel Guillaume, Eglin Véronique and Emptoz Hubert
Université de Lyon (LIRIS, UMR5205)
France

1. Introduction

Those last years, one can observe that the number of digital libraries has clearly increased but not as fast as the number of tools to promote the cultural heritage stored in those libraries. Among the great diversity of cultural inheritage we can notice that handwritten documents constitute an important part of ancient collections to valorise. In those document images, we are not interested in handwriting recognition and semantic content, but we focus on image content retrieval through visual low level characteristics of shapes (from graphemes to entire handwriting samples).

In this work, we are interested in digitized Middle-Age (composed by copyists' texts from the 9th to the 15th century), Humanistic manuscripts (essentially composed by authors' drafts from the 18th and 19th century) and overall lines based images, see Fig. 1.

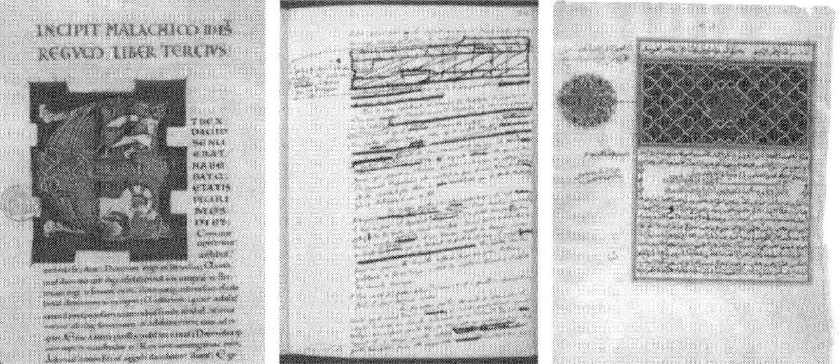

Fig. 1. Complex handwriting documents images from different periods (from 13th to 18th century)

The community of handwriting document analysis has been working for several years on the devlopment of computer-based systems for retrieval and identify handwritings from various historical periods. This begs the question whether such work can be applied to medieval writing as well. In this work, on strong constraint is to find a robust characterisation tool for writer dependent or style dependent primitives

Due to the fact that the *curvature* and the *orientation* are judged to be two fundamental dimensions of handwritings, we have searched a way to compute them on the shapes for different corpus. To compute those dimensions, we have developed a methodology that is sensitive to variations at the edges of shapes and that reveals the variability of shapes and their anisotropy at different scales. The proposed methodology has been tuned so as to be robust to disturbed environments (presence of disturbed backgrounds, of partial shapes...) without requiring prohibitive costs of process nor great storage volume for each analyzed page image. Our choice relates to a redundant multi-scale transform: the Curvelets transform that is more robust than wavelets for the representation of shapes anisotropy, of *lines segments* and *curves* in the images. Standard wavelet-based tools suffer of their incapacity to locate thin structure of lines and thin variations all along curves. Those points will be discussed in following sections.

In the literature, we have observed that mainly handwritings characterization methods may be divided into four classes:

_ The first class gathers methods that search for structural information. As examples, we can quote the average height, the width and the overall slant of the writing. Despite these methods are really simple, their efficiency in the writer identification task is not proved as far. Their main drawback is in the initial segmentation task which is rarely robust.

_ The second class is made of statistical methods. The idea behind is to accumulate information in order to be less sensitive to intrinsic variations of writings. This time the drawback is the difficulty to evaluate quantitatively the amount of information that are needed in those kinds of process.

_ The third class is made of frequency analysis that is based on a change in the representation of the signal. This time the drawback is the lack of directionality that is caused by most of multiscale frquences based representation.

_ The fourth class tries to get the best of several methods by mixing classes. Currently, we may find in the fourth class some serial arrangements of two existing methods from the first three classes.

We think that, thanks to recent works on signal processing, it is possible to mix the three first classes of methods in a single and efficient characterization approach. This mixing process is proposed and discussed in parts 0 and 0. In those sections, we will show how the curvature and the orientation of shapes are essential features that are dependent on image frequences, geometry and ditribution. The choice of these features comes from several pluridisciplinary discussions with palaeographers that we are working with. In the last part of the paper (in part 0), we will see two examples of applications based on these features: a content base image retrieval application and the analysis of the evolution process of Middle-Ages handwritings.

2. In the frequency domain

Most of the time, the structure of an image is very complex, you can find textured parts with changes more or less salient in brightness, or you can also encounter more or less overlapping objects. In all those situations it is not easy to define relevant universal features to describe objects in an image. In that context, objects are mostly defined according to various criteria such as contour, shape, texture, presence of edges more or less smooth … It is clear that a unique representation fails to take into account all these characteristics and other models should be developed to optimise the image processing that need to be done. Among these transformations we can include coding, analysis, representation or segmentation of information. These new models of representation must take into account the most appropriate information of the image without looking for secondary ones.

If these new models can take into account the most appropriate information, it is still often convenient to be able to reverse the process. Therefore, we intend to define an invertible transform to work on information not limited to greyscales. The linear transforms of Fourier and Gabor were until recently the only alternatives to the representation and modelling of greyscale images. The number of representations has today significantly increased with, for example, the Laplacian pyramid transform and the wavelet transforms, whether classical or geometrical. These new representations have led to considerable progress in applications such as compression, denoising and now characterization of the contents.

In this section, we show the way we followed to justify the choice of characterization approach based on geometrical wavelet transforms and especially on the Curvelets transform.

2.1 At the beginning, the Fourier transform

The initial work of Joseph Fourier focused on modelling the evolution of temperature through trigonometric series We call today those transforms: Fourier series. More precisely Fourier showed that for any periodic signal f of period T, we have:

$$f(t) = \frac{a_0}{2} + \sum_{k=1}^{k=\infty} \left(a_k \cos\left(\frac{2k\pi t}{T}\right) + b_k \sin\left(\frac{2k\pi t}{T}\right) \right)$$

(1)

Coefficients a_k and b_k are given by:

$$a_k = \frac{2}{T} \int_0^T f(t)\cos\left(\frac{2k\pi t}{T}\right) dt$$
$$b_k = \frac{2}{T} \int_0^T f(t)\sin\left(\frac{2k\pi t}{T}\right) dt$$

(2)

Formula (1) may be rewritten with the module r_k ($r_k = \sqrt{a_k^2 + b_k^2}$) and phase θ_k ($\cos\theta_k = \frac{a_k}{r_k}$

and $\sin\theta_k = \frac{b_k}{r_k}$) :

$$f(t) = \sum_{k=1}^{k=\infty} r_k \cos\left(\frac{2k\pi t}{T} - \theta_k\right)$$

(3)

The formulas (1) and (3) can be adapted to the case of non-periodic and integrable signals. This is called the Fourier transform.

The Fourier transform F is an operation that transforms an integrable function into another function, describing the frequency spectrum of f. If a function f is integrable, its Fourier transform is the function $F(f)$ and is given by the formula .

$$F(f) : s \rightarrow \hat{f}(s) = \int_{-\infty}^{+\infty} f(t)e^{-2i\pi st}dt$$

(4)

The departure set is the one of integrable functions f of one real variable t. The arrival set is the one of functions F (f) of one real variable s. Specifically when this transform is used in signal processing, we say that t is the time variable, f is in the time domain, that s is the frequency and F is in the frequency domain.

The Fourier transform is particularly well suited for stationary signals, so named because their properties are statistically invariant over time. If so, locating frequencies is meaningless.

The so-called natural images, especially document images, containing homogeneous zones with sharp transitions, generally located on the contours. This property makes them non-stationary signals, since the singularities appear in a non-homogenous way. The absence of localization of these singularities can be very penalizing. A solution may be found in the Gabor transform. The main well-known drawback of this approach is in the choice of the size of the sliding-window. Drawback solved with the wavelet theory.

2.2 The wavelet transform

In 1983, Morlet working on the analysis of seismic signals noted the inadequacy of the sliding-window Fourier transform due to the rigidity imposed by the fixed size of the window. He then decided to use a window of expanded or contracted size as needed. The idea of wavelets was born.

The wavelet transform uses basis functions to analyse and reconstruct a given signal. To understand this process, we shall now give a brief background on the properties of vector spaces for such reconstruction.

2.2.1 Vector and basis functions

A basis of a vector space V is a set of linearly independent vectors such that any vector v of V can be expressed as a single linear combination of these vectors in the database. There may be more of one basis for a given vector space each but each of them has the same number of vectors: this number is called the dimension of the vector space. For example, any vector of R^2 can be expressed as a linear combination of vectors (1,0) and (0,1).

Thus any vector is a linear combination of the basis of their vector space. This concept, expressed in terms of vectors, spread easily to functions by replacing the vectors of the basis with basis functions. Complex exponential functions are the basic functions for the Fourier transform.

If f (t) and g (t) are two functions of L^2 (all square integrable functions on a given interval), their scalar product can be calculated. This operation is used to calculate the wavelet transform as we recall in the following mathematical formalization:

Let f(t) a real function of real variable. Ψ is a function of zero average, centred around 0 and negligible outside a compact interval, called mother wavelet. The wavelet transform of f is:

$$g(a, b) = \frac{1}{\sqrt{a}} \int_{t=-\infty}^{t=+\infty} f(t)\Psi\left(\frac{t-b}{a}\right)$$

(5)

From the function Ψ, we can build a family of wavelets functions given by translations (coefficient b) and dilatations (coefficient a) of Ψ:

$$\psi_{a,b}(t) = \Psi\left(\frac{t-b}{a}\right)$$

(6)

where a is the frequency and b the time.

This definition shows that wavelet analysis is the similarity measure between the basis functions (wavelets) and the signal itself. Similarity is here understood as similar frequency content. The coefficients calculated in the transform indicate the degree of similarity between the signal and the wavelet at the current scale.

Unlike the Fourier transform, the mother function is not defined in the theory so that it is possible to choose the most appropriate one to the problem. However, apart from the orthogonality of the basis vectors to obtain a good reconstruction, the wavelet basis must meet two important properties to deserve the name : the admissibility and the regularity condition. We will not study those here but we will focus on what we are interested in : anisotropic structures.

2.2.2 To anisotropic structures

Within the great diversity of approaches to complement the properties of "classical" wavelets are a class of methods seeking to better characterize the anisotropic structures. These are the geometrical wavelets which can be adaptive or not.

Geometrical adaptive wavelets tries to adapt the best wavelet basis to the geometry of a given image. It becomes clear that whatever the approach chosen, a preliminary estimation of the geometry is required before decomposition. This estimation may however be done in several ways: edge detection, triangulation, regularity estimation ... We may cite, as examples of this class of methods, the Bandelets (Le Pennec & Mallat, 2003), the oriented wavelets (Chappelier & Guillemot, 2005) or the Directionlets (Velisavljevic, 2005) It appears that with such an approach, there is near no wavelets coefficients redundancy which can be an advantage for applications like compression of images.

Apart from characterizing the contours or local singularities, typically anisotropic properties, the non-adaptive geometrical wavelets share the distinction of having a fixed basis and independent of the image they represent. This allows, among other things, of not requiring additional cost for specifying, during the synthesis, the configuration used in the analysis. However this leads to many unwanted redundancy for applications such as compression. We may cite, also as examples of this class of methods, the Ridgelets (Candès & Donoho, 1999a), the Curvelets (Candès & Donoho, 1999b) and the Contourlets (Do & Vetterli, 2005)

2.2.3 The Curvelets

Due to fact that we are working with anisotropic structures, writings, we have chosen to use geometrical wavelets. The choice of a non-adaptive method is due to that we do not search to make compression of our signal but more to analyse the latter. Indeed, analysis may be better with a little redundancy in wavelets coefficients than if there was not. Finally the choice of Curvelets is due to that it has an optimal coding of information. The question now is how it is done. In the discrete domain and particularly in the case of images, we may consider that locally, there are straight contours. This is what leads to the creation of the Curvelets transform. This transform is achieved in two main stages. First we partition the image into squares of varying sizes with recovery to avoid sides effects. These squares are obtained through a finite support Fourier window. The next step is to apply a discrete Ridgelets transform within these squares with dilation of the wave function of a/a^2. Contours not captured by the separable wavelet analysis can be found in the sub-band detail. A sufficiently fine partition of the sub-bands can then obtain blocks where these contours are straight lines and are therefore suitable for Ridgelets analysis. The Curvelets transform is invertible but redundant because the analysis in discrete sub-Ridgelets core is made using a Fast Fourier Transform (FFT) of the polar plane, requiring more points than those available in the rectangular grid. Using the FFT directly from the Fourier Slice Theorem. Indeed, it indicates that the Radon transform can be obtained by applying an inverse 1-D Fourier transform along radial lines passing through the origin in the Fourier domain of the 2-D image. All these steps are illustrated in Fig. 2.

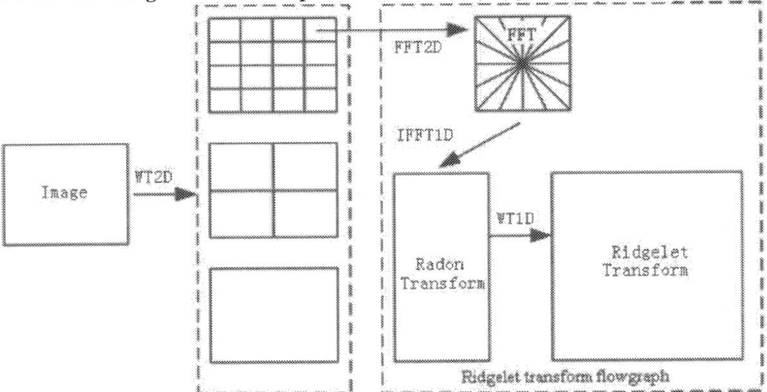

Fig. 2. Curvelets transform flow graph on an image

3. Features extraction

3.1 DCTG2

The version of the Curvelets transform introduced in section 0 uses the Radon transform. This transform is difficult to discretize. Candès and Donoho have proposed a second generation of transform that are now developed in the discrete domain. The development has been done in the software Curvelab (http://curvelet.org) The technical details related to this implementation are provided in (Candès et al, 2005) We have chosen to use in our work this implementation for the extraction of orientations and the evaluation of the curvatures on each point of the transformed image.

3.2 Orientations extraction

Curvelets coefficients are indexed in position, scale and direction. The coefficients enabled us to deduce easily the dominant orientations of strokes by retaining only the highest coefficient corresponding to processed pixel at the finest scale. We only retain the finest scale for the analysis of orientation and curvature. However, the methodology presented can be applied regardless of the scale.

In theory, for a given scale E, the number n of sub-bands created by the directional Curvelet transform is calculated using the formula :

$$n = a * 2^{\lfloor \frac{(E-1)}{2} \rfloor}$$

where a is the number of angles used for the first cutting angular frequency plane which is in our case the scale 2.

In practice we set the number of scales and a to 8 and therefore we obtain at the finest scale 64 angles: so the accuracy of the directional decomposition is around 5°. Searching for a greater accuracy requires an additional cost in terms of storage that is not necessary for our work. In addition, this implies sensitivity to slight variations in the writing which is not desired for the great variability induced by production of handwriting.

Thus, if Op is the set of coefficients of the n orientations that are analysed at the finest scale corresponding to pixel p, then the dominant orientation is o with o = *index (MaxOp)* where *Index (j)* is a function returning index $i <= n$ corresponding to Curvelet coefficient j.

We show on Fig. 3. the results of this analysis on an extract from the Washington's manuscripts library. Analysis of the circle on Fig. 4. is given as a colour reference and a zoom on a part of the orientation analysis is given on Fig. 5.

270. Letters Orders and Instructions October 1755.

only for the publick use, unless by particular Orders from me. You are to send down a Barrel of Flints with the Arms, to Winchester, and about two thousand weight of Flour, for the two Companies of Rangers; twelve hundred of which to be delivered Captain Ashby's Company, at the Plantation of Charles Sellars — the rest to Captain Cocke's Company, at Nicholas Reasmers.

October 26. GW

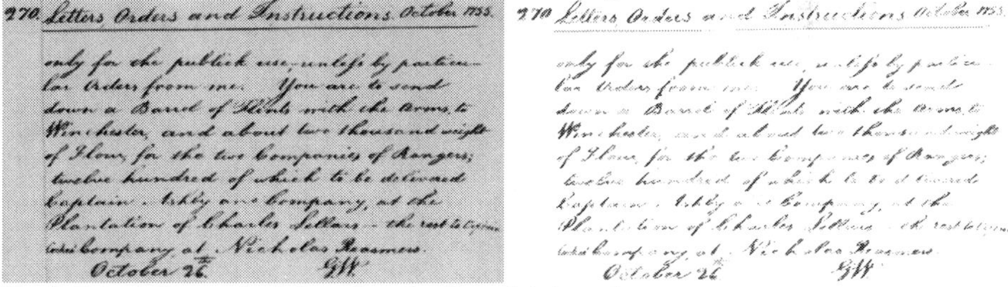

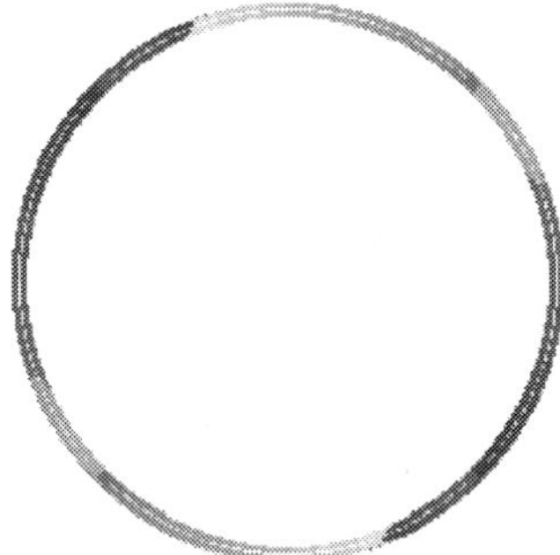

Fig. 3. Orientation analysis based on the Curvelets transform

Fig. 4. Orientation analysis of a circle

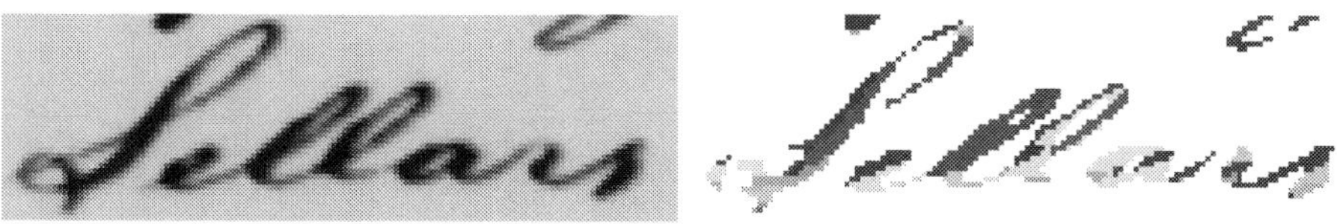

Fig. 5. Zoom on a part of the orientation analysis

3.3 Curvatures evaluation

We just show how we extract the dominant orientations. The latter, although adequate for right segments, had to be enriched for all other cases, especially for handwriting that we study but also in almost cases of images in general. This enrichment has come to the attention of the other dominant orientations for the same pixel. Indeed, it is rare for a pixel of a curve (or contour) to have a single dominant orientation and it is very common that other orientations are also carriers of information. Therefore, for each pixel, we keep a list of different dominant orientations associated with it. This list of dominant orientations has been inspired from Antoine and Jacques's works in (Antoine & Jacques ,2003)

In their work, authors use conical wavelets (Antoine et al, 2008). The support of these wavelets is strictly in a convex cone in the frequency domain which makes them very efficient in detecting objects whose orientation is marked as straight lines. From these wavelets, authors have shown that it is possible to estimate the curvature at a point in a line by estimating the number of orientations for which the wavelet coefficients corresponding to this point are significant. The main problem in our work by using this approach comes from the limitation to straight lines. Considering that conical wavelets approximate heavily Curvelet except that the parabolic scaling that is specific to Curvelets transforms allows a better selectivity of anisotropic objects. In that context, we decided to apply the same methodology but this time with the Curvelets transform. In that way we have used the list of dominant orientations that we have mentioned earlier to evaluate the curvature at the frontiers of lines and shapes. The evaluation of the curvature on each point is then simply computed by measuring the length of this list. The more long it is, the more the curvature at the point of interest is high and vice versa. Formally, we can define our evaluation of the curvature as follows:

Let's consider P as a pixel of an image I. Lp represent all significant orientations associated with it, then the level of curvature in P, Np is defined by:

$$Np = Card\ (Lp)$$

A result of this evaluation is given on Fig. 6. for the same document as for the Fig. 3. Colours used for this representation are ordered on Fig. 7. and a zoom on a part of the evaluation is given on Fig. 8.

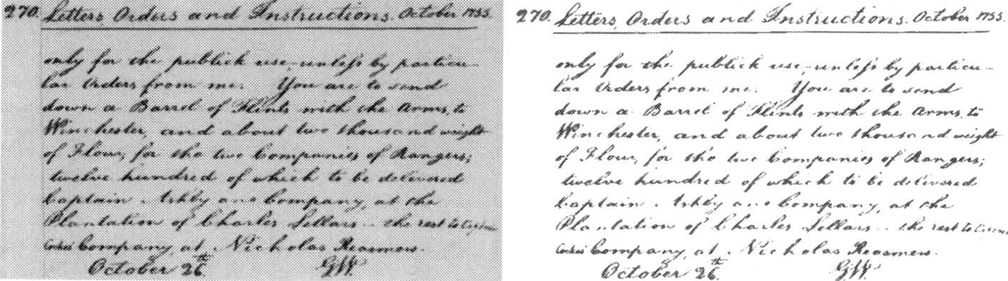

Fig. 6. Curvature evaluation based on the Curvelets transform

Fig. 7. Standard curvature scale

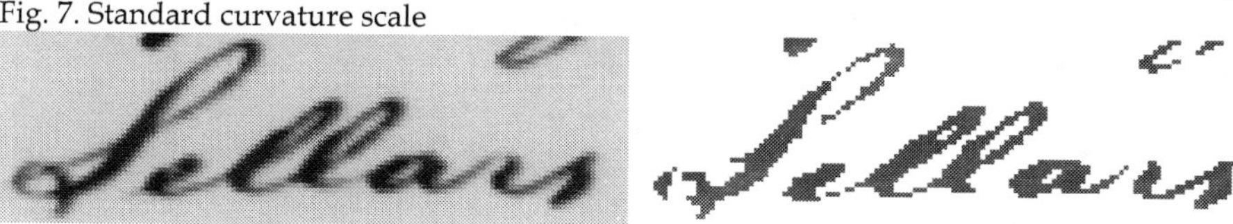

Fig. 8. Zoom on a part of the curvature evaluation

3.4 Handwriting signature design

The analysis of orientations and curvatures at the frontiers of shapes that we have presented in sections 0 and 0 provides a characterization of writing in the manuscript. However, as the amount of information contained in a manuscript may considerably vary, we have built a compact representation of this information which allows to describe a unique writing contained in the document. This representation is what we call the signature of writing and is the score matrix M of couples (curvature, orientation) extracted from the analysis of orientations and curvatures presented in sections 0 and 0.

Thus, for each pixel p on frontiers of writing, we build the couple (c, w) where c is the curvature of the line in pixel p and w is the set of c orientations retained significant for the evaluation of the curvature. We raise the values of matrix M with coordinates (c, o_i) of a value corresponding to the ratio between the coefficient o_i and the maximum of coefficients all o_i considered (see Fig. 9).

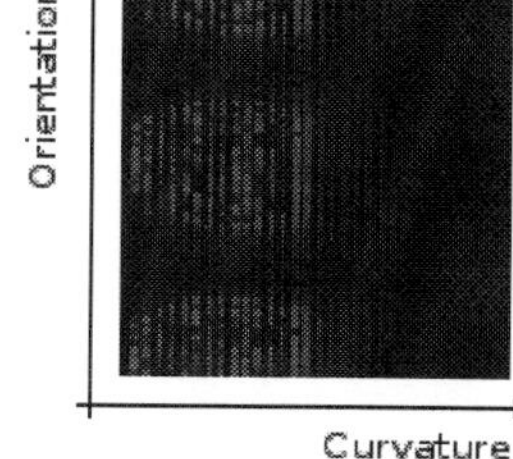

Fig. 9. Signature of Washington's handwriting

Values of this matrix of occurrences remained closely linked to the amount of information contained in the manuscript so we standardized values by keeping the ratio between the maximum value of the signature and the values of the latter. The values of the signature are then all between 0 and 1.

At the same time we have removed from our signature odd columns of the matrix. Indeed, the analysis takes into account the 360 degrees and therefore evaluates each direction twice (45 ° and 225 ° for example). This produces a curvature systematically even hence our choice (see Fig. 10). We have also removed half of the lines, but in order to illustrate and justify the symmetry, we will still represent them in the following.

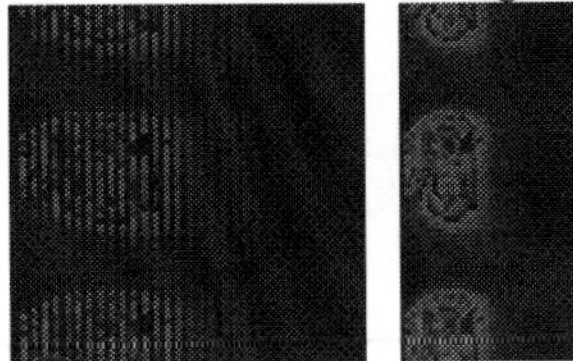

Fig. 10. Even curvatures suppression in signature

We quickly found that the standardization is not suitable for the comparisons intended for this signature. Indeed, with such an approach, significant values of the signature are, in the same language, almost invariant. For the Latin languages, for example, there are almost systematically the vertical and / or horizontal orientation considered as dominant and thus around a curvature evaluation rather low. This comes, of course, essentially from the verticality of our scripts and the horizontal alignment of our texts. To solve this problem, we have raised low values of our signature while reducing the role of orientations common to all writers. To do so, we applied a Lorentzian filter (see Fig. 11 { 2 }) before reversing the order of values in the signature (see Fig. 11 { 3 }):

$$\forall i, \forall j \rightarrow M(i,j) = 1 - L(M(i,j))$$

where L is the Lorentzian filter defined as :

$$L(x) = \frac{\Gamma}{2\pi} \frac{1}{\left(\frac{1}{2}\Gamma\right)^2 + (x - x_0)^2}$$

where x_0 is the index of the peak and Γ its width at half height.

{ 1 } Signature after even curvatures suppression   { 2 } Signature after applying Lorentzian filter   { 3 } Signature after reversing order of values

Fig. 11. Different steps of our signature changes

4. Applications

Now that features can be extracted and that if necessary those can be grouped together in a compact signature, we will now show how we used them to retrieve information from manuscripts. In section 0 we will present how we have built a CBIR (Content Based Image Retrieval) system based on our compact signature of handwritings and in section 0 we will present a word spotting system based, for the moment, exclusively on the orientations extraction.

4.1 Content based image retrieval

As every CBIR system, our one is composed of two main parts: a features extraction phase that allows a change in representation space and a comparison phase between those features which provides a list of similar images. This scheme of operation is identical to the one of a k nearest neighbours approach and is presented in Fig. 12.

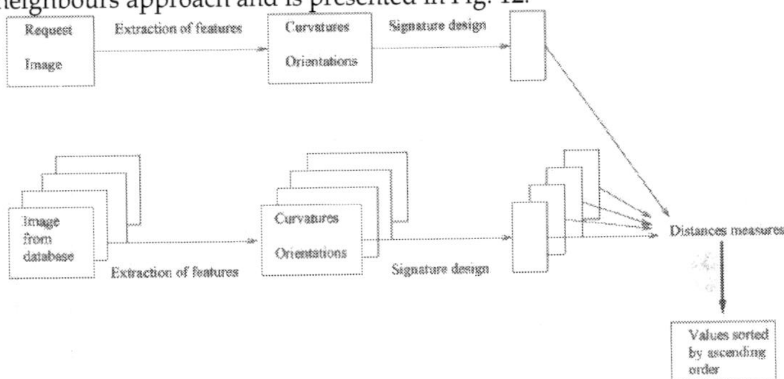

Fig. 12. Schema of a content based image retrieval system

The features extraction and the signature design steps have been presented in part 0 and we will now have a look on the similarity evaluation between signatures.

We have developed two main measures; a generic one and another one dedicated to medieval Latin manuscripts. The two measures have been integrated in our system and we have tested those on two different databases.

The evaluation process was the same for both:

_ The precision P is evaluated over all queries: $P=\dfrac{NumberOfGood\,Answers}{NumberOfAnswers}$

_ The recall R is evaluated over all queries: $R=\dfrac{NumberOfGoodAnswers}{NumberOfExpectedAnswers}$

_ The F-measure is computed from P and R: $F=\dfrac{2PR}{P+R}$

To highlight those values we have decided to compare our system to another one from the state of the art. Many of those use features based on texture, colour, ... and in our case comparison would not be very easy. So we decided to test one based on wavelets coefficients: ImgSeek (Jacobs et al, 1995)

4.1.1 Results of the generic measure

The generic measure is a linear correlation coefficient and we have tested it on a humanistic handwritings database. We present here the results obtained on the basis of manuscripts

IAM. The value of this database is that information about writers are known and the types of scripts are closed to what we call humanistic writings. We also tested our approach on images of ancient manuscripts with similar types to those in the IAM database and results were similar. However we do not present these results for rights issues on these documents. As we have mentioned, all images of the IAM database are given with accurate information about writers, the task of labelling was greatly facilitated. We provide results in Table 1 and the corresponding curves in Fig. 13.

System	Precision	Recall	F-measure
Our system	0,87	0,68	0,81
ImgSeek	0,82	0,63	0,73

Table 1. Comparison between characteristic values of our system and ImgSeek on Humanistic database

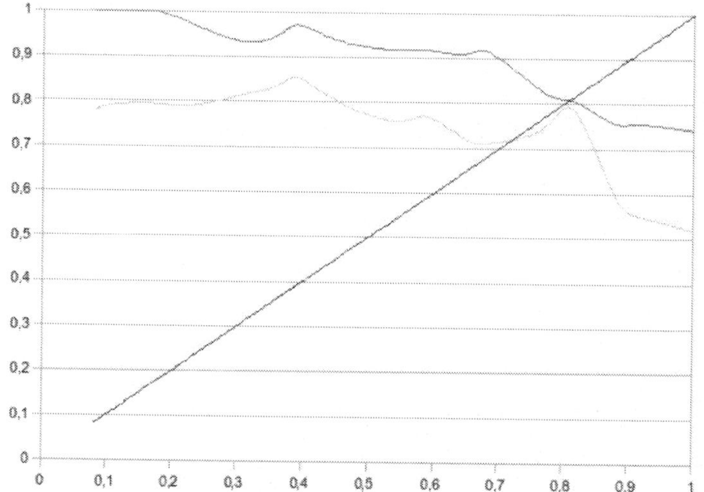

Fig. 13. Precision/Recall curves of CBIR on Humanistic database. Our system in red and ImgSeek in yellow

It appears that, despite our similarity measure do not take into account information on handwritings properties, results stay better with our system. We have also tested our approach on a natural images database and results are almost the same except that gap between the two systems is greater.

4.1.2 Specialized similarity index

We have the chance to work with palaeographers and this led us to study our linear correlation on their images. Results were clear not what they expected. By the way, we have tried to understand where could be the problem of our approach and it appears clearly that the linear correlation take to much into account some part that should not. Two Latin handwritings have clearly some common properties that should be considered in the same way that their differences. This assessment, or nearly the same, has been done by Tversky (Tversky, 1977) when he built is ratio model in the cognitive psychology field. The problem for us of this model is that it is based on binary features which is clearly not our case. We have then decided to adapt it to our specific signature. To do so, we decided to separate information of our signatures on the basis of their common and what we call the residual or distinctive parts. We shall now see how we make this separation.

For separation of values into two groups, we defined the combination of two measures that are:

_ A linear correlation based on common parts of the two signatures, which we denote $Cor_{directe}$.

_ A linear correlation based on opposition parts between the two signatures, which we denote $Cor_{residus}$.

To define common parts between the two signatures we set a threshold S between the strong and low values. This threshold is the mean of the first signature that is in our case the query signature. If for a couple of values in the signature, values of both signatures are higher (respectively lower) to S then they would be taken into account in the calculation of a direct correlation denoted Cor_{forte} (Cor_{faible} respectively) (see Fig. 14)

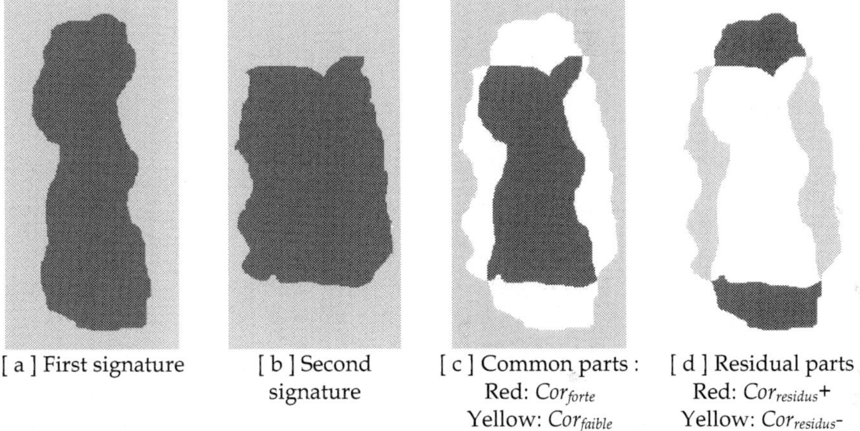

| [a] First signature | [b] Second signature | [c] Common parts :
Red: Cor_{forte}
Yellow: Cor_{faible} | [d] Residual parts
Red: $Cor_{residus}+$
Yellow: $Cor_{residus}-$ |

Fig. 14. Parts kept for the direct correlation and the residual correlation

Cor_{forte} and Cor_{faible} are grouped together in a single measure defined as follows:

$$Cor_{directe} = \alpha \times Cor_{forte} + (1 - \alpha) \times Cor_{faible} \tag{7}$$

α depends on number of values kept in each part.

In exactly the same way $Cor_{residus}+$ and $Cor_{residus}-$ are grouped together in another single measure defined as follows:

$$Cor_{residus} = \beta \times Cor_{residus+} + (1 - \beta) \times Cor_{residus-} \tag{8}$$

β also depends on number of values kept in each part.

Our index is then defined as :

$$Sim = \gamma \times Cor_{directe} + (1 - \gamma) \times Cor_{residus} \tag{9}$$

This time, the value of γ is left to the user. He may then choose between taking more into account the common parts of signatures or what makes the difference between them. On our medieval manuscripts database, curves of Precision/Recall according to the value of γ are given in Fig. 15.

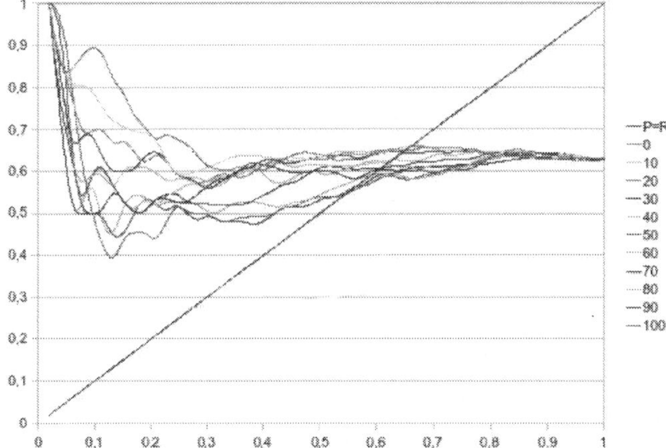

Fig. 15. Our system behaviour according to values of γ

What we can see on this curves is that, for this specific database, it is clearly more interesting to consider differences between writings more than common parts. Indeed, despite the end of curves is almost the same, for low values of recall (first answers) the precision stay higher with low values of γ

4.2 Word spotting

The word spotting is based on a similarity or a distance between two images, the reference image defined by the user and the target images representing the rest of the page or all the pages from a multi-page document. Firsts results in handwriting documents have been given by Manmatha et al. in (Manmatha & Croft, 1997). Their idea was to match words from a request and words in documents by the use of simple features such as aspect ratio's of word's bounding box. Other approaches use direct correlation methods applied on the grey levels for image similarity comparison. Those classical approaches are very sensitive to geometrical transformations and are time consuming. Moreover, correlation cannot be easily adapted to the spatial variations of the handwriting. Main solutions consist in representing the informative parts of the images with feature vectors that can be compared with other feature vectors from other images. The choice of the most discriminant features to characterize regions of interest is central. Different approaches for local image structure description have been proposed in the literature. We propose here a short overview of those methodologies. An approach proposed by Kolcz et al. in (Kolcz et al, 2000) was to search along lines of text a way to match their request in every position along this line. Several features have been used and are matched with a dynamic time warping (DTW) distance. This is a expensive way to search a match but some heuristics are used to limit the search along the lines. Moreover, results are really much better than those proposed in (Manmatha & Croft, 1997). A mix of this kind of ideas can be found in (Rath & Manmatha, 2003). The idea is to segment each documents into words with a technique given in (Manmatha & Srimal, 1999), and then to resize and realign each word so that it can be easily compared with other images. Distance between images is then computed with the DTW distance on a set of features described in this paper. The critical part of this approach is in the segmentation into words which can not be done on every documents and especially on medieval documents.

Recently, Leydier et al. in (Leydier et al., 2007) have proposed a (word, line, layout) segmentation-free method which rests on the assumption that words can be matched on a small number of guidelines. Very good results are shown but no idea is given on what happened if text is not as vertical and straight as those in manuscripts studied. However, they have proved that the strokes' orientation provide a strong piece of information in handwritten manuscripts. The hitch comes from matching distances tested which are based on the assumption that guidelines are vertical which is not necessary the case in other manuscripts. Other keyword spotting approaches very close to our proposition have been proposed those last years. Fink and Plotz in (Fink & Plotz, 2005) have tested appearance-based features for writer independent handwritten text recognition and compared it with heuristic features. Terasawa et al. in (Terasawa et al., 2006) have developed principal component analysis-based descriptors and gradient distribution features for word spotting in historical handwritten documents. The only limitation of the approach is its application to only well segmented threshold documents and very regular handwritten texts.

Our approach tries to keep the best of the different approaches presented, by searching guidelines but not necessary vertical ones. Our idea is to search for the predominant orientations of the query in documents (see Fig. 16).

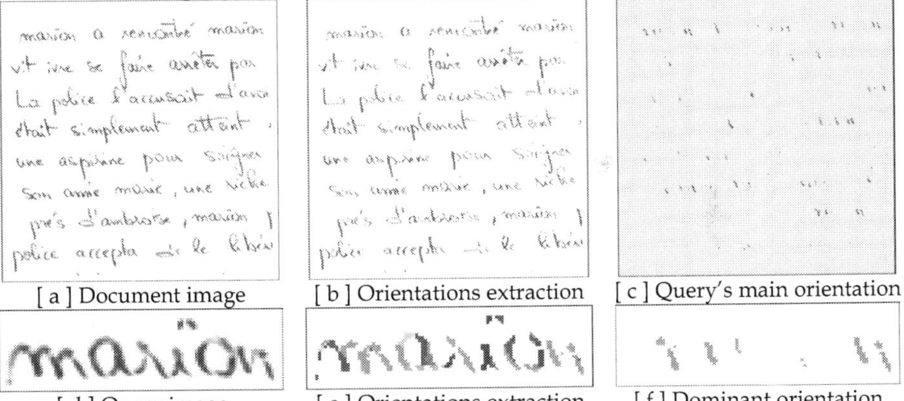

| [a] Document image | [b] Orientations extraction | [c] Query's main orientation |
| [d] Query image | [e] Orientations extraction | [f] Dominant orientation |

Fig. 16. Extraction of the dominant orientation of a query

Once orientations are extracted from the request by the use of the Curvelet transform, we search for the same organization of those orientations in a window similar to the one of the request sliding over the documents. The organization is obtained from a quad tree applied on the window in which each leaf contains the area covered by exactly the same number of pixels detected with predominant orientation of the query image (see Fig. 17).

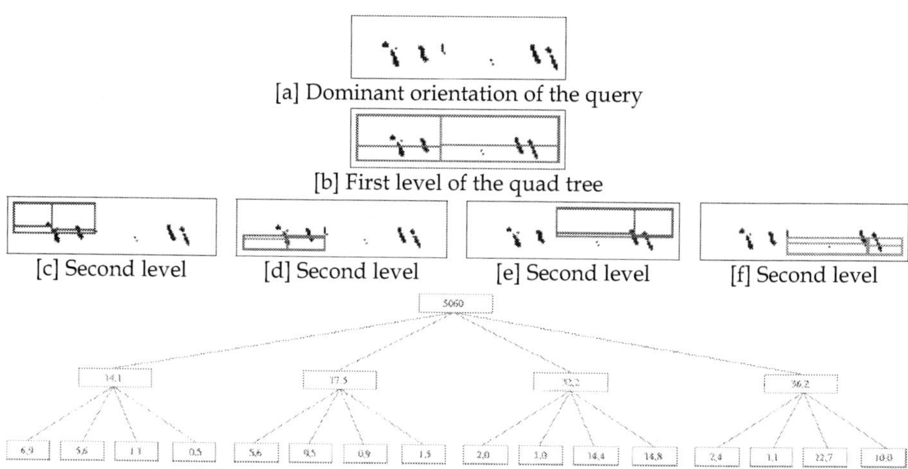

[a] Dominant orientation of the query

[b] First level of the quad tree

[c] Second level   [d] Second level   [e] Second level   [f] Second level

[g] Quad tree with area of regions stored in each leaf

Fig. 17. Dominant orientation pixels organization evaluation with a quad tree

As it is also an information retrieval system, we have computed the same value that what we have done in section 0. This time we have compared our system to the one of Leydier et al (Leydier et al., 2007) This time, it is our system which use less information than the one we compare to. Indeed, the system of Leydier et al uses information on what it searches for. For example, guidelines used to search for a word are vertical which is due to fact that this system was initially developed for Latin writings. Nevertheless, it is the closer to our system and that is why we decided to compare our system to this one.

The first database we tested is the Washington's manuscripts database. Characteristic values of this comparison are given in Table 2 and corresponding curves are given in Fig. 18.

System	Precision	Recall	F-Measure
Our system	0,8	0,42	0,55
Leydier et al.	1,0	0,53	0,69

Table 2. Comparison between characteristic values of our system and Leydier et al. on Washington's manuscript database

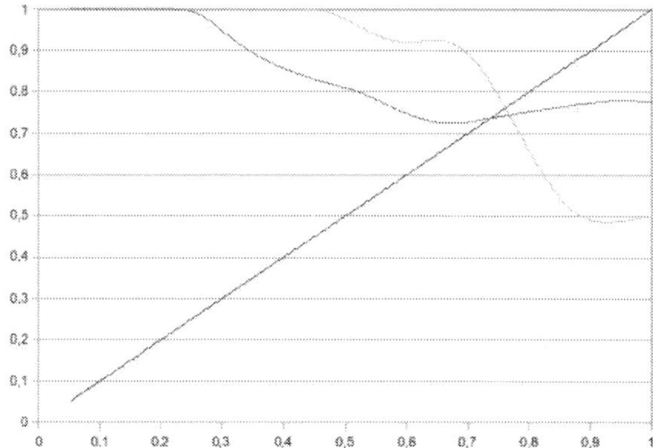

Fig. 18. Precision/Recall curves of word-spotting on Washington's manuscript database. Our system in red and Leydier et al. in yellow

Leydier et al. system is better than our one because of the use of information on shape searched. If we work on a database of comics images, which are also strokes images, the result are almoste inverted due to the generic aspect of our approach. Characteristic values are given in Table 3 and corresponding curves in Fig. 19.

System	Precision	Recall	F-Measure
Our system	1,0	0,4	0,57
Leydier et al.	0,9	0,36	0,51

Table 3. Comparison between characteristic values of our system and Leydier et al. on comics images database

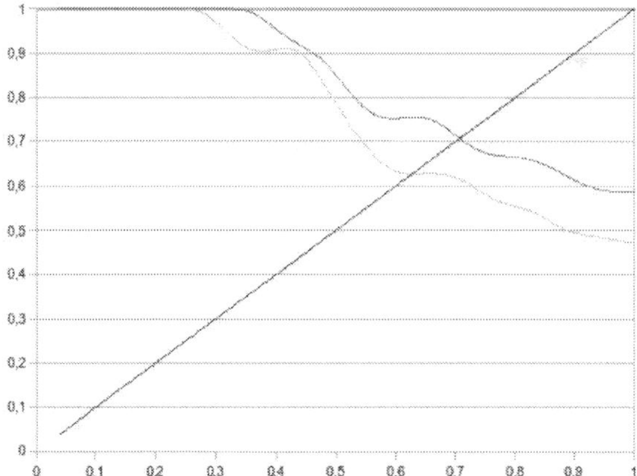

Fig. 19. Precision/Recall curves of word-spotting on comics images database. Our system in red and Leydier et al. in yellow

5. Conclusion

We have shown how one can extract features, curvatures and orientations in frontiers of shapes, from a geometrical wavelets transform. We have also shown how we can use these features to develop two applications of information retrieval. The content based information retrieval system is based on a global information about the handwriting in the document and the word spotting system is based on local information about a keyword. We have compared those systems to the state of the art and we are currently working on how to improve results.

For the word spotting system, we consider that we can use the curvature information to locate interesting points in the documents. Currently, we slide our window over all the document pixel by pixel. This is very expensive and as we can see on Fig. 20 if we reduce search to, for example, high curvatures zones the treatment cost should be greatly reduced.

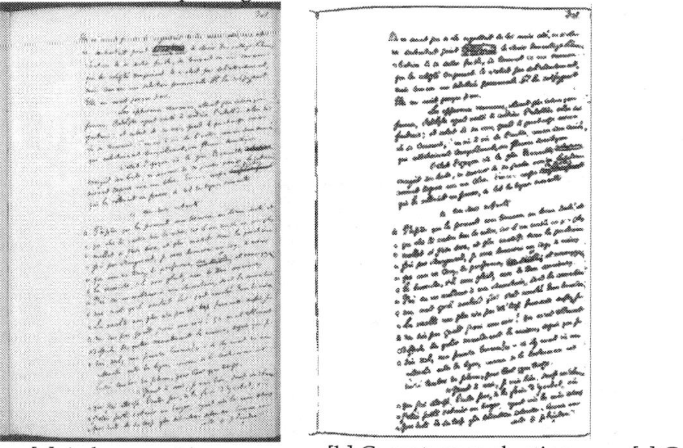

[a] A document image   [b] Curvature evaluation   [c] Curvature thresholded

Fig. 20. Example of reduction of search field thanks to curvature

We are also working on an improvement of our CBIR system. This improvement comes from a density study of writings in a new representation space. This study is closed to the Parzen window method. Once it is done, we may use this study as a preliminary index to the search in the database. We are currently working on this approach on our medieval manuscripts images database. Results still need to be evaluated by experts before we can apply it in our CBIR system.

6. References

Antoine, J-P & Jacques, L. (2003). Measuring a curvature radius with directional wavelets. Institute of Physics Conference Series, (899-904) ,(2003)

Antoine, J-P; Bogdanova, I. & Vandergheynst, P.(2008). The continuous wavelet transform on conic sections. International Journal of Wavelets, Multiresolution and Information Processing, 6,2,(137-156) ,(2008)

Candès, E. & Donoho, D., (1999). Ridgelets : a key to higher-dimensional intermittency ?, Philosophical transactions - Royal Society. Mathematical, physical and engineering sciences, 357, (2495-2509) ,(1999)

Candès, E. & Donoho, D., (1999). Curvelets : A surprisingly effective non-adaptive representation of objects with edges. Technical report

Candès, E.; Demanet, L.; Donoho, D. & Ying, L. (2005). Fast Discrete Curvelet Transforms., Technical report

Chappelier, V. & Guillemot, C.(2005). Oriented wavelet transform on a quincunx pyramid for image compression. IEEE International Conference on Image Processing, 1:I, (8-14) ,(2005)

Do, M.N. & Vetterli, M., (2005). The contourlet transform : an efficient directional multiresolution image representation. IEEE Transactions on Image Processing,14,12,(2091-2106) ,(2005)

Fink, G. A. & Plotz, T., (2005). On appearance-based feature extraction methods for writer-independent handwritten text recognition. International Conference on Document Analysis and Recognition, (1070-1074), (2005)

Jacobs, C.E.; Finkelstein, A. & Salesin, D.H.(1995). Fast multiresolution image querying. ACM, (277-286),(1995)

Kolcz, A.; Alspector, J.; Augusteijn, M.; Carlson, R. & Popescu, G., (2000). A line-oriented approach to word spotting in handwritten documents. PAA, 3,2 (153-168), (2000)

Le Pennec, E. & Mallat, S. (2003). Bandelettes et représentation géométrique des images. GRETSI, Groupe d'Etudes du Traitement du Signal et des Images

Leydier, Y. ; Lebourgeois, F & Emptoz, H., (2007). Text Search for Medieval Manuscript Images. Pattern Recognition, 12,40, (3552-3567), (2007)

Manmatha, R. & Croft, W., (1997). Word spotting: Indexing handwritten archives.Intelligent Multimedia Information Retrieval Collection.

Manmatha, R. & Srimal, N. (1999). Scale space technique for word segmentation in handwritten manuscripts. ScaleSpace99, (22-33), (1999)

Rath, T. M. & Manmatha, R., (2003). Features for word spotting in historical manuscripts. International Conference on Document Analysis and Recognition,(218), (2003)

Terasawa, K. ; Nagasaki, T. & Kawashima, T. (2006). Automatic keyword extraction from historical document images. Document Analysis Systems, (413-424), (2006)

Tversky, A., (1977). Features of similarity. Psychological Review, 84,4,(327-352), (1977)

Velisavljevic, V., (2005). Directionlets. PhD thesis, Lausanne

## 16

Bi-2DPCA: A Fast Face Coding Method for Recognition

Jian Yang [a], Yong Xu [b] and Jing-yu Yang [a]

[a] *Department of Computer Science, Nanjing University of Science and Technology, Nanjing 210094, China*
[b] *Shenzhen Graduate School, Harbin Institute of Technology, Shenzhen, China*

1. Introduction

Face recognition has received significant attention in the past decades due to its potential applications in biometrics, information security, law enforcement, etc. Numerous methods have been suggested to address this problem [1]. Among appearance-based holistic approaches, principal component analysis (PCA) turns out to be very effective. As a classical unsupervised learning and data analysis technique, PCA was first used to represent images of human faces by Sirovich and Kirby in 1987 [2, 3]. Subsequently, Turk and Pentland [4, 5] applied PCA to face recognition and presented the well-known Eigenfaces method in 1991. Since then, PCA has been widely investigated and has become one of the most successful approaches to face recognition [6-15].

PCA-based image representation and analysis technique is based on image vectors. That is, before applying PCA, the given 2D image matrices must be mapped into 1D image vectors by stacking their columns (or rows). The resulting image vectors generally lead to a high-dimensional image vector space. In such a space, calculating the eigenvectors of the covariance matrix is a critical problem deserving consideration. When the number of training samples is smaller than the dimension of images, the singular value decomposition (SVD) technique is useful for reducing the computational complexity [1-4]. However, when the training sample size becomes large, the SVD technique is helpless. To deal with this problem, an incremental principal component analysis (IPCA) technique has been proposed recently [16]. But, the efficiency of this algorithm still depends on the distribution of data.

Over the last few years, two PCA-related methods, independent component analysis (ICA) [17] and kernel principal component analysis (KPCA) [18, 19] have been of wide concern. Bartlett [20], Yuen [21], Liu [22], and Draper [23] proposed using ICA for face representation and found that it was better than PCA when cosine was used as the similarity measure (however, the performance difference between ICA and PCA was not significant if the Euclidean distance is used [23]). Yang [24] and Liu [25] used KPCA for face feature extraction and recognition and showed that KPCA outperforms the classical PCA. Like PCA, ICA and KPCA both follow the matrix-to-vector mapping strategy when they are used for image analysis and, their algorithms are more complex than PCA. So, ICA and KPCA are considered to be computationally more expensive than PCA. The experimental results in

Since the eigenvalues $\lambda_1, \lambda_2, \cdots, \lambda_n$ are sorted in decreasing order, most of the image energy is packed into a small number of column vectors of $\mathbf{B}$. In a word, 2DPCA realizes the optimal image energy compression in horizontal direction.

4. Bi-2DPCA

4.1 Idea

2DPCA can eliminate the correlations between image columns and compress the image energy optimally in horizontal direction. But, it disregards the correlations between image rows and the data compression in vertical direction. So, its compression rate is far lower than PCA and more coefficients are needed for the representation of images. This must lead to a slow classification speed and large storage requirements for large-scaled databases [27, 38].

In this section, we will suggest a way to overcome the weakness of 2DPCA. Our idea is very simple, just to perform 2DPCA compression twice: the first one is in horizontal direction and the second is in vertical direction (*Note that any operation in vertical direction can be equivalently implemented by an operation in horizontal direction by virtue of the transpose operation of matrix*). Specifically, given image $\mathbf{A}$, we obtain the feature matrix $\mathbf{B}$ after the first 2DPCA compression. Then, we transpose $\mathbf{B}$ and input $\mathbf{B}^T$ into 2DPCA, and determine the transform matrix $\mathbf{V}$. Projecting $\mathbf{B}^T$ onto $\mathbf{V}$, we obtain $\mathbf{C}^T = \mathbf{B}^T \mathbf{V}$. The resulting feature matrix is $\mathbf{C} = \mathbf{V}^T \mathbf{B}$. This process is illustrated in Figure 1.

In the whole process, the first 2DPCA transform $\mathbf{B} = \mathbf{A}\mathbf{U}$ performs the compression of 2D-data in horizontal direction, making the image energy pack into a small number of columns. While the second 2DPCA transform $\mathbf{C} = \mathbf{V}^T \mathbf{B}$ performs the compression of 2D-data in vertical direction, eliminating the correlations between columns of image $\mathbf{B}$ and making its energy further compact into a small number of rows. Ultimately, the energy of the whole image is packed into the up-left corner of the image matrix.

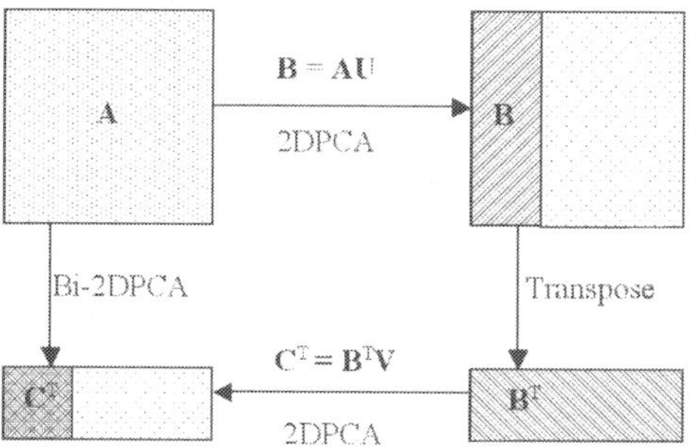

Fig. 1. Illustration of Bi-2DPCA

4.2 Algorithm

Now, let us present the detailed implementation of Bi-2DPCA. Based on the given training sample image $\mathbf{A}$, we can construct the image covariance matrix $\mathbf{G}_t$ using Eq. (12). Suppose $\mathbf{u}_1, \mathbf{u}_2, \cdots, \mathbf{u}_q$ are the orthonormal eigenvectors of $\mathbf{G}_t$ corresponding to q largest eigenvalues $\lambda_1, \lambda_2, \cdots, \lambda_q$. Let $\mathbf{U} = (\mathbf{u}_1, \mathbf{u}_2, \cdots, \mathbf{u}_q)$. Then, we get the 2DPCA feature matrix of $\mathbf{A}$, i.e.,

$$\mathbf{B} = (\mathbf{A} - E\mathbf{A})\mathbf{U} \tag{27}$$

Constructing the image covariance matrix $\mathbf{H}_t$ based on $\mathbf{B}^T$, we have

$$\mathbf{H}_t = E[(\mathbf{B} - E\mathbf{B})(\mathbf{B} - E\mathbf{B})^T] \tag{28}$$

From Eq. (27), we know $E\mathbf{B} = 0$. Thus $\mathbf{H}_t = E[\mathbf{B}\mathbf{B}^T]$. This matrix can be evaluated by

$$\mathbf{H}_t = \frac{1}{M}\sum_{j=1}^{M}\mathbf{B}_j^T\mathbf{B}_j, \text{ where } \mathbf{B}_j = (\mathbf{A}_j - \overline{\mathbf{A}})\mathbf{U}, \tag{29}$$

Suppose $\mathbf{v}_1, \mathbf{v}_2, \cdots, \mathbf{v}_p$ are the orthonormal eigenvectors of $\mathbf{H}_t$ corresponding to p largest eigenvalues $\mu_1, \mu_2, \cdots, \mu_p$. Let $\mathbf{V} = (\mathbf{v}_1, \mathbf{v}_2, \cdots, \mathbf{v}_p)$. We get the 2DPCA feature matrix of $\mathbf{B}^T$ by

$$\mathbf{C}^T = (\mathbf{B}^T - E\mathbf{B}^T)\mathbf{V} = \mathbf{B}^T\mathbf{V} \tag{30}$$

Thus

$$\mathbf{C} = \mathbf{V}^T\mathbf{B} = \mathbf{V}^T(\mathbf{A} - E\mathbf{A})\mathbf{U} \tag{31}$$

The resulting feature matrix $\mathbf{C}$ is a $p \times q$ matrix, which is much smaller than the 2DPCA feature matrix $\mathbf{B}$ and the original image $\mathbf{A}$ since p and q are always selected much smaller than m and n. We can use $\mathbf{C}$ to represent $\mathbf{A}$ for recognition purpose.

In summary of the discussion so far, the Bi-2DPCA algorithm is given below:

Bi-2DPCA Algorithm

Step 1. Construct the image column covariance matrix $\mathbf{G}_t$ using Eq. (13). Calculate $\mathbf{G}_t$'s orthonormal eigenvectors $\mathbf{u}_1, \mathbf{u}_2, \cdots, \mathbf{u}_q$ corresponding to q largest eigenvalues.

Step 2. Construct the image row covariance matrix $\mathbf{H}_t$ using Eq. (29). Calculate $\mathbf{H}_t$'s orthonormal eigenvectors $\mathbf{v}_1, \mathbf{v}_2, \cdots, \mathbf{v}_p$ corresponding to p largest eigenvalues.

Step 3. Let $\mathbf{U} = (\mathbf{u}_1, \mathbf{u}_2, \cdots, \mathbf{u}_q)$ and $\mathbf{V} = (\mathbf{v}_1, \mathbf{v}_2, \cdots, \mathbf{v}_p)$. Use the transform $\mathbf{C} = \mathbf{V}^T(\mathbf{A} - \overline{\mathbf{A}})\mathbf{U}$ to get the feature matrix of the given image sample $\mathbf{A}$.

4.3 Bi-2DPCA based image reconstruction

Bi-2DPCA allows the reconstruction of the original image pattern. Since $\mathbf{G}_t$'s eigenvectors $\mathbf{u}_1, \mathbf{u}_2, \cdots, \mathbf{u}_q$ and $\mathbf{H}_t$'s eigenvectors $\mathbf{v}_1, \mathbf{v}_2, \cdots, \mathbf{v}_p$ are both orthonormal, from Eq. (31), it is easy to obtain the reconstructed image of $\mathbf{A}$:

$$\widetilde{\mathbf{A}} = E\mathbf{A} + \mathbf{VCU}^T, \tag{32}$$

where $\mathbf{U} = (\mathbf{u}_1, \mathbf{u}_2, \cdots, \mathbf{u}_q)$, $\mathbf{V} = (\mathbf{v}_1, \mathbf{v}_2, \cdots, \mathbf{v}_p)$.

Denoting $\mathbf{C} = (c_{ij})_{p \times q}$, Eq. (32) can be rewritten by

$$\widetilde{\mathbf{A}} = \overline{\mathbf{A}} + \sum_{i=1}^{p} \sum_{j=1}^{q} c_{ij} \mathbf{v}_i \mathbf{u}_j^T \tag{33}$$

Let us denote $\boldsymbol{\varphi}_{ij} = \mathbf{v}_i \mathbf{u}_j^T$ ($i = 1, \cdots, p$; $j = 1, \cdots, q$). Obviously, $\boldsymbol{\varphi}_{ij}$ is rank-1 matrix, which is of the same size as original image $\mathbf{A}$ and called the *basis image*. Any image $\mathbf{A}$ can be approximately reconstructed by adding up the weighted *basis images* and the mean image.

4.4 Reconstruction error evaluation

Without loss of generality, the expectation of image samples generated from $\mathbf{A}$ is also supposed to be zero, i.e. $E\mathbf{A} = 0$, in the following discussion.

If we use the feature matrix $\mathbf{C}$ to represent $\mathbf{A}$, the reconstruction error of image $\mathbf{A}$ can be expressed by

$$\Delta = \mathbf{A} - \widetilde{\mathbf{A}} = \sum_{i=p+1}^{m} \sum_{j=q+1}^{n} c_{ij} \mathbf{v}_i \mathbf{u}_j^T \tag{34}$$

And, the total reconstruction mean-square error (MSE) can be characterized by

$$\varepsilon_t^2 = E \| \Delta \|_F^2 = E \| \mathbf{A} - \widetilde{\mathbf{A}} \|_F^2 \tag{35}$$

Theorem 2 Suppose $\mathbf{u}_1, \mathbf{u}_2, \cdots, \mathbf{u}_n$ are the eigenvectors of $\mathbf{G}_t$ corresponding to $\lambda_1 \geq \lambda_2 \geq \cdots \geq \lambda_n$ and $\mathbf{v}_1, \mathbf{v}_2, \cdots, \mathbf{v}_m$ are the eigenvectors of $\mathbf{H}_t$ corresponding to $\mu_1 \geq \mu_2 \geq \cdots \geq \mu_m$. Let $\mathbf{U} = (\mathbf{u}_1, \cdots, \mathbf{u}_q)$ and $\mathbf{V} = (\mathbf{v}_1, \cdots, \mathbf{v}_p)$. If we use the feature matrix $\mathbf{C} = \mathbf{V}^T(\mathbf{A} - E\mathbf{A})\mathbf{U}$ to represent $\mathbf{A}$, the total mean square error is

$$\varepsilon_t^2 = \sum_{j=q+1}^{n} \lambda_j + \sum_{j=p+1}^{m} \mu_j.$$

The proof of Theorem 2 is given in Appendix A.

Theorem 2 tells us the total MSE of Bi-2DPCA based image representation is the sum of MSEs corresponding to the two involved 2DPCA. It is easy to understand this result from the *image energy loss* point of view. After the first 2DPCA compression on $\mathbf{A}$, we obtain $\mathbf{B}$

and know that the corresponding image energy loss is $\displaystyle\sum_{j=q+1}^{n}\lambda_j$ from Theorem 1. After the

second 2DPCA compression on $\mathbf{B}^T$, we obtain $\mathbf{C}$ and know the image energy loss is

$\displaystyle\sum_{j=p+1}^{m}\mu_j$ also from Theorem 1. So, the total *energy loss* should be $\varepsilon_t^2 = \displaystyle\sum_{j=q+1}^{n}\lambda_j + \sum_{j=p+1}^{m}\mu_j$.

5. Relationship to other PCA (KLT) Techniques

5.1 Relationship to PCA and 2DPCA

Let us begin our discussion from the viewpoint of mean-square error. Unquestionably, PCA (KLT) is optimal for 1D data representation (compression) in the sense of minimal mean-square error. For 1D data $\mathbf{x}$ (vector), if the transform form $\mathbf{y} = \mathbf{\Psi}^T\mathbf{x}$ is chosen, PCA-based transform is optimal. For 2D data $\mathbf{A}$ (matrix), we can transform the data into 1D vectors by stacking the columns of $\mathbf{A}$ and then use PCA to obtain a *holistically* optimal representation. For 2D data $\mathbf{A}$, however, we can also choose another transform form $\mathbf{B} = \mathbf{AU}$. With respect to this transform form, 2DPCA turns out to be optimal; it realizes an optimal compression in horizontal direction. Bi-2DPCA provides a sequentially optimal compression mechanism with respect to the transform form $\mathbf{C} = \mathbf{V}^T\mathbf{AU}$. That is to say, if we choose such a transform form to compress the image data from horizontal to vertical, Bi-2DPCA is optimal in the sense of minimal mean-square error.

PCA, 2DPCA and Bi-2DPCA are all *image-data dependent* coding method. In contrast to PCA, a remarkable advantage of Bi-2DPCA is its low computation requirement. The computational advantage of Bi-2DPCA mainly embodies in the following three aspects:

First, Bi-2DPCA needs less computation than PCA in the construction of covariance matrices. Suppose the image size is $m \times n$ and the training sample size is M. Denote $N = m \times n$ and $l = \min\{M, N\}$. To form the covariance matrix (or the corresponding Gram matrix), PCA needs $M \times N \times l$ multiplications, while Bi-2DPCA needs $M \times m \times n^2$ multiplications to construct $\mathbf{G}_t$ and $M \times q \times m^2$ multiplications to construct $\mathbf{H}_t$. So, the total computation of Bi-2DPCA is $M \times (m \times n^2 + q \times m^2)$, which is less than $M \times N \times (m + n)$ since q is much smaller than n. Generally, $(m + n) < l$ in face recognition problems, so Bi-2DPCA needs less computation for constructing covariance matrices.

Second, Bi-2DPCA has a lower computational complexity than PCA on solving the eigen-problem. From the discussion in Section 2.1, we know that the computational complexity of PCA is $\mathcal{O}(l^3)$. Since Bi-2DPCA only needs to calculate the eigenvectors of $\mathbf{G}_t$ and $\mathbf{H}_t$, its computational complexity is $\mathcal{O}(m^3 + n^3)$. Since l is much larger than m or n in real-world applications, PCA is computationally more intensive than Bi-2DPCA.

Third, the transformation calculation of Bi-2DPCA in Eq. (31) is also smaller than that of PCA in Eq. (2). The transformation calculation of PCA is $m \times n \times d$, while the calculation of

Bi-2DPCA are $m \times n \times q + m \times q \times p$, which is smaller than $m \times n \times (p+q)$. Since $d = pq$ (if the same amounts of features are required by both methods), PCA generally needs more calculation than Bi-2DPCA in image transformation.

The foregoing discussions show PCA is computationally more intensive than Bi-2DPCA. Besides, another advantage of Bi-2DPCA is that it needs less memory requirement than PCA in face recognition systems. This is because PCA needs to save a much larger transform matrix for feature extaction. The transform matrix of PCA is sized of $N \times d = m \times n \times d$, which amounts to the size of d orginal images. While, the two transform matrices of Bi-2DPCA are only sized of $m \times p + n \times q$, which is generally less than one orginal image in size.

A comparison between PCA and Bi-2DPCA is summarized in Table 1. Here, it should be stressed that the computational advantages of Bi-2DPCA over PCA is independent of the algorithms that are adopted to calculate the eigenvectors. If an algorithm can speed up the eigenvector computation of PCA, it is certain to speed up the eigenvector computation of Bi-2DPCA in the same way.

Method	Computation Requirements			Memory Requirements
	Construction of covariance matrix	Solving eigen-problem	Image Transformation	
PCA	More	More	More	More
Bi-2DPCA	Less	Less	Less	Less

Table 1. A comparison between PCA and Bi-2DPCA in computation and memory requirements

Compared to 2DPCA, the compression rate of Bi-2DPCA is significantly improved. That is, Bi-2DPCA needs much less coefficients than 2DPCA for image representation. The advantages of Bi-2DPCA over 2DPCA are twofold. First, the storage requirements can be significantly reduced. Second, the classification speed will be increased since less computation is needed in distance (similarity) calculation.

5.2 Relationship to classical 2D-KLT

Bi-2DPCA is an *image-data dependent* coding method while 2D-KLT is *image-data independent*. The underlying difference between these two methods is that the classical 2D-KLT is based on an assumed image model while Bi-2DPCA not. The implementation of the classical 2D-KLT depends on the assumption that an ensemble of images satisfies the first-order Markov model with separable autocorrelation function. Without this assumption, the method cannot exist independently because its covariance matrices are constructed by the separable autocorrelation function rather than training samples. In contrast, Bi-2DPCA can work independently without any assumed image model. Like PCA, it relies on training samples to evaluate its covariance matrices.

Actually, the classical 2D-KLT and Bi-2DPCA have different utilities. The classical 2D-KLT is suitable for an ensemble of images and generally applied to image compression. Bi-2DPCA is suitable for a category of images that have some similar characteristics. Bi-2DPCA can be used for image representation and recognition, such as face recognition, palm identification, etc.

5.3 Relationship to ST-KLT

As discussed in Section 2.3, without the image model, the total covariance matrix is generally not equal to the outer product of the horizontal and vertical covariance matrices. Thus, the separable transform in Eq. (8) is not equivalent to KL transform. The minimal MSE property of ST-KLT cannot be guaranteed and the degree of approximation cannot be evaluated in theory. These problems are critical and not addressed by the authors in their paper [31].

2DPCA provides us theoretical insights to see through the series of problems left by ST-KLT. First of all, by the correlation analysis in Section 3.2, the intuitive meanings of the horizontal and vertical covariance matrices become clear. The horizontal covariance matrix shows the correlation between column vectors of image samples, while the vertical covariance matrix shows the correlation between image row vectors. Secondly, the transform (compression) in horizontal or vertical direction has a clear explanation. 2DPCA-based transform is the optimal transform in horizontal direction in the sense of minimal mean square error. The image energy is compacted into a small number of columns after 2DPCA transform. Similarly, if we use the transpose of image matrices as the input data, 2DPCA can realize the optimal compression in vertical direction.

Thirdly, Bi-2DPCA is a sequentially optimal technique but ST-KLT is not. It is easy to see this by analyzing their transform processes. The transform $\mathbf{C} = \mathbf{V}^T \mathbf{B} \mathbf{U}$ can be decomposed into two transforms: the column (horizontal) transform $\mathbf{B} = \mathbf{A} \mathbf{U}$ and the row (vertical) transform $\mathbf{C} = \mathbf{V}^T \mathbf{B}$. The first transform is same for the two methods but the second one is different. For the second transform, the transform matrix $\mathbf{V}$ of Bi-2DPCA is formed by the eigenvectors of the matrix $\mathbf{H}_t = E[(\mathbf{B} - E\mathbf{B})(\mathbf{B} - E\mathbf{B})^T]$, while the transform matrix of ST-KLT is formed by the eigenvectors of the matrix $\mathbf{R}_v = E[(\mathbf{A} - E\mathbf{A})(\mathbf{A} - E\mathbf{A})^T]$. These two matrices are obviously different. Since the second transform is independent of the first one, we only need to find an optimal transform to recompress the current image $\mathbf{B}$ (rather than the original image $\mathbf{A}$) after the first 2DPCA transform. From Theorem 1, it follows that the eigenvector system of $\mathbf{H}_t$ should be optimal for compressing $\mathbf{B}$. Other vector systems, for example, the eigenvector system of $\mathbf{R}_v$, must be sub-optimal and lead to a larger mean-square error. So, as a separable transform, Bi-2DPCA is better than ST-KLT in terms of energy packing performance.

In summary, Bi-2DPCA and ST-KLT are both *image-data dependent* coding method. Bi-2DPCA lays a solid theoretical foundation for a separable transform without any assumed image model. It also provides a sequentially optimal mechanism to implement this transform. In comparison, ST-KLT is sub-optimal in theory.

Besides the theoretical advantages, Bi-2DPCA is also computationally more efficient than ST-KLT. The reason is that the construction of $\mathbf{H}_t$ needs less computation than the construction of $\mathbf{R}_v$, since the image $\mathbf{B}$ (i.e., the feature matrix after 2DPCA compression on $\mathbf{A}$) is much smaller than the original image $\mathbf{A}$.

6. Experiments and Analysis

6.1 Experiments using the AT&T Database

The AT&T database contains images from 40 individuals, each providing 10 different images. For some subjects, the images were taken at different times. The facial expressions (open or closed eyes, smiling or non-smiling) and facial details (glasses or no glasses) also vary. The images were taken with a tolerance for some tilting and rotation of the face of up to 20 degrees. Moreover, there is also some variation in the scale of up to about 10%. All images are grayscale and normalized to a resolution of 92×112 pixels.

6.1.1 Image Reconstruction Analysis

In this section, we will examine the mechanism of Bi-2DPCA based image reconstruction. The first five images of each individual are drawn from AT&T database to form a training sample set. Thus, the training sample size is 200. Based on these training samples, let us form the image horizontal covariance matrix $\mathbf{G}_t$ and calculate its eigenvectors $\mathbf{u}_1, \mathbf{u}_2, \cdots, \mathbf{u}_q$ corresponding to q largest eigenvalues. Then, we construct the image vertical covariance matrix $\mathbf{H}_t$ and get its eigenvectors $\mathbf{v}_1, \mathbf{v}_2, \cdots, \mathbf{v}_p$ corresponding to p largest eigenvalues. Letting $\boldsymbol{\varphi}_{ij} = \mathbf{v}_i \mathbf{u}_j^T$ ($i = 1, \cdots, 9$; $j = 1, \cdots, 10$), we obtain 90 basis images, which are shown in Figure 2(a). As a comparison, 90 principal basis images of 2D-DCT are shown in Figure 2(b).

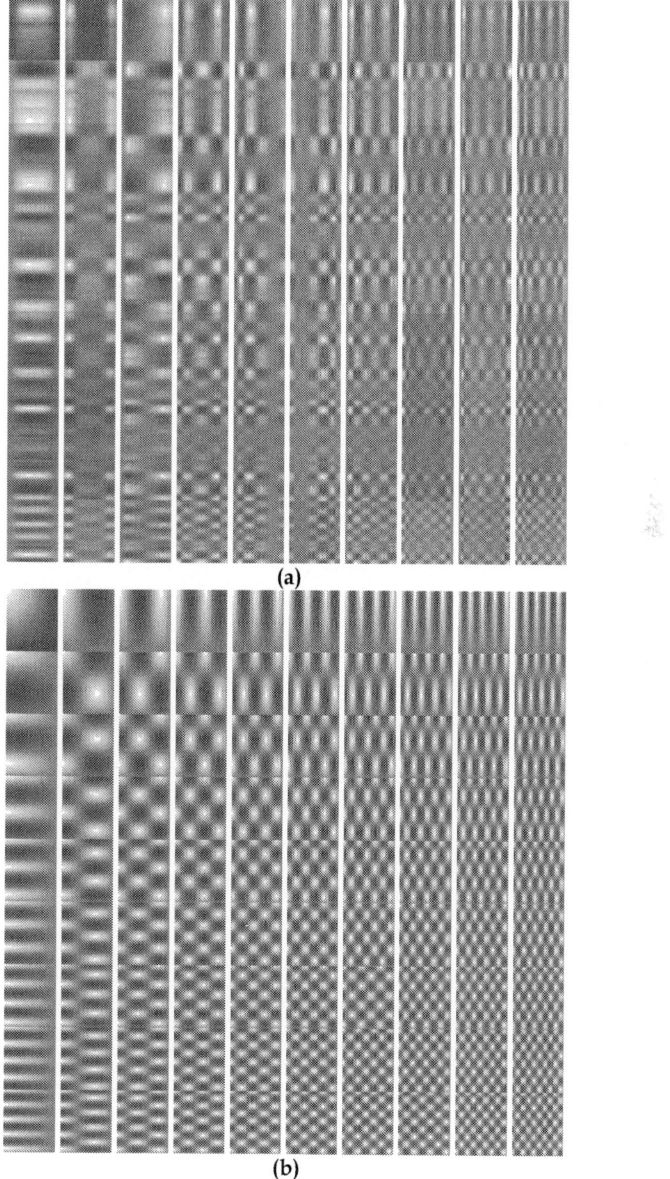

Fig. 2. Examples of basis images of Bi-2DPCA and 2D-DCT. (a) Basis images of Bi-2DPCA; (b) basis images of 2D-DCT, from up to down, $i = 1, \cdots, 9$; from left to right, $j = 1, \cdots, 10$.

From Figure 2, we can see that the basis images of Bi-2DPCA and 2D-DCT have some common properties. The lower-index (i, j are smaller) basis images φ_{ij} contain lower-frequency information and, the higher-index (i, j are larger) basis images φ_{ij} contain higher-frequency information. If we fix the column index j, the information in horizontal direction becomes more and more conspicuous with the increase of the row index i. Similarly, if we fix the row index i, the information in vertical direction becomes more and more conspicuous with the increase of the column index j. Besides, we can also see some remarkable differences between them. The basis images of Bi-2DPCA appear to be more face-image-data dependent, while those of 2D-DCT not. This is because that the basis images of Bi-2DPCA are obtained by training based on the given face images, while those of 2D-DCT are generated by a statistical model. It can be seen from Figure 2 that the first basis image φ_{11} of Bi-2DPCA is a prototype of a face, which shows some inherent information of face images. In contrast, the basis images of 2D-DCT do not embody any face-related information.

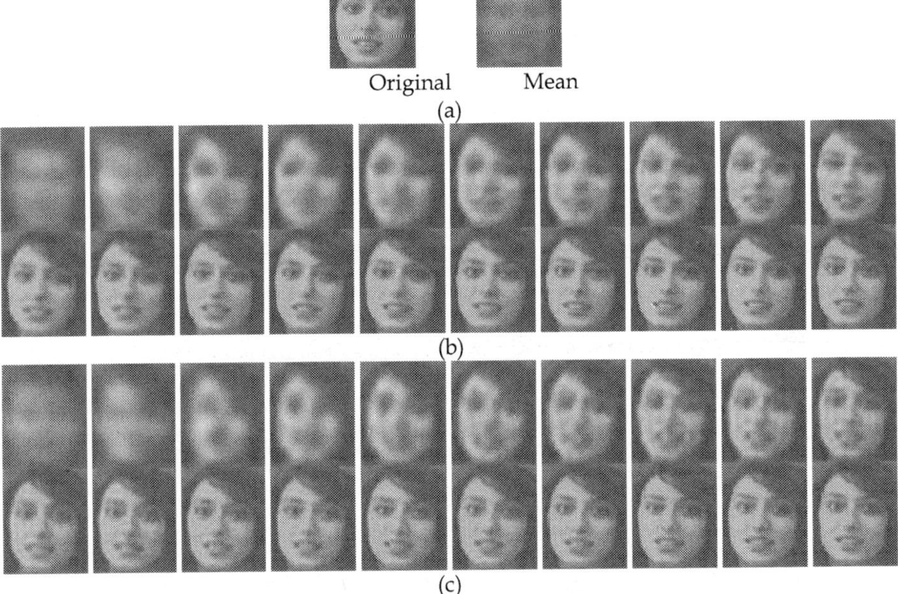

Original   Mean

(a)

(b)

(c)

Fig. 3. An original image and its reconstructed images based on Bi-2DPCA and 2D-DCT. (a) An original image and the mean image; (b) the reconstructed images based on Bi-2DPCA; (c) the reconstructed images based on 2D-DCT, when $p, q = 2, 4, \cdots, 40$ (from left to right, up to down).

Based on the basis images, Bi-2DPCA can realize the reconstruction of a given image using Eq. (33). The reconstructed image can be expressed as a superposition of a small fraction of basis images weighted by the corresponding transform coefficients. Figure 3(b) shows a series of Bi-2DPCA based reconstructed images of the original image in Figure 3(a) when p and q ($p = q$) vary from 2 to 40 with an interval of 2. In contrast, Figure 3(c) shows a series of 2D-DCT based reconstructed images as p and q ($p = q$) vary in the same way. It is obvious that the reconstructed images become clearer when more basis images are involved in the superposition. This is because the higher-index (higher-frequency) basis images φ_{ij} contain more detailed image information. It also can be seen that for each p and q, Bi-2DPCA based reconstructed image is always better than 2D-DCT based reconstructed images. This is because Bi-2DPCA transform keeps more image energy and less reconstruction loss than 2D-DCT. We will discuss this in detail in the following subsection.

6.1.2 Image Energy and Representation Error Analysis

Let us work out the horizontal covariance matrix $\mathbf{G}_t$'s all eigenvectors $\mathbf{u}_1, \mathbf{u}_2, \cdots, \mathbf{u}_{92}$ and use them to form a complete 2DPCA transform. After this transform, the original image in Figure 4 (a) is transformed into the image in Figure 4(b). Figure 4(b) shows that the image energy is compacted into a small number of columns. If we select the first $q = 10$ columns of the transformed image and compress them further using a second complete 2DPCA (the transform is determined by all eigenvectors of $\mathbf{H}_t$), we obtain an image in Figure 4 (c). Obviously, the energy of the first 10 columns is re-compacted into the up-left corner of the image. This indicates Bi-2DPCA based transform does have good energy packing property. Figure 4 (d) and (e) shows that ST-KLT and 2D-DCT based transforms are also effective for energy packing.

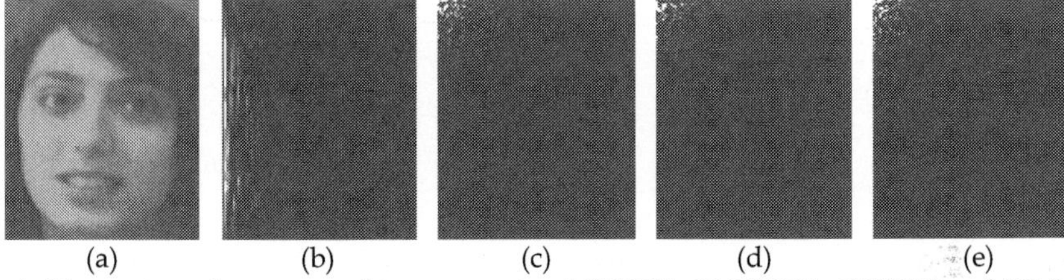

(a)   (b)   (c)   (d)   (e)

Fig. 4. Illustration of energy packing property of 2DPCA, Bi-2DPCA, ST-KLT and 2D-DCT. (a) An original image, (b) 2DPCA transformed image, (c) Bi-2DPCA transformed image (q=10), (d) ST-KLT transformed image, (e) 2D-DCT transformed image

To gain more insights into the energy packing performance of Bi-2DPCA, ST-KLT and 2D-DCT, let us analyze their mean square errors (MSEs) in image reconstruction. If we use a $p \times q$ feature matrix $\mathbf{C}$ to represent an image, the MSE of Bi-2DPCA based image reconstruction can be evaluated using the tail eigenvalues of $\mathbf{G}_t$ and $\mathbf{H}_t$ according to Theorem 2. Since there is no similar property with ST-KLT and 2D-DCT, we have to employ the definition of mean square errors, Equation (35), to calculate the MSEs of ST-KLT and 2D-DCT. The MSEs of Bi-2DPCA, ST-KLT and 2D-DCT when p and q ($p = q$) vary from 1 to 10 are shown in Table 2. Table 2 indicates the MSE of Bi-2DPCA based image representation is smaller than that of ST-KLT based. This is consistent with our theoretical analysis in Section

5.3. Also, the MSEs of the two image-data *dependent* coding methods, Bi-2DPCA and ST-KLT, are much less than that of the image-data *independent* method 2D-DCT.

Does the MSE have an impact on the recognition performance? To answer this question, let q and p ($p = q$) vary from 1 to 10. In each case, we test Bi-2DPCA, ST-KLT and 2D-DCT and list their recognition rates in Table 3. Table 3 shows, on the whole, the performance difference between Bi-2DPCA and ST-KLT is not as significant as the performance difference between Bi-2DPCA and 2D-DCT. From Table 2, we know that the MSE difference between Bi-2DPCA and ST-KLT is not as significant as the MSE difference between Bi-2DPCA and 2D-DCT. So, we can conclude that the significant MSE difference between two methods does affect their recognition rates and, the image-data *dependent* methods are more suitable for representing faces for recognition purpose. The insignificant MSE difference, however, almost has no effect on the recognition results. The recognition performances of Bi-2DPCA and ST-KLT are very close when q and p are over 3. In practice, since we always choose a larger q and p for achieving the best recognition rate, the MSE difference between ST-KLT and Bi-2DPCA has no substantial effect on their performance.

p, q	1	2	3	4	5	6	7	8	9	10
Bi-2DPCA	207.13	170.42	136.21	118.05	103.93	90.77	79.19	70.48	63.26	57.78
ST-KLT	211.69	171.03	136.89	121.86	104.84	91.06	79.39	70.56	63.35	57.96
2D-DCT	216.17	181.20	159.91	145.15	126.42	107.60	90.75	80.86	73.42	66.69

Table 2. Mean Square errors of Bi-2DPCA, ST-KLT and 2D-DCT based image representation

p, q	1	2	3	4	5	6	7	8	9	10
Bi-2DPCA	13.5	66.5	90.5	93.5	95.5	95.0	95.5	95.5	95.5	96.0
ST-KLT	12.0	64.0	90.0	93.0	95.5	95.0	95.5	95.5	95.5	96.0
2D-DCT	13.5	57.0	87.0	89.5	94.0	93.5	93.5	94.5	94.5	93.5

Table 3. Recognition rates (%) of Bi-2DPCA, ST-KLT and 2D-DCT with the variation of p and q

6.2 Experiments using the FERET Database

The FERET database is a result of the FERET program, which was sponsored by the Department of Defense through the DARPA Program [39, 40]. It has become a standard database to test and evaluate state-of-the-art face recognition algorithms.

In the FERET 1996 standard subset, the basic gallery contains 1,196 face images. There are four sets of probe images compared to this gallery: the *fafb* probe set contains 1,195 images of subjects taken at the same time as the gallery images but with different facial expression; the *fafc* probe set contains 194 images of subjects under significantly different lighting conditions; the *Duplicate I* probe set contains 722 images of subjects taken between one minute and 1,031 days after the gallery image was taken; the *Duplicate II* probe set is a subset of the *duplicate I* set, containing 234 images taken at least 18 months after the gallery images. In our experiments, the face portion of each original image is automatically cropped based on the location of eyes and resized to an image of 80×80 pixels. The resulting image is then pre-processed by a histogram equalization algorithm. Some example images after pre-processing are shown in Figure 5.

Fig. 5. Some example images of cropped images that were pro-processed by histogram equalization.

6.2.1 Performance Comparison Analysis

For consistency with other studies [23, 39], in our test, 500 images are selected from the gallery to form the training sample set. In order to reduce the effect that might be induced by the choice of the training sample set, we run the system ten times. In each time, the training sample set (containing 500 images) is randomly selected from the gallery so that the training sample sets are different for ten tests. PCA, 2DPCA and Bi-2DPCA are, respectively, employed for image representation. For PCA, 200 principal components are extracted to represent a face (this is consistent with the PCA-based baseline system in [39]). For 2DPCA, 10 principal component vectors (containing 800 features) are extracted for image representation. While for Bi-2DPCA, a 15×15 feature matrix is first obtained after image transform and then is converted into a 225-dimensional feature vector by stacking the columns in turn. Note that in our test, only the first 200 features are used by Bi-2DPCA for representation and classification purpose in accordance with the dimension of PCA. Finally, a nearest-neighbor classifier with three common distance metrics is employed for classification. These distance metrics includes: L2 (Euclidean) distance, L1 (city-block) distance, and cosine distance [23, 25]. For each method and each probe set, the average recognition rate and standard deviation (std) across ten tests with three distance metrics are listed in Tables 4-6. Taking the four probe sets as a whole testing set, the total recognition rate of each method is also calculated and listed in these tables.

Method	*fafb* (1195)	*fafc* (194)	*Duplicate I* (722)	*Duplicate II* (234)	Total (2345)
PCA	77.18 ± 0.38	14.84 ± 1.30	32.06 ± 0.43	10.15 ± 0.61	51.442
2DPCA	79.93 ± 0.29	19.35 ± 0.49	34.90 ± 0.18	11.51 ± 0.21	54.227
Bi-2DPCA	79.15 ± 0.08	16.45 ± 0.16	33.24 ± 0.12	11.42 ± 0.17	53.069

Table 4. Recognition rate (%) of PCA, 2DPCA and Bi-2DPCA with L2 distance metric

Method	*fafb* (1195)	*fafc* (194)	*Duplicate I* (722)	*Duplicate II* (234)	Total (2345)
PCA	76.49 ± 0.52	38.42 ± 1.54	33.89 ± 0.79	13.03 ± 1.55	53.892
2DPCA	81.04 ± 0.22	13.30 ± 0.46	35.90 ± 0.37	12.92 ± 0.27	54.740
Bi-2DPCA	79.65 ± 0.40	27.89 ± 1.70	35.41 ± 0.35	12.80 ± 0.53	55.076

Table 5. Recognition rate (%) of PCA, 2DPCA and Bi-2DPCA with L1 distance metric

Method	*fafb* (1195)	*fafc* (194)	*Duplicate I* (722)	*Duplicate II* (234)	Total (2345)
PCA	76.67 ± 0.42	11.06 ± 0.45	*33.80 ± 0.44*	*12.81 ± 0.48*	51.671
2DPCA	72.57 ± 0.37	16.03 ± 4.48	32.09 ± 0.66	10.13 ± 1.03	49.198
Bi-2DPCA	*79.10 ± 0.06*	*16.50 ± 0.00*	33.24 ± 0.08	11.50 ± 0.00	*53.056*

Table 6. Recognition rate (%) of PCA, 2DPCA and Bi-2DPCA with cosine distance metric

From Tables 4-6, we can draw the following conclusions. **1)** While the L2 distance metric is used, Bi-2DPCA is better than PCA for all probe sets with respect to the recognition accuracy and standard deviation. While the L1 and cosine distance metrics are employed, the recognition results are in relation to probe sets. For some probe sets, Bi-2DPCA performs better and for others, PCA perform better. However, as far as the total recognition rate is concerned, Bi-2DPCA is consistently superior to PCA, no matter what metric is used. **2)** 2DPCA outperforms Bi-2DPCA when the L2 metric is used, but its total recognition rate is worse than Bi-2DPCA with other two metrics. **3)** Every method achieves its best performance when the L1 distance metric is used. With this metric, Bi-2DPCA outperforms PCA and 2DPCA with respect to the total recognition rate.

In fact, the advantage of Bi-2DPCA over PCA is not only on its recognition accuracy, but also on its computational efficiency. In the next subsection, we will demonstrate that Bi-2DPCA is faster than PCA for face recognition system.

6.2.2 Computational Efficiency Analysis

In our experiments, we use Matlab for coding and the Matlab function *"eigs"* to calculate the eigenvectors in the implementation of PCA, 2DPCA and Bi-2DPCA. For each method, the average CPU time for training and testing (with L2 metric) across 10 random tests are listed in Table 8. It is apparent that Bi-2DPCA is much faster than PCA either for training or for testing. Although 2DPCA needs less time than Bi-2DPCA for training, it requires more time for the whole process: training and testing. To gain more insights into this, we will provide a detailed analysis on computation and memory requirements of PCA, 2DPCA and Bi-2DPCA based face recognition systems.

Method	Time for Training	Time for Testing (2345 samples)	Total
PCA	291.70	940.39	1232.09
2DPCA	97.38	912.60	1009.98
Bi-2DPCA	140.86	659.07	799.93

Table 8. The CPU time (s) for training and testing on FERET 1996 subset (CPU: Pentium IV 2.4GHz, RAM: 512Mb)

Method	Constructing covariance matrices (C_1)	Solving eigen-problems (C_2)	Transformation of an image (C_3)	Calculating distance (C_4)
PCA	$500^2 \times 80^2$	500^3	$80^2 \times 200$	$C_4 = 1196 \times 200$

	$=1.6 \times 10^9$	$= 1.25 \times 10^8$	$=1.28 \times 10^6$	$=2.392 \times 10^5$
2DPCA	500×80^3 $=2.56 \times 10^8$	80^3 $= 5.12 \times 10^5$	$80^2 \times 10$ $=6.4 \times 10^4$	1196×800 $=9.568 \times 10^5$
Bi-2DPCA	$500 \times (80^3+80^2 \times 15)$ $=3.04 \times 10^8$	$80^3 \times 2$ $= 1.024 \times 10^6$	$80^2 \times 15+80 \times 15 \times 14$ $=1.128 \times 10^5$	1196×200 $=2.392 \times 10^5$

Table 9. Calculation items of PCA, 2DPCA and Bi-2DPCA in training and testing process

Method	Training $C_1+C_2+1196 \times C_3$	Testing $(C_3 + C_4) \times 2345$	Total
PCA	3.2559×10^9	3.5625×10^9	6.8184×10^9
2DPCA	3.3306×10^8	2.3938×10^9	2.7269×10^9
Bi-2DPCA	4.3993×10^8	8.2544×10^8	1.2654×10^9

Table 10. Comparisons of computation requirements of PCA, 2DPCA and Bi-2DPCA

Method	Projector Size	Gallery Size	Total
PCA	$80^2 \times 200 = 1,280,000$	$1196 \times 200 = 239,200$	$1,519,200$
2DPCA	$80 \times 10 = 800$	$1196 \times 80 \times 10 = 956,800$	$957,600$
Bi-2DPCA	$80 \times 15+80 \times 14 = 2,320$	$1196 \times 200 = 239,200$	$241,520$

Table 11. Comparisons of memory requirements of PCA, 2DPCA and Bi-2DPCA

The computation requirements can be measured by the amount of multiplications involved in the training and testing processes. The training process includes the following calculations: (C_1) constructing covariance matrices, (C_2) learning the projector (transform matrix) by solving eigen-problems and, (C_3) transformation of an image in gallery. And, the testing process includes: (C_3) transformation of an image in probe sets and, (C_4) calculating the distances between a probe and gallery for classification. The computations involved in these items are listed in Table 9. Table 10 exhibits the computation requirements in the training, testing and the whole process.

From Tables 9 and 10, we can see that Bi-2DPCA needs much less computations than PCA in the first three items and the same computations for item C_4. So, Bi-2DPCA is computationally more efficient than PCA either for training or for testing. 2DPCA consumes less computations than Bi-2DPCA in the first three items (so that it is faster than Bi-2DPCA for training), because it deals with one covariance matrix while Bi-2DPCA deals with two. However, 2DPCA spends much more computations on item C_4 since it requires four times of features than Bi-2DPCA (or PCA) for image representation. This leads to a larger amount of computations in its testing process. In a word, Bi-2DPCA has the least computation requirements among three methods for the whole process: training and testing.

The memory requirements of a face recognition system depend on the size of projector and the total size of data in gallery. Table 11 shows these items corresponding to each method. Bi-2DPCA has the least total memory requirements among three methods. PCA has the largest total memory requirements because its projector is very large, which amounts to a total size of 200 original face images. In contrast, the projector of Bi-2DPCA or 2DPCA is much smaller; its size is less than the size of one original image. Since 2DPCA has a much lower compression rate than Bi-2DPCA, it requires more memory to save the feature vectors in gallery.

The above comparison demonstrates that Bi-2DPCA based image recognition system has advantages over PCA or 2DPCA based system on computation and memory requirements. This characteristic makes Bi-2DPCA to be a fast tool for face coding and recognition.

7. Conclusions

In this paper, two-dimensional principal component analysis (2DPCA) is first re-examined and its two properties are revealed. 2DPCA can eliminate the correlation between column vectors of image and compact the image energy onto a small number of column vectors (these vectors are used for image representation). In other words, 2DPCA realizes an optimal compression in horizontal direction. These properties are desirable and provide some theoretical supports for 2DPCA-based image representation. However, 2DPCA does not consider the correlation in vertical direction. This leads to a relative lower compression rate compared to PCA.

Bi-2DPCA technique is developed to overcome the weakness of 2DPCA. Basically, Bi-2DPCA is to perform 2DPCA twice sequentially, i.e., a first compression in horizontal direction followed by a second one in vertical direction. In this way, the correlations in both directions are eliminated and, the image energy is compacted into the up-left corner of image. The elements in this corner are chosen as features. So, Bi-2DPCA needs fewer coefficients than 2DPCA for image representation. This results in lower storage requirements and a remarkable speedup in classification. Actually, Bi-2DPCA based representation is not only economical in storage but also effective for discrimination. Our experiments on FERET database show Bi-2DPCA is comparable with 2DPCA.

In addition, the theoretical justification for Bi-2DPCA based image representation is provided. This representation mechanism is sequentially optimal in the sense of minimal mean-square error. In comparison, ST-KLT lacks this justification and is shown to be sub-optimal in theory. That is, the mean-square error (MSE) of ST-KLT is always larger than that of Bi-2DPCA. Besides, we also show that the MSEs of the image-data dependent coding methods such as Bi-2DPCA and ST-KLT are much less than the image-data independent method like 2D-DCT. Our experiments indicate that the significant MSE difference between two methods does affect their recognition performances and, the image-data dependent methods are more suitable for representing faces for recognition purpose. The insignificant MSE difference, however, almost has no effect on the recognition results.

In contrast to PCA, the most prominent advantage of Bi-2DPCA is its low computational complexity. Actually, Bi-2DPCA has lower computation requirement than PCA on almost all aspects involved, including the construction of covariance matrices, calculating the eigenvectors of these covariance matrices, and image transformation. This characteristic makes Bi-2DPCA faster than PCA in both training and testing processes. It should be mentioned that the speed advantage of Bi-2DPCA would become more remarkable with the increase of database scale and training sample size. Besides, our experiments on the FERET database also demonstrate that Bi-2DPCA is comparable with PCA in recognition performance.

8. Acknowledgements

This work was partially supported by the National Science Foundation of China under Grants No. 60632050, 60973098 and 60602038, the NUST Outstanding Scholar Supporting Program and the Program for New Century Excellent Talents in University of China.

Appendix A: The proof Theorem 2

To prove Theorem 2, a useful Lemma is first given:

Lemma A1 [41] If $\mathbf{A} \in \mathbb{R}^{m \times n}$, then $\| \mathbf{A} \|_F^2 = \mathrm{tr}(\mathbf{A}^T \mathbf{A}) = \mathrm{tr}(\mathbf{A} \mathbf{A}^T)$.

Proof of Theorem 2:

Let us denote $\mathbf{U} = (\mathbf{u}_1, \mathbf{u}_2, \cdots, \mathbf{u}_q)$ and $\mathbf{V} = (\mathbf{v}_1, \mathbf{v}_2, \cdots, \mathbf{v}_p)$. Then, $\mathbf{U}^T \mathbf{U} = \mathbf{I}_q$ and $\mathbf{V}^T \mathbf{V} = \mathbf{I}_p$.

The Bi-2DPCA based compression process contains two sequential operations, i.e. column-based (horizontal) compression $\mathbf{B} = \mathbf{A}\mathbf{U}$ and row-based (vertical) compression $\mathbf{C} = \mathbf{V}^T \mathbf{B}$.

Correspondingly, the column- and row-based reconstructions can be respectively represented by

$$\hat{\mathbf{A}} = \mathbf{B}\mathbf{U}^T, \tag{A.1}$$

$$\hat{\mathbf{B}} = \mathbf{V}\mathbf{C}. \tag{A.2}$$

From Theorem 1, we know their reconstruction MSEs are

$$\varepsilon_v^2 = \mathrm{E} \| \mathbf{A} - \hat{\mathbf{A}} \|_F^2 = \sum_{j=q+1}^{n} \lambda_j \tag{A.3}$$

$$\varepsilon_h^2 = \mathrm{E} \| \mathbf{B} - \hat{\mathbf{B}} \|_F^2 = \sum_{j=p+1}^{m} \mu_j \tag{A.4}$$

The Bi-2DPCA based reconstruction image of $\mathbf{A}$ is $\widetilde{\mathbf{A}} = \mathbf{V}\mathbf{C}\mathbf{U}^T = \hat{\mathbf{B}}\mathbf{U}^T$. The total reconstruction MSE is $\varepsilon_t^2 = \mathrm{E} \| \mathbf{A} - \widetilde{\mathbf{A}} \|_F^2$. We will prove that $\varepsilon_t^2 = \varepsilon_v^2 + \varepsilon_h^2$ as follows.

From Lemma A1, we have $\varepsilon_t^2 = \mathrm{E} \| \mathbf{A} - \widetilde{\mathbf{A}} \|_F^2 = \mathrm{E}\{\mathrm{tr}[(\mathbf{A} - \widetilde{\mathbf{A}})(\mathbf{A} - \widetilde{\mathbf{A}})^T]\}$, where

$$(\mathbf{A} - \widetilde{\mathbf{A}})(\mathbf{A} - \widetilde{\mathbf{A}})^T = (\mathbf{A} - \hat{\mathbf{A}} + \hat{\mathbf{A}} - \widetilde{\mathbf{A}})(\mathbf{A} - \hat{\mathbf{A}} + \hat{\mathbf{A}} - \widetilde{\mathbf{A}})^T$$

$$= [(\mathbf{A} - \mathbf{B}\mathbf{U}^T) + (\mathbf{B}\mathbf{U}^T - \hat{\mathbf{B}}\mathbf{U}^T)][(\mathbf{A} - \mathbf{B}\mathbf{U}^T) + (\mathbf{B}\mathbf{U}^T - \hat{\mathbf{B}}\mathbf{U}^T)]^T$$

$$= (\mathbf{A} - \mathbf{B}\mathbf{U}^T)(\mathbf{A} - \mathbf{B}\mathbf{U}^T)^T + [(\mathbf{B} - \hat{\mathbf{B}})\mathbf{U}^T][(\mathbf{B} - \hat{\mathbf{B}})\mathbf{U}^T]^T$$

$$+ (\mathbf{A} - \mathbf{B}\mathbf{U}^T)[(\mathbf{B} - \hat{\mathbf{B}})\mathbf{U}^T]^T + [(\mathbf{B} - \hat{\mathbf{B}})\mathbf{U}^T](\mathbf{A} - \mathbf{B}\mathbf{U}^T)^T.$$

Since $\mathbf{U}^T \mathbf{U} = \mathbf{I}_q$, the sum of the first two terms equals to

$$(\mathbf{A} - \hat{\mathbf{A}})(\mathbf{A} - \hat{\mathbf{A}})^T + (\mathbf{B} - \hat{\mathbf{B}})(\mathbf{B} - \hat{\mathbf{B}})^T$$

Since $\mathbf{U}^T\mathbf{U} = \mathbf{I}_q$ and $\mathbf{B} = \mathbf{AU}$, the sum of the last two terms equals to

$$(\mathbf{A} - \mathbf{BU}^T)\mathbf{U}(\mathbf{B} - \hat{\mathbf{B}})^T + (\mathbf{B} - \hat{\mathbf{B}})\mathbf{U}^T(\mathbf{A}^T - \mathbf{UB}^T) =$$
$$(\mathbf{AU} - \mathbf{B})(\mathbf{B} - \hat{\mathbf{B}})^T + (\mathbf{B} - \hat{\mathbf{B}})\mathbf{U}^T(\mathbf{AU} - \mathbf{B})^T = 0.$$

So, $(\mathbf{A} - \tilde{\mathbf{A}})(\mathbf{A} - \tilde{\mathbf{A}})^T = (\mathbf{A} - \hat{\mathbf{A}})(\mathbf{A} - \hat{\mathbf{A}})^T + (\mathbf{B} - \hat{\mathbf{B}})(\mathbf{B} - \hat{\mathbf{B}})^T$.

Thus, $\varepsilon_t^2 = \mathrm{E}\{\mathrm{tr}[(\mathbf{A} - \tilde{\mathbf{A}})(\mathbf{A} - \tilde{\mathbf{A}})^T]\}$

$$= \mathrm{E}\{\mathrm{tr}(\mathbf{A} - \hat{\mathbf{A}})(\mathbf{A} - \hat{\mathbf{A}})^T\} + \mathrm{E}\{\mathrm{tr}(\mathbf{B} - \hat{\mathbf{B}})(\mathbf{B} - \hat{\mathbf{B}})^T\}$$

$$= \mathrm{E}\|\mathbf{A} - \hat{\mathbf{A}}\|_F^2 + \mathrm{E}\|\mathbf{B} - \hat{\mathbf{B}}\|_F^2$$

$$= \varepsilon_v^2 + \varepsilon_h^2 = \sum_{j=q+1}^{n}\lambda_j + \sum_{j=p+1}^{m}\mu_j .$$

9. References

[1] W. Zhao, R. Chellappa, A. Rosenfeld, and P. Phillips, "Face recognition: A literature survey." Technical Report CAR-TR-948, UMD CS-TR-4167R, August, 2002.

[2] L. Sirovich and M. Kirby, "Low-dimensional procedure for characterization of human faces", J. Optical Soc. Of Am., 1987, vol.4, pp. 519-524.

[3] M. Kirby and L. Sirovich, "Application of the KL procedure for the characterization of human faces", IEEE Trans. Pattern Anal. Machine Intell., 1990,12(1), pp. 103-108.

[4] M. Turk and A. Pentland, "Eigenfaces for recognition", J. Cognitive Neuroscience, 1991, 3(1), pp. 71-86.

[5] M. Turk and A. Pentland, "Face recognition using Eigenfaces", Proc. IEEE Conf. On Computer Vision and Pattern Recognition, 1991, pp. 586-591.

[6] A. Pentland, B. Moghaddam and T. Starner, "View-based and mododular eigenspaces for face recognition", Proc. IEEE Conf. On Computer Vision and Pattern Recognition, 1994, pp. 84-91.

[7] A. Pentland, "Looking at people: sensing for ubiquitous and wearable computing", IEEE Trans. Pattern Anal. Machine Intell., 2000, 22(1), pp. 107-119.

[8] M.A. Grudin, "On internal representations in face recognition systems", Pattern Recognition, 2000, 33 (7), pp. 1161-1177.

[9] P.S. Penev and L. Sirovich, "The global dimensionality of face space", Proceedings of Fourth IEEE International Conference on Automatic Face and Gesture Recognition, 2000, pp. 264-270.

[10] T. Shakunaga and K. Shigenari, "Decomposed eigenface for face recognition under various lighting conditions", Proceedings of IEEE Computer Society Conference on Computer Vision and Pattern Recognition, 2001, Vol. 1, pp. 864-871.

[11] L. Zhao and Y. Yang, "Theoretical analysis of illumination in PCA-based vision systems", Pattern Recognition, 1999, 32(4), pp. 547-564.

[12] B. Moghaddam, "Principal manifolds and probabilistic subspaces for visual recognition", IEEE Trans. Pattern Anal. Machine Intell., 2002, June, 24(6), pp.780 – 788.

[13] J. Wu and Z.H. Zhou, "Face recognition with one training image per person", Pattern Recognition Letter, 2002, 23(14), 1711-1719.

[14] X. Chen, P.J. Flynn, and K.W. Bowyer, "PCA-based face recognition in infrared imagery: baseline and comparative studies", IEEE International Workshop on Analysis and Modeling of Faces and Gestures, Oct. 2003, pp. 127-134.

[15] H.C. Kim, D. Kim, S.Y. Bang and S.Y. Lee, Face recognition using the second-order mixture-of-eigenfaces method, Pattern Recognition, 2004, 37(2), pp. 337-349.

[16] J. Weng, Y. Zhang and W.-S. Hwang, Candid covariance-free incremental principal component analysis, IEEE Trans. Pattern Anal. Machine Intell., 2003, 25 (8), pp.1034-1040.

[17] A. Hyvärinen, J. Karhunen, E. Oja, Independent Component Analysis, Wiley, New York, 2001.

[18] B. Scholkopf, A. Smola, and K. R. Muller, "Nonlinear component analysis as a kernel eigenvalue problem", Neural Computation, 1998, 10(5), pp. 1299-1319.

[19] Bernhard Schölkopf and Alex Smola. Learning with kernels, MIT Press, Cambridge, MA, 2002.

[20] M.S. Bartlett, J.R. Movellan and T.J. Sejnowski, "Face recognition by independent component analysis", IEEE Trans. Neural Networks, 2002, 13(6), pp. 1450-1464.

[21] Pong C. Yuen, and J.H. Lai, Face representation using independent component analysis, Pattern Recognition, 2002, 35 (6), 1247-1257.

[22] C. Liu and H. Wechsler: "Independent component analysis of Gabor features for face recognition", IEEE Trans. Neural Networks, 2003, 14 (4), pp. 919-928.

[23] B.A. Draper, K. Baek, M.S. Bartlett, J.R. Beveridge, "Recognizing faces with PCA and ICA", Computer vision and image understanding, Special issue on Face Recognition, 2003, July, 91(1/2), 115-137.

[24] M. H. Yang, "Kernel Eigenfaces vs. kernel Fisherfaces: face recognition using kernel methods", Proceedings of the Fifth IEEE International Conference on Automatic Face and Gesture Recognition (RGR'02).

[25] C. Liu, "Gabor-based kernel PCA with fractional power polynomial models for face recognition", IEEE Transaction on Pattern Analysis and Machine Intelligence, 2004, 26(5), pp. 572-581.

[26] J. Yang, J. Y. Yang, "From image vector to matrix: a straightforward image projection technique — IMPCA vs. PCA", Pattern Recognition, 2002, 35(9), pp. 1997-1999.

[27] J. Yang, D. Zhang, A. F. Frangi, J.-Y. Yang, "Two-Dimensional PCA: a New Approach to Face Representation and Recognition", IEEE Transaction on Pattern Analysis and Machine Intelligence, 2004, 26(1), 131-137.

[28] N. S. Jayant and P. Noll, Digital Coding of Waveforms: Principles and Applications to Speech and Video. Prentice-Hall, Englewood Cliffs, New Jersey, 1984.

[29] A. Habibi and P.A. Wintz, "Image coding by linear transformation and block quantization", IEEE Trans. Communication Technology, 1971, 19 (1), pp. 50-62.

[30] A. K. Jain, Fundamentals of digital image processing, Prentice-Hall, Englewood Cliffs, New Jersey, 1989.

[31] S. Olmos, J.P. Martínez and L. Sörnmo, "Spatio-temporal linear expansions for repolarization analysis", Computers in Cardiology. IEEE Computer Society Press, Memphis, USA, September, 2002, pp. 689-692.

[32] H. Karhunen, "Uber lineare methoden in der Wahrscheinlich-Keitsrechnung", Ann. Acad. Science Fenn, Ser. A.I. 37, Helsmki, 1947.

[33] M. Loeve, "Fonctions aleatoires de seconde ordre", in P. Levy, Processus Stochastiques et Mouvement Brownien. Paris, France: Hermann, 1948.

[34] H. Hotelling, "Analysis of a complex of statistical variables into principle components", J. educ. Psychology, 1933, 24, pp. 417-441 and 498-520.

[35] Fukunaga K. Introduction to Statistical Pattern Recognition (2nd ed), Academic Press, Boston, 1990.

[36] K. Liu, Y.Q. Cheng, J.Y. Yang, et al., "Algebraic feature extraction for image recognition based on an optimal discriminant criterion", Pattern Recognition, 1993, 26 (6), 903-911.

[37] J. Yang, J.-Y. Yang, A.F. Frangi, and D. Zhang, "Uncorrelated Projection Discriminant Analysis and Its Application to Face Image Feature Extraction", International Journal of Pattern Recognition and Artificial Intelligence, 2003, 17(8), 1325-1347.

[38] D. Zhang, X. Jing, J. Yang, Biometric Image Discrimination Technologies, Idea Group Publishing, Hershey, USA, 2006

[39] P. J. Phillips, H. Moon, S. A. Rizvi, and P. J. Rauss, "The FERET Evaluation Methodology for Face-Recognition Algorithms," IEEE Transactions on Pattern Analysis and Machine Intelligence, 2000, 22 (10), pp.1090-1104.

[40] P. J. Phillips, The Facial Recognition Technology (FERET) Database, http://www.itl.nist.gov/iad/humanid/feret

[41] G. H. Golub and C. F. Van Loan, Matrix Computations, The Johns Hopkins University Press, Baltimore and London, Third edition, 1996.

## 17

A New Multimodal Biometric for Personal Identification

Pohsiang Tsai, Tich Phuoc Tran and Longbing Cao
Faculty of Engineering and Information Technology – University of Technology, Sydney
Australia

1. Introduction

Biometric technology using a single human body characteristic such as face, gait or voice has gained immerse attention with successful applications in video surveillance. Furthermore, facial recognition has been recognized as the least intrusive technology that can be implemented in many places without hazardous problems. Though existing biometric systems have been reported to be effective under certain conditions, there is a great need to improve their recognition performance. Possible alternatives to current approaches include the use of different biometric information or the combination of different biometric sources. Relevant literature indicates the possibility of using facial behavior as another behavior biometric cue. As this biometric cue reflects the internal dynamic changing factors of an individual, it also plays an important role just as the face biometric does in video surveillance. Moreover, existing research in appearance-based facial recognition always addresses the common problem of within-class variations under illumination and poses and/or facial expressions which degrades the recognition performance. Most of the algorithms (Belhumeur et al., 1997) (Chen et al., 2000) (Lu et al., 2003c) (Lu et al., 2003b) (Lu et al., 2003a) (Juwei et al., 2003) (Lu et al., 2005) (Kong et al., 2005) in facial recognition are developed to cope with the singularity problem in the presence of these variations. Some papers (Martinez, 2000) (Liu et al., 2002) (Liu et al., 2003) (Bronstein et al., 2003) (Bronstein et al., 2007) even consider facial expressions as noise that will degrade the system performance, and they attempt to build robust systems that are invariant to these variations. However, no research has been conducted to see if these intra-personal variations, especially under facial expression changes or dynamic changes of intra-personal information could help the extra-personal separation. Can within-class variation help between-class separation? Or can intra-personal facial expression variations assist extra-personal separation? We assume that "intra-personal facial expression variations could assist extra-personal separation."

In the following section, we give an overview of multimodal biometrics and soft biometrics. We discuss how multiple biometrics and soft biometric can improve classification performance. We then discuss related work that uses other biometrics in combination with facial biometric at a distance and our proposed fusion framework. Finally, we give the experimental results and conclusion.

2. Overview of Multimodal Biometrics

Biometric systems have their success in single modalities; however, there are still opportunities to improve their limitations. Jain et al. (Jain et al., 2004b) stated that these limitations include the noise in the sensed data, intra-personal variations, distinctiveness of inter-personal variations, non-universality, and spoof attacks. Furthermore, Faundez-Zanuy (Faundez-Zanuy, 2005) stated the main drawbacks in a different uni-modal biometric system. For example, in fingerprint biometrics, some people might not have their fingerprint characteristics because they were old, their fingerprints might be too oily, dry, wet or warm; or their fingerprints might be damaged temporally or permanently. These situations make it difficult or impossible for scanners to acquire their fingerprints. Facial biometrics' weaknesses are due to variations in makeup, pose or illumination variations. Therefore, it is necessary to explore other sources for performance improvement so as to achieve robustness under various circumstances.

An interesting question is "Can multiple biometrics improve performance?" Hong et al. (Hong et al., 1999) examined the possible performance improvement of a biometric system if this system integrates multiple biometrics. They proved that by integrating with other multiple biometric sources, the performance was indeed improved. Multiple biometrics also makes spoofing more difficult because of the difficulty of simultaneously spoofing multiple biometric characteristics (Jain et al., 2006).

These possible schemes of combining various biometric cues in multimodal biometrics include the fusion of 2D and 3D face images (Chang et al., 2005); the fusion of 2D image, lip motion, and voice (Fröba et al., 2000); and the fusion of 2D image, 3D facial shape and infrared facial heat pattern image (Chang et al., 2004), speech and face (Brunelli and Falavigna, 1995), faces and fingerprints (Lin and Anil, 1998), face and gait (Shakhnarovich et al., 2001). It is clear that a biometric system combining several features can achieve better recognition accuracy than a single-feature system.

Hu et al. (Hu et al., 2004) explained the three reasons for using multimodal biometrics. Firstly, it can be used in some highly secured places such as military bases or government units for visual surveillance purposes. A security system based on this can store human biometric cues such as facial appearance, gait or height in the database for access control purposes. Secondly, a police station can setup a visual surveillance system that stores criminals' biometric features in railway stations or casinos and monitor the criminal activity at a distance. Moreover, combining the various biometric cues such as facial appearance and gait can provide a more reliable alarm to the police if the facial appearance quality is low. Thirdly, it can provide reliable object recognition of either human or inanimate objects.

3. Soft Biometrics

Any physiological and behavioral human biometric cues can be used for personal identification, and these characteristics are also called 'hard biometrics'. Other human secondary information, such as gender, ethnicity, age, height, and weight and eye color are called 'soft biometrics'. These have the potential of complimenting the personal identification information provided by any hard biometrics (primary sources) and improving recognition performance (Jain et al., 2004a); however, the ancillary information may not be distinctive and permanent enough to differentiate any two individuals. "Can soft biometric traits assist user recognition?" Jain and Dass (Jain et al., 2004a) studied their usability with an example of using a fingerprint biometric system for this purpose. They provided additional personal information (gender, ethnicity, and height) to the fingerprint biometric systems and showed that it increased recognition rates about 6%.

Fig. 1 shows some examples of soft biometrics and Fig. 2 shows the general framework for integrating soft biometrics with hard biometrics.

Soft biometrics cannot be solely used for reliable personal identification because they are not distinctive and permanent. They can complement the primary biometric system. They also can be extended to multiple biometric systems. For example, Jain et al. (Jain et al., 2004a) proposed a hybrid biometric system that uses face and fingerprint as the primary biometrics and integrated with secondary biometrics (e.g. gender, ethnicity, and height). They found that the complementary secondary biometrics can help improve recognition performance significantly.

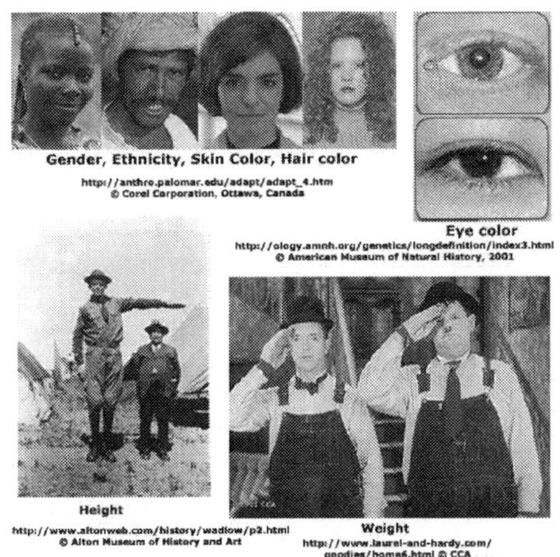

Fig. 1. Some soft biometric examples (Jain et al., 2004a)

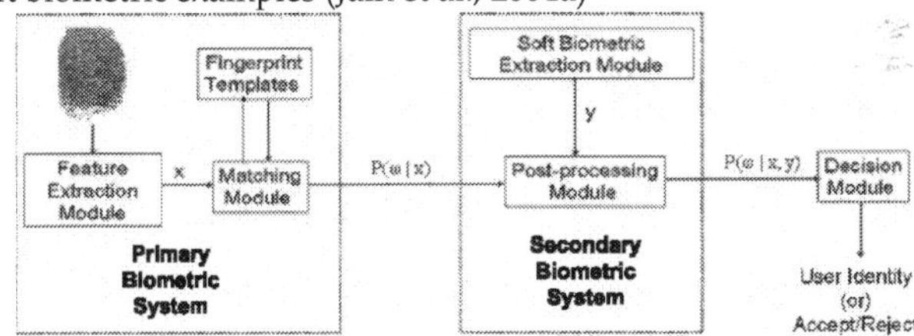

Fig. 2. General framework for soft biometric integration with hard biometrics (Jain et al., 2004a).

In the following section, we will discuss each level of fusion techniques in more detail.

4. Level of Biometric Fusion

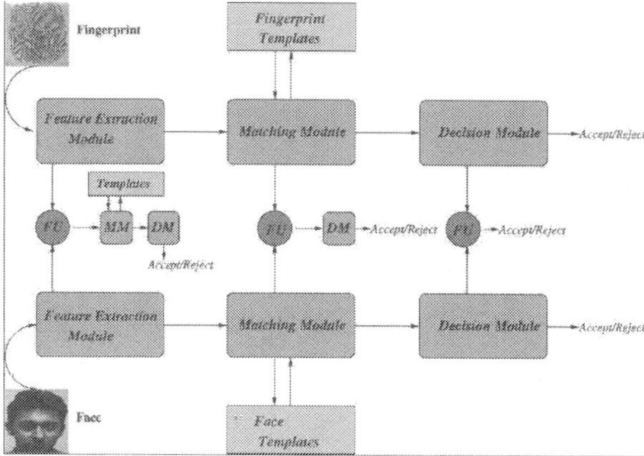

Fig. 3.The three different fusion levels in a bimodal biometric system (Ross and Jain, 2003).

The three levels of fusion techniques are described as follows:

5. Fusion at the feature extraction level

Individual biometric cues extracted from their own feature extraction module are concatenated into a larger feature vector in the fusion module. A further treatment of using feature selection or extraction methods on this new combined vector is necessary so as to avoid the curse-of-dimensionality problem.

Fusion at the feature level is more effective than fusion in other levels because more salient features are obtained. However, it has its drawbacks which include a highly correlated relationship between features which need to be removed, the high dimensional problem of the combined vectors, and privacy issues which hinder the availability of collecting multimodal biometric data(Jain et al., 2006).

6. Fusion at the matching score level

Individual matchers provide their similarity scores to indicate the proximity of the input with the template in the trained database. The scores are normalized using transformation techniques to transform the scores of the individual modalities into a common domain and an appropriate fusion strategy to combine the transformed scores (Jain et al., 2006)." This level is also called confidence or rank level. These techniques include Min-max, Z-score, or Tanh.

7. Fusion at the decision level

Individual matchers provide their own decisions based on their own feature vectors in the feature extraction module. The final decision is then made based on each individual decision by using techniques such as majority voting, behavior knowledge space, weighted voting based on the Dempster-Shafer theory of evidence, and AND and OR rules. This level is also called the abstract level.

7.1 Related Work

Uni-modal facial biometric is an un-intrusive collection of human facial characteristic that is also an important component of multiple biometric systems. This biometric can integrate with other (many) biometrics to provide a more robust identification system. A special issue in 2007 presents recent advances in biometric systems (Boyer et al., 2007) that addresses the advances in uni-modal and multimodal biometrics. It concludes that most human biometric cues such as face, fingerprint, voice, signature, and iris are large active areas while other biometric cues such as gait, ear, brain signal recordings and infrared imaging of hand vein patterns are the newer and smaller areas in uni-modal biometrics. In multiple biometrics, face and gait fusion and 2D+3D face fusion are the two active research areas.

We present literature that uses other biometrics in combination with facial biometrics at a distance. Chang et al. (Chang et al., 2003) combined the face and ear for multiple biometrics. They used the PCA method applied to these two biometrics (called Eigen-Faces and Eigen-Ears). Their results showed the potential performance increase in combination with face and ear that out-perform either face or ear. However, their limitation is that ear images were only in profile view. Chang et al. (Chang et al., 2005) fused 2D and 3D facial images for multimodal biometrics. They used the PCA method for salient feature extraction of individual modalities and score normalization method for normalizing multiple matcher scores. Their results showed that the fused 2D and 3D facial images performed better than using either 2D or 3D facial images alone. Shakhnarovich et al. (Shakhnarovich et al., 2001) integrated face and gait from multiple views for multimodal biometrics. They used a view-normalization approach to multiple views. Then, each biometric trait's matching score was combined. Their results showed the integrated face and gait biometrics had improved the recognition performance over either one alone. Zhou and Bhanu (Zhou and Bhanu, 2007) presents the latest trend in face and gait fusion. They tackled the challenging problem of using shape and intensity information of side view of the face combined with side gait information. Their approach was rather different to the traditional approaches of using a frontal view for face and a side view for gait. They used Enhanced Side Face Image (ESFI) approach and Gait Energy Image (GEI) approaches for integrating face and gait for non-cooperating human recognition at a distance. Liu and Sarkar (Liu and Sarkar, 2007) explored the possibility of using both face and gait in an outdoor environment at a distance. Toh (Toh et al., 2008) et al. proposed a weighted power series model to minimize an approximated error rate formulation for visual and infra-red fusion for facial verification. Infrared facial imaging is an additional option for multiple biometrics combining with face biometric. However, as this biometric cue requires a costly sensor, it is not applicable to a low-cost camera technology in vision-based surveillance at a distance. All the research concluded that "the performance of recognition is improved when combining multiple biometrics. Multiple biometric combination outperformed either single biometric."

In the following section, we will propose a fusion framework that integrates facial appearance and facial expression features.

8. Proposed Framework

We introduce a face coding and recognition method, the Fisher's Linear Discrimnant Classifier (FLDC), which employs the FLD Model (FLDM) (Duda et al., 2000a) for integrated facial appearance and facial expression features. The facial appearance provides textural information of a face, while the facial expression changes are geometrically encoded by distance-based facial fiducial points that capture the changes of a face when it displays facial expressions or emotions. To reduce the dimensionality of the original facial appearance and facial expression spaces, PCA, constrained by the FLDM for enhanced discriminant capability, derives low dimensional features, which are then combined using a normalization procedure in order to form integrated features accounting for both facial appearance and facial expression information. Finally, the integrated features are processed by the FLDM for face recognition.

Fig. 4 shows the proposed framework for PCA-level feature fusion. The gray level intensity of facial appearance images and fiducial point distance-based measurement of facial expression images are extracted firstly by PCA. Note that we only show the neutral expression of facial appearance and facial expression images in Fig. 4.

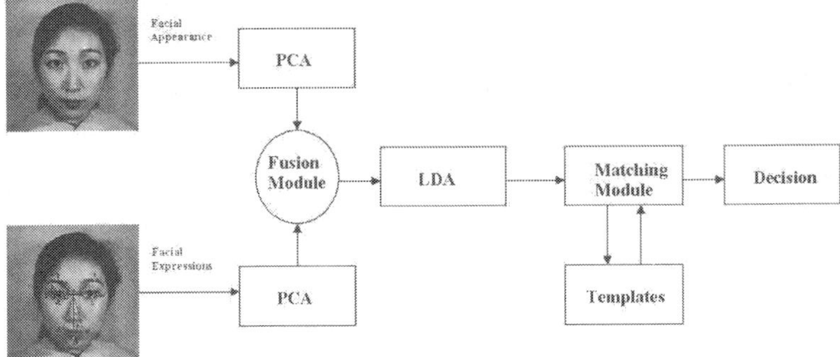

Fig. 4. The framework for PCA-level feature fusion.

For other expression images, they go through the same procedures as shown in Fig. 4.

After PCA extraction, the extracted two different biometrics are then combined together to form larger fused vectors. These fused vectors are then applied to LDA to get reduced dimensionality and the increased discriminant data distribution. Finally, the feature obtained by LDA is compared with the matching template before making the decision.

In the following sections, we discuss the feature extraction techniques used in the proposed framework.

8.1 Principal Component Analysis

Let a facial appearance or expression image X_i be a vector of dimension d. Denote the training set of n facial appearance or expression images by $X = (X_1, X_2, ..., X_n) \subset \mathbb{R}^{d \times n}$, and we assume that each image belongs to one of c classes. Define the covariance matrix X as follows :

$$\Sigma_X = \frac{1}{n}\sum_{i=1}^{n}(X_i - \overline{X})(X_i - \overline{X})^T \tag{1}$$

where $\Sigma_X \in \mathbb{R}^{d \times d}$ and $\overline{X} = (1/n)\sum_{i=1}^{n} X_i$. Then, the eigenvalues and eigenvectors of the covariance matrix Σ_X are calculated. Let $\Phi = (\phi_1, \phi_2, ..., \phi_r) \subset \mathbb{R}^{d \times d} (r \leq d)$ be the r eigenvectors corresponding to the r largest eigen-values. Thus, for a set of original facial appearance or expression images $X \subset \mathbb{R}^{d \times n}$, their corresponding eigen-based feature $Y \in \mathbb{R}^{r \times n}$ can be obtained by projecting X onto the eigen-based feature space Φ as follows:

$$Y = \Phi^T X \tag{2}$$

Hence, this reduced lower dimensional vector Y captures the most expressive features of the original data X.

8.2 Fisher Linear Discriminant Analysis

Let a facial appearance or expression image X_i be a vector of dimension d. Denote the training set of n facial appearance or expression images by $X = (X_1, X_2, ..., X_n) \subset \mathbb{R}^{d \times n}$, and we assume that each image belongs to one of c classes. Define the between-class scatter and the within-class scatter matrices as follows {Bishop, 1995 #91}:

$$S_B = \sum_{i=1}^{c} n^i (\overline{X}^i - \overline{X})(\overline{X}^i - \overline{X})^T \tag{3}$$

$$S_W = \sum_{i=1}^{c} \sum_{X_k \in X_i} (X_k - \overline{X}^i)(X_k - \overline{X}^i)^T \tag{4}$$

where $\overline{X} = (1/n)\sum_{j=1}^{n} X_j$ is the mean image of input vectors, and $\overline{X}^i = (1/n^i)\sum_{j=1}^{n^i} X_j^i$ is the mean image of the i th class, n^i is the number of samples in the i th class and c is the number of classes. Therefore, if S_W is nonsingular, the optimal projection W_{opt} is chosen as the matrix with orthonormal columns which maximizes the ratio of the determinant of the between-class scatter matrix of the projected input samples to the determinant of the within-class scatter matrix of the projected input samples. The optimal projection W_{opt} is defined as follows (Kirby and Sirovich, 1990) (Duda et al., 2000b):

$$W_{opt} = \arg\max_{W} \frac{\left| W^{T} S_{B} W \right|}{\left| W^{T} S_{W} W \right|} = \left[W_1, W_2, \ldots, W_m \right] \tag{5}$$

where $\left\{ W_i \mid i = 1, 2, \ldots, c-1 \right\}$ is the set of generalized fisher-vectors of S_B and S_W corresponding to the $c-1$ largest generalized fisher-values $\left\{ \lambda_i \mid i = 1, 2, \ldots, c-1 \right\}$, i.e.,

$$S_W^{-1} S_B W = \lambda_i W \tag{6}$$

Thus, for a set of original facial appearance or expression images $X \subset \mathbb{R}^{d \times n}$, their corresponding fisher-based feature $Q \in \mathbb{R}^{m \times n}$ can be obtained by projecting X onto the fisher-based feature space W_{opt} as follows:

$$Q = W_{opt}^{T} \cdot X \tag{7}$$

Hence, this reduced lower dimensional vector Q captures the most discriminant features of the original data X.

8.3 Fusion of Facial Appearance and Facial Expression Features

Let $X_1 \in \mathbb{R}^{d_1 \times n_1}$ and $X_2 \in \mathbb{R}^{d_2 \times n_2}$ represent the facial appearance and expression features, where d_1 and d_2 are the number of each representation's dimensionality, and n_1 and n_2 are the number of each representation, respectively. Using (1) one can derive the two covariance matrices, $\Sigma_{X_1} \in \mathbb{R}^{d_1 \times d_1}$ and $\Sigma_{X_2} \in \mathbb{R}^{d_2 \times d_2}$, and the reduced two eigenvector matrices, $\Phi_1 \in \mathbb{R}^{d_1 \times r_1}$ and $\Phi_2 \in \mathbb{R}^{d_2 \times r_2}$, of the facial appearance and expression features, respectively. Finally, one can use (2) to derive the reduced lower dimensional subspaces $Y_1 \in \mathbb{R}^{r_1 \times n_1}$ and $Y_2 \in \mathbb{R}^{r_2 \times n_2}$, of the facial appearance and expression features, respectively, to improve the generalization performance of the FLDC classifier.

The reduced lower dimensional subspaces of Y_1 and Y_2 are then integrated by using (8) of its normalization procedure to form the encoded information of these two facial appearance and expression features (Wechsler, 2007). Note that each reduced subspace is normalized to have unit norms before they are concatenated to form an augmented combined feature vector. Hence, the new fused feature matrix is defined as follows[1]:

$$U = \left(\frac{Y_1^t}{\|Y_1\|} \quad \frac{Y_2^t}{\|Y_2\|} \right)^t \in \mathbb{R}^{r_1 + r_2} \tag{8}$$

This new fused feature matrix U then replaces X in Section 0 to yield the most expressive and discriminant lower dimensional subspace Q as in (7).

8.4 Facial Recognition

The FLDC method employs the FLDM on the integrated facial appearance and expression features. When an unknown face image is presented to the FLDC classifier, the original facial appearance and expression features are firstly projected to the Y_1 and Y_2 subspaces as explained in Section 0. Then, the integrated feature U_{test} of the unknown facial image is derived using (8). Let W_{opt} be the final optimal discriminant basis matrix of the FLDA as defined by (7). The new feature space P of the unknown face image is derived as follows:

$$P = W_{opt}^t U_{test} \tag{9}$$

Let Q_c^i be the ith training data point of the class c after the FLDM transformation. The nearest neighbor classification rule is then specified as follows:

$$\left\| P - Q_c^i \right\| = \min_{j,k} \left\| P - Q_k^j \right\|, \quad P \in \omega_c \tag{10}$$

The unknown facial image is finally classified to class ω_c to whom the unknown facial feature P is the nearest neighbor.

---

[1] This method assumes the facial appearance and expression features have equal important discriminant information. According to the discussion in Chapter 5 that any human body part can be used as a biometric trait as long as it satisfies the requirement that any individual exhibits distinctive characteristics. Hence, we assume that facial expression features have equal important discriminant information as successful facial appearance-based face recognitions do.

9. Experimental Results

We evaluate the performance of the fusion framework for bi-modal biometrics using facial appearance and facial expression features. The classification performance of the framework is then compared with the uni-modalities; namely, EigenFaces, FisherFace, and the distance-based facial expression features using PCA and LDA methods; we called them EigenExpression and FisherExpression, respectively.

9.1 Experimental Design

The original images in the JAFFE database are raw facial images that include not only the facial information (neutral, angry, disgust, fear, happy, sad, and surprise), but also irrelevant information for facial recognition system. This relevant information includes hair, neck, shoulder, clothes, and background, as shown in Fig. 6.

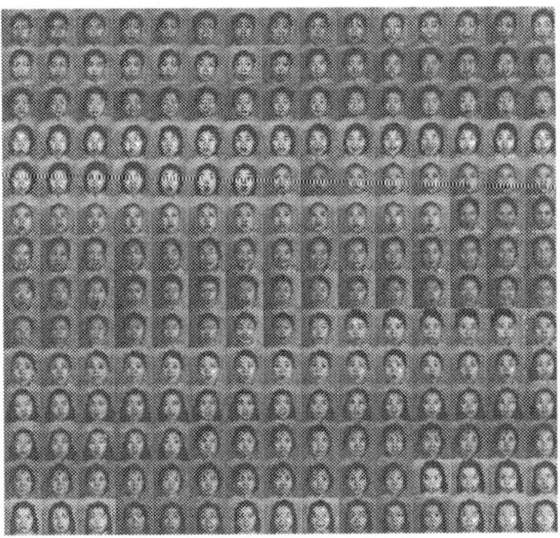

Fig. 5. Facial Expression Images from JAFFE database [74].

We use the JAFFE database for both appearance-based facial features and distance-based facial expression features. For the facial appearance features, we follow the recommended preprocessing steps (Phillips et al., 2000) so as to avoid incorrect evaluations. These steps are 1) images are registered so that the centers of the eyes are placed on specific pixels; 2) images are cropped and resized (to size 16 x 13) so as to remove the relevant non-face portions and to reduce the high dimensionality; 3) histogram equalization is performed in the resized and cropped facial pixels; 4) the final preprocessed facial data is further normalized to have zero mean and unit variance. Fig. 6 depict examples after the preprocessing stage. Finally, each image is represented as a column vector of $d = 208$.

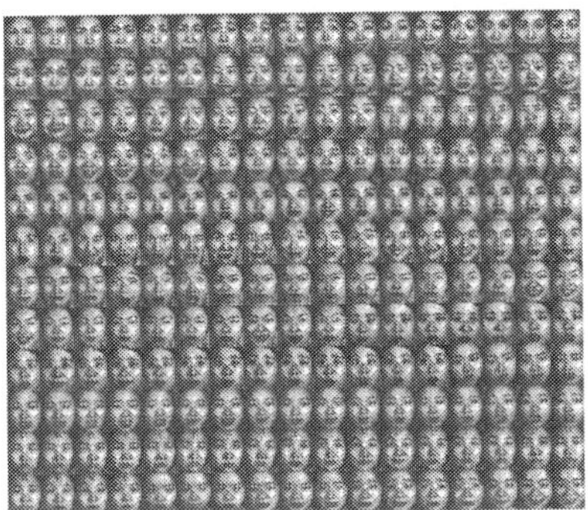

Fig. 6. Examples after preprocessing.

We design four different experiments for testing our hypothesis as follows:

I.   Neutral images in the training set and facial expression images in the testing set.
> **Training set: Only neutral images (30 images)**
> **Testing set: All facial expression images (183 images)**

II.   Facial expression images in the training set and neutral images in testing set.
> **Training set: All expression images (183 images)**
> **Testing set: Only neutral images (30 images)**

III. Using 10-fold and leave-one out cross validation for single modality. Neutral and facial expressions both are in the training and testing set.

IV.   Using 10-fold and leave-one out cross validations for bi-modalities. Neutral and facial expressions both are in the training and testing set.

Particularly, in experiment III and IV, following standard performance evaluation practices (Duda et al., 2000a), the facial expression database H, contains N images, is randomly partitioned into two subsets by using a K-fold cross-validation method: The training set Z and the testing set T. That is, the original database H is divided into K partitions[2]. In every run[3], the ith partition is used for training set Z and the remaining partitions are combined together to form the testing set T (e.g. $T = H - Z$). Any FR method evaluated here is first trained with Z, and the nearest neighbor classifier is then applied to T, so as to produce the recognition rate, which is defined as $1 - CER$ (classification error rate). Finally, all the recognition rates reported below are averaged over K runs to enhance the statistical accuracy of the assessment. Note that the nearest neighbor classifier is used for the four experiments.

---

[2] $K = 10$ (10-fold cross-validation); $K = N$ (leave-one-out cross-validation).

[3] There are 10 runs in total because of 10 folds.

9.2 The Facial Image Analysis

9.2.1 EigenFaces Versus FisherFaces

Fig. 7 and Fig. 8 shows the first 28 basis vectors of EigenFaces and FisherFaces of the facial appearance images, respectively. Each eigen-feature based faces are extracted in order to find the optimal either informative or discriminant projection axes, in which data for images lie in linear subspace. One can see from these two figures that while EigenFaces aim to extract the richest information, FisherFaces aim to extract the most discriminant classification. Note that the last five basis vectors of FisherFaces in Fig. 8 look similar and look quite different among others. One possible cause could be the training eigen-values that encode noise.

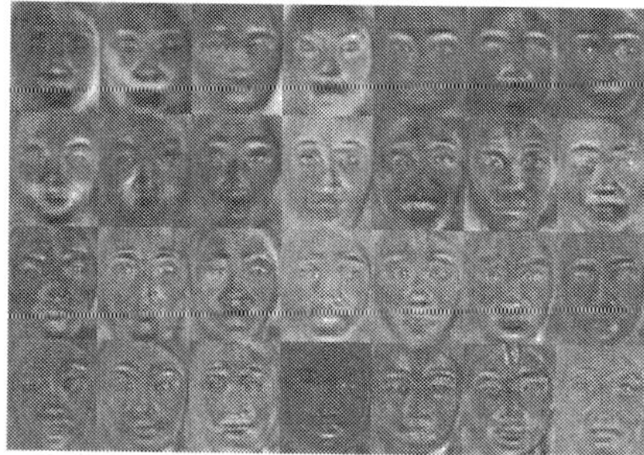

Fig. 7. First 28 basis vectors of EigenFaces of the facial appearance images.

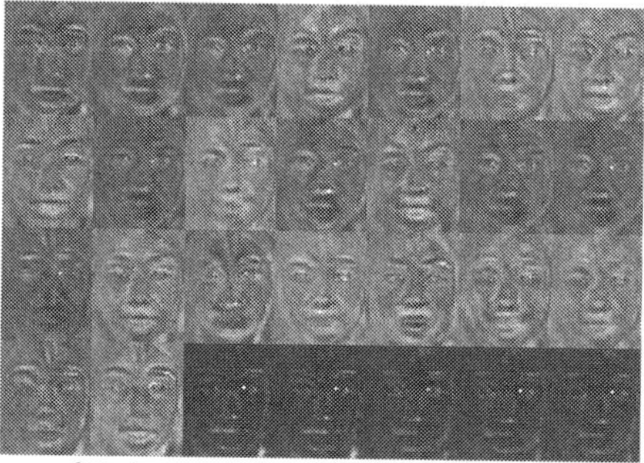

Fig. 8. First 28 basis vectors of FisherFaces of the facial appearance images.

9.2.2 Linear Subspace Analysis for Facial Appearance and Facial Expression Features

The input facial appearance and facial expression features were normalized to have zero mean and unit variance before applying them to the linear subspace analysis methods. Class labels in the following figures stand for individuals. The normalized input data were then used for extracting the first 30 and 17 dimensions of facial appearance and expression features. Note that by convention we only display the first two components of the transformed matrix of 10 individuals.

Fig. 9 demonstrates that the resultant data distribution of Eigenfaces was overlapped, yet still shows some insight on providing distinctively expressive information in the presence of facial expressions. The resultant analysis is also reflected by Eigenfaces as shown in Fig. 7. Clearly, the finding indicates that even though the resultant data distribution of the Eigenfaces in the presence of facial expression is somewhat overlapped, Fig. 7 and Fig. 9 still tend to reveal that the Eigenface method while providing the expressive information does preserve some discriminant information of individuals.

Fig. 10 demonstrates that the resultant data distribution of Fisherfaces was more overlapped than that of Eigenfaces (Fig. 9). The finding indicates that this method actually smears the classes together so that they are no longer linearly separable in the projected space. Also, this resulting projection space is not simplified for classification.

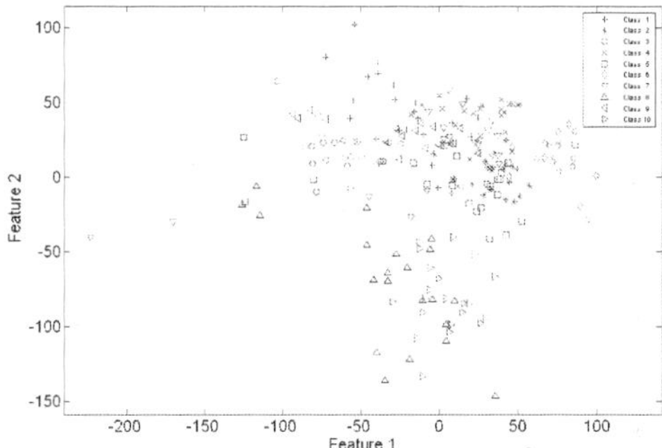

Fig. 9. Samples projected by Eigenfaces method.

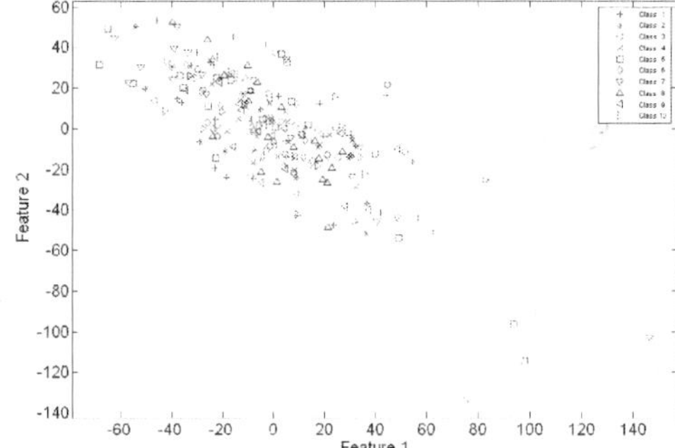

Fig. 10. Samples projected by Fisherfaces method.

Fig. 11 demonstrates the resultant data distribution of EigenExpression was worse than that of Eigenfaces (Fig. 9), but slightly worse than that of Fisherfaces (Fig. 10). The finding indicates that this method smears the classes together so that they are not linearly separable in the projected space. Note that our previous research (Tsai et al., 2005) (Tsai and Jan, 2005) also indicates that for an increase in the number of individuals the data distribution becomes more complex and intermixed.

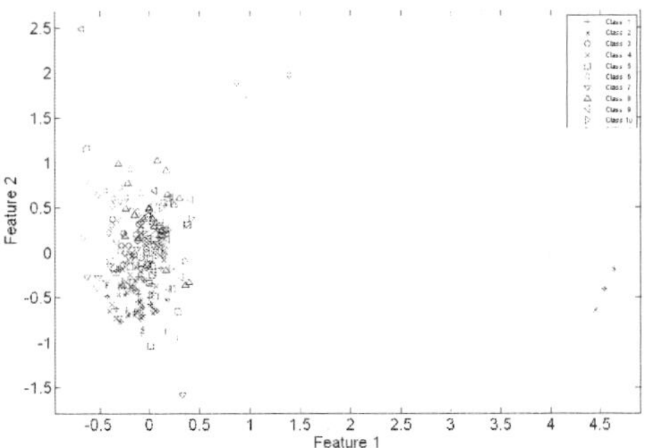

Fig. 11. Sample projected by EigenExpression method.

Fig. 12 demonstrates the resultant data distribution of FisherExpression method was less overlapped than those of Fisherfaces (Fig. 10) and EigenExpression methods (Fig. 11), but seems to be comparable to that of Eigenfaces (Fig. 9). This method promises to retain more discriminant information than that of Fisherfaces (Fig. 10). As a note of caution, it must be remembered that the resultant analyses from the above methods may be very application-specific.

The fused facial appearance and facial expression features of ten individuals were reduced to thirty features after using our method. The first two features are shown in Fig. 13. It shows that the fused features are well clustered after our method; it was far better than Eigenfaces, Fisherfaces, EigenExpression, and FisherExpression methods for classification. It indicates that the combined biometrics mutually contributed to the between-class separation.

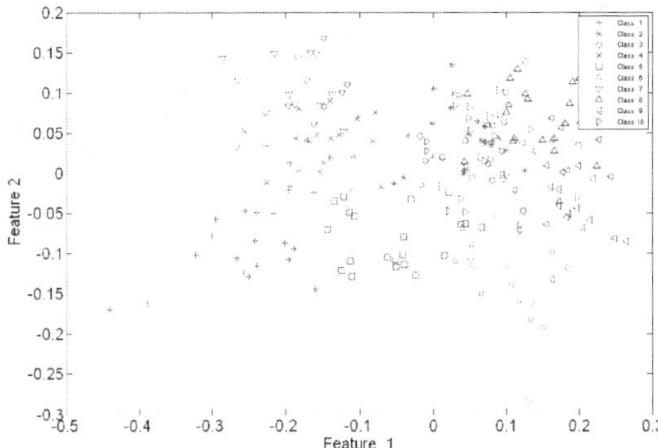

Fig. 12. Sample projected by FisherExpression method.

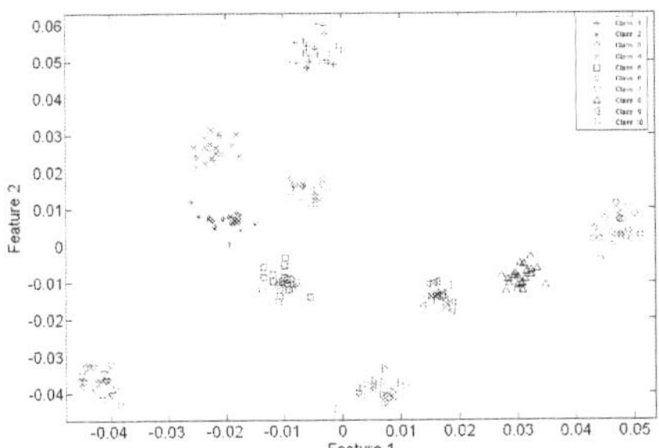

Fig. 13. Samples projected by our method of fused facial appearance and facial expression features.

9.3 Recognition Performance Comparison

9.3.1 Single Biometric Sources of Evidence: Face Versus Expressions

In this section, the assumption for the following experiments is that there is no significant difference in performance between using facial appearance or facial expressions as a biometric, given 1) use of the same PCA- and LDA-based algorithms for these two biometrics, and 2) use the different combinations for training and testing sets for experiment I and II. The recognition rates of these two experiments are computed based on the first 17 principle features. In experiment I, the baseline is the expression variation in the testing set. The experiment focuses on the recognition performance under only neutral images in the training set and facial expression images in the testing set. That is, all the neutral images were used for the training set and all the expression images were used for testing set.

Fig. 14 displays the recognition performance for experiment I. This performance is computed after 17 iterations. In terms of the facial appearance features, there was significant difference between EigenFace and FisherFace. The figure showed that the performance of EigenFace method was more stably increased than that of the FisherFace method after 17 iterations. In terms of the facial expression features, there was no significant difference between EigenExpression and FiserExpression methods. The recognition performances of these two methods were similar. Clearly, the findings indicate that if there exists facial expression changes, these changes degrade the recognition performances; as one would expect the more the facial expression changes vary from the neutral images, the worse the resulting recognition performances.

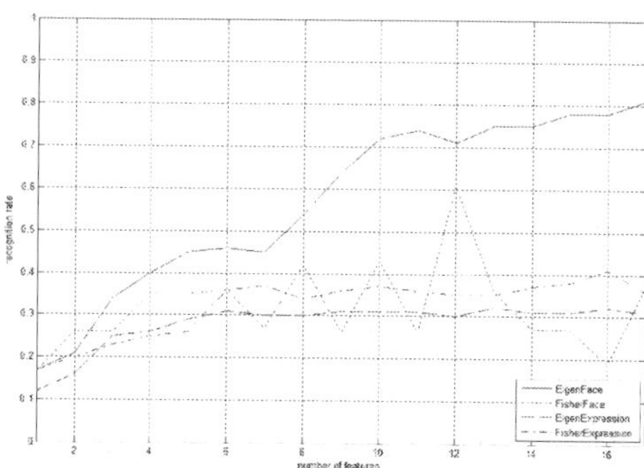

Fig. 14. Experiment I: Performance comparison - Face vs. Expressions (17 Iterations).

In experiment II, the baseline is for the only neutral faces in the testing set. The experiment focuses on the recognition performance under the condition that all the facial expression images are seen in the training stage and only neutral facial images in the testing set.

The purpose here is to determine if by knowing all the individuals' facial expression changes, could their neutral facial images be recognized during the testing stage.

Fig. 15 displays the recognition performance for experiment II. This performance is computed after 17 iterations. In terms of the facial appearance features, the EigenFace method had better performance than that of the FisherFace, and the EigenFace method still showed stability in performance increase compared to that of the FisherFace method. In terms of the facial expression features, the EigenExpression method had better performance than that of the FisherExpression method, and the EigenExpression method showed stability in performance increase compared with that of the FisherExpression

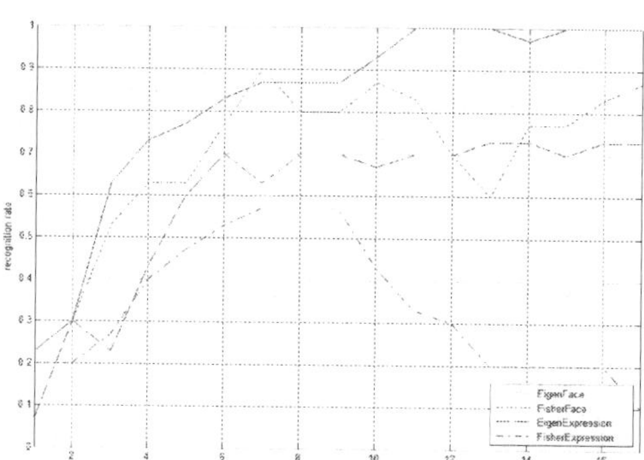

Fig. 15. Experiment II: Performance comparison - Face vs. Expressions (17 Iterations).

method. Clearly, the recognition performances of the four methods indicate the possibility that by learning individuals' facial expression changes, one can test and recognize their individual neutral faces in the testing stage. Note that the LDA-based methods here show their limitation in performance stability due to the limited training data.

In experiment III, the baseline is all the facial expressions plus neutral faces have equal chances to be seen or used either in the training or testing set. The 10-fold cross-validation is used here for performance evaluation. In addition, we also use the leave-one-out cross-validation method so as to make use of the limited size of the database as the result of providing more consolidated performance evaluation for validating our hypothesis.

This performance is computed after 17 iterations. In Fig. 16(a), in terms of the facial appearance features, the EigenFace method had better performance than that of the FisherFace, and the FisherFace method in this figure showed its dramatic instability in recognition performance. In terms of the facial expression features, the performances of EigenExpression and FisherExpression methods were quite similar; however, the performance of the FisherExpression started to decrease after the 12 features. This figure showed the limitation of the LDA-based performance instability. Clearly, the recognition performances of the four methods showed that both facial appearance and expression features can be used for biometric recognition. Note that :

(1)   Fig. 15 and Fig. 16(a) look similar, and they indicate the importance of the facial expression changes seen in the training stage.

(2) Fig. 16(b) shows similar performances to that of Fig. 16(a), except the performance of FisherFaces was increased stably. The limitation of the LDA-based method has been mitigated when the size of the training database is increased to the total number of images – 1 of the JAFFE database. This indicates the size of the JAFFE database is adequate and sufficient for validating our hypothesis in this thesis.

(3) Overall, the results of these three experiments do not provide any significant evidence for rejecting the null hypothesis that facial appearance and facial of the facial appearance-based methods, one can see that these three experiments do show the importance of both facial appearance and facial expressions.

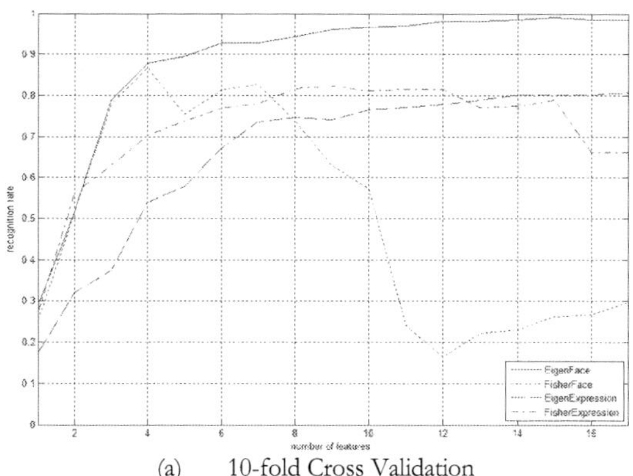

(a)   10-fold Cross Validation

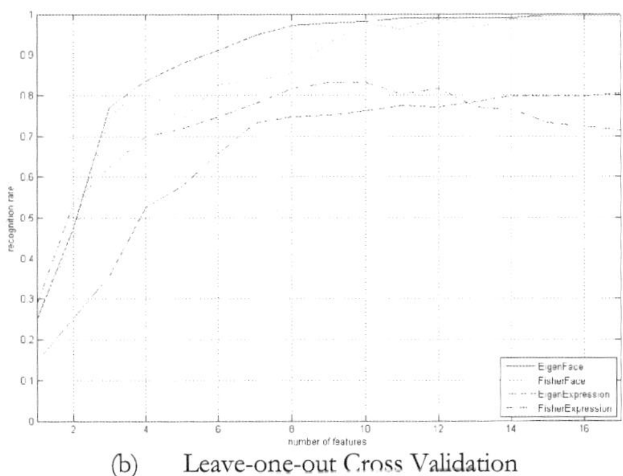

(b)   Leave-one-out Cross Validation

Fig. 16. Experiment III: Performance comparison - Face vs. Expressions (17 Iterations).

Especially, in Fig. 15 and Fig. 16, they indicate the importance of individuals' facial expressions seen in the training set. Of course, there are several reasons that would affect the recognition performance results shown here; for example, inappropriate algorithms or dissimilar quality control conditions. In the following section, we are going to investigate the potential multimodal biometric system using facial appearance and facial expression features.

9.3.2 Multiple Biometric Sources of Evidence: Face Plus Expressions

A combination scheme shown in Fig. 4 is used to investigate the value of a multimodal biometric system using the facial appearance and facial expression features. In experiment IV, the baseline is the multiple biometric sources using facial appearance and facial expression features. The 10-fold cross validation is used here for performance validation. In addition, we also use the leave-one-out cross-validation method so as to make best use of the limited size of the database.

Fig. 17 and Fig. 18 display the recognition performances between the single and multiple modalities, respectively. Fig. 17(a) shows the comparison between face-based (single modality) and proposed (multiple modality) methods after 17 iterations for experiment IV. Our method using facial appearance and facial expression features had better recognition performance than that of either EigenFace or FisherFace method. Although the performances of the EigenFace and our methods were competitive, it was apparent that our method out-performed the EigenFace and FisherFace method when the dimensionality was very low (here 9).

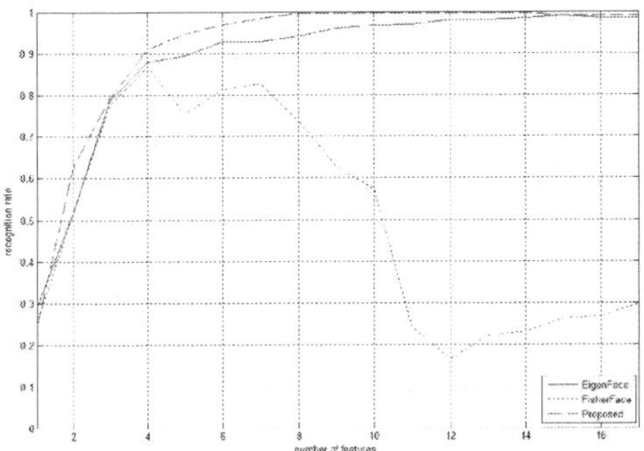

(a)   10-fold Cross Validation

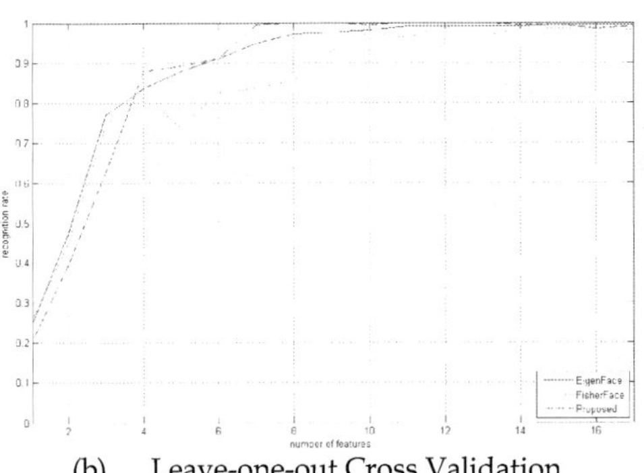

(b)   Leave-one-out Cross Validation

Fig. 17. Experiment IV: The comparison between face-based and proposed methods (17 Iterations).

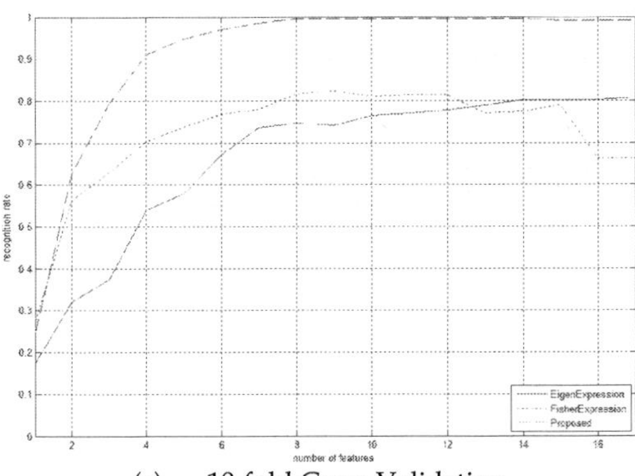

(a)   10-fold Cross Validation

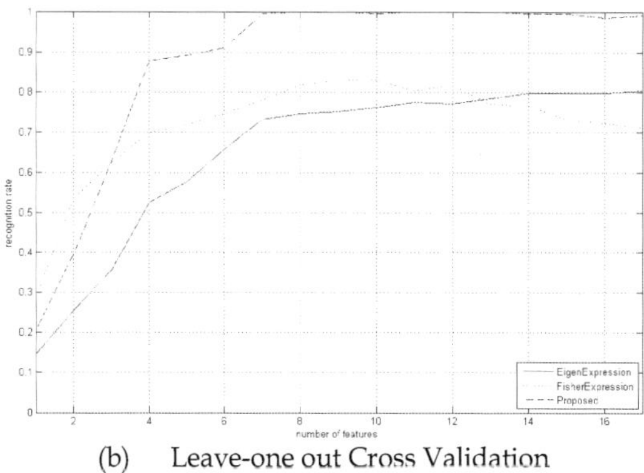

(b)   Leave-one out Cross Validation

Fig. 18. Experiment IV: The comparison between expression-based and proposed methods (17 Iterations).

Fig. 18(a) shows the comparison between expression-based (single modality) and proposed (multiple modality) methods after 17 iterations for the experiment IV. Our method using facial appearance and facial expression features had better recognition performance than that of either EigenExpression or FisherExpression method. Our method again outperformed the single modality methods when the dimensionality was very low (here 9). These two figures clearly indicate the possibility to combine the facial appearance and facial expression features for multiple biometric sources. Fig. 17(b) and Fig. 18(b) showed similar performance to those in Fig. 17(a) and Fig. 18(a), except the performance of FisherFaces was increased stably. The limitation of the LDA-based method has been mitigated when the size of the training database is increased to the total number of images – 1 of the JAFFE database. This indicates the size of the JAFFE database is adequate and sufficient for validating our hypothesis in this thesis.

9.3.3 Confidence Analysis of Prediction Performance

According to [75] , the CI metric is used for measuring how confident the estimated experimental results from experiment IV (using 10-fold and leave-one-out cross-validations) are close to the true prediction performance. In this section, we will conduct the Confidence Interval measurement of the Prediction Performance so as to consolidate and to draw our validating conclusion to prove our assumption that intra-personal variation of facial behavior can assist the separation of extra-personal separation.

The CI metric is applied to analyze the confidence degree of the two performance evaluations on evaluating our hypothesis; namely, the 10-fold cross-validation and leave-one-out cross-validation methods. We will only focus on analyzing the experimental results of comparative methods when the number of features is nine ($d = 9$)[4].

---

[4] In the literature, it is recommended the optimal number of principle components is the number of classes minus one.

Fig. 19 and Fig. 20 show the confidence interval analyses for the experimental results obtained from the 10-fold cross-validation and leave-one-out cross-validation.

In Fig. 19, there are wide ranges of confidence intervals for different comparative methods on different confidence values. For example, if we increase our confidence values from 20% to 99.8% for EigenFaces, we can see that its confidence boundaries are becoming wider and wider. Also, we can see that other methods have similar outcomes. The CI intervals tells us that the estimated experimental results obtained from 10-fold cross-validation have wide variations from the actual true experimental results. However, even though 10-fold cross-validations gave us conservative experimental results, we can still see that our method has a narrower range than any of the other methods (Please SEE Table 1). Clearly, it indicates to us that we can trust the estimated experimental results in Experiment IV. It also shows us that our method has the advantage over other comparative methods. Our result in this figure is an indication of the potential of using facial behavior combined with the facial appearance for personal identification. For further substantiation, we also use the CI metric for analyzing the leave-one-out cross-validation.

In Fig. 20, there are small ranges of confidence intervals for different comparative methods on different confidence values. We can see that after using the leave-one-out cross-validation, the ranges of confidence intervals are narrower than those in Fig. 19. Even though the confidence values are increased from 20% to 99.8%, the ranges of CI for different comparative methods are still small. This figure tells us that by using the leave-one-out cross-validation, our limited database has been maximized. In particular, we can see from the figure that our method has the smallest ranges of CI for different confidence values among other comparative methods (Please see Table 1. Estimated success rates of comparative methods and their corresponding confidence interval boundaries ($c = 99.8\%$) using 10-fold cross-validation.

).

To sum up, the CI analyses for both 10-fold cross-validation and leave-one-out cross-validation conclude that our method validate our hypothesis that the intra-personal variations of facial behavior may assist the extra-personal separations.

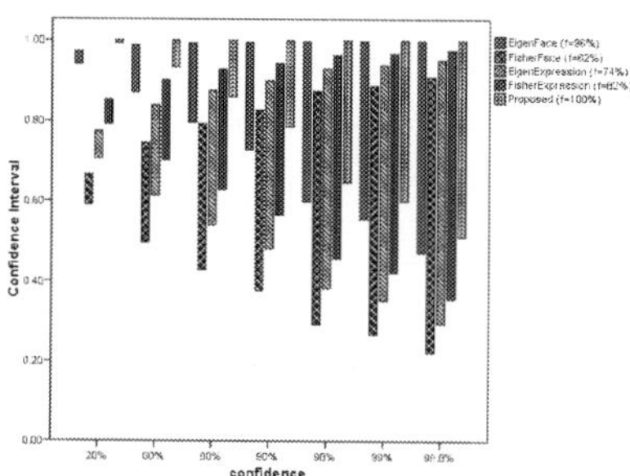

Fig. 19. Confidence Interval for the experiment IV results using 10-fold cross-validation ($N = 10 ; d = 9$).

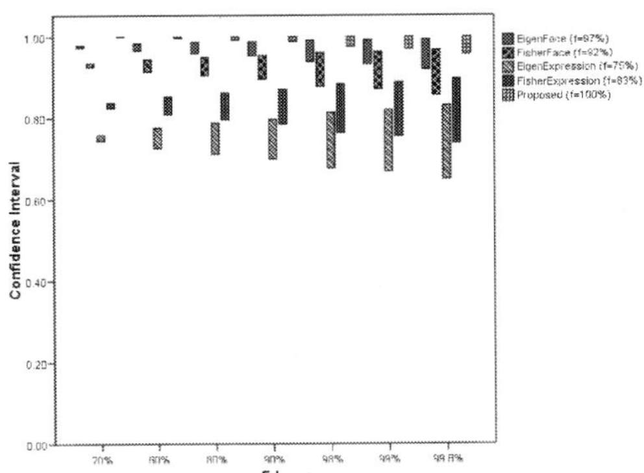

Fig. 20. Confidence Interval for the experiment IV results using leave-one-out cross-validation ($N = 213$; $d = 9$).

Methods	f	p^-	p^+
EigenFaces	0.96	0.472185	0.998449
FisherFaces	0.629	0.222549	0.909433
EigenExpression	0.742	0.29596	0.951634
FisherExpression	0.824	0.356099	0.975391
Our Method	1	0.511559	1

Table 1. Estimated success rates of comparative methods and their corresponding confidence interval boundaries ($c = 99.8\%$) using 10-fold cross-validation.

Methods	f	p^-	p^+
EigenFaces	0.976526	0.918645	0.993517
FisherFaces	0.929577	0.855038	0.967257
EigenExpression	0.751174	0.650202	0.830593
FisherExpression	0.830986	0.737872	0.895699
Our Method	1	0.957096	1

Table 2. Estimated success rates of comparative methods and their corresponding confidence interval boundaries ($c = 99.8\%$) using leave-one-out cross-validation.

9.4 Discussion

Yan (Yang, 2002) states that the PCA method aims to extract the most expressive bases in which the most optimal eigen-vectors are extracted in order to reduce the reconstruction error to the minimum. However, some unwanted variations due to illumination, poses, and/or facial expressions may be caught in the sense of this correlation-dependency method during the extraction stage. That is, these variations may increase the reconstruction error. Therefore, this method may be optimal for obtaining a good PCA projection in a correlation sense, whereas, it may be less optimal in the sense of the classification viewpoint.

Nonetheless, it is interesting to note that our experimental results shown in Fig. 17 seem to contradict the good empirical results in (Belhumeur et al., 1997). They state that "although PCA achieves larger total scatter, FLD achieves greater between-class scatter, and, consequently, classification is simplified (p.714)". In fact, the Eigenfaces method under various facial expression changes in our experiments shows its high recognition rates. It is likely that the variation of facial expressions caught in this extraction stage also provides distinctive characteristics about individuals, and PCA achieves larger total scatter; hence, yields more spaces and less overlap in data distribution. Other possible reason that causes this discrepancy from theirs is possibly because they use leave-one-out strategy to evaluate their system based on the small database[5], and it contains different variations in illumination, occlusion, and facial expressions[6]. These variations may lead to degeneration to the classification performance when applying this second-order correlated statistical method.

It has been suggested in (Adini et al., 1997) that the intra-personal variations due to illumination and viewing direction are almost always larger that the extra-personal differences. Other papers (Belhumeur et al., 1997) also address the variation due to facial expressions observes a similar effect in face identity. Therefore, it is debatable that the variation due to the internal facial changing factors could be considered as noise that affect the facial recognition or be considered as another biometric cue that could be used solely or assist in facial recognition. Note that we consider the variations due to such things as illumination, poses, or occlusions as external factors of a face and the variations due to facial expressions as internal factors of a face.

It is surprising to see from Fig. 13, that after the fusion of the facial appearance and expression features, the data distribution has become more compact and non-overlapped among individuals, in comparison with other methods as shown in Fig. 9 through Fig. 12. It seems to indicate that the internal changing factors may lead us to another interesting research area.

Moreover, the findings from Fig. 9 and Fig. 11 also demonstrate that each dimension from the single biometric may contribute some mutually discriminate information in fusion, even though the data distributions of these single methods are overlapped.

To sum up, our framework has improved recognition performance of each of facial appearance-based and facial expression-based modality. The findings also indicate the potential of using facial expression behavior for either single or multiple biometrics recognition. In particular, our method achieves almost 100% recognition rate using only 9 features.

10. Conclusion and Future Work

This chapter assessed the possibility of using facial behaviour as another individual trait for personal identification and identification improvement. Facial expression variations were previously thought of as noise that would degrade the classification performance, so

---

[5] They use sixteen subjects, and each has 10 images.

[6] The facial expressions include happy, sad, winking, sleepy, and surprised. Here, those variations are considered noise that degrades classification performance.

researchers tried to build a robust facial recognition system insensitive to facial expression changes. We took the opposite view and assumed that the dynamic information of intra-personal facial behaviour was useful not only as another behavioural biometric but could also assist the extra-personal separation for improvement of recognition performance. This innovative approach is motivated by psychophysiology regarding the way humans recognize one another from either their facial appearance or facial behaviour or both. Our findings support this hypothesis. Experiment results demonstrated that our approach outperformed other conventional methods, with highest f-value and p-values. To sum up, the research presented in this chapter opens up a new research direction that can apply to either single biometrics or multiple biometrics. More work needs to be done in this new research direction, such as implementing a larger ground truth database with spatio-temporal information of dynamic facial motion of expression for 3D modeling.

11. References

ADINI, Y., MOSES, Y. & ULLMAN, S. (1997) Face recognition: the problem of compensating for changes in illumination direction. *IEEE Transactions on Pattern Analysis and Machine Intelligence,* 19, 721-732.

BELHUMEUR, P. N., HESPANHA, J. P. & KRIEGMAN, D. J. (1997) Eigenfaces versus Fisherfaces: Recognition using class specific linear projection. *IEEE Transactions on Pattern Analysis and Machine Intelligence,* 19, 711-729.

BISHOP, C. M. (1995) *Neural Networks for Pattern Recognition,* Oxford, Oxford University Press.

BOYER, K. W., GOVINDARAJU, V. & RATHA, N. K. (2007) Introduction to the Special Issue on Recent Advances in Biometric Systems [Guest Editorial]. *IEEE Transactions on Systems, Man, and Cybernetics, Part B* 37, 1091-1095.

BRONSTEIN, A. M., BRONSTEIN, M. M. & KIMMEL, R. (2003) Expression-Invariant 3D Face Recognition. *Lecture Notes in Computer Science.*

BRONSTEIN, A. M., BRONSTEIN, M. M. & KIMMEL, R. (2007) Expression-Invariant Representations of Faces. *IEEE Transactions on Image Processing,* 16, 188-197.

BRUNELLI, R. & FALAVIGNA, D. (1995) Person identification using multiple cues. *IEEE Transactions on Pattern Analysis and Machine Intelligence,* 17, 955-966.

CHANG, K., BOWYER, K. W., SARKAR, S. & VICTOR, B. (2003) Comparison and combination of ear and face images in appearance-based biometrics *IEEE Transactions on Pattern Analysis and Machine Intelligence,* 25, 1160-1165.

CHANG, K. I., BOWYER, K. W. & FLYNN, P. J. (2005) An Evaluation of Multimodal 2D+3D Face Biometrics. *IEEE Transactions on Pattern Analysis and Machine Intelligence,* 27, 619 - 624.

CHANG, K. I., BOWYER, K. W., FLYNN, P. J. & CHEN, X. (2004) Multi-biometrics using facial appearance, shape and temperature. *IEEE International Conference on Automatic Face and Gesture Recognition.*

CHEN, L. F., LIAO, H. Y. M., KO, M. T., LIN, J. C. & YU, G. J. (2000) A new LDA-based face recognition system which can solve the small sample size problem. *Pattern Recognition,* 33, 1713-1726.

DUDA, R. O., HART, P. E. & STORK, D. G. (2000a) *Pattern Classification,* New York, Wiley

DUDA, R. O., HART, P. E. & STORK, D. G. (Eds.) (2000b) *Pattern Classification*, New York, Wiley.

FAUNDEZ-ZANUY, M. (2005) Data fusion in biometrics. *IEEE Aerospace and Electronic Systems Magazine*. Phoenix, AZ, USA.

FR BA, B., ROTHE, C. & K BLBECK, C. (2000) Statistical Sensor Calibration for Fusion of Different Classifiers in a Biometric Person Recognition Framework. *Multiple Classifier Systems*.

HONG, L., JAIN, A. & PANKANTI, S. (1999) Can Multibiometrics Improve performance? *Proceedings AutoID'99, Summit*. NJ.

HU, W., TAN, T., WANG, L. & MAYBANK, S. (2004) A survey on visual surveillance of object motion and behaviors. *IEEE Transaction on Systems, Man, and Cyernetics - Part C: Applications and Reviews*, 34, 334-352.

JAIN, A. K., DASS, S. C. & NANDAUMAR, K. (2004a) Can Soft Biometric Traits Assist User Recognition? *Proceedings of SPIE on Biometric Technology for Human Identification*. Orlando, Florida.

JAIN, A. K., NANDAKUMAR, K., ULUDAG, U. & LU, X. (2006) Multimodal Biometrics: Augmenting Face With Other Cues. IN ZHAO, W. & CHELLAPPA, R. (Eds.) *Face Processing: Advanced Modelling and Methods*. New York, Elsevier.

JAIN, A. K., ROSS, A. & PRABHAKAR, S. (2004b) An introduction to biometric recognition. *IEEE Transactions on Circuits and Systems for Video Technology*, 14, 4-20.

JUWEI, L., PLATANIOTIS, K. N. & VENETSANOPOULOS, A. N. (2003) Regularized D-LDA for face recognition.

KIRBY, M. & SIROVICH, L. (1990) Application of the Karhunen-Loeve procedure for the characterization of human faces. *IEEE Transactions on Pattern Analysis and Machine Intelligence*, 12, 103-108.

KONG, H., WANG, L., TEOH, E. K., WANG, J. G. & VENKATESWARLU, R. (2005) A framework of 2D Fisher discriminant analysis: application to face recognition with small number of training samples.

LIN, H. & ANIL, J. (1998) Integrating faces and fingerprints for personal identification. *IEEE Transactions on Pattern Analysis and Machine Intelligence*, 20, 1295-1307.

LIU, Y., SCHMIDT, K. L., COHN, J. F. & MITRA, S. (2003) Facial asymmetry quantification for expression invariant human identification. *Computer Vision and Image Understanding: CVIU*, 91, 138-159.

LIU, Y., SCHMIDT, K. L., COHN, J. F. & WEAVER, R. L. (2002) Facial asymmetry quantification for expression invariant human. *Proceedings of Fifth IEEE International Conference on Automatic Face and Gesture Recognition*.

LIU, Z. & SARKAR, S. (2007) Outdoor recognition at a distance by fusing gait and face. *Image and Vision Computing*, 25, 817-832.

LU, J., PLATANIOTIS, K. N. & VENETSANOPOULOS, A. N. (2003a) Face recognition using kernel direct discriminant analysis algorithms. *IEEE Transactions on Neural Networks*, 14, 117-126.

LU, J., PLATANIOTIS, K. N. & VENETSANOPOULOS, A. N. (2003b) Face recognition using LDA-based algorithms. *IEEE Transactions on Neural Networks*, 14, 195-200.

LU, J., PLATANIOTIS, K. N. & VENETSANOPOULOS, A. N. (2003c) Regularized discriminant analysis for the small sample size problem in face recognition. *Pattern Recognition Letters*, 24, 3079-3087.

LU, J., PLATANIOTIS, K. N. & VENETSANOPOULOS, A. N. (2005) Regularization studies of linear discriminant analysis in small sample size scenarios with application to face recognition. *Pattern Recognition Letters,* 26, 181-191.

MARTINEZ, A. M. (2000) Semantic access of frontal face images: the expression-invariant problem. *Proceedings of IEEE Workshop on Content-based Access of Image and Video Libraries.*

PHILLIPS, P. J., HYEONJOON, M., RIZVI, S. A. & RAUSS, P. J. (2000) The FERET evaluation methodology for face-recognition algorithms. *IEEE Transactions on Pattern Analysis and Machine Intelligence,* 22, 1090-1104.

ROSS, A. & JAIN, A. K. (2003) Information Fusion in Biometrics. *Pattern Recognition Letters,* 24, 2115-2125.

SHAKHNAROVICH, G., LEE, L. & DARRELL, T. (2001) Integrated face and gait recognition from multiple views. *Proceedings of the 2001 IEEE Computer Society Conference on Computer Vision and Pattern Recognition.*

TOH, K.-A., KIM, Y., LEE, S. & KIM, J. (2008) Fusion of visual and infra-red face scores by weighted power series. *Pattern Recognition Letters,* 29, 603-615.

TSAI, P. & JAN, T. (2005) Expression-Invariant Face Recognition System Using Subspace Model Analysis. *Proceedings of IEEE International Conference on Systems, Man and Cybernetics* ,Hawaii, USA.

TSAI, P., JAN, T. & HINTZ, T. (2005) Expression-Invariant Face Recognition for Small Class Problem. *Proceedings of IEEE International Conference on Computational Intelligence for Measurement Systems and Applications.* Sicily, Italy.

WECHSLER, H. (2007) *Reliable Face Recognition Methods: System Design, Implementation and Evaluation,* Springer.

YANG, M.-H. (2002) Kernel Eigenfaces vs. Kernel Fisherfaces: Face Recognition Using Kernel Methods. *Proceedings of the Fifth IEEE International Conference on Automatic Face and Gesture Recognition.*

ZHOU, X. & BHANU, B. (2007) Integrating Face and Gait for Human Recognition at a Distance in Video. *IEEE Transactions on Systems, Man, and Cybernetics, Part B,* 37, 1119-1137.

## 18

Head Pose Estimation Using a Texture Model based on Gabor Wavelets

Adel Lablack, Jean Martinet and Chabane Djeraba
Laboratoire d'Informatique Fondamentale de Lille (LIFL), Université de Lille 1
France

1. Introduction

Head pose estimation from a monocular camera or a simple image is a challenging topic. It is the process of inferring the orientation of a human head from digital imagery. Several processing steps are performed in order to transform a pixel-based representation of the head into a high-level concept of direction. The head pose is important in a lot of domains like human-computer interfaces, video conferencing or driver monitoring.

Head pose estimation is often linked with visual gaze estimation (Lablack et al., 2009) which is the ability to characterize the direction and focus of attention of a person looking to a poster (Smith et al., 2008) or to another person during meeting scenarios (Voit & Stiefelhagen, 2008) for example. The head pose provides a coarse indication of the gaze that can be estimated in situations when the eyes of a person are not visible (like low-resolution imagery, or in the presence of eye-occluding objects like sunglasses). When the eyes are visible, head pose becomes a requirement to accurately predict gaze direction (Valenti et al., 2009).

The aim of our work is to analyze the behaviour of the people passing in front of a target scene (Lablack & Djeraba, 2008) in order to extract the person's location of interest. The success of this kind of system highly depends upon a correct estimation of the head pose. In this paper, we present a template based approach which considers the head pose estimation as an image classification problem. Thus, the Pointing database (Gourier et al., 2004) has been used to build and test our head pose model. The feature vectors of different persons taken at the same pose will serve to learn a head pose classifier. The texture model is learned from feature vectors composed of the properties extracted from the real, imaginary and magnitude response of Gabor wavelets (due to the evolution of the head pose in orientation) and singular Value decomposition (SVD). The head pose estimation is then applied on the testing dataset. Finally, the classification accuracy is compared to the state of the art results that used the Pointing database.

The paper is organized as follows. First, we highlight in Section 2 relevant works in head pose estimation. We then describe the method used for the head pose estimation and the database associated in Section 3. Sections 4 and 5 provide two representations of feature vectors extracted from SVD and the 3 different responses of Gabor wavelets. We apply on them two supervised learning SVM and KNN and the Frobenius distance. We discuss the results of the head pose estimation on Section 6. Finally, we conclude and discuss the potential future work in Section 7.

2. Related Work

Head pose estimation from monocular camera or a simple image has received a lot of attention over the years. Various techniques have been proposed, and they can be categorized in two different classes:

1. Feature-based approaches: A set of specific facial features such as the eyes, nose, and mouth are used to estimate the head pose. They can use:
    - a geometric method that determines the head pose from the relative position of the eyes, mouth and nose (Pan et al., 2005).
    - a flexible model that fits a non-rigid model to the facial structure of each individual in the image plane. The estimation is the performed from feature-level comparisons or from the instantiation of the model parameters. As an example of flexible models, the Active Shape Model (ASM) (Cootes et al., 1995) which can be augmented with the texture information in order to get an Active Appearance Model (AAM) (Xiao et al., 2004).

2. Appearance based approaches: Instead of concentrating on the specific facial features, the appearance of the entire head image is modelled and learned from the training data. They can use:
    - a template based method which compares a new image of a head to a set of exemplars (each labelled with a discrete pose) in order to find the most similar view such as using multi-dimensional Gaussian distributions (Wu & Toyama, 2000).
    - a detector array method which trains a series of head detectors. Each one is adjusted to a specific pose and assigned to a discrete pose according to the detector that has the greatest support such as using SVM (Huang et al., 1998).
    - a nonlinear regression method that uses nonlinear regression tools to develop a functional mapping from the image or feature data to a head pose measurement such as using neural networks (Rae & Ritter, 1998).
    - a manifold embedding method which seeks the low-dimensional manifolds that model the continuous variation in head pose. New images can be embedded into these manifolds and then used for embedded template matching or regression such as using Pose-eigenspaces (Srinivasan & Boyer, 2002).

The above two classes may be combined (Vatahska et al., 2007) in order to overcome the limitations inherent in any single approach. The temporal information could be also introduced to improve the head pose estimation by using the results of head tracking. It is done by recovering the global head pose changes from the observed movement between video frames. A reliable and recent survey in head pose estimation can be found in (Murphy-Chutorian & Trivedi, 2009).

3. Head Pose Estimation

In the head pose estimation problem, training and testing dataset of m subjects with n poses characterized by the tilt and pan angles are pre-processed. The head image pose estimation consists of a discriminating metric learning phase, where the objective is to find a D-dimensional feature vector that allows a learning method to achieve the highest classification accuracy. The range of a head pose is divided into a limited number of exclusive classes and a classifier is trained. The number of the classes defines the accuracy of the final head pose estimation that can be achieved. In this section, we present the head pose estimation task, discuss the advantages and disadvantages of a template based approach, and present the database used for the learning and testing.

3.1 Definition

The head pose estimation consists of locating a person's head and estimating its orientation in a space using the 3 degrees of freedom (see Figure 1) which are:

- Tilt (Pitch): Corresponds to a bottom/up head movement, around the x axis.
- Pan (Yaw): Corresponds to a right/left head movement, around the y axis.
- Roll (Slant): Corresponds to a profile head movement, around the z axis.

Using a template based approach our model has the advantage to be suitable in near-field and far-field images, and learned from a training set that can be expandable to a larger size at any time without requiring any negative examples or facial feature points. However, the success of our estimation highly depends upon a correct locating of a person's head, and estimates discrete head poses only.

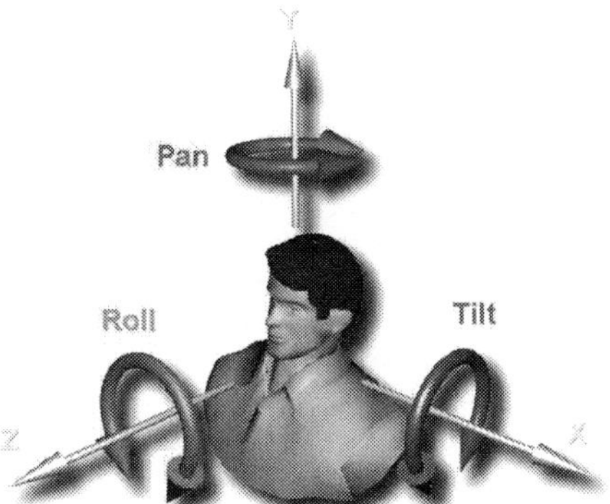

Fig. 1. Head degrees of freedom model for head pose estimation.

3.2 Head Pose Database

We use the Pointing database (Gourier et al., 2004) to build the head pose model and to test it. It consists of 93 poses for 15 persons with each pose per person taken twice (see Figure 2). We divide them into two sets:

- The training dataset: It consists of 20 images for each pose representing 11 persons (9 persons were taken twice and 2 persons were taken once).
- The testing dataset: It consists of 10 images for each pose representing 6 persons (4 persons were taken twice and the second images of the two persons left in the training dataset).

We select five poses: down-left, down-right, front, up-left and up-right which corresponds, respectively, to a pair of pan and tilt angles of {(60, -90), (-60, +90), (0, 0), (+60, -90), (+60, +90)}.

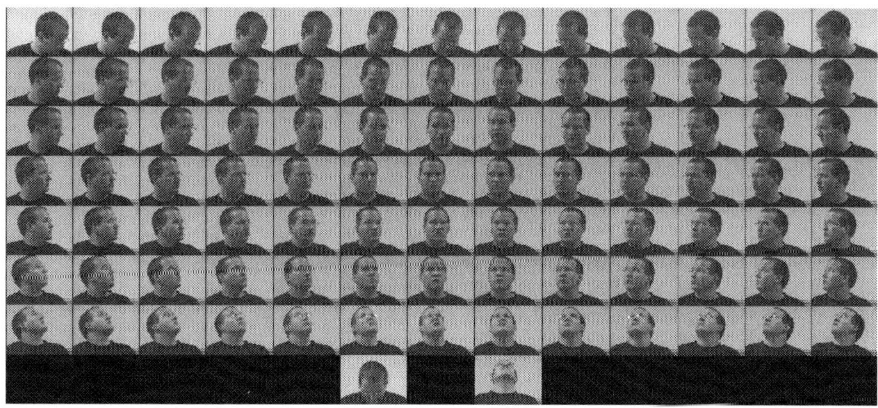

Fig. 2. The head images of the Person01 in Pointing' 04 dataset.

We make a pre-processing on these images. We start with locating a tight bounding box around the head. Then, we normalize the images in 64x64 size. Finally, we apply a histogram equalization which ensures that two faces taken under different lighting conditions are transformed into two grayscale images with similar brightness levels. We will extract different feature vectors on this transformed database.

We will extract feature vectors on the pre-processed dataset. This is based on the pose similarity assumption that different people at the same pose look more similar than the same person at different poses. Specifically two methods were chosen:

- Singular Value Decomposition: SVD is applied to the whole pose image to obtain SVD vector;
- Gabor wavelets: Gabor wavelet coefficients are sampled from the pose image in different scales and orientations;

The result is the extraction of a feature vector F_i of n elements for each head image i (with n chosen according to the specific technique used for the extraction):

$$F_i = \left(F_{i_1}, F_{i_2}, ..., F_{i_n} \right)^t$$

4. Feature Vector Extraction using SVD

The singular value decomposition (Vaccaro, 1991) of an MxN matrix A is its representation of a product of a diagonal matrix and two orthonormal matrices:

$$A = U * W * V^t$$

Where W is a diagonal matrix of singular values that can be coded as a 1D vector. All the singular values are non-negative and sorted in descending order. Applying this decomposition to a normalized head image i, it gives us a 1D vector:

$$W_i = \left(W_{i_1}, W_{i_2}, \ldots, W_{i_{64}}\right)^t$$

Every singular value W_{i_j} will be associated with two vectors U_{i_j} and V_{i_j} with $j \in \{1, \ldots, 64\}$:

$$U_{i_j} = \left(U_{i_{j_1}}, U_{i_{j_2}}, \ldots, U_{i_{j_{64}}}\right)^t$$
$$V_{i_j} = \left(V_{i_{j_1}}^t, V_{i_{j_2}}^t, \ldots, V_{i_{j_{64}}}^t\right)^t$$

Then we calculate the norm of W_i:

$$\|W_i\| = \sqrt{w_{i_1}^2 + w_{i_2}^2 + \cdots + w_{i_{64}}^2}$$

Finally, we create two kind of feature vectors of an image i:
- The first one is composed of elements obtained by dividing each element of the vector W by its norm $\|W_i\|$:

$$F_{i_j} = \frac{w_{i_j}}{\|W_i\|}, j \in \{1, \ldots, 64\}$$

- The second one is composed of the P first singular value W_{i_j} divided by the norm $\|W_i\|$ with their corresponding U_{i_j} and V_{i_j} vectors:

$$F_{i_j} - \left(\frac{w_{i_j}}{\|W_i\|}, U_{i_j}, V_{i_j}\right), j \in \{1, \ldots, P\}, P \leq 64$$

In order to select the appropriate value of P, we perform a reconstruction of the input image using the P top components (Figure 3).

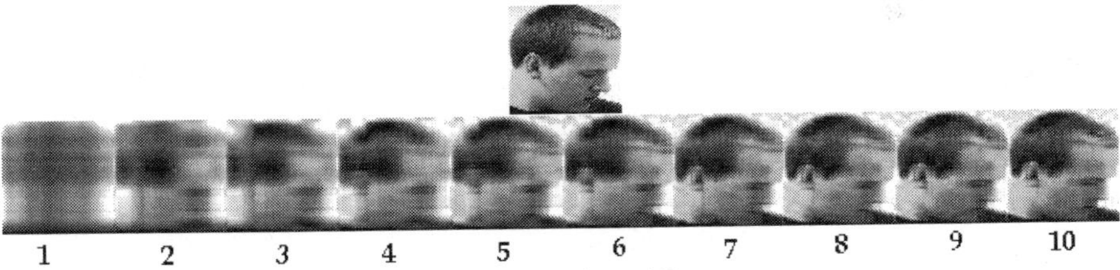

Fig. 3. Image Reconstruction according to the value of P.

The experiments were done using the two feature vectors according to the value of P and using 3 comparison methods. We have used a support vector machine (SVM) (Cristianini & Taylor, 2000) with a radial basis function kernel, a K nearest neighbor algorithm (KNN) with $K=10$ and the Frobenius distance. We report in Figures 4 and 5 the results of the classification rate of the testing dataset using the whole training dataset for learning the classifiers using SVM, KNN and Frobenius distance by varying the value of P on the two feature vectors.

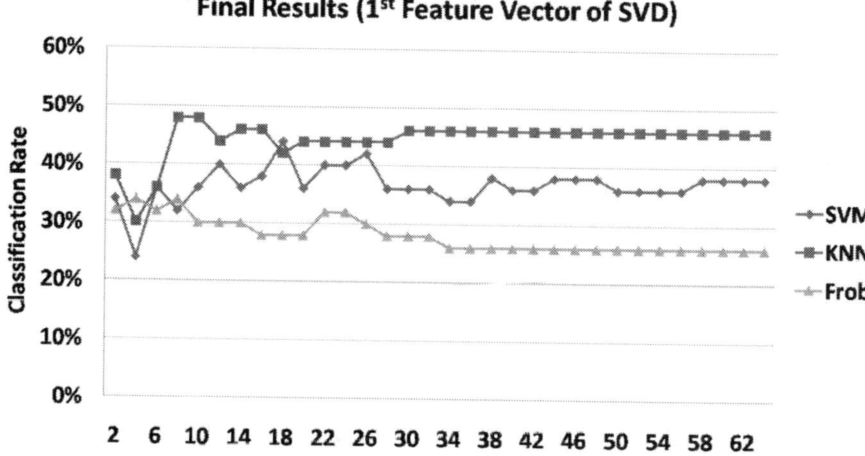

Fig. 4. Classification rate results using the 1st feature vector of SVD.

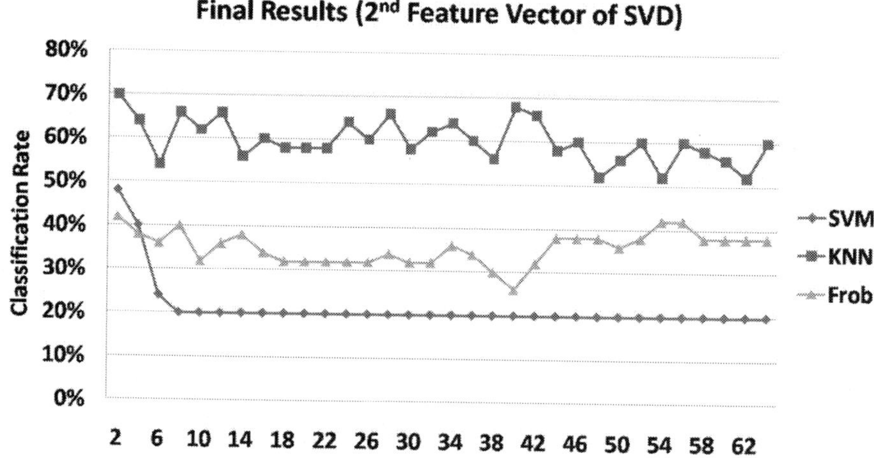

Fig. 5. Classification rate results using the 2nd feature vector of SVD.

5. Feature Vector Extraction using Gabor wavelets

We apply Gabor filters to discriminate different poses due to the evolution of the pose estimation in orientation. There is an evaluation of the pose similarity ratio at a fixed pose with varying Gabor filter orientation in (Sherrah et al., 2001). A Gabor wavelet $\varphi_{o,s}(z)$ is defined as (Zhou & Wei, 2006):

$$\varphi_{o,s}(z) = \frac{\|k_{o,s}\|^2}{\sigma^2} e^{-\frac{\|k_{o,s}\|^2 \|z\|^2}{2\sigma^2}} \left[e^{ik_{o,s}z} - e^{-\frac{\sigma^2}{2}} \right] \qquad (1)$$

where $z=(x, y)$ is the point with the horizontal coordinate x and the vertical coordinate y. The parameters o and s define the orientation and scale of the Gabor kernel, $\|.\|$ denotes the norm operator, and σ is related to the standard derivation of the Gaussian window in the kernel and determines the ratio of the Gaussian window width to the wavelength. The wave vector $k_{o,s}$ is defined as follows:

$$k_{o,s} = k_s e^{i\theta_o}$$

where $k_s = \frac{k_{max}}{f^s}$ and $\theta_o = \frac{\pi o}{S}$. k_{max} is the maximum frequency, f^s is the spatial frequency between kernels in the frequency domain, and S is the number of the orientations chosen.

For the creation of a feature vector, we use generally eight orientations $\{0, \frac{\pi}{8}, \frac{\pi}{4}, \frac{3\pi}{8}, \frac{\pi}{2}, \frac{5\pi}{8}, \frac{3\pi}{4}, \frac{7\pi}{8}\}$ at five different scales $\{0, 1, 2, 3, 4\}$ of Gabor wavelets with $\sigma = 2\pi$, $k_{max} = \frac{\pi}{2}$, and $f = \sqrt{2}$.

The Gabor wavelet representation of an image is the convolution of the image with a family of Gabor kernels as defined in Equation (1) (see Figure 6).

Fig. 6. A real response of Gabor wavelets using the 8 orientations.

The convolution of an image I and a Gabor kernel $\varphi_{o,s}(z)$ is defined as follows:

$$Conv_{o,s}(z) = I(z) * \varphi_{o,s}(z)$$

The response $Conv_{o,s}(z)$ to each Gabor kernel is a complex function with a real part $Re\{Conv_{o,s}(z)\}$ and an imaginary part $Im\{Conv_{o,s}(z)\}$ defined as:

$$Conv_{o,s}(z) = Re\{Conv_{o,s}(z)\} + i\, Im\{Conv_{o,s}(z)\}$$

The magnitude response $\|Conv_{o,s}(z)\|$ is expressed as:

$$\|Conv_{o,s}(z)\| = \sqrt{Re\{Conv_{o,s}(z)\}^2 + Im\{Conv_{o,s}(z)\}^2}$$

For each image, the outputs are $O*S$ images which record the real, the imaginary or the magnitude of the responses to the Gabor filters. As a feature vector using a specific response, we calculate for each image at a specific scale s and orientation o the mean and the deviation of its pixels intensities.

We finally concatenate the mean and deviation of each image at the O orientations and S scales in a vector. We obtain a feature vector composed of $2*O*S$ elements for each head image i:

$$F_i = (M_1, D_1, M_2, D_2 ..., M_{O*S}, D_{O*S})^t$$

We obtain 3 variations of the feature vectors using Gabor wavelets depending on the responses to the Gabor filters chosen (real, imaginary or magnitude).

In order to test the influence of the scale on the Gabor feature vectors, we conduct the experiments using 3 variations of the feature vectors using Gabor wavelets (real, imaginary and magnitude). We report respectively in Figures 7, 8 and 9 the classification rate of the testing dataset using the whole training dataset for learning the classifiers using KNN, SVM and Frobenius distance by varying the number of the selected scale s for the construction of the feature vector F_i from 1 to 5 and using the 8 following orientations: $\{0, \frac{\pi}{8}, \frac{\pi}{4}, \frac{3\pi}{8}, \frac{\pi}{2}, \frac{5\pi}{8}, \frac{3\pi}{4}, \frac{7\pi}{8}\}$.

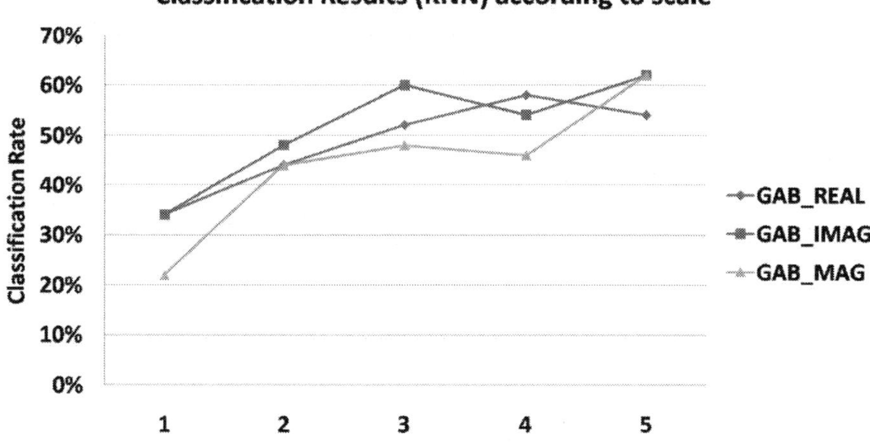

Fig. 7. Classification rate results according to the number of selected scales using KNN.

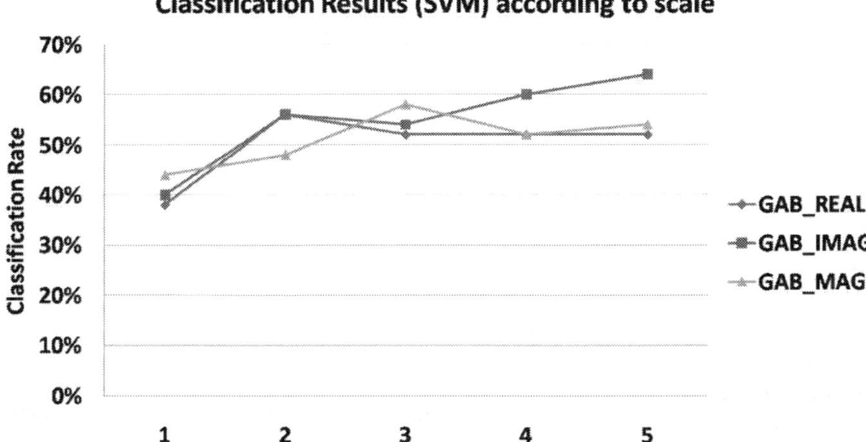

Fig. 8. Classification rate results according to the number of selected scales using SVM.

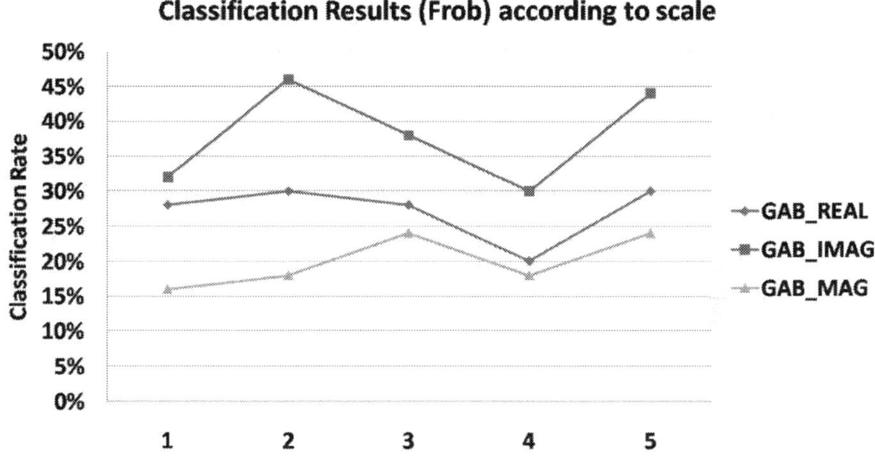

Fig. 9. Classification rate results according to the number of selected scales using Frobenius distance.

Since it appears from the last experiment that is more suitable to select five scales for the extraction of the feature vectors, we select five scales for the construction of the feature vector. We conduct another experiment by varying the selected number of orientations from 1 to 8. We report respectively in Figures 10 and 11 the classification rate of the testing dataset using the whole training dataset for learning the classifiers using KNN, SVM. We avoid reporting the results using the Frobenius distance since the classification results were weak.

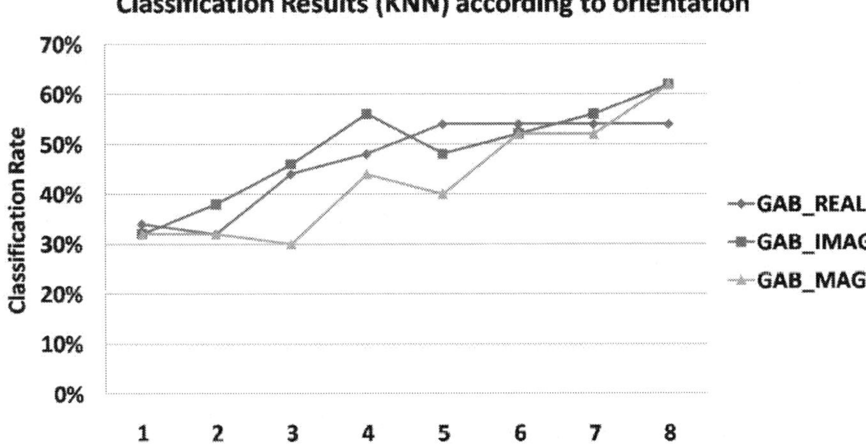

Fig. 10. Classification rate results according to the 8 selected orientations using KNN.

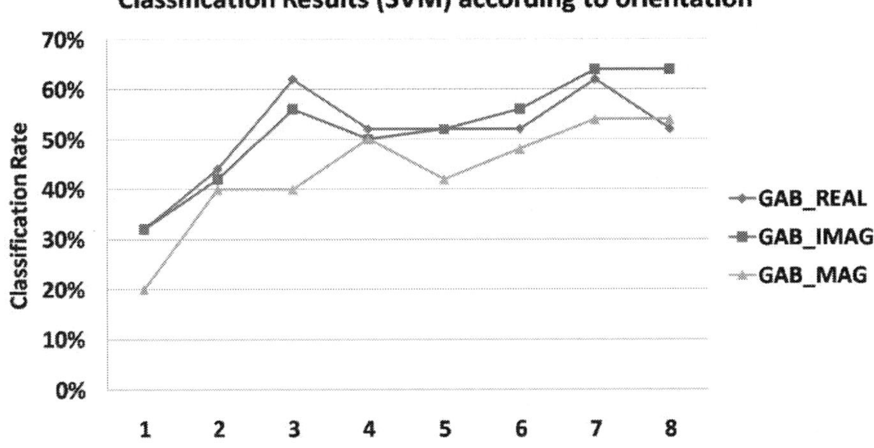

Fig. 11. Classification rate results according to 8 selected orientations using SVM.

6. Discussions

We have used a support vector machine (SVM) with a radial basis function kernel, a K nearest neighbor algorithm (KNN) with $K=10$ and the Frobenius distance for the experiments. In (Lablack & al., 2008), they note that the head pose recognition accuracies increase with the number of the training samples which is consistent with the typical supervised learning. Thus, we use the whole learning dataset for learning the classifiers in all experiments.

From the figures 4 and 5, it's clear that the information contained in the diagonal matrix of singular values is not sufficent alone. The addition of the information conatined on U and V improves the results. Since the values are ordered, the information contained in the first components is enough to perform the head pose estimation.

From the figures present in the section 5, we notice in general from the three different Gabor wavelet features that the imaginary component features are better than the magnitude and real features. This is probably due to the fact that the majority of the information is typically contained in the phase component.

We notice from the section 5 and 6 that the Gabor wavelet features perform better than the SVD features. A part of the reason is that the Gabor wavelet features are capable of handling different orientations and scales while the SVD features are not. Even if the 2nd feature vector of SVD get the best result of the experiments using KNN.

7. Conclusions

In this paper, we have presented a comparison of 3 learning methods (SVM , KNN, and Frobenius distance) applied to feature vectors extracted from head images. These vectors were extracted from the real, imaginary, and magnitude responses of Gabor wavelets, and from SVD of the image in order to make a head pose estimation. We choose different values for the parameters used for the creation of these feature vectors in order to select the most suitable. Our future work will focus on the combination of different feature vectors using the whole Pointing'04 database.

8. Acknowledgments

This work has been supported by the European Commission within the Information Society Technologies program (FP6-IST-5-0033715), through the project MIAUCE (http://www.miauce.org).

9. References

Cootes, T. F.; Taylor, C. J.; Cooper, D. H. & Graham, J. (1995). Active shape models - their training and application. *Computer Vision and Image Understanding* (61): 38-59

Cristianini, N. & Shawe-Taylor, J. (2000). An introduction to support vector machines and other kernel-based learning methods. *Cambridge University Press*

Gourier, N.; Hall, D. & Crowley, J. L. (2004). Estimating face orientation from robust detection of salient facial features, *Proceedings of ICPR Workshop on Visual Observation of Deictic Gestures (Pointing)*, Cambridge – UK

Huang, J., Shao, X. & Wechsler, H. (1998). Face pose discrimination using support vector machines (SVM). *14th International Conference on Pattern Recognition (ICPR)*, Vol 1, (154–156), Brisbane – Australia

Lablack, A. & Djeraba, C. (2008). Analysis of human behaviour in front of a target scene. *19th International Conference on Pattern Recognition (ICPR)*, Tampa, Florida – USA

Lablack, A.; Maquet, F., Ihaddadene, N. & Djeraba, C. (2009). Visual gaze projection in front of a target scene. *2009 IEEE International Conference on Multimedia and Expo (ICME)*, New York City, NY – USA

Lablack, A.; Zhang, Z. M. & Djeraba, C. (2008). Supervised learning for head pose estimation using SVD and Gabor Wavelets. *1st International Workshop on Multimedia Analysis of User Behaviour and Interactions (MAUBI) in conjunction with the 10th IEEE International Symposium on Multimedia (ISM)*, Berkeley, California - USA

Murphy-Chutorian, E. & Trivedi, M. M. (2009). Head pose estimation in computer vision: A survey. *IEEE Transactions on Pattern Analysis and Machine Intelligence (TPAMI)*, Vol 31, No 4, (607–626)

Pan, Y.; Zhu, H. & Ji, R. (2005). 3-D Head Pose Estimation for Monocular Image. *Fuzzy Systems and Knowledge Discovery*. Springer, (293-301)

Rae, R. & Ritter, H. (1998). Recognition of human head orientation based on artificial neural networks. *IEEE Trans. on Neural Networks*, Vol 9, No 2, (257–265)

Sherrah, J.; Gong, S. & Ong, E. J. (2001). Face distributions in similarity space under varying head pose. *Image and Vision Computing*, Vol 19, No 12, (807–819)

Smith, K.; Ba, S., O.; Odobez, J-M. & Gatica-Perez, D. (2008). Tracking the Visual Focus of Attention for a Varying Number of Wandering People. *IEEE Transactions on Pattern Analysis and Machine Intelligence (TPAMI)*, Vol 30, No 7, (1212–1229)

Srinivasan, S. & Boyer, K. (2002). Head-pose estimation using view based eigenspaces. *16th International Conference on Pattern Recognition (ICPR)*, Quebec City - Canada

Vaccaro, R., J. (1991). SVD and Signal Processing II: Algorithms, Analysis and Applications. *Elsevier Science Inc.*

Valenti, R., Yucel, Z. & Gevers, T. (2009). Robustifying eye center localization by head pose cues. *International Conference on Computer Vision and Pattern Recognition (CVPR)*, Miami, FL – USA

Vatahska, T.; Bennewitz, M. & Behnke, S. (2007). Feature-based Head Pose Estimation from Images. *IEEE-RAS 7th International Conference on Humanoid Robots (Humanoids)*, Pittsburgh - USA

Voit, M. & Stiefelhagen, R. (2008). Deducing the visual focus of attention from head pose estimation in dynamic multi-view meeting scenarios. *10th International Conference on Multimodal interfaces (ICMI), (173-180)*, Chania – Grece

Wu, Y. & Toyama, K. (2000). Wide range illumination insensitive head orientation estimation. *Automatic Face and Gesture Recognition (AFGR), (183–188)*, Grenoble - France

Xiao, J.; Baker, S.; Matthews, I. & Kanade, T. (2004). Estimating face pose by facial asymmetry and geometry. *IEEE International Conference on Computer Vision and Pattern Recognition (CVPR)*, Vol 2, (535-542)

Zhou, M. & Wei, H. (2006). Face Verification Using GaborWavelets and AdaBoost. *18th International Conference on Pattern Recognition (ICPR)*, Vol 1, (404–407), Hong Kong

## 19

Embedded Intelligence on Chip: Some FPGA-based design experiences

Félix Moreno*, Ignacio López† and Ricardo Sanz‡
(*CEI, †TAII , ‡ASLab)Universidad Politécnica de Madrid
Spain

1. Introduction

The following FPGA-based (*Field Programmable Gate Array*) experiences stem from a broader line of research investigating methodologies for scaling cognitive/intelligent architectures into limited-resource implementations. Some of these architectures were designed for solving problems involving abstract concepts and uncertain environments, without regarding resource requirements: their original implementations are cluster-based, PC-based or other.

Commercial, embedded applications have afforded being independent from them for years. However, today there exists a drive towards new functionalities which put conventional technologies to their limit. From the point of view of the user, these functionalities stand, for instance, for HMI capable of interacting with the user in natural language, perception systems capable of detecting objects in the environment and reacting to their presence and automatic control systems capable of replacing human operation in complex scenarios.

A representative field of application of these functionalities is the automotive industry. Active research is being carried out to develop highly dependable, low-cost real-time systems that may predict forthcoming accidents, may assess risk situations when driving or that may take control of the vehicle when collision is detected as inevitable (for example some PSSIS: Primary and Secondary Interaction Systems).

From the point of view of the engineer, many of these functionalities involve complex tasks as object recognition, decision making and action planning, supported by enriched models of the environment and the system itself, capable of representing concepts, abstract properties and uncertainty. All of these tasks are carried out as part of the operation of existing cognitive architecture-based systems.

2. What are cognitive or intelligent architectures?

Although there exists certain debate regarding the meaning of cognitive architectures, we can accept two main senses of the term:

- Architectures which base their operation in exploiting knowledge.
- Architectures that are designed to operate depending on their recognition of the environment.

What is done with that recognition that the system gathers from its environment? The representation of information fluxes and processes from sensors to actuators is the definition of a cognitive architecture. Given the broadness of these definitions, we may revise techniques and grossly categorize cognitive architectures as follows:

- Control architectures: An elementary type of architecture is the classical feedback control loop, from the basic PID implementation, including the wide varieties of topologies derived from it. The basic idea is that the controller tries to maintain the difference between a required variable value and the actual measured one null.

- Reactive and behaviour-based architectures: Control architectures are adequate to operate executing simple, well defined tasks in environments with limited uncertainty and limited sources of perturbance, as the controlled environments in industrial settings. However, other systems such as those designed to move autonomously in an unknown, dynamic environment require more complex control schemes. Reactive architectures are designed to make systems act in response to their environment in such a way that the action of the system appears as a direct reaction to a certain combination of input values. Entire sequences of tasks may be executed as a reaction to a certain input pattern. When the inputs change, ongoing tasks may be interrupted and replaced by new ones, according to a task allocation hierarchy which is also pre-designed in the system architecture as a function of the system inputs. This combination of task sequences and allocation hierarchies allow reactive architectures to operate within a range of conditions suitable for some basic functionalities (explorer robots, automatic hoovers). A system out of this range, due to inadequate design or to unexpected environmental events would lead to undetermined or undesired actions.

- Goal-driven architectures: This type of architectures are designed to operate in highly uncertain environments, typically where some kind of analysis is required to assess the conditions of operation, prior to the system executing any action. Uncertainty emerges from a mismatch between the system and its scenario of operation: the system not being configured for a particular environment, so that it ignores what may happen next and therefore the consequences of a potential action. Goal–driven architectures are designed to achieve their objectives in these circumstances by first analyzing the situation, then building a model, and finally designing and executing the appropriate actions. The major difference from the other types of architecture is that environment models and possible actions, which are static in control and in reactive architectures, are built in run time and changed by the system itself. In general, goal driven architectures operate following a common, basic sequence of processes executed in cycles: a) Build an objective, b) Analyze the environment, c) Design a task to achieve the objective within the given environment. If this cannot be done, build a sequence of lower level targets aimed at progressing toward the higher level objective.
These processes may imply highly developed perceptive, deliberative and actuation functions. In parallel to them, these architectures may implement learning algorithms that help optimize the system for future or eventual conditions of operation. As a result, these architectures may achieve high levels of autonomy. However, some limitations have been met when implementing them in actual systems, relative to resource consumption. Some deliberative, learning and

perceptive processes would require extremely large memory and computational resources for real time operation, especially in fast-evolving environments, or when dealing with highly abstract tasks.

There exist hybrid approaches which combine and integrate devices and elements of the three categories above. In particular, PID controllers are used by the majority of implementations dealing with mechanical systems, although they may be reconfigured in real time by complex goal-driven architectures.

The ultimate goal of the research line which will be illustrated by the FPGA experiences described in subsequent sections is to build systematic methodologies in order to engineer all aspects of scaling high level goal architectures to low cost, real time devices.

3. Scaling high level architectures to low-cost FPGAs

We may realize that the process of designing a low cost, embedded cognitive architecture implies a wide range of problems motivated by two major properties of the triad system-environment-desired functionality:

- **Complexity** of the desired functionality, the given system and especially the environment in which it will be operating.
- **Uncertainty**, derived from the vast range of possible scenarios of operation that may emerge.

3.1 Managing complexity

There exist two main techniques for reducing model complexity:

- Excluding or ignoring variables: Not measuring or evaluating them.
- Coarsening measurement: Reducing resolution enough to be representative but avoiding unnecessary detail.

These two techniques must be applied repeatedly until a reasonable degree of representativeness is reached.

In practice, eliminating uncertainty completely from an environmental model is either impossible or would make the system useless. We have to bear in mind that many of the functionalities that we shall be trying to implement have to do with making the system predict events or analyze scenarios, in which it is difficult to know precisely what is going to happen or how intense it will be. In other words: uncertainty will be intrinsic to our own application, so our model should be able to represent it in some way. In conclusion, when a certain optimal is achieved in complexity, uncertainty may and must not be completely eliminated from the model of the environment. The problem now is managing uncertainty.

3.2 Managing uncertainty

As it has been pointed out, uncertainty may appear in two ways: not knowing what is going to happen or not knowing how intense it will be. More formally, we can say that there are two types of uncertainty:

- Qualitative uncertainty: Ignoring the nature of the actual event that may occur or that is already taking place. This type of uncertainty is the specialty of goal driven architectures.

- Quantitative/intensive uncertainty: Given a certain event, ignoring its intensity. A typical example of this is ignoring the actual value that will be measured the next instant.

There exist well known, established techniques which allow dealing with both types of uncertainty. Knowing which variable to measure and how to act upon it, it is only a matter of estimating how intense the action must be. This problem can be successfully managed by classical control. Enhancements of the classical PID loop such as some non-linear controllers or model reference adaptive control (MRAC) even achieve a limited range of reaction to qualitative uncertainty.

In general, managing qualitative uncertainty is a much deeper and broader problem. Classical artificial intelligence techniques as neural networks, fuzzy logic and expert systems offer basic tools. Expert systems and fuzzy logic in combination may analyze uncertain scenarios provided that their dynamics fall within the range covered by the rule databases, variables and member functions are well designed. Neural networks may analyze sensor readings in raw and extract patterns within the limitations of their own type (ie. perceptron, cognitron), number of neurons, etc.

However, some new functionalities require wider ranges of qualitative uncertainty management than those provided by these techniques. Complex environmental analysis, complex action selection processes and advanced learning mechanisms, exceeding typical neural network ones, are some examples. This is the use of cognitive architectures.

The role of a cognitive architecture is to define a sequence of operation and to assign roles to the resources of the system, these resources and processes being implemented by expert systems, neural networks, PIDs or whatever other technique, hardware or software. Scaling cognitive architectures equals to selecting which parts of their original specification are really needed and how could they be simplified, which stages of the operating cycles are indispensable and how to integrate both while preserving functionality.

3.3 Perception, deliberation, action

The operation of any system, can, in general, be explained in terms of perceptive, deliberative and actuating processes. Sometimes the processes are not designed thinking of any of those three roles, though inevitably they end up performing one when functioning. Complex realizations of any of them may rely on the use of extensive memory resources, which may also be classified in roles: long-term memory and short-term memory. While the first contains information that may stay in the system during long periods of activity, short term memory contains transiting variable values or sensory measurements as such. It can be observed that, as a general rule, goal-driven architectures tend to exploit long term memory (which stores knowledge) as intensely as short term memory, while reactive architectures, with simpler design, may even have none.

For scaling cognitive architectures (Albus, 1995), it is useful to have a clear idea of the character of the system to be designed: whether it will be mainly perceptive, deliberative or actuating. This will allow a gross idea of the necessary resources. In general, systems centered in action processes will demand little or none deliberative processing (action selection, planning, decision making), while problem solving systems will demand little action processes.

Of course, it is not only the type of processing we are interested, but mainly the type and quantity of resources each type of process has associated. Sometimes, the designer is able to choose the nature of the system, or it is given by the application itself. For example, in the case of ADAS (Advanced Driver Assistance System), the target is to warn or inform the driver about a variety of risks, options for driving, etc. This case is expected to require little or none actuating functions except, perhaps, some kind of HMI. On the contrary, perceptive functions are expected to become quite developed, if analyzing risk for example. On the other hand, an autonomous driving vehicle may rely on extensive perceptive and deliberation processes for analyzing the environment, possible action and tradeoffs.

4. The process of scaling an architecture

Scaling a cognitive architecture adds up to finding a match between functionality, architecture and implementation. The process is simple: given a certain functionality, a certain architecture must be designed, by iteration, coupling capacities and resources with the implementation design. During the process, the engineer must continuously work for optimization of resource use. There is no general formula as to how to optimize. The two ways of dealing with complexity which were mentioned above apply, however: first, to eliminate any parts, elements or functions of the architecture that are not strictly needed to achieve the desired functionality. Second, to eliminate any excess of resolution in measurements, calculations and precision.

Exaggerated examples of these rules help to understand their meaning. If you have the necessary information to make your application work by only adding and subtracting, do not build a cognitive architecture to do the same job. It will consume more resources and take more time, and may even do it wrong sometimes. If your artificial vision system must detect spots between 1 and 2 cm² at 1 m distance, do not spend money in 1920x1200 resolution cameras and image processing algorithms. A low resolution camera will do the filtering for free, quicker and cheaper. If your system will always operate with objects A, B and C, you may spare designing learning algorithms that will enable it recognizing any new object around.

Naturally, there might not always exist a solution to a scaling problem, due either to an exceedingly complex functionality or to insufficient resources. Logically, the more strict the functionality specifications or the higher the system flexibility they demand, the more difficult it will be to simplify any architecture into low cost hardware. Any scaling process should begin with dividing functionality specifications, to ensure that parts may be achieved progressively in spite of possible overall failure.

When a solution is possible, however, a good approach is to start assuming the best of cases, when resources are unlimited, designing the basic architecture for it, and proceed simplifying the design in each iteration. The process ends when a certain match is achieved between the three. That is, when the desired functionality has yielded a simplified architecture that can be implemented in the available resources. Over-optimizing the architecture is, nevertheless, good for two reasons. First, it may allow implementing the system in lower cost hardware, or may leave free resources in your board for other purposes. Second, it reduces the probability of errors. In general, the bigger the system –and therefore, its architecture- the higher its probability of failure; so keep it as small as possible. While resource optimization derives from minimizing architectural complexity, there are overall factors to be taken into account during the design stage. A basic collection of criteria could be:

- The automatic process admits drastic optimization in time and resources. When possible, make things automatic.
- The higher the uncertainty in the environment, the more flexible the system, the less automatic it can be, the more resources necessary. The better the modeling of the environment, the lesser the uncertainty.
- There is a tradeoff between memory and computational power: in general designing memory-based processes may simplify run time computation and vice versa. If you have enough memory and information to store, use it. It makes things more automatic.
- In general, there is also a tradeoff between deliberation and perception: the more developed the perceptive processes, the simpler the deliberative processes may be and vice versa. But here there is no general rule, for perceptive processes may be as complex and demanding as purely deliberative ones.

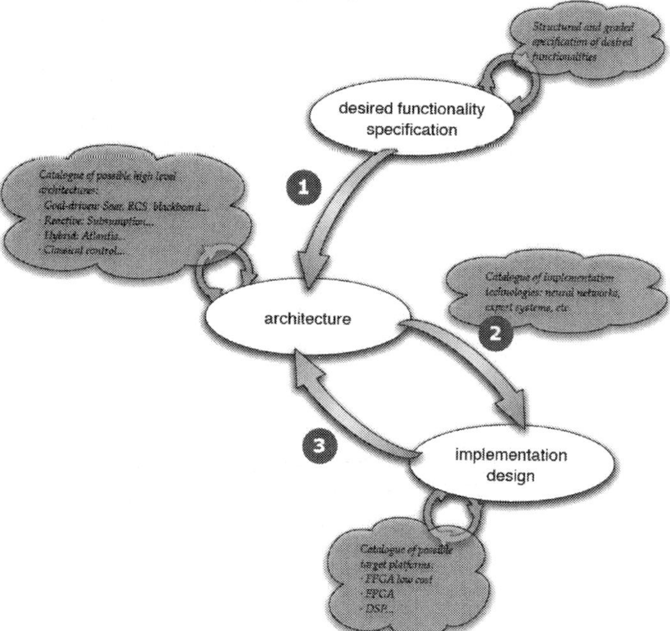

Fig. 0. General process of scaling cognitive architectures

5. A low-cost Real-Time FPGA solution for driver drowsiness detection

In this work some of the most recent advances in digital image processing techniques have been used to make vehicle drivers face analysis by detecting symptoms of tiredness and distraction in order to prevent sudden risk situations.

The results of the experiments show (Moreno et al., 2003) that a large number of car or trucks accidents can be avoided by detecting real-time physical and psychological states of the drivers in normal driving conditions. There are three main objectives in this design: To detect the driver eyelid movements, to detect the number of frames the driver has his eyes closed and to detect when the driver turns right or left (or bows) his head for a long time. Thus, several well known algorithms have been used and optimized for this field of application, such as spatial and temporal filtering, motion detection, optical flow analysis, etc.

Digital signal and image processing techniques have been used together. Furthermore, a low-cost Real-Time solution based upon both FPGA (ALTERA FLEX 10K30 and ALTERA Cyclone Device EP1C3) have been achieved.

Figure 1 shows the flexibility of the system, because it can be used for driver drowsiness detection or road lane markers, both in real-time.

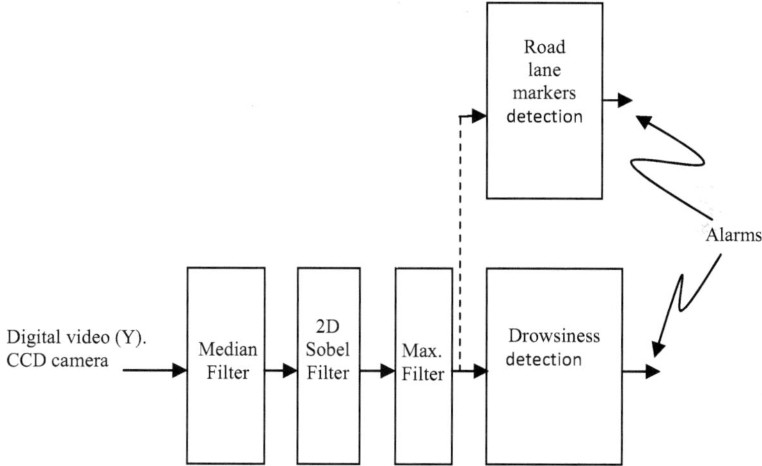

Fig. 1. FPGA architecture

Median filtering is used to minimize the effect of the Gaussian noise. It is very well suited for this type of application; however, the trade-off between the number of gates (FPGA logic elements, LE) used and the benefit obtained is very poor. For this reason, and in order to get a very low-cost solution, removal from the final design must be considered; at the same time a high quality digital video signal coming from a CCD camera must be employed containing an infrared system suitable for low-light conditions (0 lux) must be employed. Some experiments were carried out with very low-cost CMOS cameras; but, unfortunately they do not work properly in low-light situations.

Next, the 2D Sobel filtering uses two matrices applied sequentially over 9x9 pels (picture element) blocks:

$$\begin{Bmatrix} -1,-2,-1 \\ +0,+0,+0 \\ +1,+2,+1 \end{Bmatrix} \quad \begin{Bmatrix} -1,+0,+1 \\ -2,+0,+2 \\ -1,+0,+1 \end{Bmatrix} \tag{1}$$

Then, the final result is calculated by the equation:

$$|Ysob| = \sqrt{|y_{1d}^2 - y_{2d}^2|} \qquad\qquad (2)$$

Finally, Ysob is compared to a configurable threshold value (UMB_SBL):

> *If Ysob > UMB_SBL then*
> > *Ypel = White_value (235d);*
>
> *else*
> > *Ypel = Black_value(16d);*
>
> *end if;*

This pseudo-code is not exactly a Sobel algorithm because we assign the White_value or Black_value instead the |Ysob| (Sobel parameter/luminance_pel). This allows us to simplify the calculations just suitable for the case of the driver drowsiness detection or road lane markers detection, without introducing a noticeable error. It also allows us to save a large amount of FPGA logic elements (making the fitter process much easier) and as a result of that we get a significant speed up (in terms of logic depth reduction).

Once the image has been filtered (median and 2D Sobel filtering), Maximum filtering is used usually to enlarge the edges of the objects detected by the Sobel filtering. However, this is not really necessary, because the algorithm for driver drowsiness detection and the algorithm for road lane markers detection are both based upon differential optical flow analysis, instead of traditional motion estimation algorithms.

The algorithm designed is able to detect: driver eyelid movements, number of frames the driver has his eyes closed and when the driver turns right or left (or bows) his head for a long time (this is a configurable parameter). In our system, a long time means 12 frames because at 25 frames/sec (PAL video rate) the elapsed time is 480msec. So, if the car speed were 120km/h, the distance covered would be 16 meters.

The implemented algorithm consists in comparing the number of white pels in the current frame with two parameters (maximum and minimum white pels values) previously calculated. When the current number of white pels is greater than the maximum value or smaller than the minimum one, the algorithm automatically calculates those new parameters over the next 12 frames, and the process would start again. This is very useful in order to adapt system sensitivity to light conditions.

According to ITU-R 601 Recommendation for PAL systems, each frame is formed by 720x576pels, which produces a very large amount of luminance information to be processed (414,720 pels/frame). The key factor of our system is to process only the area where the driver eyes would be located. We have tested algorithms for eyes detection but the trade-off between cost and performance is very poor. We propose to adjust the camera to the drivers'head in a comfortable driving position previously and to set the image area to be processed (configurable parameter) at the beginning (Figure 2 shows the result when processing the whole frame, no real-time and Figure 3 shows the result when processing only a specific frame area, in real-time).

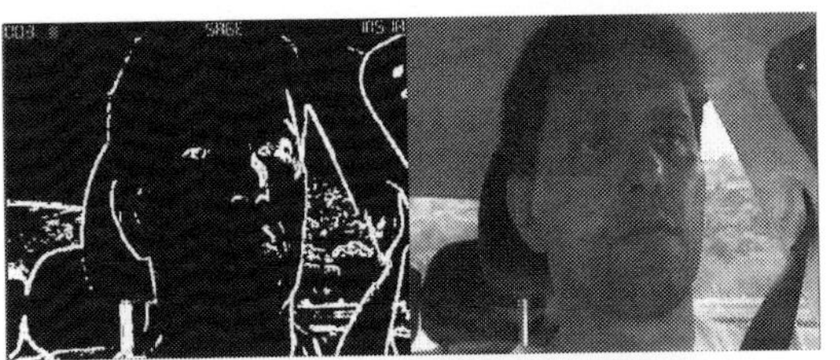

$$(2)$$

Fig. 2. Drowsiness detection

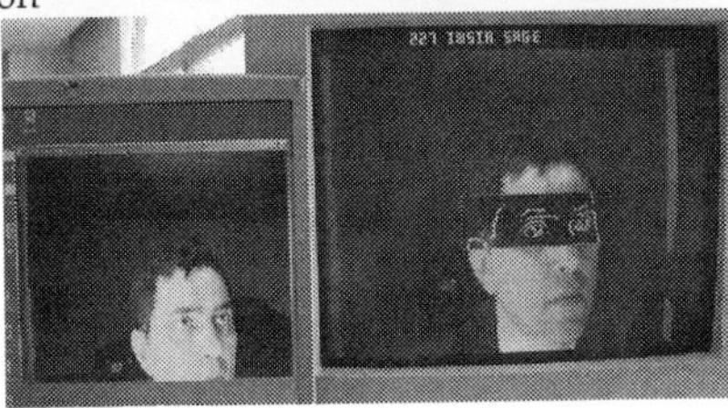

Fig. 3. Real-time drowsiness detection

The reduction of the number of pels to be processed is very significant: 20,400pels for 100 lines x 204 pels area (see Figure 3). Nevertheless, Median and Sobel filtering work over 9x9pels blocks in order to yield a processed pel; so only by means of a pipeline architecture would real-time processing be achieved.

In the case of road lane markers detection algorithm only the 24 lines of the bottom of each frame are processed, because only those lines are really relevant to detect if a car is leaving its tracks due to a driver distraction. On the other hand, in our system only one video camera is employed, so, no 3D image analysis algorithm can be used at all. We have used a very simple approach that consists on fitting the camera zoom to the car width. In this way, while driving along, the lane markers "disappear" just through the right side and/or the left side of the image. In case of the car is out of the track, the lane markers would "disappear" through the bottom side of the image and the system would warn the driver (see Figure 4). Some experiments have been carried out on real roads and we have obtained very satisfactory results.

The algorithm consists in obtaining the difference between the present frame and the frame immediately before. The difference is calculated over all the pels belonging to the last 24 bottom lines of each frame. If the result is zero and the pel processed is a White_pel, this means that a lane marker probably starts in this frame. The process continues over the next frames. The algorithm is able to detect if the object detected is really a lane marker or just a shadow or other disturbance on the road.

Fig. 5. Road line tracks detection

6. A new Real-Time Hardware Architecture for Road Line Tracking Using a Particle Filter

In this work a new real-time hardware architecture based on real time image processing and the use of a Particle Filter, as the fundamental element for tracking lines of a road, is presented. To this end a hardware system has been designed based on the use of low-cost high-reliability FPGA integrated circuits (ALTERA-Cyclone and ALTERA-Cyclone II). For this purpose, a multilevel pipeline architecture (at pixel block - 3x3- and pixel level), which aims to guarantee the processing of the 8-bit digitized images obtained from a single video camera (SONY in PAL format, ITU-R 601, ITU-R 656), has been developed. The entire processing and prediction system has been developed in VHDL-93, simulated and synthesized with ModelSim and Quartus-II respectively (Alarcon et al., 2006).

Although many systems have been proposed for detecting involuntary lane departure of motor vehicles, based on vision systems (or based on other technologies), they have not had the expected success. System reliability is limited by weather conditions and visibility, as well as those imposed by the state of the highway. In general, it can be said that these systems basically perform three functions: 1) image feature extraction, 2) matching and 3) taking decisions. Moreover, all of them should be considered deterministic functions, except in some approaches, real time in most cases and, to a lesser extent, implemented in application specific hardware.

A new model to represent lane lines and the relative position of the vehicle with respect to the lane boundaries is proposed. The position of the lane lines is tracked on the successive images obtained from the camera (25 fps, PAL frame rate), by projecting the model. Model parameters are updated by superimposing the image, with the projection of the model on the following image. In the model, a search area of the lane boundaries is defined on the image, which allows processing time to be reduced, and the problems caused by false lane detections resulting from the inherent noise in the images to be reduced or eliminated. The parameters of the model are processed and updated by means of the Particle Filter.

A robust, artificial vision based system for detecting involuntary lane departure which depends only on the processing speed and the frame rate of the camera has been developed. This system allows road line position to be predicted with a bounded error.

The Particle Filter, in Artificial Vision applications, is used for tracking objects in an image sequence. The Particle Filter models the probability function a posteriori of a stochastic process, by means of an N particle distribution and their associated probabilities in State Space. This type of filter needs a dispersed search to properly track the features sought in the image sequence. It is a model used to calculate the state of a time-variant system or, in other words, a sequential estimation algorithm.

In this study, artificial vision techniques have been applied with no restriction on the incoming images. Hence no type of marker is used on the highway. So the system, after the acquisition of the monochrome images of a camera, is able to process the information and to track the lane lines in a reliable and robust manner.

The VHDL implementation of the proposed system, shown in Figure 6, required an image preprocessing stage. Median filtering, a non linear filter, is used to minimize the effect of Gaussian noise, and Sobel filter is used to detect edges in the image.

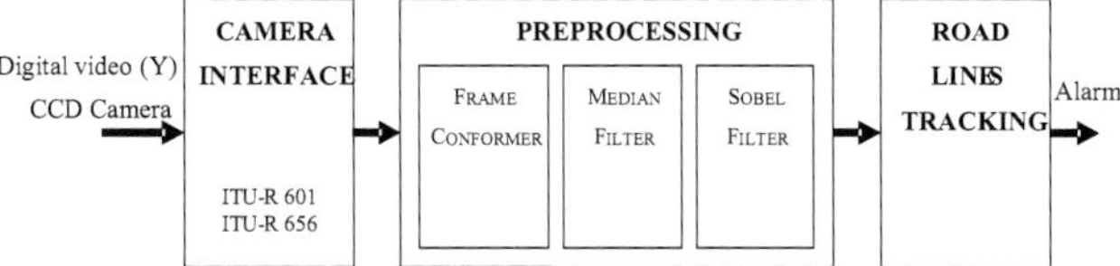

Fig. 6. System architecture

For the system to work optimally, several morphological operations must be carried out on binary images to obtain the necessary information in filter processing. The reason for this is based on the computational load reduction necessary for the hardware implementation, since not all the information in the image is pertinent for the reference application. As it has been mentioned, only the bottom part of the image is relevant, as shown in Figure 7; and, inside that part, the image has been segmented into three regions, left, center and right, of 37x102 (rows x columns) pixels, corresponding to the Regions of Interest (RoI), where the corresponding lanes are located.

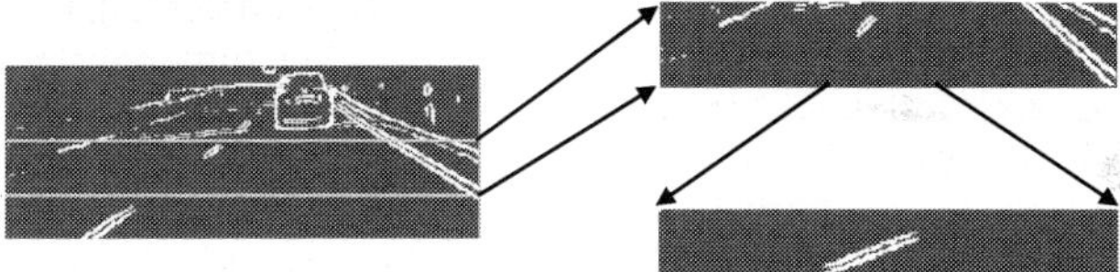

Fig. 7. Image Segmentation

From an algorithmic point of view, the Particle Filter (Arulampalam et al., 2002) is detailed in Figure 8. The Line Model Detection (L_M_D) carries out line detection in the image by means of a morphological line model. Next, particle weights computation is done in the Survival Model (S_M), checking if the error made in the prediction of the Center of Mass done in the previous image, is delimited as explained in Hardware Architecture section. At the same time, in Particle Displacement (P_D), the displacement speed of the particles is computed. By means of the Movement Model (explained in Hardware Architecture section) in Prediction Update (P_U), the position of the new particles is predicted and updated.

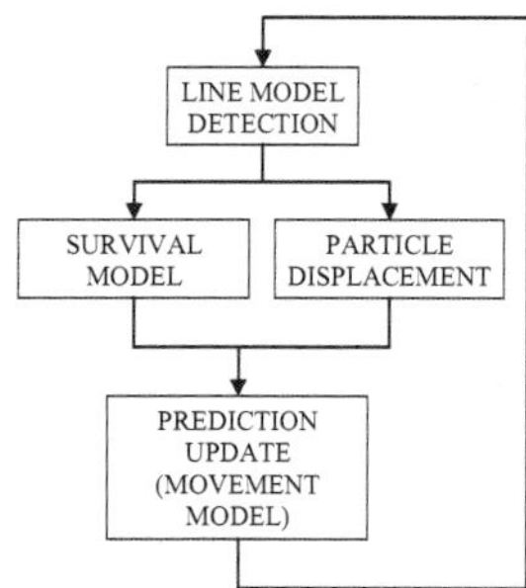

Fig. 8. Diagram of the Particle Filter designed

Some of the results obtained with the proposed architecture are shown in Figure 9. It can be observed that the 12 initially generated particles (Figure 9.a) predict the position of the lane line in accordance with the established deviation parameters (deviation = 0.1) (see Figure 9.b), and how they converge in the last 2 images (Figure 9.c and 9.d) toward the real position of the Center of Mass of the line.

One of the essential objectives of the hardware implementation of the algorithms was to achieve a high processing speed to get a real-time low-cost system. The hardware system implemented in the FPGA, Figure 6, corresponds to a linear multilevel pipeline architecture. These hardware modules implement the first pipeline level of the architecture adapting perfectly to the requirements of the image prefiltering algorithms:

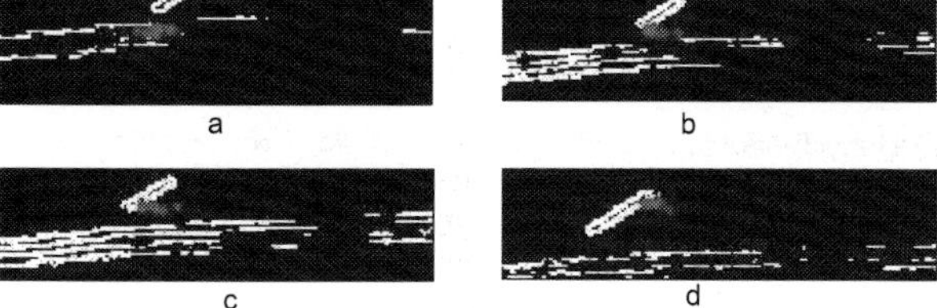

Fig. 9. Prediction of the lane line using 12 particles

a) Median Filter, to suppress the Gaussian noise and b) Sobel Filter, to extract the boundaries. Furthermore, all the submodules that constitute the complete system are also based on a pipeline architecture and are capable of delivering a valid result in each clock cycle during their stable operating cycle. The hardware design methodology employed in the second module, Preprocessing, is directed to minimizing both the use of large memory banks for storage of complete frames and the complexity of the control system. Figure 10 shows a more detailed design of the 3 submodules that make up this Preprocessing Block. The use of FIFO buffers allows a relaxation in memory restrictions, by not having to store a whole image. In short, it is only necessary to store two lines of an image in the corresponding FIFO. The Filter Control, implemented in a distributed manner, together with the adaptation of the information obtained from the camera via the Camera Interface and Frame Conformer blocks, Figure 6, guarantees a minimum use of hardware resources, at the same time as total independence of the camera and of the Particle Filter model used respectively. This is possible by adding a header (sync embedded bits) to each of the pixels coming from the camera, which indicates the type of pixel being handled at all times: SoFrm (Start of Frame), SoLn (Start of Line), PoLn (Pixel of Line), EoFrm (End of Frame) and NoPix (No Pixel). At the same time some discrete synchronization signals are created in the system. This results in a Datapath width of 11 bits.

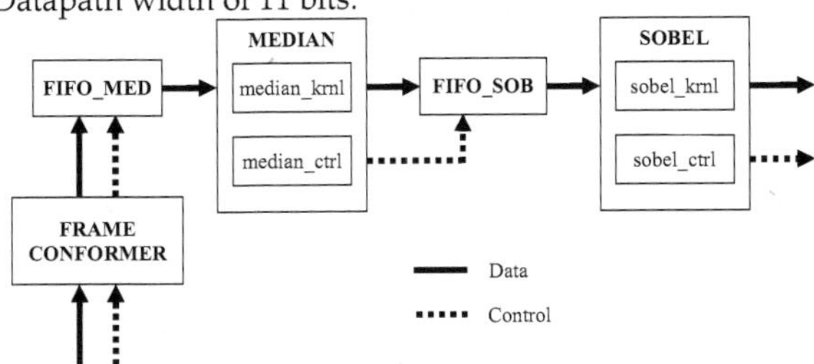

Fig. 10. Preprocessing Module

The data frame so formed has allowed each of the filters to be structured in two major submodules: the filter Kernel and the filter Control, respectively, both in the Median and in the Sobel filter. The Kernel responds to a linear pipeline structure at pixel level and 3x3 pixel block whilst the Distributed Control in each of the blocks guarantees a maximum throughput for a minimum consumption of logic.

As for the most important module in the system, the Particle Filter, Figure 11 shows the hardware implementation of the architecture which, written in VHDL, operates over the RoI, Figures 6 and 7.

In each image the presence of lane lines is established and their Center of Mass is calculated, thereafter predicting their position by application of the Movement Model which can be seen before. Until all terms present in this equation are available, three consecutive images (frame0, frame1 and frame2) are needed for prediction and full tracking.

To functionally explain the hardware implementation of the algorithm, it must be assumed that the Centers of Mass of the lane lines for the initial and successive frames have been found, and that the predictions are correct. In such a case, the algorithm is processed as indicated previously. The procedure, in other case, will be explained later.

$$
\begin{aligned}
t = 0 &\qquad X_1 = MC + RND_{init} \\
t = 1 &\qquad X_2 = X_1 + \left[RND_\sigma \right] \\
t = 2 &\qquad X_3 = X_2 + \left[\left(X_2 - X_1 \right) + RND_\sigma \right] \\
\forall t \geq 2 &\qquad X_{t+1} = X_t + \left[\left(X_t - X_{t-1} \right) + RND_\sigma \right]
\end{aligned}
\tag{3}
$$

where $X = \{x_0, x_1, ..., x_{n-1}\}$ is the set of all the particles, MC the centers of mass detected, RNDinit the initialization random function, and RNDσ the random function that represents the variance term of the Particle Filter. Each increment of t is assumed to be in whole multiples of TFrame (TF, 40 ms, PAL rate). The design of the architecture has been carried out so that each particle is evaluated and appropriately updated, independently of the rest. This allows each of them to be found in one of the three states described before, and which are explained below.

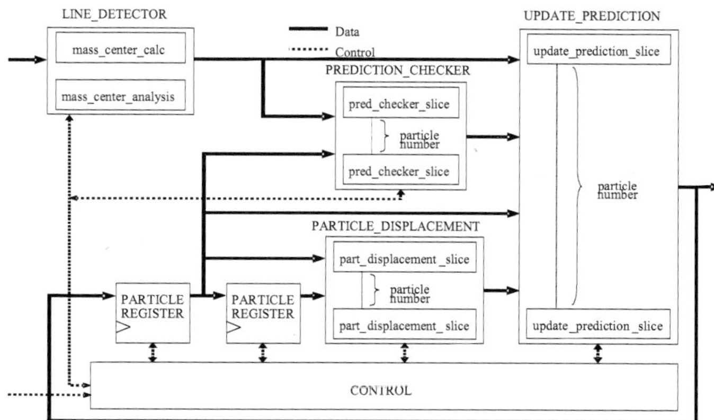

Fig. 11. Functional Description of the Particle Filter Hardware Implementation

The equation shown below, which represents the so called Movement Model, governs the overall behavior of the filter:

$$X_{t+1} = X_t + \left[(X_t - X_{t-1}) + RND_\sigma \right]$$

1) init_state → t = 0. frame0 is analyzed, so there is no initial information at all. After finding the Centers of Mass of the line, the particles are distributed around the same with a dispersion given by RNDinit, the latter constituting the prediction of the position of the Center of Mass in the following image made from that detected in the current image.

2) transitory_state → t = 1. The prediction consists on applying the variance term to the prediction made in the previous image.

3) steady_state → t ≥ 2. All data is now available to apply the equation of the filter completely, that is, the previous prediction Xt, the particle displacement term (Xt – Xt-1), which represents the speed at which the lines are moving in the real scenario, and the variance RNDσ.

This routine is followed for the case in which the error committed in the prediction, measured with respect to the Center of Mass of the current image, is delimited within a margin of error defined by the maximum value of RNDinit. At this point, steady_state, two situations can arise:

1. A new line is detected. Depending on the error made, two further situations can arise.

   • The error is bounded. This is the general case, steady_state, which operation process has been explained above, (1).

   • The error is not bounded. The calculation sequence begins again for the three following frames, considering this as init_state, t = 0.

2. It is in the case where no line is detected that the prediction makes most sense, being the prediction validated when a new line is found in the following frames. Thus, when the line appears again, its position will have been predicted, and it will be possible to evaluate the correctness thereof, proceeding again as in point 1.

The Particle Filter subsystem implemented uses 4 particles for each video line analyzed, resulting a total of 12 particles, operating only on the horizontal axis of the image. The dynamic margin (range) of the pseudo random numbers generated, RNDinit (4-bit LFSR) and RNDσ (3-bit LFSR), as well as the number of particles and the number of bits used for their encoding, are closely related to the number of video lines used for detecting the lane lines, the width of the RoI and the number of frames necessary to establish a good prediction in real time (PAL frame rate = 25 fps). The impact in dimensioning the DataPath of the pipeline architecture and its control, have constituted one of the main challenges in implementing the total system. The number of bits used to encode the particles is 10, representing integers with sign, whereby this coding could be employed for RoIs of up to 512 pixels in width.

Synthesis results for different low-cost FPGAs were obtained, trying to compare the different architectures. This Module is composed of two FIFO memories that store 2 video lines for the implementation of the Median and Sobel Filters respectively. The Distributed Control of this Module has the responsibility of ensuring that the information at pixel level reaches the Particle Filter Module, Figure 11, in optimum conditions. A Cyclone EP1C20F400C7 FPGA has been taken as the reference low-cost development system.

The FIFO memories were implemented making use of internal RAM resources available in the FPGA (294912 bits distributed in 64 blocks of 4608 bits, known as M4Ks). The results obtained with Quartus II "MegaWizard Plug-in Manager", an assistant that helps in the instantiation of architecture-specific resources, have been compared with the direct instantiation of the *scfifo lybrary* component. This has been the design decision made since errors were detected in the assistant that made the creation of the desired FIFO memory impossible.

The Median and Sobel Filters FIFOs -11 bits per word- (Figure 10) differ in two positions. It must be pointed out that, as far as synthesis is concerned, this has a relative importance. After several synthesis tests, it was observed that the design of the LPM component of Altera *scfifo* (single-clock fifo) and the mapping process of the memory in HW, always produce a FIFO with a power of two number of positions. Thus, a FIFO of 126 positions would occupy the same resources (memory and LEs) as one of 128. On the other hand, one of 129 positions will occupy the same as one of 256. The difference probably rest in the generation of the FIFO control signals. Besides, it also must be pointed out that the proposed architecture for both the Sobel and the Median filter, as regards the number of FPGA resources employed, is completely independent of the size of the image to be processed. The key point in the architecture that makes such synthesis results possible is the series communication protocol implemented at pixel level. This protocol makes that the Submodules that implement the filters do not need to know the RoI size. This information is managed by the Frame Conformer block, being the insignificant increase in the size of the Preprocessing Module due to this submodule, as well as to the FIFOs.The synthesis of the Particle Filter, as well as its fitting in different types of FPGA with a different architecture, number of logic elements (LE), availability of internal RAM memory, etc., have allowed a comparison to be carried out among all of them and some final conclusions to be reached. This Filter is the module in the architecture of the system developed that consumes most logic element (LE) resources.

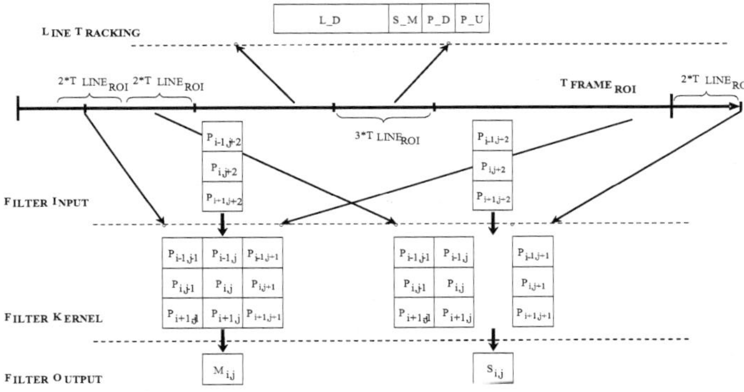

Fig. 12. System Pipeline Processing

7. FPGA Implementation of an Image Recognition System based on Tiny Neural Networks and on-line Reconfiguration

Neural networks are widely used in pattern recognition, security applications and robot control. We propose a hardware architecture system; using Tiny Neural Networks (TNN) specialized in image recognition. The generic TNN architecture allows expandability by means of mapping several Basic units (layers) and dynamic reconfiguration; depending on the application specific demands. One of the most important features of Tiny Neural Networks (TNN) is their learning ability. Weight modification and architecture reconfiguration can be carried out in run time. Our system performs shape identification by the interpretation of their singularities. This is achieved by interconnecting several specialized TNN (López et al., 2007).

There are several levels of parallelism in the neural network recognition system that we are proposing: Parallelism among networks, among the layers of a network, among neurons and among connections. All of them are shown on the General Architecture of the system (Figure 13).

We can classify the ANN hardware implementation in two main categories: that based on microprocessors by using Digital Signal Processors (DSP) or general purpose processors, and that using an Application Specific Integrated Circuit (ASIC) or Field Programmable Gate Array (FPGA).

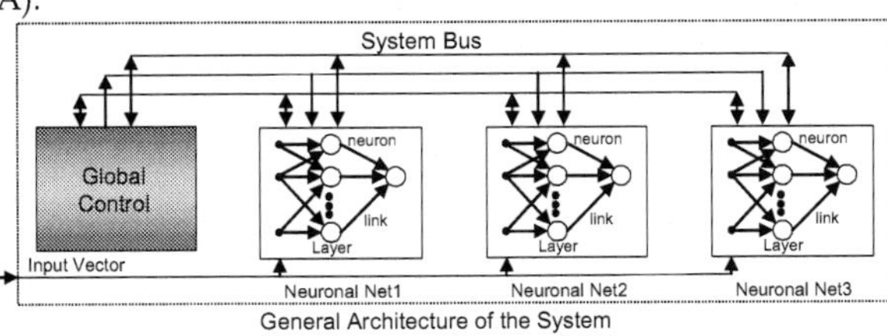

General Architecture of the System
a) Net, b) Layers, c) Neurons, d) Links

Fig. 13. System Architecture

The first one based on microprocessors, is more flexible and relatively easy to implement. However, when the network becomes larger (for example, in a fully connected network), it is not the best option: general purpose computers are required, and the usage and application depend on power and area characteristics available.

The number of "synapses" and multipliers included in a fully interconnected network is proportional to the squared total number of neurons. The speed slows down due to the increase in the number of multipliers, and the chip size or chip area increases significantly, which becomes one of the critical points in ANN design. In order to solve this problem, the use of hardware multipliers seems to be an option to resolve the chip size problem; as well as the design of neural networks without multipliers or reusable ones. Our work explores multiplier re-usability based on an internal bus structure. Taking into account the parallelism of the neural network model, it is possible to map the architecture on array processors, obtaining a linear growth in the number of multipliers. Figure 14 shows a network interconnected by mean of an array processor model.

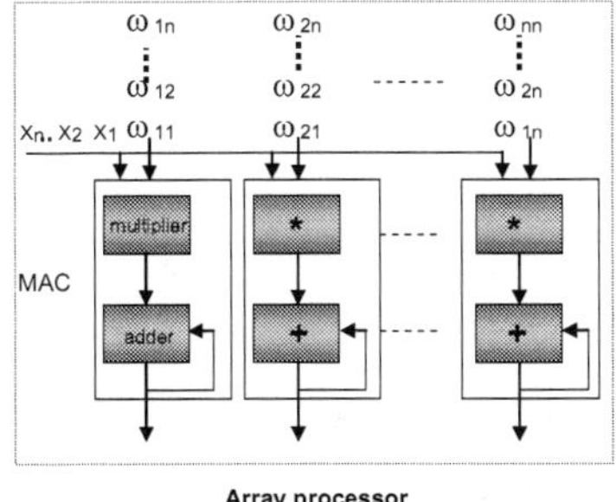

Fig. 14. Network Example

The main objective of this research is the design of a reconfigurable, efficient, low cost architecture for shape recognition. Robust methods for the analysis of images, and the implementation of a system based on specialized TNN have been developed for shape recognition by means of the analysis of some characteristics of the image (singularities). Traffic signal recognition and/or pedestrian recognition are two of the most relevant applications. These networks work cooperatively to obtain the classification of the image.

The main restriction comes with the complexity of the information contained in the image data, because they are sensible to changes of the environment. It is then necessary to have a recognition system that allows dynamic reconfiguration. It is necessary to develop an architecture that allows optimum usage of hardware resources, due to the limitations in power and available area. The suggested system is formed by small Perceptron multilevel networks, and it was implemented in an Altera Cyclone II FPGA.

The requirements of recurrent learning processes can be satisfied by the reconfiguration and flexibility of FPGAs. Weight modification and architecture reconfiguration can be carried out during run time.

When talking about ANN implementation, the following considerations should be taken into account: frequency, precision, configuration issues, and ANN parallelism. In order to improve general design characteristics, there are two units: Basic units and Control units.

Basic units (specialized neural networks) are in charge of signal processing and weight and bias data storage, including the multiplication of the weights by the inputs, the accumulation and the nonlinear function activation. Control units work on the basic of signal transmission including parallel processing and the algorithm work. By considering those units, the proposed design (as shown in Figure 15) has an efficient architecture based on specialized neural networks by recognition, to be implemented in FPGAs.

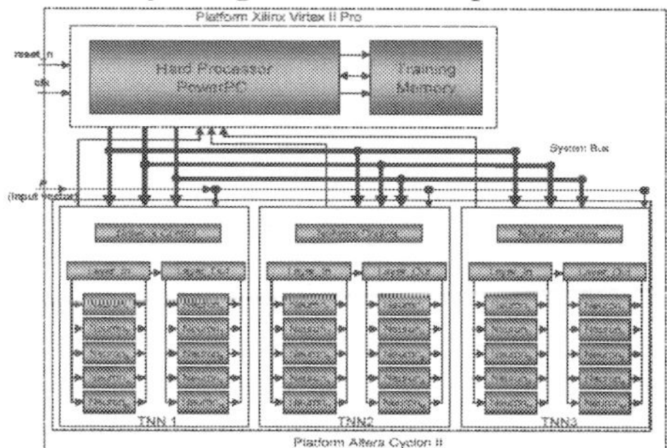

Fig. 15. System Architecture

For achieving the learning operation the algorithm is divided in three phases, known as: feed-forward, back-propagation and up-date. In the feed-forward phase the input signals propagate through the network layer by layer, eventually producing some response at the output of the network. This response is compared with the desired (target) response, generating error signals that are propagated in backward direction through the network. In this backward phase of operation, the free parameters of the network are adjusted so as to minimize the sum of square error. Finally, weights and biases are updated using the data obtained in the previous phase. The process is repeated as many times as necessary in order to have a trained network. The three phases of algorithm are shown in Figure 16.

Since the proposed architecture is auto-reconfigurable during the execution time, separated modules where developed. So that the system carries out an on-line reconfiguration, the same learning rules should be applied concurrently over a new pattern. When the network is reconfigured, the Control unit executes the learning process concurrently, using the training patterns stored along with the new pattern to be recognized.

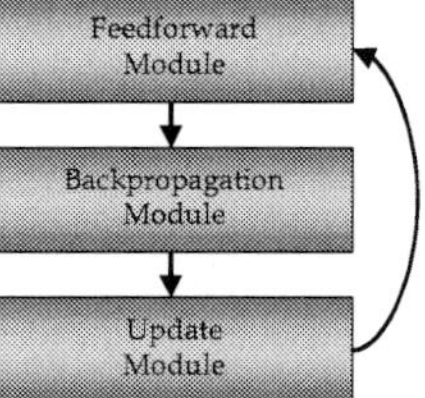

Fig. 16. Sequential Algorithm for Learning Operation

When the learning processes finishes, collected data are transmitted to the weights and bias network memories, by means of the control unit and pass through the backpropagation level, which checks the reconfiguration and learning of it.

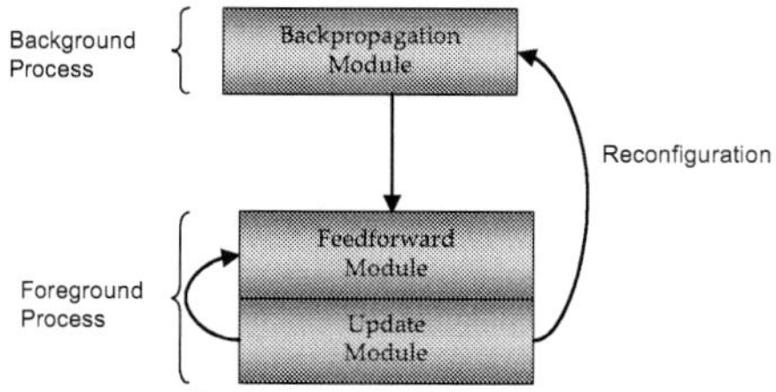

Fig. 17. Algorithms Segmentation for Learning Operation

Figure 17 shows the implementation of the different levels of the learning algorithm. The feed-forward and update modules corresponding to the Basic unit were implemented directly in the same FPGA (Altera Cyclone II), and they are executed concurrently in a foreground Process.

At that moment, the uncertainty module determines if there is a new pattern and sends a request to the control unit to reconfigure the network. The backpropagation module corresponding to on line learning was implemented in the PowerPC processor XILINX (Virtex II), background process. By means of a state machine, three modes of operation of the system were defined. In the Initialization mode, the system loads the initial values of the weights and biases, and begins the Classification mode. In this mode, the network works in feed-forward, and when it detects that a new pattern has arrived it changes to the Reconfiguration mode. When this mode finished, the update is carried out in other to begin again with the classification mode. The different modes of operation and the states machine will be explained later.

Considering the problems of size and scalability, we propose a design based on the mathematical model of the neural networks, similar to the model shown in figure 18(a).

As explained above, the synapse number is limited (network size) by the size of the internal memory of FPGA. In addition, the network architecture (number of neurons and number of layers) is also limited by the hardware resources. In order to avoid these difficulties, a Basic Processing Unit is suggested as the central component of the network. This unit is called the Knowledge Unit (KWU) and can be modified to configure a neuron or a number of them in order to create one of the layers of the network, obtaining different topologies according to the programming of the internal registers of the system.

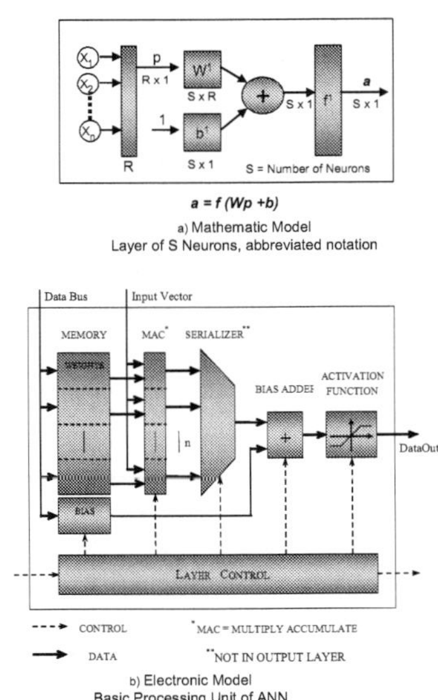

a) Mathematic Model
Layer of S Neurons, abbreviated notation

b) Electronic Model
Basic Processing Unit of ANN

Fig. 18. Specialized Tiny Neural Networks Model

Figure 18b shows the model of a Basic Learning Unit. The hardware architecture is obtained by mapping the high level algorithmic model of the Perceptron neural network into the equivalent module hardware. A data input vector (coming from the acquisition and pre-processing levels) and the external buses system (address, data and control) is used to interconnect the knowledge units with the general control of the system.

According to our research it is necessary to know the degree of parallelism (taking into account the hardware resources) of the algorithm, in order to trade off the development and hardware resources consumption when implemented. With the suggested model, the Basic Learning Unit architecture has an almost complete parallel functionality, providing the best development with the minimum resources.

All hardware neurons (Basic Units), are formed by a MAC Unit (multiplier and accumulator), a Serial Unit (multiplexer), and the Non-lineal Functions calculator, all of them interconnected by a parallel system bus as shown on figure 18b.

MAC Units are connected through the internal data bus to their weight memories and to the series of input data (input vector). Let us suppose that we have an input layer of N neurons. By means of this architecture it is possible to carry out N operations in parallel with serial input data because of the simultaneous access of the memories, through the internal structure of bus. Therefore, the weight and bias memories have been implemented in the RAM modules embedded in the FPGA. These modules allow being accessed independently, so faster memory accesses are achieved thanks to this distributed memory scheme.

The design of the Basic Unit should include a level in which output data are obtained (output vector) in order to balance cost and development. This internal output contains the results of the first layer neurons and it is used as an input vector on the network's hidden or the output layers.

All of the MAC units makes parallel calculations ending up into an architecture with a high hardware resources consumption, so resources are optimized by an adder and a block which activates the non-lineal function used into the Basic Unit design; this way, the Learning Unit architecture has an input vector and an output vector for the information transfer (feed-forward), through the different network layers, being able to implement several neural networks, Perceptron Multilayer (PM).

As a special case, when talking about a Perceptron Multilayer network and due to the little number of neurons on the exit layer, it is not necessary to use a Serial Unit because cost and development trade off does not have a negative impact on the architecture. There is an adder and an activation function by output neuron; the bias memory has been implemented with registers in the same adder, reducing the RAM cost and achieving resource optimization. We can see the architecture of an exit layer unit on figure 19.

Having the Learning Unit, it is easy to have a neural network interconnecting two or more Basic Units; depending on the number of layers those neurons have (Modular and Scalable features of the Architecture). The interconnection is performed by an internal bus that transfers the data vectors of the previous stage. The data flow is controlled by a control unit through a protocol which indicates to the next layer on the network, the beginning and end of the information vector.

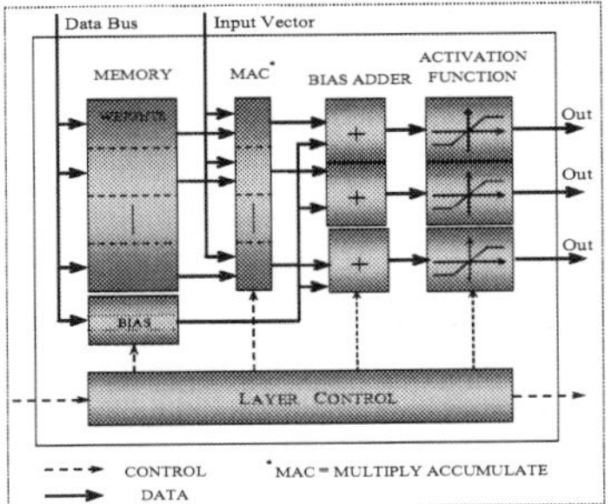

Fig. 19. Basic Unit Output Layer

With the Basic and Control units designed, a new layer of the neural network, which we will call the Learning Generic Unit can be designed. This is the basic module in the network and gives the modular characteristic to the system, which enables the Perceptron networks with several neurons and layers to be implemented.

These units are also the basic modules on the huge architectures on FPGAs platforms, having a growing system on internal networks and the whole one. A growing and modular system is achieved when the modular control unit is designed.

The modular design of the Control unit of the network layers avoids the need for global control and a completely modular and scalable system is obtained. The main activities carried out by the Control Unit are signal transmission and learning algorithm execution.

The state machine of the Control Unit has been designed to improve the system performance. This state machine has been carefully created and has three different ways of implementing the algorithm (figure 20) as explained previously.

The characteristics of the design allow that several networks execute the classification process in parallel, and meanwhile concurrently the training process could be executed in another one TNN.

In order to maintain the processing speed of a TNN in hardware and its versatility in simulations, the reconfiguration of the neural network on its different hardware levels has to be possible (Reconfiguration features). Different researches have revealed that general purpose processors can be used in order to reprogram the neural network. We could also use FPGAs to modify the bus structure and the Basic Unit possessing by means of the change in the configuration registers.

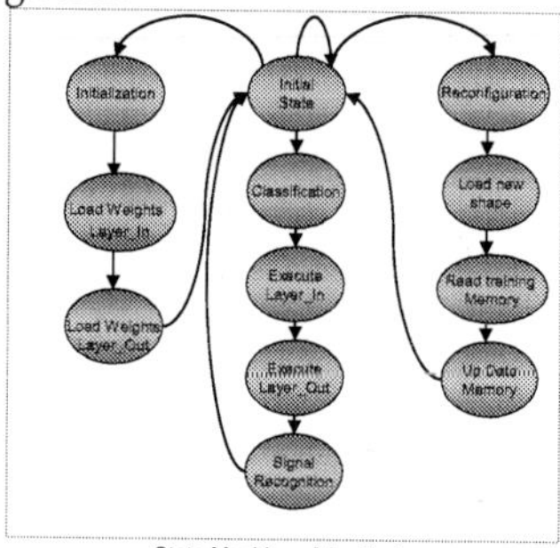

State Machine of the System
a) Initialization b) Classification c) Reconfiguration

Fig. 20. System Operation

The characteristics of the design allow that several networks execute the classification process in parallel, and meanwhile concurrently the training process could be executed in another one TNN.

In order to maintain the processing speed of a TNN in hardware and its versatility in simulations, the reconfiguration of the neural network on its different hardware levels has to be possible (Reconfiguration features). Different researches have revealed that general purpose processors can be used in order to reprogram the neural network.

The way in which general purpose processors are used is better although it is not completely successful with regard a the processing speed and required areas; in any case, the reconfigurable hardware networks are limited when programming but they have more processing speed, they use a smaller area and they can be included in an integrated circuit (system on-chip). Due to the characteristics of the suggested system, it can be considerate to be a heterogeneous architecture, combining the activities from the general purpose processors (programming availability) and those of the FPGAs (parallel processing and execution speed).

The specialized network design has an Uncertainty stage (module). The basic function of the module is to determine if the output data sequence corresponds to the training pattern or if it is similar to it, generating a valid signal for the recognition. On the other hand, if the Uncertainty module detects similar points on a probability range between 50% and 75%, a signal for reconfiguration is produced. Uncertainty stages are visible on Figure 21.

When the reconfiguration takes place, the global control system executes several processes concurrently: input vector acquisition, data attachment to training memory, new training vectors (target) and on-line training execution (including the new learning pattern). When training is finished, the hardware stages have been reconfigured: training memories (content and dimensions), and weight and bias memories have been updated, with new values obtained at the end of the process.

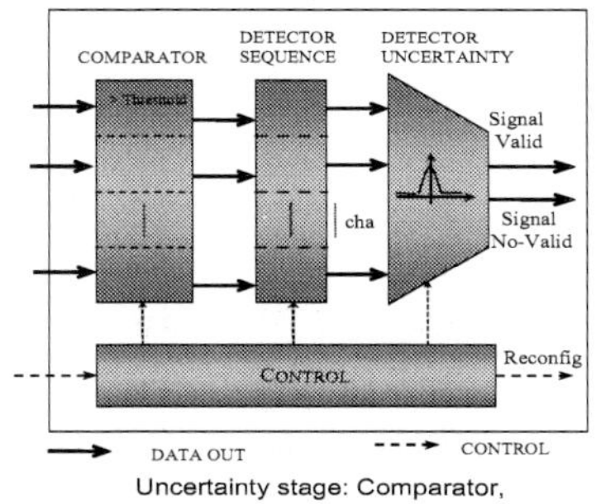

Fig. 21. Uncertainty Module

The system designed is highly parallel and able to execute several tasks at the same time. The networks in our system are also cooperative in order to solve complex issues through small networks. As an example of the system application, the networks can be trained to identify special points on an image. These points are characteristic elements of shape (singularities) such as right-angled corners, round segments and acute-angled corners. These singularities are used for the recognition of rectangular, circular and triangular shapes. Autonomous robots or intelligent systems for cars use this kind of system.

The decision to have the communication of the global control system through a bus structure was taken after consideration of the efficiency level that we wanted to achieve. In this way the memory blocks share the same space on the system and can be accessed with a logic address, having as a result a distributed system of the memories on the networks with a centralized control. The addressing mode was considered to be the optimum model because it does not require a redundant memory for the networks, and only during the reconfiguration process can exists a redundancy in the network memories that have to be reconfigured, achieving a more rapid convergence of the algorithm. See figure 22, for the networks interconnection to the global control.

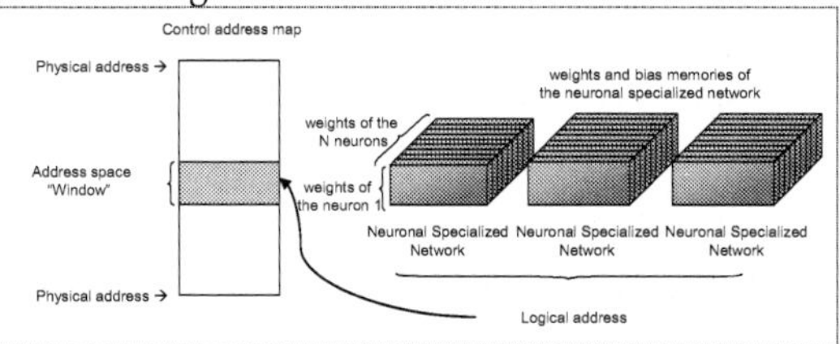

Fig. 22. System Memory Map

The reconfiguration takes place at the moment at which a new image must be recognized. Therefore, the architecture has to be modified, and the new training patterns and the targets added to the memory. When the training process ends, the memories are updated and the network has the recognition connections.

According to the research, there are different forms of reconfiguration on a neural network. During the execution time, the number of neurons on the input layer can be modified or we can give enough knowledge to the network by changing the training memory content. The either of both methods leads us to the image recognition.

Depending on available hardware resources and the applications of the system, a dynamic reconfiguration is possible when the image is part of the same group. Specialized cooperative networks, where installed for reconfiguration to be held in the control section, acquire more knowledge as new images are recognized.

The weight and bias data stored in the memory modules were obtained by the previous off-line learning, using a backpropagation algorithm. Simulation software was developed using Matlab and Simulink, Neural Network Toolbox. In order to obtain the data of the memories of weights, 450 patterns of training with different characteristics have been used, taking into account the fact that all correspond to an image of the same class (rectangular, circular and triangular shapes)

The training method works in batch mode, which means that once all the entries were presented, the learning stage updates the weights and bias according to the decreasing moment of the gradient and an adaptive learning scale.

A region of 6x5 (columns*rows) pixels has been used to detect the singularities. The classification mode has been implemented as a series of regions processing. First, the ROI extractor detects the RoI (Region of Interest), figure 23, sized 60x45 pixels, and stores it in the internal embedded RAM memory. Then, successive vector of characteristic are extracted from the RoI, and sent to the TNN to be processed. So, dividing the RoI in 6x5 sized-regions, results in 10x9 data input vector in one RoI. This is the actual amount of data being processed in each image field, resulting in 90 vectors of 30 pixels each one. This has been accomplished by sweeping the RoI, and by sending each vector of characteristics to the TNN, and by storing the result associated to each region. In this way, probability maps of possible detected singularities are obtained so that the uncertainty stage can decide whether a signal has been detected or not.

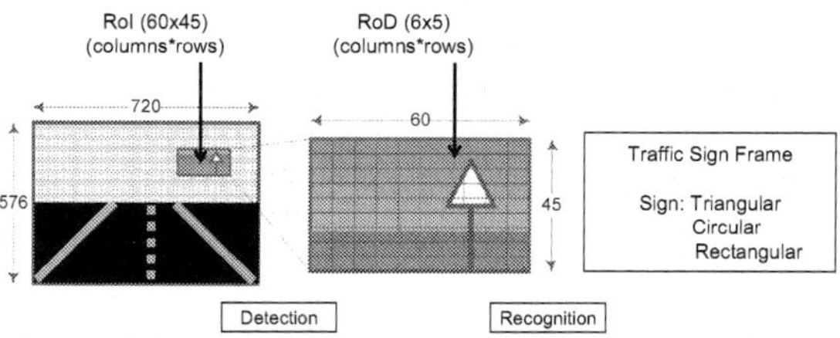

Fig. 23. Traffic Sign Recognition

In addition, further simulations in MATLAB, have established that a Q8.16 format is accurate enough to quantify weights and biases. This reduction in the bit width leads to a reduction in the resources consumed by the network. But more importantly, a great increase in the maximum operating frequency is also achieved. This is a key factor if we want to enhance the system.

As a design premise we have always had in mind a design for reuse methodology. Therefore, a big effort has been made to specify as many generic hardware modules as possible. For this reason, the architecture and VHDL description of the TNN has been improved so that later versions, apart from the basic functionality mentioned above, make possible their building N-layer, m-output perceptrons in the easiest and most-automated way possible. These features have been incorporated so that we shall be able, in the future, to test the system architecture on larger FPGAs.

Preliminary synthesis (no synthesis effort or optimizations directed to the synthesizer) results for Altera CYCLONE EP1C20F400C6 and CYCLONE-II EP2C35F672C6 devices have been obtained with the Altera Quartus II (v. 6.0) software package. The proposed architecture (Q8.16) fits in one CYCLONE device, but remaining resources, mainly memory, are a bit scarce. Therefore, the system has also been implemented in the CYCLONE-II device. Functional and post-fitting simulations with Mentor Graphics ModelSim simulation environment show how the real-time restrictions imposed on the system and the functional specifications are met.

8. Dynamic reconfigurability for scalability in multimedia environments

Multimedia products and services (Alsolaim et al., 2000) must face nowadays to different situations in terms of variable parameters like the available bandwidth, Quality of service (QoS), display size, or battery life, among others. In order to deal with these new scenarios, the standardization committee known as Joint Video Team (JVT), initiated in 2003 the development of a new video coding standard named Scalable Video Coding (SVC), conceived as a scalable solution for different users that may have different needs. The SVC standard represents an extension of the successful H.264/AVC (Advanced Video Coding) standard, as it maintains the video coding techniques introduced in the H.264/AVC encoding loop but incorporating a set of novel tools in order to provide video encoders and decoders with three levels of scalability: temporal scalability, spatial scalability, and video quality scalability. The use of dynamic reconfiguration technology is the main key factor to deal with these exigent characteristics, even more stringent for real-time applications. In particular, the use of an ad-hoc scalable network of reconfigurable nodes able to cope with the requirements imposed by the SVC standard will be proposed. The reconfigurability concept is envisioned within the scope of this research project in a threefold manner:
a) The nodes are composed by a set of reconfigurable Processing Elements (PEs) in charge of performing the computations demanded by the SVC standard. b) PEs communicate among them throughout a reconfigurable Network-on-Chip (NoC); and c) These nodes are communicated by a reconfigurable off-chip wireless network.

Reconfigurable architectures offer a good balance between implementation efficiency and flexibility because they combine post-fabrication programmability with the spatial (parallel) computation style of ASIC platforms and the flexibility of the GPPs (General Purpose Processors).

Embedded and networked systems must perform progressively more complex functions, which require a high level of embedded intelligence. This rise in intelligence force an increase in the level of information processing that the embedded systems carry out, giving as result a significant increase in the complexity of the hardware and software. Due to this, the conception and design of embedded systems for digital signal (video) processing applications in real-time have to face two major points, in many cases opposed one to each other. On one side, a higher level of intelligence is demanded day by day to the systems, and, on the other side, these systems have requirements of real-time operation and reliability, which are difficult to meet in complex systems. The way to be explored in whatever research activity is a) to exploit high-level cognitive architectures in embedded systems, b) to develop systems by model-based processes and c) to develop scalable architectural models that allow maintaining properties of intelligence and reliability across a wide spectrum of implementation platforms. This drives our work necessarily to evolvable hardware. We are carrying on some preliminary studies for using discrete wavelets implemented in hardware in order to achieve embedded intelligence on chip for dynamic reconfigurability for scalability in multimedia environments.

9. Acknowledgement

This work was developed funded by the Spanish Ministry of Science under the National R&D Plan: PROFIT, FIT 110100-2001-10, TRA2004-07441-C03-03/AUT, TEC2008-06846-C02-01/TEC; and by the European Commission ARTEMIS-2008 program: SMART (Secure, Mobile visual sensor networks Architecture). The authors wish also to thank Teresa Riesgo, Ruben Salvador and Jaime Alarcón. Without them all, this document would not have been possible.

10. References

Alarcón, J.; Salvador, R.; Moreno, F. and López, I. A new real-time hardware architecture for road line tracking using a particle filter. *Proceedings of 32nd annual Conference of the IEEE Industrial Electronics Society, IECON'06*, Paris 2006, pp 736-741.

Albus J.S. RCS: A Reference Model Architecture for Intelligent Systems, 1995. In *Working Notes: AAAI 1995 Spring Symposium on Lessons Learned from Implemented Software Architectures for Physical Agents*.

Alsolaim, J.; Beker, M.; Glesner and Starzyk, J. Architecture and Application of a Dynamically Reconfigurable Hardware Array for Future Mobile Communication Systems. *Simposium on Field-Programmable Custom Computing Machines*, Ref: 0-7695-0871-5/00, pp. 205-214, IEEE 2000.

Arulampalam, M.S.; Maskell, S.; Gordon, N. and Clapp, T. A Tutorial on Particle Filters for Online Nonlinear/ Non-Gaussian Bayesian Tracking. *IEEE Transactions on Signal Processing, vol. 50, No. 2 February 2002*.

López, I.; Salvador, R.; Alarcón, J. and Moreno, F. Architectural design for a low cost FPGA-based traffic signal detection system in vehicles. *Volume 65900, pages 65900M. SPIE, 2007*. Gran Canaria. Spain.

Moreno, F.; Aparicio, F.; Hernández, W. and Páez J. A low-cost real-time FPGA solution for driver drowsiness detection. In *Proc. 29th Annual Conference, IEEE Ind. Elect. Society, IECON'03*. Virginia (USA), ISBN:0-7803-7906-3/03.

## 20

Hessian Matrix-Based Shape Extraction and Volume Growing for 3D Polyp Segmentation in CT Colonography

Mark L. Epstein, MS, Ivan Sheu, BS and Kenji Suzuki, PhD
Department of Radiology, Division of Biological Sciences, The University of Chicago
USA

1. Introduction

The size of a lesion is one of the most important features for medical decision-making. The lesion size is usually measured by a clinician, and existing practice relies on size representation using the single longest dimension. There are, however, established variations among clinicians in manual measurement of lesion size, and a recent study implies volume measurement to be more clinically informative than the linear representation (Pickhardt et al., 2005). Volume metrics captures the real growth, and changes in size are amplified compared to those in one dimension. As a further hurdle, modern medical imaging systems produce images on which a polyp appears in a series of 2D slices -- measuring a lesion volume by drawing contours on many medical images is labor-intensive, poorly reproducible, and subjective. An automated volume measurement scheme has the potential to improve efficiency, consistency, and objectivity, avoiding problems of fatigue, variations in hand-eye coordination and subjective decision-making.
Colon cancer is the second leading cause of cancer deaths in the United States (Jemal et al., 2008). In the screening for this disease, lesion size plays an especially important role in determining malignant potential and the need for intervention. In particular, tracking a change in polyp size is an important marker for the clinician. Computed tomography colonography (CTC) is a diagnostic examination that radiologists use for detecting colonic polyps (precursor of colon cancer) (Macari & Bini, 2005). Significantly, the measured size of a polyp at CTC directs clinical treatment, by determining whether results of screening require intervention (Pickhardt et al, 2003). For instance, the current clinical standard is to weigh polyps $\geq$ 10 mm more highly. However, current measurement of the single longest dimension of a polyp is subjective and has variations among radiologists. As evidence of the variability of manual linear measurement of polyps at CTC, studies reported interobserver and intraobserver variations between 16 to 40% (Yeshwant et al., 2006; Taylor et al., 2006; Jeong et al., 2008). As stated earlier, volume measurement could be more clinically informative than longest linear dimension, and this holds true in CTC. However, manual measurement of polyps at CTC suffers from the same inherent problems as lesions in general (labor intensity, poor reproducibility, and subjectivity), and similarly would benefit from automation. As a medical sign frequently occurring in the population, a consistent and

efficient volume metric for polyps at CTC to inform clinical decisions is especially important.

Our purpose in this study was to develop a computerized scheme for segmenting 3D polyps in CTC and evaluate its accuracy and efficiency relative to "gold-standard" volumes determined by manual segmentation.

2. CT Colonography Database

Our CTC database (Table 1) was obtained from a multi-center clinical trial (DC Rockey, et al., The Lancet 2005). Our database consisted of 34 polyp views (17 polyps) in CTC scans from 15 patients. Each patient was scanned in both supine and prone positions with collimations of 1.0-2.5 mm. The image matrix size is 512 x 512 pixels with pixel sizes of 0.5 – 0.7 mm/pixel. Polyp locations were confirmed with reference to optical colonoscopy reports. Polyps were selected by a radiologist with the inclusion criteria of no fuzzy border and being visible in both supine and supine. The mean polyp size at optical colonoscopy was 10 mm, with 10 polyps in a 6-9 mm range, and 7 polyps in a 10-18 mm range.

Table 1. CT Colonography Database (DC Rockey, et al., The Lancet 2005)

Institutions	6 hospitals in the U.S.
Patients	15
Polyps	17 (34 views)
CT system	Multi-detector-row CT system
Slice thickness	1.0 – 2.5 mm
Image matrix size	512 x 512 pixels (0.5 – 0.7 mm/pixel)
Polyp location confirmation	With reference to optical colonoscopy reports
Inclusion criteria	No fuzzy border, visible on supine & prone
Polyp size	Mean 10 mm, 6 – 9 mm (n = 10), 10 – 18 mm (n = 7)

3. Establishment of the "Gold Standard"

Here is our protocol for establishing the "gold standard". A radiologist manually outlined the polyp in each 2D axial slice. High quality magnification enabled drawing precise contours. Volumes were calculated by summation of the enclosed areas. Three measurements were made, each at least one week apart, to reduce a memory effect bias. The average of the three trials was used as the "gold standard". Furthermore, the prone and supine volumes were averaged for the purposes of results analysis. An example of a manually outlined polyp is shown in Fig. 1.

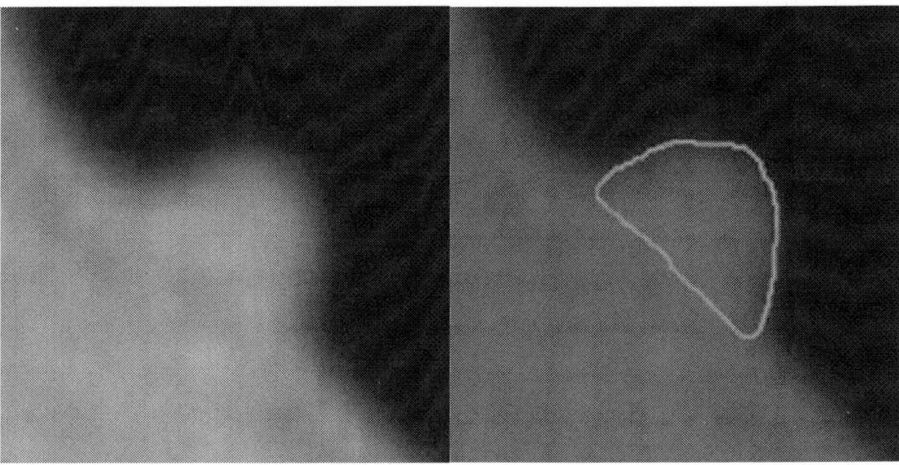

Fig. 1. Example of manually outlined polyp.

4. Automated Segmentation

A high-level flow chart of our automated polyp segmentation scheme is shown in Fig. 2. The scheme takes as input the CTC image data. The steps are: segmentation of the colon; extraction of a highly polyp-like seed region based on the Hessian matrix; segmentation of polyps by use of a 3D volume-growing technique; and sub-voxel refinement to reduce a bias of segmentation.

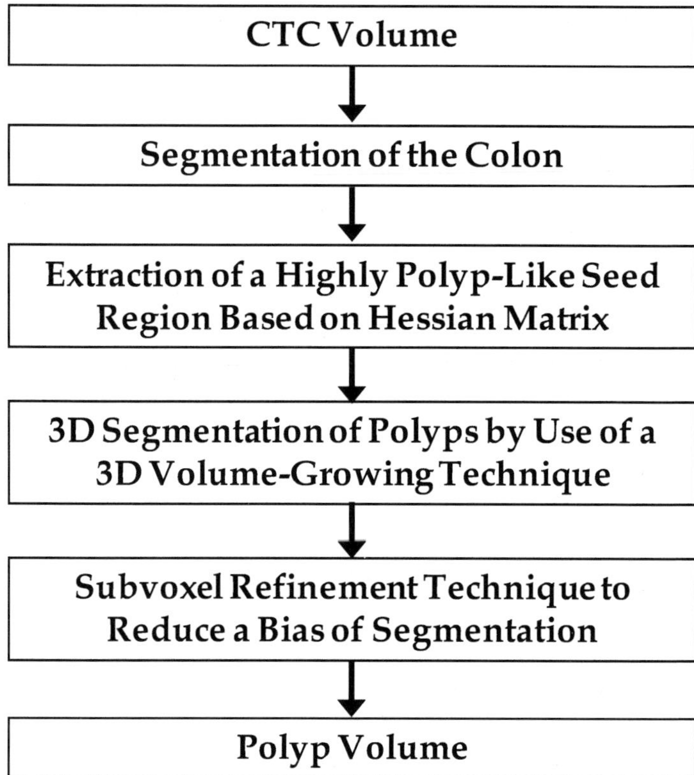

Fig. 2. Flow chart of our automated segmentation scheme.

A more detailed map of our segmentation scheme, showing sub-step intermediates, is given in Fig. 3. The reader is encouraged to refer to both the high-level flow chart and the detailed map while following the description of the scheme.

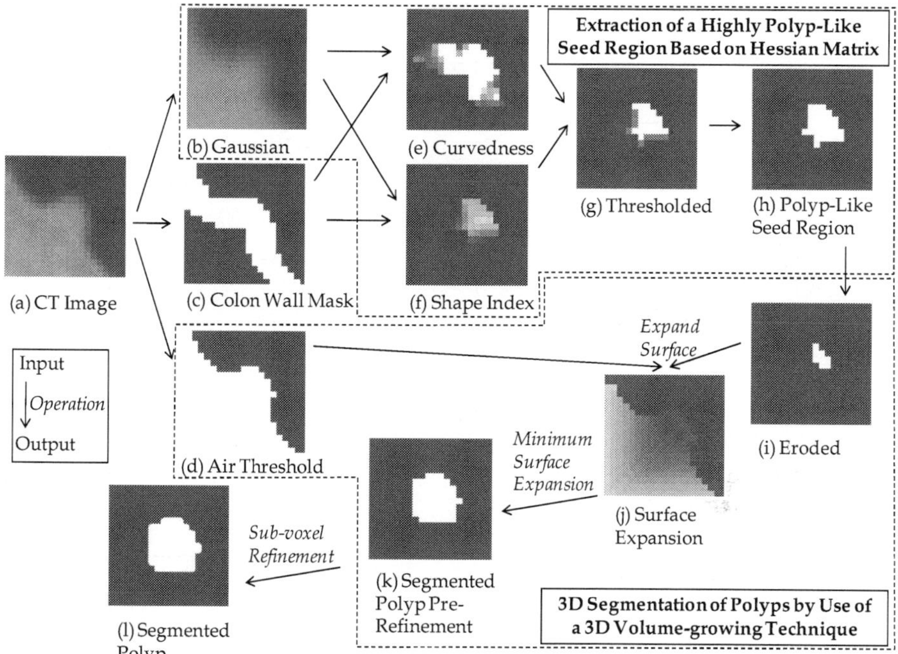

Fig. 3. Pictorial diagram of our segmentation algorithm.

The original 3D CT data are anisotropic such that an image voxel (i.e., a 3D pixel) is longer in the z direction than it is in the x and y directions. We account for this by generating isotropic 3D data (Fig. 3a). The isotropic volumes are generated by resampling the original 3D CT data through linear interpolation.

To confine our initial stages of polyp segmentation to the appropriate anatomical region, i.e., the colon, we next segment the colon wall with uniform thickness by using anatomical knowledge-based segmentation (Masutani et al., 2001; Yoshida et al., 2001) (Fig. 3c).

The next step of the scheme leverages the characteristic rounded shape of a bulbous polyp (Fig. 4 through Fig. 6). To reduce the effect of image noise, we apply a Gaussian smoothing filter (Fig. 3b). Our detection scheme relies on shape features; as an intermediate step, we apply a Hessian matrix operator which quantifies the local curvature in the 3D image (Dorai & Jain, 1997). The principal curvatures at a point describe the maximum and minimum rates that the local surface deviates from a plane. Two feature images can be derived from the principal curvatures, that together provide a measurement of the local shape and the "degree of the shape" at a point. These are known as shape index (Fig. 3f) and curvedness (Fig. 3e) (Yoshida et al., 2001). Shape index and curvedness are defined as

$$SI(p) \equiv \frac{1}{2} - \frac{1}{\pi} \arctan \frac{\kappa_1(p) + \kappa_2(p)}{\kappa_1(p) - \kappa_2(p)}, \tag{1}$$

$$CV(p) \equiv \sqrt{\frac{\kappa_1(p)^2 + \kappa_2(p)^2}{2}} \tag{2}$$

where κ_1, κ_2 represent the maximum and minimum curvatures, respectively. In this step, two feature images are created, whose quantities represent shape index and curvedness.

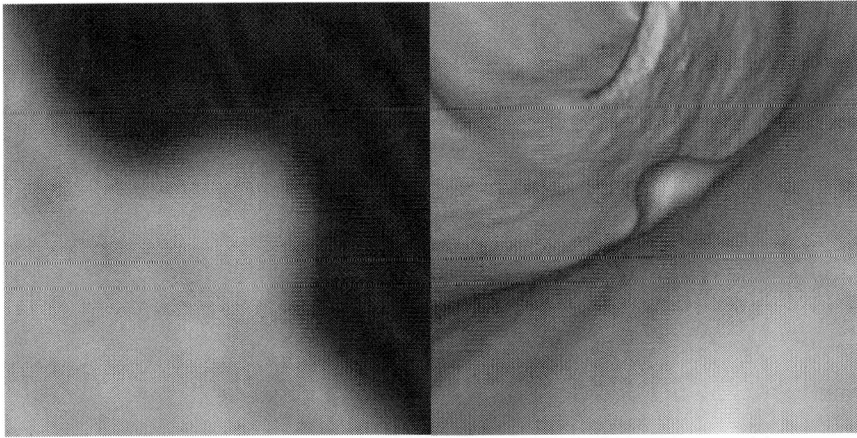

Fig. 4. Case 1 – polyp displayed in 2D axial and 3D endoluminal views.

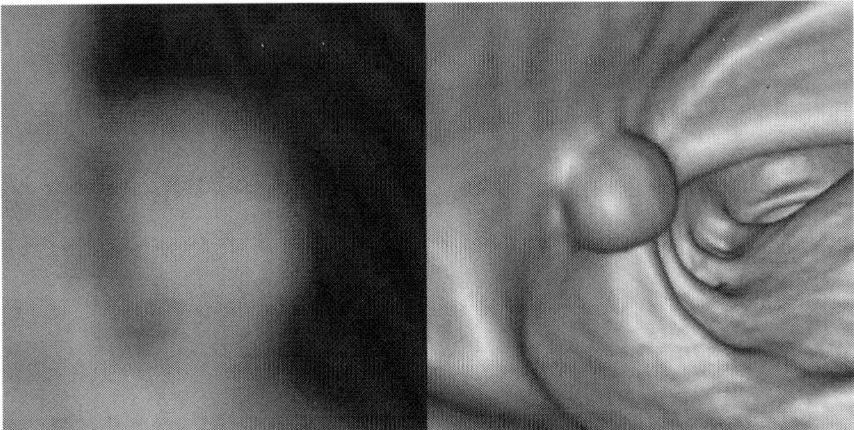

Fig. 5. Case 2 – polyp displayed in 2D axial and 3D endoluminal views.

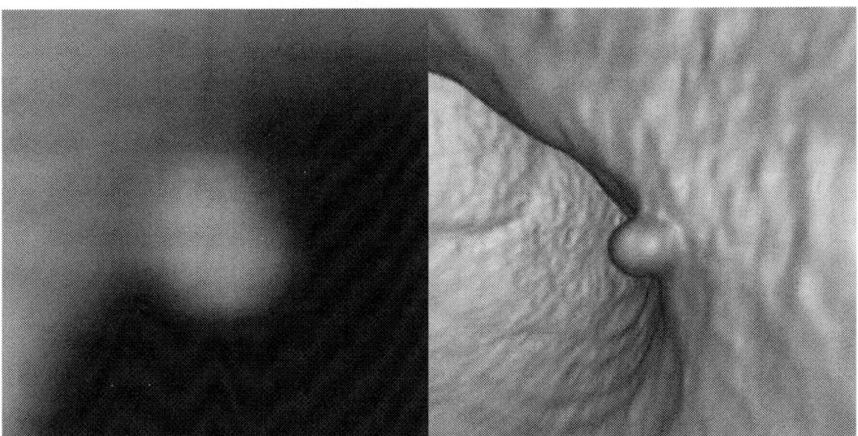

Fig. 6. Case 3 – polyp displayed in 2D axial and 3D endoluminal views.

The two Hessian matrix-based feature images are used together to extract a cap-shape
structure that is typical of a bulbous polyp. To achieve this, first we run two range threshold
operations on each feature images. The first range threshold is narrower than the second.
The narrow range threshold operation results in a set or sets of very highly polyp-like
voxels. The two narrow range threshold images are combined by a Boolean logical
multiplication; the two wide range threshold images are similarly combined (Fig. 3g). We
then perform a connectivity analysis based on a connected-component labeling algorithm,
e.g., (Suzuki, Horiba et al., 2003; He, Chao, Suzuki et al., 2008) to allow the narrow range
threshold region to grow to include any connected wider range threshold voxels. The result
is a set of highly polyp-like regions localized on the cap-shape parts of polyps (Fig. 3h). A
seed point may be manually provided by the user to select a single region of interest.
Another way to envision the feature thresholding process is to think of the more relaxed
range threshold operation as running first, and then eliminating regions which do not
contain any voxels with values in the stricter range.
The polyp segmentation is still incomplete at this stage because the current region only
includes the cap-shape region voxels that have the shape index and curvedness values
within the designated range, such as the peripheral region of the polyp. For the next stage,
we developed a segmentation technique based on region growing (Shapiro and Stockman
2001) to segment the remaining, non-cap-shape region. This stage of our segmentation
algorithm is called 3D volume growing based on rate of lumen-prohibited expansion. First
we employ an air threshold of the original CT image to distinguish the lumen from non-
lumen (Fig. 3d). Second we load our seed region of highly polyp-like voxels obtained from
the previous process (Fig. 3h). Third, we iteratively expand within the *non-lumen* for a
predetermined 'k' number of iterations, while tracking the volume (Fig. 3j). Finally we find
the region in which the volume expansion rate was the minimum (Fig. 3k). Expressed in set
notation, the minimum volume expansion point occurs at the xth iterative expansion when
$\{W_x\} < \{W_i\}$ for i = 1, 2, ... k, where W is the set of expanded pixels.
The volume expansion rate minimum is chosen because this is the state where the polyp has
been more completely segmented and it occurs before over-segmentation dominates. Up to

the volume expansion rate minimum, the surface expansion iterations are including nearby non-cap-shape voxels of the polyp. After the volume expansion rate minimum is reached, an ever-increasing volume expansion rate is observed while non-polyp voxels are added to the growing region. Therefore, the volume expansion rate minimum conveniently marks the transition in mode from inclusion of mainly polyp voxels to mainly non-polyp voxels. This point is best suited for capturing a region to proceed to the next stage of segmentation.

After collecting the gold standard and automated volumes, we determine that the automated volumes are on average smaller than the gold volumes. To reduce this bias of segmentation, we uniformly apply a 3D sub-voxel refinement technique (Fig. 3l and Fig. 7). The binary image shown represents a computer-segmented polyp. The grid lines indicate the original voxel size. First we resample the image to a higher resolution; a resampling factor of X, therefore, means that one original voxel is converted to X^3 voxels in the resampled image. Next we dilate the image by a specified radius, using a spherical kernel. The radius chosen was determined by the magnitude of the segmentation bias. The resulting region represents our computer-segmented polyp. Finally we calculate the volume, accounting for the resampling.

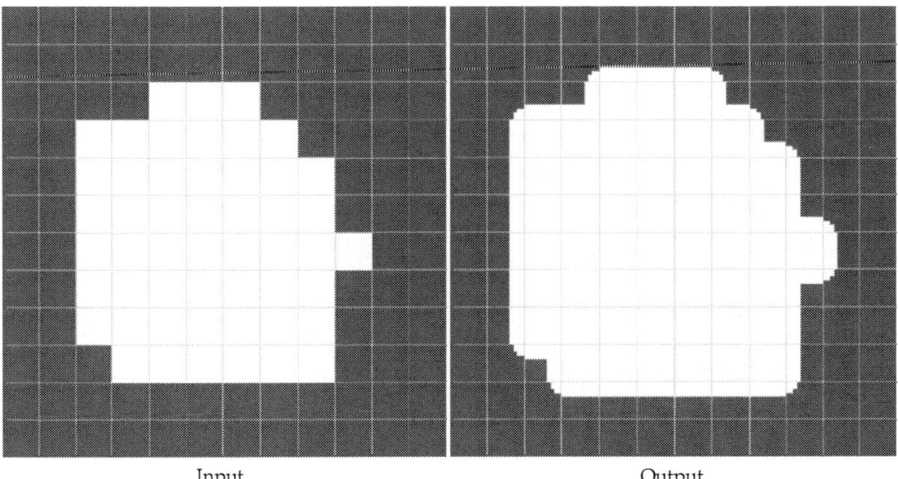

Fig. 7. Illustration of the sub-voxel refinement.

5. Quantitative Analysis

Our measurement scheme yielded a mean polyp volume of 0.36 cc with a range of 0.15 to 1.24 cc, whereas the mean "gold standard" manual volume was 0.38 cc with a range of 0.14 - 1.08 cc (Table 2). The mean differences between automated and manual volumes for polyps ranging from 6-9 mm and those 10 mm or larger (by optical colonoscopy) were 23.4% and 17.5% with standard deviations (SD) of 19.2% and 17.6%, respectively (Table 3). These differences were comparable to the intra-observer variation of 14.0% with SD of 13.1%. The two volumetrics reached excellent agreement (intra-class correlation coefficient was 0.79) with no statistically significant difference (P = 0.61).

Table 2. Mean and range of volumes by automated and "gold-standard" manual segmentation

	Mean	Range
Manually traced volumes	0.38 cc	0.14 – 1.08 cc
Automated volumes	0.36 cc	0.15 – 1.24 cc

Table 3. Volume comparison between manual and automated segmentation; comparable to intra-observer variation of manual segmentation

	Mean ± SD
Absolute percent difference between automated and manual volumes for polyps 6-9 mm	23.4% ± 19.2%
Absolute percent difference between automated and manual volumes for polyps ≥ 10 mm	17.5% ± 17.6%
Intra-observer variation for manual volumes	14.0% ± 13.1%

6. Case Examples

Computer vs. manual contour comparison for Case 1 is shown in Fig. 8 for both supine and prone views. In this case, the automated volume is very close to the gold standard volume.

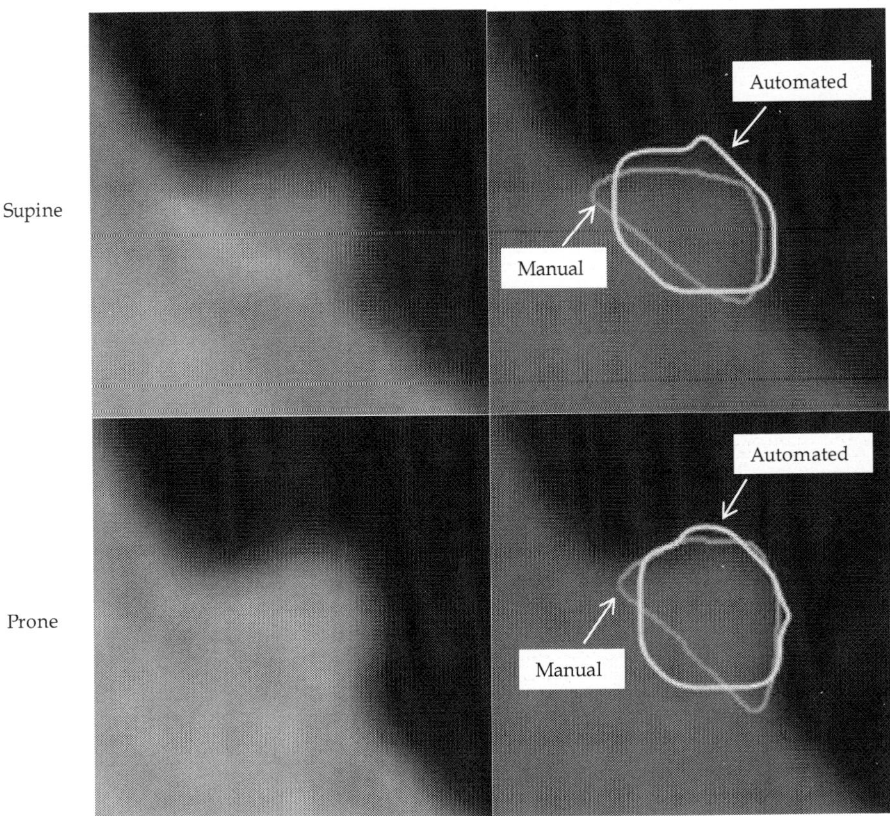

Fig. 8. Case 1: Comparison between automated and manual segmentation (prone "gold standard" manual volume = 0.21 cc; prone automated volume = 0.19 cc; supine "gold standard" manual volume = 0.15 cc; supine automated volume = 0.17 cc).

Computer vs. manual contour comparisons for two additional cases are shown in Fig. 9 and Fig. 10. The automated segmentation tended to include more of the low-intensity border at the colon-air interface, whereas it included less of the polyp's base than did the manual segmentation. The automated segmentation is fairly accurate for Cases 1 through 3.

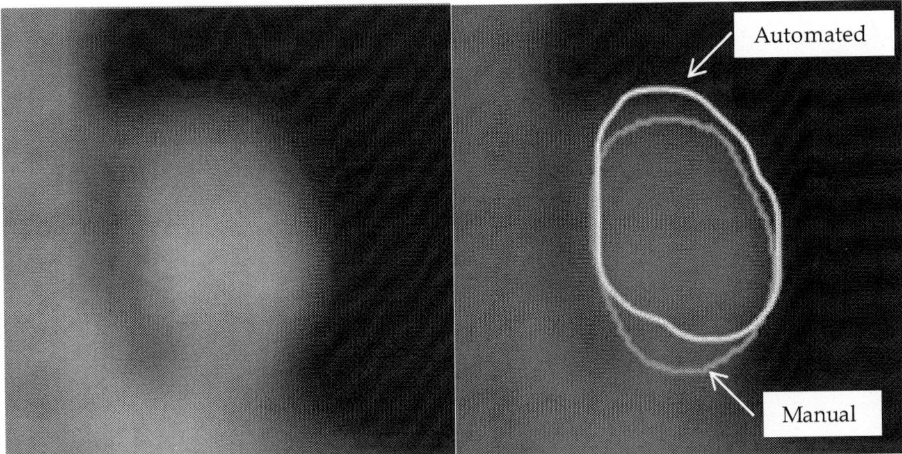

Fig. 9. Case 2 Prone: Comparison between automated and manual segmentation ("gold standard" manual volume = 0.34 cc; automated volume = 0.27 cc).

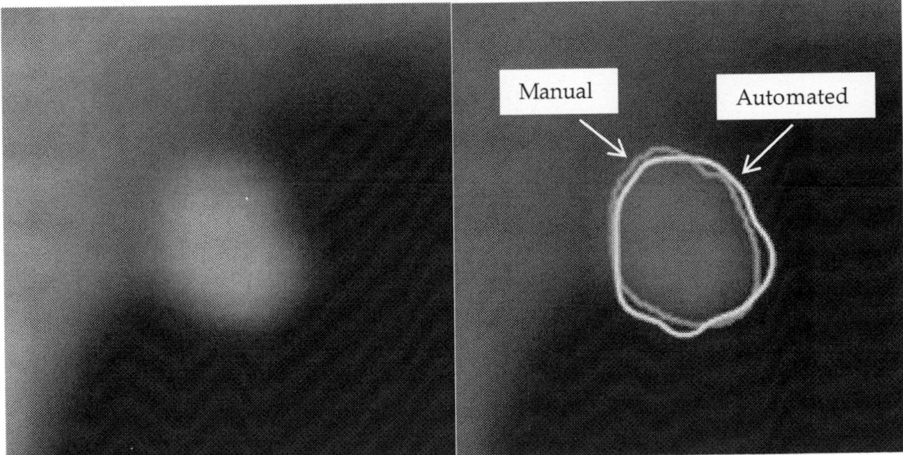

Fig. 10. Case 3 Supine: Comparison between automated and manual segmentation ("gold standard" manual volume = 0.17 cc; automated volume = 0.15 cc).

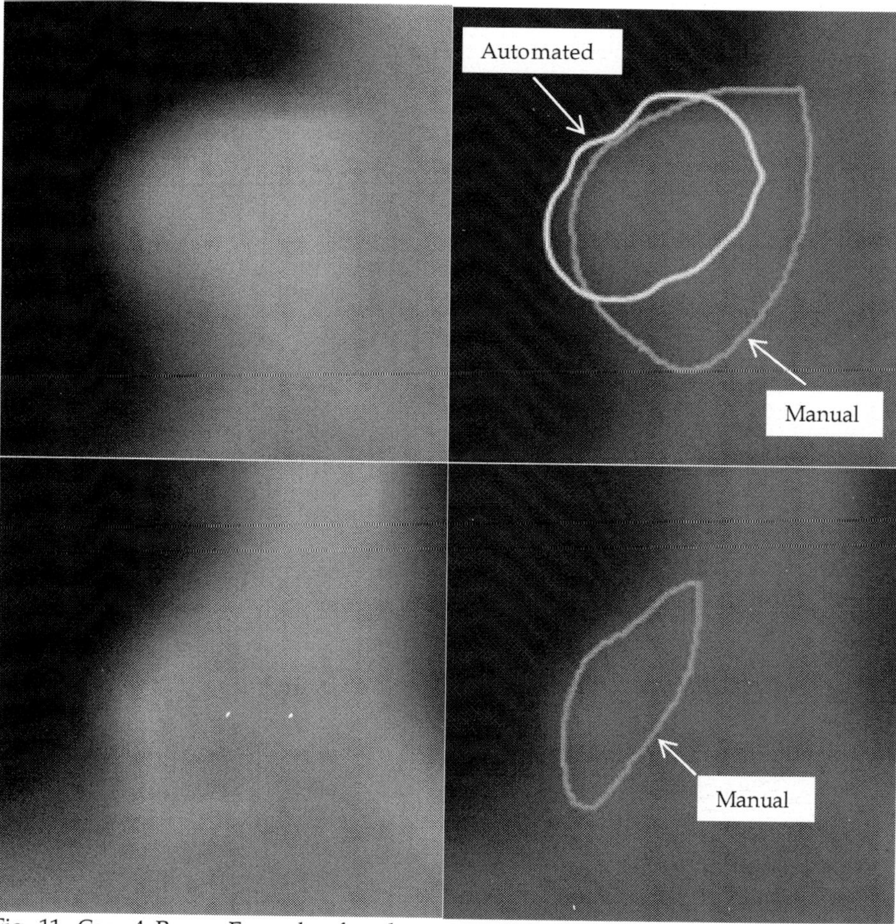

Fig. 11. Case 4 Prone: Example of under-segmentation by the automated segmentation, showing two slices ("gold standard" manual volume = 0.36 cc; automated volume = 0.19 cc).

Our algorithm may leave out parts of a polyp with indefinite borders or subtle morphology. An example of under-segmentation is represented by two slices of Case 4 in Fig. 11. In this polyp view, the computer under-segmented by missing part of the base and subtle peripheral regions.

We compared computer volumes against gold standard volumes and prone volumes against supine volumes and found generally good correlation. In the comparison of automated (computer) volume vs. "gold standard" manual volume, two outliers exist as a result of morphological features of the polyps: over-segmentation and under-segmentation. In the under-segmentation case, the bulb of a large, pedunculated polyp rested on the colon wall. In the over-segmentation case was an oblong, sessile polyp on a haustral fold.

In the comparison of prone vs. supine volumes of computer-segmented polyps, although the correlation is generally good, the two most significant outliers are caused by a change of polyp shape between the two patient positions. These polyps appear more bulbous in one view, and thus the segmentation is more accurate, but they appear subtler in the other view, which results in under-segmentation.

7. Conclusion

To put it in perspective, the advantages over manual volumetry are that an automated process is efficient, objective, and consistent, with one mouse click versus five minutes of manual drawing.

A limitation of automated volumetry is that the process occasionally results in mis-segmentation. This requires manual modification to fix, but it may retain some efficiency benefit within a semi-automated approach.

Polyp volumes obtained by our automated scheme agreed excellently with "gold standard" manual volumes. Our fully automated scheme efficiently can provide accurate polyp volumes for radiologists; thus, it would help radiologists improve the accuracy and efficiency of polyp volume measurements in CTC. Our scheme is potentially applicable to accurately segmenting 3D bulbous objects in 3D volumes.

Combining automated volume measurement with computer-aided detection of polyps (Suzuki, Yoshida et al., 2006; Suzuki, Yoshida et al., 2008) would provide radiologists even more efficient and accurate way of detection of polyps in CTC.

8. Acknowledgements

This study was supported by: The University of Chicago Cancer Research Center Support Grant; Grant Number R01CA120549 from the National Cancer Institute/National Institutes of Health, and SIRAF Cluster Funding in research.

9. References

Dorai, C; Jain, A.K (1997). "COSMOS – A Representation Scheme for 3D Free-Form Objects", *IEEE Transactions on Pattern Analysis and Machine Intelligence* 19(10):1115-1130.

He, L., Y. Chao, et al. (2008). "A run-based two-scan labeling algorithm." *IEEE Trans Image Process* 17(5): 749-56.

Jemal, A.; Siegel, R.; Ward, E.; Hao, Y.; Xu, J.; Murray, T.; Thun, M.J. (2008). "Cancer Statistics, 2008", *CA – A Cancer Journal for Clinicians* 58(2):71-96.

Jeong, J.Y.; Kim, M.J.; Kim, S.S. (2008). "Manual and Automated Polyp Measurement: Comparison of CT Colonography With Optical Colonoscopy", *Academic Radiology* 15(2):231-239.

Macari, M.; Bini, E.J. (2005). "CT colonography: Where have we been and where are we going?" *Radiology* 237(3):819-833.

Masutani, Y.; Yoshida, H.; MacEneaney, P.M.; Dachman, A.H. (2001). "Automated Segmentation of Colonic Walls for Computerized Detection of Polyps in CT Colonography", *Journal of Computer Assisted Tomography* 25(4):629-638.

Pickhardt, P.J.; Choi, J.R.; Hwang, I.; Butler, J.A.; Puckett, M.L.; Hildebrandt, H.A.; Wong, R.K.; Nugent, P.A.; Mysliwiec, P.A.; Schindler, W.R. (2003). "Computed Tomographic Virtual Colonoscopy to Screen for Colorectal Neoplasia in Asymptomatic Adults", *The New England Journal of Medicine* 349(23):2191-2200.

Pickhardt, P.J.; Lehman, V.T.; Winter, T.C.; Taylor, A.J. (2005). "Polyp Volume Versus Linear Size Measurements at CT Colonography: Implications for Noninvasive Surveillance of Unresected Colorectal Lesions", *Gastrointestinal Imaging* 186(6):1605-1610.

Shapiro, L. G. and G. C. Stockman (2001). Computer Vision. New Jersey, Prentice-Hall: 279-325.

Suzuki, K.; I. Horiba; Sugie, N.. (2003). "Linear-time connected-component labeling based on sequential local operations." *Computer Vision and Image Understanding* 89(1): 1-23.

Suzuki, K., H. Yoshida, et al. (2006). "Massive-training artificial neural network (MTANN) for reduction of false positives in computer-aided detection of polyps: Suppression of rectal tubes." *Med Phys* 33(10): 3814-24.

Suzuki, K., H. Yoshida, et al. (2008). "Mixture of expert 3D massive-training ANNs for reduction of multiple types of false positives in CAD for detection of polyps in CT colonography." *Med Phys* 35(2): 694-703.

Taylor, S.A.; Slater, A.; Halligan, S.; Honeyfield, L.; Roddie, M.E.; Demeshski, J.; Amin, H.; Burling, D. (2006). *Radiology* 242(1):120-128.

Yeshwant, S.C.; Summers, R.M.; Yao, J.; Brickman, D.S.; Choi, J.R.; Pickhards, P.J (2006). "Polyps: Linear and Volumetric Measurement at CT Colonography", *Radiology* 241(3):802-811.

Yoshida, H. and J. Nappi (2001). "Three-dimensional computer-aided diagnosis scheme for detection of colonic polyps." *IEEE Trans Med Imaging* 20(12): 1261-74.

## 21

3D Reconstruction of Brain Tumors from Endoscopic and Ultrasound Images

Ruben Machucho-Cadena and Eduardo Bayro-Corrochano
CINVESTAV, Unidad Guadalajara,
Department of Electrical Engineering and Computer Science
Jalisco, México
rmachuch,edb@gdl.cinvestav.mx

1. Introduction

1.1 Statement of the Problem

Endo-neuro-sonography (ENS) has gained special attention in recent years. Its major advantages over traditional brain surgery are that it is a minimally invasive surgical technique and the endoscopic camera and ultrasound images provide useful information. Ultrasound images are inexpensive compared to tomographic and resonance magnetic images (which are very hard to obtain in an intraoperative setting) and allow surgeons to see beyond the tissues within the brain. Another way would be to extract three-dimensional (3D) information from the combined endoscopic and ultrasound images to help surgeons better locate brain structures (such as tumors). Some work has been done in this direction, mainly in the replacement of classic ultrasound (2D imaging methodology) by 3D ultrasound equipment (Unsgaard et al., 2006). We have focused our attention on using classic ultrasound techniques and endoscopic images to extract 3D information. We propose tracking the ultrasound probe in the endoscopic images and then computing the ultrasound probe's pose in 3D space without an external method (optical or magnetic). We tested two alternative methods to track the ultrasound probe in endoscopic camera images as well as two methods to segment brain structures in ultrasound images, and then we compared the latter two types. We used conformal geometric algebra for the necessary geometric calculations and to put the results in 3D space.

1.2 Outline of Our Method

The equipment setup is as follows: The ultrasound probe is introduced through a channel in the endoscope and is seen by the endoscopic camera. With visual tracking equipment (Polaris), we can calculate the 3D position of the endoscope tip; we want to know the ultrasound (US) probe's pose in order to have the exact location of the US sensor. This is important because the US probe is flexible and rotate on its own axis. It can also move back and forth, and since the channel is wider, there is also random movement around the channel (Fig. 1). The US probe is connected to a drive unit for a micro-tip transducer; the transducer is rotated to generate a $360°$ beam at 10 MHz. By tracking the US probe in the endoscopic image in successive video frames, we can use multiple-view 3D estimation techniques to find the pose of the US probe's axis. With this pose and the exact location of the endoscope's tip, we can estimate the 3D coordinates of the US probe's tip. This is fundamental since the US image is orthogonal to the US probe's axis (see Fig. 2). We know that in one small interval of time x, the ultrasound probe is fixed, and the endoscopic camera undergoes a movement that is equivalent to an inverse motion, that is, the endoscopic camera is fixed, and the ultrasound probe undergoes a movement. In Figs. 1 and 2, we showed the 3D virtual representation of the phantom brain used for the experiments. This model was constructed with magnetic resonance images of the phantom.

1.3 Structure of the Chapter

This chapter is organized as follows. Section 2 describes the techniques used to track the ultrasound probe in the endoscopic images. Two alternative methods are presented: saturation thresholding and particle filtering. Section 3 is devoted to ultrasound image processing. We present a method based on morphological operators to segment brain structures and compare its performance versus level-set methods. Section 4 describes how to calculate the 3D pose of the probe using conformal geometric algebra (CGA) and multiple-view methods. We present our conclusions in Section 5.

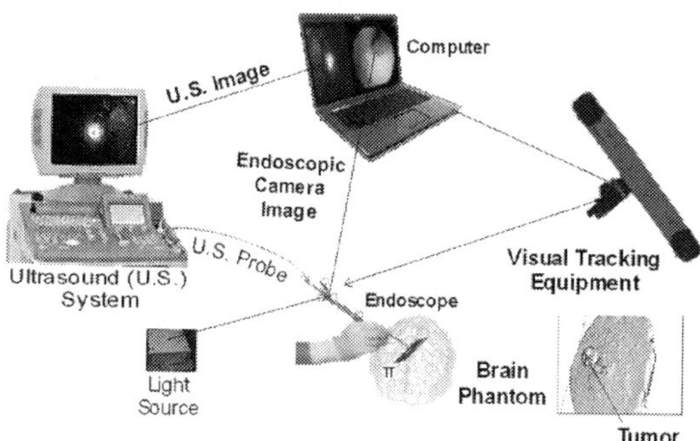

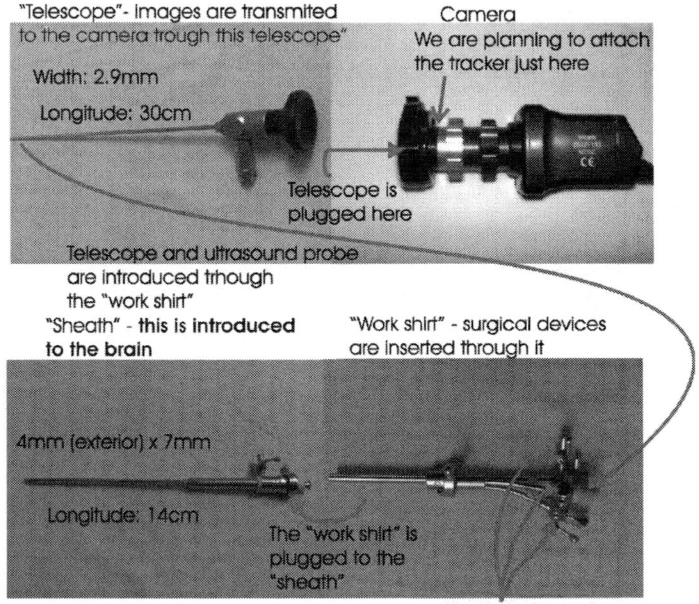

Fig. 1. ENS equipment setup.

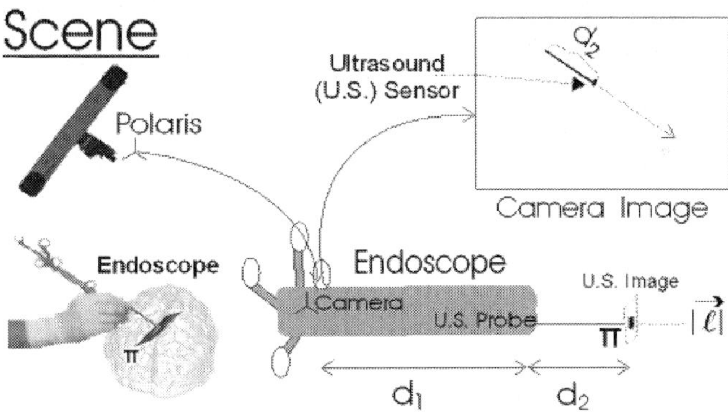

Fig. 2. Scene for the virtual representation. The plane π that is to be calculated contains the US image to be segmented and is orthogonal to the unit vector $\bar{\ell}$.

2. Endoscopic Image Processing

2.1 Tracking the Ultrasound Probe

The goal here is tracking the US probe that is seen in the endoscopic camera images. To achieve this, we use two alternative techniques: saturation thresholding and particle filters. The goal is to track the axis line of the US probe throughout the images. Knowing this line is important because it allows us to compute its 3D coordinates using the camera's projection matrix. Such a projection is done as follows: Every line is backprojected to form a plane in the space, which contains the line and the camera's center. Using two consecutive images, the intersection of its respective planes will yield the line in 3D (Hartley & Zisserman, 2004). To obtain a more accurate result, we take only the unitary vector of this line (because the calculation of the translation in the projection matrix is up to a scalar factor). We translate the first point (the tip of the endoscope) obtained by the Polaris lecture by a distance d_2 (see Fig. 2) along the direction of the unitary vector in the direction of the previously obtained line, and this translated point will be the position of the US sensor in 3D, making it possible to obtain the plane π to make the virtual representation. The d_2 distance is taken from two retroprojected points of the US probe in the 3D space, these points are begin and end of the tracked US probe in each pair of images. Polaris gives us the linear transformation between its frame and the attached tracker to the endoscopic camera and, to calculate the linear transformation between the tracker and the image frame, we use the hand–eye calibration method (Bayro-Corrochano & Daniilidis, 1996). Now we give a brief overview of the saturation thresholding and particle filter methods that were independently used to track the axis of the US probe.

2.2 Saturation Thresholding

The saturation thresholding method can help segment objects like ultrasound probes. Images are converted from RGB (Red, Green, Blue) format to HSV (Hue, Saturation, Value). $V = \max(R,G,B)$; $S = 255*(V - \min(R,G,B))/V$ if $V \neq 0$; otherwise, $S = 0$. Figure 3(a) and (b) show the saturation histogram and saturation image, respectively. Selecting all values inside [58, 255] yields the binary image in Fig. 3(c). We use the chain code to calculate the smallest and largest areas that should be eliminated, as shown in Fig. 3(d). The ultrasound probe can be described by two line segments indicating its contour. The main axis is calculated as the average segment. We cast rays from the region support endpoints and select the two rays that best encompass the segmented region [see Fig. 4(a)]. A good candidate is the ray containing more background pixels than segmented pixels. The results are shown in Fig. 4(b), which displays the main axis of the ultrasound probe.

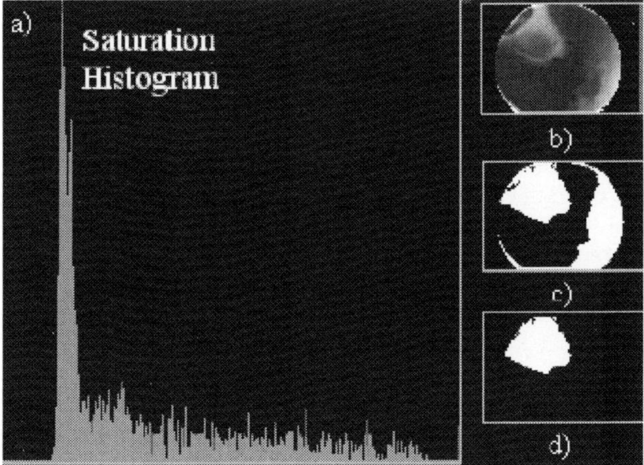

Fig. 3. Saturation histogram.

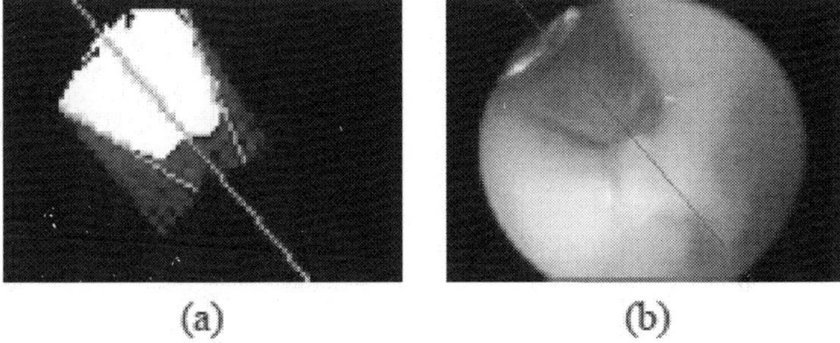

Fig. 4. Estimated line using saturation thresholding.

2.3 Tracking with Particle Filters

Another approach to perform visual tracking is to use a Bayesian tracker, thus treating motion tracking as a Bayesian state-estimation problem. In order to use a Bayesian framework, one must model the object being tracked as a state vector. Also needed is a method to evaluate how well the predicted states of the state vector fit the observation. The most widely used Bayesian tracker is the Kalman filter. However, Kalman filters require a Gaussian observation probability and a Gaussian posterior probability density. Our observations show that the random movement of the ultrasound probe can hardly be described as Gaussian. This situation made us look for a more general tracker: the particle filter.

2.3.1 The Particle Filter

Particle filters emerged from the pioneer work of Isard and Blake (1998). These filters were introduced to track objects in visual clutter and can handle multimodal observation probabilities.

Let's assume that x_t represents the state (state vector) of the object at time t and that $X_t = \{x_1,\ldots,x_t\}$ represents its history over time. The vector $Z_t = \{z_1,\ldots,z_t\}$ encloses all the observations z_i up to time t. In our framework, z_t represents an endoscopic image at time t. The particle filter approximates the posterior $p(x_t|Z_t)$ of the probability distribution. The key idea in particle filtering is to approximate the probability distribution (and consequently the posterior) by a weighted finite set of samples, the particles. Let $S = \left\{\left(s_t^{(n)}, \pi_t^{(n)}\right)\middle|\, n = 1,\ldots, N\right\}$ be a weighted set of N different samples. Every sample $s^{(i)}$ represents a possible object state, and a weight $\pi^{(i)}$ is associated with it. This weight represents the likelihood for the associated particle to be the true location of the target object. The weights are normalized so that $\sum_{i=1}^{N} \pi^{(n)} = 1$.

By applying Bayes' law, the posterior $p(x_t|Z_t)$ can be recursively expressed as

$$p(x_t|Z_t) = k_t\, p(z_t|x_t)\, p(x_t|Z_{t-1}). \tag{1}$$

With the state vector at time $t-1$, the posterior $p(x_{t-1}|Z_{t-1})$ can be obtained by marginalizing over x_{t-1}, making it possible to obtain the distribution $p(x_t|Z_{t-1})$:

$$p(x_t|Z_{t-1}) = \int_{x_{t-1}} p(x_t, x_{t-1}|Z_{t-1}) = \int_{x_{t-1}} p(x_t, x_{t-1})\, p(x_{t-1}|Z_{t-1}), \tag{2}$$

where the chain rule was applied [$p(x_t|x_{t-1})$ is the dynamic model]. To perform the filtering operation, a new set of particles is created by selecting with replacement N particles from the N particles created at time $t-1$. The probability of selecting a particle $s^{(i)}$ is proportional to its normalized weight $\pi^{(i)}$. Then the new particles are updated using the system's evolution model. The new weights for the updated particles are calculated, measuring how well the object position represented by each particle fits with the observation z_t at time t. After the weights are normalized, the mean state is estimated at each time by $E[S] = \sum_{n=1}^{N} \pi^{(n)} s^{(n)}$.

Subsequent locations of the probe can be represented as a rotation and translation with respect to the initial line estimate. A state vector can be represented as $s^{(i)} = \left[d_x^{(i)}, d_y^{(i)}, d_\theta^{(i)}\right]$, with its components describing this translation and rotation. This model evolves in each stage according to

$$S_t = S_{t-1} + N_t,\tag{3}$$

where N_t is white Gaussian noise.

To obtain the weight of each particle, the image of the area selected in the first picture is obtained and rotated and translated according to the particle's (state vector) components. The transformed image is then compared to the observed image by means of the Bhattacharyya distance between their color histograms, as described by Nummiaro et al. (2003).

2.4 Tracking Results

The saturation thresholding (ST) method was applied as explained, and the particle filter was applied using up to $N = 300$ particles, but little difference is observed in the results when $N > 100$. Several images and sequences have been tested. Figure 5 shows the results for the particle filter method. Both tracking methods described performed well in practice. However, we prefer the ST method (Section 2.2) because it is faster and also because the particle filter method is nondeterministic. We obtained an accuracy of 94% with the ST method.

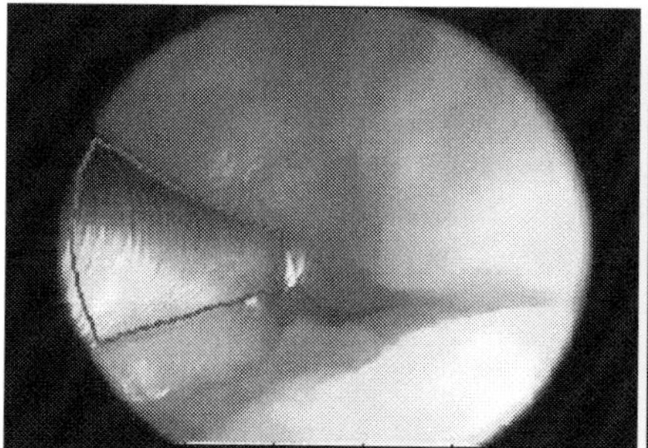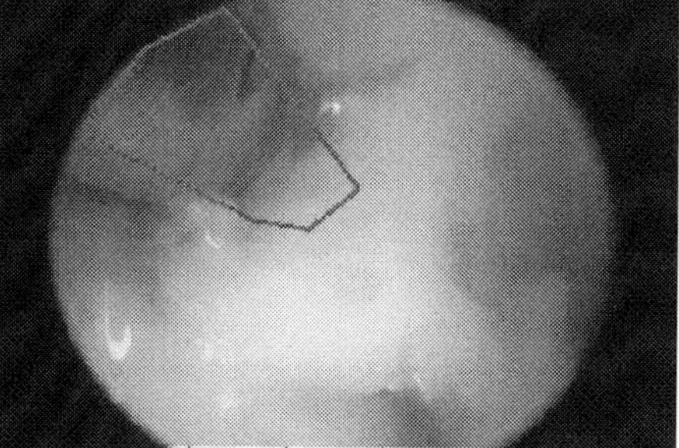

Fig. 5. The results for the particle filter method.

3. Ultrasound Image Processing

The goal in this stage is to segment interesting structures in the brain images, such as tumors. We used two methods in order to process the ultrasound images; the first is based on morphological operators (Castleman, 1996), and the second is the level-set method.

3.1 Segmentation of the Tumor Using Morphological Operators

We are using morphological operators in order to fill small holes that appear due to the subsampling provided by the Aloka ultrasound system. The closing morphological operator of image I with subimage M (structuring element) is defined as $I \cdot M = (I \oplus M) \otimes M$, where $\oplus$ and $\otimes$ represent the dilatation and erosion morphological operators, respectively.

We process the ultrasound images in the following way:

Copy the original image (do not modify it); select a region of interest (ROI); otherwise, the ROI will be the complete image. The ROI will be the same for all images.

If the ROI contains either a section of or the entire central part of the image, we exclude that part of the ROI because it only contains noise.

Normalize the ROI to minimize the contrast/brightness influence.

Apply a threshold to the gray levels of the ROI, to select only the highest levels.

Apply a closing morphological operator to fill the holes of the ROI.

Use the chain code to calculate the smallest areas of the ROI, and eliminate them.

Apply a logical AND operation between the ROI and the original image. The result is the segmented tumor, which is to be represented in 3D.

To normalize image I_0 and to obtain $I(x, y)$, we used the following equations:

$$I_p(x, y) = \frac{I_0(x, y) - \bar{I}_0}{\max(I_0) - \min(I_0)},$$

$$I(x, y) = 255 * \frac{I_p - \min(I_p)}{\max(I_p) - \min(I_p)}, \tag{4}$$

where $\bar{I}_0$ is the mean of the image intensity and the number 255 represents the maximum gray level in the image. Figure 6 shows an example of the segmented tumor in ultrasound images.

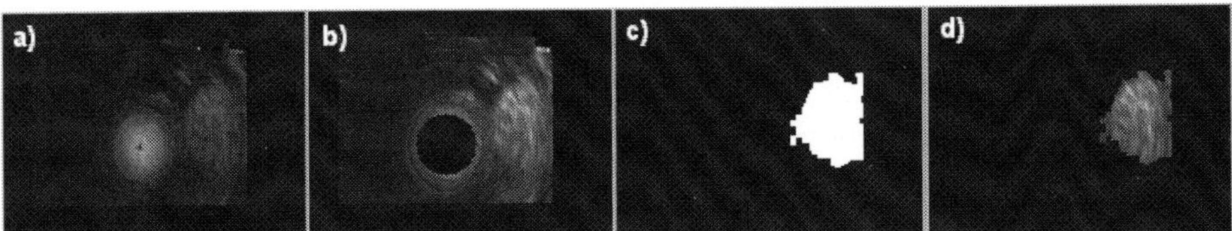

Fig. 6. Isolating the tumor. (a) Original US image to be segmented. (b) The central part of the image is excluded and the image is normalized. (c) ROI. (d) Result of segmentation.

3.2 Segmentation of the Tumor Using the Level-Set Method

The level-set method uses an initial seed on the image. This seed evolves with time until a zero velocity is reached or the curve has collapsed (or the maximum number of iterations is reached). To evolve the curve, the method uses two lists, called L_{in} and L_{out} (Shi, 2005).

Figure 7 shows the results obtained using the level-set method. Figure 7(a) is an original ultrasound image. Figure 7(c) shows the selected and normalized ROI. Figure 7(d) shows the initial seed applied to Fig. 7(c). Figure 7(e) shows the collapsed curve. Figure 7(f) is the binary mask obtained from Fig. 7(e). This mask is applied to the original image, and we thus obtained the result of the segmentation [Fig. 7(b)]. The figures were obtained from Aloka ultrasound equipment using a phantom brain.

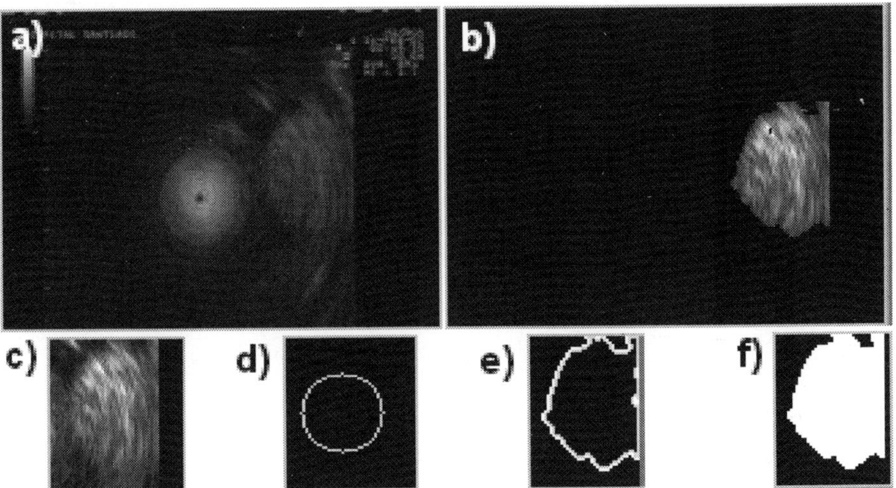

Fig. 7. Segmentation using the level-set method.

3.3 Comparison of the Methods

We obtained a processing time of 0.005305 seconds for the morphological operators method versus 0.009 seconds for the level-set method, that is, 188 fps vs. 111 fps. We recommend both methods for inline implementation, because they are fast and reliable.

4. Calculating the Ultrasound Probe's Pose

4.1 An Outline of Conformal Geometric Algebra

Conformal geometric algebra (CGA) has been used in many areas such as medical image processing, robotics, and artificial vision (Li et al., 2001). CGA represents geometric entities such as points, lines, planes, and spheres in an economical and compact form. CGA preserves the Euclidean metric and adds two basis vectors: e_+, e_-; $e_+^2 = 1$, $e_-^2 = -1$, which are used to define the point at the origin $e_0 = \frac{1}{2}(e_- - e_+)$ and the point at infinity $e = e_- + e_+$. The points in CGA are related to Euclidean space by $p = p + \frac{p^2}{2}e + e_0$. A sphere in dual form is represented as the wedge of four conformal points that lie on sphere $s^* = a \wedge b \wedge c \wedge d$; its radius ρ and its center p in R^3 can be obtained using $\rho^2 = \frac{s^2}{(s \cdot e)^2}$, $p = \frac{s}{-(s \cdot e)} + \frac{1}{2}\rho^2 e$. To know if a point p is into/out/on a sphere s^*, we use the normalization $e \cdot s = -1$ to represent the sphere as a single vector. In this way, if $p \cdot s > 0$, then p is into the sphere; if $p \cdot s < 0$, then p

is out of π^*; if $p \cdot s = 0$, then p is on the sphere π^*. A plane in dual form is defined as a sphere, but the last point is at infinity: $\pi^* = a \wedge b \wedge c \wedge e$; the normal n to this plane is its dual π if the coefficient e_+ of π is positive, else $n = -\pi$, so we can get the signed distance from p to π^* as $p \cdot n$. Figure 8 shows these concepts. A line in dual form is represented as the wedge of two points and the infinity point: $L^* = a \wedge b \wedge e$. A line can also be calculated as the intersection of two planes: $L = \pi_1 \wedge \pi_2$. This equation is used to calculate the 3D line that represents the ultrasound probe's axis. As mentioned, we are taking only the unit vector of this line. To achieve a translation by a distance d_2 from a point p_1 in the direction of a line,

we obtain p_2: $T = \exp\left(\frac{1}{2} d_2 L\right)$, $p_2 = T p_1 \tilde{T}$.

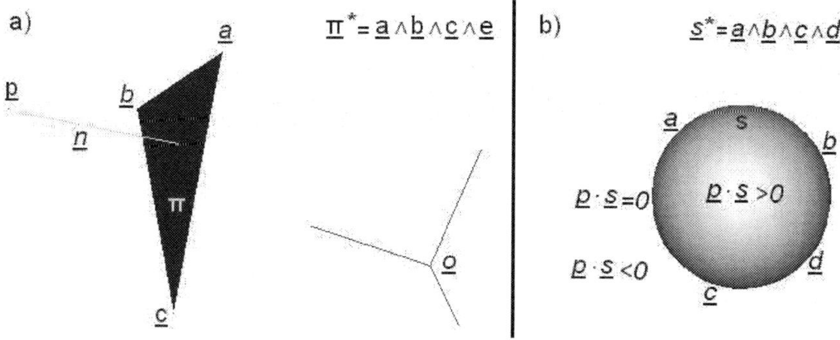

Fig. 8. Conformal entities used in the geometric tests. (a) The plane and (b) sphere.

4.2 Putting the Results in 3D Space

Figure 9(a) shows a slice of a tumor in 3D space; we can see the frame of the Polaris system and the calculated axis of the ultrasound probe. Figure 9(b) shows a convex hull applied to a set of slices of tumors, that is, the minimal convex set containing all the slices. This convex hull was built by using conformal geometric algebra to the geometric tests, as explained in Section 4.1. Figure 10 shows the tumor in a phantom brain model.

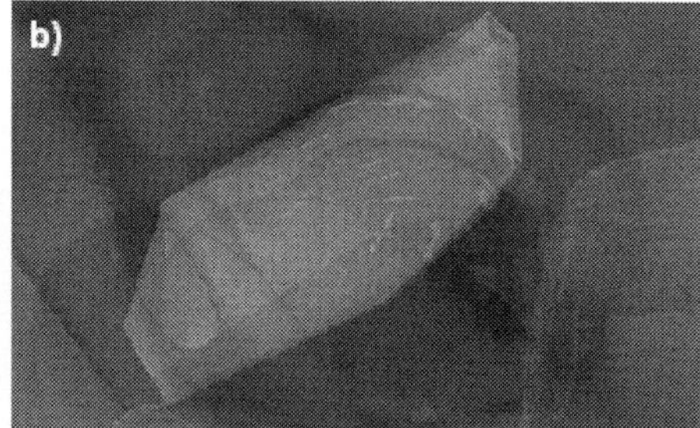

Fig. 9. (a) Virtual representation of the segmented US image. (b) Applying a convex hull to the results.

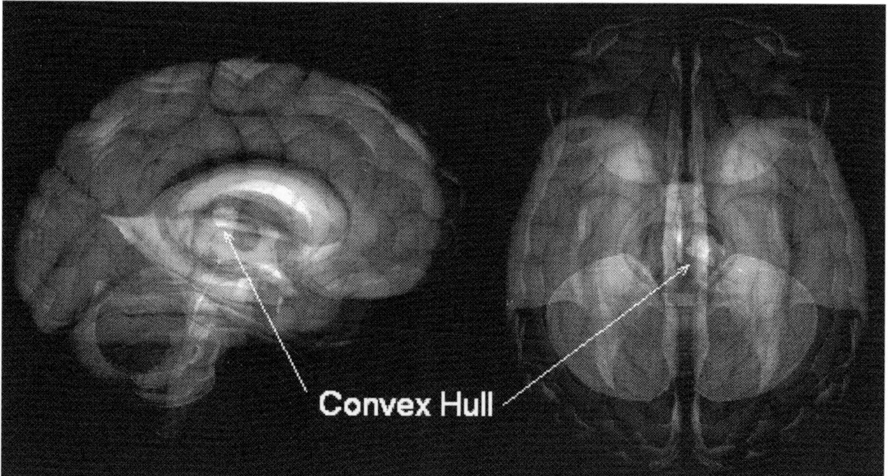

Fig. 10. The tumor in a phantom brain model.

5. Conclusions

In this chapter, we addressed the problem of obtaining 3D information from joint ultrasound and endoscopic images obtained with ENS equipment. In order to register both sources, we developed two alternative methods to locate the US probe's tip in endoscopic images: using saturation thresholding and a particle filter. Some preliminary results were shown. As for the ultrasound image, we presented two methods to segment interesting brain structures: morphological operators and level sets. In order to find the better method to track the ultrasound probe in the endoscopic camera images and to segment the tumor in the ultrasound images, we compared the results obtained with both methods. The results were shown in 3D space; the 3D information was calculated from the results obtained by the tracking process in endoscopic images.

The performance of the proposed approach was demonstrated using several images that were subject to occlusions and changes in illumination and contrast. The results indicated that the proposed approach is robust.

6. References

Bayro-Corrochano, E.; Daniilidis, K. 1996. The dual quaternion approach to hand-eye calibration. In *International Conference on Pattern Recognition (ICPR '96)*, Vienna, Austria, Vol. 1, pp. 318–322. IEEE Computer Society.

Castleman, K. 1996. *Digital Image Processing*, Prentice Hall, Englewood Cliffs, NJ.

Hartley, R.I.; Zisserman, A. 2004. *Multiple View Geometry in Computer Vision*, 2nd ed., Cambridge University Press, New York.

Isard, M.; Blake, A. 1998. CONDENSATION—Conditional density propagation for visual tracking. *International Journal of Computer Vision*, 29:5–28.

Li. H.; Hestenes, D.; Rockwood, A. 2001. *Geometric Computing with Clifford Algebras: Theoretical Foundations and Applications in Computer Vision and Robotics*, Springer-Verlag, New York, 2001.

Nummiaro, K.; Koller-Meier, E.; Van Gool, L. 2003. An adaptive color-based particle filter. *Image and Vision Computing*, 21(1):99–110.

Shi, Y. 2005. Object-based dynamic imaging with level set methods. Ph.D. thesis, Boston University.

Unsgaard, G.; Rygh, M.; Selbekk, T.; Müller, T.; Kolstad, F.; Lindseth, F.; Nagelhus Hernes, T. 2006. Intra-operative 3D ultrasound in neurosurgery. *Acta Neurochirurgica*, 148(3):235–253.

Automatic Recognition of Emotional States From Human Speeches

Ling Cen[1], Wee Ser[2], Zhu Liang Yu[3] and Wei Cen[4]
[1]Institute for Infocomm Research
Singapore
[2]School of Electrical and Electronic Engineering,
Nanyang Technological University
Singapore
[3]College of Automation Science and Engineering,
South China University of Technology,
Guangzhou, China
[4]Elektrotechnik GmbH, Postfach, Kassel, Germany

1. Introduction

As computer-based applications receive increasing attention in the real world and in our daily life, the Human-Computer Interaction (HCI) technology has also advanced rapidly over the recent decades. One essential enabler of natural interaction between human and computers is the computers' ability to understand the emotional states expressed by the human subjects (so that personalized responses can be delivered accordingly). This is not surprising as it is well known that emotion plays an important role in human-human communications. Emotions are mental and physiological states associated with feelings, thoughts, and behaviors of human subjects. The emotional state expressed by a human subject reflects not only the mood but also the personality of the human subject.

Automatic recognition of emotional states from cues expressed by human subjects, such as face expression or tone of voice, has found increasing applications in security, learning, medicine, entertainment, etc. For example, detecting abnormal emotions, such as stress or nervousness, helps to detect lie or identify suspicious human subjects. Emotion recognition in automatic tutoring systems, such as web-based e-learning, can adjust the tutoring content and delivery speed according to users' responses. Automatically recognizing emotions from patients could also be helpful in clinical studies as well as in psychosis monitoring and diagnosis assistance. Emotion classification has been applied in the customer service sector

This work was supported in part by the National Natural Science Foundation of China under Grant 60802068, and Guangdong Natural Science Foundation under Grant 8451064101000498, Program for New Century Excellent Talents in University under Grant NCET-10-0370 and the Fundamental Research Funds for the Central Universities, SCUT under Grant 2009ZZ0055.

too, where machines at call centers adjust their responses automatically according to the emotions expressed by the customers (e.g. anger, frustration, satisfaction, etc.). In the entertainment sector, interactive games have been developed that can interact adaptively with human players too. All these examples clearly illustrate that the demand for natural human-like machines is the major motivation or driving factor for the increasing research effort invested in automatic identification of the emotional states of human subjects.

Speech conversation is an important way for natural and effective communications between humans and computers. Over the past decades, advancement in robust speech recognition and synthesis techniques has contributed significantly in making such communications natural and effective. Human speech conveys not only the linguistic content but also the emotion of the speaker. Although the emotion does not alter the linguistic content, it carries important information on the speaker's desire and intent (Cowie et al., 2001; Ververidis & Kotropoulos, 2006). As such, it is important that computers understand the emotional states conveyed in human speech for effective human-computer interaction applications.

Modeling and analysis of emotions from human speech span across several fields, including psychology, linguistics, and engineering. As there is a lack of precise definition and models for emotions, automatic recognition of emotions has been a challenging task to researchers. Indeed, research on speech based emotion recognition has been undertaken by many for around two decades (Amir, 2001; Clavel et al., 2004; Cowie & Douglas-Cowie, 1996; Cowie et al., 2001; Dellaert et al., 1996; Lee & Narayanan, 2005; Morrison et al., 2007; Nguyen & Bass, 2005; Nicholson et al., 1999; Petrushin, 1999; Petrushin, 2000; Scherer, 2000; Ser et al., 2008; Ververidis & Kotropoulos, 2006; Yu et al., 2001; Zhou et al., 2006). In engineering, speech emotion recognition has been formulated as a pattern recognition problem that involves feature extraction and emotion classification. This is the model adopted in this chapter. In particular, this chapter discusses the designs and performances of several popular classification techniques namely, the Probabilistic Neural Network (PNN), the Universal Background Model - Gaussian Mixture Model (UBM-GMM), the Support Vector Machines (SVMs), and the Hidden Markov model (HMM), for emotion classifications. For completeness, a hybrid technique that combines the strengths of multiple classifiers (Ser et al., 2008) will also be discussed. Experimental results using the LDC database (University of Pennsylvania) will be presented and discussed in the chapter too, to provide a feel of the recognition accuracies for the various emotion recognition techniques described above.

The remaining part of this chapter is organized as follows. Some related works are briefly presented in Section 2. The acoustic feature extraction process is discussed in Section 3. In Section 4, several popular classifiers, including a hybrid method, for emotion recognition are discussed. Experimental results and performance comparison are shown in Section 5 and the concluding remarks are given in Section 6.

2. Related Works

Speech emotion recognition can be formulated as a pattern recognition problem. Such pattern recognition machines consist of two major modules, i.e. feature extraction (including speech signal pre-processing) and emotion classification. Fig. 1 shows a typical structure of the speech emotion recognition system.

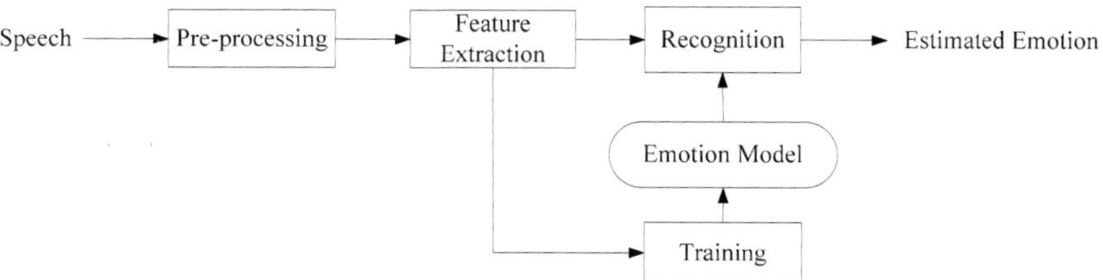

Fig. 1. Typical structure of a speech emotion recognition system

Feature extraction is an important module that provides the acoustic correlates of emotions in human speech for emotion classification. The basic acoustic features extracted directly from the original speech signals, e.g. pitch and intensity related features, are widely used in speech emotion recognition (Ververidis & Kotropoulos, 2006; Lee & Narayanan, 2005; Dellaert et al., 1996; Petrushin, 2000; Amir, 2001). Some features derived from mathematical transformation of basic acoustic features, e.g. Mel-Frequency Cepstral Coefficients" (MFCC) (Specht, 1988; Reynolds et al., 2000) and Linear Prediction-based Cepstral Coefficients (LPCC) (Specht, 1988), are also employed in some studies. The pitch of speech is the main acoustic correlate of tone and intonation, which represents the highness or lowness of a tone as perceived by the ear. It depends on the number of vibrations per second produced by the vocal cords. As the pitch is related to the tension of the vocal folds and the subglottal air pressure, it can provide the information about the emotions of speakers (Ververidis & Kotropoulos, 2006). The energy related features are also commonly used in emotion recognition. As the pitch and energy are calculated on a frame basis, statistics of the extracted features are usually used, such as mean, median, range, standard deviation, maximum, minimum, and linear regression coefficient (Lee & Narayanan, 2005; Ververidis & Kotropoulos, 2006). Speech rate and ratio of duration of voiced and unvoiced are considered to indicate emotional states of speakers too (Lee & Narayanan, 2005; Ververidis & Kotropoulos, 2006).

The behavior of the acoustic features in different emotional states has been studied in the literature (Davitz, 1964; Huttar, 1968; Fonagy, 1978; Moravek, 1979; Van Bezooijen, 1984; Havrdova & McGilloway et al., 1995, Ververidis & Kotropoulos, 2006). Anger is associated with the highest energy and pitch level among anger, disgust, fear, joy and sadness. Disgust has a lower mean pitch level, a lower intensity level and a slower speech rate than the neutral state. Low levels of the mean intensity and mean pitch are measured with sadness. A high pitch level and a raised intensity level are found in speech expressed with fear. The pitch contour trend separates fear from joy. A downwards slope in the pitch contour can be observed in speech expressed with fear and sadness, while the speech with joy shows a rising slope. Observable variance on speech rate is found in different emotions. More detailed information can be found in (Ververidis & Kotropoulos, 2006). However, even though many researches have been carried out to find acoustic features suitable for emotion recognition, there is still no conclusive evidence to show which set of features can provide the best recognition accuracy (Zhou, 2006).

After the acoustic features are extracted and processed, they are sent to emotion classification module. Many popular classifiers are employed in the literature. Dellaert et al. (1996) used K-nearest neighbor (k-NN) classifier and majority voting of subspace specialists for the recognition of sadness, anger, happiness and fear and the maximum accuracy achieved was 79.5%. Neural network (NN) was employed to recognize eight emotions, i.e. happiness, teasing, fear, sadness, disgust, anger, surprise and neutral and an accuracy of 50% was achieved (Nicholson et al. 1999). The linear discrimination, k-NN classifiers, and SVM were used to distinguish negative and non-negative emotions and a maximum accuracy of 75% was achieved (Lee & Narayanan, 2005). Petrushin (1999) developed a real-time emotion recognizer using Neural Networks for call center applications, and achieved 77% classification accuracy in recognizing agitation and calm emotions using eight features chosen by a feature selection algorithm. Yu, et.al. (2001) used SVMs to detect anger, happy, sadness, and neutral with an average accuracy of 73%. Scherer (2000) explored the existence of a universal psychobiological mechanism of emotions in speech by studying the recognition of fear, joy, sadness, anger and disgust in nine languages, obtaining 66% of overall accuracy. Two hybrid classification schemes, stacked generalization and the un-weighted vote, were proposed and accuracies of 72.18% and 70.54% were achieved respectively, when they were used to recognize anger, disgust, fear, happiness, sadness and surprise (Morrison, 2007). Hybrid classification methods that combined the Support Vector Machines and the Decision Tree were proposed (Nguyen & Bass, 2005). The best accuracies for classifying neutral, anger, lombard and loud was 72.4%.

3. Acoustic Feature Extraction for Emotion Recognition

In this section, the features used in our work and the process involved are briefly described. In the experiments given below, three short time cepstral features are extracted, which are Perceptual Linear Prediction (PLP) Cepstral Coefficients, Mel-Frequency Cepstral Coefficients (MFCC), and Linear Prediction-based Cepstral Coefficients (LPCC). Before extracting the raw features, the speech data are first high-pass filtered by a FIR filter given by

$$H(z) = 1 - 0.9375z^{-1}.$$

(1)

Signal frames of length 25 msec are then extracted from the filtered speech signal at an interval of 10 msec. A Hamming window is applied to each signal frame to reduce signal discontinuity. The list below shows the feature set used in this chapter.

1) PLP - 54 features
18 PLP cepstral coefficients
18 Delta PLP cepstral coefficients
18 Delta Delta PLP cepstral coefficients.

2) MFCC - 39 features
12 MFCC features
12 delta MFCC features
12 Delta Delta MFCC features
1 (log) frame energy
1 Delta (log) frame energy
1 Delta Delta (log) frame energy

3) LPCC – 39 features
13 LPCC features
13 delta LPCC features
13 Delta Delta LPCC features

Fusing the PLP, MFCC and LPCC features, a vector with dimension of R^M is achieved, where $M = 132$ is the total number of the features extracted for each frame.

4. Classifiers for Emotion Recognition

The features extracted from the speech samples as described in the previous section, are sent to the emotion classification module. The module output is the estimated emotion category of an utterance. Before a classifier can be used to automatically label the emotion categories, a training process has to be carried out. The speech samples in the whole database are divided into two parts. One is used to train the classifiers, and the other is for the test use. In the below sub-sections, we will introduce several popular classification methods used in emotion classification.

4.1 Probabilistic Neural Network (PNN)

The Probabilistic Neural Network (PNN) (Specht, 1988) has been employed as an excellent pattern classifier in many applications due to its excellent characteristics such as simple training, quick convergence and easy implementation. The PNN solves classification problems using Bayesian classifiers. A basic structure of a PNN is shown in Fig. 2. It consists of 4 network layers, i.e. input layer, pattern layer, summation layer and output layer.

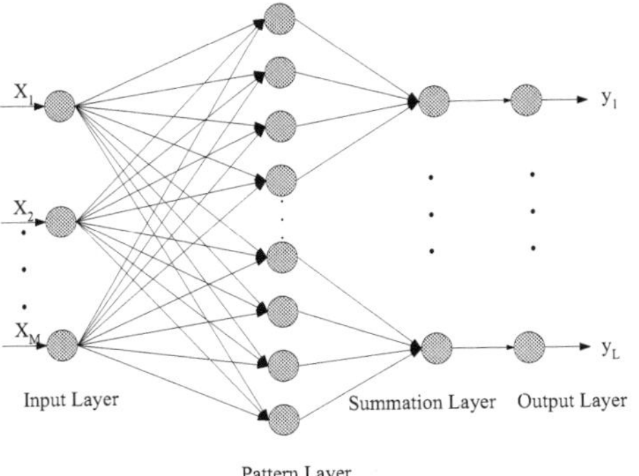

Fig. 2. Structure of a Probabilistic Neural Network

As shown in Fig. 2, the input of the PNN, $\mathbf{x} = [x_1, x_2, ..., x_M]^T$ is the M-dimension feature vector. The distribution function that estimates the likelihood of an input feature vector belonging to a learned category is developed in the pattern layer via supervised training using a given training set. This layer works in the same way as a Bayes classifier, where the class dependent Probability Density Functions (PDF) are approximated using a Parzen estimator. Each unit in the pattern layer represents an exemplar in the training set. The activated function in this layer can be a Gaussian function given by

$$f(z_j) = \exp\left[(z_j - 1)/\sigma^2\right], \text{ for } j = 1, 2, ..., N, \tag{2}$$

where σ, which is also called smoothing factor, is the variance of the Gaussians, N is the number of the exemplars in the training set (equal to the number of the units in this layer), and z_j is the weighted input of the jth unit expressed as

$$z_j = \mathbf{x} \cdot \mathbf{w}_j. \tag{3}$$

Here, $\mathbf{w}_j = [w_{j1}, w_{j2}, ..., w_{jM}]^T$ is the M-dimensional weighting vector for the jth exemplar in the training set. Let $\mathbf{x}_j^{c_i}$ for $j = 1, ..., N_i$ denote the N_i training exemplars belonging to emotion c_i ($c_i \in C$, where C is the vector of class labels under reorganization). The probability density function, $p(\mathbf{x}|c_i)$, is expressed as

$$p(\mathbf{x}|c_i) = \frac{1}{\sqrt{(2\pi)^M}\sigma^M} \cdot \frac{1}{N_i} \cdot \sum_{j=1}^{N_i} \exp\left(\frac{\left(\mathbf{x} - \mathbf{x}_j^{c_i}\right)^t \left(\mathbf{x} - \mathbf{x}_j^{c_i}\right)}{2\sigma^2}\right). \tag{4}$$

Via training process, the outputs from the units that belong to one emotion category are combined in the summation layer. Each unit in the summation layer is associated to one emotion category. The output layer works in a competitive way, where only one category is generated for any given input vector. The output $\mathbf{y} = [y_1, y_2, ..., y_L]^T$ is an L-dimension vector, where L is the number of emotion categories. The output of the unit related to the predicted category has the value of "1" and the others have "0".

4.2 Universal Background Model - Gaussian Mixture Model (UBM-GMM)

The Gaussian Mixture Model (GMM) assumes that the observed variables are generated via a probability density distribution that is the weighed linear combination of a set of Gaussian PDF. It is considered as a single-state HMM with a Gaussian mixture observation density and has been shown to be the most successful probability density function in text-independent speaker recognition, where no *prior* knowledge is available on what the speaker will say (Reynolds, 2000).

In the GMM, the distribution of a random variable $\mathbf{x} \in R^M$ is a mixture of G Gaussians given as

$$p(\mathbf{x}|\lambda_{c_i}) = \sum_{g=1}^{G} w_g p_g(\mathbf{x}), \tag{5}$$

where λ_{c_i} is the density model related to the class, c_i, G is the number of the Gaussian components, and w_g is the mixture weights satisfying the constraint $\sum_{g=1}^{G} w_g = 1$. The Gaussian densities, p_g, is shown as

$$p_g(\mathbf{x}) = \frac{1}{\sqrt{(2\pi)^M |\Sigma_g|}} \cdot \exp\left(-\frac{(\mathbf{x}-\mu_g)^T (\mathbf{x}-\mu_g)}{2\Sigma_g}\right), \tag{6}$$

where μ_g and Σ_g are the M-dimension mean vector and $M \times M$-dimension covariance matrix, respectively. The density model, λ_{c_i} is denoted as $\lambda_{c_i} = \left\{w_g, \mu_g, \Sigma_g\right\}_{g=1}^{G}$, which represents the probability density distribution of the feature vectors ($\mathbf{x}$) for the category c_i. The optimum set of parameters of λ_{c_i} can be identified in an iterative manner using the Maximal likelihood Principle (MLP) and Expectation-Maximization (EM) algorithm. The likelihood of $\mathbf{x}_1, \mathbf{x}_2, ..., \mathbf{x}_{N_i}$ is defined as

$$L(\mathbf{x}_1, \mathbf{x}_2, ..., \mathbf{x}_{N_i} \mid \lambda_{c_i}) = \prod_{j=1}^{N_i} \sum_{g=1}^{G} w_g p_g(\mathbf{x}_j), \tag{7}$$

where $\left\{\mathbf{x}_1, \mathbf{x}_2, ..., \mathbf{x}_{N_i}\right\}$ are the exemplars in the training set belonging to the category, c_i. The EM algorithm iteratively updates w_g, μ_g, Σ_g for $g = 1, ..., G$, in order to monotonically increase the likelihood in (7).

The EM algorithm consists of two steps: Expectation Step and Maximization Step. In the Expectation Step, we calculate

$$e_{jg} = p(g \mid \mathbf{x}_j) = \frac{w_g p_g(\mathbf{x}_j)}{\sum_{t=1}^{G} w_t p_t(\mathbf{x}_j)}, \text{for } g = 1, ...G. \tag{8}$$

Then in the Maximization Step, w_g, μ_g, Σ_g for $g = 1, ..., G$, are updated as

$$\hat{a}_g = \frac{1}{N} \sum_{j=1}^{N_i} e_{jg},$$

$$\hat{\mu}_g = \frac{\sum_{j=1}^{N_i} e_{jg} \mathbf{x}_j}{\sum_{j=1}^{N_i} e_{jg}},$$

$$\hat{\Sigma}_g = \frac{\sum_{j=1}^{N_i} e_{jg} \left(\mathbf{x}_j - \mu_g \right)^T \left(\mathbf{x}_j - \mu_g \right)}{\sum_{j=1}^{N_i} e_{jg}}.$$

$$(9)$$

By iteratively performing the above steps, the EM algorithm is able to find an optimum set of parameters for the GMM.

In order to handle mismatches more effectively, the Universal Background Model (UBM) is incorporated into the GMM, and the resultant model is denoted as UBM-GMM (Reynolds, 2000). In the UBM-GMM, not only the hypothesis that an utterance belongs to an emotion category, but also the hypothesis that it does not belong to this category, are tested. Each of the categories is trained with two models. The emotion model, λ_{c_i} is trained using the training samples belonging to the emotion class c_i, and a background model, $\lambda_{\bar{c}_i}$ is meantime trained using those samples that do not belong to c_i. When the emotional state of a new utterance with feature vector $\mathbf{x}$ is recognized, both λ_{c_i} and $\lambda_{\bar{c}_i}$ are used to generate the PDF of the feature vector, $p\left(\mathbf{x} | \lambda_{c_i} \right)$ and $p\left(\mathbf{x} | \lambda_{\bar{c}_i} \right)$ as illustrated in Fig. 3. The emotion category of the utterance is determined using the likelihood ratio

$$\frac{p\left(\mathbf{x} | \lambda_{c_i} \right)}{p\left(\mathbf{x} | \lambda_{\bar{c}_i} \right)} \geq \eta,$$

$$(10)$$

where η is a predetermined threshold. In UBM-GMM, the log-likelihood ratio, S_{c_i}, is often used, given as

$$S_{c_i} = \log p\left(\mathbf{x} | \lambda_{c_i} \right) - \log p\left(\mathbf{x} | \lambda_{\bar{c}_i} \right) \geq \eta', \eta' = \log \eta.$$

$$(11)$$

Highest S_{c_i} determines the emotion class of $\mathbf{x}$, which implies higher $p\left(\mathbf{x} | \lambda_{c_i} \right)$ and lower $p\left(\mathbf{x} | \lambda_{\bar{c}_i} \right)$.

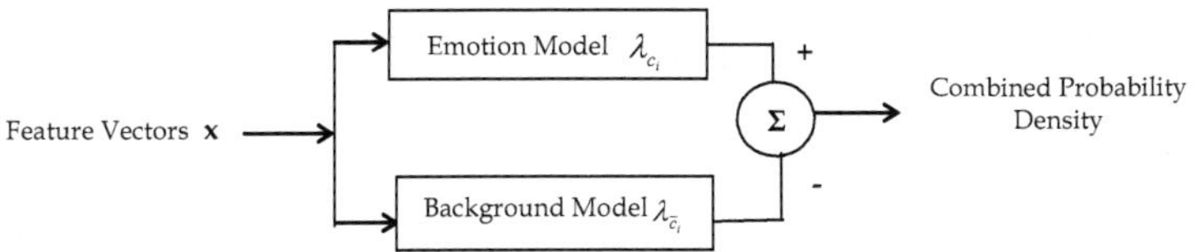

Fig. 3. Output Probability Density of UBM-GMM

4.3 Hidden Markov Model (HMM)

The HMM has a good representation of the temporal behavior of signals being modeled. As such, it is commonly used in temporal based pattern recognition applications (e.g. speech recognition, handwriting recognition, gesture recognition, etc.). In HMM, the system to be modeled is assumed to be a Markov process with a finite set of concatenated states. The states cannot be observed directly, while the observation that is generated in the states according to the associated probability distribution is visible, from which the model is named as Hidden Markov Model.

Assume that there are N states, $S=\{S_1, S_2, ..., S_N\}$, and M distinct observation symbols per state, $V=\{v_1, v_2, ..., v_M\}$, in the model. Each of these states is associated with a probability distribution over the possible outcome. Transition among the states is controlled by a set of transition probabilities. Let $\Lambda = \{a_{ij}\}$ represent the state transition probabilities given as

$$a_{ij} = p\{q_{t+1} = S_j | q_t = S_i\}, \text{ for } 1 \leq i, j \leq N, \tag{12}$$

where q_t is the state at time t and a_{ij} satisfies

$$a_{ij} \geq 0, \ \sum_{j=1}^{N} a_{ij} = 1, \text{ for } 1 \leq i, j \leq N. \tag{13}$$

The observation symbols correspond to the physical output of the system being modeled. Let $B = \{b_j(k)\}$ denote the observation symbol probability distribution in state j, where

$$b_j(k) = p\{O_t = v_k | q_t = S_j\}, \text{ for } 1 \leq j \leq N, \ 1 \leq k \leq M, \tag{14}$$

and O_t is the observation in time t and v_k is the kth observation.

The distribution $b_j(k)$ satisfies

$$b_j(k) \geq 0, \ \sum_{k=1}^{M} b_j(k) = 1, \text{ for } 1 \leq j \leq N, \ 1 \leq k \leq M. \tag{15}$$

Assume that the initial state distribution $\pi = \{\pi_i\}$ is given as

$$\pi_i = p\{q_1 = S_i\}, \text{ for } 1 \leq i \leq N. \tag{16}$$

An HMM can then be represented as $\lambda = (\Lambda, B, \pi)$. Given a suitable set of the values of N, M and the initial state distribution, the model can be trained to solve the three fundamental problems (Rabiner, 1989). The process involved is summarized below.

1) Given an observation sequence with the following T observations

$$O = O_1 O_2 ... O_T, \ O_t \in V, \ t = 1, 2, ..., T, \tag{17}$$

and the model $\lambda = (\Lambda, B, \pi)$, evaluate $p(O|\lambda)$, i.e. the probability of the observation sequence. As the calculation of enumerating every possible state sequence of length T for calculating $p(O|\lambda)$ involves on the order of $2T \cdot N^T$ calculations, the problem can be solved efficiently using the forward algorithm that requires on only the order of $N^2 T$ calculations. Consider forward variable $\alpha_t(i)$ that is defined as the probability of the partial observation sequence (until time t), $O_1 O_2 ... O_t$, and the state S_i at time t, given the model λ, expressed as

$$\alpha_t(i) = P(O_1 O_2 ... O_t, q_t = S_i \mid \lambda). \tag{18}$$

This can be solved inductively, as follows:

Initialization

$$\alpha_1(i) = \pi_i b_i(O_1), \ 1 \leq i \leq N. \tag{19}$$

Induction

$$\alpha_{t+1}(j) = \left[\sum_{i=1}^{N} \alpha_t(i) a_{ij} \right] b_j(O_{t+1}), \ 1 \leq t \leq T-1, \ 1 \leq j \leq N. \tag{20}$$

Termination

$$P(O \mid \lambda) = \sum_{i=1}^{N} \alpha_T(i). \tag{21}$$

2) Given the observation sequence $O = O_1 O_2 ... O_T$ and the model λ, determine the optimum sequence of the model states. There is no exact and unique solution for this problem. Optimality criteria are applied to find optimal state sequence. The Viterbi algorithm (Viterbi, 1967; Forney, 1973) that finds the single best state sequence based on dynamic programming methods is commonly used to solve this problem.

3) Estimate the model parameters $\lambda = (\Lambda, B, \pi)$ that best match the observed signal, i.e. maximizing the probability of the observation sequence given the model, $p(O|\lambda)$. As there is no analytical approach to solve the problem, λ is usually chosen such that $p(O|\lambda)$ is locally maximized using an iterative procedure such as the Baum-Welch method.

In the above, we have briefly introduced the algorithm for solving the first problem as speech emotion recognition belongs to this problem and can be solved efficiently using HMMs. The observation sequence is the feature vector of an utterance. Through training process, one HMM is established for each emotion category. If an individual training is carried out for each speaker, S HMMs are trained for each emotion, where S is the number of speakers. With the trained HMMs, estimating the emotion category of an utterance is equivalent to calculating the probability of $p(O|\lambda)$ for the given observation sequence. It can be solved using the forward algorithm described above. The HMM with the highest probability determines the emotion category of the utterance.

4.4 Support Vector Machines (SVMs)

SVMs that developed by Vladimir Vapnik (1995) and his colleagues at AT&T Bell Labs in the mid 90's, have become of increasing interest in classification (Steinwart and Christmann, 2008). It has shown to have better generalization performance than traditional techniques in solving classification problems. In contrast to traditional techniques for pattern recognition that are based on the minimization of empirical risk learned from training dataset, it aims to minimize the structural risk to achieve optimum performance.
It is based on the concept of decision planes that separates the objects belonging to different categories. In the SVMs, the input data are separated as two sets using a separating hyperplane that maximizes the margin between the two data sets. Assuming the training data samples are in the form of

$$\{\mathbf{x}_i, c_i\}, \ i = 1, ..., N, \ \mathbf{x}_i \in \mathbf{R}^M, c_i \in \{-1, 1\} \tag{22}$$

where $\mathbf{x}_i = [x_1, x_2, ..., x_M]$ is the M-dimension feature vector of the ith samples, N is the number of samples and c_i is the category to which $\mathbf{x}_i$ belongs. Suppose there is a hyperplane that the separates feature vectors $\phi(\mathbf{x}_i)$ with positive category from the negative one, here $\phi(\bullet)$ is a nonlinear mapping of the input space into higher dimensional feature space. The set of points $\phi(\mathbf{x})$ that lie on the hyperplane is expressed as

$$\mathbf{w} \cdot \phi(\mathbf{x}) + b = 0, \tag{23}$$

where $\mathbf{w}$ and b are the two parameters. For the training data that are linearly seperable, two hyperplanes are selected to yield maximum margin. Suppose $\mathbf{x}_i, \ i = 1, ..., N$ satisfies

$$\phi(\mathbf{x}_i)\cdot\mathbf{w}+b\geq 1, \text{ for } c_i=1,$$
$$\phi(\mathbf{x}_i)\cdot\mathbf{w}+b\leq 1, \text{ for } c_i=-1. \tag{24}$$

It can be re-written as

$$c_i\left(\phi(\mathbf{x}_i)\cdot\mathbf{w}+b\right)-1\geq 0, \ \forall i=1,2,...,N. \tag{25}$$

Searching a pair of hyperplanes that gives the maximum margin can be achieved by solving the following optimization problem

$$\text{Minimize } \|\mathbf{w}\|^2 \tag{26}$$
$$\text{subject } c_i\left(\phi(\mathbf{x}_i)\cdot\mathbf{w}+b\right)\geq 1, \forall i=1,2,...,N.$$

where $\|\mathbf{w}\|$ represents the Euclidean norm of $\mathbf{w}$. This can be formulated as a quadratic programming optimization problem and be solved by standard quadratic programming techniques.

Using the Lagrangian methodology, the dual problem of (26) is given as

$$\text{Minimize } W(\alpha)=\sum_{i=1}^{N}\alpha_i-\frac{1}{2}\sum_{i,j=1}^{N}c_ic_j\alpha_i\alpha_j\phi(\mathbf{x}_i)^T\phi(\mathbf{x}_j), \tag{27}$$
$$\text{subject } \sum_{i=1}^{N}c_i\alpha_i=0, \ \alpha_i\geq 0, \ \forall i=1,2,...,N.$$

where α_i is the Lagrangian variable.

The simplest case is that $\phi(\mathbf{x})$ is a linear function. If the data cannot be separated in a linear way, non-linear mappings are performed from the original space to a feature space via kernels. This aims to construct a linear classifier in the transformed space, which is the so-called "kernel trick". It can be seen from (27) that the training points are appeared as their inner products in the dual formulation. According to Mercer's theorem, any symmetric positive semi-definite function $k\left(\mathbf{x}_i,\mathbf{x}_j\right)$ implicitly defines a mapping into a feature space

$$\phi:\mathbf{x}\rightarrow\phi(\mathbf{x}) \tag{28}$$

such that the function is an inner product in the feature space given as

$$k\left(\mathbf{x}_i,\mathbf{x}_j\right)=\phi(\mathbf{x}_i)\cdot\phi(\mathbf{x}_j) \tag{29}$$

The function $k\left(\mathbf{x}_i,\mathbf{x}_j\right)$ is called kernels. The dual problem in the kernel form is then given as

$$\text{Minimize } W\left(\alpha\right)=\sum_{i=1}^{N}\alpha_i-\frac{1}{2}\sum_{i,j=1}^{N}c_ic_j\alpha_i\alpha_jk\left(\mathbf{x}_i,\mathbf{x}_j\right),\tag{30}$$

$$\text{subject }\sum_{i=1}^{N}c_i\alpha_i=0,\ \alpha_i\geq 0,\ \forall i=1,2,...,N.$$

By replacing the inner product in (27) with a kernel and solving for α, a maximal margin separating hyperplane can be obtained in the feature space defined by a kernel.   Choosing suitable non-linear kernels, therefore, classifiers that are non-linear in the original space can become linear in the feature space. Some common kernel functions are shown in below:

Polynomial (homogeneous) kernel: $k\left(\mathbf{x},\mathbf{x}'\right)=\left(\mathbf{x}\cdot\mathbf{x}'\right)^d$,

Polynomial (inhomogeneous) kernel: $k\left(\mathbf{x},\mathbf{x}'\right)=\left(\mathbf{x}\cdot\mathbf{x}'+1\right)^d$,

Radial basis kernel: $k\left(\mathbf{x},\mathbf{x}'\right)=\exp\left(-\gamma\left\|\mathbf{x}-\mathbf{x}'\right\|^2\right)$, for $\gamma>0$,

Gaussian radial basis kernel: $k\left(\mathbf{x},\mathbf{x}'\right)=\exp\left(-\dfrac{\left\|\mathbf{x}-\mathbf{x}'\right\|^2}{2\sigma^2}\right)$.

A single SVM itself is a classification method for 2-category data. In speech emotion recognition, there are usually multiple emotion categories. Two approaches are commonly used to solve the problem, namely one-versus-all and one-versus-one (Fradkin and Muchnik, 2006). In the first approach, one SVM is built for each emotion. In the second approach, one SVM is built to distinguish between every pair of categories. The final classification decision is made according to the results from all the SVMs with the majority rule. In the one-versus-all way, the emotion category of an utterance is determined by the classifier with the highest output based on the winner-takes-all strategy. In the one-versus-one way, every classifier assigns the utterance to one of the two emotion categories, then the vote for the assigned category is increased by one vote, and the emotion class is the one with most votes based on a max-wins voting strategy.

4.5. A Hybrid Classification Method

In the previous studies, most emotion recognition schemes use a single classifier, and very few have considered hybrid classification methods (Morrison, 2007). Intuitively, if the individual schemes can be suitably combined, an improvement in accuracy can be expected. This section describes a recently reported hybrid scheme that combines the strengths of multiple classifiers (Ser et al., 2008).

The structure of the hybrid scheme is shown in Fig. 4, which consists of two basic classifiers, i.e. the PNN classifier and the UBM-GMM classifier. The outcomes of these two classifiers are fused together to generate the final result by the Fusion Look-Up Table (LUT) approach.

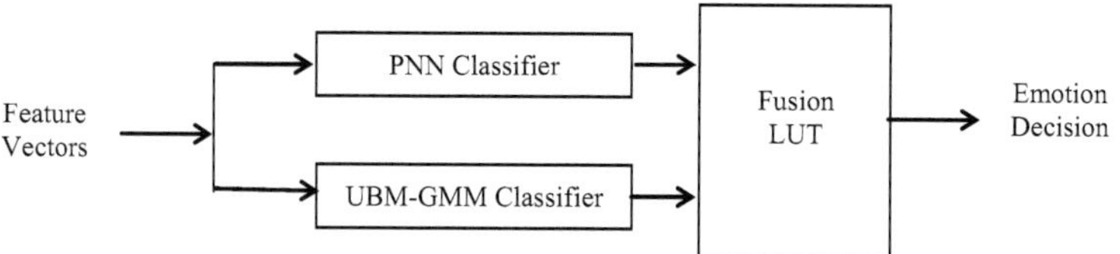

Fig. 4. Structure of Proposed Hybrid Scheme (LUT: Look Up Table)

In the training stage, the PNN and the UBM-GMM classifiers are firstly trained individually. Then the confusion matrices for the two base classifiers and a LUT that is denoted as F, is formed using a different part of training data from that used to train the base classifiers. Let L be the total number of emotional states to be classified. The L-by-L confusion matrix for each of the base classifier takes the following form:

$$\begin{pmatrix} p_{11} & \cdots & p_{1L} \\ \vdots & \ddots & \vdots \\ p_{L1} & \cdots & p_{LL} \end{pmatrix}$$

In the matrix, $p_{i,j}$ is the probability that the estimated class is c_j given that actual class is c_i. For an effective classifier, the values of the diagonal entries are expected to be much higher than those of the non-diagonal entries.

The Fusion LUT, F, a matrix with dimension of $L^3 \times 4$, records all possible emotional states estimated by the two classifiers, the actual emotional states, and the conditional probability of the actual emotion being one of the emotional states. This is elaborated below.
Let c_{PNN} and c_{GMM} be the emotional states estimated by PNN and UBM-GMM respectively, and c_r be the actual emotional state. A typical row of F takes the form,

$$[\,c_{PNN} \quad c_{GMM} \quad c_r \quad p(c_r)\,]$$

where $p(c_r)$ is the conditional probability of the emotional state c_r given by

$$p(c_r) = prob(c = c_r \mid c_{PNN}, c_{GMM}). \tag{31}$$

It can be approximated as

$$p(c_r) \approx N_{c_{PNN}-c_{GMM}} / N_{c_r}, \tag{32}$$

where $N_{c_r-c_{PNN}-c_{GMM}}$ represents the number of utterances whose emotions being c_r given that the estimated emotion from the PNN and GMM classifiers being c_{PNN} and c_{GMM}, respectively, and N_{c_r} denotes the number of utterances expressed in the emotion c_r. Note that $N_{c_r-c_{PNN}-c_{GMM}}$ and N_{c_r} count only the utterances used to calculate the LUT. In the ideal situation when the recognition accuracy of every single classifier is 100%, $p(c_r)$ becomes

$$p(c_r) = \begin{cases} 1, & \text{for } c_{PNN} = c_{GMM} = c_r \\ 0, & \text{otherwise} \end{cases}. \tag{33}$$

In the testing stage, the emotion of a speech sample is determined by either the Fusion LUT or the confusion matrices.

The training-testing process can be summarized into the following 6 steps.

Step 1 Train each of the two classifiers, PNN and UBM-GMM, independently using the training data.

Step 2 Use the trained classifiers to recognize the emotions of the utterances extracted from another speech data training set.

Step 3 Calculate the confusion matrices for both the base classifiers.

Step 4 Calculate the fusion LUT, F, according to the process described before.

Step 5 Apply the two base classifiers to the test data separately, and obtain the estimated emotional states, c_{PNN} and c_{GMM}, respectively.

Step 6 Compare the values of $p(c_r)$ in the fusion LUT where the first 2 indices are c_{PNN} and c_{GMM}. Determine the fusion output as $c_{fus} = c_r$ where the value $p(c_r)$ is the highest. In the case when $p(c_r) = 0$ (which can happen when the training sample size is too small), compare the values of $p_{i,i}$ in the two confusion matrices, where i corresponds to c_{PNN} and c_{GMM}, for the respective confusion matrices. The final decision of the emotional state, c_{fus} is then taken to be the c_r corresponding to the highest $p_{i,i}$.

5. Experiments

5.1 Database

The speech emotion database used in this study is extracted from the Linguistic Data Consortium (LDC) Emotional Prosody Speech corpus (catalog number LDC2002S28), which was recorded by the Department of Neurology, University of Pennsylvania Medical School. It comprises expressions spoken by 3 male and 4 female actors. The speech contents are neutral phrases like dates and numbers, e.g. "September fourth" or "eight hundred one", which are expressed in 14 emotional states (including anxiety, boredom, cold anger, hot anger, contempt, despair, disgust, elation, happiness, interest, panic, pride, sadness, and shame) as well as neutral state. The number of utterances is approximately 2300.

5.2 Experiment Description

The PNN, UBM-GMM, HMM, SVM and the hybrid classification method are employed to automatically recognize emotional states from speech samples. In our experiment, we consider the different characteristics of speech among the speakers. The speech data are trained in speaker dependent training mode, in which an individual training process is carried out for each speaker. In the experiment, the database is divided into two parts, i.e. training dataset and testing dataset. For the PNN, GMM, HMM and SVM classifiers used individually, three quarters of the data are employed to train the classifiers; for the hybrid classification method, half of the data are employed to train the base classifiers, a quarter of the data are used to calculate the Fusion LUT and the confusion matrices. The rest quarter of data are used for testing purpose in our methods.

5.3 Results and Discussion

Numerical results obtained by the PNN, UBM-GMM, HMM, SVM, and the hybrid scheme are shown in Tables 1. The average accuracies achieved by PNN, UBM-GMM, HMM, SVM and the hybrid scheme are 68.60%, 72.73%, 69.60%, 62.67%, and 75.13%, respectively.

	PNN	UBM-GMM	HMM	SVM	Hybrid
Anxiety	79	77	82	76	80
Boredom	71	79	76	81	76
Cold Anger	64	69	58	59	71
Contempt	73	80	79	58	82
Despair	65	79	76	71	79
Disgust	78	89	81	65	84
Elation	59	81	68	73	72
Hot Anger	75	85	85	74	77
Happiness	61	76	49	60	68
Interest	64	70	63	51	73
Neutral	80	54	82	61	81
Panic	62	75	70	52	75
Pride	72	53	53	54	72
Sadness	74	63	51	46	74
Shame	52	61	71	59	63
Average	68.60	72.73	69.60	62.67	75.13

Table 1. Recognition accuracies (%) of the PNN, UBM-GMM, HMM, SVM, and the hybrid scheme

The accuracies for individual emotion recognition achieved by the PNN, UBM-GMM, HMM and SVM are plotted in Fig. 5. It is shown from the experiment results that among the 4 classifiers, the UBM-GMM has achieved highest average accuracy. The recognition performance of the HMM in this experiment is similar to that of the UBM-GMM. For each of these emotion categories, the highest recognition accuracy is achieved by different classification method, e.g. for anxiety, the highest accuracy of 82% is achieved by the HMM; for despair, the accuracy of 79% obtained by the UBM-GMM is the highest; for Neutral, the highest accuracy of 82% is achieved by the HMM; and for Pride, the PNN gives the highest accuracy of 72%. It indicates that one cannon simply make a conclusion that one classifier is better than another classifier.

It can be seen from Table 1, the hybrid scheme is able to improve the recognition accuracy compared to the classification methods used individually. The average accuracy is 75.13%, which is 6.53% and 2.40% higher than the PNN and UBM-GMM individually used, respectively. In the literature, usually only 2-6 different emotional states are classified. Considering the difficulties encountered due to the facts that the number of emotional states is as large as 15, the results are rather satisfying.

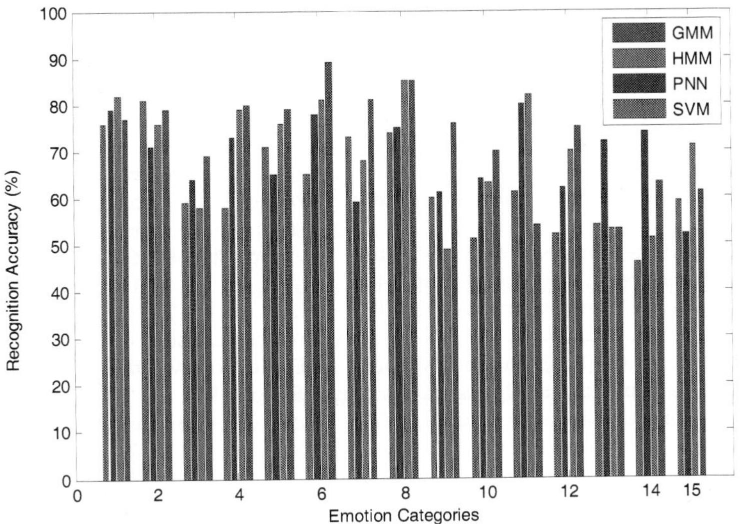

Fig. 5. Recognition accuracies of PNN, UBM-GMM, HMM and SVM

6. Conclusions

Over the recent decades, automatic recognition of emotional states has attracted increasing interest among the researchers. This chapter addresses the problem of emotion recognition from human speech cues. The processes involved and some popular methods for feature extraction and emotion classification have been discussed in the chapter. In particular, acoustic features such as the short time cepstral features, i.e. Perceptual Linear Prediction (PLP) Cepstral Coefficients, the Mel-Frequency Cepstral Coefficients (MFCC), and the Linear Prediction-based Cepstral Coefficients (LPCC), have been discussed in the chapter. Several popular classification methods, including the Probabilistic Neural Network (PNN), the Universal Background Model -Gaussian Mixture Model (UBM-GMM), the Hidden Markov model (HMM), the Support Vector Machines (SVMs), and a recently proposed hybrid method have been discussed too. Experimental results, in terms of recognition accuracies, obtained by using the LDC database (University of Pennsylvania) have been included and discussed in the chapter too.

7. References

Amir, N. (2001), Classifying emotions in speech: A comparison of methods, *Eurospeech*, 2001.
Clavel, C., Vasilescu, I., Devillers, L.& Ehrette, T. (2004), Fiction database for emotion detection in abnormal situations, Proceedings of International Conference on Spoken Language Process, pp. 2277-2280, 2004, Korea.

## 23

Intelligence Computing Approaches for Epileptic Seizure Detection Based on Intracranial Electroencephalogram (IEEG)

Tsu-Wang Shen and Xavier Kuo

Department of Medical Informatics, Tzu Chi University
Taiwan

1. Introduction

Epilepsy is a neurological disorder and can be defined as a symptom where a sudden and transient disturbance occurs in the normal electrical activity of the brain (İnan & Kuntalp, 2007). Multiple factors can trigger epilepsy, such as brain injury, disease, light stimulation, and genetics. People may be born with the disorder; however, the exact underlying epilepsy mechanism is still uncertain.

Epilepsy affects four to five percent of the world's population at some point in their lives and 1% of the world's population suffer from chronic epilepsy (Betts, 1998). According to the Epilepsy Foundation of America, more than two million people in the United States have a seizure disorder. In Taiwan, about 200 thousand people suffer from this disorder (Wang, 1998). Alarmingly, the death rate is unacceptably high, as epilepsy increases a person's risk of premature death by about two to three times that of the non-epileptic population. The epilepsy-related death rate among patients is about 40%. Causes of death include the underlying disease in symptomatic epilepsy, sudden unexpected death in epilepsy (SUDEP), accidents during an epileptic attack, status epilepticus, suicide, and treatment-related death (Nouri & Balish, 2006). Hence, the unpredictability of seizures still overshadows the lives of most epilepsy patients.

Treatment options for epilepsy may include surgery, a special diet, or a surgically implanted device which delivers electrical stimulation to the brain. According to the Epilepsy Foundation of America, seizures can be successfully controlled by appropriate medication such as anti-epileptic drugs or anti-convulsants in about 50% to 80% of cases. However, for patients who do not respond well to medication, surgery is the next best option.

Due to the risks associated with the unpredictability of epilepsy, epileptic seizure detection is critically important to physicians. Nowadays, video- Electroencephalogram (EEG)-monitoring is the gold standard for the diagnosis of epilepsy. EEG is the recording of electrical activity produced by the firing of neurons within the brain, and has long been used as a clinical test in the diagnosis and monitoring of epilepsy. Prior to surgery, intracranial electroencephalogram (IEEG) needs to be monitored in order to confirm the seizure zone. Unfortunately, analyzing these EEG recordings is a time-consuming task for neurology physicians, and patterns indicating epilepsy can sometimes be confused with those of other disorders producing similar seizure-like activity (Kalaycı & Oʻzdamar, 1995). Hence, there is a strong need to develop an artificial intelligent (AI) system for epileptic seizure detection.

Osorio et al. (Osorio, Frei, & Wilkinson, 1998) developed an algorithm for real-time detection of epileptic seizures based on the fast wavelet transform with the Daub 4 family of wavelets and a median filter to detect seizures. In their algorithm, power spectral density (PSD) in a time sequence played an important role in distinguishing seizures. Their real-time method achieved high sensitivity and specificity when tested on 125 seizures in short time segments from 16 subjects. Tezel (Tezel & oʻzbay, 2009) presented three neural network models with different adaptive activation functions (NNAAF) within hidden neurons to detect epileptic seizures. Activation functions included the sigmoid function, sum of sigmoid function and sinusoidal function, and Morlet Wavelet function. Previous research (Wongsawat, 2008) also demonstrated the use of phase congruency to robustly detect epileptic seizure, calculated using Log-Gabor wavelets. The number of spikes detected from the phase congruency of two classes of EEG data (epilepsy and seizure-free) were used as distinctive features. In addition, Worrell et al. (Worrell et al., 2004) suggested that high frequency epileptiform oscillation signatures appear highly localized in the seizure onset zone. The authors noted that the brief spikes of low amplitude and high frequency energy were clinically useful for localizing the seizure onset zone. Kaiser's (Kaiser, 1990, 1993) proposed the Teager energy operator (TEO) to estimate the energy of an oscillating signal. Choi et al. (Choi, Jung, & Kim, 2006) modified Kaiser's TEO method with an improved multi-resolution Teager energy operator (MTEO) detector that employs smoothing windows normalized by noise power derived from mathematical analyses. Their experimental results prove that this detector achieves higher detection ratios at a fixed false alarm ratio than both the TEO detector and the discrete wavelet transform detector.

In response to the need for detecting seizure onset more efficiently, the development of spike or seizure detection algorithms has grown rapidly. Abnormal spikes under certain conditions in EEG recordings are indicators used for the diagnosis of epilepsy (Kiloh, McComas, Osselton, & Upton, 1981; Niedermeyer & Silva, 1993), so abnormal spike detection plays a crucial role in epileptic seizure detection. İnan et al. (İnan & Kuntalp, 2007) applied the fuzzy C-means (FCM) clustering algorithm on certain epileptic spike features, such as time durations. The FCM based two-stage system provides a 93.3% sensitivity and 74.1% specificity to detect spikes (a total of 166 individual waves with 15 epileptic spike and 151 non-epileptic spike activities). However, the selectivity of spikes was only 26.4%, which means that just over 1/4 of all waves labelled as epileptic spikes were truly epileptic spikes. Xu et al. (Xu, Wang, Zhang, Zhang, & Zhu, 2007) tried to solve the same problem by using an improved morphological filter and comparing it to the traditional morphological filter and wavelet analysis using the Mexican hat function. Their method results in a 7.52% overall false detection rate based on 957 spikes.

2. Fusion System Structure of Epileptic Seizure Detection

In this chapter, the goal is to use fusion technology (Hall & McMullen, 2004) to develop an intelligence computing approach to detect seizure onset from intracranial EEG (IEEG), which is different from pure spike detection (İnan & Kuntalp, 2007; Xu et al., 2007). The fusion technology indicates levels of the Joint Directors Of Laboratories (JDL) data fusion process through source preprocessing, object refinement, situation refinement, impact assessment, process refinement and cognitive refinement (optional (Bosse, 2007)).

The system structure of seizure detection for the above fusion processing begins with Level 0 processing, which includes EEG signal processing and filtering. Because of the high correlation between EEG channels, Level 1 processing evaluates the number of spikes and TEO energy on multiple EEG channels. Back propagation artificial neural network (BPNN), fuzzy C-means (FCM), ant colony k-means (AK) and TEO provide for feature extraction. In Level 2 processing, the above values are interpreted to mean seizure onset by meeting a certain number of thresholds. Level 3 processing utilizes the expert system to make a decision. Level 4 processing measures the performance. However, fusion control is optional in this system. The block diagram is shown is fig. 1. In Level 1, Either BPNN, FCM or AK was applied and compared to the framework to extract spike patterns in EEG signals indicating different types of epileptic conditions.

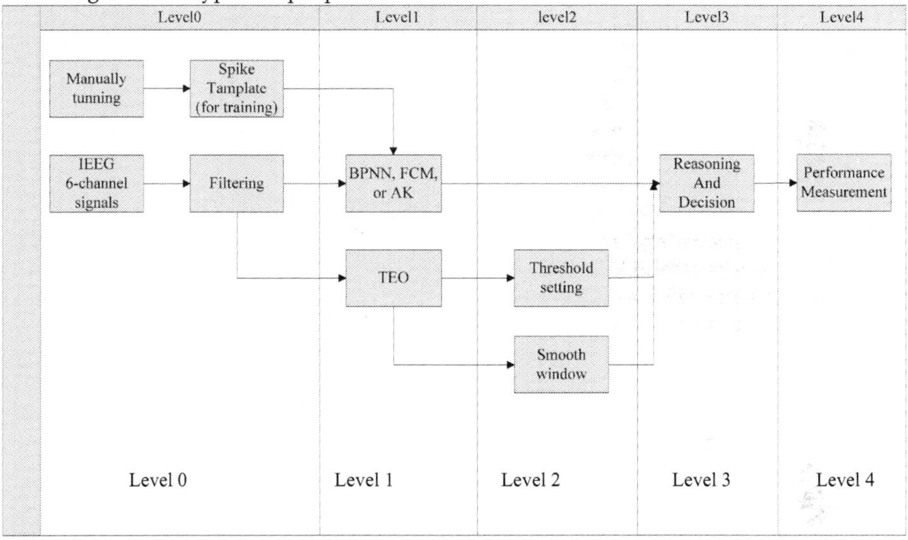

Level0	Level1	level2	Level3	Level4
Manually tunning → Spike Tamplate (for training)				
IEEG 6-channel signals → Filtering	BPNN, FCM, or AK		Reasoning And Decision	Performance Measurement
	TEO	Threshold setting		
		Smooth window		
Level 0	Level 1	Level 2	Level 3	Level 4

Fig. 1. Fusion system structure of seizure detection

3. Methodology

The methods for implementing the above system structure are listed as follows:

3.1 Experiment Databases

Our experimental data came from two sources. The training data for spike detection came from Tzu Chi Hospital in Taiwan. The raw data of electrocorticography (ECoG) and depth EEG from patients who underwent epileptic surgery with chronic intracranial recordings were analyzed. The program developers were blind to these files.

The testing electroencephalography came from the FSPEEG database (Aschenbrenner-Schiebe et al., 2003; Maiwald et al., 2004; Winterhalder et al., 2003) with authorization. The data were recorded during invasive pre-surgical epilepsy monitoring at the Epilepsy Center of the University Hospital of Freiburg, Germany. The EEG database contains invasive EEG recordings of 21 patients suffering from medically intractable focal epilepsy. Of the 21 patients, 11 have their epileptic focus locations in neocortical brain structures, 8 in the hippocampus, and 2 in both. Detailed information on the 21 subjects is listed in Table 1. The database has a sampling rate of 256 Hz with 16-bit resolution without notch or band pass filters applied at the beginning. Matlab 7.x (Mathworks Inc.) and Visual Studio 2008 C# (Microsoft Inc.) were used for implementation.

Patient	Sex	Age	Seizure Types	Regions	Seizures Analyzed
1	F	15	SP	Frontal	4
2	M	38	SP,CP,GTC	Temporal	3
3	M	14	SP,CP	Frontal	5
4	F	26	SP,CP,GTC	Temporal	5
5	F	16	SP,CP,GTC	Frontal	5
6	F	31	CP,GTC	Temporo/ Occipital	3
7	F	42	SP,CP,GTC	Temporal	3
8	F	32	SP,CP	Frontal	2
9	M	44	CP,GTC	Temporo/Occipital	5
10	M	47	SP,CP,GTC	Temporal	5
11	F	10	SP,CP,GTC	Parietal	4
12	F	42	SP,CP,GTC	Temporal	4
13	F	22	SP,CP,GTC	Temporo/Occipital	2
14	F	41	CP,GTC	Fronto/Temporal	4
15	M	31	SP,CP,GTC	Temporal	4
16	F	50	SP,CP,GTC	Temporal	5
17	M	28	SP,CP,GTC	Temporal	5
18	F	25	SP,CP	Frontal	5
19	F	28	SP,CP,GTC	Frontal	4
20	M	33	SP,CP,GTC	Tempro/Parietal	5
21	M	13	SP,CP	Temptral	5

SP=simple partial CP=complex partial GTC=generalized tonic-clonic
Table 1. Summary of 21 subjects on FSPEEG database

3.2 Level 0: Filtering and Spike Template Selection for Training Process

Unlike other databases, the database: was recorded directly from focal areas, benefiting from the advantage of a high signal-to-noise ratio. Nonetheless, there was still a need to remove power-line interference, signal-line stretch, and baseline wonder artifacts for signal quality assurance. Hence, three digital filters were applied, including a 50/60Hz notch filter, a 0.1-70Hz band pass filter, and a median filter.

In general, there are about 10 types of epileptiform discharges. Fig. 2 lists the most common types of spikes (spike, sharp wave, spike-and-wave complexes, and polyspike complex). Fifty of the most common spike templates and fifty background normal IEEG templates were manually selected for training purposes.

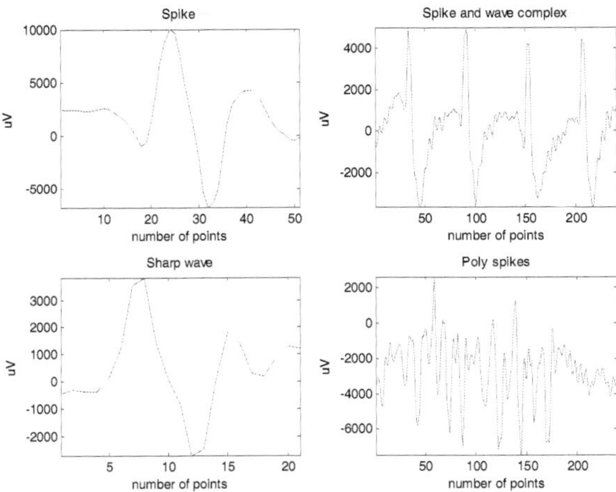

Fig. 2. Four most common types of spikes (spike, sharp wave, spike-and-wave complexes, and polyspike complex)

Our neurology expert carefully marked typical epilepsy spikes and non-spikes for algorithm development. In Fig. 3, three types of feature waves were extracted from templates, including up waves and down waves from epileptic spikes and background normal IEEG waves were extracted, as well as up waves and down waves from epileptic spikes and background normal IEEG waves.

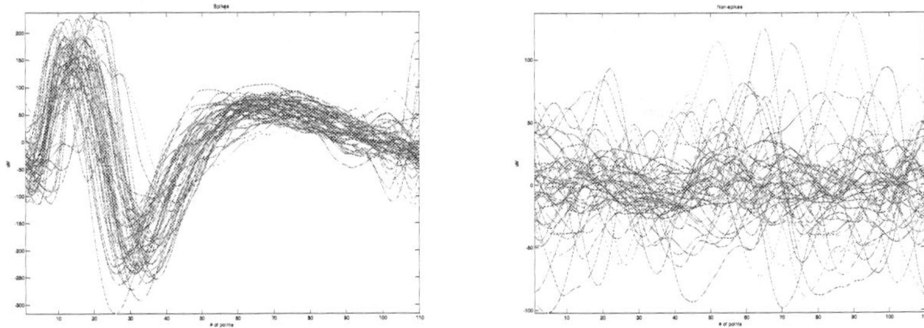

Fig. 3. Training templates typical spikes (left) and non-spikes (right)

For the following sections, three intelligent computing techniques (BP, FCM and AK) are introduced.

3.3 Level 1: Spike Pattern Recognition

As mentioned, epileptic spike detection methods can be categorized as: (1) morphology-based and (2) feature-based. The concept of the morphology-based method is to compare the entire spike waveform to a spike template. Any spike waveforms close to the template are classified as epileptic spikes. The other distanced waveforms are distinguished as normal IEEG. In comparison, the concept of the feature-based method is to extract possible spike features from IEEG waveforms for classification. The following computational intelligence methods are able to be applied on both categories.

3.3.1 Back propagation neural network

Back propagation neural network (BPNN) (Haykin, 2008) is a supervised neural network. BPNN is a well-known artificial neural network. BPNN includes three layers: the input layer, hidden layer, and output layer as show in fig. 4.

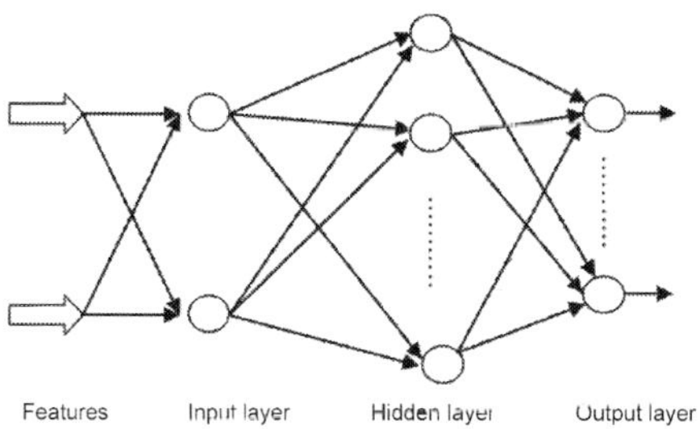

Fig. 4. Three layers in BPNN

The sigmoid function was used as an activation function. The output of the j-th neuron in the output layer is given by

$$Y_j = f\!\left(net_j^Y\right) \tag{1}$$

where net_j^Y is the sum of the j-th neuron in the output layer

$$net_j^Y = \sum_h W_{hj}^{HY} H_h + \theta_j^Y \tag{2}$$

where W_{hj}^{HY} is the weight between the h-th neuron in the hidden layer and the j-th neuron in the output layer, H_h is the output of the h-th neuron in the hidden layer, θ_j^Y is the bias of the j-th neuron in the output layer. One output neuron indicates epileptic spikes, and the other output neuron represents normal EEG rhythms. The output of the h-th neuron in the hidden layer is given by

$$H_h = f\!\left(net_h^H\right) \tag{3}$$

where net_h^H is the sum of the h-th neuron in the hidden layer

$$net_h^H = \sum_h W_{ih}^{XH} x_i - \theta_h^H \tag{4}$$

where W_{ih}^{XH} is the weight between the i-th neuron in the input layer and the h-th neuron in the hidden layer, x_i is the i-dimensional input data, θ_h^H is the bias of the h-th neuron in the hidden layer. Our BPNN structure for epileptic spike detection is N-15-2, meaning that the template length is N with 15 neurons in the hidden layer and 2 neurons in the output layer.

3.3.2 Fuzzy C-means clustering

Fuzzy C-means is an algorithm that follows the same steps as the k-means (Haykin, 2008) algorithm. However, instead of binary indicators, FCM applies degrees of memberships as indicators. This method finds the minimum distance D between input vector x and specific classes.

$$D = \frac{1}{M}\sum_{i=1}^{M} d_{min}(x_i) \tag{5}$$

The main procedures are as follows,
1.   Initialize the indicators to make the sum of indicators equal to one

$$\sum_{j=1}^{M} I_{ji} = 1, \forall j = 1,....,n \tag{6}$$

2.   Calculate the codebook w_i by using indicators and input vector x

$$w_i = \frac{\displaystyle\sum_{j=1}^{n} I_{ji}^{m} x_j}{\displaystyle\sum_{j=1}^{n} I_{ji}^{m}} \tag{7}$$

3.   Re-compute the new indicators by using new codebook w_i

$$I_{ji} = \frac{1}{\displaystyle\sum_{s=1}^{k}\left(\frac{\left\|x_j - w_i\right\|}{\left\|x_j - w_s\right\|}\right)^{\frac{2}{m^*-1}}} \tag{8}$$

where m* is set as 2.
4.   The distance of fuzzy C-means is calculated by

$$D = \sum_{i=1}^{M}\sum_{j=1}^{n} I_{ji}^{m}\left\|x_j - w_i\right\|^{2} \tag{9}$$

Then run steps 1 through 4 until all codebooks are convergent.

3.3.3 Ant K-means clustering (AK)

Ant colony optimization (ACO) is a recently proposed metaheuristic approach for solving hard combinatorial optimization problems (Dorigo & Stiitzle, 2000). In particular, the ant k-means (AK) clustering method is one branch of the biomimetic approach proposed by R.J. Kuo (Kuo, Wang, Hu, & Chou, 2005). Instead of using general clustering methods, biomimetic computing is a biology-inspired technology which is flourishingly used in system modeling, social science, and artificial intelligence (AI). This method simulates the interaction of an ant society to solve clustering problems without using any machine training processes. This self-organized structure is based on a certain probability, so-called pheromone, and results in a robust clustering method. It is proved that this method can be applied to many different kinds of clustering problems, or combined with data mining techniques to achieve more promising results in other industries (Kuo et al., 2005).

Ants exhibit many characteristics that solve different problems. As mentioned, ACO is an approach for solving optimization problems, and the ant k-means deals with clustering problems. The main idea behind the ants algorithm depends on a chemical material called "pheromone." A higher pheromone concentration guides ants toward their clustering targets. On the other hand, pheromone naturally evaporates over time, so that longer travel paths can cause low pheromone concentration. Hence, the optimal path is guaranteed. This kind of self-organized social behavior is applied to solve clustering problems by constructing the best pathway for clustering. The AK algorithm assigns each data point to a specific cluster (class) and each ant gives its own clustering solution. Ants aggregate to centers of classes by a probability P.

$$P_{ij}^{k} = \frac{\tau_{ij}^{\alpha}\eta_{ij}^{\beta}}{\sum_{c}^{nc}\tau_{ic}^{\alpha}\eta_{ic}^{\beta}} \tag{10}$$

where τ is the pheromone, η is the inverse of the distance between the two points, α is the relative importance of the trail $(\alpha \geq 0)$, β is the relative importance of the visibility $(\beta \geq 0)$, c is the cluster, and nc is the number of clusters. After m ants have done their clustering, the best solution is chosen and assigned a new pheromone.

$$\tau_{ij}(n+1) = (1-\rho)\tau_{ij}(n) \times \frac{Q}{TWCV} \tag{11}$$

where ρ is the pheromone decay parameter $(0 < \rho < 1)$, Q is a constant, TWCV is the total within cluster variance. By continuing this process, the clusters are distinguished. The new centers are calculated by Eq. 13.

$$\sum_{k=1}^{nc}\sum_{i\in K}(O_i, O_{center}(T_k))^2 \tag{12}$$

where O_i is the i-th data, and T_k is the ant set T within class k.

The steps of the algorithm are described below::
1. Initialize pheromone (equal to 1), the number of clusters (k) and number of ants (m).
2. Initialize m ants to k different random cluster centers.
3. For each ant, let each input vector x belong to one cluster with the probability given in Eq. 10.
4. Calculate new cluster centers.
5. If the TWCV is changed, go to next step. Otherwise, go to Step 3.
6. Update the pheromone level in all data according to the new solution.
7. Update cluster centers according to the new solution.
8. If the distances of cluster centers to zero or less than ε, merge the centers.
9. If the termination criterion is satisfied, go to the next step. Otherwise, go to Step 3.
10. Output the clustering results.

Various clustering techniques with no training process required have been widely applied in many fields, including gene selection and expression (Liu, Wan, & Wang, 2006; Tseng & Kao, 2005), artificial intelligence, and epileptic spike detection. Thus, it is necessary to understand the advantages and limitations among various clustering techniques (k-means, FCM, and

AK). Hence, the UC Irvine Machine Learning Repository database was tested to compare three clustering algorithms (kmeans, FCM, and AK). Table 2 lists the investigated databases and their descriptions and Table 3 compares the accuracy among various clustering algorithms. Promisingly, the results show that the AK method provided the best overall results in those datasets.

Machine learning datasets	Number of instances	Number of attributes	Number of classes
Iris	150	4	3
Lung Cancer	32	56	3
Breast Cancer Wisconsin (Diagnostic)	569	32	2
Wine	178	13	3
Pen-Based Recognition of Handwritten Digits	10992	16	10

Table 2. Machine learning database description

Name of dataset	AK	Kmeans	FCM
Iris	90.66%	70.88%	84.64%
Lung Cancer	62.34%	50%	48.15%
Breast Cancer Wisconsin (Diagnostic)	90.54%	85.41%	88.05%
Wine	70.22%	65.36%	69.67%
Pen-Based Recognition of Handwritten Digits	71.48%	45.24%	28.69%

Table 3. Accuracy comparison on various clustering algorithms

The Iris dataset, which contains 3 classes, can be used to illustrate an example. One class is linearly separable, while the others are non-linearly separable. In this dataset, the AK method demonstrated the best performance compared to the k-means and FCM algorithms. Both the AK and FCM algorithms process non-linear datasets with a high degree of accuracy. Fig. 5 plots the Iris dataset with two attributes (1&2) for visialization. The k-means algorithm works well when handling linearly separable distributions, but the AK and FCM algorithms have an advantage by being able to separate non-linearly separable data. Due to the pheromone factor, performance of AK improved dramatically.

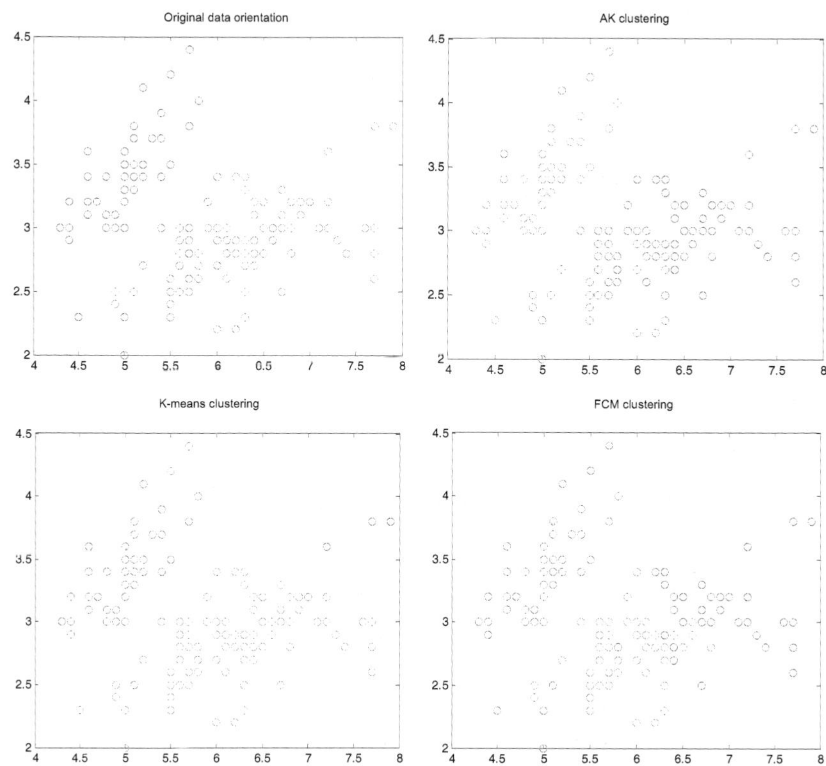

Fig. 5. Comparison of the cluttering results among AK, K-means, and FCM methods

3.4 Level 1 & 2 Teager Energy Operator (TEO) And Smooth Window

Multi-resolution teager energy operator (MTEO)(Choi et al., 2006) as shown in Eq.13 is one kind of filter to enhance action potential.

$$x^*(n) = \psi(x(n)) = x^2(n) - x(n+k)x(n-k) \tag{13}$$

where x(n) is an IEEG signal and k is a constant. MTEO is used here because some properties of action potential waves are similar to spikes. It can also change the value of k to reduce noise. In addition, smoothing window is used to the enhance signal x* after MTEO as follows,

$$y(n) = \frac{\sum_{i=1}^{sw} x^*(i)}{sw} \tag{14}$$

where sw denotes length of window (here sw=50). The method is used for distinguishing seizure onset by setting the threshold to 1900 μV^2.

3.5 Level 3: Reasoning for Data Fusion

The reasoning behind data fusion is based on the following five principles: 1) sudden desynchronization of background EEG pattern, 2) changing of frequency into a distinct rhythm, 3) showing the spiky phase of the oncoming rhythmical waves, 4) increasing in voltage of the new rhythm, and 5) propagation of the new EEG activity into adjacent regions or channels were encoded into the program for seizure onset detection and description of the seizure zone.

4. Level 4. Performance Measurement and Results

Using the training dataset, an accuracy rate of 86.37% and 97.33% for seizure onset detection and seizure zone illustration was obtained with the BPNN-based and AK-based systems, respectively. It must be noted however, that BPNN was under supervised learning and AK was a non-supervised learning process, so the training dataset for the AK-based system is for comparison purposes only. Adding more training samples for BPNN is expected to increase the system performance.

In the testing data, all seizure durations within the FSPEEG database were given. There were a total of 21 IEEG recordings from different subjects, each with different types of epilepsy and varying seizure onset times. For the preformance evaluation purpose, our extracted the 2 minutes before and after seizure occurrence (4 minutes total). The data was then divided into 10-second segments for evaluating performance of seizure detection. After arranging the data, there was a total of 348 minutes of EEG for processing, including 107 minutes of seizure onset. The ratio of seizure onset time to non-seizure onset time is about 1/3. Table 4 shows the morphology-based system performance as an example by evaluating each individual' s data.Accuracy, sensitivity, and specificity are general indexes for performance measurement.

$$\text{Sensitivity} = \frac{TP}{TP+FN} \times 100\% \tag{15}$$

$$\text{Specificity} = \frac{TN}{TN+FP} \times 100\% \tag{16}$$

where, TP-true positive is the number of epileptic seizure (ES) waves correctly detected by the system, TN-true negative is the number of non-ES waves correctly detected by the system, FP-false positive is the number of waves incorrectly labeled as ES activity by the system, and FN-false negative is the number of waves incorrectly labeled as non-ES activity by the system.

Patient #	Sensitivity		Specificity		Accuracy	
	BPNN	AK	BPNN	AK	BPNN	AK
1	50%	66.67%	80%	68.89%	78.13%	68.75%
2	70.97%	54.84%	95.12%	92.68%	84.72%	76.39%
3	65.21%	62.79%	100%	97.26%	86.67%	84.48%
4	53.13%	69.77%	85.71%	87.01%	85.71%	80.83%
5	0%	15.79%	99.01%	95.05%	83.33%	82.5%
6	57.89%	35%	100%	100%	88.89%	91.94%
7	48%	33.33%	95.74%	80.43%	79.17%	59.76%
8	25%	50%	70.83%	70.83%	47.92%	60.42%
9	66.67%	16.67%	92.31%	91.03%	83.33%	65%
10	0%	34.09%	100%	90.79%	63.33%	70%
11	85%	80%	58.93%	69.64%	69.79%	73.96%
12	52.38%	45%	78.67%	88.16%	72.92%	79.17%
13	25%	50%	100%	92.86%	68.75%	75%
14	46.51%	30.23%	98.11%	90.57%	75%	63.54%
15	61.11%	19.44%	100%	81.67%	85.42%	58.33%
16	7.96%	28.85%	100%	97.06%	60%	67.5%
17	85.71%	33.33%	53.85%	96.15%	65%	47.17%
18	80%	80%	60.87%	80%	61.67%	80%
19	20%	40%	91.21%	89.01%	87.5%	86.46%
20	83.33%	40%	97.62%	95%	93.33%	76.67%
21	0%	13.95%	100%	93.51%	65%	65%
Overall	**47.3%**	**40.1%**	**87.7%**	**88.2%**	**74.6%**	**73.2%**

Table 4. System performance of ten-second window periods for two morphology-based methods.

Based on our results, the morphology- AK based method performs the promising results. In Fig. 6, upper and lower figures show the spike and normal templates in sequence (250, 500, and 1000 epochs if thirty ants were chosen), respectively. Each process loop includes random data selecting, centers computing, and pheromone updating.

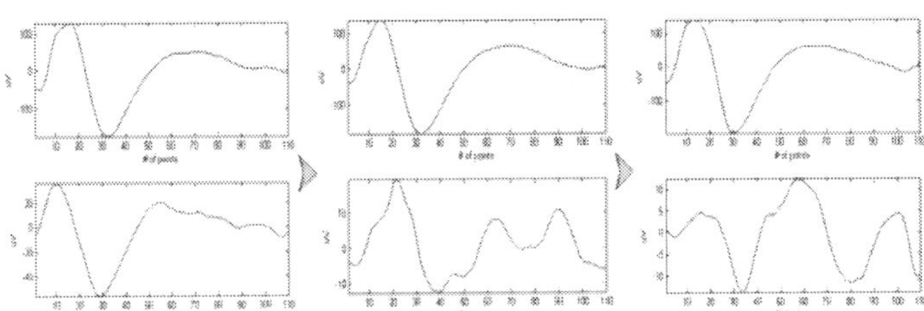

Fig. 6. In AK process, from left to right, it shows the results when 250, 500, and 1000 epochs applied.

Hence, the method is also applied on FSPEEG database and the method detects epileptic spikes accurately in Fig 7.

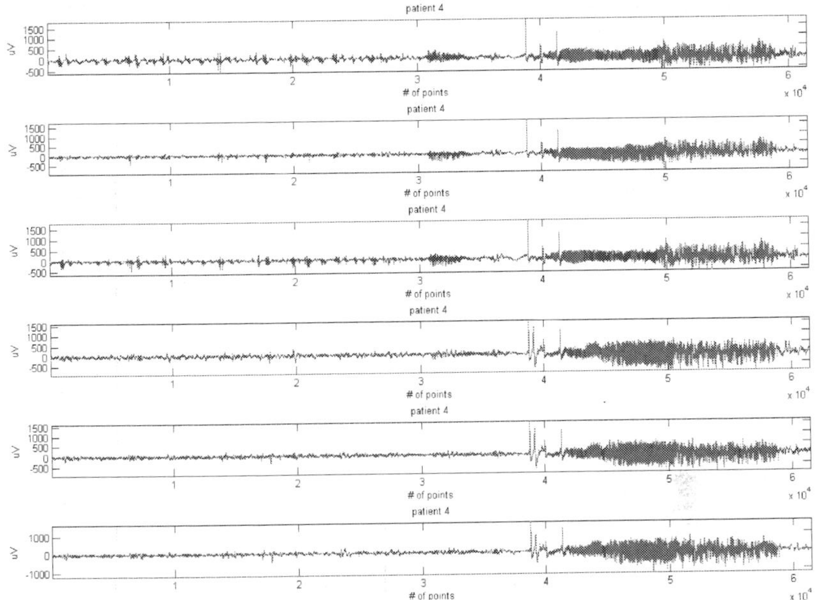

Fig. 7. Applied morphology-AK based method on FSPEEG database for six-channel IEEG: The red waveforms indicate spikes which are detected accurately.

The BPNN based system has an overall accuracy of 74.6%, with a specificity and sensitivity of 87.7% and 47.3%, respectively. The AK based system has an overall accuracy of 73.2%, with a specificity and sensitivity of 88.2% and 40.1%, respectively. The reason behind low sensitivity could be due to the lack of EEG channels. The FSPEEG database provided 6 channels (instead of the full 20 channels) - 3 infocus and 3 outfocus channels. Because epileptic discharges spread, it is hard to make a decision based on just a few channels. However, the 74.9% accuracy and 87.7% specificity means that our method can be used as a non-seizure eliminator. If the system preformance only considers whether the seizure is detected during the ictal stage, the BPNN-based and AK-based systems provide a detection rate of 90.5% (19 out of 21) and 100% (21 out of 21), respectively. Fig.8. shows that the fusion system for epileptic seizure detection is implemented by Visual Studio 2008 C#.

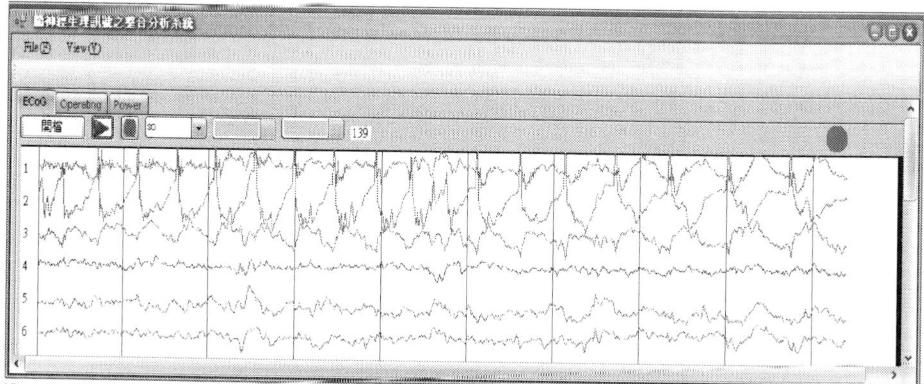

Fig. 8. System interface: Once seizure is detected, the circle on the right top turns into red with sound alert. Spikes also are marked as red.

5. Conclusion and Discussion

It has to be noted that the BPNN-based system has 0% sensitivity and almost 100% specificity for patients #5, 10, and 21. This means that the system missed the seizure completely and marked it as a non-seizure. However, in the AK-based system, no 0% sensitivity cases appeared. This means that although the system may not detect seizure onset during its entire time period, the epileptic seizure can be detected at some point during the seizure occurrence. Overall, the two systems have different characteristics in seizure detection. Overall, the ant k-means (AK) provide an effective, accurate, and adaptive method for spike detection. In addition, no training or pre-knowledge is required on AK algorithm. However, unlike traditional k-means, ant k-means reaches higher accuracy because ant k-means has the pheromone probability to jump out of the local minima. The result shows that AK worked successfully well in our epilepsy patient data.

In the BPNN training phase, the selected spikes should be increased to improve system performance. However, the TEO plus smooth window can detect energy change well, and therefore, the non-seizure part is easy to identify. Background EEG must be used for calibration to avoid outliers with small background EEG. Small EEG amplitudes cause high FP because of the subtle energy change. This caused our system to label all small amplitude EEG data as non-seizure events. Moreover, the baseline wander would cause high TN due to the sensitivity of TEO. However, the system marked input data with heavy baseline wander as seizures.

6. Future research

Although the epileptic seizure detection system still has room for improvement, the preliminary results are encouraging. Future research may focus on predicting anatomic seizure in the context of an epilepsy surgical plan. Seizure prediction (Aschenbrenner-Schiebe et al., 2003; Winterhaider et al., 2003) is essential because of the various aspects associated with the disorder, including diagnosis, treatment options, physical risks, social implications, loss of self-efficacy, depression and anxiety. Risks of delaying a correct diagnosis through this method occur among patients who meet a physician infrequently in the interictal state. In addition, seizure prediction provides a new way for drug treatment to maximize intended drug effects, minimizes possible side-effects, and can serve as a guide toward developing an effective acute intervention in the early phase (Schelter, Timmer, & Schulze-Bonhage, 2008); Early diagnosis is beneficial, because long-term antieplieptic treatment increases a person's risk of premature death, can have hormonal effects on fertile females, trigger liver failure, and cause mood disorders. Unfortunately, seizure prediction with a time horizon of minutes to hours remains a challenge and a clinically applicable solution is still not available. The tools developed for seizure identification should serve in future neurological expert system development, brain computer interface (BCI), or investigation of mental tasks by a patient.

7. Acknowledgements

This research is supported by Tzu Chi University / General Hospital and the project serial number is TCMRC-P-97006. Thanks to Dr. Yue-Loong Hsin and Dr. Tomor Harnod in the Department of Neurology of Tzu Chi Hospital for providing the necessary support. Also special thanks to group researchers of the University Freiburg and the University Hospital Freiburg in providing the EEG database (https://epilepsy.uni-freiburg.de/) for this research.

8. References

Aschenbrenner-Schiebe, R., Maiwald, T., Winterhalder, M., Voss, H. U., Timmer, J., & Schulze-Bonhage, A. (2003). How well can epileptic seizures be predicted? An evaluation of a nonlinear method. *Brain, 216*(2616-2626).

Betts, T. (1998). What is epilepsy? Electrical Engineering and Epilepsy: A Successful Partnership, *IEEE Trans. on Biomed. Eng.* Savoy Place,London.

Bosse, E. (2007). *Concepts, Models, and Tools for Information.* Norwood,MA: Artech House Inc.

Choi, J. H., Jung, H. K., & Kim, T. (2006). A New Action Potential Detector Using the MTEO and Its Effects on Spike Sorting Systems at Low Signal-to-Noise Ratios. *IEEE Trans. on Biomed. Eng, vol. 53*(No. 4), p.p.738-746.

Dorigo, M., & Stiitzle, T. (2000). The Ant Colony Optimization Metaheuristic: Algorithms, Applications, and Advances. *Technical Report IRIDIA.*

Hall, D. L., & McMullen, S. A. H. (2004). *Mathematical Techniques in Multisensor Data Fusion* (2nd ed ed.). Norwood, MA,: Artech House Inc.

Haykin, S. (2008). *Neural Networks and Learning Machines* (3rd ed.): Prentice Hall.

İnan, Z. H., & Kuntalp, M. (2007). A study on fuzzy C-means clustering-based systems in automatic spike detection. *Comput Biol Med, 37*(8), 1160-1166.

Kaiser, J. F. (1990, April 3-6). *On a simple algorithm to calculate the energy of a signal.* Paper presented at the ICASSP, Albuquerque, New Mexico.

Kaiser, J. F. (1993, April). *Some useful properties of Teager's energy operators.* Paper presented at the IEEE ICASSP, Minneapolis, Minnesota.

Kalaycı, T., & Oˇ zdamar, O. (1995). Wavelet preprocessing for automated neural network detection of EEG spikes. *IEEE Engineering in Medicine and Biology*, 160 - 166.

Kiloh, L. G., McComas, A. J., Osselton, J. W., & Upton, A. (1981). *Clinical Electroencephalography* (4th ed ed.). London, UK,: Butterworths Inc.

Kuo, R. J., Wang, H. S., Hu, T.-L., & Chou, S. H. (2005). Application of ant K-means on clustering analysis. *Computers & Mathematics with Applications, 50*(10-12), 1709-1725.

Liu, B., Wan, C., & Wang, L. P. (2006). An efficient semi-unsupervised gene selection method via spectral biclustering. *IEEE Transactions on Nano-Bioscience, 5*(2), 110-114.

Maiwald, T., Winterhalder, M., Aschenbrenner-Scheibe, R., Voss, H. U., Schulze-Bonhage, A., & J., T. (2004). Comparison of three nonlinear seizure prediction methods by means of the seizure prediction characteristic. *Physica D, 194*(357-368).

Niedermeyer, E., & Silva, F. L. D. (Eds.). (1993). *Electroencephalography, Basic Principles, Clinical Applications and Related Fileds* (3rd ed ed.). Baltimore,MD: Williams & Wilkins.

Nouri, S., & Balish, M. (2006). Sudden Unexpected Death in Epilepsy. from http://www.emedicine.com/neuro/topic659.htm

Osorio, I., Frei, M. G., & Wilkinson, S. B. (1998). Real-time automated detection and quantitative analysis of seizures and short-term prediction of clinical onset. *Epilepsia, 39*(6), 615-627.

Schelter, B., Timmer, J., & Schulze-Bonhage, A. (Eds.). (2008). *Seizure Prediction in Epilepsy From Basic Mechanisms to Clinical Applications* (1 ed.). Berlin: Wiley-VCH.

Tezel, G., & o¨zbay, Y. (2009). A new approach for epileptic seizure detection using adaptive neural network. *Expert Systems With Applications, 36*(1), 172-180.

Tseng, V. S., & Kao, C. P. (2005). Efficiently Mining Gene Expression Data via a Novel Parameterless Clustering Method. *IEEE/ACM Transactions on Computational Biology and Bioinformatics, 2*, 355 - 365.

Wang, P.-J. (1998). Comphrehensive Therapy of Refractory Epilepsy. In T. E. Association (Ed.), (Vol. 2-4).

Winterhalder, M., Maiwald, T., Aschenbrenner-Schiebe, R., Voss, H. U., Timmer, J., & Schulze-Bonhage, A. (2003). The seizure prediction characteristic: A general framework to assess and compare seizure prediction methods. *Epilepsy and Behavior, 4*, 318 - 325.

Wongsawat, Y. (2008). Epileptic seizure detection in EEG recordings using phase congruency. *Conf Proc IEEE Eng Med Biol Soc. 2008*, 927 - 930.

Worrell, G. A., Parish, L., Cranstoun, S. D., Jonas, R., Baltuch, G., & Litt, B. (2004). High-frequency oscillations and seizure generation in neocortical epilepsy. *Brain, 127*(Pt 7), 1496-1506.

Xu, G., Wang, J., Zhang, Q., Zhang, S., & Zhu, J. (2007). A spike detection method in EEG based on improved morphological filter. *Comput Biol Med, 37*(11), 1647-1652.

## 24

Pattern Recognition Using Time Statistic Classification

Rodolfo Romero Herrera
National Polytechnic Institute (ESCOM IPN)
México, D.F.

1. Introduction

A pattern recognition system should be composed of a sensor that gathers the observations to classify such a digital camera, a feature extraction system that transforms the information captured in numerical or symbolic, and a system of classification or description of the information measure.

A pattern recognition system must have a sensor in charged of getting the data to classify for example a digital camera, a characteristic collector system that changes the captured information to numeric or symbolic values, and a classification system of the measured information.

In this chapter we focus on the statistical classification. Its main classifier is based on probability theory. It is historically the first approach and that there was probably the most developed, but it does not mean that its development and research has been finished yet.

We begin with the moments used in statistics and which are basic, which can be used to find patterns within a data base by applying the statistical patterns in the recognition of particular facial expressions in digital video processing. Despite the good results that give us the recognition of patterns using the moment , these are not enough in many cases, so we need to use other mathematical operations such as correlation and covariance as well as other concepts derived from these equations.

Most of the processes studied have historically been analyzed in an instant of time, but I really did not occur in a second. Any experiment is deterministic; all have a degree of uncertainty. Researchers have developed a theory of probabilities, although again apply with respect to a viewpoint determistico. On why we must return to stochastic processes and add a clear perspective toward randomized experiments. Although there are many phenomena which can be applied the probability, we will focus on the affective computing, for the recognition of facial expressions, because it is a process that must be treated with this efoque. To accomplish this, first locate the face and then the characteristic points of the face; Once done, apply the statistical analysis with the expectation and variance in a process that varies in time, and therefore change these values. These functions can be characterized with Gaussian or Rayleigh. Although results are promising. It is evident that with increasing the number of stored data, requires more resources or more efficient implementation of algorithms for analysis and interpretation of data.

2. Procedures for classification of patterns

The statistical approach extracts quantitative properties. The syntactic approach is based on relations associated with the geometric shape of objects. objects and the appearance-based approach considers ways to view them(Gonzalez, 2002).There are many applications of statistical pattern recognition such as finite state machine translation (Vincent alabu, 2007). Statistical pattern recognition is characterized by the use of vectors for the representation of patterns (x1 ... xn) € Rn, while the arrangement or, more generally, graphs are attacked in structural recognition. The recognition process is based on assuming that the patterns of the same class are located in a compact region Rn. The representation of objects given in terms of the vector has several properties such as the similarity of objects or Euclidean dintancia (Kaspar Reisen).

3. Statistical classification

Many new applications for developing models from data have been inspired by the capabilities of biological systems, particularly in the human biological system. Indeed, biological systems learn to accommodate the statistical nature of the environment. Both humans and animals have excess capacity on the recognition of faces, voices or smells but learn through interaction with the environment. The pattern recognition systems are based on the principles of engineering and statistics rather than on biology, however, there is an attempt to imitate the human brain or animal (Gonzalez 2002).

4. Moments

4.1 Probability density function

Much of the Japanese success is due to the use of statistical methods, which implies a large collection of information or scientific data. However, there is a big difference between collecting scientific information and inferential statistics. The use of techniques that allow us to move beyond data support; rather we infer conclusions. The information is collected as samples or groups of observations. Samples are collected from populations, which are groupings of all individuals or individual elements of a particular type. Obtaining these data is an experiment; therefore it must be repeatable and conclusions as well, however just a small change to the data change; but, in the statistical analysis, despite this small change the conclusion remains.

4.2 Random Variables

Suppose that each point in space we assign a sample number. Then we have a defined role in the sample, called stochastic variable or stochastic function. It is usually denoted by a capital letter, like X or Y. A random variable that takes a finite number of values is called discrete random variable, while one that takes an infinite number of values not accounting is called a random variable not discrete (Murray, 2001).

X is a discrete random variable, and suppose that the possible values that it can have are given by x1, x2, x3, ..., with certain order. Assume further that these values are taken with probabilities given by:

$$P(X = x_k) = f(x_k) \qquad k = 1,2,\ldots \qquad (1)$$

Then the probability distribution is given by:

$$P(X=x) = f(x) \qquad (2)$$

For $x = x_k$, is reduced to the equation (1), while for other values of x, $f(x) = 0$.
In general, $f(x)$ is a probability function if

$$f(x) \geq 0 \qquad (3)$$
$$(4)$$

$$\sum_x f(x) = 1$$

4.3Dimensional distribution

Consider two discrete random variables, we define the joint probability function of X and Y given by:

$$P(X=x, Y=y) = f(x,y) \qquad (5)$$

Where:

$$f(x,y) \geq 0 \qquad (6)$$

$$(7)$$

$$\sum_x \sum_y f(x,y) = 1$$

That is to say, the sum of all values is equal to one X yY.
Equation 7 gives us the most complete information about a two-dimensional random variable.
Suppose that X can assume any of the m values $x_1, x_2, x_3, \ldots \ldots x_m$ and Y can take any of the values $y_1, y_2, y_3 \ldots \ldots, y_n$. Then the probability of event $X = Y = x_j$ and y_k is given by

$$P(X=x_j, Y=y_k) = f(x_j, y_k) \qquad (8)$$

If we want the distribution of probability for each cardinal separately, it is clear that the probability of y_k must add all possible values in x_j

$$P(y_k) = \sum_j P(x_j, y_k) \qquad (9)$$

Similarly:

$$P(x_j) = \sum_k P(x_k, y_j) \qquad (10)$$

In many situations the two random variables X and Y, taken together, are a very natural result of a single experiment (L Paul).

5. Mathematical expectation

Moments are called the "expectation of some important types of functions. The Mathematical expectation is defined as (Elmer, 2005):

$$< x > = \sum x_i\, P(x_i) \tag{11}$$

Considering the multitude of central moments, That is to say, moments with respect to base, we have that:

$$< \dot{x}^n > = \sum (x_{i_-} < x >)^n\, P(x_i) \tag{12}$$

The second central moment is then defined as:

$$< \dot{x}^2 >= \sum (x_{i_-} < x >)^2 P(x_i) \tag{13}$$

An analysis of the second central moment, this results in increased when the distance of possible values increases and the mathematical expectation increases. Then we can conclude that him second central moment evaluates the dispersion of the possible values with respect to the mathematical expectation, it is called the variance σ^2. The standard deviation is defined as $\sigma = \sqrt{\sigma^2}$. The deterministic variables do not have standard deviation; that is to say:

$\sigma 2$ of constant $=0$

In the case of a bidimensional random variable is twice the initial and central moments with respect to the unidimensional random variable, and it is possible to introduce mutual initial and central moments:

$$< x^n y^y > = \iint x^n y^n f(x, y)\, dx\, dy \tag{14}$$

$$< \dot{x}^n \dot{y}^n > = \iint \dot{x}^n\, \dot{y}^n f(x, y)\, dx\, dy \tag{15}$$

6. Relations in the random variables

x, y are independent
Means that the result of the experiment a random variable does not influence the experiment of another random variable.
If

$$P(AB) = P(A)\, P(B\,|\,A) \tag{16}$$

but are independent, then:

$$P(AB) = P(A)\, P(B) \tag{17}$$

Functional dependence
The result of an experiment of a random variable affecting the likelihood of the values of another variable.

Statistical dependency
This result should be a measurement mathematics which can be evaluated and that is within the mutual moments.

7. Moment of Covariance

We propose $< \dot{x}\dot{y} >$ $\square$ with n = m = 1
Case 1 x and y are independent
In the continuous case we have:

$$< \dot{x}\dot{y} >= \int \dot{x}\dot{y}f(x,y)dxdy \tag{18}$$

We must:
P(AB)= P(A)P(BIA) as similarly $f(x,y) = f(x)f(yIx)$

But x and y are independent so that: $f(x,y)=f(x)f(y)$
Substituting in the formula ()

$$< \dot{x}\dot{y} > = \int \dot{x} f(x)dx \int \dot{y} f(y)dy = 0 \tag{19}$$

Because the expectation of the first moment is zero by definition.
Case 2 dependence.
We propose y = kx + a
Where "k" and "a" are constants
Let us now consider a discrete case.

$$< \dot{x}\dot{y} > = \sum_i \sum_j \dot{x}_i\dot{y}_j P(x_i)P(x_i)P(y_i|x_i) \tag{20}$$

Of equation (20) we will analyze:

$$\sum \dot{y}_j P(y_j|x_i) \tag{21}$$

Because it is a line we must:

$$P(y_j|x_i) = \begin{cases} 0 & j \neq i \\ 1 & j = 1 \end{cases} \tag{22}$$

Therefore the equation (21) is equal to $\dot{y}_j$
Substituting into (20) we have

$$< \dot{x}\dot{y} > = \sum_i \dot{x}_i\dot{y}_j P(x_i) \tag{23}$$

On the other hand we have:

$$\dot{y} = y - <y>$$ (25)

$$<y> = <kx + a> = <kx> + <a> = k<x> + a$$ (26)

Substituting in (24)

$$\sum \dot{x}_i \dot{y}_j P(x) = \sum \dot{x}_i k \dot{x}_i P(x_i) = k \sum \dot{x}_i^2 P(x_i) = k\sigma_x^2 = <\dot{x}\dot{y}>$$ (27)

Therefore we have:

$$0 \leq <\dot{x}\dot{y} \leq k\sigma_x^2$$ (28)

8. Random process

When we have many achievements and chose a time t1, in this section we have many points which are traces of each realization. that is to say, in this section we have a variate, this variate depends on the phase. See Figure 1. To have multiple signals and therefore data, while it is very difficult to describe analytically through each realization and their probabilities. Meaning that, we must determine a number for each function of time; this number is known as functional. However, there are few processes which are known for their function

We will try to describe our random process with a lot of f (p)-dimensional.

9. The function mathematical expectation and the covariance function

There is a section of time and a one-dimensional random variable xi, so you can get a lot of initial and central moments of any order, thus producing the mathematical expectation for each section. Join these points and we obtain a deterministic function(Romero, 2005). It is possible to calculate for each section, many high-order moment and again unite the charts. For example, you can calculate its variance for each section. This function is called the function of the variance of our random process.

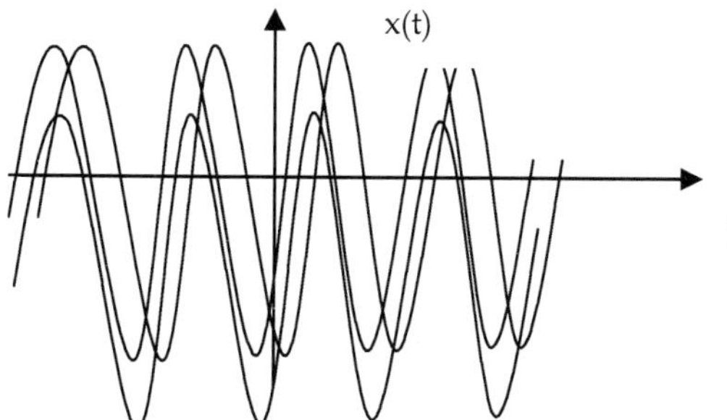

Fig.1. Functions of a complex process aletorio

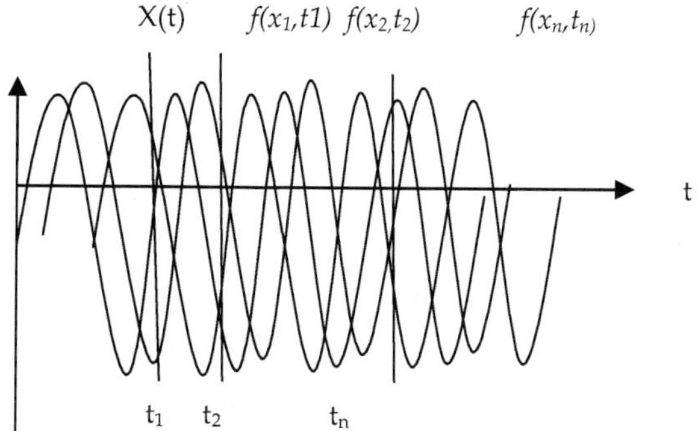

Fig. 2 Segmentation of random process

The processes may have the same function of mathematical expectation and of variance; however these processes may be different, reason why the functions moment of first order are not sufficient. Because they do not find the difference within the structure of two-time random processes different. it is by this, that considers the bidimensional variates; for example at the time t1tenemos the random variable X_1 (t_1) and at the time t_2 we have the random variable X_2 (t_2). These two random variables forming a two dimensional random variable. Each two-dimensional random variable can be described with two-dimensional function f (X_1 (t_1), X_2 (t_2)). Can be calculated many mutual initial and central moments of any order. We chose the momnet $< \dot{X}_1(t_1)\dot{X}_2(t_2) >$, which we know as the moment covariate. This moment is a number deterministic and evaluates the statistical dependence between two linear sections in the random process. This moment is called a covariance function.

$$Kx(t_1, t_2) = < \dot{X}_1(t_1)\dot{X}_2(t_2) >\big|_{t_2 \to t_1} = < \dot{X}_1^2(t_1) >= \sigma_x^2(t_1) \qquad (29)$$

Where this result is the maximum of the covariance function, where there is total dependence. When we increase the distance between two sections, the covariance function tends to zero. So if a process is smooth covariance function tends to zero slowly, if the process is very chaotic then the covariance function tends to zero too fast, that is to say, that the covariance function reflects the difference between the structures of the time in the random processes.

10. Stationary Random Process

The random process is called stationary when its mathematical hope does not depend on the time, its variance does not depend on the time and its function of covariance does not depend on its section fixes (time) and only depends on the distance between two sections (τ).

Here it is important to note that the covariance function is equal to the variance when the distance τ is equal zero, this means that the function of covariance includes information about the variance.

When two random processes X (t) y Y(t) are different, but have statistical dependence, then we characterize the role of mutual covariance with the expression:

$$< \dot{x}(t)\dot{y}(y + \tau) = K_{xy}(\tau) = \iint \dot{x}(t)\dot{y}(t + \tau)f(x(t), y(t + \tau)dx(t)dy(t + \tau) \tag{30}$$

If the function compares with itself with retardation we have:

$$K_x(\tau) = < \dot{x}(t)x(t + \dot{\sigma}) > \tag{31}$$

Which is called autocovarianza function.

There are other moments in the initial and central base dimensional but it's very complicated to calculate; however when the process is Gaussian, is sufficient to characterize K_x (t2-t1). So if you find that the process is Gaussian then simply calculate the value of a parameter for K_x for learning.

11. Method Viola & Jones.

In this application, first use a technique for locating the face, with the purpose of applying statistical methods. There are many different techniques for the detection and location of the face in an image, each one whit special characteristics. Most of the techniques have problems such the detection of a high number of false positives with no uniform background or a time high in the analysis of the image, because by nature of the project is essential image processing time Real is considered a technical proposal by Paul Viola and Michael J. Jones, with which the faces are detected at a speed of 24 frames per second tested in a conventional machine with an Intel Core Duo 1.8 Ghz.

This method is basically the location of the face using a group of rectangular features which are seeking a set of features a combination of clear parts and dark rectangles distributed within the face (Viola & Jones, 2001).

The main reason for using these features rectangular is that a system based on characteristics operates faster than a system based on pixels

We use three kinds of characteristics: the two rectangles, three rectangles and four rectangles. These features rectangular (CRs) are 10 different types shown in Figure 3

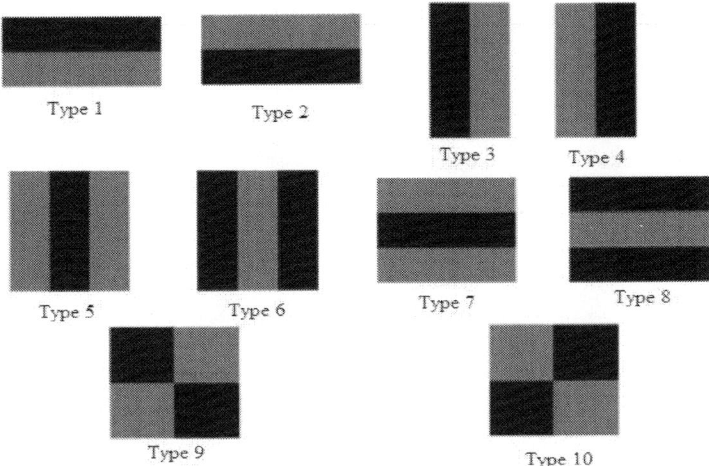

Fig. 3. Set of ten rectangular features used in the process of locating faces

The ways to use these CRs, is placing them in a certain position within the image and calculate the difference between the amounts of pixels within the clear part the dark side of the CR, gaining an integer value that it must overcome a certain threshold to be considered as being on the facial feature that should locate. This phase of training is to find the CRs that in a certain scale and position within a window of size 142 * 116 pixels, as well as its threshold, can pinpoint a feature of a human face, and this CR receives name classifier.

In Figure 4 you can appreciate a package of 16 classifiers where all classifiers figure locate a feature of the face.

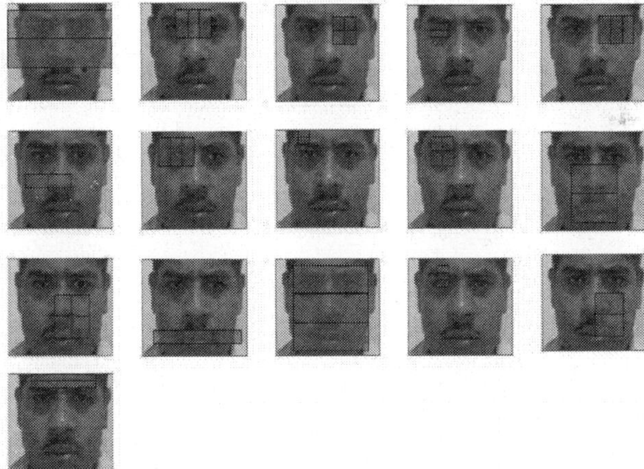

Fig. 4.- 16 rectangular features.

Once you have all these classifiers with their thresholds are placed cascading to expedite the processing power and do it in real time. Each waterfall has a number n binder and has a total of m levels of the waterfall. The more levels of the waterfall will take more processing time.

To calculate the CRs very quickly at various scales using a representation of the image called comprehensive picture. The comprehensive picture can be calculated with a couple of operations per pixel. Once calculated, any of the CRs can be calculated at any scale and location in a time constant. The image in a comprehensive position (x, y) contains the sum of the pixels above and left of (x, y), including it.

$$ii(x,y) = \sum_{x' \leq x, y' \leq y} i(x',y') \tag{32}$$

Where ii (x, y) is the holistic picture yi (x, y) is the original image (Figure 4). Using the next couple of recurrences:

$$s\ (x,\ y) = s\ (x,\ y\text{-}1) + i\ (x,\ y) \tag{33}$$
$$ii\ (x,\ y) = ii\ (x\text{-}1,\ y) + s\ (x,\ y)$$

Where s (x, y) is the cumulative sum of the values of the pixels of the row, s (x -1) = 0, and ii (-1, y) = 0) the integral image can be calculated in one pass on the original image [7].

Fig. 5 .- The value of a comprehensive picture at one point (x, y) is the sum of all pixels up and left

In Figure 6 the red rectangle shows the position in which the system has made the location of the face with a size of 142 * 116 pixels.

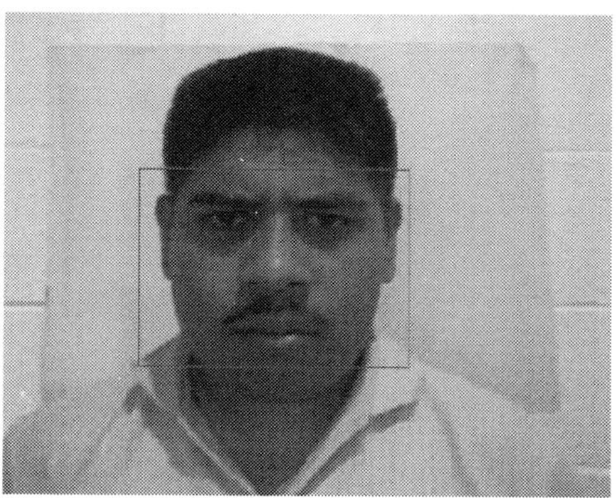

Fig. 6.- Detector of the face

12. The operator Nitzberg

Nitzberg proposes an operator making it possible to estimate the magnitude of the gradient and its orientation, as well as evidence of the presence of points corner. It uses the information in the gradient at a particular neighbourhood and combines it with a gradient operator to reduce noise. The first thing that is done is to calculate the partial derivatives in x and y throughout the image (Nitzberg & Shiota, 1993):

$$I_x(x,y) = \frac{I(x+1,y) - I(x-1,y)}{2} \qquad 34$$

$$I_y(x,y) = (I(x,y+1) - I(x,y-1))/2 \qquad (35)$$

Here is defined as follows 2X2 matrix:

$$Q(x) = \int dx'\rho(x-x')\nabla I(x')^T = \int dx'\rho(x-x')\begin{pmatrix} I_x^2(x') & I_xI_y(x') \\ I_xI_y(x') & I_y^2(x') \end{pmatrix} \qquad (36)$$

where $\nabla I(x)$ is a vector column and $\rho(x)$ is a function of decreasing weight with maximum value is 0.

The matrix Q(x) have an auto-value associated with the $\lambda_1(x)$, associated to the auto-vector $e_1(x)$ and a ato-value minor$\lambda_2(x)$. magnitude of the self-vector is give for $I_e(x) = \lambda_1(x)$ and them orientation for the orientation of a auto-vector associated $\theta_1(x) = e1$ (x) direction of self-associated vector calculation fot of points corner is used the value of the second self-worth or self-worth less than $I_c(x) = \lambda_2(x)$.

The role of weighting $\rho(x)$ allows us to soften to a greater or lesser ρThe role of weighting extent. In the experiments, and for simplicity, we selected the following function :

$$\rho(x) = \begin{cases} \dfrac{1}{w^2} & -\dfrac{w}{2} \le x \dfrac{w}{2} \; y - \dfrac{w}{2} \le y \le \dfrac{w}{2} \\ \\ 0, & \textit{in other case} \end{cases} \tag{37}$$

This descriptor contour allowed analyse frames taken by a video capture system, which provides the result is a frame that represents the pixels characteristic of it. [10].

It is an estimate of the location of the eyes, nose and the mouth which applies the operator Nitzberg this helps only get the information most important Figure 7.

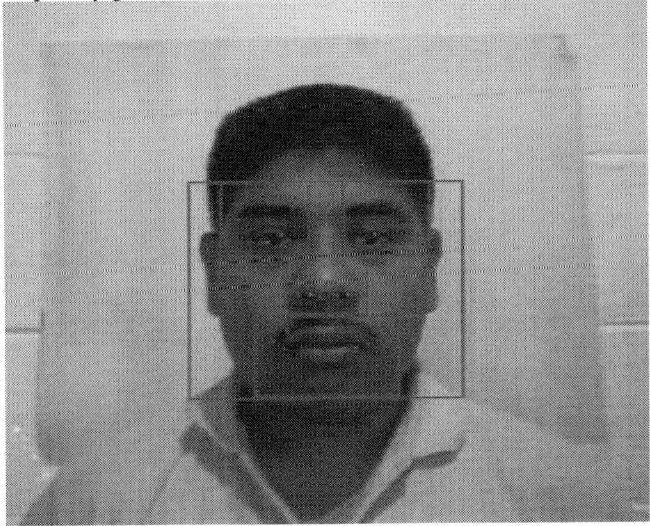

Fig. 7. Implementation of the operator Nitzberg

13. Applications.

To apply the reasoning, we obtained graphs of a system for detecting bodily emotions , and other of recognition of facial expressions, and a simulation system that uses emotional states "Cathexis" (Velazquez, 1996).

The graphs are shown in Figures 8, 9; Show the behavior of the recognition of bodily expression. The mathematical expectation shows curves similar to Gauss and Rayleigh.

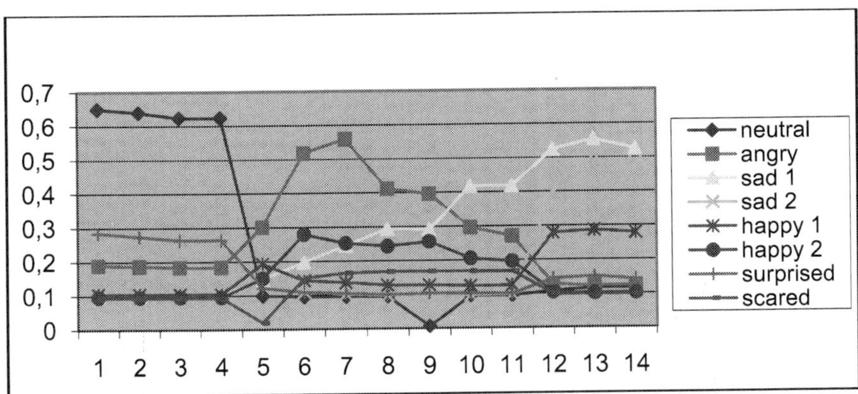

Fig. 8 Expectation of recognition of bodily expressions

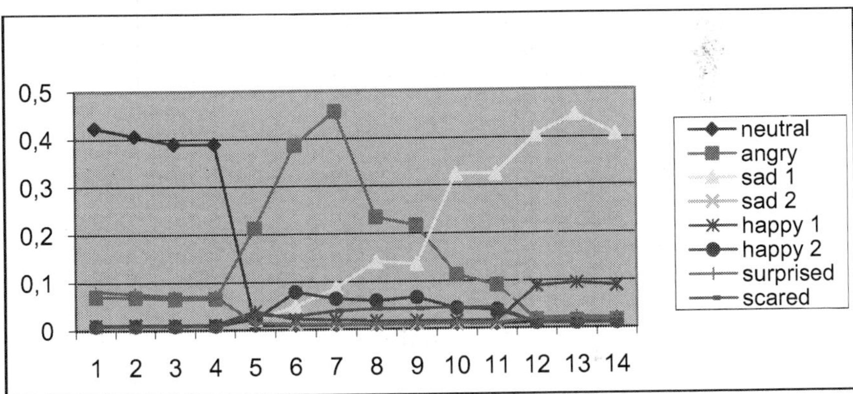

Fig. 9 Variance for the recognition of bodily expressions

In Figure 10 and 11 shows the result of recognition of facial expressions and again shows that the expectation tends to be Rayleigh or Gaussian

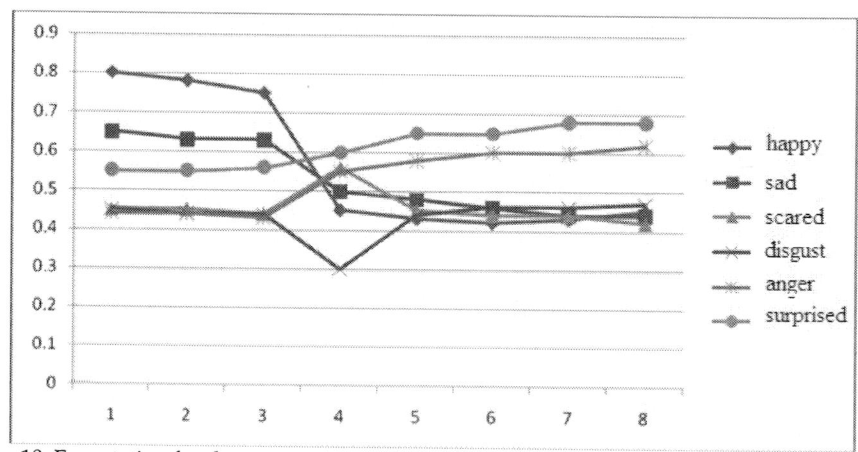

Fig. 10. Expectation for the recognition of facial expressions

For the simulation is used ecuasión of cathexis (Velazquez, 1996). The result is the same Gaussian behavior.

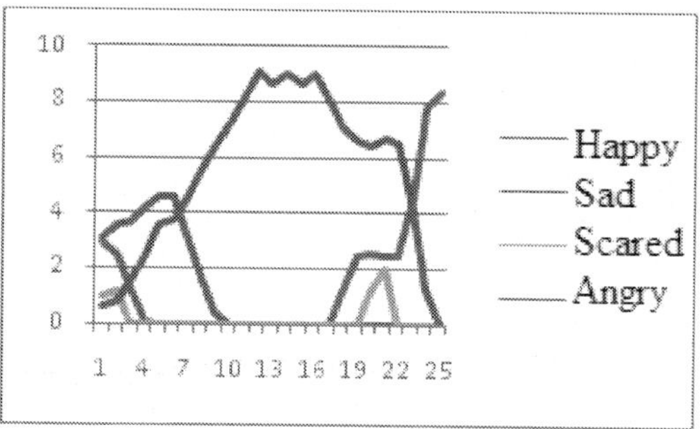

Fig. 11. Mathematical Expectation for the simulation of cathexis.

Influence emotional behavior among themselves, thus changing the graphic Gaussian perfect, and for this very reason also has a tendency to Rayleigh curves. Gaussian function is defined by the equation (Osborn 2007) (Van 2008):

$$f(x) = ae^{-(x-b)^2/2c^2}$$

Where a, b and c are real constants (a> 0). The graph of the function is symmetrical bell-shaped. The parameter "a" is the height of the campaign centered on the point b, determining the width C of the same. For this particular case f (x) is the expectation for figures 1, 3 and 4. If the case of Figure 4 f (x) is the variance.

The function is defined by the Rayleigh equation (Vanek & Albright, 2008) (Kalimuthu, 2006):

$$f(x|\alpha) = \frac{x\, e^{\frac{-x^2}{2\alpha^2}}}{\alpha^2}$$

Where α is the height of the graphs of Rayleigh and therefore the parameter of interest. Therefore if the system takes the parameter α or the maximum height, we can store this information and if the value is repeated with a certain tolerance of it as part of learning within a knowledge base. In probability theory and statistics, the Rayleigh distribution is a continuous distribution function. When a file is usually two-dimensional vector has two components, orthogonal and independent and follow a normal distribution. That is where Rxx tends to zero.

Therefore, the value of Kxx does not help to determine whether a Gaussian or Rayleigh. That is, if Kxx tends to 1 then it is a Gaussian function with a linear dependence.

14. Conclusion

There are many phenomena whose processes are not significant, practically everything in nature. It is essential for this in-depth analysis and generation of methods that take into account the random processes, and within those involving such time as a variable (stochastic processes). We present a method that is efficient for learning commands, based on the recognition of emotional expressions. The correlation was not a measure to infer whether it was random or a linear dependence, and on this basis to determine the possible plot to use. The processing time depends on how successful it is to be learning. It is clear that more data are obtained will be more efficient learning, but as long as it learns to be a higher order.

The effectiveness of the methodology was tested in a simulation, it would need to use a robot for example, or industrial machines, but the results promise good projection Asia all stochastic processes with Gaussian or Rayleigh graphs. The implementation of the system within a robot is part of future work, as well as implements inference techniques.

15. References

Vicente Alabu, Francisco Casacuberta, Enrique Vidal, Alfons Jua (2007) Inference of stochastic Finite-state Traducers Using N Gram mixture; *Pattern recognition and Image Analisys*; Thrid Iberian Conference, Proceedings part IILNCS 4478; Springer Girona Spain

Kaspar Reisen, Michel Neuhaus, Horst Bunke (2007) Graph Embedding in vector spaces by means of prototype selection ; Graph Based Representations in Pattern recognition; *6th IAPR –TC-15 International Workshop* , *GbRPR* Proceedings; LNCS 4538, Springer , Alicante Spain.

González Pajares, Jesús M. de la Cruz (2002) Visión por computador Imágenes digitales y aplicaciones; Alfaomega Ra-Ma; pp. 373-418; México D.F; ISBN 970-15-0804-1;

Murray R. Spiegel, John Schiller, R. Alu Srinivasan (2001) Probabilidad y estadística; *Mc Graw Hill*, Colombia, ISBN: 958-41-0133-1

Elmer B. Mode, R. García Garza (2005). *Elementos de probabilidad y esatadística,* Reverte, ISBN: 8429150927, Barcelona

Romero Villafranca Rafael, Zunica Ramajo Luisa Rosa (2005). *Métodos estadisticos en Ingeniería* ;Ed. Univ. Politecnica de valencai ; 334 pp ; ISBN : 849705279 ; Spain.

Viola, Paul & Jones, Michael (2001) Robust Real-Time Object Detection, *International Journal of Computer Vision,* 57, 2, December 2004, 137-154, ISSN: 0920-5691 (Print) 1573-1405 (Online Siegwart, R. (2001). Name of paper. *Name of Journal in Italics,* Vol., No., (month and year of the edition) page numbers (first-last), ISSN

Nitzberg M., DMumford, TShiota (1993) Filtering, Segmentation, and Depth, Springer-Verlag New York, Inc, 143pg, ISBN: 3540564845, USA

Velásquez J D.. (1996)"Cathexis: a computational model for the generation of emotions and their influence in the behavior of autonomous agents". *S. M. Thesis. Department of electrical engineering and computer science,* Massachusetts institute of technology, 1996.

Osborn Carol E.(2007) *Basic Statistics for Health Information Management Technology;* Jones & Bartlett Publishers, ISBN: 0763750344, 9780763750343; USA

Van Vliet Caroyne M.(2008) *Equilibrium and Non-Equilibrium Statistical Mechanics;* World Scientific, ; ISBN: 9812704779, 9789812704771; USA, UK

Vanek Francis M., Albright Louis D.(2008) *Energy Systems Engineering: Evaluation and Implementation;* McGraw-Hill Professional, ISBN: 0071495932, 9780071495936; USA

Kalimuthu Krishnamoorthy(2006) *Handbook of statistical distributions with applications;* CRC Press; ISBN: 1584886358, 9781584886358; USA

## 25

Pattern Recognition based Fault Diagnosis in Industrial Processes: Review and Application

Thomas W. Rauber, Eduardo Mendel do Nascimento,
Estefhan D. Wandekokem and Flávio M. Varejão
Universidade Federal do Espírito Santo
Brazil

1. Introduction

The detection and diagnosis of faults in complex machinery is advantageous for economical and security reasons (Tavner et al., 2008). Recent progress in computational intelligence, sensor technology and computing performance permit the use of advanced systems to achieve this objective. Two principal approaches to the problem exist: model-based techniques and model-free techniques. The model-based line of research (Isermann, 2006; Simani et al., 2003) needs analytical model of the studied process, usually involving time dependent differential equations. One advantage is that the faults are an intrinsic part of the model. Deviations from the expected values are recorded in a residual vector which represents the state of health of the process. Frequently, the post-processing of the residual vector is approached by computational intelligence based techniques like statistical classifiers, artificial neural networks, and fuzzy logic. The use of these techniques however should not cause the impression that the classification of the process state is based solely on knowledge extracted from example data. An important drawback of model-based approaches is the necessity to establish an analytical model of the process which is a nontrivial problem. An experimental process setup in a controlled laboratory environment can be described by a mathematical model. Often the process is embedded in a control loop which naturally demands that inputs, controlled variables, and sensor outputs are modeled. In real-world processes the availability of an analytical model is often unrealistic or inaccurate due to the complexity of the process, so that false diagnosis can be caused by inappropriately designed models. Hence, the model-free techniques are an alternative method in case where an analytical model is not available.

In this chapter we describe model-free fault diagnosis in industrial process by pattern recognition techniques. We use the supervised learning paradigm (Bishop, 2007; Duda et al., 2001; Theodoridis & Koutroumbas, 2006) as the primal mechanism to automatically obtain a classifier of the process states. We will present a pattern recognition methodology developed for automatic processing of information and diagnostic decision making on industrial process. The fundamental drawback of the model-free approach is the necessity to provide a statistically significant number of labeled example data for each of the considered process classes. If only a small number of patterns are available in the training phase, the statistical classifiers might be misled and very sensitive to noise. Nevertheless, the extraction of knowledge about the process states principally from a set of example patterns has some attractive properties and permits the application of well studied pattern recognition paradigms to this important problem of fault detection and diagnosis. Sometimes in the model-free approach a partial model of the faults is used (for instance in bearing fault diagnosis, where the expected frequency features are calculated from the specification of the bearing and the shaft frequency (Li et al., 2000)). This fact however should not mislead the reader that a model-based approach to fault diagnosis is used in that case. The central mechanism to describe a process situation is a d-dimensional feature vector $\mathbf{x} = (x_1 \cdots x_j \cdots x_d)^\mathsf{T}$ together with a class label ω_i. This feature vector is the result of an information processing pipeline depicted in Fig. 1. A similar information processing philosophy was proposed by Sun et al. (2004), however without any feature selection which we consider fundamental for an optimized performance of the fault diagnosis system. Some raw measurements delivered from sensors attached to the process can be immediately used as features x_j without any pre-processing. For instance a thermometer or manometer attached to some chemical reactor tank will provide the continuously valued temperature or pressure which can be passed to the next information processing stage without further treatment. The health of an electrically powered machine can often be characterized by its current consumption. In vibration analysis (Scheffer & Girdhar, 2004), the accelerometer is the main sensor and delivers displacement values $X(t)$ in the time domain which can mathematically be derived to velocity $\dot{X}(t)$ and acceleration $\ddot{X}(t)$ values. Usually the raw time domain signal is submitted to statistical processing (Samanta & Al-Balushi, 2003), Fourier transform (Li et al., 2000), wavelet coefficient extraction (Paya et al., 1997), envelope analysis (McFadden & Smith, 1984), or any other method that provides stationary values. This process is known as feature extraction on the measurement level. For instance, an accelerometer velocity signal $\dot{X}(t)$ of a motor transformed to the frequency domain by a Fourier transform produces frequency values $F(u)$ which can be considered extracted features at each of the frequencies u. This leads us to an essential problem of feature extraction, namely the production of large amounts of features. We need subsequent steps after the feature extraction on the measurement level to reduce the dimension of the finally used feature vector $\mathbf{x}$ to a reasonable size. This can be achieved again by feature extraction, this time on the information processing level, and finally by feature selection, to retain only a relatively small amount of features which additionally are the most discriminative ones. For instance, all frequencies u of a Fourier spectrum could be submitted to Principal Component Analysis (a linear feature extractor based on statistics) to reduce the dimensionality of the data (Jolliffe, 2002). Finally, the retained principal components could be fed to a feature selection algorithm in order to produce, for instance, a unique feature vector $\mathbf{x}$ to describe the whole process situation.

The basic strategy of obtaining a highly discriminative, low dimensional process state descriptor in the form of a single feature vector can be resumed in the following main steps:

1. Get as many raw measurements from as many sensors of a process as possible;

2. Submit the raw measurements to as many feature extraction techniques as possible, plausibly applicable to the specific problem;

3. Reduce the high dimensional data to only a few final features which simultaneously are the most discriminative descriptors of the process;

4. Induce a classifier for fault diagnosis.

The first item is usually restricted by the available sensors which can be used for data acquisition. For instance a motor pump produces electrical, acoustic, and vibrational patterns (Al Kazzaz & Singh, 2003) which all could be used if appropriate sensors are available. The second methodology opens up a huge variety of signal processing techniques which are only

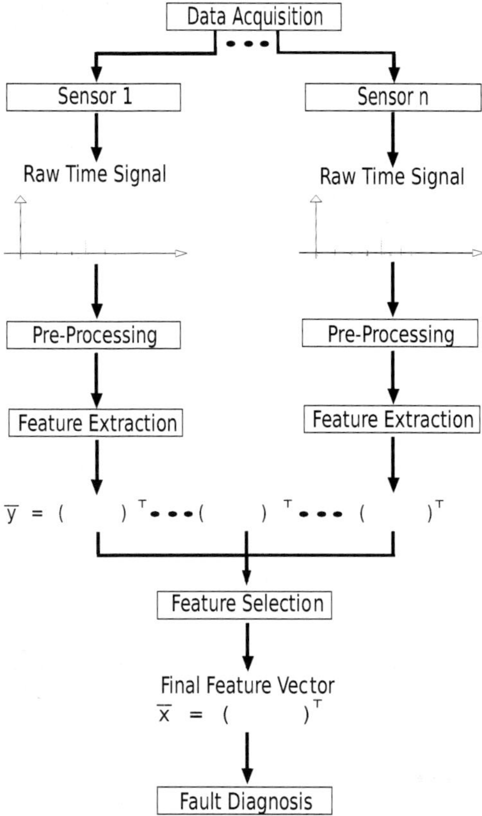

$$\overline{y} = (\quad)^T \bullet\bullet\bullet (\quad)^T \bullet\bullet\bullet (\quad)^T$$

$$\overline{x} = (\quad)^T$$

Fig. 1. Information processing pipeline to obtain a feature vector **x** which is of relatively low dimension and contains the most discriminative information about the state of a process.

restricted by the nature of the signal, the available software, and computing resources. From a vibration signal one might calculate wavelet coefficients (Paya et al., 1997), Fourier coefficients (Li et al., 2000), statistical measurements (Samanta & Al-Balushi, 2003), and frequencies obtained from envelope analysis (McFadden & Smith, 1984).

A review of some well-known processing techniques, such as statistical features in the time and frequency domain, to extract detailed information for induction machine diagnosis will be presented. Fourier methods to transform the time-domain signal to the frequency domain, where further analysis is carried out, is also discussed in this chapter. Using these techniques the state of machine can be constantly monitored and detailed analysis may be made concerning the health of the machine. The use of as many feature extraction methods as possible raises the chances that the most discriminative information is somehow captured by some of these features. If a prior restriction to only a limited set of features is defined, one might loose valuable aspects hidden in the signal. Finally, we use feature selection techniques to emphasize the importance of each feature for the classification task and this information could be used for instance to retain the most discriminative information in a low dimensional vector.

The final stage of the construction of the monitor of the process condition is the training of a classifier, using labeled examples. Different strategies for the construction of the final classifier based on the result of the feature selection stage can be followed. The simplest one is to use the selected feature set as a filter for training and classification. More sophisticated techniques determine the final classification as the result of a multi-level decision process based on an *ensemble* of distinct classifiers (Duda et al., 2001). The goal is to elevate the performance of the final classifier relative to the individual classifier performances. The individual classifiers might differ for instance in the feature set that is used.

The chapter is organized in the following manner: Section 2 gives an overview of existing techniques to calculate features from raw signals. Then the calculus of new features from existing ones by information processing methods is approached in section 3. Special attention is given to the information filtering done by feature selection in section 4. When the feature model has been defined, we are interested in the expected quality of our fault classifier. This question is analyzed in section 5. As a practical benchmark of some of the presented techniques, section 6 illustrates their application to an interesting real-world, complex diagnosis task in the context of oil rig motor pump fault diagnosis. We investigate the described fault diagnosis methodology using pattern recognition techniques using real examples of rolling element bearing fault and misalignment fault of rotating machines. Final conclusions are drawn in section 7.

2. Measurement level feature extraction

Any conclusion about the condition of a process is based on the patterns which are obtained from sensorial devices attached to the dynamic system that in general constantly changes its state. Which sensors will be used should be considered as an integral part of the design of the whole diagnostic system. An ideal situation is a continuous on-line monitoring with many distinct sensors which deliver the data about the electrical, acoustic, and vibration activities. Usually this ideal situation is not encountered due to technical or budget restrictions or since the specificity of the application requires particular sensors. After preprocessing, the sensor patterns are available as digital information that can be processed by a specialized hardware or general purpose computer. A principal distinction is made with respect to the domain of the signal. The original continuous signal $s(t)$ in the time domain is discretized into n samples $s_1, \ldots, s_n$ that were acquired during a finite sampling interval. The number of samples depends on the duration of the acquisition and the sampling frequency. The Fourier transform provides the signal in the frequency domain. A mixed time-frequency domain is encountered when time dependent signals are processed by short-term Fourier transforms or wavelet transforms. In the following we compile some representative feature extraction methods that are widely used in the literature related to pattern-recognition based fault diagnosis.

2.1 Statistical features in the time domain

When we consider the original discretized time domain signal, some basic discriminative information can be extracted in the form of statistical parameters from the n samples $s_1, \ldots, s_n$ (Stefanoiu & Ionescu, 2006).

2.1.1 Root Mean Square (RMS)

One of the most important basic features that can be extracted directly from the time-domain signal is the RMS which describes the energy of the signal. It is defined as the square root of the average squared value of the signal and can also be called the *normalized energy* of the signal:

$$\text{RMS} = \sqrt{\frac{1}{n}\sum_{i=0}^{n-1} s_i^2}. \tag{1}$$

Especially in vibration analysis the RMS is used to perform fault *detection*, i.e. triggering an alarm, whenever the RMS surpasses a level that depends on the size of the machine, the nature of the signal (for instance velocity or acceleration), the position of the accelerometer, and so on. After the detection of the existence of a failure, fault *diagnosis* is performed relying on more sophisticated features. For instance the ISO 2372 (VDI 2056) norms define three different velocity RMS alarm levels for four different machine classes divided by power and foundations of the rotating machines.

2.1.2 Peak-to-Valley (PV) alias Peak-to-Peak (PP)

Another important measurement of a signal, considering a semantically coherent sampling interval, for instance a fixed-length interval or one period of a rotation, is the peak-to-valley value which reflects the amplitude spread of a signal:

$$\text{PV} = \frac{1}{2}\left(\max_{i=0}^{n-1} s_i - \min_{i=0}^{n-1} s_i\right). \tag{2}$$

2.1.3 Peak

If we consider only the maximum amplitude relative to zero $s_{ref} = 0$ or a general reference level s_{ref}, we get the peak value:

$$\text{peak} = \max_{i=0}^{n-1} s_i - s_{ref}. \tag{3}$$

Often the peak is used in conjunction with other statistical parameters, for instance the peak-to-average $\left(\text{peak}\middle/\frac{1}{n}\sum_{i=0}^{n-1} s_i\right)$ or peak-to-median $\left(\text{peak}\middle/\underset{i=0}{\overset{n-1}{median}}\, s_i\right)$ rates (Ericsson et al., 2005).

2.1.4 Crest factor

When we relate the peak value to the RMS of the signal, we obtain the crest factor:

$$\text{CF} = \text{peak}/\text{RMS}, \tag{4}$$

which expresses the *spikiness* of the signal. The crest factor is also known as peak-to-average ratio or peak-to-average power ratio and is used to characterize signals containing repetitive impulses in addition to a lower level continuous signal. The modulus of the signal should be used in the calculus.

2.1.5 Kurtosis

The analytic definition of the kurtosis is $\kappa = -3 + \mu_4/\sigma^4$ with $\mu_4 = E\{(s - E\{s\})^4\}$ being the fourth moment around the mean and σ^4 being the square of the variance. Considering the n samples $s_1, \ldots, s_n$, we determine the sample kurtosis as:

$$\kappa = -3 + \frac{\frac{1}{n}\sum_{i=0}^{n-1}(s_i - \bar{s})^4}{\left[\frac{1}{n}\sum_{i=0}^{n-1}(s_i - \bar{s})^2\right]^2}, \tag{5}$$

where $\bar{s}$ denotes the estimated expected value of the signal (average). The kurtosis expresses an aspect of *spikiness* of the signal, although in a higher order than the crest factor, and describes how peaked or float the distribution is. If a signal contains sharp peaks with a higher value, then its distribution function will be sharper.

2.1.6 Further statistical parameters

Besides the RMS, variance, and kurtosis, Samanta & Al-Balushi (2003) further present the skewness (normalized third central moment) $\gamma_3 = \mu_3/\sigma^3$ and the normalized sixth central moment $\gamma_6 = \mu_6/\sigma^6$ as statistical features in bearing fault detection. In the context of gearbox fault detection, Večeř et al. (2005) describe further statistical features frequently used as condition indicators: the energy operator

$$\text{EO} = \frac{n^2 \sum_{i=0}^{n-1}\left((s_{i+1}^2 - s_i^2) - \bar{s}\right)^4}{\left[\sum_{i=0}^{n-1}\left((s_{i+1}^2 - s_i^2) - \bar{s}\right)^2\right]^2} \; ; \tag{6}$$

energy ratio, that is, ratio of the standard deviations of the difference signal and the raw signal

$$\text{ER} = \sigma(d)/\sigma(s), \tag{7}$$

where difference signal d is defined as the remainder of the vibration signal after the regular meshing components are removed; sideband level factor (sum of the first order sideband about the fundamental gear mesh frequency divided by the standard deviation of the time signal average), sideband index (average amplitude of the sidebands of the fundamental gear mesh frequency); zero-order figure of merit

$$\text{FM0} = \text{PV} \Big/ \sum_{i=0}^{M} A_i, \tag{8}$$

where A_i is the amplitude of the i-th gear mesh frequency harmonics; kurtosis of the differential signal (FM4 parameter); kurtosis of the residual signal (a synchronous averaged signal without the gear mesh frequency, its harmonics, drive shaft frequency, and its second harmonics) or envelope normalized by an average variance (NA4 parameter and NB4 parameter). The reader interested in more details is referred to (Lei & Zuo, 2009; Večeř et al., 2005).

2.2 Statistical features in the frequency domain

Especially when leading with signals from processes that produce periodic signals, like rotating machinery, the Fourier transform (Bracewell, 1986) of a one-dimensional signal is an information conserving fundamental analytic functional $\mathscr{F}\{s(t)\} = F(u)$ that decomposes the signal into additive sine and cosine terms in the complex domain, i.e. $F(u) = \Re(u) + j\Im(u)$. The phase angle information $\phi(u) = \arctan\left(\Im(u)/\Re(u)\right)$ is a valuable source of information when for instance the relative movement of different parts of a rotating machine at a given frequency u should be analyzed (Scheffer & Girdhar, 2004). The vast majority of analytic work is however done with the magnitude $|F(u)| = \sqrt{\Re^2(u) + \Im^2(u)}$ of the Fourier transform, also known as the Fourier spectrum or generally the frequency spectrum or simply the spectrum of $s(t)$. The Fourier spectrum will be symmetric and hence only one half has to be kept. Usually the discrete signal buffer of $n\prime$ samples is interpolated to a length n which is a power of two in order to be able to apply the Fast Fourier Transform algorithm of complexity $O(n\log n)$. The spectrum constitutes a new discrete signal of $n/2$ samples $f_1, \ldots, f_{n/2}$ which serves as the basis to extract more features. For the sake of simplicity we once again presume that we have n samples, instead of $n/2$. The Root Mean Square (RMS) can also be calculated in the frequency domain. Often we are interested on RMS of particular bands interest, for instance the bands around the harmonics in rotating machinery, i.e. the multiples of the fundamental shaft rotation frequency. In order to calculate the features of specific bands, the interval of the particular spectra has to be considered, either as absolute intervals or as percentages (for instance 2% of the frequency value to lower and higher frequencies).

It should be clear that in terms of statistical pattern recognition, the features x_j can assume any of the numerical descriptors that can be obtained from the frequency domain, such as: single frequencies, RMS of bands or the whole signal, and all conceivable functional mappings of the signal. We do not question the information content of the obtained features at this moment. Surely, some features will contain much more valuable discriminative power than others. Some features may even contaminate the descriptive behavior of the feature vector that describes that condition of the process. The information filtering will later be done by the feature selection step.

Especially for the analysis of acoustic signal which might for instance represent the noise emissions caused by a fault, the *Cepstrum* is the inverse Fourier transform of the logarithm of the magnitude of the Fourier transform of signal s, i.e. $\mathscr{F}^{-1}\{\log\left(|\mathscr{F}\{s(t)\}|\right)\}$, (Theodoridis & Koutroumbas, 2006).

2.3 Time-frequency domain features

There are analytic techniques that try to capture frequency content at different time instances, as it were a hybrid representation of the signal regarding the changing intensities over time and simultaneously looking at repetitive patterns during limited time intervals because the signal is non-stationary. In fault diagnosis there certainly exist fault signatures that respond adequately to these techniques, for instance the brush seizing faults in a DC servo motor described by Sejdić & Jiang (2008).

2.3.1 Short-time Fourier transform (STFT)

When we multiply a signal with a finite window function and take the Fourier transform of the product, we calculate the STFT. For instance, Al Kazzaz & Singh (2003) used the STFT to obtain the spectra of overlapping signal segments of a vibration signal and then averaged the set of spectra in order to reduce random vibration and the noise in the signal. When the window function is a Gaussian, we obtain the Gabor transform (Gabor, 1946).

2.3.2 Wavelet transform

The wavelet transform (Chui, 1992) has the advantage of a flexible resolution in the time and frequency domains when compared to the short-time Fourier transform which has a fixed window size. Like in the case of the Fourier transform, we can distinguish among continuous wavelet transform, wavelet series expansion, and the discrete wavelet transform. The latter is used in software implementation in digital signal processing to obtain the wavelet coefficients which describe the signal in terms of multiples of wavelet basis function. An important distinction is between orthogonal and non-orthogonal basis functions. The dyadic wavelet family furthermore facilitates the efficient implementation of the discrete wavelet transforms, since the translations and scales are powers of two. In the majority of research work, the orthogonal dyadic wavelet basis is used (Loparo & Lou, 2004; Paya et al., 1997; Singh & Al Kazzaz, 2004; 2008). A good introduction to the theory of wavelets with an application of gearbox fault detection can be found in (Wang & McFadden, 1996). In that application non-orthogonal wavelet basis functions are used to capture the transients of a fault signal, justified by two drawbacks of the orthogonal bases, namely not having enough scales to describe the scaled versions of the transients and the different calculated coefficients describing the same transients at different time instants. We restrict the definition to the discrete orthogonal dyadic wavelet transform (Castleman, 1995). Given a basis function, or mother wavelet $\psi(s)$ of the signal function s, the set of functions which are scaled and translated versions of the mother wavelet $\psi_{l,k}(s) = 2^{l/2}\psi_{l,k}\left(2^{l}s - k\right)$ that form an orthonormal basis of $L^2(\mathbb{R})$, with $-\infty < l, k < \infty$, $l, k \in \mathbb{N}$, are the dyadic orthogonal wavelet functions. The coefficients of the discrete dyadic wavelet transform can be obtained as:

$$c_{l,k}(s) = \sum_{i=0}^{n-1} s(i\Delta t)\psi_{l,k}(i\Delta t), \qquad (9)$$

where the signal s is sampled at n discrete instances at intervals Δt and $l = 0, 1, \ldots, \log_2 n - 1$, $k = 0, 1, \ldots, 2^l - 1$. In the context of signal analysis this transform can also be viewed as a multiresolution recursive filter bank for different scaled and translated versions of the same signal signature. Dyadic wavelets that furthermore have a compact support are for instance the Haar or Daubechies wavelets (Castleman, 1995).

2.3.3 Other time-frequency analysis techniques

Recently, Yan et al. (2009) have presented the Frequency Slice Wavelet Transform (FSWT). It constitutes a parameterized generalization, and can be specialized into the Fourier transform, the Gabor transform, the Morlet wavelet transform (Goupillaud et al., 1984), and the Wigner-Ville distribution (Wigner, 1932).

2.4 Final Considerations of feature extraction on the measurement level

It should be clear that from a raw signal a variety of features can be extracted, starting from simple statistical parameters, like the RMS, until sophisticated mathematical transforms. The envisaged application is of course the main motivation to use a certain feature extractor or another. On the other hand, we could adopt a strategy to obtain a great variety of new, possibly useful information from the original signal, sending it to a battery of feature extractors. Why should it not be reasonable to use some statistical features from the time domain together with a few wavelet coefficients, possibly from different wavelet types, then further joining some RMS value from several different bands of a frequency spectrum ? One could argue that this produces a huge amount of features, possibly worthless for diagnostic purposes, introducing features that contaminate the valuable parameters of our system. The answer to this objection is the use of subsequent information filtering steps in the processing pipeline. Later we will describe the use of feature selection to retain only the most useful features that finally characterize the process states. For now we can think of merging all available features produced by the procedures described above in to a new feature vector $\mathbf{x} := (x_1 \cdots x_j \cdots x_d)^{\mathsf{T}}$ that will be processed by the next information processing methods.

3. High level feature extraction

In the previous section we gave a slight overview for methods which can calculate features from a raw signal acquired from a technical process with the intention to use it for fault diagnosis. There exist a series of methods which take existing feature vectors and transform them into other feature vectors eventually reducing the dimension of the original descriptor and/or improving its discriminative behavior with respect to the fault classes. One principal distinction can be made between linear and non-linear methods.

3.1 Linear methods

When the components y_l, $l = 1, \ldots d'$ of the new feature vector $\mathbf{y}$ are all linear combinations $y_l = \sum_{j=1}^{d} m_{lj} x_j = \mathbf{m}_l^{\mathsf{T}} \mathbf{x}$ of the components x_j of the original feature vector $\mathbf{x}$, then we obtain a linear feature extractor. The m_{lj} are the real valued elements of a matrix $\mathbf{M}$ that implements the extraction easily as $\mathbf{y} = \mathbf{M}^{\mathsf{T}} \mathbf{x}$. Linear methods have the advantage that they are mathematically tractable by well studied applied linear Algebra. Linear feature extraction is an unsupervised technique, working without the knowledge to which class a pattern belongs. This can easily destroy discriminative information. For instance in Principal Component Analysis it can happen that the variance in a newly extracted component is higher than in another, ranking it before the lower variance component, although the class separability in the second less important component might be better.

3.1.1 Principal Component Analysis

Principal Component Analysis (PCA) (Jolliffe, 2002) is the most well studied technique to map the existing feature vectors $\mathbf{x}$ to linearly uncorrelated and lower dimensional feature vectors $\mathbf{y}$, eventually sacrificing new components with a small variance. The first two or three principal components additionally can be visualized, exposing the mutual relationship of the patterns. From the total of n d-dimensional pattern samples $\mathbf{x}^{(1)}, \ldots, \mathbf{x}^{(n)}$ that describe process situations we estimate the mean $\hat{\mu} = \frac{1}{n} \sum_{k=1}^{n} \mathbf{x}^{(k)}$ and covariance matrix $\hat{\Sigma} = \frac{1}{n-1} \sum_{k=1}^{n} (\mathbf{x}^{(k)} - \hat{\mu})(\mathbf{x}^{(k)} - \hat{\mu})^{\mathsf{T}}$. The symmetric $d \times d$ matrix $\hat{\Sigma}$ is then submitted to an eigenanalysis which delivers d eigenvalues λ_j and the corresponding eigenvectors ϕ_j which are ordered following a descending order of the corresponding eigenvalues to form the feature extractor $\mathbf{\Phi} = (\phi_1, \ldots, \phi_d)$. If we extract $\mathbf{y} = \mathbf{\Phi}^{\mathsf{T}} \mathbf{x}$ we obtain a linearly uncorrelated feature vector $\mathbf{y}$ of the same dimension d. If we delete the columns $d' + 1, \ldots, d$ from $\mathbf{\Phi}$ with $1 \leq d' < d$, we obtain the $d \times d'$ matrix $\mathbf{\Phi}'$ that extracts the d' principal components as $\mathbf{y}' = \mathbf{\Phi}'^{\mathsf{T}} \mathbf{x}$. The approximation error $\mathcal{E}$ committed by discarding the $d - d'$ low variance components is $\mathcal{E}(d') = \sum_{j=d'}^{d} \lambda_j$. Synonymous for PCA are Karhunen-Loève Transform (KLT),

Hotelling transform, or Proper Orthogonal Decomposition (POD). When the data has been centered to its global mean and all components are preserved, PCA is also equivalent to Singular Value Decomposition (SVD).

3.1.2 Independent Component Analysis

Another linear feature extractor is Independent Component Analysis (ICA) (Hyärinen et al., 2001) which has the task to separate independent signals from mixed signals. This could be interesting to recognize the contributions of different faults in a signal, or find the latent independent variables that mix together to the observable variables (features) in a process. Again, from the original feature vector $\mathbf{x}$ a new feature vector $\mathbf{s}$ is extracted by a linear transform (matrix multiplication) as $\mathbf{s} = \mathbf{W}\mathbf{x}$, where the extractor $\mathbf{W}$ is a $d' \times d$ matrix, called the demixing matrix. The d' independent components s_j are maximized with respect to their non-Gaussianity, an information based criterion for independence, often measured by kurtosis or negentropy. A few representative applications of ICA in the context of fault diagnosis are for instance (Jiang & Wang, 2004; Lee et al., 2006; Pöyhönen et al., 2003).

3.2 Non-linear methods

Any non-linear mapping $\mathbf{y} = \mathbf{\Phi}(\mathbf{x})$, where the original d-dimensional feature vector $\mathbf{x}$ is transformed to the H-dimensional extracted feature vector $\mathbf{y}$ can be considered a non-linear generator of new features that might be more discriminative than the original information. As an example take the classical XOR problem, linearly not separable, where the mapping

$$\mathbf{\Phi}\left(\begin{pmatrix} x_1 \\ x_2 \end{pmatrix} \right) = \begin{pmatrix} \phi_1\left(\begin{pmatrix} x_1 \\ x_2 \end{pmatrix} \right) \\ \phi_2\left(\begin{pmatrix} x_1 \\ x_2 \end{pmatrix} \right) \\ \phi_3\left(\begin{pmatrix} x_1 \\ x_2 \end{pmatrix} \right) \end{pmatrix} = \begin{pmatrix} x_1 \\ x_2 \\ x_1 x_2 \end{pmatrix} \tag{10}$$

from the original bi-dimensional space enables linear separability in the mapped tri-dimensional space. When a classifier $g(\mathbf{x}) = \mathbf{w}^\mathsf{T}\mathbf{\Phi}(\mathbf{x})$ is a linear combination of the basis functions ϕ_h we deal with a Generalized Linear Discriminant Function (GLDF) (Duda et al., 2001). A great variety of feature extraction techniques falls in this category, for instance polynomial combinations of the original features, radial basis functions, Multilayer Perceptrons (when omitting the activation function in the output layer), or any other calculus of new features not definable as a matrix multiplication of a linear extraction matrix with the original feature vector (Theodoridis & Koutroumbas, 2006). When we need only a similarity measure between two mapped feature vectors $\mathbf{\Phi}(\mathbf{x})$ and $\mathbf{\Phi}(\mathbf{x}')$ without having to define the mapping explicitly, but only its dot product, we define a *kernel* $k(\mathbf{x}, \mathbf{x}')$. Examples are the polynomial mapping $k(\mathbf{x}, \mathbf{x}') = (\mathbf{x} \cdot \mathbf{x}' + 1)^r$ calculating all monomials up to degree r and the Gaussian radial basis function $k(\mathbf{x}, \mathbf{x}') = \exp(-\gamma||\mathbf{x} - \mathbf{x}'||^2)$ with shape parameter γ. These kernels are especially needed in Support Vector Classification and Regression (Theodoridis & Koutroumbas, 2006).

If we solve a regression problem by replicating the input vector $\mathbf{x}$ as the target vector in a Perceptron with one hidden layer, and if the number of neurons H in the hidden layer is smaller than the dimension d of $\mathbf{x}$, we have an auto-associative feedforward neural network, applied for example by (Skitt et al., 1993) in the context of machine condition monitoring. The extracted feature vector is composed by the components $y_h = z(\mathbf{w}_h^{\mathsf{T}}\mathbf{x})$, $h = 1, \ldots, H$, where $z(.)$ is the activation function, usually the logistic function:

$$z(a) = \frac{1}{1 + e^{-a}} \tag{11}$$

or the hyperbolic tangent:

$$z(a) = \tanh a = \frac{e^a - e^{-a}}{e^a + e^{-a}}. \tag{12}$$

Kohonen's Self-Organizing Map (SOM) (Kohonen, 1998) organizes neurons in a 1-D, 2-D, 3-D, or higher-dimensional topological map. After the map is trained there is a single responding neuron (the winner) inside the maps lattice. The discrete position could be taken as an extracted feature vector. High-dimensional patterns can be mapped to a lower dimensional map by the Sammon plot (Sammon Jr., 1969) which tries to preserve the mutual distances among all patterns in the original and mapped pattern space. Although the mapping is principally conceived for visualization in two or three dimensions, theoretically any dimension lower than the original d can be chosen for feature extraction. The auto-associative feedforward neural network, Kohonen map, and Sammon map have been applied to non-linear feature extraction by (De Backer et al., 1998), besides a collection of methods called multidimensional scaling.

4. Feature selection

In the previous two sections we gave a slight overview of methods which can calculate features from a raw signal acquired from a technical process with the intention to use it for fault diagnosis. There exist a series of methods which take existing feature vectors and transform them into other feature vectors eventually reducing the dimension of the original descriptor and/or improving its discriminative behavior with respect to the fault classes. This was called high level feature extraction. On the other hand, we can filter out some of the existing features and retaining others, such forming again a new feature vector, without modifying the original individual features. This is feature selection. This stage is of great importance because the feature extraction by several distinct extraction methods probably generates a large quantity of features that can have a marginal importance for classification or even jeopardize the classifier performance if they are used. Hence, the objective of this stage is to express the importance of the features in the classification task. The quality criterion can be individual, but the multidimensional nature of the process descriptors demands the analysis of feature sets, because of the interdependency relations within a feature set.

An early excellent compilation of feature selection techniques is given by Devijver & Kittler (1982). Guyon & Elisseeff (2003) give an introductory treatment about this subject in the field of Machine Learning. A paper collection about computational methods of feature selection is Liu & Motoda (2007). A feature selection algorithm is basically composed of two ingredients, namely a search strategy algorithm and a selection criterion. The search strategy is about which of the feature subsets are analyzed and the selection criterion associates a numerical value to each of these subsets, thus permitting the search for the subset that maximizes the criterion.

Kudo & Sklansky (2000) do an extensive experimental comparison on standard machine learning databases with basically all existing algorithms at the time of the publication. The simplest evaluation of a quality criterion of features is by individually calculate the criterion and then rank the whole set of available features. This strategy of course ignore completely the multidimensional nature of the descriptors of the process. Nevertheless, when the original feature set is very large, it is a useful preprocessing step. If, for instance, the classification performance of a single feature is not better than random classification, this suggests that it contains no information at all and can be discarded prior to a more sophisticated search. We call this search strategy Best Features (BF).

Sequential Forward Selection (SFS) and Sequential Backward Selection (SBS) are greedy algorithms that add or delete a feature at a time without permission to later on eliminate or join it again relative to the currently selected feature set. Their generalized version that permit an exhaustive search within a small candidate set added or deleted at a time are Generalized Sequential Forward Selection (GSFS) and Generalized Sequential Backward Selection (GSBS). The Plus-L-Take Away-R (PLTR) strategy permits backtracking for a fixed number of steps, thus allowing to eliminate previously selected features or joining previously deleted features. When allowing backtracking as long as it improves the quality criterion of the currently selected feature set, we have the floating versions of PLTR, called Sequential Forward Floating Selection (SFFS) and Sequential Backward Floating Selection (SBFS) (Pudil et al., 1994).

When the criterion always increases monotonically when joining an additional feature, we are able to apply the Branch-and-Bound (BB) strategies. The most prominent algorithm is the original of Narendra & Fukunaga (1977) which was refined later to the improved BB (Yu & Yuan, 1993) and relaxed BB methods (Kudo & Sklansky, 2000). The biggest drawback of BB methods is that the most natural selection criterion is the error rate and this is *not* monotonically increasing or its complement decreasing. Besides, even with the exhaustive implicit visit of all leaves of the search tree, the algorithm is computationally still expensive. Another line of research for search strategies are Genetic Algorithms (GA) (Estevez et al., 2009; Oh et al., 2004; Pernkopf & O'Leary, 2001). The basic idea is to combine different feature subsets by a crossover procedure guided by a fitness criterion. The advantage of GAs for feature selection is the generation of quite heterogeneous feature sets that are not sequentially produced.

Each feature selection subset search strategy must define a criterion J which defines the quality of the set. When a classification or regression task will be performed based on the features, and the very performance of the system is used as the quality criterion, the whole feature selection is called a *wrapper*. The most common wrapper methods use the estimated classification accuracy of the subsequent classifier as the quality criterion. This implies that a classification architecture and an error estimation algorithm must be defined. For instance a 10-fold cross validation together with a Support Vector Machine could be used. A regression wrapper would probably take the expected approximation error as J. A *filter* selection algorithm defines the selected subset before a regression of classification is done by the set. Selection criteria related to filters can principally be grouped into interclass distances, probabilistic distances and information-based criteria (Devijver & Kittler, 1982). A more detailed description for search strategies and selection criteria is given in the following sections.

4.1 Search algorithms in feature selection

If we want to select d features $X_d = \{x_{k_i} | i = 1, \ldots, d; k_i \in \{1, \ldots, D\}\}$, from an available pool of D features $Y = \{x_j | j = 1, \ldots, D\}$, an exhaustive search would take $\binom{D}{d}$ iterations which is computationally unfeasible for even moderate number of features. So we have to rely on suboptimal search strategies. Let us suppose that we a have a selection criterion J that is able to evaluate the quality of a candidate set Ξ_k, composed of k features. We are interested in that candidate set of cardinality k that maximizes the criterion, hence we are looking for the set X_k with

$$J(X_k) = \max_{\{\Xi_k\}} J(\Xi_k). \tag{13}$$

For $k = d$ we obtain a satisfactory feature set that maximizes the selection criterion for d features.

Best Features (BF) is simply evaluating $J(\{x_j\})$ for each feature $j = 1, \ldots, D$, ordering the features in descending order relative to J and setting the selected set X_d to the first d features of the ordered set. This mechanism ignores the multidimensionality of the problem, but on the other hand in an $O(D)$ complexity selects a feature set. As it was already mentioned the application of BF is recommended as a preprocessing step if an extremely large number D of features is available.

Sequential Forward Selection (SFS) (Devijver & Kittler, 1982) starts with an empty set. Consider that k features have already been selected by SFS which are included in the feature set X_k. If Y is the total set of all D features $Y \setminus X_k$ is the set of $D - k$ candidates ξ_j. Test each candidate together with the already selected features and rank them following the criterion J, so that $J(X_k \cup \{\xi_1\}) \geq J(X_k \cup \{\xi_2\}) \geq \ldots \geq J(X_k \cup \{\xi_{D-k}\})$. Then the updated selected feature set is given as $X_{k+1} = X_k \cup \{\xi_1\}$. The algorithm is initialized by $X_0 = \emptyset$ and stops at X_d. Although SFS is an algorithm that considers mutual dependencies among the involved features, it has the main drawback of not allowing the posterior elimination of a feature ξ_j, once it has been selected.

Sequential Backward Selection (SBS) (Devijver & Kittler, 1982) which starts with all features Y as being selected and then discards one feature at a time, until $D - d$ features have been deleted, i.e. d features have been retained as the selected ones. Consider that k features have already been discarded from $\bar{X}_0 = Y$ to form feature set $\bar{X}_k$. In order to obtain the feature set with one more feature discarded, rank the features ξ_j contained in set $\bar{X}_k$, so that $J(\bar{X}_k \setminus \{\xi_1\}) \geq J(\bar{X}_k \setminus \{\xi_2\}) \geq \ldots \geq J(\bar{X}_k \setminus \{\xi_{D-k}\})$. Then the updated selected feature set is given as $\bar{X}_{k+1} = \bar{X}_k \setminus \{\xi_1\}$, i.e. the worst feature ξ_1 is discarded. The SBS strategy is computationally more demanding than the SFS algorithm, since the criterion J has to be evaluated with generally more features. As in the case of SFS, the SBS does not allow the posterior reintegration of a feature ξ_j, once it has been discarded.

The Plus L-Take Away R selection algorithm (Devijver & Kittler, 1982; Pudil et al., 1994) tries to overcome the drawbacks of the SFS and SBS methods by allowing to discard a feature that has already been selected and reintegrate a feature into the selected pool after it has been discarded thus avoiding the nested nature of the sets chosen by SFS and SBS. If the parameter L is greater than R then the we start with the SFS algorithm to join L features to the selected pool. Then R features are discarded by the SBS procedure to get a set X_{L-R}. We repeat the joining L features by SFS and discarding R features by SBS until d features have been reached in X_d. The parameters L and R must appropriately be chosen to match d and not overreach the minimum 0 and maximum D. If $L < R$ then we start with the whole feature set Y and the SBS algorithm to first discard R features. Then L features are joined again by SFS. The SBS-SFS pair is repeated until reaching d features. PLTR in contrast to the greedy forward and backward algorithms SFS and SBS allows a backtracking step, although with a fixed size that can discard already selected or include already discarded features.

If we allow the backtracking for an arbitrary number of times as long as the quality criterion J is improving, we arrive at the *floating* techniques (Pudil et al., 1994). As a representative for a complete sequential search strategy algorithm, we present the Sequential Forward Floating Search (SFFS) in algorithm 1. The second condition in line 9 is a very simple mechanism to avoid looping. It remembers the last included feature by SFS and does not allow the immediate exclusion by SBS. More sophisticated looping prevention techniques could be conceived.

Algorithm 1 is easily simplified to the SFS algorithm by omitting the inner loop between line 6 and line 14.

Algorithm 1 SFFS

Input: A set Y of D available features $Y = \{x_j | j = 1, \ldots, D\}$, the number of desired features d.

Output: The feature set X with cardinality $|X| = d$ that maximizes the selection criterion.

1: Select one feature x_{SFS} from Y by Sequential Forward Selection (SFS)
2: $X \leftarrow \{x_{\mathrm{SFS}}\}; Y \leftarrow Y \setminus \{x_{\mathrm{SFS}}\};$
3: **repeat**
4:     {Select one feature x_{SFS} from Y by SFS}
5:     $X \leftarrow X \cup \{x_{\mathrm{SFS}}\}; Y \leftarrow Y \setminus \{x_{\mathrm{SFS}}\};$
6:     **repeat**
7:         conditional_Exclusion $\leftarrow$ **false**;
8:         Determine best candidate for exclusion x_{SBS} from X using SBS
9:         **if** $J(X \setminus \{x_{\mathrm{SBS}}\}) > J(X)$ AND x_{SBS} not included in the last SFS step **then**
10:           conditional_Exclusion $\leftarrow$ **true**;
11:           {Excluding the feature improves criterion J}
12:           $X \leftarrow X \setminus \{x_{\mathrm{SBS}}\}; Y \leftarrow Y \cup \{x_{\mathrm{SBS}}\};$
13:         **end if**
14:     **until** (NOT conditional_Exclusion OR $|X| = 1$)
15: **until** $|X| = d$

All search algorithms previously presented in this section are based on the idea of building a unique feature set that presents an optimal classification performance, and in each iteration the set is improved by the insertion or removal of some features. The output of such method leads naturally to the idea of a order of importance (ranking) among the selected features. However, one may be interested in obtaining several potentially good feature sets, in order to assign the final classification label after the inspection of the performance of each of those sets, rather than relying on a unique set. *Genetic Algorithms* (GA) (Opitz, 1999) can naturally be used to meet this requirement. They are is inspired by Darwin's biological natural selection, in which different individuals combine and compete among themselves in order to transmit their winner genes to future generations. In GA-based feature selection, each individual is a feature set, and their individual quality (fitness) can be measured, for example, as the error rate of a classifier built on the corresponding features. If $|Y|$ is the cardinality of the global pool of features to be selected, a natural way of representing an individual is as a binary string composed of $|Y|$ bits, so that the value 1 in the i-th bit indicates the presence of the i-th feature in the feature set represented by that individual, and the value 0 indicates its absence. The algorithm starts with the creation of the initial individuals (by a random or heuristic-based method), and in each generation, the best individuals are more likely to be selected to transmit their bits (genes) to future generations. This transmission involves the combination of the bits of each "parent" in order to create a "child", which will have, for instance, the first half of its bits coming from the first parent, and the second half coming from the second parent. To increase the diversity of individuals, the mutation operator can be used, so that each bit has a small probability of being flipped. Finally, after the passage of several generations, the population will be composed of distinct individuals with a high fitness value, or equivalently several feature sets that possibly present good classification results and diversity among themselves with respect to the chosen features.

4.2 Selection criteria in feature selection

The previously defined selection algorithms all need to define a multivariate selection criterion J which judges the quality of the candidate feature set. One of the obvious choices in a classification context is to choose those features that minimize the error of the classifier, thus creating the basic wrapper feature selector. Since we do not have any parametric description of the class specific stochastic processes, we have to estimate the error rate. To do that we need first to define the classifier architecture and then the error estimation method. As a simple rule of thumb one can use the 1-Nearest Neighbor classifier together with the Leave-One-Out error estimation procedure (Devijver & Kittler, 1982; Duda et al., 2001; Theodoridis & Koutroumbas, 2006). The use of a multilayer perceptron as the classifier together with a cross-validation error estimation method is computationally unfeasible, since during selection, for discarding of a single feature or joining another, we would have to completely train the network and estimate its classification accuracy.

Filter criteria $J(X)$ of a feature set X allow to obtain the selected feature set before a regression or classification is done. One can expect that there is a strong correlation between a high value of a filter criterion and a good regressor or classifier. For instance when we have two classes and the distances among the samples of the same class (intraclass distance) is low and the distances between each sample of one class and the samples of the other class are high (interclass distance), we can expect a low error rate of a classifier.

For the definition of an interclass feature selection criterion, one has to define first a metric $\delta(x_i^{(k)}, x_j^{(l)})$ between a sample $x^{(k)}$ which belongs to class ω_i and sample $x^{(l)}$ which belongs to class ω_j. Usually the Euclidean distance $||x_i^{(k)} - x_j^{(l)}||$ is used. Other choices are Minkowski of order s as $\left[\sum_{f=1}^{F} |x_{if}^{(k)} - x_{jf}^{(l)}|^s \right]^{1/s}$, City Block (i.e. Minkowski of order 1), Chebychev $\max_f |x_{if}^{(k)} - x_{jf}^{(l)}|$ or some other nonlinear metric. The index $f = 1, \ldots, F$ is over the current candidate set X. The selection criterion is then the average interclass distance among all data points of all classes $J(X) = \frac{1}{2n^2} \sum_{i=1}^{c} \sum_{j=1}^{c} \sum_{k=1}^{n_i} \sum_{l=1}^{n_j} \delta(x_i^{(k)}, x_j^{(l)})$.

Consider two probability density functions $p_a(\mathbf{x}; \boldsymbol{\theta}_a)$ and $p_b(\mathbf{x}; \boldsymbol{\theta}_b)$ of a d-dimensional continuous random variable $\mathbf{x}$, defined by their functional forms p_a, p_b and parameter vectors $\boldsymbol{\theta}_a, \boldsymbol{\theta}_b$ respectively. A probabilistic distance measure J between the two probability density functions is a functional that measures the difference Δ integrated over the domain $\mathbb{R}^d$ of $\mathbf{x}$:

$$J(p_a, p_b, \boldsymbol{\theta}_a, \boldsymbol{\theta}_b) = \int_{\mathbf{x}} \Delta[(p_a, p_b, \boldsymbol{\theta}_a, \boldsymbol{\theta}_b)] d\mathbf{x}. \tag{14}$$

The metric Δ should be positive, zero if the values of the two functions coincide, and correlated to the their absolute difference (Devijver & Kittler, 1982). In the context of classification the a priori probabilities $P_a = Pr[\mathbf{x} \in \omega_a]$, $P_b = Pr[\mathbf{x} \in \omega_b]$ for the two classes ω_a, ω_b can additionally be incorporated into the probabilistic distance, hence in this case we have $J = J(P_a, P_b, p_a, p_b, \boldsymbol{\theta}_a, \boldsymbol{\theta}_b)$. In general J is defined for probability density functions (pdf) that could come from distinct functional families, for instance a univariate Normal distribution $p_a(x; \mu, \sigma^2)$ and a Gamma distribution $p_b(x; k, \theta)$. In practice however only pdfs with the same functional form $p_a = p_b$ are compared. Hence the pdf p under consideration becomes implicit and the functional forms are dropped from the argument list, so we have a function of the parameters $J(\theta_a, \theta_b)$. For instance the distance between two Gaussians in the univariate case with their means and variances given is $J([\ \mu_a\quad \sigma_a^2\ ],[\ \mu_b\quad \sigma_b^2\ ])$. The probabilistic distance between two multivariate Gaussian is the best studied distance. Assuming that the data obey this distribution one can obtain closed form distance measure based only on the means μ_i and covariance matrices Σ_i of the classes ω_i. For an overview of probabilistic distances see for instance Rauber et al. (2008).

Information based criteria for feature selection, especially mutual information was applied by Estevez et al. (2009). The idea is to measure the increment of information that a feature produces and rank the feature candidate sets following this information gain.

5. Performance estimation

A very important step in the design of a fault diagnosis system that is based on supervised learning of an automatic classifier is to estimate the quality of the resulting diagnosis system. Once again, like in the case of feature selection we can devise performance criteria and cross validation algorithms that give us an idea what we can expect from the fault classifier.

5.1 Data partition for performance estimation

If we had knowledge about the class-conditional probability distributions, an analytic calculus of the error rate would be possible. Since in practice only data is available, we divide the complete data set of n samples into at least a training set and a test set. Another division divides the data into three sets, where the additional validation set is normally used to either tune system parameters and/or serve as a test set. When the final classifier is defined the totally isolated test set that neither has be used to obtain good features, nor tune classifier parameters is used to estimate the performance.

The *Hold-out* method arbitrarily divides the n samples into $n - t$ training samples and t test samples, trains the classifier and submits the training samples to it. Eventually the splitting is repeated and the mean of the runs is taken as the final score of the performance criterion. *K-fold cross validation* also known as *rotation* divides the n samples arbitrarily into k sets of cardinality $\frac{k}{n}$. Then k times each of the sets with $\frac{n}{k}$ samples is retained as the test set, and the remaining $(k - 1)\frac{n}{k}$ samples are used for training the classifier. Then the performance measure is obtained by submitting the training samples to the trained classifier. The accumulated individual criteria obtained by the k runs is the final estimated performance criterion. If we set $k = n$ we have the *leave-one-out* estimation. A further estimation method is the over-optimistic *resubstitution* where the same set of n samples is used for training and test. The early textbook of Devijver & Kittler (1982) gives a more profound analysis of the data set division methods.

5.2 Classifier performance criteria

The estimated accuracy of a classifier by using the above mentioned data partition techniques is the classical and most obvious quality label of a classifier. A 100% accuracy is the ideal goal but in practice can only be envisioned due to the innumerous sources of uncertainty of a real world application. Especially in fault diagnosis a high classification accuracy might be misleading. Imagine a two-class condition monitoring system where the fault has an a priori occurrence of 1%. If we can detect normal situations in 98% of the time, our system is not a very good predictor.

An alternative way to compare the performance of a classifier is the Receiver Operating Characteristic (ROC) graph (Fawcett, 2006). This is a technique for visualizing, organizing and selecting a two-class classifier based on its performance in a two-dimensional space where the true positive rate (*tpr*) (also called hit rate or recall) is plotted on the Y axis and the false positive rate (*fpr*) is plotted on the X axis. The inference method of the classifier must provide a numerical continuous *score*, ideally the a posteriori probability of the positive class $P(\omega_{POS}|\mathbf{x})$. Each point in the ROC graph represents one specific classifier. One classifier is supposed to be better than the other if its position is to the northwest of the first. Any classifier on the diagonal is said to follow a random guessing strategy whilst a classifier below the diagonal performs worse than random guessing and may be said to have useful information, but applying it in an incorrect way. The ROC analysis is very important to compare classifiers considering unbalanced classes problem, such as a machine fault diagnosis since the number of negative class examples is almost always greater than the positive ones. Metrics such as accuracy are sensitive to changes in class distribution. In the context of fault diagnosis often two-class problems are tackled, allowing the direct counting of the false positives and false negatives. For several different fault classes a specialist for each class can be created, merging all other classes into the negative class. The performance criterion derived from the ROC graph employed in our research is the area under the ROC curve (AUC). For details on how to efficiently calculate the AUC parameter, see (Fawcett, 2006).

A final comment could be made about the classifier used to make the final decision about the diagnosed fault. An aspect in fault detection and diagnosis which in our opinion is often exaggerated in its importance is the classifier architecture. Frequently in conference proceedings and journal papers the part that realizes the classification stage of the diagnosis system is emphasized too much, for instance artificial neural networks (Duda et al., 2001). A sophisticated classifier cannot compensate for a poorly modeled feature description of the process. In our understanding it is worth to invest more in the signal processing and feature extraction and selection part of the system. This in general permits the use of a simpler classifier, for instance from the family of Nearest-Prototype (Devijver & Kittler, 1982), or Quadratic Gaussian (Duda et al., 2001). We often use the K-Nearest Neighbor classifier due to its non-parametric nature and ability to give good qualitative performance estimates, justified by the Cover and Hart Inequality in Nearest Neighbor Discrimination (Duda et al., 2001). The Support Vector Machine (Theodoridis & Koutroumbas, 2006) is an interesting alternative and also often used in our work.

6. Real-world application

Several publications have also discussed the detection of faults in industrial processes but only using well behaved data from a controlled laboratory environment. When an experimental benchmark is used, the fault classes are perfectly known permitting a doubtless labeling of the data sample for supervised learning. Machine simulations can assist in several aspects of system operation and control, being useful to do preliminary investigations about the capability of the method, though it cannot completely simulate all real-world situations. There are a number of factors that contribute to the complexity of the failure signature that cannot be simulated. Most industrial machinery contains components which will produce additional noise and vibration whereas a simulated environment is almost free from external vibrations. To investigate the performance of the previously presented fault diagnosis method using pattern recognition techniques, real acquisitions were obtained from various oil extraction platforms. We will apply some of the previously presented methods to diagnosis two of the most common defects in rotating machines of oil extraction rigs: bearing fault and misalignment fault. A statistically significant amount of real examples were available. Measurements were regularly taken during five years from 25 different oil platforms operating along the Brazilian

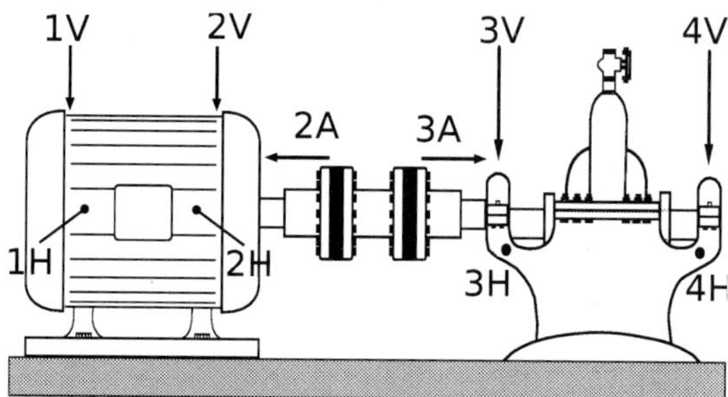

Fig. 2. Motor pump with extended coupling between motor and pump. The accelerometers are placed along the main directions to capture specific vibrations of the main axes. (H=horizontal, A=axial, V=vertical.)

coast. A total amount of 3700 acquisitions was collected. Of this total, only 1000 examples had some type of defect attributed by a human operator relying on his experience. The remainder of the examples represented normal operational conditions. Each acquisition labeled as a fault presents some kind of defect that can be divided into electrical, hydrodynamic, and mechanical failures, and may present several types of defects simultaneously. Normal examples, that is, examples without any defect were not used in this experiments. An example is called "normal" when the level of overall RMS is less than a pre-set threshold. In this way we could distinguish a faulty example from an example in good condition without training a sophisticated classifier, doing only a simple pre-processing.
The considered motor pumps are composed of one-stage horizontal centrifugal pumps coupled to an AC electric motor. Accelerometers strategically placed at points next to bearings and motors allow the displacement, velocity or acceleration of the machine over time to be measured, thus generating a discrete signal of the vibration level. Fig. 2 shows a typical positioning configuration of accelerometers on the equipment. In general, the orientations of the sensors follow the three main axes of the machine, that is, vertical, horizontal, and axial. Vibration signals are collected by means of a closed, proprietary vibration analyzer equipped with a sensor in the time domain and vibrational signal techniques were applied within the system.

6.1 Bearing fault diagnosis

We are interested in investigating a well-known method for monitoring the bearing condition applied to real world data obtained from rotating machines of oil extraction rigs using automatic pattern recognition techniques. A basic model of a bearing usually has rolling elements, inner and outer raceways, and a cage. The bearings, when defective, present characteristic frequencies depending on the localization of the defect (Mobley, 1999). Defects in rolling bearings can be foreseen by the analysis of vibrations, detecting spectral components with the frequencies (and their harmonics) typical for the fault. There are five characteristic frequencies at which faults can occur. They are the shaft rotational frequency F_S, fundamental cage frequency F_C, ball pass inner raceway frequency F_{BPI}, ball pass outer raceway frequency F_{BPO}, and the ball spin frequency F_B. The characteristic fault frequencies equations, for a bearing with stationary outer race, can be found in Mobley (1999). Whenever a collision between a

Class	A priori class distribution
Negative (without bearing fault)	69.43%
Positive (with any bearing fault)	30.57%

Table 1. Class distribution of the examples

defect and some bearing element happens, a short duration pulse is produced. This pulse excites the natural frequency of the bearing, resulting in an increase of the vibrational energy. The defect diagnosis based on the characteristic fault frequencies follows a set of consecutive stages usually denominated as envelope detection (or amplitude demodulation) (Harris & Piersol, 2002; McFadden & Smith, 1984). The envelope is an important and indicated signal processing technique that helps in the identification of the bearing defects, extracting characteristic frequencies from the vibration signal of the defective bearing, because the mechanic defects in components of the bearing manifest themselves in periodic beatings, overlapping the low frequency vibrations of the entire equipment, for instance caused by unbalance of the rotor of the pump. The objective is to isolate these frequencies and their harmonics, previously demodulated by the Hilbert transform (Čížek, 1970). With this analysis it is possible to identify not only the occurrence of faults in bearings, but also identify possible sources, like faults in the inner and outer race, or in the rolling elements.

The first step in amplitude demodulation is signal filtering with a band-pass filter to eliminate the frequencies associated with low frequencies defects (for instance unbalance and misalignment) and eliminating noise. The frequency band of interest is extracted from the original signal using a FIR filter (Harris & Piersol, 2002; Oppenheim et al., 1998) in the time domain. The envelope can be calculated by the Hilbert transform (Čížek, 1970). Given a signal $h(t)$ in the time domain, the Hilbert transform is the convolution of $h(t)$ with the signal $\frac{1}{\pi t}$, that is,

$$\tilde{h}(t) := \mathscr{H}\{h(t)\} := h(t) * \frac{1}{\pi t} = \frac{1}{\pi}\int_{-\infty}^{\infty} h(t)\frac{d\tau}{t-\tau}. \tag{15}$$

The envelope of the signal in the discrete form is then given by

$$\mathscr{E}[k] = \sqrt{h^2[k] + \tilde{h}^2[k]}. \tag{16}$$

Since each considered example always presents at least one kind of defect (not only bearing defect), the approach to deal with this multilabel classification problem was to generate a binary rolling bearing classifier in the following way: all examples without any bearing fault constitute the negative class while the examples containing at least one kind of bearing defect belong to the positive class. The training base was created considering that each acquisition is formed by all signals collected by each sensor placed on each bearing housing of the motor pump. Table 1 shows the proportion of positive and negative examples where the positive class means the class of examples containing any rolling element bearing defect and the negative class is the class of examples that have no bearing fault.

There are two important steps in the fault detection process. The first is to perform signal processing to generate the feature vector used in the subsequent classification step and the second step consist of inducing a classifier. In this experiment we extract features from some important bands of the envelope spectrum. We consider narrow bands around the first, the

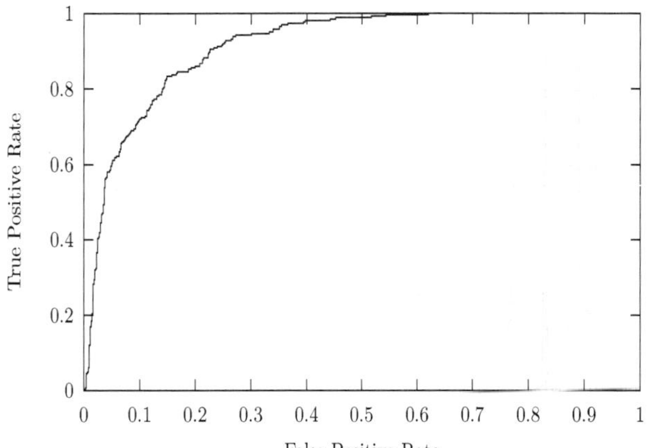

Fig. 3. SVM classifier performance (AUC=0.92).

second, the third, the fourth, and the fifth harmonic of each characteristic frequency. Another useful information used was the RMS calculated from the spectrum of acceleration and from the envelope spectrum of each measurement point. In this experiment we use the Support Vector Machine (SVM) (Bishop, 2007; Theodoridis & Koutroumbas, 2006) classifier trained with its best number of selected features so its performance is maximized. We used the radial basis as the kernel function with the spread parameter gamma equal to 8, and set the cost parameter C of the C-SVM to 0.5.

A detailed description about the real bearing fault examples and the mentioned classification approach can be found in (Mendel et al., 2009). Fig. 3 shows a ROC graph generated for the SVM induced classifier. Cross-Validation (10-fold) was used to estimate the classifier performance using the area under the ROC curve (AUC) as the performance criterion. With these experiments we are able to conclude that envelope analysis together with pattern recognition techniques really provide a powerful method to determine the condition that a bearing is defective or not.

6.2 Misalignment fault diagnosis

Misalignment is a mechanical problem with a high probability of occurrence. This kind of fault refers to problems related to the coupling between the shaft of the motor and the shaft of the pump, and occurs when they are parallelly oriented but do not coincide (parallel misalignment), or when they are not parallel but do coincide (angular misalignment). Both situations usually occur simultaneously, with a characteristic signature of a high vibration at the first, the second and the third harmonic of the main shaft rotation frequency, in both radial and axial directions. Fig. 4 shows the frequency spectrum of the velocity signal obtained from an accelerometer positioned near of the main shaft of a defective motor pump, in the case of misalignment and no other fault simultaneously.

An experiment of misalignment diagnosis that is done inside a well controlled laboratory environment enables the emergence of the characteristic signature of the fault, and the induced classifiers can achieve a very high accuracy in the misalignment detection. In a real world situation, however, the complexity increases considerably. Many other types of mechanical

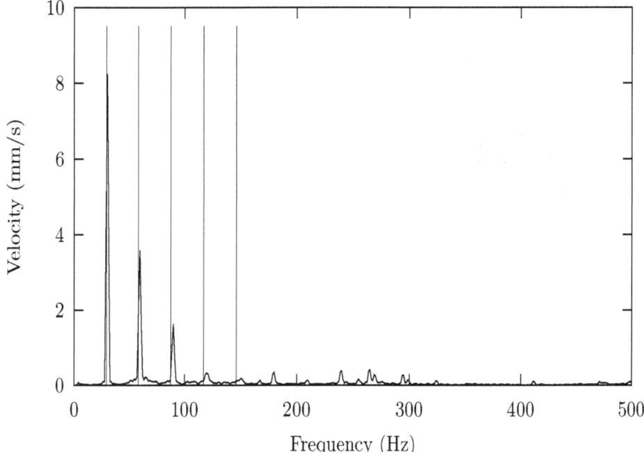

Fig. 4. Manifestation of the misalignment fault in the first three harmonics of the vibration signal spectrum

defects generate vibrations in the same frequencies as misalignment, for instance unbalance and mechanical looseness, and in that cases the total RMS energy in such frequencies tends to accumulate in a manner that is difficult to predict. The possibility of correct diagnosis then depends on the analysis of the situation in other frequency bands in which the signature of other defects should be sought, as well as the absence of misalignment influence. Based on that, it is clear that the determination by a human expert which are the relevant frequency bands to be analyzed by the classifier is a non-trivial task. Therefore, an interesting approach to this problem is the methodology outlined in section 1, namely the extraction of a large amount of features (which are mostly the RMS energy of some important bands of the frequency spectrum), followed by the feature selection stage in order to seek for feature sets that maximize the misalignment diagnosis performance.

Our experiments with the above presented motor pump faults database showed that the use of a single specific feature set to describe the whole process for the misalignment detection gives marginal results. A better approach has proved to be the training of several different misalignment classifiers, each one using a different feature set, and obtain the final classification of an unknown example combining the class result given by each one of these classifiers. This approach permits to alleviate the occasional presence of noisy information in a specific feature set, as other sets are also used for classification. The simplest approach to determine which are the different feature sets, each one generating a distinct classifier, is to perform the feature selection process by using an incremental selection algorithm, which gives as output the order in which each feature was selected (the feature rank). So, different feature sets can be obtained distinct from each other by the amount of features they have (for instance, a set composed of the first 15 selected features). Though sets with a greater number of features completely contain the sets with fewer features in a sequential search algorithm like SFFS, the classifiers still present different results, and this difference is emphasized by the usage of a cross-validation method in order to automatically tune the numerical parameters for each of the final selected feature sets. This approach was described in (Wandekokem et al., 2009) and the final classifier results will be shown here.

Experiment	Number of positive (defective) examples	Accuracy of the Final Classifier
First pair of training and test data	200 (61.9% of total)	71.45%
Second pair of training and test data	201 (64.0% of total)	74.22%
Third pair of training and test data	152 (47% of total)	74.76%

Table 2. Class distributions and the final classifiers accuracies for the test databases of the misalignment experiments.

To perform the experiments, we divided the complete database into a pair of training data and test data, each one with data obtained from oil rigs that are not used in the complementary base, and keeping the approximated proportion of 2/3 of the examples in the training database and the remaining 1/3 in the test database. We repeat that division process three times, evaluating three different experiments. While it is necessary to use data obtained from some oil rigs in more than one training database, the test databases for these experiments are disjoint. The first step in our evaluation is to select features with the SFS algorithm for each training database, using as the selection criterion the estimated accuracy of a SVM classifier by a 10-fold cross-validation, with the fixed parameters cost $C = 0.5$ and $\gamma = 8.0$. Selecting as the feature sets to be used in the final classifier ensemble are the 20 feature sets that maximize the criterion of the feature selection, and automatically tuning the values of their C and γ parameters by a cross-validation method. The final score value assigned to a test example can be calculated as the arithmetic mean of the scores assigned to by each of these 20 SVM classifiers. The scores are continuous values ranging from 0 to 1, and can be seen as the probability estimates of the example belonging to the positive class (defective pattern). Hence, as we used 0.5 as the score threshold value, an example with a final score below 0.5 was classified as the negative (non-defective) class. Table 2 presents, for each one of the three pairs of training and test databases, the class distributions and accuracies achieved by the final classifier architecture.
A more robust approach should explicitly seek different classifiers, which will produce a high quality classifier ensemble, a desired situation in which the performance of the ensemble surpasses the performance of each one of its individual classifiers. The use of genetic algorithms can meet this requirement, as individuals that represent very distinct feature sets can be individually searched and developed. However, this approach still poses challenges, such as the determination of which classifiers (individuals) among the available ones will be used to compose the final classifiers ensemble and is left for future research.

7. Conclusion

We first gave an overview of feature models that can be used for fault diagnosis, obtained from sensors attached to an industrial process. We distinguished between feature extraction on the measurement level that provide the principal descriptors of the process condition like spectra or statistical parameters, and feature extraction on the information level, like Principal Component Analysis. In order to filter out the enormous amount of features, possibly generated by the extractor techniques, we employ feature selection to obtain the final set of characteristic descriptors for the process situation. Besides, we discussed performance criteria of a diagnosis system relevant to a specific application in fault diagnosis, like the area under the ROC curve. As an example application we pointed out a automatic fault diagnosis system for motorpump defects in a real-world environment of oil rigs. Given the variety of processes in which faults may occur, it is impossible to cover all relevant techniques that are useful for their detection. Our intention was to transmit our experience derived from a concrete problem in this very interesting and challenging field of research. We will try to further study sophisticated methods and apply them to automatic fault detection and diagnosis in order to improve the quality even more.

Acknowledgment

We would like to thank COPES-Petrobras for the financial support given to the research from which this work originated (grant *Convênio Específico nr. 05 (4600225485) do Termo de Cooperação 0050.0023457.06-4 Petrobras-UFES*).

8. References

Al Kazzaz, S. A. S. & Singh, G. K. (2003). Experimental investigations on induction machine condition monitoring and fault diagnosis using digital signal processing techniques, *Eletric Power Systems Research* **65**: 197–221.

Bishop, C. M. (2007). *Pattern Recognition and Machine Learning*, Springer, Berlin.

Bracewell, R. N. (1986). *The Fourier Transform and Its Applications*, 2nd edn, McGraw-Hill, New York.

Castleman, K. R. (1995). *Digital Image Processing*, 2nd edn, Prentice Hall, New Jersey.

Chui, C. K. (1992). *An Introduction to Wavelets*, Academic Press.

De Backer, S., Naud, A. & Scheunders, P. (1998). Non-linear dimensionality reduction techniques for unsupervised feature extraction, *Pattern Recognition Letters* **19**(8): 711–720.

Devijver, P. A. & Kittler, J. (1982). *Pattern Recognition: A Statistical Approach*, Prentice/Hall Int., London.

Duda, R. O., Hart, P. E. & Stork, D. G. (2001). *Pattern Classification*, 2nd edn, John Wiley and Sons, New York.

Ericsson, S., Grip, N., Johansson, E., Petersson, L. E. & Strömberg, J. O. (2005). Towards automatic detection of local bearing defects in rotating machines, *Mechanical Systems and Signal Processing* **19**(3): 509–535.

Estevez, P., Tesmer, M., Perez, C. & Zurada, J. (2009). Normalized mutual information feature selection, *Neural Networks, IEEE Transactions on* **20**(2): 189–201.

Fawcett, T. (2006). An introduction to ROC analysis, *Pattern Recognition Letters* **27**: 861–874.

Gabor, D. (1946). Theory of communication, *Journal of the IEE* **93**(26): 429–457.

Goupillaud, P., Grossman, A. & Morlet, J. (1984). Cycle-octave and related transforms in seismic signal analysis, *Geoexploration* **23**: 85–102.

Guyon, I. & Elisseeff, A. (2003). An introduction to variable and feature selection, *J. Mach. Learn. Res.* **3**: 1157–1182.

Harris, T. A. & Piersol, A. G. (2002). *Harris's Shock and Vibration Handbook*, 5th edn, McGraw-Hill.

Hyärinen, A., Karhunen, J. & Oja, E. (2001). *Independent Component Analysis*, Wiley, New York.

Isermann, R. (2006). *Fault-Diagnosis Systems: An Introduction from Fault Detection to Fault Tolerance*, Springer, Berlin.

Jiang, L. Y. & Wang, S. Q. (2004). Fault diagnosis based on independent component analysis and fisher discriminant analysis, *Proceedings of the Third International Conference on Machine Learning and Cybernetics*, pp. 3638–3643.

Jolliffe, I. T. (2002). *Principal Component Analysis*, 2nd edn, Springer, Berlin.

Kohonen, T. (1998). The self-organizing map, *Neurocomputing* **21**(1-3): 1–6.

Kudo, M. & Sklansky, J. (2000). Comparison of algorithms that select features for pattern classifiers, *Pattern Recognition Letters* **33**: 25–41.

Lee, J. M., Qin, J. S. & Lee, I. B. (2006). Fault detection and diagnosis based on modified independent componente analysis, *American Institute of Chemical Enginners Journal* **52**(10): 3501–3514.

Lei, Y. & Zuo, M. J. (2009). Gear crack level identification based on weighted knearest neighbor classification algorithm, *Mechanical Systems and Signal Processing* **23**(5): 1535–1547.

Li, B., Chow, M. Y., Tipsuwan, Y. & Hung, J. C. (2000). Neural-network-based motor rolling bearing fault diagnosis, *IEEE Transactions on Industrial Electronics* **47**(5): 1060–1069.

Liu, H. & Motoda, H. (2007). *Computational Methods of Feature Selection (Chapman & Hall/Crc Data Mining and Knowledge Discovery Series)*, Chapman & Hall/CRC.

Loparo, K. A. & Lou, X. (2004). Bearing fault diagnosis based on wavelet transform and fuzzy inference, *Mechanical Systems and Signal Processing* **18**(5): 1077–1095.

McFadden, P. D. & Smith, J. D. (1984). Vibration monitoring of rolling element bearings by the high frequency resonance technique - a review, *Tribology International* **17**: 1–18.

Mendel, E., Rauber, T. W., Varejao, F. M. & Batista, R. J. (2009). Rolling element bearing fault diagnosis in rotating machines of oil extraction rigs, Glasgow.

Mobley, R. K. (1999). *Root Cause Failure Analysis (Plant Engineering Maintenance Series)*, Butterworth-Heinemann.

Narendra, P. & Fukunaga, K. (1977). A branch and bound algorithm for feature subset selection, *Computers, IEEE Transactions on* **C-26**(9): 917–922.

Oh, I.-S., Lee, J.-S. & Moon, B.-R. (2004). Hybrid genetic algorithms for feature selection, *Pattern Analysis and Machine Intelligence, IEEE Transactions on* **26**(11): 1424–1437.

Opitz, D. W. (1999). Feature selection for ensembles, *AAAI '99/IAAI '99: Proceedings of the sixteenth national conference on Artificial intelligence and the eleventh Innovative applications of artificial intelligence conference innovative applications of artificial intelligence*, American Association for Artificial Intelligence, Menlo Park, CA, USA, pp. 379–384.

Oppenheim, A. V., Schafer, R. W. & Buck, J. R. (1998). *Discrete-Time Signal Processing*, 2nd edn, Prentice-Hall.

Paya, B. A., Esat, I. I. & Badi, M. N. M. (1997). Artificial neural network based fault diagnosis of rotating machinery using wavelet transforms as a preprocessor, *Mechanical Systems and Signal Processing* **11**(5): 751–765.

Pernkopf, F. & O'Leary, P. (2001). Feature selection for classification using genetic algorithms with a novel encoding, *in* G. Goos, J. Hartmanis & J. van Leeuwen (eds), *Computer Analysis of Images and Patterns*, Springer Berlin / Heidelberg, pp. 161–168.

Pöyhönen, S., Jover, P. & Hyötyniemi, H. (2003). Independent component analysis of vibrations for fault diagnosis of an induction motor, *Proceedings of the IASTED International Conference on Circuits, Signals, and Systems*, Cancun, Mexico, pp. 203–208.

Pudil, P., Novovičová, J. & Kittler, J. (1994). Floating search methods in feature selection, *Pattern Recognition Letters* **15**(11): 1119–1125.

Rauber, T. W., Braun, T. & Berns, K. (2008). Probabilistic distance measures of the dirichlet and beta distributions, *Pattern Recognition* **41**(2): 637–645.

Samanta, B. & Al-Balushi, K. R. (2003). Artificial neural network based fault diagnostics of rolling bearings using time-domain features, *Mechanical Systems and Signal Processing* **17**(2): 317–328.

Sammon Jr., J. W. (1969). A nonlinear mapping for data structure analysis, *IEEE Transactions on Computers* **C-18**(5): 401–409.

Scheffer, C. & Girdhar, P. (2004). *Pratical Machinery Vibration Analysis and Predictive Maintenance*, 1st edn, Elsevier, Oxford, U. K.

Sejdić, E. & Jiang, J. (2008). Pattern recognition in time-frequency domain: Selective regional correlation and its applications, *in* P.-Y. Yin (ed.), *Pattern Recognition*, IN-TECH, Vienna, pp. 613–626.

Simani, S., Fantuzzi, C. & Patton, R. J. (2003). *Model-Based Fault Diagnosis in Dynamic Systems using Identification Techniques*, Springer, Berlin.

Singh, G. K. & Al Kazzaz, S. A. S. (2004). Vibration signal analysis using wavelet transform for isolation and identification of electrical faults in introduction machine, *Eletric Power Systems Research* **68**(1): 119–136.

Singh, G. K. & Al Kazzaz, S. A. S. (2008). Develpment of an intelligent diagnostic system for induction machine health monitoring, *IEEE Systems Journal* **2**(2): 273–288.

Skitt, P. J. C., Javed, M. A., Sanders, S. A. & Higginson, A. M. (1993). Procee monitoring using auto-associative, feed-forward artificial neural networks, *Journal of Intelligent Manufacturing* **4**(1): 79–94.

Stefanoiu, D. & Ionescu, F. (2006). *Fuzzy-Statistical Reasoning in Fault Diagnosis*, Springer, London.

Sun, Q., Chen, P. & Xi, F. (2004). Pattern recognition for automatic machinery fault diagnosis, *Journal of Vibration and Acoustics* **126**(2): 307–316.

Tavner, P. J., Ran, L., Penman, J. & Sedding, H. (2008). *Conditiong Monitoring of Electrical Machines*, The Institution of Engineering and Technology, London.

Theodoridis, S. & Koutroumbas, K. (2006). *Pattern Recognition*, 3rd edn, Academic Press, Inc., Orlando, FL, USA.

Čížek, V. (1970). Discrete Hilbert transform, *IEEE Transactions on Audio and Electroacustics* **18**(4): 340–343.

Večeř, P., Kreidl, M. & Šmíd, R. (2005). Condition indicators for gearbox condition monitoring systems, *Acta Polytechnica* **45**(6): 35–43.

Wandekokem, E. D., Franzosi, F. T. A., Rauber, T. W., Varejão, F. M. & Batista, R. J. (2009). Data-driven fault diagnosis of oil rig motor pumps applying automatic definition and selection of features, *Proceedings of the 7th IEEE International Symposium on Diagnostics for Electric Machines, Power Electronics and Drives*, Cargèse, France, pp. 1–5.

Wang, W. J. & McFadden, P. D. (1996). Application of wavelets to gearbox vibration signals for fault detection, *Journal of Sound and Vibration* **192**(5): 927–938.

Wigner, E. (1932). On the quantum correction for thermodynamic equilibrium, *Phys. Rev.* **40**(5): 749–759.

Yan, Z., Miyamoto, A. & Jiang, Z. (2009). Frequency slice wavelet transform for transient vibration response analysis, *Mechanical Systems and Signal Processing* **23**(5): 1474–1489.

Yu, B. & Yuan, B. (1993). A more efficient branch and bound algorithm for feature selection, *Pattern Recognition* **26**(6): 883 – 889.

## 26

Every Color Chromakey

Atsushi Yamashita, Hiroki Agata and Toru Kaneko
Shizuoka University (Japan)

1. Introduction

Image composition is very important to creative designs such as cinema films, magazine covers, promotion videos, and so on. This technique can combine images of actors or actresses in a studio and those of scenery taken in other places (Porter & Duff, 1984). Robust methods are needed especially for live programs on TV (Gibbs et al., 1998, Wojdala, 1998).

To perform image composition, objects of interest must be segmented from images, and there are a lot of studies about image segmentation (Ful & Mui, 1981, Skarbek & Koschan, 1994), e.g. pixel-based, area-based, edge-based, and physics-based ones. For example, Snakes (Kass et al., 1988) was proposed as an effective technique based on edge detection. However, there have not been developed practical methods which are accurate and automatic, while methods with high accuracy are proposed that are realized by human assistance (Mitsunaga et al., 1995, Li et al., 2004). Qian and Sezan proposed an algorithm that classifies the pixels in an input image into foreground and background based on the color difference between the input image and a pre-recorded background image (Qian & Sezan, 1999). The classification result is obtained by computing a probability function and the result is refined using anisotropic diffusion. However, the algorithm does not work well when foreground objects share regions of similar color and intensity with background. It has also restriction of requiring a stationary camera.

As to camera motion, Shimoda et al. proposed a method in which the background image alters accordingly as the foreground image is altered by panning, tilting, zooming and focusing operations of the camera (Shimoda et al., 1989). This method is a fundamental technique of virtual studios (Gibbs et al., 1998, Wojdala, 1998).

As a method that takes the advantage of three-dimensional information, Kanade et al. proposed a stereo machine for video-rate dense depth mapping that has a five-eye camera head handling the distance range of 2 to 15m using 8mm lenses (Kanade et al., 1996). Kawakita et al. proposed the axi-vision camera that has up-ramped and down-ramped intensity-modulated lights with an ultrafast shutter attached to a CCD probe camera (Kawakita et al., 2000). These systems can obtain the ranges from the camera to the objects in the scene and extract the objects from the images by using the range information. Yasuda et al. proposed the thermo-key extraction technique that measure thermal information for keys based on that the high temperature region is the human region (Yasuda et al., 2004).

However, since these systems consist of special devices, it is difficult for ordinary users to realize image segmentation by employing this information.

Chromakey, which is also referred to as color keying or color-separation overlay, is a well-known image segmentation technique that removes a color from an image to reveal another image behind. Objects segmented from a uniform single color (usually blue or green) background are superimposed electronically to another background. This technique has been used for long years in the TV and the film industries.

In image composition, the color $I(u,v)$ of a composite image at a pixel (u,v) is defined as:

$$I(u,v) = \alpha(u,v)F(u,v) + (1 - \alpha(u,v))B(u,v) \qquad (1)$$

where $F(u,v)$ and $B(u,v)$ are the foreground and the background color, respectively, and $\alpha(u,v)$ is the so-called alpha key value at a pixel (u,v) (Porter & Duff, 1984).

The color at a pixel (u,v) is the same as that of the foreground when $\alpha(u,v)$ equals to 1, and is the same as that of the background when $\alpha(u,v)$ equals to 0. In chromakey, it is very important to determine the alpha value exactly. Methods for exact estimation of the alpha value have been proposed in applications of hair extraction, transparent glass segmentation, and so on (Mishima, 1992, Zongker et al., 1999, Ruzon & Tomasi, 2000, Hillman et al., 2001, Chuang et al., 2001, Sun et al., 2004).

However, conventional chromakey techniques using a monochromatic background have a problem that foreground objects are regarded as the background if their colors are similar to the background color, and the foreground regions of the same color are missing (Fig. 1(a)).

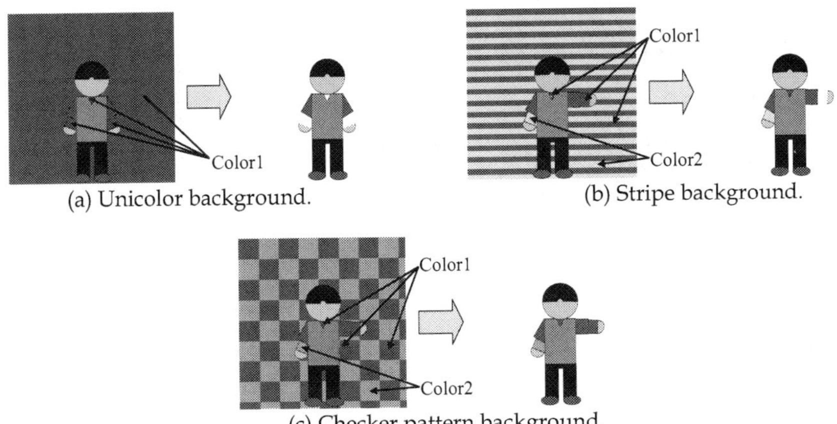

(a) Unicolor background.

(b) Stripe background.

(c) Checker pattern background.

Fig. 1. Region extraction with chromakey.

To solve this problem, Smith and Blinn proposed a blue screen matting method that allows foreground objects to be shot against two backing colors (Smith & Blinn, 1996). This method can extract the foreground region whose colors are the same as the background color. This alternating background technique cannot be used for live actors or moving objects because of the requirement for motionlessness within a background alternation period.

In order to solve the above problem, we proposed a method for segmenting objects from a background precisely even if objects have a color similar to the background (Yamashita et al., 2004). In this method, a two-tone stripe background is used (Fig. 1(b)). As to foreground extraction, the boundary between the foreground and the background is detected to recheck the foreground region whose color is same as the background. To detect the region whose color is same as the background, the method employs the condition that the striped region endpoints touch the foreground contour. If the foreground object has the same color as the background and has parallel contours with the background stripes, endpoints of the striped region do not touch the foreground contour. Therefore, it is difficult to extract such foreground objects (Fig. 1(b)). To solve this problem, we also proposed a chromakey method for extracting foreground objects with arbitrary shape in any color by using a two-tone checker pattern background (Fig. 1(c)) (Agata et al., 2007).

Basically, these two methods (Yamashita et al., 2004, Agata et al., 2007) only decide the alpha values as 0 or 1 discretely, and exact alpha value estimation is not considered. In other words, these methods mainly treat segmentation problems, not composition problems.

In this paper, we propose a new chromakey method that can treat foreground objects with arbitrary shape in any color by using a two-tone checker pattern background (Fig. 1(c)). The proposed method estimates exact alpha value and realizes natural compositions of difficult regions such as hair (Yamashita et al., 2008).

The procedure consists of four steps; background color extraction (Fig. 2(a)), background grid line extraction (Fig. 2(b), (c)), foreground extraction (Fig. 2(d), (e)), and image composition (Fig. 2(f)).

2. Background Color Extraction

Candidate regions for the background are extracted by using a color space approach. Let R_1 and R_2 be the regions whose colors are C_1 and C_2, respectively, where C_1 and C_2 are the colors of the two-tone background in an image captured with a camera (Fig. 2(a)). Then region R_i ($i = 1, 2$) is represented as

$$R_i = \{(u,v) \mid I(u,v) \in C_i\} \tag{2}$$

where $I(u,v)$ is the color of an image at a pixel (u,v).

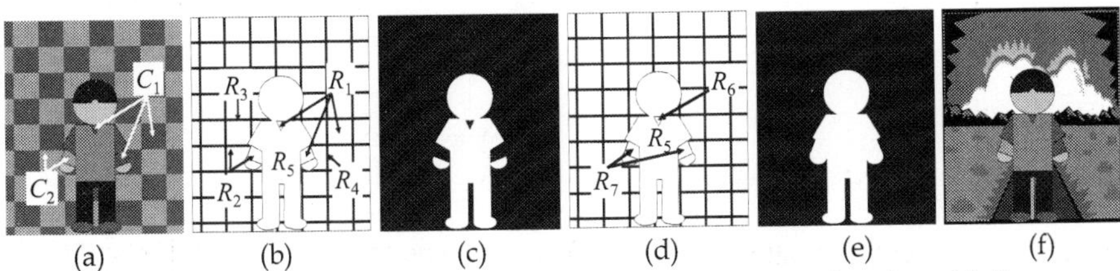

Fig. 2. Procedure.   (a) Original image.   (b) Region segmentation 1.   (c) Foreground extraction 1.   (d) Region segmentation 2.   (e) Foreground extraction 2.   (f) Image composition.

In addition to regions R_1 and R_2, intermediate grid-line regions between R_1 and R_2 are also candidates for the background. Let such regions be denoted as R_3 and R_4, where the former corresponds to horizontal grid lines and the other to vertical ones, respectively (Fig. 2(b)). The color of R_3 and R_4 may be a composite of C_1 and C_2, which is different from C_1 and C_2. Here, let C_3 be the color belonging to regions R_3, R_4 or foreground region, and we have the following description:

$$C_3 = \{I \mid I \notin (C_1 \cup C_2)\} \tag{3}$$

Figure 3 illustrates a relation among background regions R_1, R_2, R_3, R_4, and pixel colors C_1, C_2, C_3. It is necessary to estimate C_1 and C_2 in individual images automatically to improve the robustness against the change of lighting conditions. We realize this automatic color estimation by investigating the color distributions of the leftmost and rightmost image areas where the foreground objects do not exist as shown in Fig. 4(a). The colors in these reference areas are divided into C_1, C_2, and C_3 in the HLS color space by using K-mean clustering. Figure 4(b) shows the distribution of C_1, C_2, and C_3 in the HLS color space, where the H value is given by the angular parameter. The HLS color space is utilized because color segmentation in the HLS color space is more robust than in the RGB color space against the change of lighting conditions.

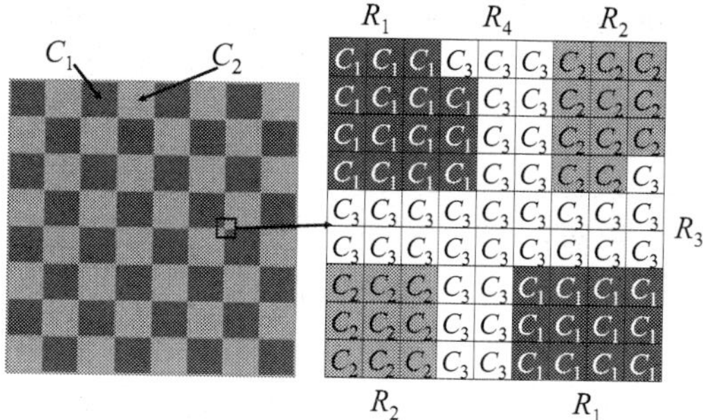

Fig. 3. Background regions and their colors.

(a) Reference areas.

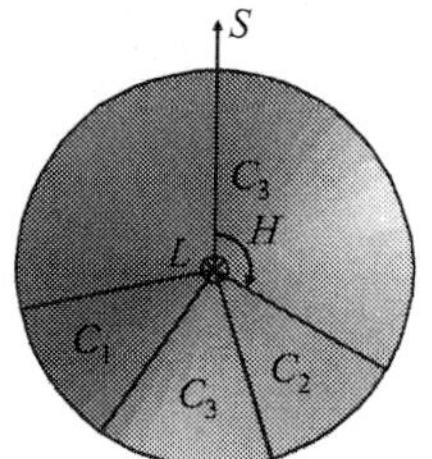

(b) HLS color space.

Fig. 4. Background color estimation.

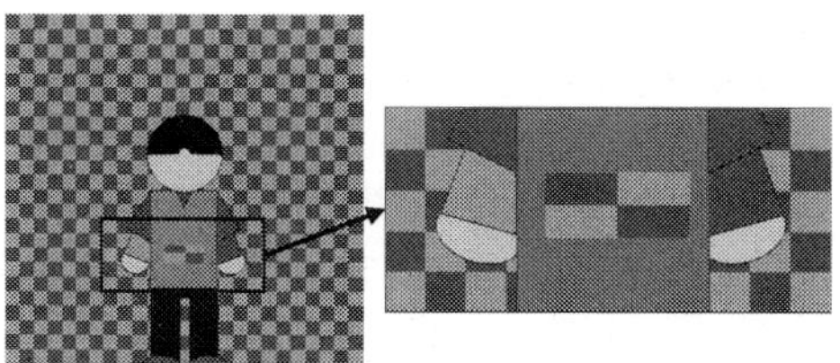

Fig. 5. Checker pattern in the foreground object.

Let H_i (i = 1, 2) be the mean value of the H values of C_i (i = 1, 2) in the reference areas, and let h_j (j = 1, 2, ..., N) be the H value of each point in the image, where N is the total number of pixels of the image. Pixels are regarded as background candidate pixels if they satisfy the following condition, where T is a threshold:

$$|H_i - h_j| \leq T \qquad (4)$$

3. Background Grid Line Extraction

Background grid lines are extracted by using adjacency conditions between two background colors. Background grid line regions R_3 and R_4 contact with both R_1 and R_2. The colors of the upper and lower regions of R_3 differ from each other, and also the colors of the left and right regions of R_4 differ from each other. Therefore, R_3 and R_4 are expressed as follows:

$$R_3 = \{(u,v),(u,v+1),\cdots,(u,v+l+1) \mid I(u,v+1) \in C_3,\cdots,I(u,v+l) \in C_3,$$
$$((I(u,v) \in C_1, I(u,v+l+1) \in C_2) \text{ or } ((I(u,v) \in C_2, I(u,v+l+1) \in C_1))\} \qquad (5)$$

$$R_4 = \{(u,v),(u+1,v),\cdots,(u+l+1,v) \mid I(u+1,v) \in C_3,\cdots,I(u+l,v) \in C_3,$$
$$((I(u,v) \in C_1, I(u+l+1,v) \in C_2) \text{ or } ((I(u,v) \in C_2, I(u+l+1,v) \in C_1))\} \qquad (6)$$

where l is the total number of the pixels whose color is C_3 in the vertical or horizontal direction.

However, if R_3 and R_4 are included in foreground objects, e.g. when a person wears in part a piece of cloth having the same checker pattern as the background as shown in Fig. 5, these regions can not be distinguished whether foreground or background. Therefore, we apply a rule that background grid lines should be elongated from those given in the reference area where foreground objects do not exist. If grid lines in foreground objects are dislocated from background grid lines as shown in Fig. 6, they are regarded as foreground regions. Elongation of the background grid lines is realized by the following method.

In the case of horizontal background grid lines, continuous lines exist at the top of the image as shown in Fig. 7 (a). At any part of the left and right reference area of the image, foreground objects do not exist. Therefore, it is possible to match any horizontal lines between the left end of the image and the right one by making correspondence from top to bottom one by one. We approximate the horizontal background grid lines behind the foreground object by applying a least mean square method to visible grid-line pairs.

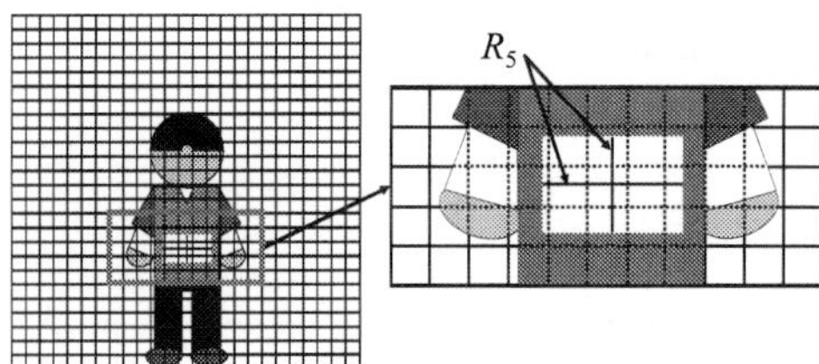

Fig. 6. Background grid line approximation.

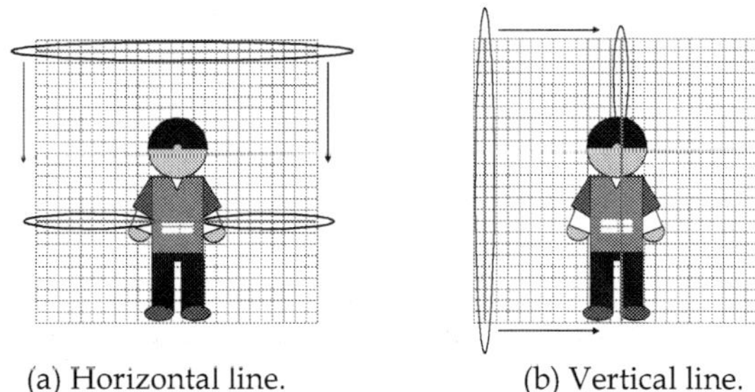

(a) Horizontal line.   (b) Vertical line.

Fig. 7. Background grid line estimation.

In the case of vertical background grid lines, continuous lines exist at the left and the right end of the image as shown in Fig. 7(b). However, if a foreground object is a standing person, it is not always possible to match the vertical lines between the top end of the image and the bottom one. In this case, we estimate the vertical background grid line behind the foreground object by applying a least mean square method only to the line at the top end of the image.

When applying a least mean square method to estimate either horizontal or vertical grid lines mentioned above, we should take into account the influence of camera distortion as a practical problem. Then we should fit higher-order polynomial curves instead of straight lines to the background grid lines. Here, we may have another approach; i.e. if we use a perfect checker pattern background consisting of squares or rectangles each of which has exactly the same shape, and a distortion-free camera whose image plane is set perfectly parallel to the checker pattern background, the background grid-line extraction procedure will become a very easy one. Comparing to this situation, our procedure seems to be elaborate, but it has such advantages as a camera with an ordinary lens can be used, the camera is allowed to have some tilt, and a checker pattern background which is somewhat distorted is available.

In this stage, all regions whose colors are same as the background are extracted as the background candidates, which may include mis-extracted regions as illustrated in Fig. 2(c). Those are regions which belong to the foreground object but have the same color as the background. As shown in Fig. 2(d), we define foreground regions whose colors are different from the background as R_5, and we define mis-extracted regions isolated from the background and neighboring to the background as R_6 and R_7, respectively. These errors are corrected in the next step.

4. Foreground Grid Line Extraction

Background candidate regions corresponding to R_6 and R_7 should be reclassified as the foreground, although their colors are same as the background. This reclassification can be realized by adopting the following rules concerning to adjacency with background grid lines.

1. If there is a background region candidate that does not connect with the background grid line regions R_3 nor R_4, it is reclassified as the foreground region R_6 (Fig. 8, top).
2. If there is a background region candidate which has an endpoint of a background grid line in its inside, it is divided into two regions; one is a foreground region and the other is a background (Fig. 8, right). The dividing boundary of the two regions is given by a series of the interpolation lines each of which is a connection of neighboring background grid-line endpoints (Fig. 9(a), (b)). The region containing the background grid line is regarded as the background, and the other is regarded as the foreground region R_7.

Figure 9 illustrates the above 2nd rule. Background grid-line endpoints shown in Fig. 9(a) produce the dividing boundary as a series of interpolation lines as shown in Fig. 9(b).

By completing the above procedures, the image is divided into seven regions R_1 - R_7. Regions R_5, R_6 and R_7 are the foreground regions (Fig. 2(d), (e)). The contours of the foreground objects may not be exact ones, because the interpolation lines do not give fine structure of the contours owing to the simplicity of straight line connection. Therefore, we need to execute post processing for contour refinement which is realized by Snakes (Kass et al., 1988) (Fig. 10).

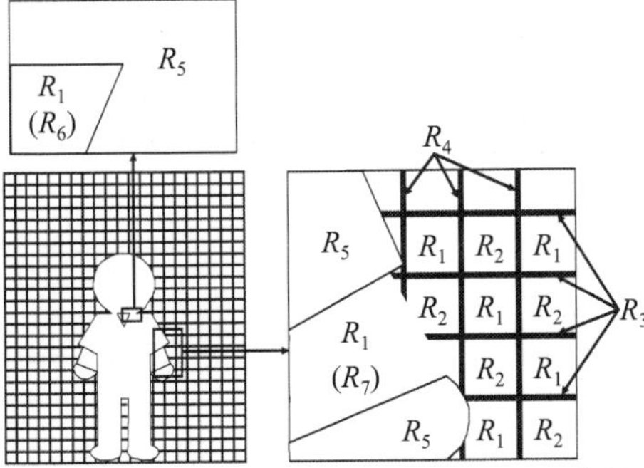

Fig. 8. Foreground region whose color is same as the background. Top: Inside the foreground (R_1 is reclassified to R_6). Right: Neighboring to the background (R_1 is reclassified to R_7).

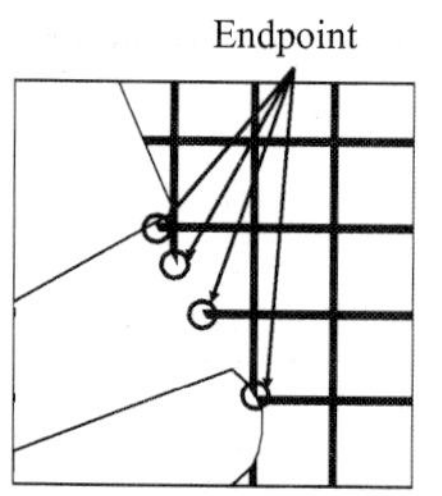

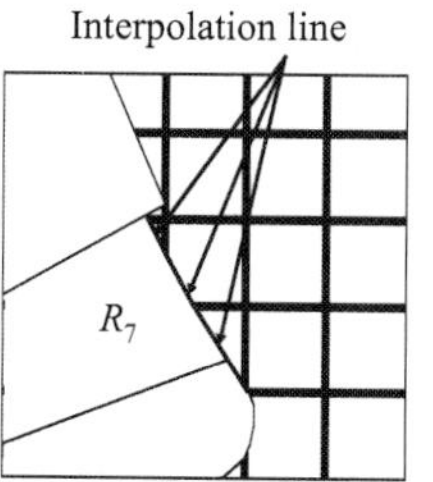

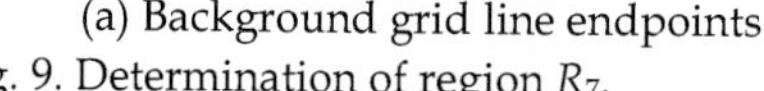

(a) Background grid line endpoints.   (b) Interpolation lines.

Fig. 9. Determination of region R_7.

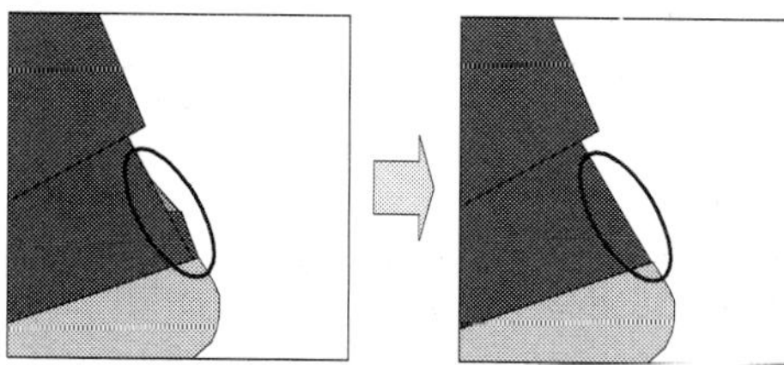

Fig. 10. Region extraction using Snakes.

Let $\mathbf{s}_i = (u,v)$ $(i = 1, 2, \ldots, n)$ be closed curves on the image plane (u,v), and we define Snakes energy as:

$$E_{snakes}(\mathbf{s}_i) = E_{spline}(\mathbf{s}_i) + E_{image}(\mathbf{s}_i) + E_{area}(\mathbf{s}_i) \tag{7}$$

where $E_{spline}(\mathbf{s}_i)$ is the energy to make the contour model smooth, $E_{image}(\mathbf{s}_i)$ is the energy to attract the contour model to the edge, and $E_{area}(\mathbf{s}_i)$ is the energy for the contour model to expand to fit to the reentrant shape (Araki et al., 1995).
These energies are defined as:

$$E_{spline}(\mathbf{s}_i) = \sum_{i=1}^{n}(w_{sp1}\,|\mathbf{s}_i - \mathbf{s}_{i-1}|^2 + w_{sp2}\,|\mathbf{s}_{i+1} - 2\mathbf{s}_i + \mathbf{s}_{i-1}|^2) \tag{8}$$

$$E_{image}(\mathbf{s}_i) = -\sum_{i=1}^{n}(w_{image}\,|\nabla I(\mathbf{s}_i)|) \tag{9}$$

$$E_{area}(\mathbf{s}_i) = \sum_{i=1}^{n} w_{area}\{u_i(v_{i+1} - v_i) - (u_{i+1} - u_i)v_i\} \tag{10}$$

where w_{sp1}, w_{sp2}, w_{image}, and w_{area} are weighting factors, respectively. $I(\mathbf{s}_i)$ is a function of image intensity on $\mathbf{s}_i$.

Therefore, $|\nabla I(\mathbf{s}_i)|$ is the absolute value of image intensity gradient. In the proposed method, $|\nabla I(\mathbf{s}_i)|$ is given by the following equations depending on what region the pixel belongs to.

$$|\nabla I(\mathbf{s}_i)| = \begin{cases} |I(u_i+1,v_i)-I(u_i,v_i)|+|I(u_i,v_i+1)-I(u_i,v_i)|, & \text{if } (u,v) \notin R_3, R_4 \\ |I(u_i+1,v_i)-I(u_i,v_i)|, & \text{if } (u,v) \in R_3 \\ I(u_i,v_i+1)-I(u_i,v_i)|, & \text{if } (u,v) \in R_4 \end{cases} \qquad (11)$$

Equation (11) shows that the contour model should not be attracted to the edges belonging to the background grid lines. The horizontal and the vertical background grid lines are regarded as edges that have large intensity gradients along the vertical and the horizontal directions, respectively. Therefore, we make directionally selective calculation of intensity gradients for pixels belonging to region R_3 or R_4 in Equation (11).

5. Image Composition

The extracted foreground image and another background image are combined by using Equation (1) (Fig. 2(f)).

The alpha values for the background pixels are decided as 0 (black regions in Fig. 11(b)), and those for the foreground pixels are decided as 1 (white regions in Fig. 11(b)) by using Snakes. It is important to decide binary alpha values for region extraction, however, alpha values of boundary regions between foregrounds and backgrounds are neither 0 nor 1. Therefore, we estimate alpha values by using Bayesian approach to digital matting (Chuang et al., 2001).

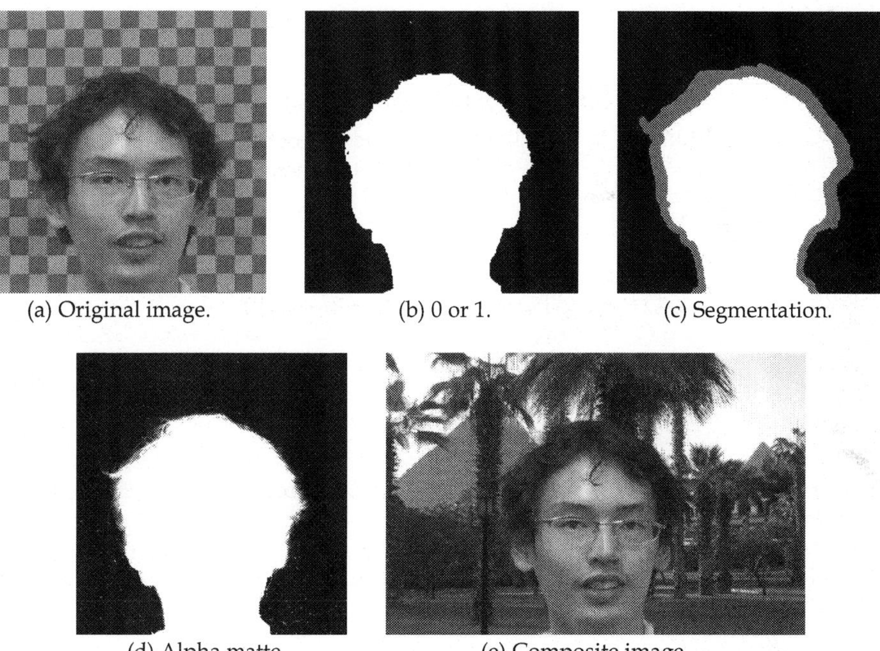

(a) Original image.   (b) 0 or 1.   (c) Segmentation.

(d) Alpha matte.   (e) Composite image.

Fig. 11. Image composition.

Conservative foregrounds (white regions in Fig. 11(c)), conservative backgrounds (black regions in Fig. 11(c)), and unknown regions (grey regions in Fig. 11(c)) are segmented from the region extraction result by using foreground extraction results by Snakes.

Alpha value, in other words, opacity for each pixel of the foreground element, is estimated by using a modified Bayesian matting method that can extract same color regions with backgrounds (Fig. 11(d)), and a natural composite image is generated by using the opacity (Fig. 11(e)). Note that Snakes is essential to our method for deciding initial foreground regions and dividing image into three regions. Our method cannot work well without Snakes, because initial foreground contours is important for estimating opacity for same color regions with backgrounds.

6. Experiment

Experiments were performed in an indoor environment. In the experiments, we selected blue and green as the colors of the checker pattern background, because they are complementary colors of human skin color and generally used in chromakey with a unicolor background.

The pitch of the checker pattern was 30mm x 30mm to interpolate the boundary of R_6 region precisely. Note that we have also compared the patterns of the background, e.g. triangle, quadrate, hexagon, and so on (Matsunaga et al., 2000). Checker pattern (quadrate) was selected from the simulation results of the optimization by considering the accuracy of foreground extraction (the numbers of the endpoints of region R_7 can be increased) and the computation time.

The sizes of still images were 1600 x 1200 pixels, and those of the moving image sequence were 1440 x 1080 pixels, respectively.

The threshold value T for a color extraction in Equation (4) was 20. The length l of regions R_3 and R_4 was 4. The weighting factors w_{sp1}, w_{sp2}, w_{image}, w_{area} for Snakes were 30, 3, 2, 1, respectively. In approximation of the background grid lines by a least mean square method, we used quartic equations to fit. All parameters were determined experimentally by manual search for optimal ones to give good results. These parameters were unchanged throughout the experiments.

The method has been verified in an indoor environment with a lot of people whose clothes were diverse in color.

Figure 12 shows an experimental result, where Fig. 12(a) shows a foreground image, Fig. 12(b) shows a background extraction result, Fig. 12(c) shows a foreground extraction result before contour refinement, Fig. 12(d) shows a foreground extraction result after contour refinement (Snakes), Fig. 12(e) shows opacity for alpha matte, and Fig. 12(f) shows a result of the image composition, respectively.

Figure 13(a) shows a composite result without alpha estimation and Fig. 13(b) (enlarged result of Fig. 12(f)) shows a result with an alpha estimation. From these results, it is verified that natural compositions of difficult regions such as hair can be realized.

Figure 14 shows the results of region extraction using a unicolor, a stripe and a checker pattern background, respectively. Figures 14(a), (b) and (c) are original images to segment, where sheets of the same paper used as the background are put on the foreground person in order to confirm the validity of the proposed method. Figure 14(d) shows that the foreground regions whose colors are the same as the background color can not be extracted. Figure 14(e) shows that if the foreground regions have the same colors as the background and have parallel contours with the background stripes, they can not be extracted. Figure 14(f) shows that the foreground regions whose colors are the same as the background color are extracted without fail.

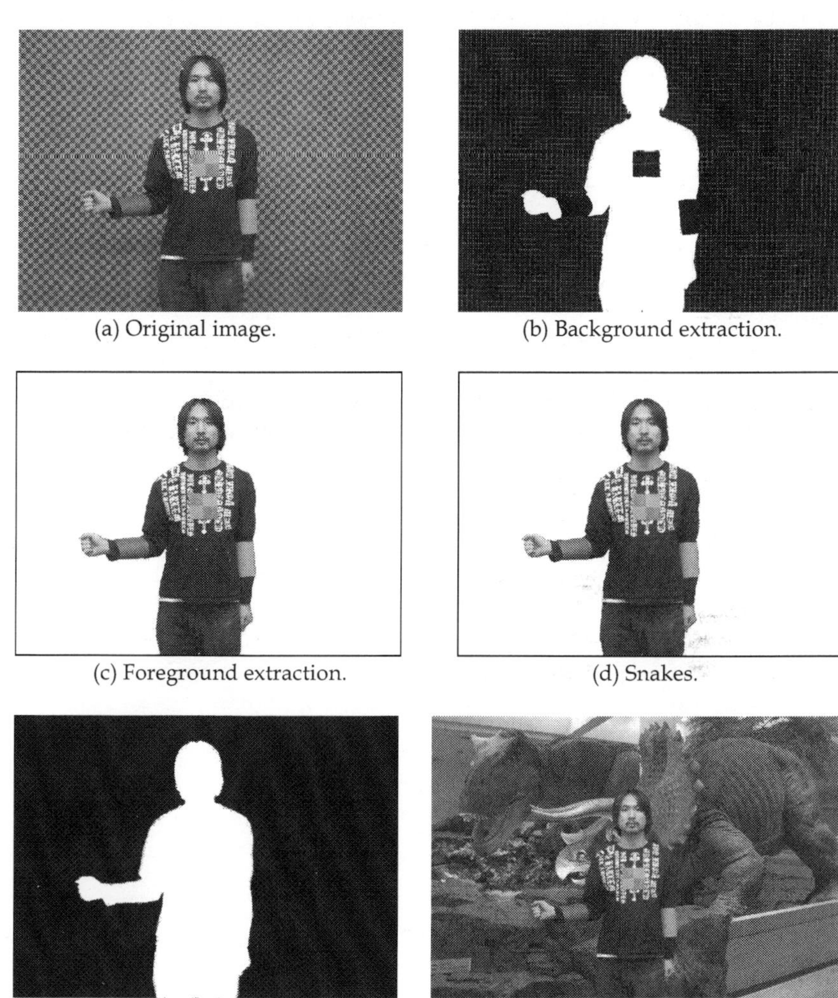

(a) Original image.

(b) Background extraction.

(c) Foreground extraction.

(d) Snakes.

(e) Alpha matte.

(f) Image composition.

Fig. 12. Experimental result 1.

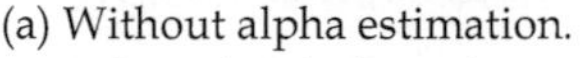

(a) Without alpha estimation.   (b) With alpha estimation.

Fig. 13. Experimental result 2 (enlarged image of Fig. 12).

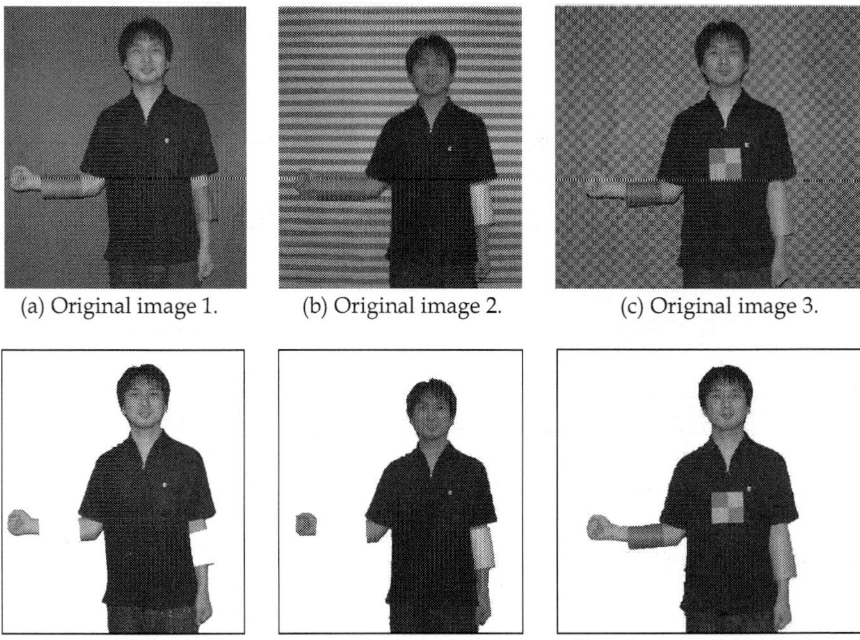

(a) Original image 1.   (b) Original image 2.   (c) Original image 3.

(d) Result image 1.   (f) Result image 2.   (g) Result image 3.

Fig. 14. Experimental result 3.

Figure 15 shows other experimental result. In Fig. 15(a), sheets of the same paper used as the background are put on the foreground person. In Fig. 15(b), same color checker pattern are put inside the foreground person. In Fig. 15(c), the foreground person holds his pelvis with his left hand, and there is a hole inside the foreground person. From these results, it is verified that foreground objects can be extracted without fail regardless of colors and shapes of foreground objects whose colors are same as the background colors.

(a) Same colors as background.

(b) Same color checker pattern as background.

(c) Hole (Person who holds his pelvis with his left hand).

Fig. 15. Experimental result 4.

Figure 16 shows results for a moving image sequence, where (a), (b) show foreground images, and (c) shows results of image composition, respectively.

From these experimental results, the effectiveness of the proposed method is verified.

 Pattern Recognition, Recent Advances

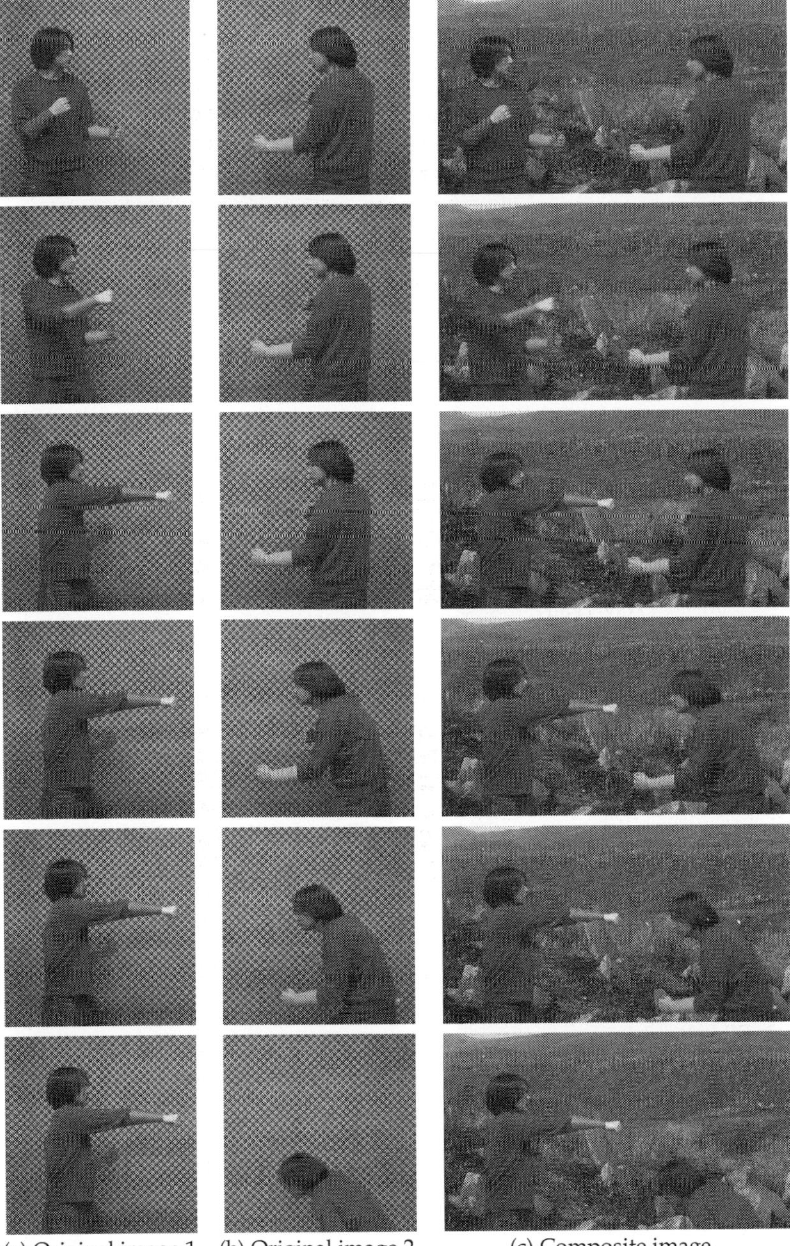

(a) Original image 1. (b) Original image 2. (c) Composite image.

Fig. 16. Experimental result 5.

7. Conclusion

In this paper, we proposed a new chromakey method using chromakey with a two-tone checker pattern background. The method solves the problem in conventional chromakey techniques that foreground objects become transparent if their colors are the same as the background color. The method utilizes the adjacency condition between two-tone regions of the background and the geometrical information of the background grid lines.

Experimental results show that the foreground objects can be segmented exactly from the background regardless of the colors of the foreground objects.

Although our proposed method can work successfully, parameters for image processing should be determined automatically based on appropriate criteria to improve our method. When applying the method to a video sequence, we should take the advantage of interframe correlation. The parameters and the background grid-line geometry obtained in the first frame can be utilized in processing of succeeding frames so that the total processing time will be much shorter.

8. References

Porter, T. & Duff, T. (1984). Compositing Digital Images, *Computer Graphics* (*Proceedings of SIGGRAPH1984*), Vol.18, No.3, pp.253-259, 1984.

Gibbs, S., Arapis, C., Breiteneder, C., Lalioti, V., Mostafawy, S. & Speier, J. (1998). Virtual Studios: An Overview, *IEEE Multimedia*, Vol.5, No.1, pp.18-35, 1998.

Wojdala, A. (1998). Challenges of Virtual Set Technology, *IEEE Multimedia*, Vol.5, No.1, pp.50-57, 1998.

Fu, K.-S. & Mui, J.K. (1981). A Survey on Image Segmentation, *Pattern Recognition*, Vol.13, pp.3-16, 1981.

Skarbek, W. & Koschan, A. (1994). Colour Image Segmentation - A Survey, *Technical Report 94-32, Technical University of Berlin, Department of Computer Science*, 1994.

Kass, M., Witkin, A. & Terzopoulos, D.(1988). Snakes: Active Contour Models, International *Journal of Computer Vision*, Vol.1, No.4, pp.321-331, 1988.

Mitsunaga, T., Yokoyama Y. & Totsuka, T. (1995). AutoKey: Human Assisted Key Extraction, *Computer Graphics* (*Proceedings of SIGGRAPH1995*), pp.265-272, 1995.

Li, Y., Sun, J., Tang, C.-K. & Shum, H.-Y. (2004). Lazy Snapping, *Computer Graphics* (*Proceedings of SIGGRAPH2004*), pp.303-308, 2004.

Qian, R. J. & Sezan, M. I. (1999). Video Background Replacement without A Blue Screen, *Proceedings of the 1999 IEEE International Conference on Image Processing (ICIP1999)*, pp.143-146, 1999.

Shimoda, S., Hayashi M. & Kanatsugu, Y. (1989). New Chroma-key Imagining Technique with Hi-Vision Background, *IEEE Transactions on Broadcasting*, Vol.35, No.4, pp.357-361, 1989.

Kanade, T., Yoshida, A., Oda, K., Kano, H. & Tanaka, M. (1996). A Stereo Machine for Video-Rate Dense Depth Mapping and its New Applications, *Proceedings of the 1996 IEEE Computer Society Conference on Computer Vision and Pattern Recognition (CVPR1996)*, pp.196-202, 1996.

Kawakita, M., Iizuka, K., Aida, T., Kikuchi, H., Fujikake, H., Yonai, J. & Takizawa, K. (2000). Axi-Vision Camera (Real-Time Distance-Mapping Camera), *Applied Optics*, Vol.39, No.22, pp.3931-3939, 2000.

Yasuda, K., Naemura, T. & Harashima, H. (2004). Thermo-Key: Human Region Segmentation from Video, *IEEE Computer Graphics and Applications*, Vol.24, No.1, pp.26-30, 2004.

Mishima, Y. (1992). A Software Chromakeyer Using Polyhedric Slice, *Proceedings of NICOGRAPH92*, pp.44-52, 1992.

Zongker, D.E., Werner, D.M., Curless, B. & Salesin D.H. (1999). Environment Matting and Compositing, *Computer Graphics (Proceedings of SIGGRAPH1999)*, pp.205-214, 1999.

Ruzon, M.A. & Tomasi, C. (2000). Alpha Estimation in Natural Images, *Proceedings of the 2000 IEEE Computer Society Conference on Computer Vision and Pattern Recognition (CVPR2000)*, pp.18-25, 2000.

Hillman, P., Hannah J. & Renshaw D. (2001). Alpha Channel Estimation in High Resolution Images and Image Sequences, *Proceedings of the 2001 IEEE Computer Society Conference on Computer Vision and Pattern Recognition (CVPR2001)*, Vol.1, pp.1063-1068, 2001.

Chuang, Y.-Y., Curless, B., Salesin, D.H. & Szeliski, R. (2001). A Bayesian Approach to Digital Matting, *Proceedings of the 2001 IEEE Computer Society Conference on Computer Vision and Pattern Recognition (CVPR2001)*, Vol.2, pp.264-271, 2001.

Sun, J., Jia, J., Tang, C.-K. & Shum, H.-Y. (2004). Poisson Matting, *Computer Graphics (Proceedings of SIGGRAPH2004)*, pp.315-321, 2004.

Smith, A.R. & Blinn, J.F. (1996). Blue Screen Matting, *Computer Graphics (Proceedings of SIGGRAPH1996)*, pp.259-268, 1996.

Yamashita, A., Kaneko, T., Matsushita S. & Miura, K.T. (2004). Region Extraction with Chromakey Using Stripe Backgrounds, *IEICE Transactions on Information and Systems*, Vol.87-D, No.1, pp.66-73, 2004.

Agata, H., Yamashita, A. & Kaneko, T. (2007). Chroma Key Using a Checker Pattern Background, *IEICE Transactions on Information and Systems*, Vol.90-D, No.1, pp.242-249, 2007.

Yamashita, A., Agata, H. & Kaneko, T. (2008). Every Color Chromakey, *Proceedings of the 19th International Conference on Pattern Recognition (ICPR2008)*, pp.1-4, TuBCT9.40, 2008.

Araki, S., Yokoya, N., Iwasa, H. & Takemura, H. (1995). A New Splitting Active Contour Model Based on Crossing Detection, *Proceedings of the 2nd Asian Conference on Computer Vision (ACCV95)*, Vol.2, pp.346-350, 1995.

Matsunaga, C., Kanazawa Y. & Kanatani, K. (2000). Optimal Grid Pattern for Automated Camera Calibration Using Cross Ratio, *IEICE Transactions on Fundamentals*, Vol.E83-A, No.10, pp.1921-1928, 2000.